18th Annual Edition

KNIVES '98

D1611026

Edited by
Ken Warner

DBI BOOKS
a division of Krause Publications, Inc.

CONTENTS

TRENDS

STATE OF THE ART

FACTORY TRENDS

DIRECTORY

STAFF

EDITOR
Ken Warner

ASSOCIATE EDITORS
Robert S.L. Anderson
Harold A. Murtz

ASSISTANT TO THE EDITOR
Lilo Anderson

PRODUCTION MANAGER
John L. Duoba

EDITORIAL/PRODUCTION ASSOCIATE
Karen Rasmussen

ELECTRONIC PUBLISHING MANAGER
Nancy J. Mellem

ELECTRONIC PUBLISHING ASSOCIATE
Laura M. Mielzynski

COVER PHOTOGRAPHY
John Hanusin

MANAGING EDITOR
Pamela J. Johnson

PUBLISHER
Charles T. Hartigan

THE COVER KNIVES

At the top of our handsome heap is the jewelled folder in gold and pearl and Damascus, all the work of Dellana Warren; next, clockwise, is a massive angularity in ivory and steel, a straight-edged fighter by Scottie H. White. At bottom, in abalone and ATS-34, is a graceful Ron Gaston dagger; above that is a Peter Martin hunter with a remarkable filled cactus grip. That blue and pearl folder, in titanium and ATS-34, has two blades and was made by Gerald E. Corbit. And finally, with its carved wood grip surmounted by an ivory rose, there's Larry Sandlin's dagger, four-bar blade beautifully matched.

Ken Warner

Copyright © 1997 by Krause Publications, Inc., 700 E. State St., Iola, WI 54990. All rights reserved. Printed in the United States of America.

No part of this book may be reproduced, stored in a retrieval system, or transmitted in any form or by any means, electronic, mechanical, photocopying, recording or otherwise, without prior written permission of the publisher.

The views and opinions of the authors expressed herein are not necessarily those of the publisher, and no responsibility for such views will be assumed.

ISBN 0-87349-195-5 **Library of Congress Catalog Card #80-67744**

INTRODUCTION

THIS IS THE eighteenth of these volumes, which adds up to nearly 5000 pages of material all prepared on the subject of mankind's oldest tool, a device that has no moving parts when at work. It's amazing.

Your reporter here is probably the only fellow on the planet who has written 150,000 words in captions for pictures of knives. And it will be a while yet before other publications catch up to the sheer number of photos of knives published here—we're getting close to 10,000.

This is one of those moderately peculiar publishing situations where the publication has just kept on keeping on while all the practitioners in its subject field sprinted off in all directions. None of them actually got clear out of sight, but have there been changes? You bet.

We have quicker craftsmanship than ever. With all those blazed trails to follow, new guys get going in a hurry.

We have better businessmen amongst our artistes than ever. Now they make deals with the factories. As this is written, one stout lad is juggling three major company offers for his designs.

Hearing about a knifemaker getting into customer trouble is a much rarer thing now, though it never was what you could call rampant. Now, it's the customers most often diddling the makers.

Every niche of knifemaking has what we'd have thought a hell of a stout organization eighteen years ago. The Guild is a monster; the ABS has its own college; the state groups are pretty heavy-duty.

We get into and out of trends faster and faster. What happened to dangle knives and to Swedish steel, for instance?

What I'm saying is it better be exciting over there on the reader's side of this book because what we're putting in here is hot stuff. Please enjoy it.

Ken Warner

The London Hunting Knife

HUNTING? IN LONDON? The notion of a "London" hunting knife could baffle a modern reader at the outset, especially if he has studied enough history, or read enough Sherlock Holmes, to know London was the greatest metropolis of the 18th and 19th centuries—not just the greatest city in Britain, but the greatest metropolis of the whole world. It was exactly the sort of place a sportsman would leave when he set out to go hunting.

And that, of course, was the point. British merchants, sea captains, military officers, colonizers, planters, missionaries and adventurers of every stripe would outfit themselves for overseas journeys in London. In London was made, or at least was sold, the best of everything.

High on this list was London cutlery. London's preeminence in cutlery dated back to the Middle Ages. Its Cutlers' Guild was founded in the 12th century, organizing and regulating a craft that had been practiced there at least back to Roman times.

By the 18th century, both Sheffield and Salisbury were striving to compete with London, but Salisbury cutlery was already in decline by then, while Sheffield had as yet only garnered a high reputation among the credulous provincials of North America. When Sheffield cutlery merchants sold their wares in London—and nearly all of them had showrooms or agents there—they would do everything the law allowed, and sometimes more, to convey the impression to customers that their blades had been forged and hafted in the metropolis.

By the 19th century, most of the ordinary cutlery sold in London was indeed Sheffield-made, although the makers', factors' or merchants' marks on the blades did not actually say so. In fact, if a knife is old and says SHEFFIELD on the blade, it was probably exported to the United States.

In 1814, it became legal for an English cutler or cutlery merchant to spell out his name, business name, and address on his blades, in lieu of just the cutler's registered guild mark. In 1819, London forbade its merchants to include the word LONDON in such blade markings, unless the blade had in fact been made in London. So collectors today should learn that a London street address on a blade that is not followed by LONDON means that the blade was contract-made elsewhere, usually in Sheffield.

Premium cutlery was another story. By the 19th century, London cutlers could no longer compete with Sheffield in mass production, so they focused their efforts on custom and high-grade work for the carriage trade: aristocrats, professional men and prosperous merchants. The same was then true of big city cutlers in America and Western Europe—make the best, and market the rest.

And the best of the best, when it came to cutlery, were surgical instruments. London's 19th-century surgical-instrument makers enjoyed, and deserved, an exalted reputation, a reputation that endures to this day. A handful of their successors are still in business.

Not only surgeons appreciated this fact. Most of the best London-made hunting knives were made and signed by prominent surgical-instrument makers. When wealthy sportsmen wanted the best knife that money could buy, they followed their doctors' advice and went to see crafts-

Those big British knives aren't always Bowies.

by BERNARD R. LEVINE

11-1
A few London hunting knives, like this one, have clip-point blades. Both the ricasso of the blade and the spring clip on the scabbard are stamped LUND/FLEET ST/LONDON. This one has a $12^{1}/_{8}$-inch blade, steel guard and butt, stag handle and leather scabbard with nickel silver mounts. (Floyd Ritter collection, Bruce Voyles photo, courtesy Bill Adams.)

Some liked the hunt up close and personal—very close, very personal. Samuel Baker and his younger brother, John, use their knives to kill a 400-pound Ceylonese boar.

men like John Savigny, Richard Paget and John Weiss, artisans who were then as well known as any of the surgeons who employed their gleaming instruments, and as any of their custom knifemaking counterparts are today.

London was also home to the most distinguished sword manufacturer in Britain. Wilkinson of Pall Mall was not the only, nor even the largest, English sword firm, but its reputation was the very highest. In the 19th century, some sportsmen turned to Wilkinson for their hunting knives, and the old-line firm did not disappoint them.

The Hunting Knives

Hunting knives are as old as human hunting. To Stone Age man, as to modern hunters, the knife was mainly a tool for opening and dismembering the quarry once it was slain. But with the advent of metal blades in the Bronze Age, long knives and short swords could be used as primary hunting weapons, much as they were used in battle.

Of course, large wild animals are a good deal stronger, and a good deal quicker, than any human. Most hunters preferred to keep their distance, using deadfalls and traps, spears and bows, and later firearms, to bring their quarry down. Venison might be tasty, and deerskin useful, but neither, for most men, was worth risking the loss of life or limb.

However, a few bold and strong men in every generation seek out contests with nature that are up close and personal. Armed with knife or short sword, and abetted by a pack of fearless hounds, such men would close with wild beasts like a gladiator in the arena. And the London hunting knife resembles the Roman gladius, the thrusting short sword with which the legions of ancient Rome conquered much of the known world, more than any other weapon.

Samuel Baker

The best known English hunter with knife and hounds was Samuel White Baker—best known because he wrote extensively and well about his fabulous adventures. Nine books by Baker were published, two of them collections of his wide-ranging articles, essays and stories.

Sam Baker's life was packed with more drama and adventure than most works of fiction. He hunted just about every sort of big game there is, using both hunting knives and pioneering high-powered, muzzle-loading rifles of his own design. As a diversion, he led major Egyptian military expeditions in the Sudan and sought out the sources of the Nile.

Samuel Baker was born June 1821, in Enfield, Middlesex, into a very wealthy commercial family. Even as a boy he was an ardent naturalist, fist-fighter and hunter (for more about Baker's fascinating life, see the bibliography).

In 1845, when he was twenty-four, Sam Baker orga-

A London hunting knife much like Sam Baker's. Its 12½-inch spear-point blade, 1⅞ inches wide, is stamped V crown R/PAGET/185 PICCADILLY/LONDON. It has crown stag handle, steel guard and ferrule, and leather scabbard with steel mounts (throat replaced). (Bob Chicca collection, Bruce Voyles photo, courtesy Bill Adams.)

This is an 1866 engraving of Sir Samuel White Baker and his second wife, Lady Baker (nee Florence Barbara Maria Finnian von Sass), whom he bought at a Turkish white slave auction in Vidin, Bulgaria, in 1858.

nized a large-scale hunting expedition to Ceylon (now Sri Lanka), in pursuit of elephant, buffalo and stag. This proved so successful that he decided to stay. He then started one of the first major tea plantations on the island, but his main interest there was always hunting. His first book of hair-raising hunting tales, *The Rifle and Hound in Ceylon*, was published in 1853 and remained in print more than fifty years. His second book, in 1855, *Eight Years' Wandering in Ceylon*, proved even more popular.

In his last book, *Wild Beasts and Their Ways*, published in 1890, Samuel Baker described in detail the methods of hunting large animals with dogs and a hunting knife. Most remarkable were tales he told of slaying leopards and water buffalo, but these exploits were exceptional. The usual quarry was stag or boar. He wrote:

> When using the hunting-knife, extreme dexterity is to be observed in delivering the stab, and instantaneously recovering the weapon. There is no object to be gained by keeping the knife within the wound, and there is considerable danger of injury to the hand. If the knife is used by an expert it will never be held with the point downwards like a dagger, but the handle will be grasped for a direct thrust, as though the weapon were a

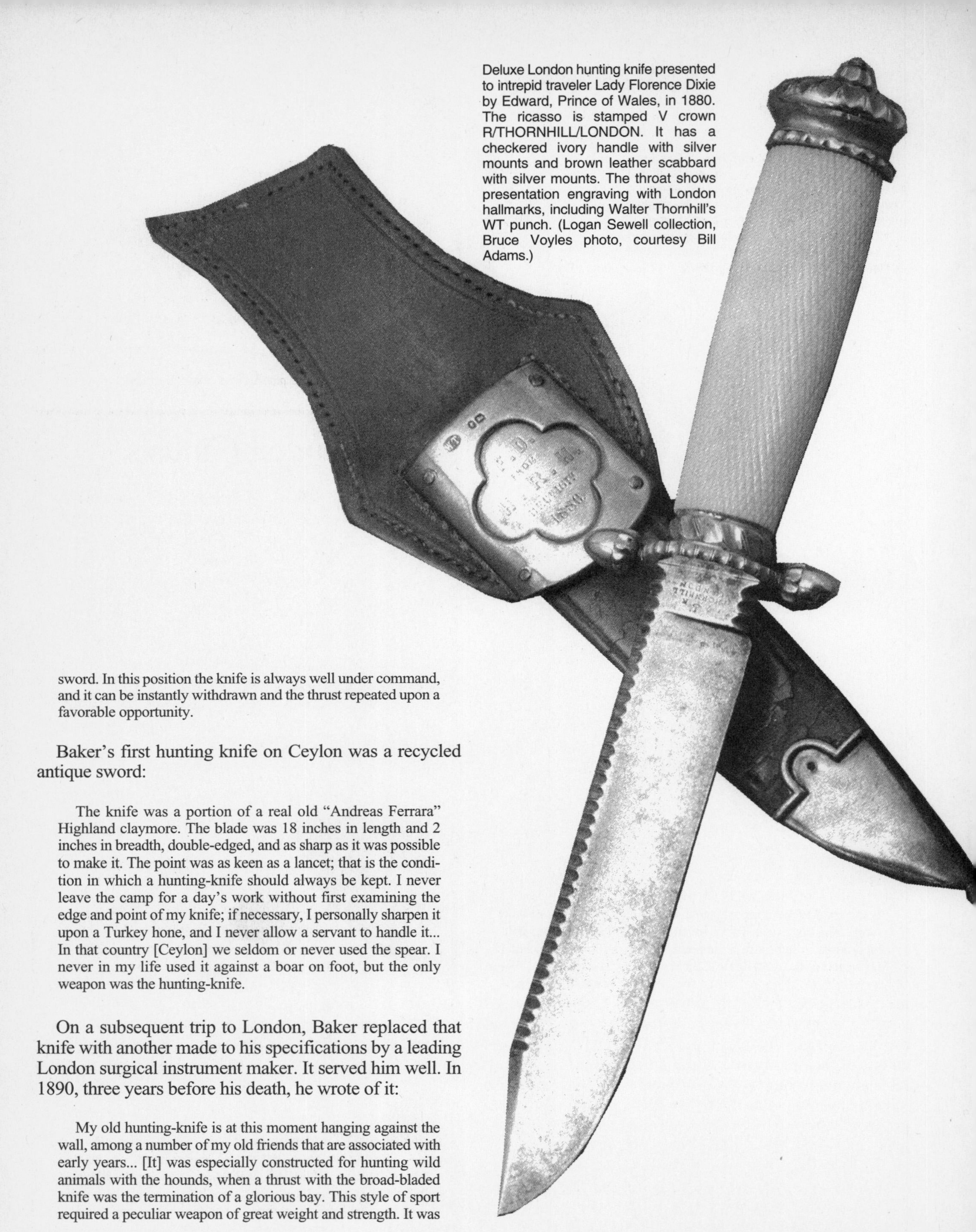

Deluxe London hunting knife presented to intrepid traveler Lady Florence Dixie by Edward, Prince of Wales, in 1880. The ricasso is stamped V crown R/THORNHILL/LONDON. It has a checkered ivory handle with silver mounts and brown leather scabbard with silver mounts. The throat shows presentation engraving with London hallmarks, including Walter Thornhill's WT punch. (Logan Sewell collection, Bruce Voyles photo, courtesy Bill Adams.)

sword. In this position the knife is always well under command, and it can be instantly withdrawn and the thrust repeated upon a favorable opportunity.

Baker's first hunting knife on Ceylon was a recycled antique sword:

The knife was a portion of a real old "Andreas Ferrara" Highland claymore. The blade was 18 inches in length and 2 inches in breadth, double-edged, and as sharp as it was possible to make it. The point was as keen as a lancet; that is the condition in which a hunting-knife should always be kept. I never leave the camp for a day's work without first examining the edge and point of my knife; if necessary, I personally sharpen it upon a Turkey hone, and I never allow a servant to handle it... In that country [Ceylon] we seldom or never used the spear. I never in my life used it against a boar on foot, but the only weapon was the hunting-knife.

On a subsequent trip to London, Baker replaced that knife with another made to his specifications by a leading London surgical instrument maker. It served him well. In 1890, three years before his death, he wrote of it:

My old hunting-knife is at this moment hanging against the wall, among a number of my old friends that are associated with early years... [It] was especially constructed for hunting wild animals with the hounds, when a thrust with the broad-bladed knife was the termination of a glorious bay. This style of sport required a peculiar weapon of great weight and strength. It was

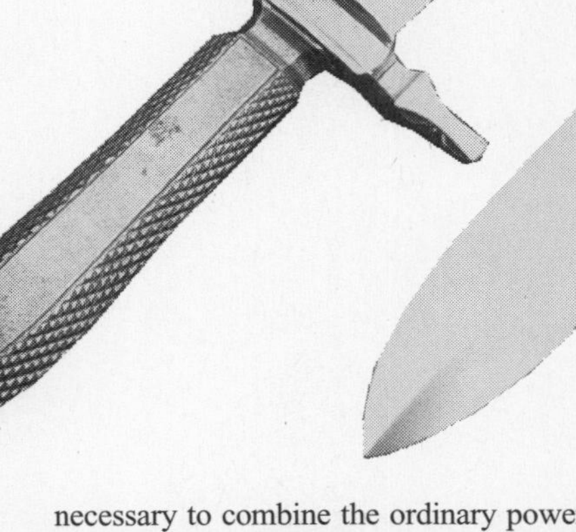

The surgical-instrument heritage of this London hunting knife is obvious. Its intricately cut guard and its faceted handle with alternate panels of checkering are all steel. The ricasso of the 11¼-inch double-edged blade is stamped EVANS & Co./12 OLD FISH ST./LONDON. (Roger Baker collection, Bruce Voyles photo, courtesy Bill Adams.)

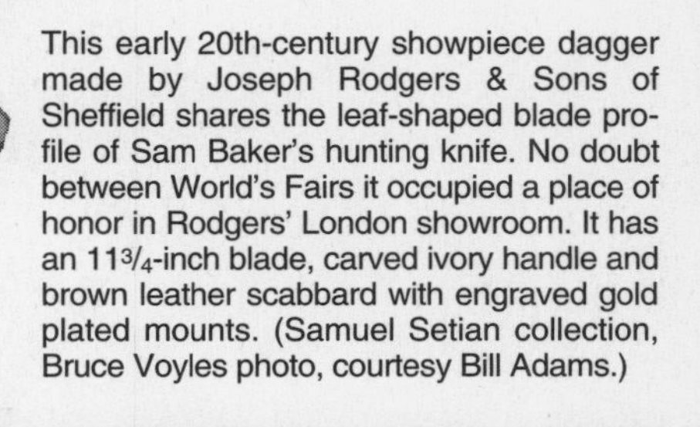

This early 20th-century showpiece dagger made by Joseph Rodgers & Sons of Sheffield shares the leaf-shaped blade profile of Sam Baker's hunting knife. No doubt between World's Fairs it occupied a place of honor in Rodgers' London showroom. It has an 11¾-inch blade, carved ivory handle and brown leather scabbard with engraved gold plated mounts. (Samuel Setian collection, Bruce Voyles photo, courtesy Bill Adams.)

necessary to combine the ordinary power of a knife with the efficiency of a bill-hook, for clearing jungle when necessary; for cutting poles, to carry home the heads and horns of sambar deer, etc.; to fell the young trees for building an impromptu hut; and for the hard work of cutting up large animals into quarters, for conveyance by coolies where no roads existed, either for pack animals or for carts.

It was difficult to arrange a knife that would comprise all these desiderata, but Mr. Paget, of Piccadilly (long since dead), was a first rate cutler, and he produced the perfection of a blade. [Richard Paget began his cutlery business at 184 Piccadilly, London, in 1822.] The knife weighed exactly 3 pounds, including the sheath. It weighs 2¼ pounds now without the cover, being reduced by constant grinding during many years of hard work. The blade was 1 foot in length, 2 inches wide, and doubled-edged 3 inches from the point, slightly hollow in the center (1¾-inch wide), and again 2 inches wide at the base, and 5/16-inch thick at the back... When sharpened to as keen a point and edge as could be obtained, this highly tempered steel would pierce a hole right through one of the old rim pennies, and would cut the same coin into two halves, when placed upon a block of oak, without in the least degree either turning the point or damaging the edge...

This was the perfection of a weapon for the purpose required; it was the companion of every hunt where no firearms were permitted, and, whatever the game might be that was discovered by the pack, it was brought to bay and killed by the hounds and hunting-knife. Sometimes it might be a sambar deer, which was the recognized object of pursuit; at other times it might be the small red deer; frequently a wild boar; and sometimes, but rarely, a buffalo...such a knife, in the hand of any person who knew how to use it, would have been

London Cutlers

LIST OF LEADING London cutlers who made hunting knives. (*W means an example was included in the January 1997 Williamson auction in San Francisco, followed by the lot number and price realized, courtesy Butterfield & Butterfield; dates from Bennion.)

Briggs (*W 3511, $2875)
Evans & Co., 12 Old Fish Street
Hill & Co., 4 Haymarket (*W 3600, $1725)
Lund, Fleet Street, Cornhill (*W 3608, $1092.50)
Richard Paget, 185 Piccadilly, 1822-?. Made a hunting knife for Samuel White Baker
Savigny & Co., c1720-c1850 (*W 3702, $747.50)
- Paul Savigny, worked c1720-1726, was the successor to Widow How (Ephraim How, d. 1720, was the most famous London cutler in the early 18th century)
- John Tessier Savigny, worked c1726-1784
- John Horatio Savigny, worked c1789
- John Henry Savigny, worked c1794-1810
- Savigny, Everill & Mason, worked c1810-1850
- Successors used "Late Savigny" until c1896

Savory & Moore, c1794-present
Simpson, c1788-1863
Stodart, c1787-1839
Walter Thornhill (*W 3513, $3450)
Underwood, c1820-?. Successor to Yeeling Charlwood
Thomas Weedon, c1789-1856
John Weiss, 1787-present (*W 3650, $1380; *W 3651, $1092.50)
Wilkinson Sword, Ltd. Made Shakespear knife, others (unmarked example, replaced sheath: *W 3548, $1725)

The Shakespear Knife by Wilkinson of London was produced in a variety of sizes, but all the same style, often marked with serial numbers and the etched name. (Courtesy Steve Eisner)

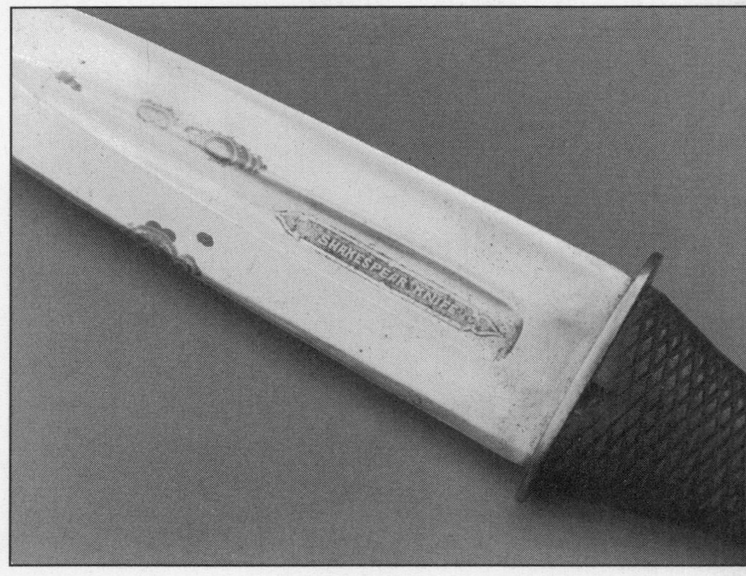

> nearly as formidable as the old Roman sword. I have on more than one occasion stood against the charge of a sambar stag at bay, and met the attack with the point of the knife in the face, held firmly at arm's length. This requires great strength of arm and a firm footing, but, above all things, a blade that is more dependable than the British bayonet [which in that period was scandalously defective].

Baker kept a game book in Ceylon from October 1851 to March 1854. In those thirty months, he slew with his London hunting knife 138 sambar deer, 14 wild hogs, and 8 red deer. Then he added, "Although many wild boars were killed, they were never objects of the hunts, but on the contrary, they were if possible avoided, as an encounter invariably resulted in the sacrifice of hounds..."

Of course once the hounds had caught the scent of a boar, there was no calling them off. The boar would lead them on a desperate chase for ten minutes or so, then go to ground in a thicket of thorns or bamboo where its rear and flanks would be shielded. Then the biggest hounds, the "seizers," would go in after it. Smart seizers would wait for an opportunity to seize the pig over the shoulder by its opposite ear. Stupid ones would rush in headlong and be tusked to death for their rashness.

> There was then no time to lose, and, with the hunting-knife drawn, a few struggles through the tangled brake brought me upon the scene. One hound would have assuredly secured his hold... upon the opposite ear, and would endeavor to turn the boar's head upwards, by pulling back. Another would have seized the ear next to him, while the remaining seizers would have tackled the boar in every direction, one hanging beneath its throat, another by the thigh just above the joint. Without a moment's hesitation it was then necessary to close, and drive the long knife up to the hilt behind the shoulder...

> The large and heavy hunting-knife was an admirable weapon for this style of hunting, as both point and edge could always be depended upon. The skin of a boar is tough, and requires an acute point...

Henry Shakespear

Henry John Childe Shakespear was a contemporary of Baker's, though nearly a generation older. He, too, gained renown through his own writing about his adventures, most particular his 1850s volume, *Wild Sports of India*. As a serving army officer in British India, Major Shakespear did most of his big game hunting on the subcontinent.

Shakespear's claim to fame was that he created his own hunting knife design, which resembles most nearly a 17th-century Scottish dirk. This "Shakespear Knife" was manufactured in a variety of sizes and configurations by Wilkinson Sword. Here is how Major Shakespear described the version that he carried himself, and that he furnished to his hunting companions:

How to Tell One

SINCE MOST LONDON hunting knives were custom-made, it is rare to see two alike. Even "standard" patterns, such as the Wilkinson Sword "Shakespear Knife," exhibit wide variation. However, there is an overall similarity in design to London Hunting Knives that makes them easy to recognize. Here is how I describe the type in *Levine's Guide to Knives and Their Values*, 4th Edition (page 465):

England—London Hunting Knife

At least 12 inches overall. Stout spear-point blade. Stag, boxwood, ebony, or ivory handle with steel, nickel silver, or sterling mounts. Brown or black leather sheath, usually with matching mounts. Late 18th to early 20th centuries. Stouter than most Bowie knives, these hunting weapons were used by English gentleman adventurers to kill large game, mainly deer and boar. Examples marked LONDON were made there, usually by surgical instrument makers, and of the highest quality. Those with just a London street address were made in Sheffield for a London retailer... Example shown made circa 1815-1830 by the London surgical instrument firm of John Weiss (1787-present), ebony and nickel silver...

The very knife shown, which I used to own, was sold at auction in January 1997 for a bit over $1000.

In its basic spear-point form, the London Hunting Knife is something of a hybrid between two ancient and traditional European hunting weapons, the boar spear and the hanger, or hunting short sword. It is shaped like a spear blade, only larger, while it is mounted like a sword, only smaller. Here is how I describe the related but more traditional German hunting sword in *Levine's Guide to Knives and Their Values*, 4th Edition (page 467):

Germany—Hanger or Hunting Sword

12 inches long up to short sword size. Usually stag handled. Usually has cross guard (with hoof-shaped quillons) and counter-guard like a sword. Leather sheath with metal fittings. 18th-20th centuries. Value $200-750 depending on quality and embellishment. Example shown from 1914 catalog, has side-knife... Used for killing large game animals, for disjointing game, and for personal defense. Also serve as a badge of rank among professional German foresters. Stag and boar are still hunted with spear and short sword.

Each of us is armed with a shikar or hunting knife, the sheath of which fits into the breast of the shooting coat. Thus the knife is ready to hand, and can be used in a moment—to save or lose life. My hunting knives are some seven inches long and one and a half broad in the blade, partly double-edged, fluted, coming to a keen point, and kept as sharp as possible. There is a spring in the sheath which catches the handle of the blade when it is down in the sheath; when required for use, this spring is pressed open with the finger, at the same time the hilt is grasped. It requires no buckle or other fastening; the steel button in the side of the sheath fitting into a button hole in the pocket of the hunting-coat...

I have examined a number of actual or pictured Shakespear knives, and though they differ in detail, they are all evidently of the same manufacture. One I have here at the moment is etched SHAKESPEAR KNIFE in a panel in the front fuller of the stout, double-edge, 7-inch blade. The steel guard is minimal in size. The wasp-waisted handle is checkered hardwood, probably box. The brown leather scabbard with patinated steel tip is much as Shakespear described, with spring catch and button. However on this example, a brown leather frog is buttoned to the sheath, so the knife can be worn suspended from a belt.

An example sold at auction in January 1997 for $1725 had a longer blade (10 1/8 inches) with smaller fullers, a wider lobed guard, and a checkered hardwood handle of slightly different proportion The blade is etched with a small crest or coat of arms, and the plated guard is stamped with a serial number—as are many Wilkinson Shakespear Knives. Its minimalist sheath is evidently a later replacement.

Today, fine antique London hunting knives, used by thousands of adventuring Englishmen who read Baker and Shakespear, sell for fractions of the prices of antique Bowies—about the price of a mid-range modern hunting rifle. This puts them well within the reach of most arms collectors. ●

Bibliography

Baker, Samuel W., *The Rifle and Hound in Ceylon*. Longmans, 1854.

Baker, Samuel W., *Wild Beasts and Their Ways*. Macmillan, 1890.

Bennion, Elisabeth, *Antique Medical Instruments*. Sotheby, 1979.

Blackmore, Howard L., *Hunting Weapons*. Walker, 1971.

Butterfield & Butterfield, *The William R. Williamson Bowie Knife Collection*. January 28, 1997 auction catalog.

Casada, Jim, "Samuel Baker, Victorian Adventurer." *Gray's Sporting Classics*.

Levine, Bernard, *Levine's Guide to Knives and Their Values*, 4th Edition. Vernon Hills, IL: DBI Books, 1997.

Levine, Bernard, "Knife Lore," *National Knife Magazine*. November 1994; February 1995.

Middleton, Dorothy, *Baker of the Nile*. 1949

Shakespear, Henry J.C., *Wild Sports of India*.

Stephens, Frederick J., *Fighting Knives*. Arco, 1980.

Welch, Charles, *History of the Cutlers' Company of London, Vol. II, From 1500 to Modern Times*. Cutler's Company, 1923.

Williamson, William R., "The Shakespear Knife," *Guns & Ammo*. November 1977.

EVEN THOUGH THE tragedy took place more than thirty-five years ago in November of 1961, I still remember it vividly. It was around the time of my birthday, and everyone with a thirst for adventure was following the news accounts of Michael Rockefeller, son of Nelson Rockefeller, governor of New York, on his second art collecting trip to western (Dutch) New Guinea. This collection is now housed in the Rockefeller wing of the Metropolitan Museum of Art. I was just out of high school, and a friend had spent a year in Australia with a trip to the eastern half of the island—Papua New Guinea—where he had obtained a drum, a bow and several wickedly carved barbed arrows. He was the envy of our crowd. Australia administered PNG at the time, and it was among the last primitive and dangerous places on earth.

found, killed and dined on an exhausted Michael Rockefeller after a tidal bore swamped his catamaran at the mouth of the Betsj or possibly the Siretsj river and forced him to swim for shore.

While there has been much controversy surrounding this over the last three and a half decades, the Asmat themselves claim to have done the deed—killing and eating a half-drowned white man who wore glasses. Rockefeller was the only missing white man; he was in the area; and he wore glasses.

The Reverend Cornelis Van Kessel claimed the Asmat killed him as payback for two Asmat being killed by white Dutch police. The concept of payback and the associated feuds run throughout the entire island. Allegedly, these Asmat were from the village of Otsjanep.

The Daggers

The Dutch side of the island was even more so. And it still is.

Headlines screamed the disappearance of Michael Rockefeller to a shocked world. It seemed impossible: Born to wealth, privilege and the social elite, he was thought by many to be immune to the dangers of the untamed world. He wasn't. At first, he was feared drowned as his double canoe (catamaran) had overturned. However, he was a strong swimmer, and rescue expeditions were sent out—to no avail. Crocodiles and sharks live in the waters, so rumors of his being eaten by them began to circulate. As time dragged on, more rumors of him being eaten surfaced, but they were far more sinister. This time, local headhunting cannibals were blamed.

Because of this, the area's borders were shut down to most all of the outside world and the land became even more mysterious. Dutch rule was passed to Indonesia, and that half of the island is now known as Irian Jaya.

Vast tidal swamps of southwest Irian Jaya reveal stinking, steaming flats of mud that are flooded twice a day. Thick mangroves, palms, vines, orchids and sago trees line the rivers that flow south down from the mountains—first fresh, then brackish as they drain into the swamps. Malarial mosquitoes add their own special touch to the scene.

This is the land of the Asmat, the fierce native Melanesian peoples, some 65,000 strong, who—it is claimed—

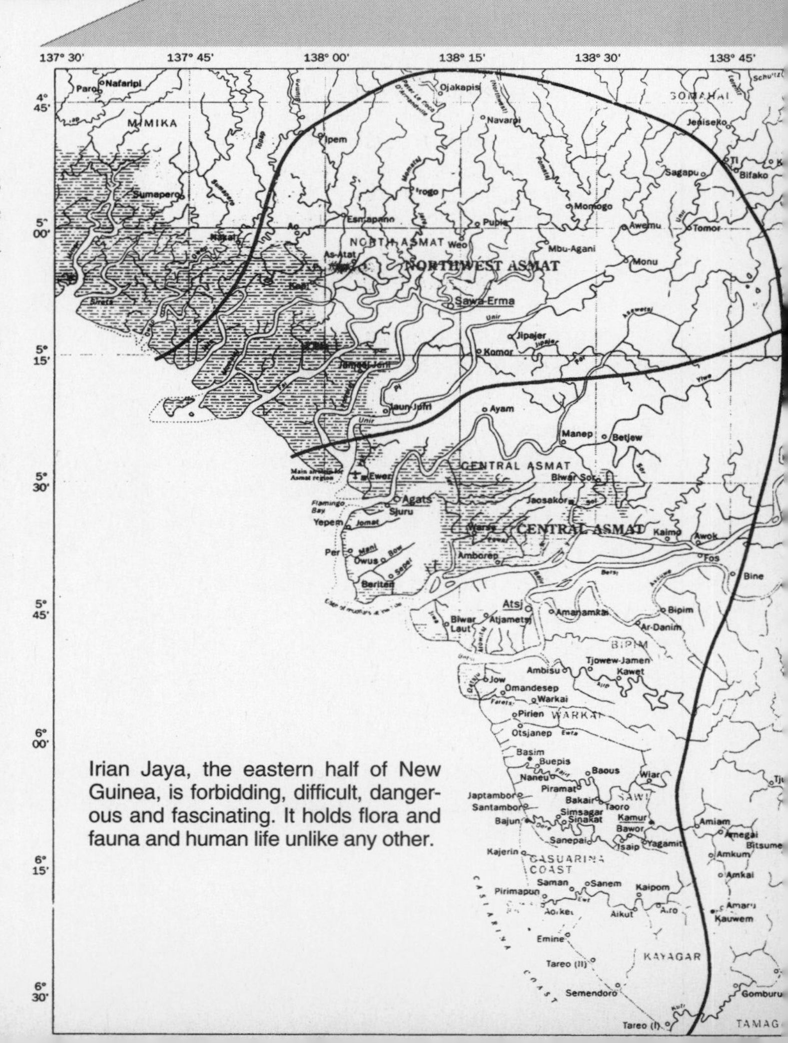

Irian Jaya, the eastern half of New Guinea, is forbidding, difficult, dangerous and fascinating. It holds flora and fauna and human life unlike any other.

by LANCE STRONG

of the Asmat

This Asmat warrior is in his house, holding a cassowary bone dagger. The armband on his left bicep serves as a sheath. The man on the far left is an Indonesian guide; the explorer's hat and water bottle are on the right.

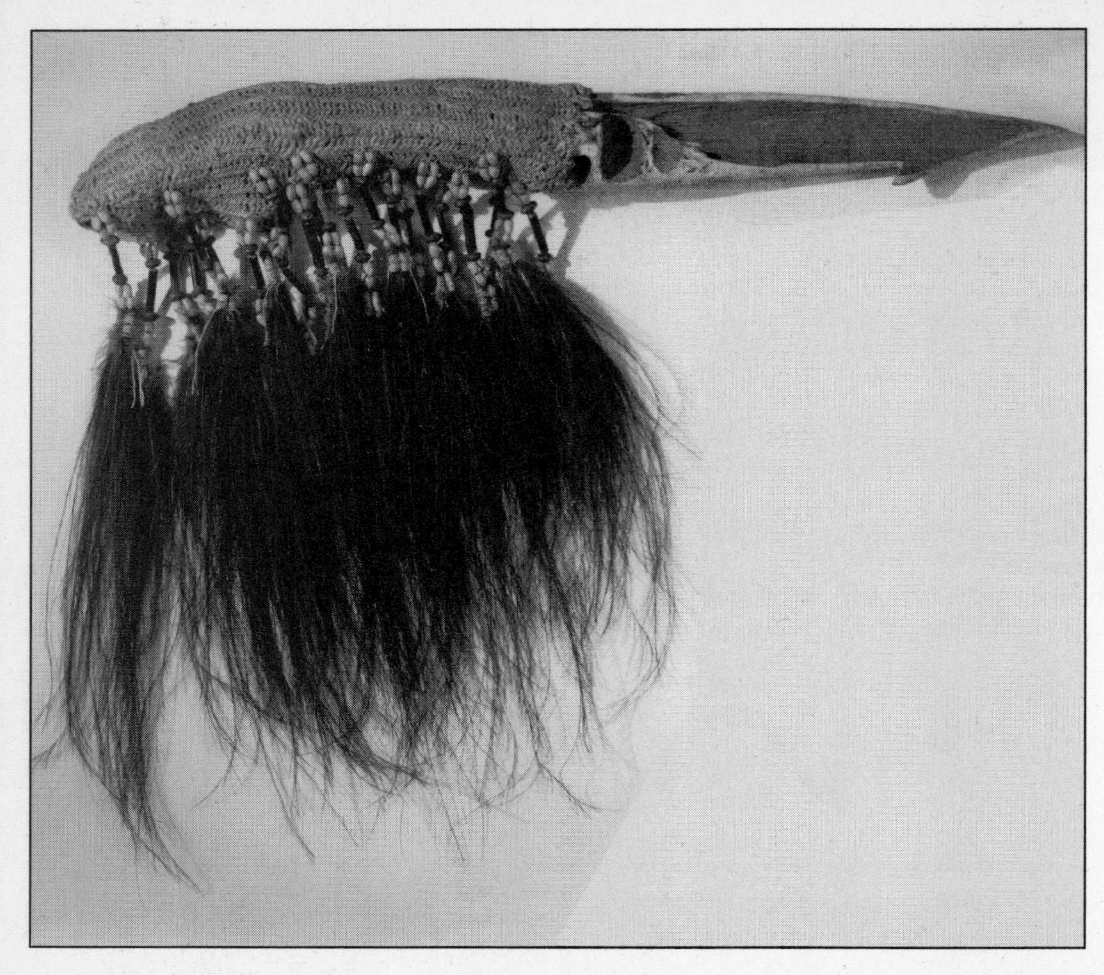

This Asmat dagger is made from a crocodile jawbone with finely woven sago fiber over the handle area, cassowary feathers and quills, and silver-grey coix and red abrus seeds—22 inches.

Even Captain James Cook, one of the finest explorers of the world, ran afoul of the Asmat. In 1770, he landed a party looking for fresh water and/or coconuts when a fight ensued. One account states he lost twenty men, but Cook's own records show only that they were driven back to the ship. Cook always tried to avoid bloodshed and restrained his men from opening deadly aimed fire wherever he went. He, of course, met his own demise nine years later when he was killed and partially eaten in Hawaii under conditions of stress, illness, and religious and cultural misunderstandings.

Not long ago, I visited the Museum of Fine Arts on the campus of the University of Utah and was delighted to find Asmat art carvings. The piece that most interested me was the cassowary thigh-bone dagger. The cassowary is a large bird related to the ostrich, rhea and emu. Unlike the ostrich, however, it has three toes instead of two, and one of these has a lethal claw that reportedly could be used to eviscerate a man. It also has a casque of horn-like (or beak-like) material on the top of its head that is claimed to allow the bird to crash head first through the thick forest.

I don't know about you, but the idea of a bird the size of an ostrich with a red and blue head and a built-in crash helmet running at me in the jungle with the ability to tear at my guts with its clawed foot sends chills down my spine. And the possible use for a dagger made from its bone—and sometimes its claw—creates additional fear.

The dagger I looked at was about 15 inches long with a knotted string sago fiber cover over the rounded joint end. It had carved barbs near the tip. Cassowary hair-like feathers and quills along with grey coix and red abrus seeds decorated the fiber cover. The museum shop director kindly gave me the name of Steven C. Chiaramonte, a Salt Lake City businessman, as the donor.

Mr. Chiaramonte generously agreed to meet with me and acquaint me with research books on the Asmat, as well as show me pieces in his collection and tell me of his personal experiences among the people from his several visits. I was surprised to learn that the bone dagger is the primary killing tool of the headhunters; I had assumed that the arrow and the spear are the killing weapons of choice.

They seem to be most used to wound and capture the enemy, who is taken to one of the magnificent long war canoes, bent over and tied to a crosspiece in the canoe, and dispatched with the dagger. The head is cut off using a bamboo knife and cooked with much ritual in the village. A hole is punched in the side, and the brains eaten. The skull then becomes a trophy skull for the successful warrior. In contrast with an ancestor skull that most usually has the jawbone attached and is often used as the warrior's pillow to maintain the intimate talisman contact, the enemy skull's jawbone is discarded or given to the women to make into a necklace and the skull is used for a boy's initiation into manhood ceremony.

Daggers are carried in a woven rattan band, point down, on the left upper arm (for a right-handed warrior) and may be made from cassowary thigh bone or even human femur! Some are lightly engraved with a rat's tooth, and all have sharp pointed ends. The point may be plain, carved with barbs or tipped with a cassowary claw held in place with beeswax and sap. This can slip off to fester in a wound.

The most prized daggers are very rare and hard to find. They are made from the lower jaw of a crocodile and can be about 24 inches in length. Far too large and heavy to be carried in an arm band, they are extremely important possessions of the Asmat warrior.

It is still possible to travel to the bush and obtain your own dagger. According to Chiaramonte, one can fly to Singapore or Jakarta or Denpasar. Then to Ujung Pandang on Sulawesi. Next it's Biak and then Jayapura—Hollandia of MacArthur's time for you WWII buffs. A permit (suratjala) is needed from the police-military for the dangerous and restricted areas. You may have to bargain for it. It's necessary to show that you're worthy, that you have a reason to be there, and have enough money to take care of yourself, and *can* take care of yourself.

The staging area is Agats. Three possible ways of getting there include (1) Fly to Wamena in the highlands. There, catch a missionary flight to the south coast. This entails crossing 16,000-foot peaks, and one day in ten may provide a break in the clouds. Land on any of the WWII steel runways still extant. (2) Fly to Merauke on the coast or Senggo in the foothills. From Senggo canoe downstream, or from Merauke take a freighter along the coast and then canoe—motorized or paddle—to shore. The water here is shallow, about 3 feet deep. You may be able to avoid Agats with these routes. (3) Fly to Timika (copper mine) and hire a canoe to the Asmat area. It is

These are all thought to be of cassowary bone. The small one in the middle is *not* human. The other two need to be X-rayed through the sago fiber covers to determine their origin. At left: From Central Asmat, this cassowary bone has carved barbs near the point with woven sago fiber cap in two colors with cassowary feathers, quills and silver-grey coix seeds. It is 16 inches. At middle: From Northwest Asmat, this cassowary bone has finely carved barbs near the point with woven band, white cockatoo feathers, cassowary quills and red abrus and silver-grey coix seeds. It is 14 inches. At right: From the Fayit River, village of Buepis, this cassowary bone has a cassowary claw held in place with beeswax. The decorations are engraved with rat's tooth, woven sago fiber cap, cassowary feathers, quills and silver-grey coix seeds embedded in the beeswax near the claw. It is 16 inches.

This small crocodile jawbone dagger has a woven and string sago fiber handle, cassowary feathers and silver-grey coix seeds. From Bajun Village, Southwest Asmat, it is 16 inches.

(Below) An Asmat warrior with a dagger. The carvings on the wall and rafters are also sought-after genuine primitive art.

about 12 hours at sea in a motorized canoe and costs about $700. This is perhaps the most reliable way to go, but the least cost effective.

At Agats, "the county seat of the Asmat area," as Chiaramonte calls it, hire a canoe. *Warning:* Any place within two days of Agats has impact from the outside. After about two days you begin to enter the hinterlands.

So, if all goes well, Agats can take about eleven days. You can find daggers in Agats—or Jayapura or even Jakarta for that matter—and they are probably Asmat, but made-for-sale items, *not* made-for-use. Remember that two-day rule. North and inland is a good area, but a "displeasing" place. Sounds like mud and bugs and ugly to me. South and inland is better, but go at least two days or the items will have price tags!

Excellent art areas are to be found on the Fayit river and the villages of Basim or Buepis. I asked about trade items to take such as lighters, monofilament and hooks, stuff I've used on the Amazon. Not much good. They want tobacco—Indonesian—or sometimes Indonesian cash if they can get to where they can buy tobacco. Best travel times are around the end of October, and March and April. Maybe I'll see you there.

Many areas are now "pacified," but the fact that others are closed and permits are required for those that open leads me to believe that not all headhunting has ceased. Whenever I see a picture of a human femur dagger, or a warrior with his trophy skull, I think of Michael Rockefeller and I wonder. So maybe I won't see you there. ●

SUBSTANCE OVER SYMBOLISM

This Survival Dirk by Kevin Hoffman features an edge-and-a-half, integral crossguard, grip-framed full-tang, concealed slot in tang, scored haft, lanyard hole and non-reflective finish. The ventilated Kydex sheath includes a screwdriver tip.

For a soldier, knife choices are all personal

by PAUL BRUBAKER

IT IS A military maxim that battles are fought by men who'll use every resource to achieve their mission. Weapons are only the tools or implements used to accomplish the mission. Weapons may be used well or used badly, but they cannot achieve what spirit will not attempt. The knife in war demonstrates this.

The basic characteristics of a good combat knife are almost independent of style and preference, which is not what most critics say. There is a school of thought for anything and everything, and only a little experience will begin to inform the participant. The only question is whether a soldier can survive long enough to learn, or unlearn, all the important things; this is why most combat commands establish their own orientation or preparation courses to supplement the fundamentals. But one cannot always prepare for the unanticipated or altered circumstance. During WWI, soldiers fashioned crude but effective trench knives from barbwire anchors because the tactics changed faster than the supply system could adjust to urgent need. These improvised trench knives wouldn't have qualified for the experts, but they worked in the trenches.

More often, the situation confronting the modern soldier is deciding which item to procure from the vast array of acceptable alternatives. This selection is complicated since assignments and environments vary widely in the interdependent commitments of geopolitics. A combat knife selected for desert operations may not be suitable for alpine maneuvers. A knife intended for jungle survival may not fulfill urban combat expectations. So, if one is not going to get new weapons issued upon each relocation, then some categorical decisions must be made.

The first categorical limitation is mission and self assessment. If one's specialty sets limits, then certain considerations needn't be calculated and others must be emphasized. Operating around fuel, salt water or other caustics may define the prime characteristics. Fitting the leg-pocket of a flight-suit may limit size. Working with magnetic mines may determine composition. Field utility may eliminate some refinements. And personal preference for a style or material may abrogate a more reasonable selection. A leather handle and carbon steel blade may be poor choices for waterborne operations, but preventive maintenance can limit the damage for a while. One's self-image is a crucial factor in sustaining confidence and fighting spirit, so consider it when selecting a combat knife.

The considerations for categorical limitations include mission/self, style, metal, construction, handle, sheath and price. Just as one may have preferences within the logistical system, such as desiring a certain type of radio when operational parameters are optional, the final decision for any choice must remain consistent and compatible with the specialized objectives. If mission specialization requires weapon concealment, then size and weight become significant factors. The style of the blade tip, belly or back may be influenced by the individual's specialization. If a medic's combat-utility knife should be single-edged for safety, then the conventional dictate is superseded. If stainless steel or non-ferrous alloys or ballistic plexiglas is required, then the composition priority is elevated. The handle material is usually optional, but should always be reliable and comfortable. The rule governing price is to buy the best one can afford to replace, because knives are not indestructible and are often lost without any possibility of recovery.

Of the categorical limitations, sheaths or scabbards are the most neglected. One should never purchase a knife because of its holster, but most manufacturers pay very little attention to this essential item. When a knife's sheath needs replacing, it is a good idea to commission a custom model that will fit its special niche. Such customizing may stipulate the material, from leather to ABS, and include unique keepers or combination pockets for hone and accessories. Although custom knives will often offer better sheaths, they, too, may not be ideal; so it is important to remember that sheaths will wear out and are replaceable.

The categorical limitation that generates the most expert advice is knife construction. This presumes that the buyer has both the knowledge and expertise to discriminate among the various technical possibilities. The truth is that factory knives don't offer construction options, and custom knifemakers are usually too intelligent and experienced to sign their name to an inferior product simply to satisfy a sale. The specific hardness of any knife is not critical, because most knives will function without any heat-treatment at all, and every metal has an optimal temper for its composition. Few soldiers know the construction particulars of their issue weapons, but they must become expert in their care and use. Unless there is some extraordinary requirement, one should forget about the variable nomenclature of the blade—from forte to foible, from bevel to choil, from swedge to ricasso—because application and restoration will be sufficiently preoccupying. Most people cannot distinguish among the various metals when bevel and mass are equalized, and most of the complaints about metallic performance are attributable to improper sharpening. Given the extremely high quality of industrial alloy available, and the potential for a bladesmith to impair or contaminate barstock by inattention or inexperience, one can depend upon satisfaction from almost all factory products. Custom knifemakers are the artistic element that improves creative production, and they are the major source of innovative ideas.

The definition of a combat knife is debatable. For some, it is a highly refined weapon with no other application, an argument similar to the definition of an assault rifle being uncompromised. Others believe a combat knife must justify its existence by serving field or utilitarian functions, since it will probably never be used, if statistics remain consistent, as a weapon of stealth or last resort. Throughout my military career, I always carried a knife, never used it in combat, and often regretted its presence...however, I would carry one again. My selection would still be exclusive, but I'd never object to anyone electing practical function. Regardless of style or preference, there are a baker's dozen of characteristics that should guide the selection of a combat knife.

In order of importance, the basic characteristics are manual access, silence, grip, tang, crossguard, blade strength, edge, size, weight, balance, security, finish and options. This list will not recommend integrated tools (from screwdrivers and wrenches to can-openers and cap-lifters), ancillary instruments (from compass and range-finder to inclinometer and sundial), or permanent camouflage patterns. One's military specialization may dictate some reordering of these priorities, which is entirely appropriate. Nonetheless, the priorities of this list acknowledge that actual knife combat is very rare, but will be exceedingly swift and fiercely violent.

A combat knife must be swiftly accessible to just one hand, and it must also be properly restored with one hand. A combatant usually doesn't have the opportunity to encourage the knife's cooperation, since drawing it is often a statement of emergency. Some soldiers mount their knives so they may be drawn and replaced with either hand, but that isn't always possible or even desirable, given its limited application. Wherever it is mounted, from belt or harness to pouch or pack, it should remain there for automatic or reflex action when needed.

Not every combat knife needs to be stealthy, but they all need to be quiet. They shouldn't rattle in their scabbard, echo or rebound when accidently knocked, signal alert when unsecured and drawn, or contain telltales and shifts. Knifework is always close, and there is advantage in surprise, so one's knife should not telegraph the move.

A knife without a secure grip is more dangerous to the owner than to the opponent. A hard smooth handle is easier to maintain and may last longer, but a textured grip will help ensure survival. A toothed or scored edge along the exposed tang will contribute, but sweat-grooves in the haft are also essential. The grip should also be a true guide to blade position. The actual material selected for the handle will depend upon personal preference or specific need, but it should be tough enough not to leave the knife with an exposed tang. Some people prefer a skeletonized treatment, in which the tang is actually the haft, but this minimalism will probably benefit from at least a para-cord wrap to insulate and dim the exposed metal. The handle should fit the user's hand, being neither too large nor too small. A fair guide is that the addition of side-scales should not quadruple the total thickness of the haft; the maximum measure of handle breadth or width should not exceed 1-inch. To reiterate Fairbairn's guide, make a loose fist and compute the opening—it'll be smaller than you think.

The tang on a combat knife should be full-width and full-length. Smaller tangs threaten the integrity of the whole knife, due to the extreme stress of military applications. Some custom knifemakers will adjust the knife's balance and enhance its decoration by brass-wrapping a stub-tang. A slotted-tang sacrifices some central bulk to include some internal stowage of small survival items without the loss of function. Any tang-extension that protrudes beyond the haft or butt should be functionally blunt so as to avoid inadvertent self-injury.

A combat knife needs a full double-guard, which is called a crossguard. It may be added as perpendicular to the blade's plane, or integral with the plane from the same barstock. It need not be large, but it should be textured on the haft side to increase its resistance. Although some manuals have recommended advancing a finger forward to wrap around the quillon of the crossguard for enhanced grip, this is extremely risky. A single guard is reserved for single-edged blades. A sub-hilt, which is a single-guard set behind the crossguard into the haft, can make changing hand positions difficult and dangerous.

The blade strength of a combat knife should extend all the way to the tip by means of plane or bevel geometry. One of the strongest blade constructions is of triangular cross-section which can be enhanced by the addition of a fuller along the spine; however, few knives are so configured. For eccentric rising-point blades, the blade back lends strength to the spine. On symmetrical blades, the spine of intersecting bevels must approach as near the tip as possible. Some blades are hexahedral in cross-section and derive their strength from the massive plane making the blade's sides. Fullers—wide grooves—are introduced to the blade to add rigidity while reducing weight, and they may be discontinuous or isolated.

Unless there is a good reason not to have it, a combat knife should be either double-edged or offer an edge-and-a-half. This has nothing to do with style and everything to do with efficiency. A double-edged blade tends to assist itself on penetration and saves time on rotational reversal during slashes. A double-edged blade can also become specialized, with one edge honed finer than the other, or one edge serrated and the other plain...which reminds us again that the grip must orient the knife in the hand. However the edges are arranged, they should be easily maintained in the field; therefore sawteeth are not recommended.

The standard S.O.F. (top) has a bright finish with a single finger-groove full tang; the modified Dirk has a non-reflective finish with a grip-framed full tang, both by Kevin Hoffman, whose knives suit the author.

In making my earliest choices, I made the mistake of equating blade length with combat stand-off or fighting distance. It is possible that an additional inch in length may enable a near-miss to make contact, but it is also possible that a too lengthy blade will not respond well during movement. One must not only consider the optimum performance length—to get to vital points through winter clothing or protective armor—and the most practical size to carry. As photo-analysts and map-readers know, nature has no straight lines or square angles, so putting a 12- to 15-inch rigid bar somewhere on the multi-curved human body is a problem. Most experts agree that an anti-personnel combat knife should have at least a 6-inch blade to reach all the vital areas. Requirements for concealment or compactness may reduce this to an absolute minimum of

These combat knives the author likes include the fully toothed Amphibious S.O.F., an all-out survival dagger and the survival Dirk. It's all personal, he says, and he says any will do.

5 inches. Experience has shown that a blade longer than 8 inches is unwieldy. I am most comfortable with a 7-inch blade, but size must be factored with considerations of weight and balance.

Every True Son of the Macho Masculine Mystique believes himself to be incredibly strong and invincible, but continuous or serial operations eventually take their toll. An exhausted or enervated soldier is not alert and cannot react or perform as well as one who is rested and ready. The objective is not to test endurance, but to accomplish the mission. A too heavy knife, no matter how irresistible or attractive, will eventually become a burden. A well-designed product considers the influence of weight on the entire system during miserable and inclement operation. Weight reduction may focus on excess blade size, improper blade or hilt, materials, inappropriate haft material or improper sheath material. It is important to achieve the best possible combination of size and materials in appropriate weights without any loss of potential performance, because a knife that's unreliable isn't worth the bother of carrying.

Mixed among the mysterious and arcane lore of true knife perfection is the issue of proper balance. It is only significant if the combat knife is drastically distorted, which probably indicates poor design or construction. Pommels were added to edged weapons to counter-balance them, but have since been refined into other functions. Even throwing knives and combat knives are not suitably tempered for such abuse, and don't require perfect mid-point tuning, since one finds the proper balance point for the distance and throwing style employed. The basic rule is that utility knives are blade-heavy to improve their working efficiency, and combat knives are hilt-heavy to keep them stable in the hand. If everything else about the knife and its sheath are acceptable, then the balance will be serviceable, if not absolutely perfect.

The requirement for knife security is basic common sense—if it isn't there when you need it, then it isn't worth owning. The retention method must not interfere with the need for one-hand access, and it must not be too complicated. I always test the retainer by pulling on the knife to attempt to draw it without releasing the keeper system. Keepers that allow the knife to shift out of position or to rattle about are as useless as those that release their contents without unlocking. A soldier may have to travel through hostile terrain without the opportunity to protect his gear and accessory weapons, so they must stay put without assistance. The security retention system must not compromise tactical noise-discipline, so silence is a very important corollary.

The most obvious thing about any combat knife is its finish, and too many people judge a knife's potential by its appearance. As with any type of camouflage, the best is that which blends with one's immediate surroundings. And the appearance of a knife is easily changed. A non-reflective finish is a nice feature, but it's not essential. Some experts recommend a polished treatment because the reflection will be of psychological benefit in the forthcoming fight, but that is debatable. A good polish helps to maintain the weapon in good working order, especially if exposed to corrosives, but one can always apply a permanent or temporary coating to reduce unwanted flash. As with the scabbard, a knife's finish is not a sufficient cause for acquisition or avoidance.

The combat knife can be a combination system. The new M-9 bayonet is a field utility knife as well as a wire-cutter, and it will serve when nothing better is available. The purist may want to add a hone or accessory folder to the sheath of his precious combat knife, so as to preserve it. A combat swimmer or parachutist will want to tether the knife with a lanyard to prevent its loss during air or water use. Accessory items, like survival or first-aid, or supplemental tools, like pliers or saws, may be desired by some specialists. Hollow-handle and slotted-tang knives accommodate the need for internal stowage of small items, but these knives are usually more expensive models. It should be remembered that options are not essential, and that the gear pouches or backpack of the combatant may serve as well as a modified total knife system.

Another military maxim states that combat consists of periods of boring routine interrupted by moments of frightful horror and chaotic terror. Many troops actually work harder and longer in training than in genuine combat. War-game scenarios are not always strategically valid, but the simulated tactical application of weapons and gear can teach valuable lessons. There is time in the field to work on weapons, equipment and positions, so there's time to clean and sharpen the combat knife, to use it as a field aid, and to cook with it. If the knife doesn't perform well in training, then it won't perform any better in authentic reality. It doesn't matter who designed it or who endorsed it, because they aren't using it in the precise manner you are employing it. You are the sole arbitrator of this decision, and few things are more personal than the selection of a combat knife. ●

John Russell's ROMANTIC ADVENTURE

by RALPH MROZ

THE GREEN RIVER knives of J. Russell & Company have a legendary reputation as the knives of the Western expansion and settlement during the 1840s through the 1870s. What is not so well known, however, is the fact that J. Russell & Company was founded on little more than a dream and was the first American cutlery company of any merit.

As a young man in his early thirties, John Russell of Greenfield, Massachusetts, made his fortune in Georgia during the great cotton expansion of 1824 to 1828. He married and returned to Greenfield in 1832. Being of a restless and enterprising nature, he decided, at age thirty-seven, to enter a new business, one in which he had no experience whatsoever. Spurred by nothing but romantic descriptions of cutlery making in Sheffield, England, he

In the 1830s, creating a cutlery factory like this in the United States was an incredibly romantic idea—but it worked.

bought land on the Green River in Deerfield, Massachusetts, erected a shop, and began the manufacture of chisels. The shop's site is now in present-day Greenfield. Two years later, in 1834, the shop began to produce knives stamped with the trademark *Green River Works*.

From the beginning, this factory was different. Russell invested in then-innovative trip-hammers and a steam engine, the power of which was distributed by leather belts throughout the building. The factory's forges, quenching vats, furnaces and work stations were laid out in a manner which anticipated the assembly-line efficiency of Henry Ford in the next century. Hampered by a lack of skilled cutlery craftsmen, Russell compensated by investing in the best possible steel. The fact that he put the same attention and craftsmanship into such basic articles as chisels, and later ax heads, astonished most people of the day and earned the J. Russell & Company a very favorable reputation that carried over to its knives.

In the early 1800s, all quality cutlery in America came from the Sheffield area in England. At that time, even the cutlers of Solingen in Germany considered Sheffield knives as the world's best. The English guild system controlled the cutlery industry, and the cutlers', bladesmiths', hafters' and sheathers' guilds protected their membership with strict rules regarding the manufacture of knives. Factories were non-existent, and all work was done in small shops. The work was slow, tedious and expensive, but the knives produced were of very high quality. By contrast, American cutlery up to that point had been of very low quality, and cutlery customers, especially woodsmen and pioneers who depended on a good, reliable knife as an indispensable tool, knew it. The Green River Works had foremost to overcome this prejudice against native-made cutlery if it was to succeed.

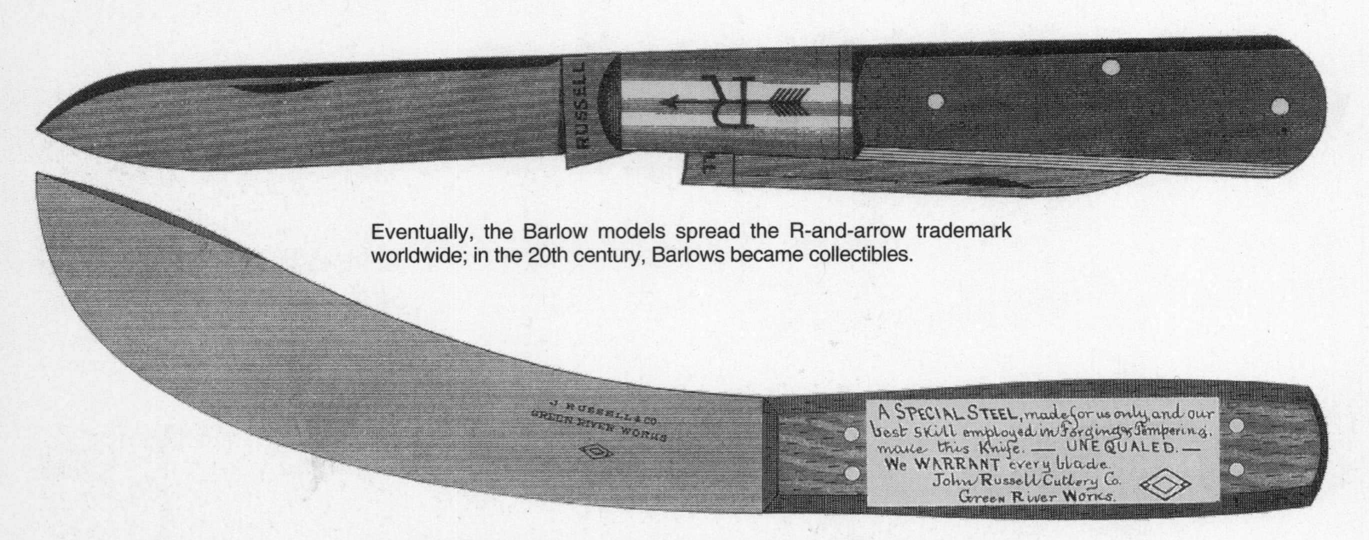

Eventually, the Barlow models spread the R-and-arrow trademark worldwide; in the 20th century, Barlows became collectibles.

Bread and butter in cutlery were high-quality knives like this skinner, the Green River Works label plain to see.

Russell invested tens of thousands of dollars in his quest—a very considerable sum in those days—and overcame floods that ruined his original shop. Consequently, his factory could easily produce fifteen times as many knives as the Sheffield guilds in the same amount of time. The efficiency of the factory, the high quality of its knives, Russell's skill at picking employees and partners, and the international trading and monetary difficulties resulting from the Panic of 1837 gave J. Russell & Company a foothold in the American cutlery market.

And then, there was the Westward Expansion of 1840-1850.

In the early 1840s, J. Russell & Company began to produce an American hunting knife. The hunting knives of England were fancy and lightweight—totally unsuited for the large game, rough country and everyday chores of the Western pioneers. The original Green River Knife was a plain hunting knife with an 8$^3/_4$-inch blade and a simple wood handle. It was often shipped dull so that it could be sharpened by the owner appropriately for the its intended task—scraping skins, for example, called for one-sided sharpening so as not to gouge the hide.

The reputation of the Green River Knife grew rapidly during the 1840s as settlers, mountain men and Indians alike used it as a hunting, camp and utility knife, and as a weapon. In the days before repeating firearms, a man's knife was usually the quickest weapon at hand. Everyone is familiar with the battle cry of the day, "give it to 'em up to the Green River." This use of the knife was colorfully illustrated by John L. Hatcher in his telling of an encounter with a group of Indians who had robbed him: "Sez I, hyar's a gone coon eft they keep my gun, so I follers thar trail an' socks my big knife up to the Green River—first dig!"

The demand for Russell knives only grew as gold was discovered in California. Between 1840 and 1860, some 60,000 Green River Knives were sent to the frontier. Following on the heels of the original Green River hunting knife, J. Russell & Company introduced an abruptly curved skinner and a butcher-style knife that became known as the "Dadley." The success of these knives, and the vindication of John Russell's original dream, is perhaps best indicated by the fact that cutlers from England and Germany now routinely counterfeited them, stamping their own knives with the famous Green River trademark.

The success of J. Russell & Company was built on two factors: The market created by the great Western settlement and the business acumen of John Russell and his partners. This success continued through the Civil War years and beyond. In 1865, for example, the company's 400 employees produced sales of $411,000, and J. Russell & Company was profitable and grew through the rest of the century.

But bull markets eventually end, and mortal men die. Additionally, J. Russell & Company and its successor companies suffered the usual frequent fires, labor troubles and other calamities that plagued early factories. In 1933, after a series of ups and downs, and a move to the neighboring town of Turners Falls, the John Russell Cutlery Company (the successor to J. Russell & Company) was sold to the Harrington Cutlery Company of Southbridge, Massachusetts, some 50 miles to the south. The new company was known as the Russell-Harrington Cutlery Company, and it still produces knives under the Dexter name. Within a few years, all former Russell cutlery operations had moved from the Green River area to Southbridge, and that chapter of American history was closed.

On the banks of the Green River, on the original site of the J. Russell & Company, another company was soon founded. Greenfield Tap and Die (GTD) was for decades the largest manufacturer of taps and dies in the world, and it, like J. Russell & Company before it, was part of the industrial bedrock of the community. GTD provided stable employment for the waves of European immigrants—the author's grandfather was one—who came to the area. But by the 1970s, it, too, had run its course. Eventually bought by big-city conglomerates, GTD operations were moved, downsized and finally closed. Its old, pre-war edifice still stands, a testament to an earlier manufacturing era. The structure has recently been bought by a developer who hopes to use it as incubator space for high-tech spinoffs from the nearby University of Massachusetts.

Another new technology, another talented entrepreneur, another dream.

A new cycle begins.

The ordinary butcher pattern was a Green River staple for 100 years or more.

This is the Dadley-pattern shape, a 19th-century hunting knife and so cataloged by Russell.

Editor's Note

The careful reader will see that there is no claim here that Green River knives dominated the beaver trade, only that when they did arrive on the frontier they were successful.

Postscript

The material for this article was taken from a little-known book, *The History of the John Russell Company*, which was compiled by the American Studies Group at Deerfield Academy, Deerfield, Massachusetts. Printed in 1976 by a local Deerfield publisher, the Channing L. Bete Company, the book is now out of print. ●

AT ONE TIME—actually for a very long time—I was enamored of boot knives. One might say I had an affaire with boot knives. Webster's defined "affaire" as "a romantic or passionate attachment typically of limited duration." A well-known advice columnist has stated that there is no affaire if there is no penetration. OK, this affaire qualifies on both counts, something I prefer not to dwell on, but nevertheless true.

allowed sufficient room for the butt of the knife to oscillate and thereby osculate my leg on a repetitive basis, like with every step, until the beating I was taking was more than the beating from which the presence of the knife was intended to protect me. Yes, I know I've never been beaten up, but just because I'm paranoid doesn't mean they aren't after me!

Well, maybe I could wear different boots and make this concept viable. Lace-up boots would negate the beating, but do nothing to increase accessibility, unless they were significantly shorter. That's cool, I prefer boots about 6 or 7 inches high, anyway. Take a 4-inch, or even 3-inch, boot knife and stick it (with scabbard, of course—I may be

My Affaire with BOOT KNIVES

I have owned knives for at least fifty-seven years that I can recall. I have not yet used any effectively as a weapon, although their potential use as such has been a continuing awareness on my part. Any knife can be used as a weapon, and I suspect one would be hard put to find a type of knife that has never been so used (or misused, depending on your point of view).

Most of my early knives were pocketknives, and up until about a decade ago, that pretty much defined the limits on their use as weapons. At some point, I became smitten with boot knives. I think there are few pieces of cutlery prettier than a well-executed boot knife. I'm not going to get embroiled in defining boot knives; better men than I have failed. If you are reading this book, you probably have a picture, definition or image that "boot knife" conjures up for you, and that will do nicely for our purposes, thank you very much.

For me, a boot knife is double-edged, concealable, and probably fairly flat (to aid in its concealability, of course, and no, I don't think that's redundant.) Many are furnished with sheaths that allow clipping or otherwise affixing the knife to one's boot (*Voila!*). I could never get this to work. Oh, the clip worked alright (well, most of the time), but I never found a manner that was both comfortable and accessible.

In Western boots or Wellingtons, the daggone thing was too far up my leg to be readily accessed if pants were worn outside my boots. If you tuck your pants inside your boots, the whole purpose is obviated, and besides people think you are going square dancing. I would have speedier access by dropping my drawers than by hiking up one leg thereof. Also, I found that my state of muscular development, or rather the lack thereof, led to a loose fit of the boot shaft on my calf. The resulting space

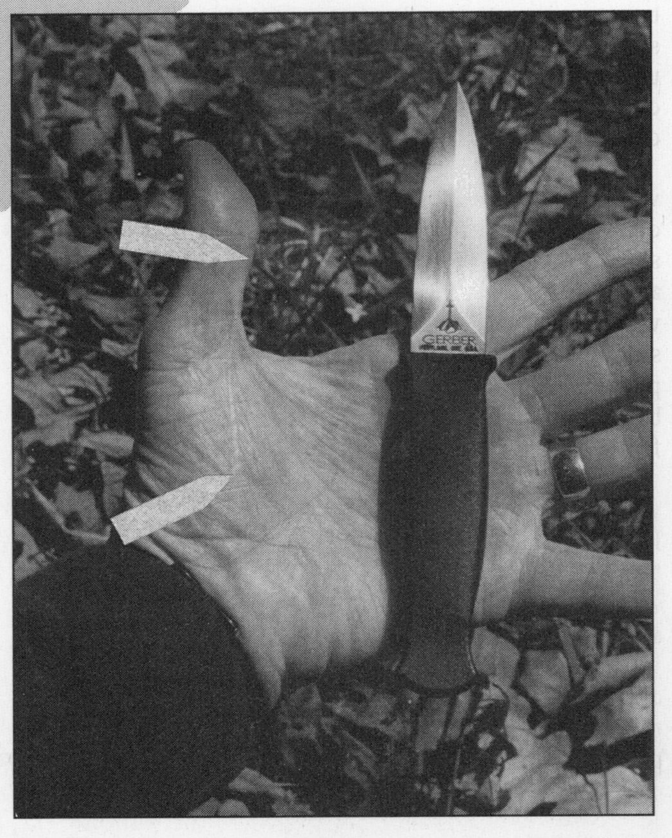

After fifteen years, the scar has faded, but the memory remains vivid—the affaire is over.

by JACK COLLINS

(Left) I flirt a lot with these nowadays: apart from the boot knife (far left); Benchmade models AFCK, mini-AFCK, Emerson 975 and Emerson 970; and Spyderco models designed by Howard Viele and Wayne Goddard; and the Spyderco Endura.

paranoid but I'm not masochistic) into a 6-inch boot, lace it up and go for a walk. I guarantee that within 50 yards people will think you're trying to imitate Grandpa McCoy.

I've owned knives made by a number of noted makers and a number of factory boot knives, and I've enjoyed looking at and petting them all, but none served as desired. At least, not for me. I admit it was my shortcomings that led to failure.

The next step was to seek another location on my person where (what the heck do you call a boot knife when you don't wear it in your boot?) the knife could be worn unobtrusively. Why sure, inside the waistband of my trousers. First, be well aware that you must remove the sheath in order to reinsert the knife once drawn, unless....no, there's no unless. Second, be sure that you can withdraw the knife without incident. What is an incident? Let me tell you...

About fifteen years ago, before I decided that walking was just as good as running, only slower, I habitually ran on a path through a wooded area near my home. Although surrounded by houses, the path was relatively deserted, and so I carried a Gerber boot (?) knife tucked into the waist of my running shorts at the small of my back. The shorts were tight enough that I was not abused by this position. A large dog, a great big dog, a *huge* dog, often barked at me, but he was secured behind a chain-link fence...usually.

On the day in question, there were no barks. All I heard were his toenails scratching on the path behind me, rapidly approaching. I was prepared. Knowing that the clip on the sheath did not hold very well on the nylon of my shorts, I had practiced jerking on the handle of the knife, slapping the assembly into my left hand, and withdrawing the knife, leaving the sheath in my left hand. Don't get ahead of me here. I turned on the dog, implementing the practiced maneuver. This time, however, upon slapping the knife and sheath into my hand, it was painfully obvious the sheath had separated from the knife somewhere between my shorts and my thumb. The resulting cut required thirteen stitches to close, and the scar serves today to remind me why I don't like boot knives anymore. The dog? He took off like he was shot, figuring, I guess, that he had just encountered the original cast of *Edward Scissorhands*, or someone so stupid that biting was not that challenging. Everyone I know agrees with the dog. A witty friend (at least half-witty) suggested that I not attempt to use a chainsaw as I might cut off my own leg and expect the tree to fall down. Ha, ha, ha.

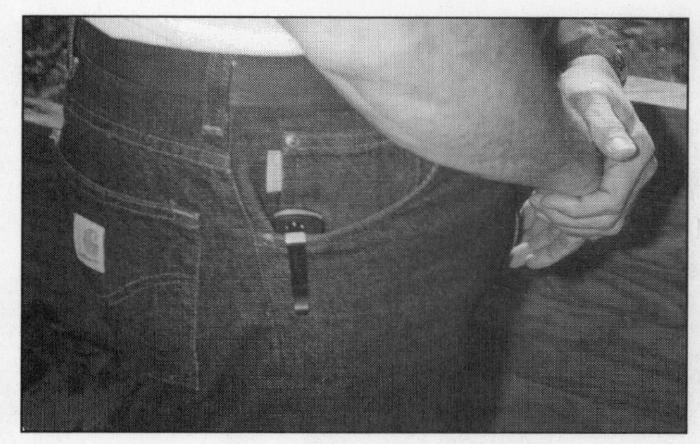
(Below) The Emerson-designed CQC7, like most such, is very unobtrusive in a jeans' pocket, but handy for any use.

These days, I find my need for a knife that *might* be pressed into defensive use very well served by products from Spyderco and/or Benchmade. Cold Steel also provides a number of folders designed with similar intent. I have grown particularly fond of the Benchmade AFCK and the CQC7, made by the same firm and designed by Ernest Emerson. Other favorites are the Spyderco Endura and the Howard Viele-designed folder, also by Spyderco.

All of the above are equipped with pocket clips and open with one hand. They are very comfortable and unobtrusive in the pocket of my everyday jeans, and are extremely versatile as general utility knives. Should the need arise for a fixed-blade knife in a covert situation, I have a Pesh Kabz with multi-carry system from Bud Neely that is a dandy piece of work, absolutely secure in its carry modes, which are several. I don't miss boot knives at all. Maybe I miss the affaire. ●

NEAR HERE, LAST year, we presented some thoughts on sharpness, most centered on the virtues of the convexly ground knife edge. This effort is not about that, but about the other kinds of edges and the kind of cutting most knives provide.

In plain truth, most knives with any pretension toward quality can be sharp enough; some of these can be keen indeed. In large measure, sharpness of such blades in use is a function of the user's cutting skills and of his (her?) diligence in restoring the edge regularly.

I knew a distinct gent of the old school, a bit rural in background. He wore 'em out, lost 'em, busted 'em, but he never complained about the edges of his knives. K.B. Albritton bought his pocketknives, mostly in hardware stores, by making a clerk get 'em all out and open, and then K.B. picked the sharpest one.

"If they can't make it sharp, why should I even try?" were his sentiments.

And out in his farm's toolshed there was a bench for sharpening stuff—boxes of files for hoes, a rack of scythe stones, a two-sided oilstone mounted on the bench. K.B. didn't have a whole lot of use for dull tools. And a farmhand who'd work with a dull hoe could go work elsewhere, too. K.B. sent him there.

If his own personal knife was sharp the first time he tried it, then K.B. would keep it that way. He did spend a certain amount of time with a whetrock, which he expected.

That's half of most folks' sharpness problem these days. Even farmers seem to find it hard to find five minutes every couple weeks. Nobody takes the time. The other half of the problem is knowing what to do with a whetrock or a moonstick or an oilstone or crocksticks or a diamond hone—all those grinder things. Just what you are supposed to wind up with eludes an awful lot of us, apparently. That's because we're not looking, I reckon.

A serviceable edge is created when two slanting plane (flat) surfaces meet at the center of the blade—that's the center of the thin part, of course. This is the simple theory of it all, but maybe we should define some of those terms.

Serviceable means, at a minimum, the edge will cut a business card in half easily, slice a tomato without tearing it, cut meat into chunks cleanly, whittle or point up a stick smoothly, sharpen a pencil without breaking the lead too many times. Such an edge, and therefore its knife, is serviceable.

Slanting means that from wherever this edge starts, its two sides are converging.

Plane means flat, unrumpled, smooth, not wavy. A good one is shiny, and you can see it as a clean, bright streak along the blade when you tilt it to the light.

Thinking About The SERVICEABLE

Meet means come together, intersect, join. Where the planes don't meet, there's a flat spot; when they meet off center, there's a wiggle. So they have to meet correctly.

Center means middle, and it means middle all the way from the handle to the point. You can work with an off-center edge, or even a crooked one, but only if you know the knife.

So that's pretty simple, right? We got this solid flat object that can't run away and we got these other solid grinder things and we have opposable thumbs, barring accident, and most of us will test out with higher IQs than even the above-average knife. So why do so many put up with unserviceable edges?

I believe it's because some of us don't know what to look for and the rest don't even look. It's all there, plain to see. In nearly infinite variety, those intersecting surfaces are there.

You just use your grinder things, whatever sharpening device you have, to restore those surfaces—or change them some if that suits you better. You look to see what you got and then fix it. And then stop.

This reporter has been one of those people with a "knack" for sharpening. I could and can make the average knife sharper than the average bear can.

The immaculate blade of a hollow-ground J.D. Clay skinner shows the serviceable edge as a black line here. (Long photo)

EDGE

by KEN WARNER

This premium Schatt & Morgan stock knife, quite sharp, shows its edge as a bright line.

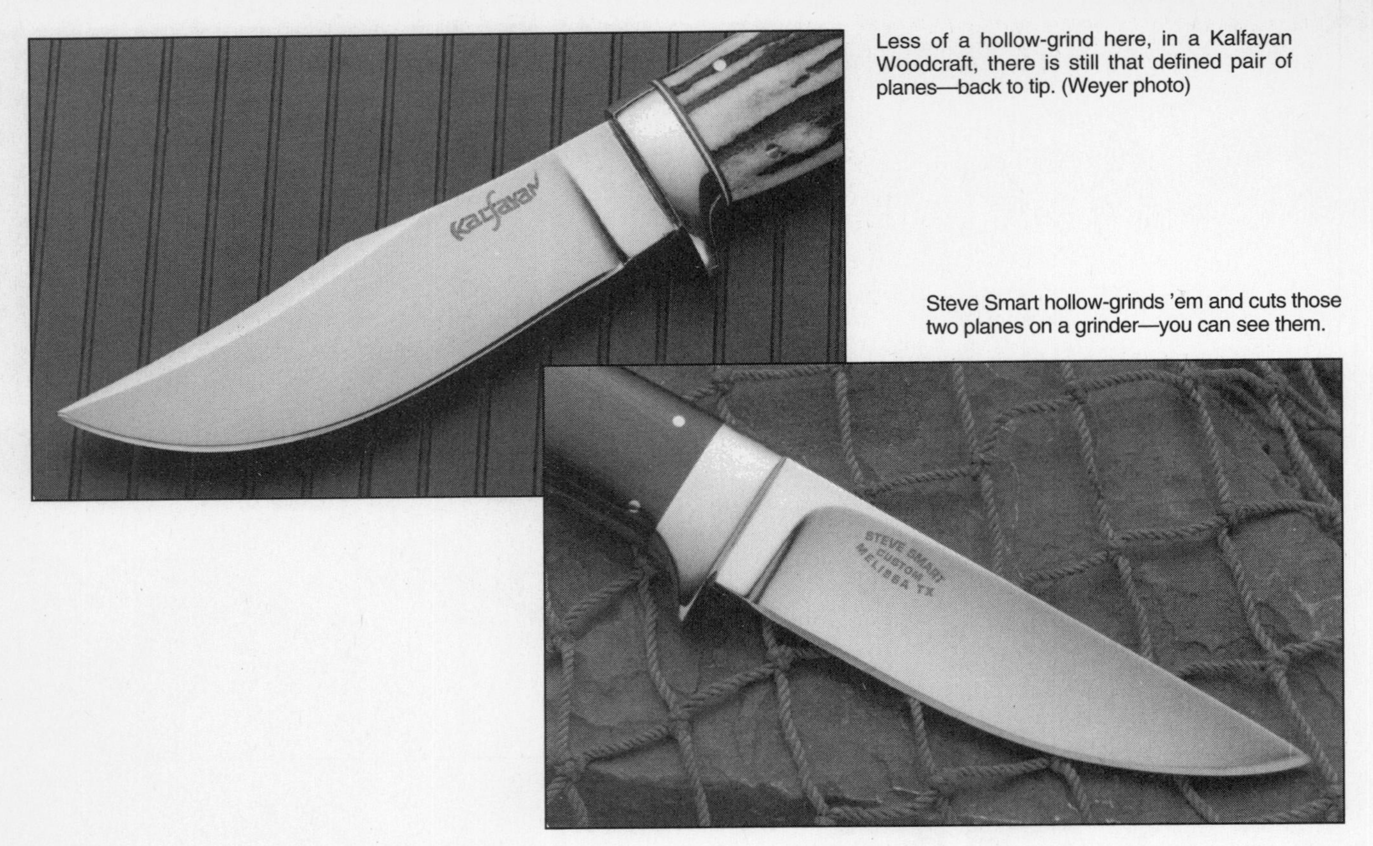

Less of a hollow-grind here, in a Kalfayan Woodcraft, there is still that defined pair of planes—back to tip. (Weyer photo)

Steve Smart hollow-grinds 'em and cuts those two planes on a grinder—you can see them.

Back some years, some of the highest priced gun writing talent we have would get quite peeved when I hit a knife a couple of licks and pronounced it sharp—and it was.

In most cases, we were on a hunt and it was the guy's personal knife and he had followed the directions and spent a lot of time and still had a dull knife. In almost every such instance, the guy had gone past the sharp part. Me, I looked first and just refined whatever pair of intersecting planes he had. And I quit as soon as they were aligned.

It worked like magic. Made 'em mad, but they stood for it.

It is *not* magic. Anybody's set of directions for sharpening will work if you follow them. All that stuff about angles and such is OK, I guess. You don't have to study sharpology very long to figure out that a "thin" edge, one where the plane surfaces meet at an acute angle, will slice stuff easier—while it lasts—than a beefier edge. You do have to study yourself and your knife to figure which suits you best.

There's a lot more, of course. And most of it is called geometry. In the average dictionary, *geometry* is defined as a branch of mathematics that deals with the measurement, properties and relationships of points, lines, angles, surfaces and solids. Every knife has almost all of that, and how those are arranged makes a knife serviceable or not.

In broad terms, the general geometry of a knife should be employed to present the point and the edge to their work in the most efficient way. It doesn't matter whether the knife is opening clams or lambs, slicing beets or beef,

In the last few decades, this old-time whetrock probably didn't accomplish much, but think of the miles of sharp before that.

Over on the "just in case" side, the same edge works, as on this Tom Watson Model UF4 blade.

Here we get a little more complex—there are two planes on each side to form the edge—in a John W. Walker hunter.

chopping brush or heads, the whole idea is the shape makes it possible to let the edge do its work. And that's why there are so many patterns—everybody has an opinion.

However, we're supposed to be talking *edge* here, the *serviceable edge*, in fact. And we will.

We have to pay attention to the shape of a blade in three dimensions if we want a serviceable edge on it. A pretty thick blade, for instance, generally has to be thinned toward the edge, and that will make a wide cutting bevel. Thin blades can be beveled quicker and still work out.

So what's thick and what's thin? A vernier caliper tells me thick serviceable blades are .10- to .15-inch, up 5/16-inch or so from the actual edge. A thin blade will be .060- to .080-inch, at the same place. That's the place to start your thinking about edge bevels.

There's more.

For instance, the smoother and shinier the edge—and the blade near the edge—the better it cuts. A sandblasted blade, for instance, will not cut with the same ease the same blade could manage if it were bright and well-polished. Same goes for blueing, hard-coating, whatever. Smooth is best.

The face—the *plane*, we have called it—of the edge is big enough to see. If it is roughly ground—120 grit—you can see that roughness. Get a smooth one. Or smooth the roughness yourself—at the same angle on the same plane.

A great many knifemakers do just that. They shape their knives to look good, in patterns that are popular, and take the edge geometry to slimness—a nice, straight thin blade, so far as the 3/8-inch above the edge is concerned, and then they break a clean, shiny bevel on each side to

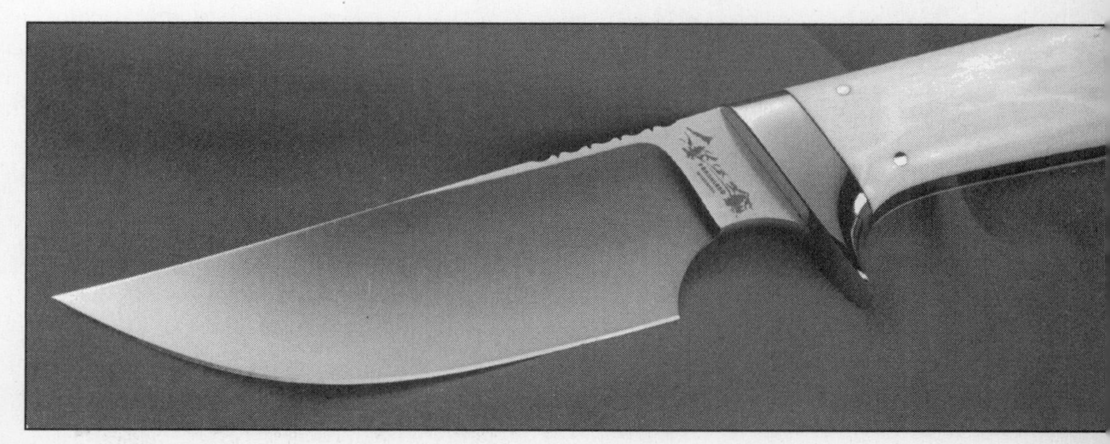

On this Frankland knife is some very handsome hollow-grinding, delicately thinned out in symmetry—then the two sides of the edges are cut. (Mumford photo)

Stay Sharp in Your Old Age

by JOE RYCHETNIK

WORKING ON MY 70th year has been a revelation to me. I knew sex was history; then staying up all night sipping good Scotch single malts with old hunting and fishing buddies was ruled out by the medics; then one of the things I found most relaxing over the years—sharpening our family knives—was coming to an end. The anthropologists say arthritis has been a plague of man since he crawled into a cave for shelter, and my doctors say it's my turn.

First, I found myself waking up in the middle of the night with severe pain in my right arm and especially my hand. My right hand is my shooting hand, and my right arm my shooting arm, and my great pleasure is to spend hours out on the range doing everything from benchrest shooting to rolling Bud cans with my old Colt Woodsman. But my hand could not hold anything tightly or push hard as it once did. So, along with shooting, even with super pain killers, the once-strong right hand can't cope with the usual chores, like sharpening the family knives.

These eyes have seen dull knives come and sharp knives go for a long time.

This short Randall shows the same serviceable edge plane. In the old days at Randall, producing that bright line was called "honing."

meet in the center and create a serviceable edge, very likely sharp, and very likely to be easy to maintain.

This is the edge, for instance, you see on the big blade of almost any Victorinox Swiss Army Knife, when it comes out of the box. It is the edge once seen on all U.S.-made standard-make folders out of the box, and still to be found there pretty often. It is the edge K.B. Albritton looked for on the hardware store counter when he bought a new knife.

This is the edge you see on quality kitchen cutlery—food preparation knives. (Which is not the same as the edge on professional kitchen and butcher's cutlery.) It is how hollow-ground and flat-ground knives are sharpened—the knife's blade is brought to thinness along the edge and then beveled to make the two planes meet.

Uncharitable persons, meaning those who buff wedge and convex edges onto *their* blades, say these—the standard, serviceable edges—are "dubbed off." It ain't fair to say that, indeed, it's disparaging. Of the dozen or so dictionary definitions for *dub* and *dubbing* and *dubbed*, exactly none apply, except very negatively. That is, the poorly done buffed edge is as "dubbed" as a poorly done ground edge.

The width of that "streak of light" you can see when you tilt the blade varies not only with the thickness of the blade it's on. In blades of the same thickness, it varies according to the angle we mentioned, so it's wider when a *very* acute angle is reached. Conversely, in a hard use chopping blade, the visible edge bevel should be narrow-

I always used to set up my knife laboratory on the butcher block table. I'd haul out and clamp down a foot-long Soft Arkansas stone I bought from A.G. Russell twenty-five years ago, set up a crock stick set, and get out the Gerber and the Dick MultiCut steel. I generally put a scratch pad in the corner because I gave every sharpened knife the paper curl test. My No. 4 wife found some curly hair on one of her French knives once, so I quit the arm hair test a while back.

My old friend Craig Claiborne, the *New York Times* cooking authority, has had his picture taken standing by one of those fancy Chef's Choice sharpeners, and I trust his judgment, so I gave the Edge Craft people a call and found that the electric sharpeners started at about $200. But they offered me an alternative that didn't need an electric plug—their Chef's Choice Manual Diamond Hone No. 45.

This neat kitchen gadget is solidly built and will float if you happen to drop it in the lake. Here in the Mojave Desert, the only liquid near my knives is a kitchen sink. No worry there. This heavy-duty plastic device weighs all of 4 ounces.

It has six tiny rubber feet, which means no slippage while sharpening. All you have to do is place the No. 450 on the table or bench, place your left hand on the handle, which secures down the sharpener, and run your dull knife back and forth twenty to twenty-five times in the left slot, and about a dozen times in the right slot. Not a great deal of pressure is needed. The roller guides help reform the blade edge angles in the first slot and the second slot grind puts a very sharp and fine edge on the knife at a somewhat more acute angle. Kitchen knives are easy to sharpen, hunting knives, because of their thickness, take a bit more effort, but in the end, a sharp blade from tip to hilt is the final product. They are so sharp I have stopped whacking them on my Gerber and seldom on the Dick MultiCut steel. Each knife is tested on the scratch pad, wiped with a towel, and stored safely. I still put a box of Band-Aids out when I am finished as the Lady of the House tends to forget and often nicks herself.

I am back in the sharpening business. I will get another one of these for deer camp as those guys seldom have a sharp knife on Opening Day. I bored a hole in the handle to hang it by. I am back in the sharp business.

er, because that wider angle will put more metal behind the cutting edge and therefore bolster it.

There was once a company named Track Knives. Their knives were sharp but different. The edge bevel—the streak of light—was nearly half an inch tall. It was very wedgy, but it worked like a charm as a meat-cutting hunter's edge. They photograph well, too. The one Ithaca Gun Co. gave me has been on two book covers so far.

The ground edge on a good kitchen knife is normally not too obvious, but it's there. Virtually all food preparation knives are on 1/8- or 3/32-inch stock, then ground from the back of the blade to be quite thin at the edge. Small bevels at the edge of such a blade can produce good cutting qualities.

Sometimes a given blade's geometry puts obstacles in the edge's way. If there's a sort of shoulder above the edge, it can't get very far into the cut. If the blade is just too thick, a guy with a stone is looking at a lot of work to achieve sharpness. The worst thing—and you see one once in a while—is a careless grind, one that is thick here, thin there.

Given an edge like we have described, any blade will cut pretty well at least once. If it is soft metal—we once used copper, you know—it won't stay keen. If it is hard, the edge, once you get it, should last a good while. There are other factors, but that's metallurgy. Geometry, remember, is what makes an edge.

Mostly, though, any blade with flat sides that taper to the edge can be made sharp. It just takes, for serviceability, those two flat planes that meet at the center. ●

This is a high-ticket heavy-duty titanium blade—configured to serviceable sharpness by the pair of intersecting planes at the edge.

A Jones knife with improved handle, Sigman sheath, and Gerber Multiplier is the answer for the writer.

by JACK COLLINS

IN SEARCH OF OUR HOLY GRAIL

THE CRUSADES OF the Middle Ages were, at least ostensibly, fought to recover the Holy Grail, that being the chalice used by Jesus Christ to serve the Last Supper to the twelve disciples. As such, it was considered to be the symbol of perfection and the most significant icon of the Christian faith. The crusaders were not successful in their quest, although many secondary motives were undoubtedly served.

Similar searches have been undertaken for equally elusive objects over the intervening years. A case in point is the search for the fabled "all-around rifle." This has often taken the form of arguments as to whether or not said ideal arm has already been discovered by one or more of the participants, together with attempts to convince dissidents of the validity of the arguments. Few subjects seem to stir men's souls around a campfire or in a hunting cabin as readily as this eternal question.

For the past three years, John Yankoviak and I have been engaged in a similar, if not equally futile, search for a Holy Grail of knives, to wit: The Only Knife You'll Ever Need. In part, this venture was triggered by the realization that the mountain men of yore set off into the then-uncharted wilderness with a rifle, an axe and a knife. And with these implements, and their considerable wits, those men lived nearly solitary, but apparently satisfying, lives.

What kind of knife would be desirable for such use? John and I have discussed this subject so often and so earnestly we have just about beaten it to death. We have, however, arrived at some conclusions that I believe merit consideration.

Now, our criteria that we have developed/recognized are very subjective. I invite you to substitute your own ideas and follow wherever that takes you. You will not be bored, rest assured, however frustrated.

The knife we envision is one that can be used for a great variety of purposes with a high degree of efficacy. It is not, by any stretch of the imagination, the absolute best tool for each job it may be called upon to undertake. It is simply a knife with which one could perform most, if not all, of the chores one would normally assign a knife.

For me, it is not etched, engraved or scrimshawed. A knife with beauty of line and execution does not require decoration to make it beautiful. I appreciate the time and talent required to execute such art on a knife, and if that is your taste and your pocketbook can handle it, then that is what you should have. But not me.

These are the functions that must be performed at least acceptably in order meet our demands for an all-around knife:

Field dressing—gutting and skinning a deer or other big game animal. We both hunt, so this naturally comes high on the list.

Kitchen or camp chores—slicing an onion, a loaf of bread, spreading peanut butter, cutting a pizza, butchering, etc.

Clearing light brush—cutting a field of fire around one's deer stand, trimming twigs up to and including small branches the size of one's thumb around camp, and such.

Minor surgery—though often defined as that performed on someone else, in this case, we mean splinter removal, blister opening, trimming broken fingernails.

Defense—no knife is a primary defensive weapon, but a good one sure beats the heck out of a loud scream or a weak whimper.

In addition to being suitable for these uses, there are several characteristics any ideal knife must have:

Convenience—it can be carried safely on the person in such a manner as to be readily available for use under any atmospheric conditions.

Durability—able to withstand serious, heavy-duty use bordering on abuse.

Good knife features—edge holding, ease of sharpening, minimum care requirements.

Good ergonomics—feels good in the hand, usable with one hand in the dark or other unseen places, and such.

Intangibles—pride of ownership, eye appeal and other long-lasting intangibles.

The knife that embodies these characteristics and enables the user to perform the listed functions will have a drop- or spear-point, flat- or convex-ground blade of suitable stain-resistant steel (154CM, ATS-34, 440C, etc.) with sufficient heft to allow chopping small limbs; it will be single-edged and well-balanced; the Micarta handle will have a thong hole; it will have a Kydex sheath and probably go under 6 inches for the blade.

Single-edged drop- or spear-point blades allow the user to "choke up" on the blade if required for delicate work such as caping or picking out splinters. Stain-resistant steel simply requires less care over long periods than that which is not stainless. We are not talking about discoloration here, folks. We are talking about edge retention when one cannot or does not clean and oil the knife after each use.

In such an environment, corrosion may well ruin the edge long before use has taken its toll. Well balanced is "in the hand of the beholder," if I may mangle a quote. Micarta handle slabs are merely the most durable slabs in common use on full-tang knives, and Micarta is also available in suitable form for hidden tangs. G10 may serve as well, but is mostly seen on folders and is said to become slippery when wet. I personally love stag handles, but their use must be foregone on the basis of durability.

The thong hole, an often-overlooked feature, and a thong are absolutely essential when using a knife over water, on extremely steep terrain, or when in a tree stand. Additionally, they also enable the user to employ a more efficient chopping stroke by allowing only enough handle to be retained in the hand to guide the blade, thereby giving the effect of a longer blade.

Flat or convex grinds result in less fragile edges for the chopping function than do hollow-ground blades. Kydex

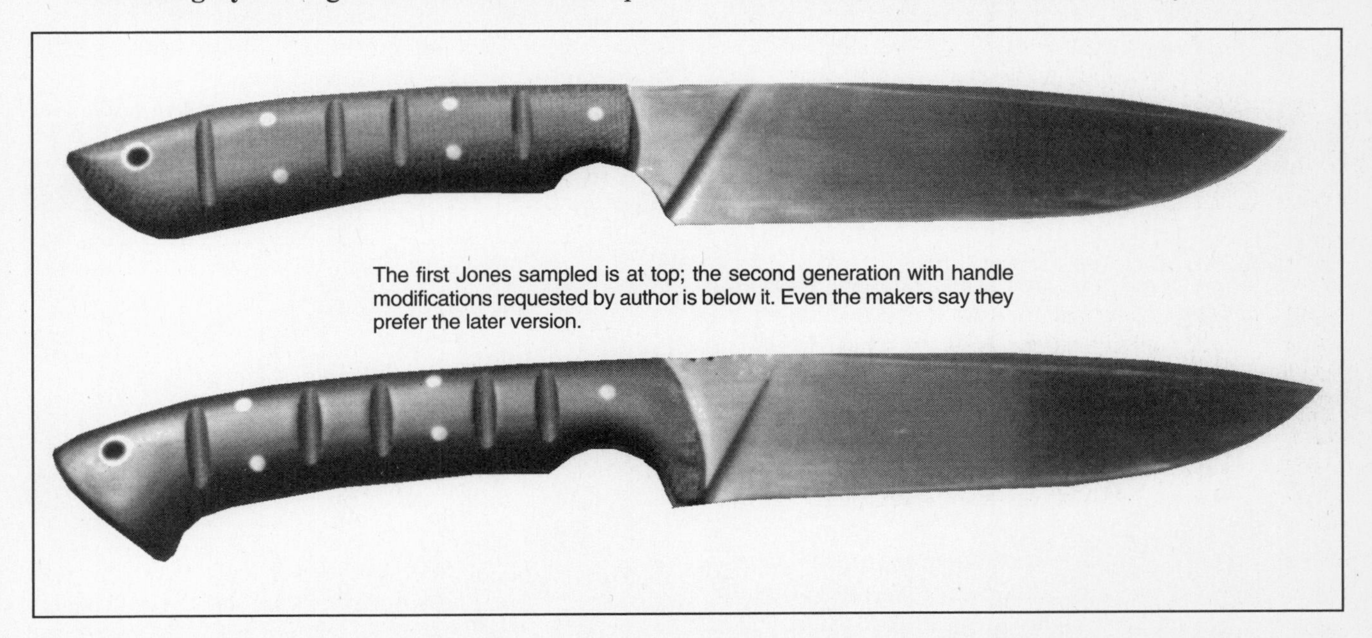

The first Jones sampled is at top; the second generation with handle modifications requested by author is below it. Even the makers say they prefer the later version.

SOME WE TRIED

WE CONCOCTED A list of candidate knives, but money reared its ugly head—it's ugly when you don't have enough—and prevented us from examining each blade on the list. Let's look, anyway, at the ones we did. What follows is a highly opinionated critique of some excellent knives. All are top drawer.

Chris Reeve Shadow IV—An outstanding knife, perhaps the sharpest delivered blade we examined. While talking to John on the phone, I absentmindedly shaved most of the hair from one leg before I realized what I was doing. One would not be handicapped by this or any other Reeve knife, except for two factors: One, the handle is necessarily round in order to accommodate the one-piece design with the hollow handle, and this removes or reduces the tactile knowledge of blade position when in the dark or wrist deep in blood; two, dip this knurled handle in blood and one is faced with a severe cleaning problem, probably requiring hot water and a brush. The fact that this knife is not made from a rust-resistant steel compounds the problem. A superior choice if big game hunting is not high on your list.

Emerson SPECWAR by Timberline—This is perhaps the most beautiful knife I have ever owned. The fit and finish are far, far above factory knives in general and surpass most custom makers. The first few days I owned it, I could only fondle and admire it ("fondling" John calls it.) When trying to use it, two "faults" became apparent. First and foremost, this is a left-handed knife. The bevel grind is on the wrong side for a right-handed person. Try to whittle a stick or chop a sapling and you'll see that the blade grind is perfect for slipping off unless held at an uncomfortable angle. Second, while the sheath is a masterpiece of engineering, *for our purposes* it is one of the most over-engineered pieces of outdoor equipment I have encountered. If one intends to jump from airplanes in flight, bungee jump, swim long distances underwater or other such violent activities, this sheath may well be just what the doctor ordered, but please notice that none of the above were listed under our heading of

sheaths offer the user (and the knife) more protection under difficult weather conditions. Leather, even in a properly fitted sheath, will go to pot if exposed to extreme wet weather for extended periods. We just have to learn to live with the noise Kydex can make when struck or brushed. Any length beyond 6 inches gets kind of awkward when you have both hands inside a deer and covered with blood.

We looked at a lot of knives—some reported nearby—but I found just two knives, both by custom makers, which will do very nicely, thank you very much. One is a standard model that I spied in KNIVES '96, and one is a slightly modified example of a standard model. The search will continue, but two of the Grails are in hand.

The standard model was made by A.T. Barr and is called his Camp/Combat knife. It has a 5¾-inch flat-ground drop-point blade of ¼-inch ATS-34 with contoured Micarta slabs on a tapered tang. It is a thing of beauty—a field-grade knife with a bead blasted finish; it's what I wanted, and my eye says it's a beauty. There is no choil, and no doubt where the point or edge is when holding it. At 11 ounces (14 with the supplied Kydex sheath), it will definitely chop, and it's sharp enough to shave with. It is a little thick for optimum slicing, but I was able to slice and dice an onion effectively and without mishap, and, boy, will that sucker chop! Come deer season we'll check out some other functions.

The second knife was made by Barry and Philip Jones of Danville, Virginia. I first bought one of their standard models, a JK-16A Fighter. After using it for cleaning

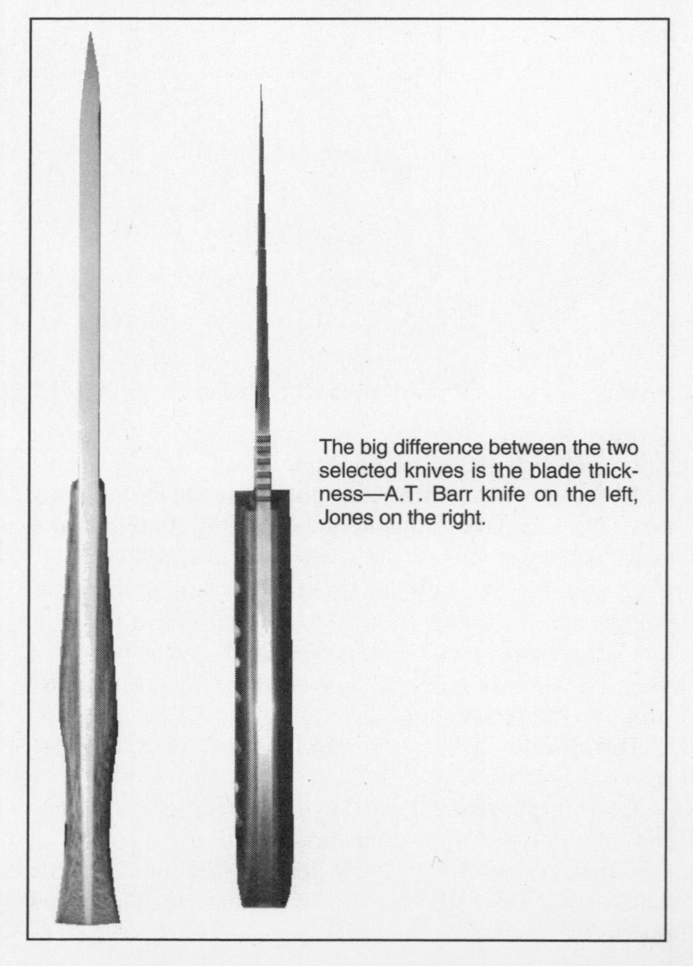

The big difference between the two selected knives is the blade thickness—A.T. Barr knife on the left, Jones on the right.

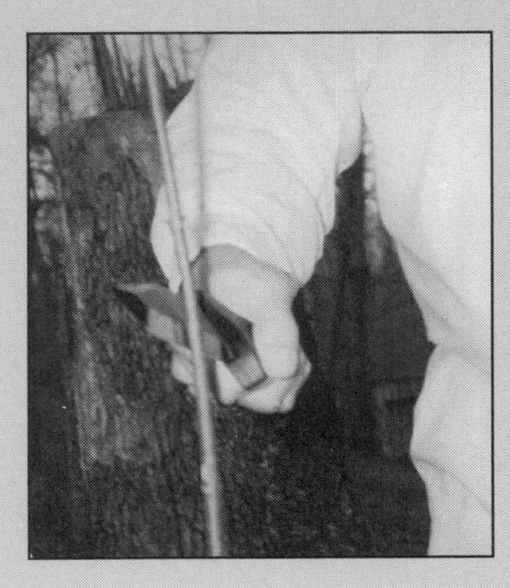

Timerline's SPECWAR will not cut for the right-handed user at this angle, though very sharp.

necessary functions. If you are or might become engaged in such activities, then you must judge the merits of the sheath for yourself. If you are left-handed, there's good news and bad news. The knife will work much better, but the sheath is still right-handed. Tough!

Randall Pathfinder—The very name Randall bespeaks high quality (I have three put away for my grandsons.) I thought this was going to be "the one," until I gutted a deer with it. Everything went fine up to the splitting of the brisket. Maybe you don't do this when cleaning a deer. I do. The choil manifest in almost all Randall knives hung up on the brisket, leading to a very frustrating process. Since I am a deer hunter and this is my practice, scratch the Randall. If you prepare your game differently, or are more adept than I, this could be a great knife for you.

Rafter Apache—I had Kevin Kimsey of Rafter Kustom Knives make me one of his knives, and it is a beauty, with one of the most ergonomic handles I have found on a knife. It is, however, too small for effective chopping. That is my fault, not his, as I specified the knife I wanted. It also came with an excellent Kydex sheath.

Greco Tanto—I bought a large tanto from John Greco at the Blade Show in 1995. It was very good for chopping and heavy work, but really too big for splinter removal or use inside a deer. Again, my fault, but a great knife for the money.

Great knives, all these, but the Grail is an individual quest. I had to keep looking.

Jack Collins

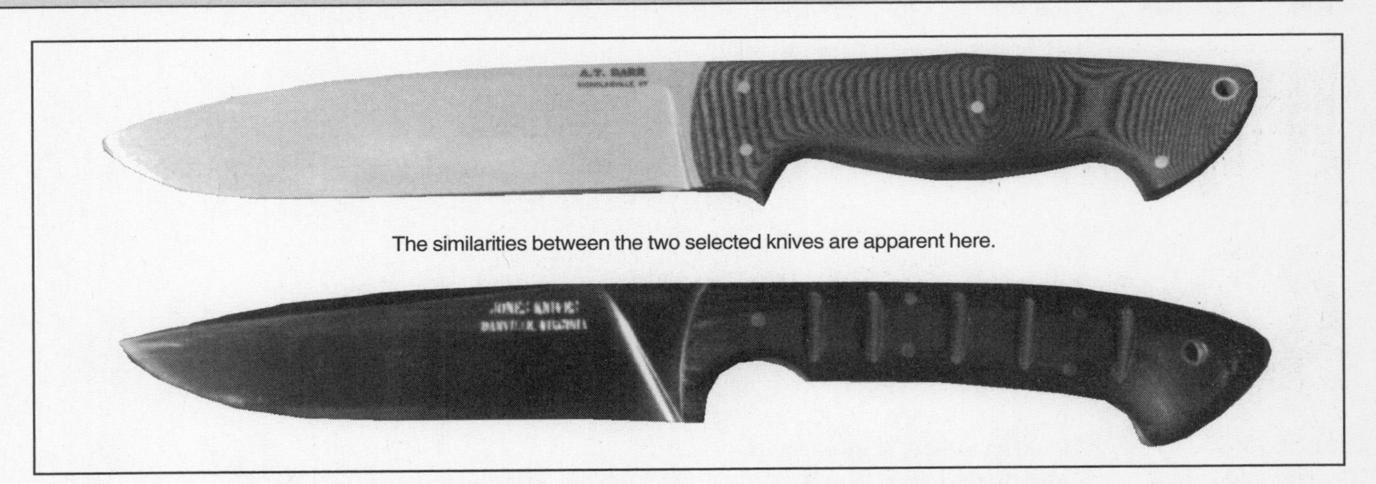

The similarities between the two selected knives are apparent here.

deer, slicing onion, removing splinters (actually my partner, Tom Lovelace, did that) and chopping small branches from a tree-stand location, I knew I had a winner. After one season of use, I had them make a second-generation version with a handle modified to my liking. And it meets my needs perfectly. It has a $5^{1}/_{4}$-inch flat-ground drop-point blade of ATS-34 with a hand-rubbed finish, no choil and a very positive feel concerning the location of the point and edge. It weighs 8 ounces, and the Kydex-lined nylon sheath adds 5 ounces. The sheath has a pocket that neatly accommodates a Gerber Multiplier (as I requested) and that brings the weight of the total package to 21 ounces. The sheath was made by Frank Sigman's S&S Enterprises. I can think of no way to improve upon this knife.

I believe any good knifemaker can make a knife to meet almost any requirements one can postulate. I do think, however, that one is better served in the long run if one finds a maker doing something close to the desired product, then you can go from there. Both these knives have a combat design origin, and weapon use is certainly a viable option with either. Even more important is the general "attitude" of knives designed for combat, or perhaps more correctly, knives designed for use in a combat zone. They just start off being very close to what was wanted.

Even owning the Only Knife You'll Ever Need does not preclude *owning* other knives. So, yes, I bought a new deer knife yesterday, and there's a fishing trip coming, too. ●

by JOE RYCHETNIK

To keep the right stuff handy...

HANG IT ON YOUR BELT

AMONG THE GREAT inventions of history, I assign the belt somewhere in the top ten, along with knives, clubs, and maybe brandy and soda. The belt not only holds the pants up and the clothing tight to the body, but allows the outdoorsman, if no one else, to hang various items of equipment on his body, conveniently handy yet out of the way. While the military is into suspenders holding up the kits of war, the belt can do it all for the rest of us. A stout 2-inch leather belt will support your kit and your pants, and do it comfortably. Narrow belts are painful, and the G.I. web belt can twist when loaded. Experience has shown that it makes good woods sense to have certain items on your person, and belted gear of various types can offer a lot of utility and often safety.

As for combination tools, I mean knives in sheaths that hold two or more items in a handy way. Not an open lineman's tool pouch, but still secure and ready at hand. I have hunted most of my adult life and have gone through many styles and kinds of belt-carried gear, the type having more to do with the kind of hunting I am doing and where. Part of every hunt seems to be an experiment on

The Marine Corps corpsmen's bolo has a heavy blade and will take almost an axe edge, ideal for "bush whacking."

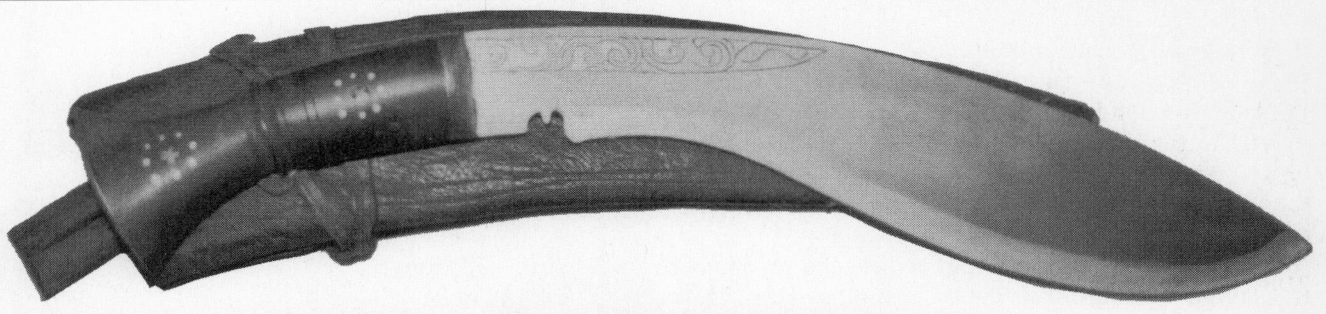

(Opposite page) This leather work was done nearly forty years ago by Brice Safespeed Holster Works, Portland, Oregon. It holds a Herter's skinning blade and an ex-G.I. bush knife—very useful.

(Above) Used for seven weeks in the High Terai of Nepal, this kukri was effective while clearing a campsite. The bull hide sheath allows belt carry.

how something new will work out when taken afield. That sort of test means a lot to my way of thinking about outdoor gear. I once tested sleeping bags for Eddie Bauer when I lived on the edge of the Bering Sea at Nome. They used to set a temperature factor for each bag, and I soon decided those estimates were liberal and very subjective. I finally bought the best and thickest and longest bag they offered, complete with fuzzy inner liner, and found it was life-preserving at -40 degrees F, but not exactly comfortable. We were hunting moose where there were no trees.

One of the knife experiences that came out of that weekend hunt in the Bendeleben foothills of the Seward Peninsula was that a very sharp and stout knife was needed to shave enough butter into the pan to cook anything to eat. The butter had the consistency of glass—we finally ended up melting the whole quarter pound and spent more time chopping up "wooden" bacon. The deep cold—and I have worked at -72 degrees F one time up in Isabell Pass—requires very sharp tools that can take a lot of stress.

When considering combination tools, I like to feel that there won't be anyone else to help, that the situation will be worse than planned, and sharp items may save your life, if not just make a hunt successful. I recall once in Alaska hunting moose in the Chugach Mountains where the entry into the moosy area (we had scouted the region by Super Cub a week before) was through a mile or so of thick alders. From the air, it looked a bit tight going, but from the ground, with Kelty backpack and a rifle, and knowing that what goes up must come down, we found the wall of saplings and inch-thick-or-more alders almost impenetrable. It was a wall of greenery that stopped us cold.

With just hunting knives, we would have been hacking our way through that jungle for a week. I had my trusty Hudson Bay axe and, in the outfit I carried then, a large bush knife made from a WWII Marine jungle knife coupled into a sheath with a Herter skinner. The axe was OK, but what really saved the day was whacking away with the bush knife. We were able to cut a trail open enough for us to get through, and we widened it somewhat when we packed out two moose, which is pure hard work even on smooth open ground.

Later on, I ran into a similar belt of young trees hunting

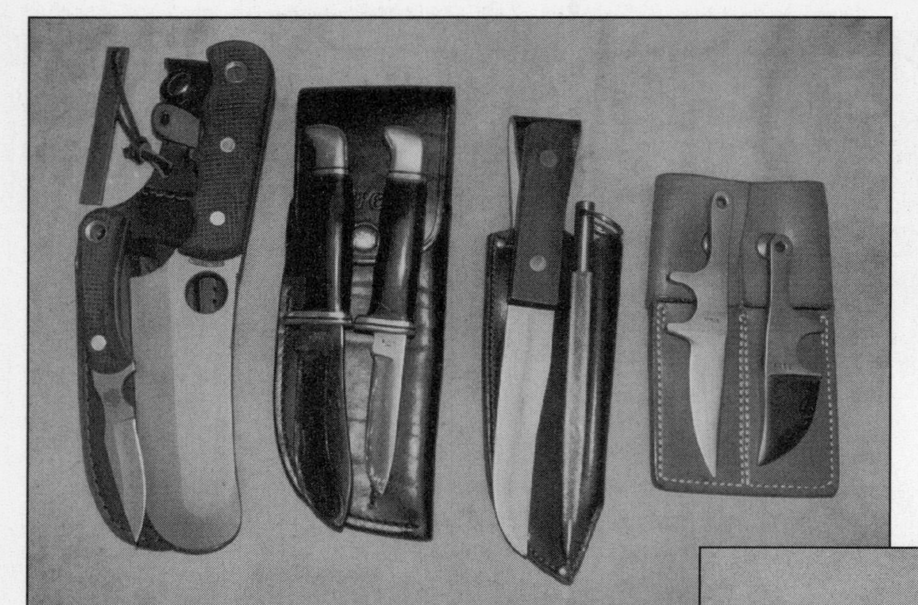

Four combination belt knife outfits, all practical and used by the writer over the years (from left): A Knives of Alaska sheath has a fine caping knife and a cleaver/skinner; Buck Knives once offered this set of hunting knives that were very popular with Alaska big game guides—a caper and a skinner made game work fast and easy; a Sheffield-made combination called The Bushman was very popular in East and South Africa just after WWII—a 7-inch butcher-type knife of medium hardness and a round steel; the last by custom maker G.W. Stone offers the minimum size of dressing tools—a caper and a skinner of 440C—and will slip into the back pocket of jeans.

a hill just west of Fairbanks. We had landed on a dirt strip and saw no sign of game there, but noticed two moose just below the top and had to chop out a path. I was carrying my Napalese kukri, and it worked like a charm. That curved blade with the weight at the pointy end was just the tool to do it. The moose didn't seem to mind that noise.

I had used the kukri in Nepal earlier, and on another trip there, working for a few weeks in the High Terai seeking to do some studies of the endangered Asian rhino, I found that tool useful again. The grass in the High Terai is 17 to 18 feet tall. It towers above some of the elephants we were riding around that jungle. To make room on the ground for a campsite, we cut down this giant grass, and nothing works as well as a kukri. I imagine this large curved knife would find many uses here if outdoorsmen would give it a try.

I have two examples from my Nepal days and was very happy to learn that some U.S. factories provide fine modern kukris that handle even better that the originals. Better steel, for certain, but this is not to condemn the Nepalese and knives. Those jungle knives are both weapons and tools. They must have a mild steel blade that will allow it to be sharpened in the field with a file. The Cold Steel version in their Carbon V steel holds an edge longer than the Nepalese knives, and the handle, of a rubber composition, is much easier to grip. The Nepalese kukris have two smallish knives tucked in the back in separate pouches. These are for eating and preparing food. The traditional rule back in that hill country is that kukri must not be drawn unless it is used to kill—to draw blood in some way. If some utilitarian task must be done, the kukri blade has a "prick" on it to allow the user to draw his own blood to maintain tradition. The Cold Steel kukri is not so-equipped.

[Editor's Note: That's a rational explanation for that cutout design on the traditional kukri. Of course, I never found one with a sharp sticker.—KW]

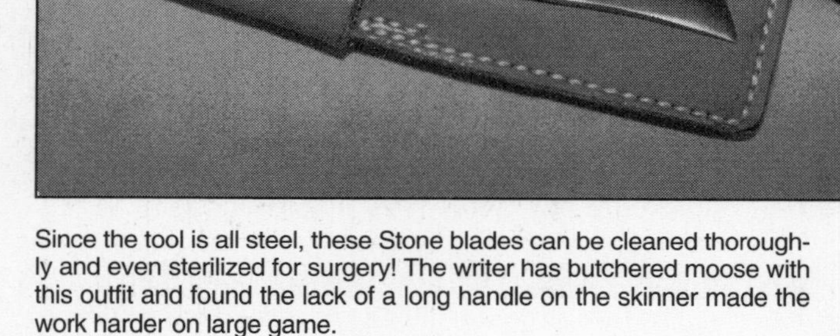

Since the tool is all steel, these Stone blades can be cleaned thoroughly and even sterilized for surgery! The writer has butchered moose with this outfit and found the lack of a long handle on the skinner made the work harder on large game.

I like knife sets that put together a super-sharp caping-style blade—for the fine work of skinning game, particularly if a trophy has been taken and is to be mounted—and a large-size skinner with a nice belly or sweep to the blade. The longer blade area of the big skinner will make the tedious task of removing an acre or so of heavy hide from an elk or moose so much easier. These jobs are really better done with two men. One holding the hide and pulling it away, and the other carefully separating the hide from the meat. One man can do it, but it's no fun!

It always pays to carry a spare knife along. I think more knives are lost falling in the snow, being buried under leaves and pine needles, or being stuck into a tree and then forgotten than any other way. A good sheath is seldom going to lose your knife, but using it and leaving it behind

Gerber's Bolt Action three-bladed hunter's tool is an excellent product and has worked well on the ranch. Stainless steel blades snap in and out by manipulating the thumb slide, and it all packs into a Cordura belt pouch.

(Below) For the bird hunter, a pair of game shears are worth their weight in gold. Buck Shears have several tools built in. The Puma hunters pocketknife was made prior to WWII and offers a locking main blade, a gut hook, a sharp saw with screwdriver tip and a bird gutting hook.

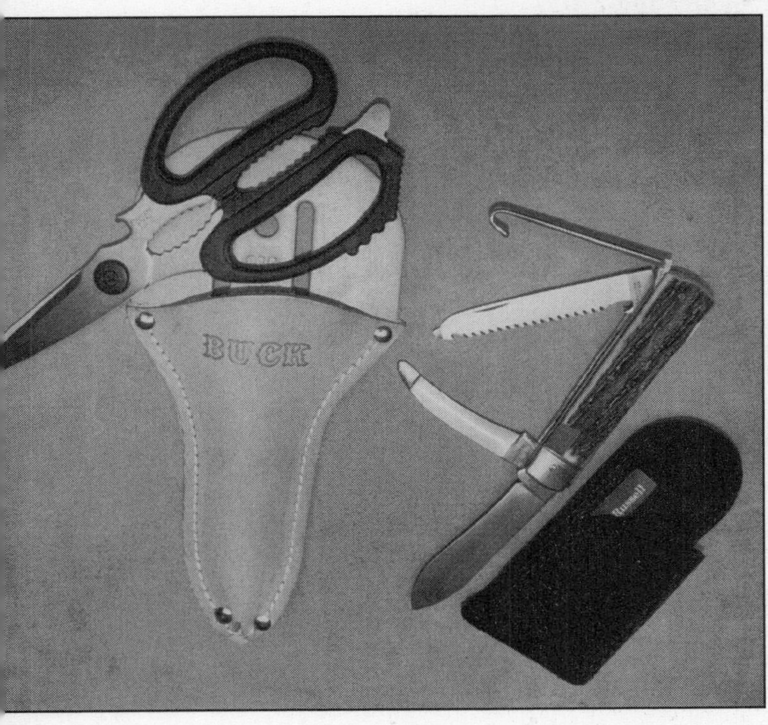

Coast Cutlery offers the Sport Mechanic for hunters and campers, and the well-designed stainless steel tools are most useful around any bush operation.

is more likely to happen. I prefer the pouch sheath, because keepers are often sliced off trying to return the blade with one hand.

When I started in scouting, I was given for Christmas a Marble's sheath knife that was my pride and joy until I dropped it from a boat while fishing. It was inexperience that did it, but many good knives are lost the same way. Cleaning fish and letting the current grab the blade, or just plain dropping it into some place too deep to retrieve, is typical sorrow. I like the fishing knives that float!

Many Alaska big game guides carry nothing but a folding knife on their belt or in their pocket. I guess it is a matter or pride with them to be able to do "the whole job" with a 3-inch blade from some super-sharp, long-carried Case or Buck folder. The most impressive job of small-knife butchery I have ever seen was some years ago when my hunting friend Jack Fahs and I were driving to a fancy dress party in his brand-new Oldsmobile convertible. We hit a small deer that jumped right into the path of the speeding car and was dead on arrival with the pavement. Jack and I both had hunting licenses in our wallets, but we were not ready to dress that deer and had nothing to do it with. In front of the headlights, Jack's eyes lit up. He always carried a small ornamental knife that hung from a key chain and was decorated with the Masonic Order symbol. The blade was perhaps an inch long, but in just a few minutes he had that deer cleaned and ready to go into the trunk. We were, of course, covered with blood up to our elbows, having removed the fine jackets and rolled up our sleeves. Rather than arrive looking like grisly murderers, we stopped at an all-night filling station and washed ourselves in the bathroom. We left from there more or less prepared to party, but the fellow cleaning up that men's room must have thought a murder had taken place near

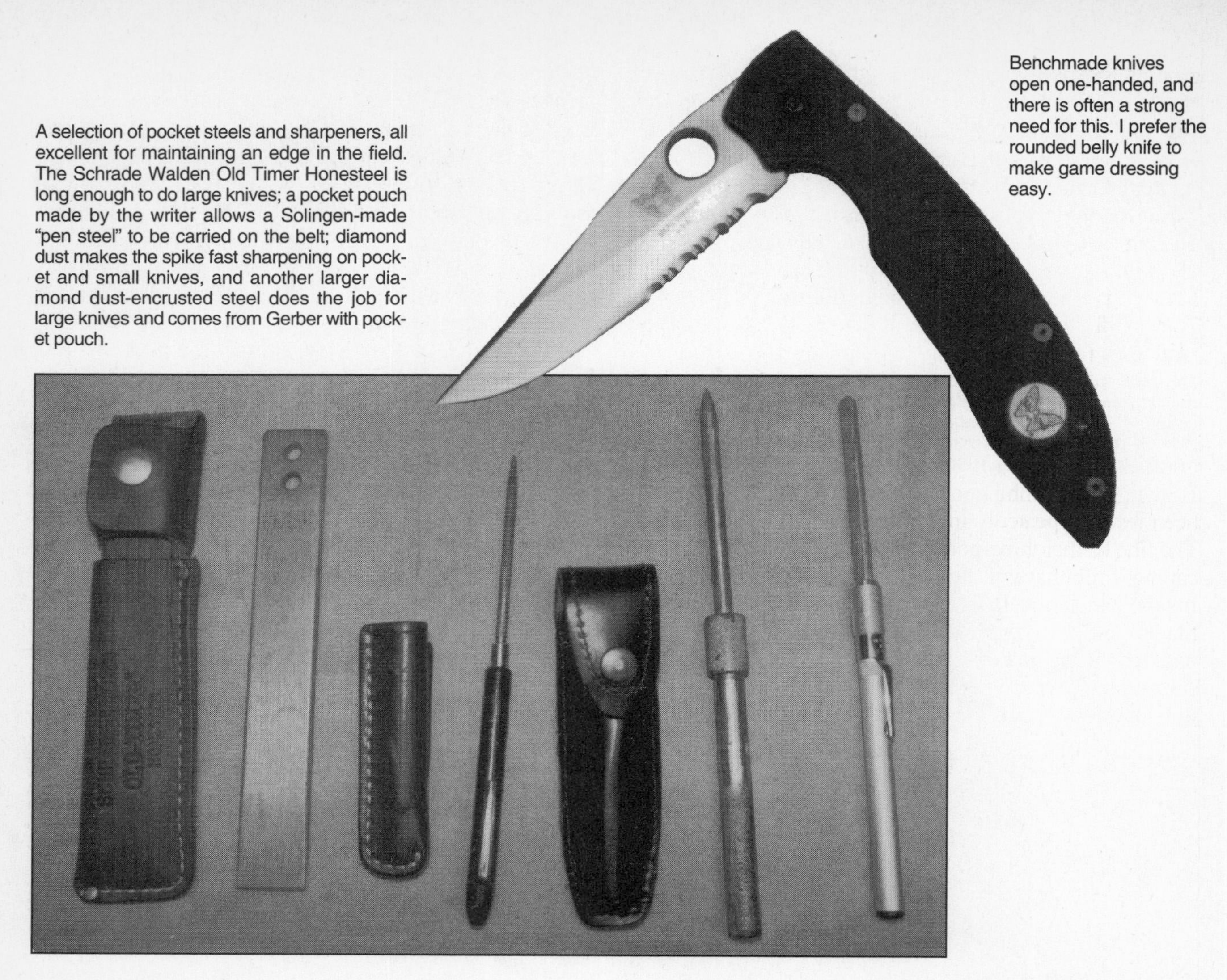
A selection of pocket steels and sharpeners, all excellent for maintaining an edge in the field. The Schrade Walden Old Timer Honesteel is long enough to do large knives; a pocket pouch made by the writer allows a Solingen-made "pen steel" to be carried on the belt; diamond dust makes the spike fast sharpening on pocket and small knives, and another larger diamond dust-encrusted steel does the job for large knives and comes from Gerber with pocket pouch.

Benchmade knives open one-handed, and there is often a strong need for this. I prefer the rounded belly knife to make game dressing easy.

the sink. The point I make is that any good sharp knife in the hands of an experienced game dresser can do the job. Our ancestors used sharp rocks to get the job done.

The two-knife kit offers a lot of versatility. I found the new Gerber Bolt Action Three-Blade to have a lot of convenience and utility. It packs into a small pouch on your belt and weighs almost nothing. My test knife stayed sharp through a whole wild boar, and those critters have dirt-encrusted hides that will defeat a lot of cutlery. I like the idea of having a small saw blade that really cuts. Getting a branch just the right size to hold open game or providing any number of small wood jobs around the camp is much easier with such a blade. I carry a folding sportsman's saw in my hunting kit, but often that bag of tricks is not where I am. The handy sawtooth pocketknife blade will do the job. I don't recommend the pocketknife saw for firewood. There are several handy folding timber saws that will do that job more efficiently. In fact, today, great thought has been applied to every piece of camping gear to make it lighter, more portable and easier handling. In the case of the bush-whacking tool, many would prefer a machete, but in the woods I was dealing with, the thin and long blade would not do as well as the kukri.

My old friend and former hunting editor for *Sports Illustrated* for twenty-five years, Virginia Kraft, was nearly put down by a wild machete while hunting jaguar in Central America. The blade went wild from a trail-cutting crew member and bounced off a tree and hit her, blade first, at the Achilles tendon. This would have been the end of her career and would have meant a long and painful pack-out, but she was wearing Gokey Bottes that covered the area above the ankle and saved her. The guide had suggested tennis shoes that day! Always give a bush whacker enough room to do his job and expect the occasional accidental loss of the knife. It happens. We wore hard hats when I worked for the Forest Service in Alaska, and it was for that reason—wild bush knives and machetes released accidentally. A flying knife can spoil your whole day!

It is easier to do camp work and field game dressing with a good grip on your knife. The sheath knife with a "sticky" handle is just the best way to go at the messy job. What shouldn't happen when you are working with a sharp knife deep inside an animal is for the knife to get away from you and cut you.

There is an argument about finger grooves or no finger

grooves on hunting knife handles. I have tried all the variations and found that deep finger grooves are in the way with half the game and camp jobs I did. I have very shallow finger grooves on a hunting knife I designed and had created in stainless by George Herron. The grooves don't get in the way, yet offer some additional control when making long strokes with the knife. That Herron knife, by the way, offers a grooved thumb purchase at the top of the blade at the hilt and also a small choil for finer control. The handle has a large hole at the end for hanging the knife on a nail in the camp. Nothing worse than having to clean a knife every time it is used so you can store it in the sheath.

The new kid on the block when it comes to combination belt kits is the Knives of Alaska creation called The Brown Bear Combination. It is well thought out and has been tested repeatedly in Alaska, where animals are big. The fine leather three-pocket sheath contains a very handy caping knife that will find use as a camp paring knife, it fits the hand so well. The big mother of this set is a wide bladed and very nicely designed cleaver/skinner. Both handles have a material called "Suregrip," and they are sure-gripped when you take one up. I would love to put this set to work, but I won't be up in Alaska until August this year, too late for test results to make this article. I did get a test report from my ranching cousin, who does some butchering on his place. He said it was the best set he has seen, and the blades worked well on his pig and calf jobs. The third item in the sheath is the steel, and it's large enough to use easily and safely.

Rychetnik showing off his George Herron "Alaskan" model knife in 440C with shallow-grooved linen Micarta handle.

With more than 200 knives in my collection that goes back at least forty years (I have lost my share and, when the soup was thin, had to sell some real nifty knives; the Bob Loveless Delaware Maid 4-inch drop-point made me cry when I parted with it, but we had medical problems, and owning that knife was not as useful as having the $1000), I have tried to test and use purposefully every one.

I seldom go into the field without something new. I am really getting the feel for the serrated-edge blade, and some of the folders today have both a serrated- and straight-edge blade that is the best of both worlds. Swiss Army Knives came out with a larger pocketknife called The Picnic, which offers a 4-inch serrated blade and a shorter straight blade, plus some other tools, with a composition red handle that grips easily. The keyring at the end means it can be attached to a lanyard, and I like to keep my good knives safe. It is a lockblade, as well. I was a hero at a recent picnic when I could whip out that sharp blade and slice the Italian dried salami in just a few seconds. I carry a knife everywhere, except to bed. It sort of dates me, but our generation found it hard to live without a knife. I must use my pocketknife a dozen times a day, and my No. 4 wife can't move without her Swiss Army multi-bladed purse knife.

I will never forget the time I was hunting with now-gone Jack McPhee, who saw me unpack my field cutlery and pushed me aside. He had a long-bladed Trapper's Muskrat knife that was kept razor-sharp. In less than an hour, with my assistance, he had a "freezer-bull" moose cleaned, skinned and reduced to twelve parcels, mainly boneless, for packing out. I never got that good, but then I never took as many of the giant deer as he had. He was a wizard with the folding German knife he always carried. His wife gave me the Henckel's when Jack died.

People always ask me about a proper survival kit, and almost always they fail to bring that kit along when they go for their walk in the woods. I say that a best-quality multi-blade and tool pocketknife like the Swiss Army or the Wenger-Buck (no cheapo Chinese copies) is the main item. One of the new pocket tools in a pouch like the Coast Cutlery Sport Mechanic will work well. A waterproof match case, some variety of Band-Aids, a compass if you know how to use one—the Swiss Army Recta is just 2 ounces with lanyard—about 25 yards of nylon parachute cord, a small AA flashlight, a cheap plastic police whistle and a roll of fruit-flavored LifeSavers should get you by most problems, like being stuck out overnight. Along with a $10 Space Blanket and sleeping bag, these items will fit in a belt pouch you can pick up at a mountaineer and ski supply shop. Take them with you. I bet you use the knife more than anything else! ●

Uncelebrated and unappreciated, the Cattaraugus 225Q was...

THE CATTARAUGUS 225Q was possibly the most widely used and best performing U.S. military-issue combat knife in World War II. You would not know that from its publicity.

Instead, in a major cutlery reference book, you can read: "Cattaraugus and Case made utility knives with heavy 6-inch blades and steel butts for the Army Quartermaster Department. Their main use was for opening and re-closing wooden crates, though as surplus they were advertised as 'Commando Knives.'" Several other recent references on U.S. military knives give pretty much the same information, often adding that the heavy buttcap is for hammering nails in crates and that the knives were specifically intended for use by Quartermaster troops.

That is all blatant nonsense. The Cattaraugus 225Q was a dyed-in-the-wool combat knife that saw a tremendous amount of action and deserves a lot better place in history. A sharp pry bar for Quartermaster troops to use for opening and closing crates it was not.

As is the custom for the United States, we entered WWII grossly short of the equipment necessary to wage war, including knives. The only "combat" knife on hand in any quantity was the Mark 1 Trench Knife from WWI, the double-edged dagger with a cast brass knuckle. Extremely effective in a close-quarters melee, it was not particularly practical, it was poorly balanced and excessively heavy, and it used large amounts of brass.

So military procurement agencies quickly purchased a variety of large commercial hunting knives. Such knives are excellent tools and generally adequate weapons. The orders placed with a large number of cutlery manufactures were for a generic combat utility knife with a single-edged 6-inch blade with fullers (blood grooves). This approximated the 6-inch Marble's Ideal hunting knife. It

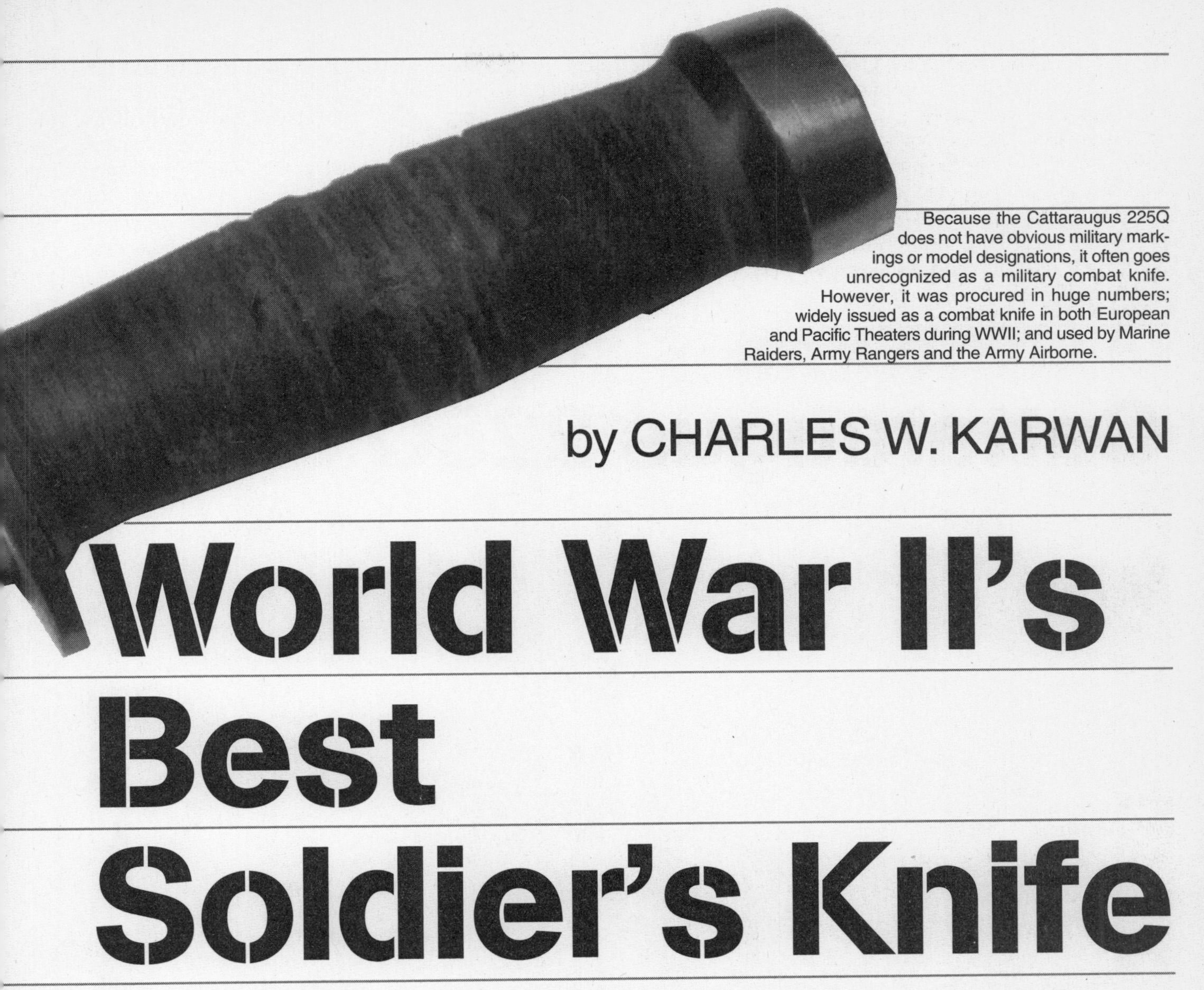

Because the Cattaraugus 225Q does not have obvious military markings or model designations, it often goes unrecognized as a military combat knife. However, it was procured in huge numbers; widely issued as a combat knife in both European and Pacific Theaters during WWII; and used by Marine Raiders, Army Rangers and the Army Airborne.

by CHARLES W. KARWAN

World War II's Best Soldier's Knife

is not known whether the Marble's knife was used as a model, but the fact that most of the manufacturers already made a copy of the Marble's knife brought about the strong similarity.

These knives were always intended to serve as combat knives, and most were issued to front-line combat soldiers and Marines. They saw a lot of action, particularly early in the war before the standardized combat knife models were available in quantity. There is no standard model designation for these knives since they were purchased by the government on individual contracts with general specifications, though they were often referred to generically as "6-inch combat utility knives."

Such knives were made during WWII by Case, Cattaraugus, Ka-Bar, Kinfolks, Kingston, Kutmaster, Pal, Queen, Robeson, Western and probably others. Many were purchased for issue, and some were purchased for resale at post and base exchanges and at ship's stores. Cattaraugus and Pal made by far the largest number (probably in the millions each), while Ka-bar made about a half-million. The rest are fairly uncommon in comparison.

By 1943, the Army had standardized and adopted the M3 Knife, the Navy had done the same with the Mark 2 knives, and the Marines had adopted their Fighting Utility (F-U) knife. Interestingly, the Navy Mark 2 and USMC F-U knives, which are the same knife with different markings, are little more than thinner versions of the Marble's 7-inch Ideal hunting knife. Regardless, the 6-inch knives were still supplied on government contracts at least into 1944 and made for resale until the war ended.

The Case 337 6-inch Q and Cattaraugus 225Q variations are more stoutly built than most of the rest, and they are the only ones with "Q" in their markings. According to several references, the Q stands for "Quartermaster," though after years of looking I have not found a single bit of written evidence that verifies that assumption. However, for the sake of discussion, let us say that the Q does stand for Quartermaster. Does that mean that the knife was procured for use by Quartermaster troops? Not hardly!

The Quartermaster branches of the various services have as their mission the procurement of all supplies of standard manufacture and supplies standard to two or more of the other branches of that service. This includes practically everything from beans to buildings, but does not include ordnance and items specific only to a certain

are normally opened by members of the using unit, not by Quartermaster personnel. Furthermore, no matter how dumb you may think the military is, ever since crates were invented they have known the best way to open nailed-shut crates is with a pry bar, not a knife. Consequently, pry bars have been procured and issued for that purpose since Julius Caesar was a corporal. While it is entirely likely that a combat knife might be made stout enough to serve as a pry bar in an emergency, it is ludicrous to think that knives would be issued specifically for that purpose when pry bars were already in the supply system.

Many envision a combat knife being suitable for dueling, though such encounters are practically unknown in military conflicts. The knife must be capable of being used as an emergency weapon, but most of its use will be as a tool. The versatile blade shape of the 225Q and its robust construction make it likely the best combat knife issued during WWII.

branch. Certainly, knives of most kinds fit into the Quartermasters' procurement domain.

A good example were the butcher knives and bread knives procured by the Quartermaster branch of the Army for use in the mess halls of all the Army branches. Even though they were specifically designated Quartermaster butcher knives and Quartermaster bread knives on their procurement contracts, the only time they were actually used by Quartermaster personnel was in a Quartermaster unit mess hall.

It is also important to know that, while the Quartermaster branch may procure supplies that are in crates, such crates

Cattaraugus called their Model 225Q a "Commando Knife" throughout the war. Every one of their many wartime advertisements that mention the 225Q does so as a combat knife used by combat troops. Indeed, even though there are no units designated as Commando units in the U.S. military, the 225Q was issued to several Commando-like elite American fighting units, including the Marine Raider Battalions, the Army Rangers and the Army Airborne. They were also widely issued to regular Marine and Army combat units before the F-U and M3 knives were adopted and procured, and even well afterward. The 225Q has the additional distinction of appearing to be the

An American artillery forward observer (FO) operating out of an observation post near the crest of Chiunzi Pass in Italy, which had been captured by Darby's Rangers. He is carrying a Cattaraugus 225Q combat knife. Rest assured that he is not a Quartermaster soldier concerned with opening crates. (Photo credit Robert Capa, Imperial War Museum, London)

only WWII combat knife issued in quantity to both Army and Marine fighting units.

Going over WWII combat pictures that I have, I find the 225Q seems to show up more in the Pacific Theater than in Europe, but there is no question it saw a great deal of service in both places, including even by Airborne troops dropping in at Normandy. In all cases, they were issued for use as combat knives. In one particular photo series showing Marine Raiders training in close combat with knives, the knives are very clearly Cattaraugus 225Qs.

A number of things set off the Cattaraugus 225Q from the rest of the WWII combat knives. First, they are incredibly strong. Not only have I never seen a broken specimen, I have never even heard of one breaking. That is far from the case with most WWII combat knives. Custom knifemaker Wayne Goddard says the Cattaraugus 225Q was the only military knife he never succeeded in breaking as a kid. Wayne grew up when surplus U.S. military knives were plentiful and cheap, and any male kid worth his salt owned at least one. The surplus knives that did break were often broken by misusing them for prying, but nothing broke more knives than throwing them. I am a few years younger than Wayne, but I can remember those days quite well and can readily recall being in on breaking my share of surplus knives, usually by throwing them at a tree stump or similar target. However, like Wayne, I never managed to break or even significantly damage a 225Q.

For a long time, I conjectured that the 225Q must have been made from a special alloy steel. Several things caused me to think this. First, I noticed that, even though the blades are bright steel, they do not rust as readily as most other military knives, and when they do rust they only get very shallow pitting. Also, they always seemed to take a very keen edge and hold it particularly well. Their ability to absorb abuse without breaking or chipping was also endearing.

One time after reading about a bladesmith test that required cutting through a free-hanging 1-inch manila rope with one stroke, chopping through a fir 2x4, and then

The Cattaraugus 225Q, the Case 337-6″Q, and some others procured by the military in WWII had scabbards oriented like this, with the edge facing the opposite to the norm. When drawn by a right-handed person, the blade is edge upward, precisely how Marines were then taught to hold a combat knife. It is unlikely a sharpened pry bar would be thus used.

The 225Q had a wider and thicker tang than other WWII knives, with a unique and extremely strong assembly system. Three steel discs form the buttcap—the first goes straight onto the tang; the second goes over the tang and is turned 90 degrees to lock; the third goes onto the end and two twisted shank nails are driven in through all three disks into the leather. At right is the knife with the middle disc in place.

shaving hair, I sharpened my 225Q to a hair-popping edge and gave it the test. To everyone's surprise but mine, it easily passed the test. This demonstrates that the 225Q has good edge geometry and excellent edge retention.

Certainly, this is exceptionally good performance for any production knife, let alone a wartime-manufactured production military knife. When my research indicated that Cattaraugus had made some kitchen cutlery with chrome moly alloys before WWII, I was sure I was on to something that accounted for the superior performance of the 225Q.

Working with Wayne, we had two 225Qs Rockwell tested, and both had blade edges with an Rc of 60, which is fully 2 to 6 points harder than the other U.S. military knives. Then Wayne had a 225Q blade spectroscopically analyzed and broke my bubble. The steel was the same common 1095 high carbon tool steel used by many other knife manufacturers. It was not some exotic alloy.

It would seem the rust resistance and superior edge holding of the 225Q are functions of the high blade hardness. The fact that the blades are not brittle and do not chip is a testament to the high quality of the heat-treatment and the use of differential hardening, such as making the tang softer than the blade.

The brute strength of the 225Q comes partially from that superior heat-treatment of good blade material and partially from the fact that the blade is thicker, and the tang is both thicker and wider, than the other military knives. And then there is the unique way the knife is put together.

Most WWII U.S. military knives have leather washer handles with a buttcap pinned on with a cross pin, screwed on directly or with a nut, or riveted on. The 225Q uses a system that is stronger than those. The buttcap is actually made up of three stacked oval steel disks. The end of the blade's tang has a notch cut into each side that is the exact thickness of one of these disks and is placed the thickness of one disk from the end of the tang. The first disk has a rectangular hole to match the tang plus a small round hole on each side of the tang hole. This disk was forced down over the tang under hydraulic pressure to compress the leather washer handle material down until the tang notches are exposed. The second disk has the tang hole cut at 90 degrees from the normal along with a crosscut that allows the disc to be put over the tang and turned a quarter-turn to lock the disc into the notches on the tang. The last disc is put on so that the butt is flush with the rear of the tang, and then two high-grip nails are driven in, one on each side of the tang. These nails go through all three discs into the leather of the handle and also serve to prevent the middle disc from rotating, thereby keeping the whole assembly securely locked together.

This assembly system is strong and secure, lends itself to mass production, and has the advantage of allowing relatively easy disassembly for repair or adjustment. While leather washer-handled military knives are notorious for having the leather shrink and the handle getting loose, such problems are rare with the 225Q.

Another clue to the original intended purpose of the 225Q is revealed by its scabbard. It is made with the edge of the knife oriented so that when the knife is drawn by a right-handed person the edge is upward. This is precisely the way the Marines were taught to hold a combat knife for knife fighting during WWII. I do not think it was an accident that this sheath orients the knife the opposite way from the norm. Interestingly, the sheaths of the Case 337 6-inch Q, the Kingston 6-inch, and several others of the WWII 6-inch combat utility

The Navy Mark 2 butt (right) is held on by a simple through-pin, and it has a much smaller and thinner tang. There is no question that the construction of the 225Q (left) is vastly stronger.

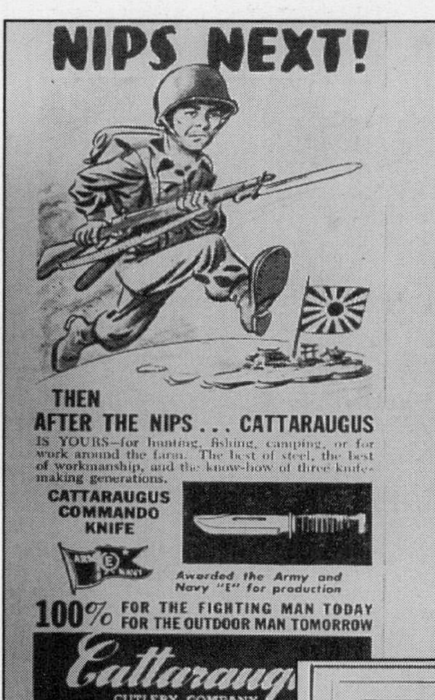

This advertisement came out after the surrender in Europe, but before the Japanese surrender. Note "Commando Knife" is used for the 225Q, and also note the Army-Navy "E" production award.

knives of the same type have sheaths constructed with this same unorthodox orientation.

Cattaraugus was one of a small percentage of the American cutlery companies that received special awards for the excellence of their production efforts during WWII. The award was based on a combination of factors, including the volume of production, the quality control and timely delivery based on the contract specifications. The Army and Navy "E" for excellence in production was awarded to Cattaraugus in November of 1944 for its production of folding survival machetes, Signal Corps folding knives and their "Commando" knives.

I well remember as a young lad chatting with a friend

An early war advertisement by Cattaraugus featuring their 225Q "Commando Knife" that is "in the fighting lines." It wasn't a tool for opening crates.

Cattaraugus was a prominent advertiser in WWII outdoor magazines. When they learned their 225Q jumped into Normandy, they were happy to point it out.

A late war Cattaraugus advertisement picturing the 225Q "Commando Knife."

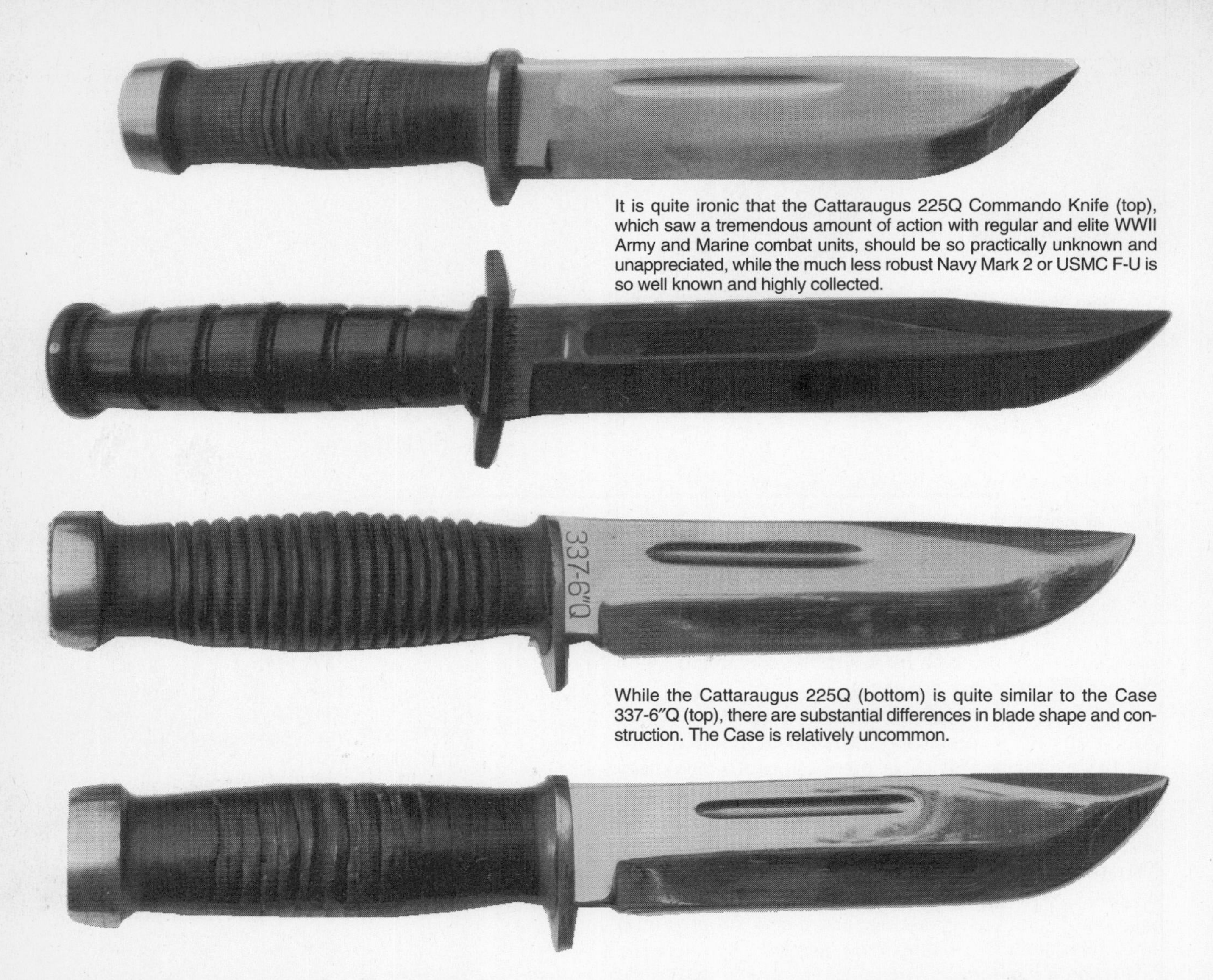

It is quite ironic that the Cattaraugus 225Q Commando Knife (top), which saw a tremendous amount of action with regular and elite WWII Army and Marine combat units, should be so practically unknown and unappreciated, while the much less robust Navy Mark 2 or USMC F-U is so well known and highly collected.

While the Cattaraugus 225Q (bottom) is quite similar to the Case 337-6"Q (top), there are substantial differences in blade shape and construction. The Case is relatively uncommon.

of my father who was a veteran WWII Marine gunnery sergeant in Carlson's Raiders. He had seen action in at least three major amphibious landings in the Pacific and was pretty salty. Having heard about the special knife that the Carlson's Raiders were known for (a Collins Bowie), I asked him if he still had the knife he was issued. He said he did, went to a cupboard and pulled out a Cattaraugus 225Q that he said was issued to him and was his constant companion through most of his combat service. He was quite fond of that knife and even demonstrated its keenness by shaving hair off of his arm. My later research confirmed the Raider Battalions did issue the 225Q along with the more famous but less practical Collins Bowies.

The 225Q has never been popular with collectors, mostly because it is surrounded by those misconceptions and that misinformation. First; there is no obvious military designation marking on it, so they often go unrecognized as military or are dismissed as private-sale knives. Second, they do not fit many people's mistaken idea of what a combat knife should look like—there is no large double crossguard nor a partially or fully sharpened top edge. Then, there is that nonsense about it being a knife for Quartermaster troops to use for opening crates, which causes many to classify the 225Q with such things as military kitchen cutlery and such. Few modern collectors have actually ever used these knives, so they do not know about the 225Q's superior performance in cutting, edge holding or strength.

For my money, the Cattaraugus 225Q was the premier combat utility knife of WWII. It wasn't perfect. It would have been even better if it had a slightly longer handle with a little drop in it. Also it needed a provision for a lanyard. However, its superior performance and strength more than made up for these deficiencies.

My war was Vietnam. My combat knife in Vietnam was a handmade knife by a famous maker, and, sadly, it was a major disappointment. I would have been happier if I had taken my Cattaraugus 225Q to Vietnam because it has better edge geometry, is stronger, is more rust resistant, and has a more practical blade configuration than the knife I did take. The Cattaraugus 225Q deserves a lot more credit and a better place in history than it has ever received. ●

TRENDS

Someone decides to put all these photos in here, and that someone also decides to not put all those other photos in here.

That would be a problem—or a worse problem—except there is a sort of system. There are several categories; indeed, there are a couple of kinds of categories. So what you see are the best photos of the best examples that got to the choice, category by category.

The big ones—Bowies, hunters and locking folders—are there to give very nearly any nifty knife a shot. And then it seems to make sense to have some types compete against each other, comparing perfectly good knives that take a day or less to make with creations with weeks in them is hardly fair, for instance.

That's the system here. This is the eighteenth time we've done this and maybe the third system. It will probably change, because not only do the Trends change, but *how* they change changes.

What's a Trend? We find out when the photos show up. And we get a few clues at shows. And we talk to an occasional knifemaker. Some hit hard, like folders; some sneak in, like titanium.

Enjoy.

Ken Warner

THE BOWIE BURGEONS

IT DOESN'T GO away. There are very big names, high-class smiths mostly (but not, emphatically not, all) who build hardly anything else. For a little break, such a fellow might make a camp knife.

They're all looking for the ultimate Bowie, and since James Bowie was careless enough to leave no precise prescription for us, most anyone might find it this very week. And that explains the wondrous variety.

In fact, that explained the wondrous variety of original 1830s-1840s Bowies. Nobody knew what a Bowie was—the material, physical object, that is—but they all wanted one anyway. And here they came—spear-pointed, clip-pointed, straight-backed, curved, relatively heavy, more usually pretty light. They had broad blades and narrow, big crossguards and none.

It was a mess—just not orderly. And so, of course, splendid. Bowie was a game anyone could play, and everybody did, and an awful lot still do.

All the main lines are still around. They make some in every flavor every year. And more and more they're trending toward what this writer thinks of as *real*—a largish very quick knife, a slasher and sticker, not a chopper.

There's a lot of fellows specializing in pattern-welded blades on their Bowies (though not so many seen here this year) for reasons hard to fathom. They're darned handsome, but the pretty blades are ..... well, the precise word is anomalous. They don't exactly fit the picture.

Variety and shape and finish aside, the essence of the Bowie idea, its reason for being, is that it's a weapon, a sidearm. The essence of *that* is that it's *there*. You have it with you.

▲*Don R. Broughton:* Sixteen inches of classic profile in 1084 and nickel silver. (Weyer photo)

▶*Roger Massey:* The famous "No.1" Bowie replicated in a 13½-inch 5160 blade. The shape is deliberate. (Gallagher photo)

▶*Jerry Fisk:* A 9-inch forged 1084 blade with coffin handle in stag and ivory. (Gallagher photo)

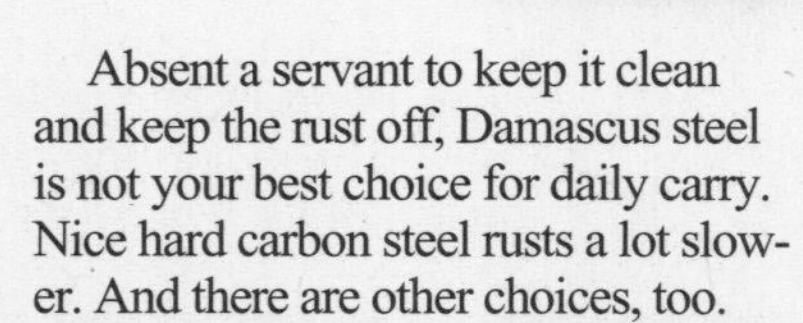

Absent a servant to keep it clean and keep the rust off, Damascus steel is not your best choice for daily carry. Nice hard carbon steel rusts a lot slower. And there are other choices, too.

In the closing years of the 20th century, your stainless steel Bowie makes a lot of sense. Among other things, that virtually ensures that the knife will be on hand for the closing years of the 21st century. Given decent care—mostly kept dry, that means—the thing could make it to the 25th century.

What will they say then of such as we see here? How about, "Those were the days!"

Ken Warner

▲*Steven J. Rapp:* Called Philadelphia style, this one in 440C goes 15 inches overall. (Weyer photo)

◀*Steven J. Rapp:* Schively style in 440C and mastodon ivory and stainless fittings throughout—just under 16 inches. (Weyer photo)

▲*Vincent K. Evans:* Meticulous detailing and a fancy-backed ladder Damascus blade at 8 inches. (Weyer photo)

▶*Edmund Davidson:* A massive job—an integral Bowie in 15-inch-long hand-rubbed A2 steel, flat-grooved. (Slobodian photo)

▼*James Batson:* Coffin-handled, just over a foot long, this one's set up as a "carry piece." (Weyer photo)

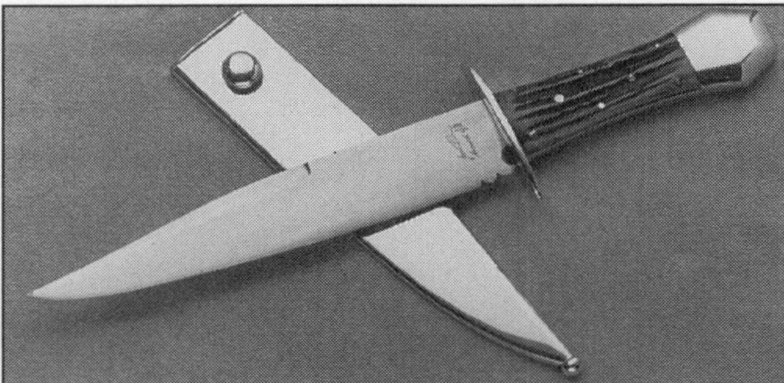

◀*Tim Hancock:* This knife—this one—has become a Bowie knife poster boy—it's $14^{1}/_{2}$ inches overall in Damascus and ironwood. (Weyer photo)

▲*Clay Gault:* The Bowie newly interpreted in two sizes—hand-rubbed with fleur-de-lis checkering panels. (B. Gault photo)

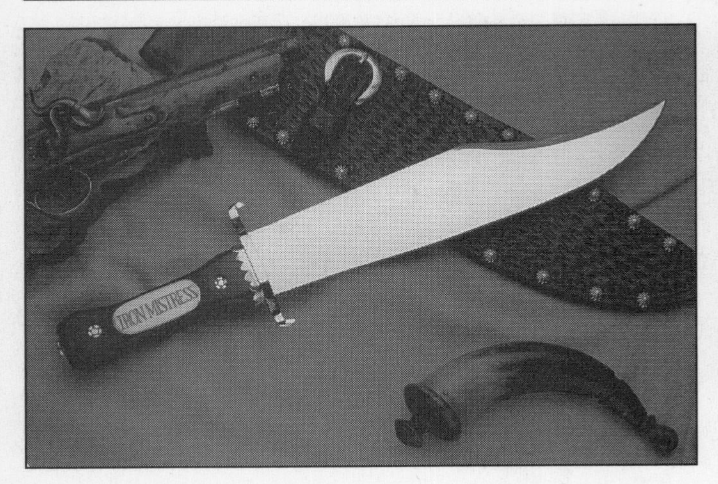

▲*Dennis Des Jardins:* In case you did not recognize the style, this one is labeled. (Chan photo)

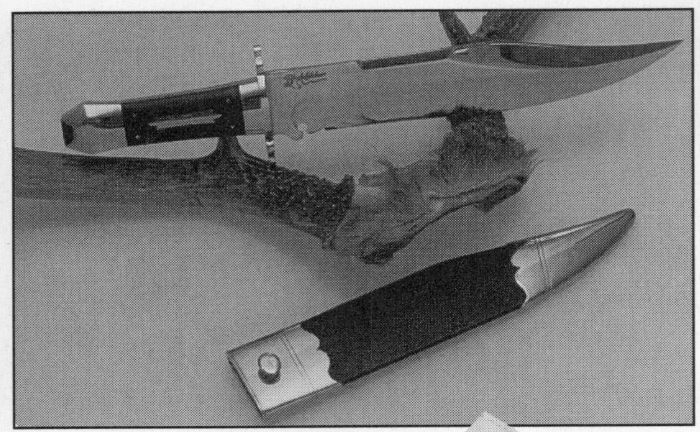

▲*Joe D. Huddleston:* There are $1\frac{1}{3}$ edges here in ATS-34, hollow-ground, all ebony and stainless. (Leviton photo)

▼*Norman L. Beckett:* Big Mistress styling with mokume, German silver trimmings, ebony grip and 440C blade. (Weyer photo)

▶*Judson Brennan:* The artistic Bowie in carbon steel and ivory, chastely engraved. (Weyer photo)

▼*Steven J. Rapp:* Prolific production of replicas of well-known historical Bowies, all in 440C up to 16 inches overall. (Weyer photo)

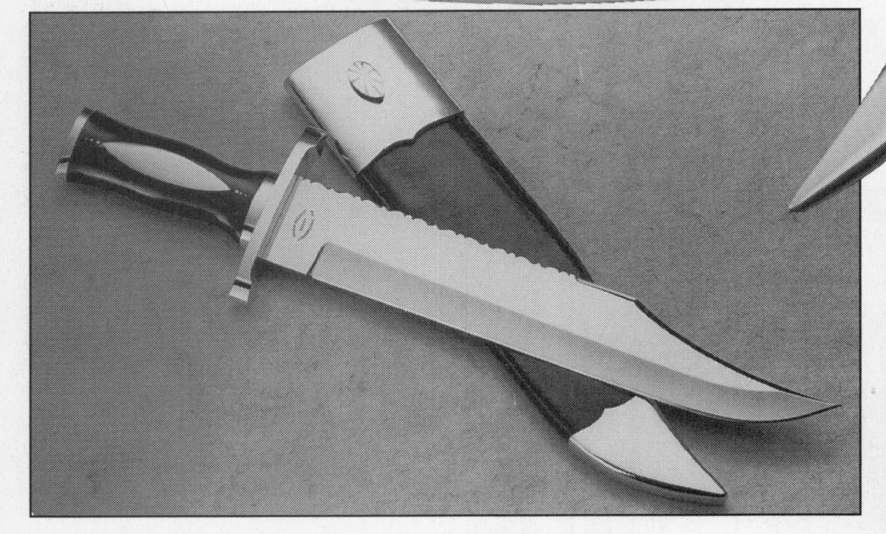

▼*Kim Thomas:* Significant S-guard over a 7-inch blade, trimmed in browned steel.

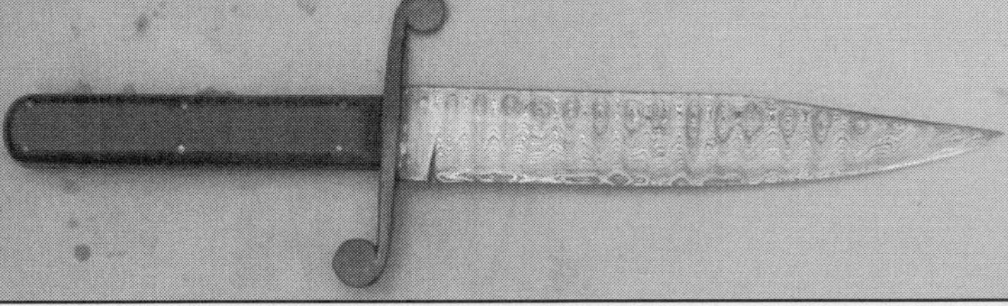

▲*Ed Halligan:* Curly maple and 1085 at 14 inches overall—stainless steel fittings. (Weyer photo)

▲*Timothy F. Potier:* Cleanly ground forged 1080 in a hidden tang blackwood grip—15 inches overall. (Gallagher photo)

▶*Roger M. Green:* Stag rabbet handle, horsehead pommel—14 inches overall with 440C blade. (Weyer photo)

▶*Tim Lively:* Up from the forks of the creek—boldly forged southwest style in antiqued finish.

▼*Michael Roberts:* Robust style in green bone and forged W2, iron-fitted with brass accents. (Weyer photo)

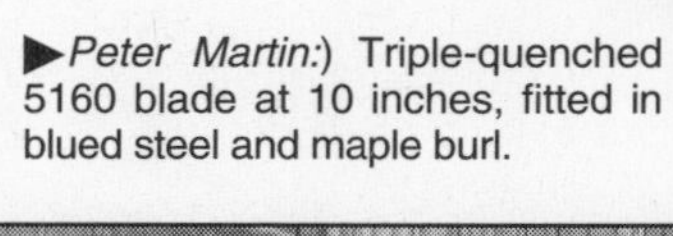

▶*Peter Martin:*) Triple-quenched 5160 blade at 10 inches, fitted in blued steel and maple burl.

▲*Don R. Broughton:* Southwest style with backwood trimmings for a 10-inch forged 1084 blade. (Weyer photo)

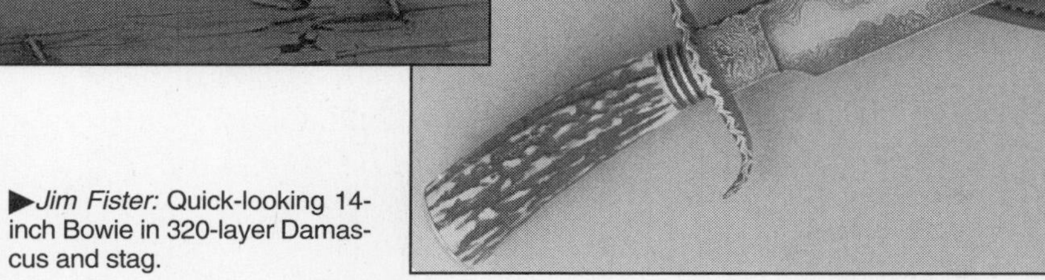

▶*Jim Fister:* Quick-looking 14-inch Bowie in 320-layer Damascus and stag.

TRENDS

SMALL AND NIFTY

SOME SAY IT'S easier to work big than small. That's particularly true, in your reviewer's eyes at least, if the worker at small is going for proportion as well as for cute and for function and for portability.

There is a functional design problem involved in small knives. Every once in a while, regardless of planning, the little guys wind up boys in a man's world, forced into cutting jobs properly meant for, say, 6-inch blades, but for which they're the only tool at hand.

That's when you find out about workmanship and solid materials. It is rare, of course, for a handmade knife to be *frail*, though some tiny factory knives are relatively weak—plenty strong for *their* designed chores, mind you, but not for emergency pry bar use or whatever.

There has been a relatively famous and deliberately small knife on the market one can assume passed the emergency test OK. It had several names, but I liked Rudy Ruana's best. He called it the Smokejumper, and he called it that because he knew smokejumpers and because the smokejumpers knew that knife. It was a skinner shape, hand-forged and shrunk to about 5 inches *overall*. It worked, and it works today. A little knife can do it.

They shouldn't have to, of course. The fellow who makes and the fellow who uses a small knife may be far more interested in tuckability, light weight, good small cuts and moves than in King Konging. You can see that in a lot we show here.

We're not looking at wood-carving tools, or caping sets, or bird-and-trout knives here. They're all small, of course, but not, if you'll excuse me, SMALL. They're, actually, as big as their designed jobs permit.

Nope. We're talking pure small, and that's what you're looking at. Enjoy.

Ken Warner

▲*Francesco Pachi:* Small boot knife in Damascus, abalone and gold—niftier than average.

▲*Hank Ishihara:* Called the Whale, it's just a bitty thing in ivory and nickel silver and, yes, frogskin. (Weyer photo)

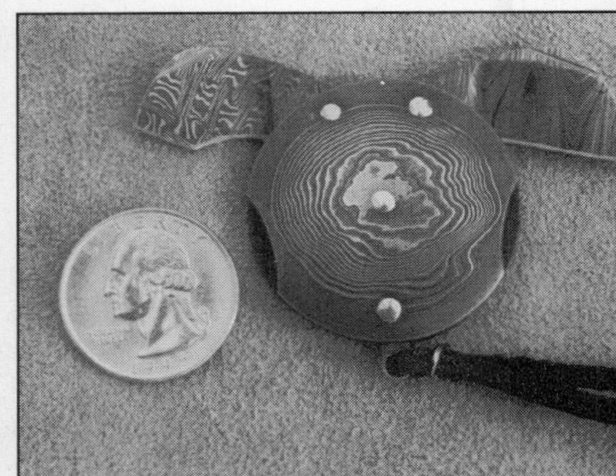

▲*Peter Martin:* Two blades in a half-dollar size, all manner of steel and gold.

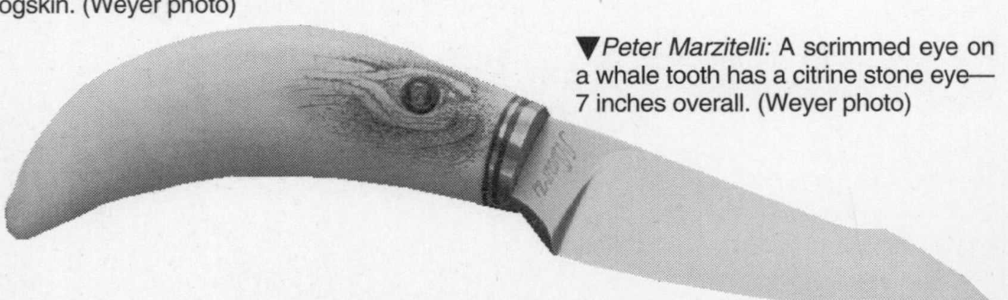

▼*Peter Marzitelli:* A scrimmed eye on a whale tooth has a citrine stone eye—7 inches overall. (Weyer photo)

▲*Marvin Solomon:* O1 steel and Micarta, 6½ inches overall, for an eye-catching utility knife. (Gallagher photo)

▲*Owen Dale Wood:* Gent's knife in 440C and ivory, 7¼ inches overall, engraved by Simon M. Lytton. (Weyer photo)

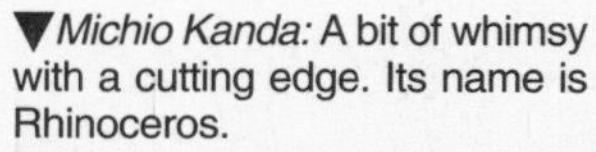

▼*Michio Kanda:* A bit of whimsy with a cutting edge. Its name is Rhinoceros.

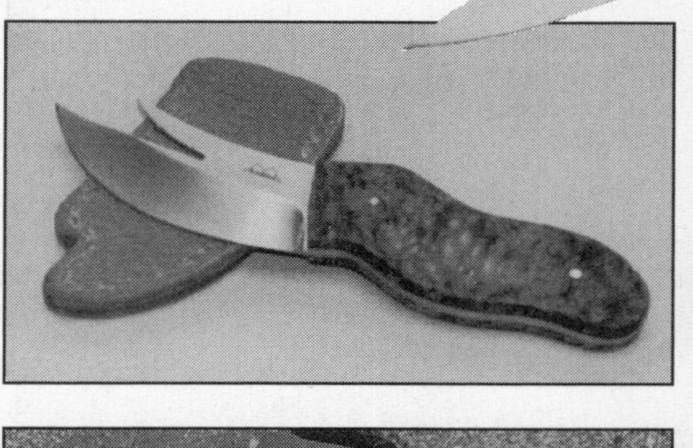

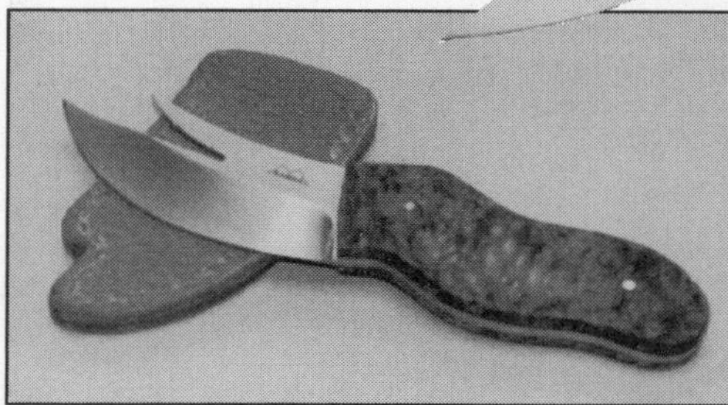

▲*Paul M. Jarvis:* Blackwood and heavily patterned Damascus, set off with sterling and a Chris Kravitt sheath. (Weyer photo)

▲*Don Cowles:* It's Corian and O1 steel and straightforward leather for a working ooloo.

▶*Wally Hayes:* Pearl—carved—and Damascus—filed—make a clean personal knife just 7 inches long. (Weyer photo)

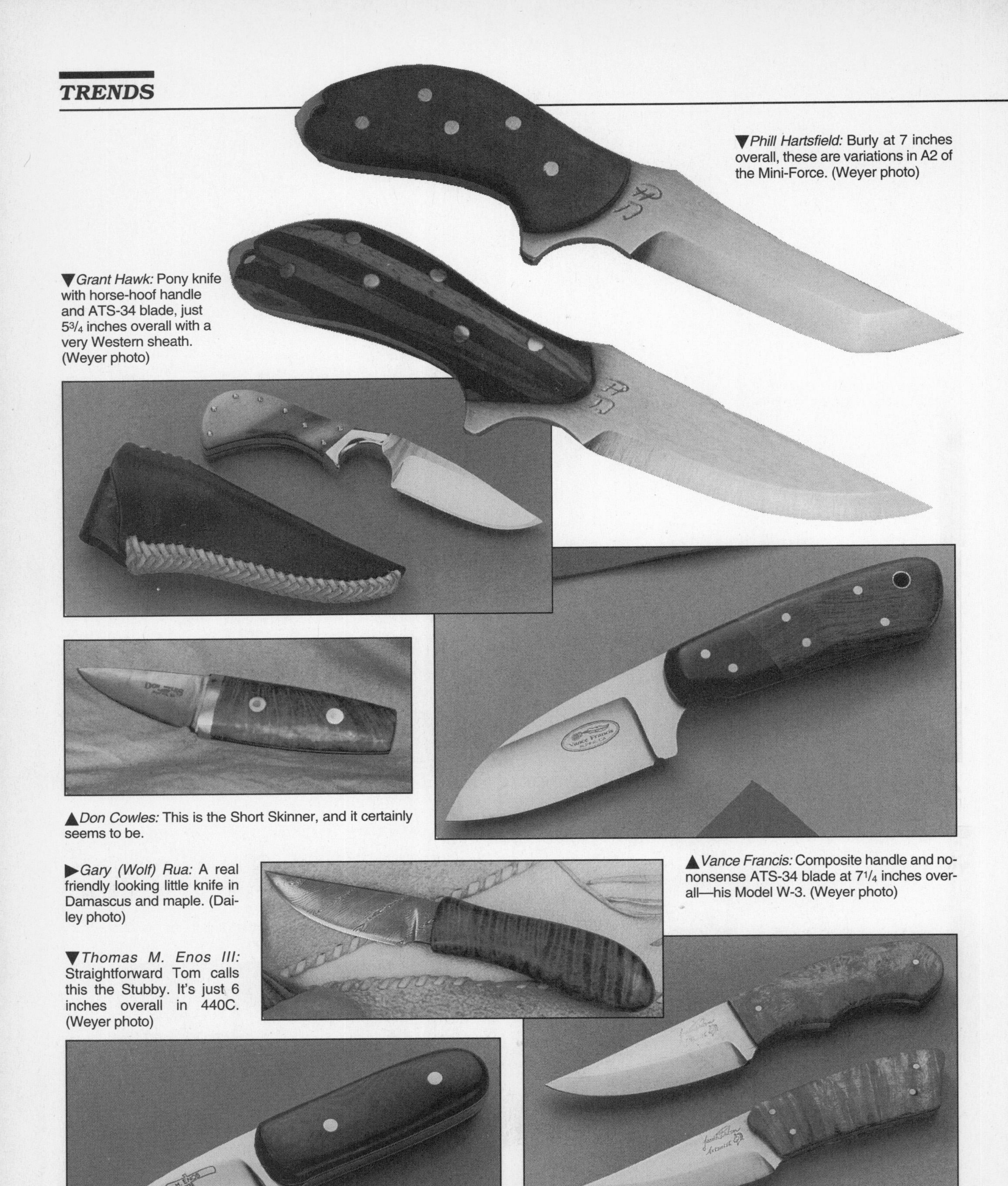

▼*Phill Hartsfield:* Burly at 7 inches overall, these are variations in A2 of the Mini-Force. (Weyer photo)

▼*Grant Hawk:* Pony knife with horse-hoof handle and ATS-34 blade, just 5¾ inches overall with a very Western sheath. (Weyer photo)

▲*Don Cowles:* This is the Short Skinner, and it certainly seems to be.

▲*Vance Francis:* Composite handle and no-nonsense ATS-34 blade at 7¼ inches overall—his Model W-3. (Weyer photo)

▶*Gary (Wolf) Rua:* A real friendly looking little knife in Damascus and maple. (Dailey photo)

▼*Thomas M. Enos III:* Straightforward Tom calls this the Stubby. It's just 6 inches overall in 440C. (Weyer photo)

▲*James Batson:* These are desk knives, forged from 1084, set off with burl maple. (Weyer photo)

◀*Carl S. Zakabi:* Called the Chicken Bone, because of its handle shape, it's a short utility piece. (Long photo)

▼*Vincent K. Evans:* Really small, a usable miniature at 4½ inches overall, it's koa and Damascus. (Weyer photo)

◀*Gerd Jorgensen:* In the shape of new Scandinavia—new materials and the old lines smoothed up.

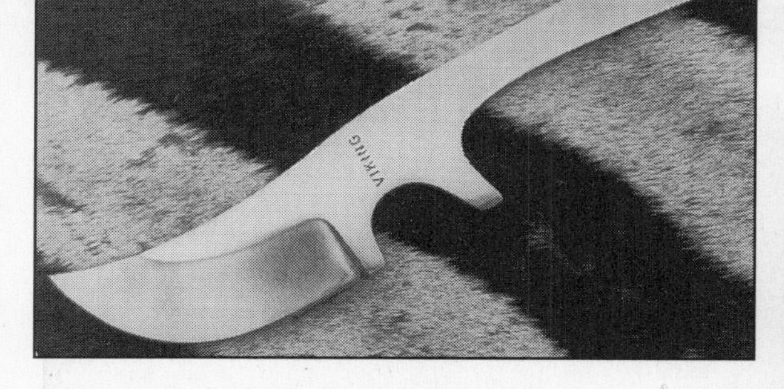

▲*James Thorlief Eriksen:* Mini-skinner by Viking cut in 440C right down to minimum—7¼ inches overall.

◀*Guenter Boehlke:* Small and curvy, with ironwood grip and Balbach Damascus.

▲▼*Pat Crawford:* This is a titanium Knech knife—the blade is 3 inches and can be made in ATS-34, too.

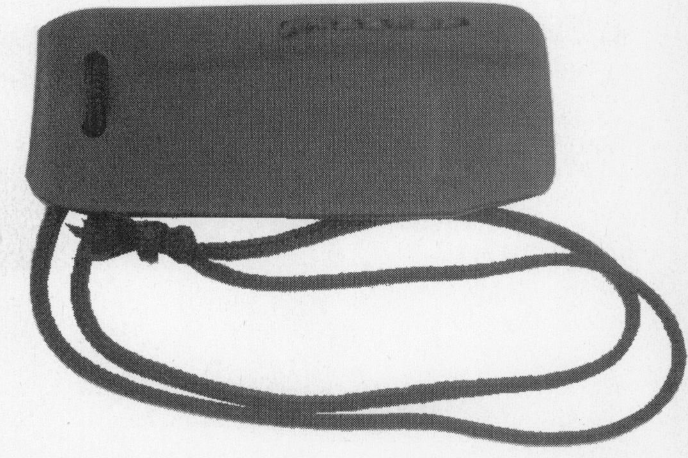

▲*A.W. Dippold:* These dual-purpose deluxe cigar cutters will open all the way for other cutting.

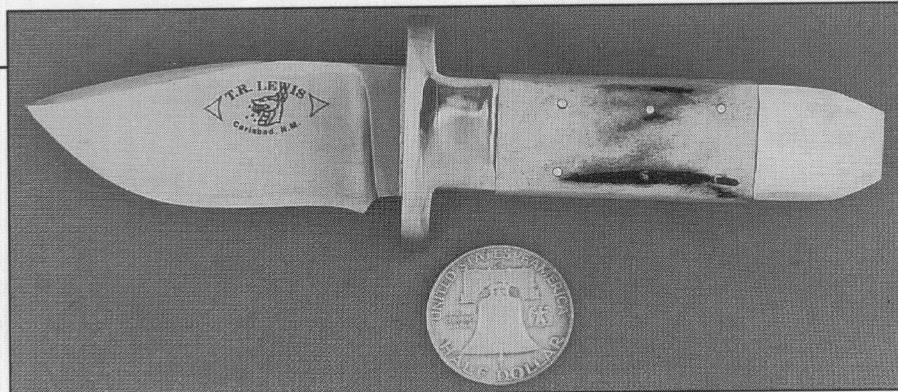

▲*Tom R. Lewis:* The blade is 3 inches of ATS-34, bolstered and pommeled with a stag inset.

▶*Lynn Maxfield:* This one's called Bobcat; made in 154CM and Pakkawood, it's shaped to work well from cross-draw.

▼*Lowell C. Lockett:* Serious cutting tool with a hefty ivory handle—big enough.

▲*Harald Sellevold:* Celtic, Norse, Scots: It's all there in maple, a laminated blade and sterling silver. (Blaha photo)

▲*Mike Yurco:* Neck knife in claw style, ground from 440C—the sheath is Kydex on a chain.

▼*J.E. Sinclair:* Stout fellow in stainless, nickel silver and buffed antler.

▲*J.E. Sinclair:* It takes a really small crowned antler chunk to pull this off, but here it is.

THE ELEGANT KNIFE AGAIN

ELEGANCE IS THERE or not. It, like other stuff, happens. There are, oh, maybe twenty knifemakers out there known to this writer who achieve elegance almost every time, but I'm pretty sure they're not setting out to do so.

For guys who do it, words like "nice" or "neat" or even "slick" cover the subject. Critics like your reporter use words like "elegance."

Regardless, for the knowledgeable, elegance is almost always desirable. It may be that occasionally the elegant line is a little weaker than, say, a stylized line or a customary line in the same place. But that's hard to tell without the knife in hand.

Price isn't really part of elegance, except that the knifemaker who grinds a little deeper, finishes more meticulously and takes greater pains is likely to be a fellow who believes in his knives. And that fellow will, often as not, ask for more money.

You absolutely cannot send out for elegance. It is either in the knife or you'll never get it this time. Engravers and scrimmers and etchers and such have to be careful when they meet elegance. Any sort of mislick by an embellisher on an elegant piece sticks out like a black eye on a beauty queen.

Really pricey knives are often elegant. If his things seem naturally to come out clean and clear of line, a fellow can do for the top of the market, and some do.

It's fascinating to examine the elegant knife, to try to see the difference, which is almost always in a line. We have fixed it so you can try your hand right here.

Ken Warner

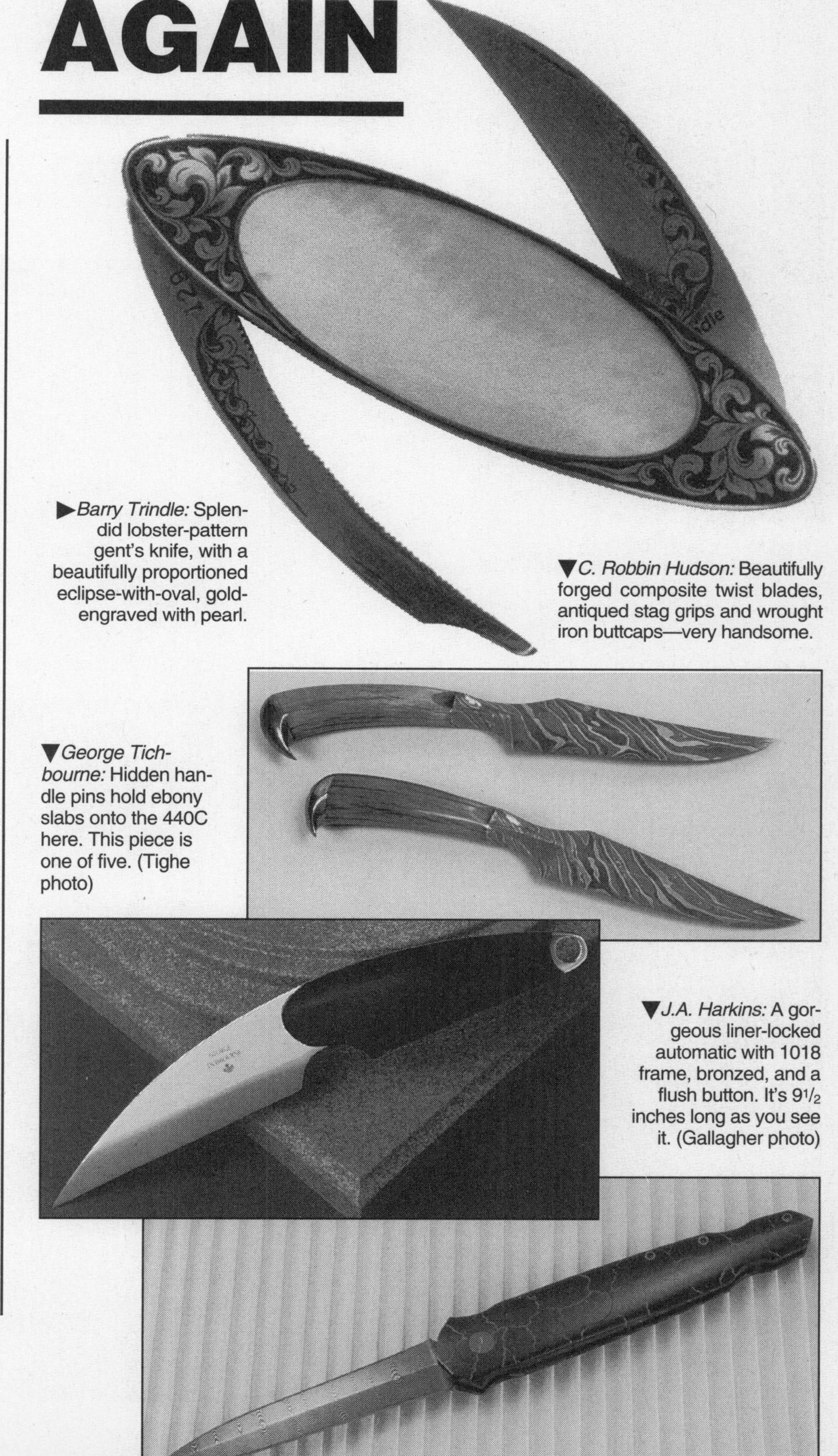

▶*Barry Trindle:* Splendid lobster-pattern gent's knife, with a beautifully proportioned eclipse-with-oval, gold-engraved with pearl.

▼*C. Robbin Hudson:* Beautifully forged composite twist blades, antiqued stag grips and wrought iron buttcaps—very handsome.

▼*George Tichbourne:* Hidden handle pins hold ebony slabs onto the 440C here. This piece is one of five. (Tighe photo)

▼*J.A. Harkins:* A gorgeous liner-locked automatic with 1018 frame, bronzed, and a flush button. It's 9½ inches long as you see it. (Gallagher photo)

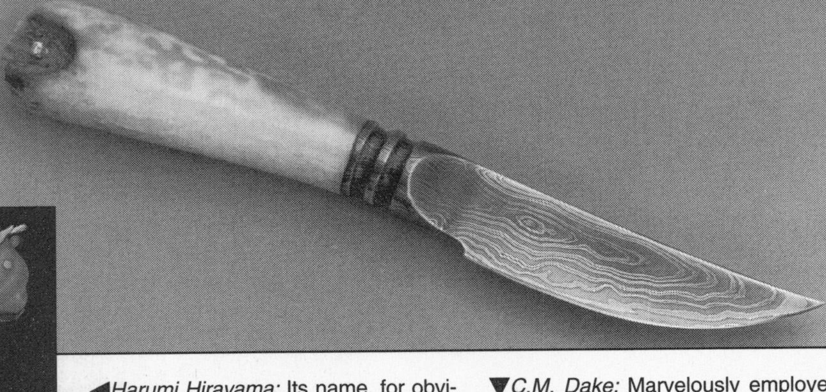

▶*Alex Chase:* It's a tad over 5 inches in 01/L6 Damascus, the handle is a fossil walrus tooth and the spot of light is a diamond—wonderful. (Weyer photo)

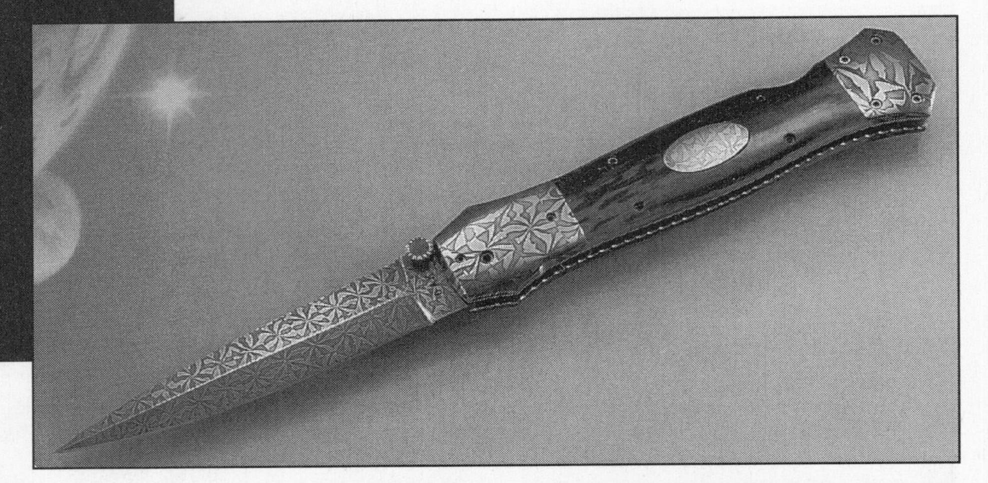

◀*Harumi Hirayama:* Its name, for obvious reasons, is Bouquet; the scales are luminous pink shell; pins and shackle are gold. It locks open.

▼*C.M. Dake:* Marvelously employed Meier Damascus set off with mammoth ivory from the 19th century and a 20th-century automatic lock. (Gallagher photo)

▼*George Koutsopoulos:* Splendid Old World sort of package, engraved by Don Norton.

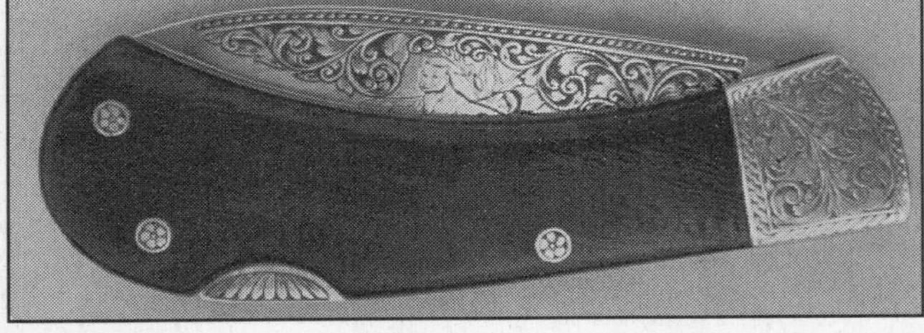

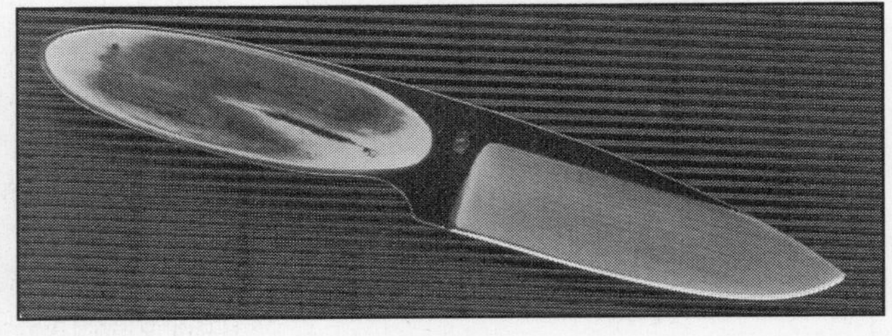

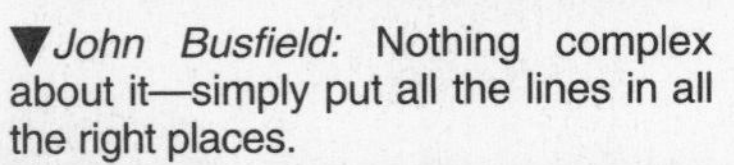

▼*John Busfield:* Nothing complex about it—simply put all the lines in all the right places.

▲*Wolfgang Dell:* Hand-rubbed steel, hand-rubbed blue mammoth ivory—just under 8 correctly proportioned inches.

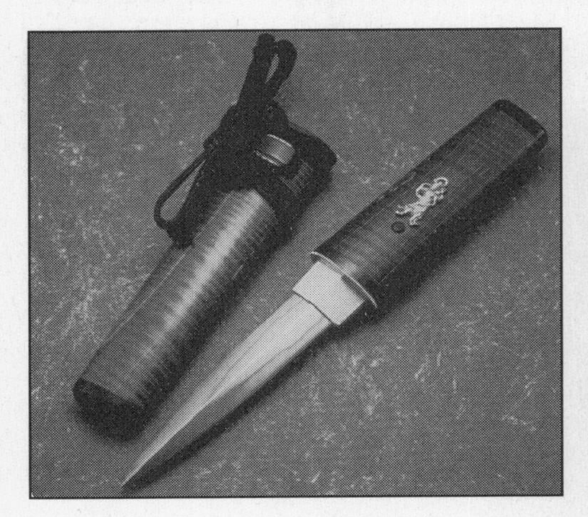

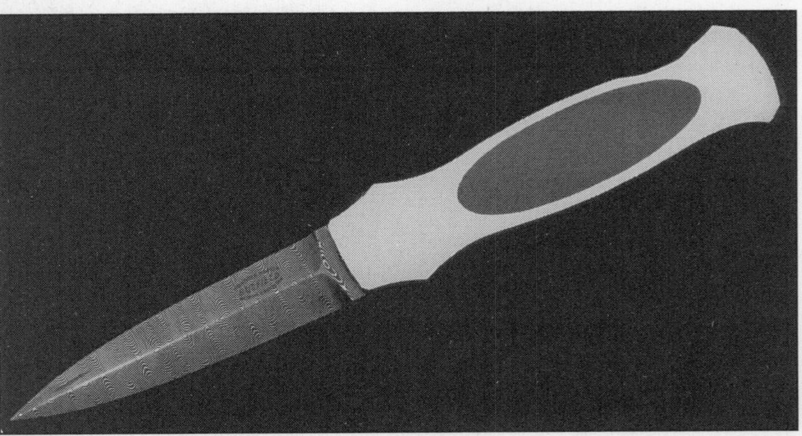

▲*Don Polzien:* Traditional or not, this is a tasteful ensemble in Japanese style.

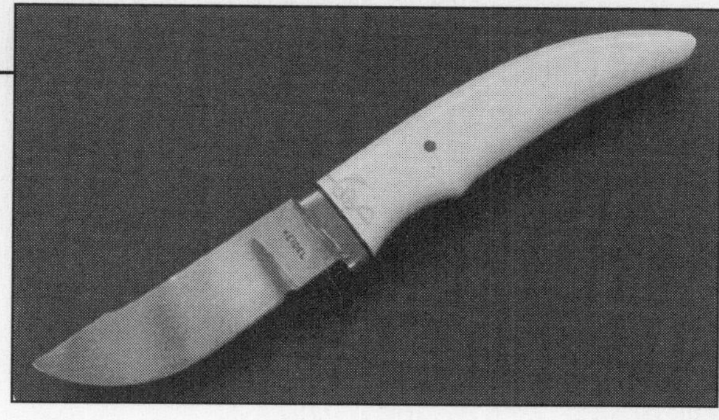

▲*Gene W. & Scott J. Keidel:* An elegant skinner? Yep. It's 440C, brass and ivory Micarta, but it's still elegant.

▶*Barry Gallagher:* A full coppery mokume shell underlaid with brown-lip pearl holding a Meier Damascus blade and other touches—4 inches closed. (Self photo)

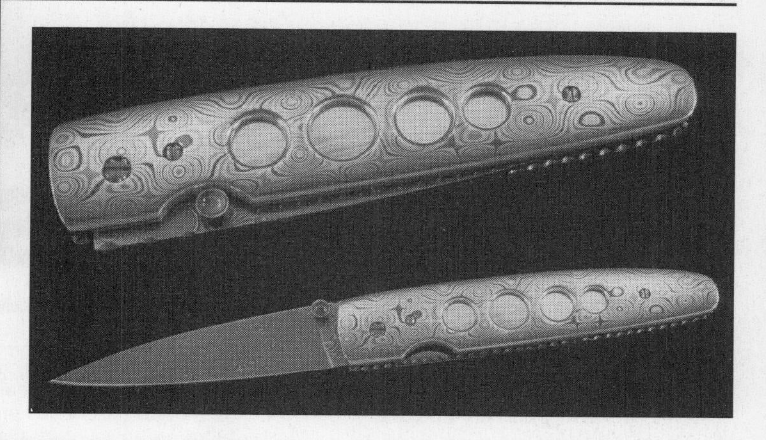

◀*Andrew Frankland:* The blade is 9 inches; the shape is Zulu assagai; the execution in Damascus, titanium, nickel silver wire and ivory is impeccable. (Reinders photo)

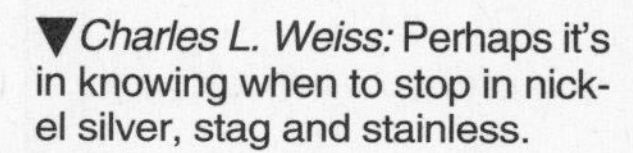

▼*Charles L. Weiss:* Perhaps it's in knowing when to stop in nickel silver, stag and stainless.

▶*Kouji Hara:* A nifty conception carved from the steel, called the Stone Step.

▶*Harvey J. Dean:* Immaculate 6-inch Bowie hunter immaculately proportioned in $^3/_{16}$-inch 1095, nickel silver and India stag. (Gallagher photo)

◀*Larry Newton:* Looks good open or closed—it's the lines and the mix of patterns that does it.

SWORDS, LOTS OF SWORDS

THEY'RE GAINING ON us again. The handmade sword is getting into a sort of cycle. They ebb a while, then flow a while. Right now, it's flow.

We got your Katanas, your broadswords and knightly stuff, and your Vikings, of course. We also are seeing hunting swords and hangers and basket-hilted Scottish broadswords and some swept-hilt rapiers, and some darned good-looking Persian yataghans and such.

There are cutlasses for sailing ships and, apparently, spaceships. And a lot of swordly large daggers are shown here, too.

We still don't have sword fights, although that may change. There are plenty of commercial swords—more than ever—and some of them are said to be battle-worthy.

And Ontario has announced a whole bundle of Black Wind swords for Everyman. There are seven models in 3/16-inch black, probably of 1095 steel. They're one-piece swords in Kydex sheaths at 18 to 30 inches overall and are unlikely to break when they hit something.

They probably will hit something. It's been some time since you could buy a sound sword, brand-new, for the price of a classy hunting knife or deluxe folder. So a lot of people will. And then what?

Ken Warner

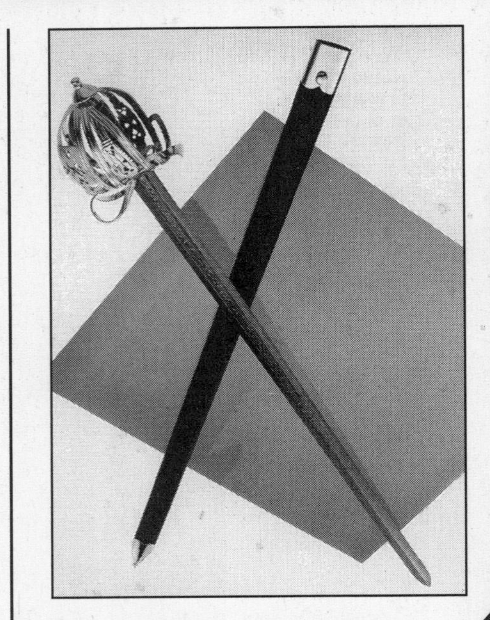

▲*Vincent K. Evans:* All-out Scottish basket-hilt sword in Damascus, horn and nickel silver at 41 1/2 inches overall. (Weyer photo)

▲*Vincent K. Evans:* Not Japanese, but Chinese, we have here a 36-inch saber in Damascus and browned steel. (Weyer photo)

▶*Craig A. Steketee:* Ladder Damascus, fitted in cast bronze, silk and ironwood at 30 inches overall. (Weyer photo)

▼*Michael Bell:* Unerringly Japanese in look, construction and execution, this all-out Katana was made in Washington state. ((Weyer photo)

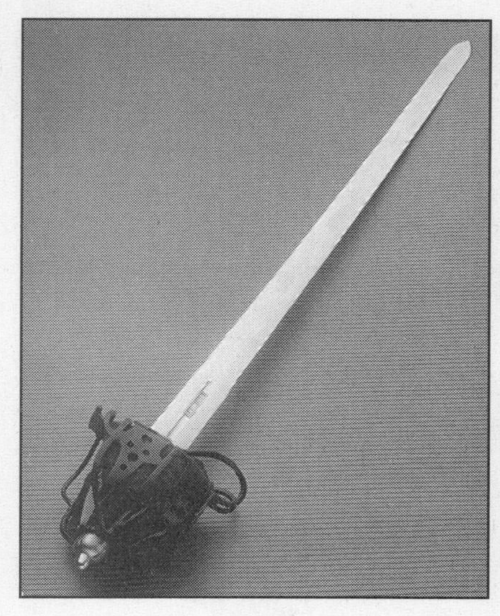

▲*Al Massey:* Basket-hilted in steel, leather-gripped, this Highlander sword has 1084 blade and a full length of 37 inches. (Weyer photo)

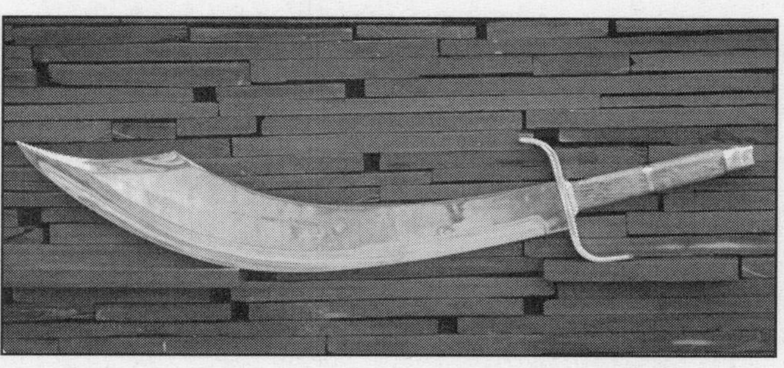

◀*Ricardo Villar:* A scimitar—a BIG scimitar—in 420 stainless, wood and brass—45 inches overall.

▼*J.W. Townsend:* Rag Micarta and 440C in 33½ imaginative inches—equipment for other worldly dragonslaying. (Weyer photo)

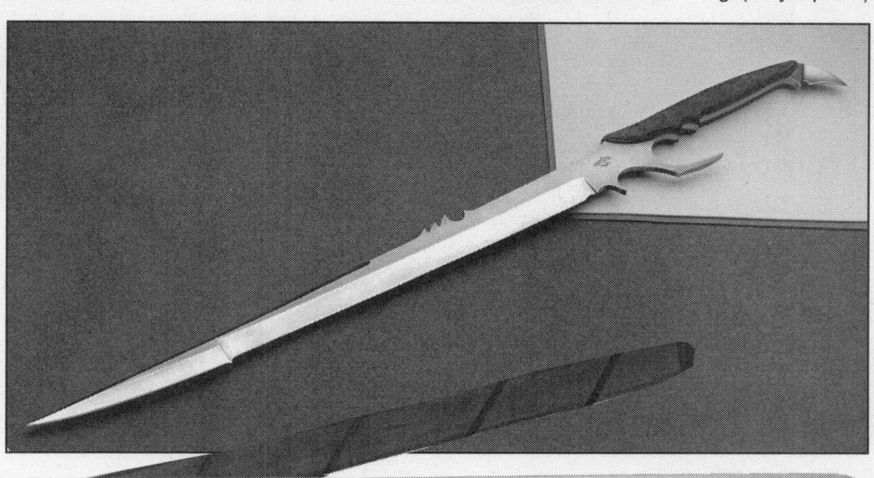

▼*Mike Lewis:* This big guy has 37½ inches of ATS-34 blade (54 Rc) set up with leather wrap and redwood scabbard.

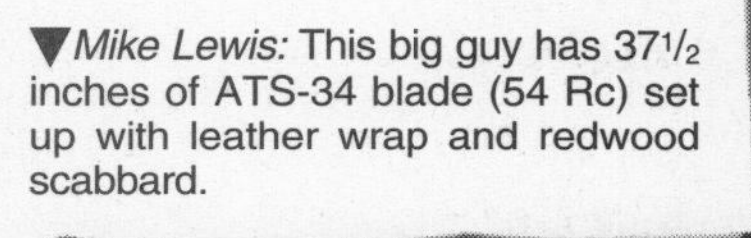

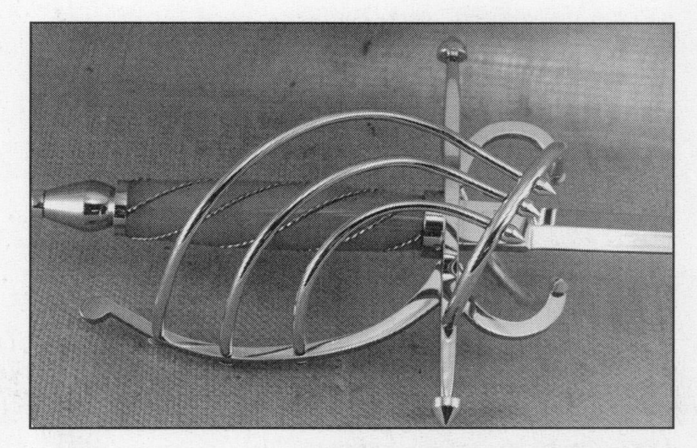

▲▶*Larry Mensch:* Good-looking swept-hilt rapier is perhaps a style they should have tried back then.

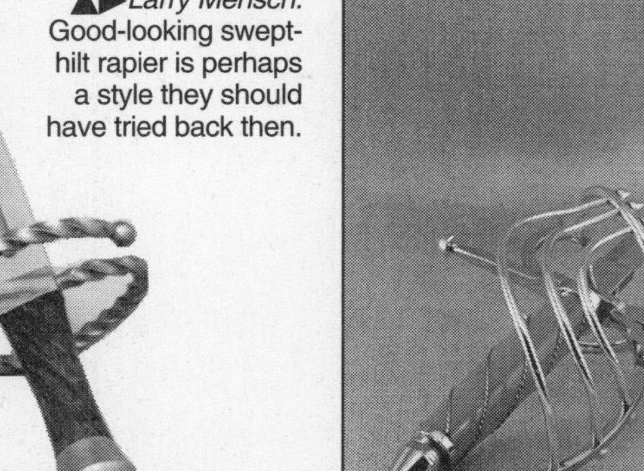

▲*Kevin R. Cashen:* All welded Damascus, 27½ inches overall, in the Viking style with composite blade. (Weyer photo)

▶*Mike Lewis:* This Dragon Steel *Katzbalger* in 440C (at 54 Rc) would have delighted a 16th-century German mercenary.

▼*Wolfgang Loerchner:* Blued steel grip and stainless blade, bead-blasted here and there for texture—very nice at 20 inches overall. (Weyer photo)

▲*James R. Cook:* Hunting sword with 21-inch carbon steel blade, stag grip and copper/silver fittings. (Hughes photo)

▼*Steve Dunn:* Simple and elegant 19th-century foot officer's sword in Damascus (for rich officers, of course). (Weyer photo)

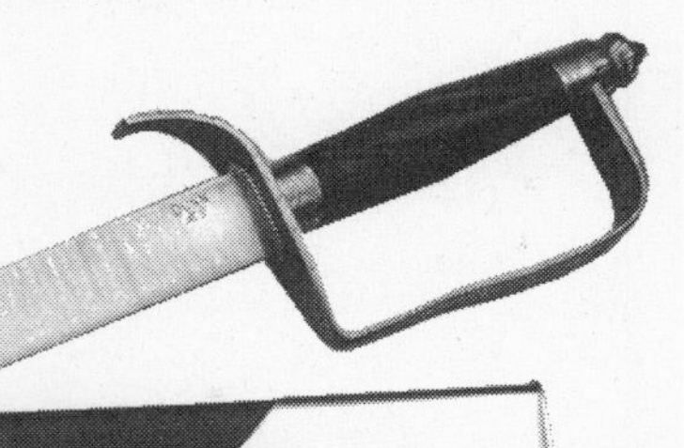

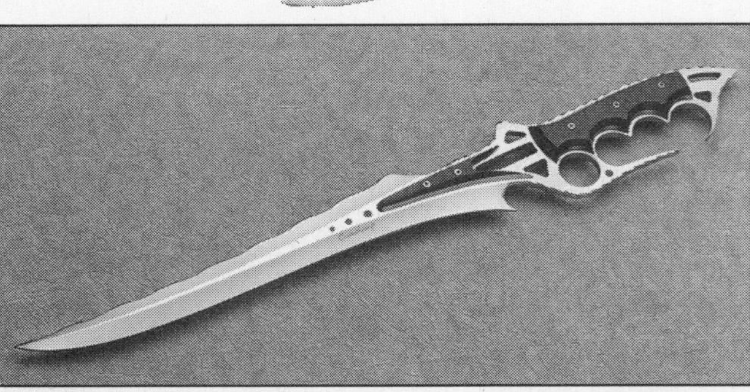

▲*Gaetan Beauchamp:* Short boarding cutlass for on-board spaceship battles—20 inches overall. (Weyer photo)

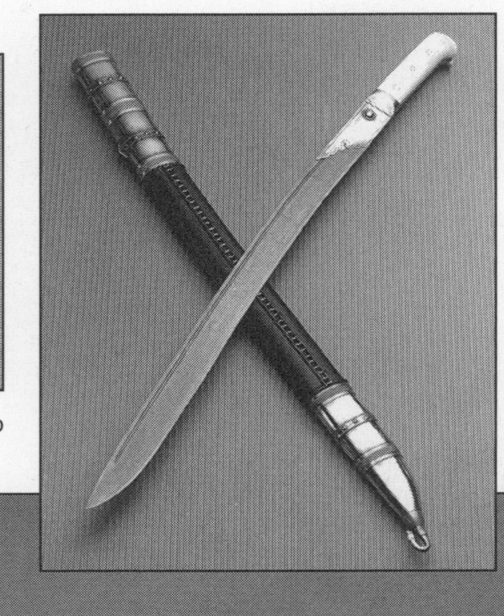

◀*Vincent K. Evans:* Yataghan, 28½ inches overall, in Damascus, ivory, silver—most subtle, most handsome. (Weyer photo)

▼*Paul M. Jarvis:* Maker calls it a Ko-Dachi. It goes about 21 ornate inches overall in Meier Damascus, ivory, sterling, gold wire and garnets. (Weyer photo)

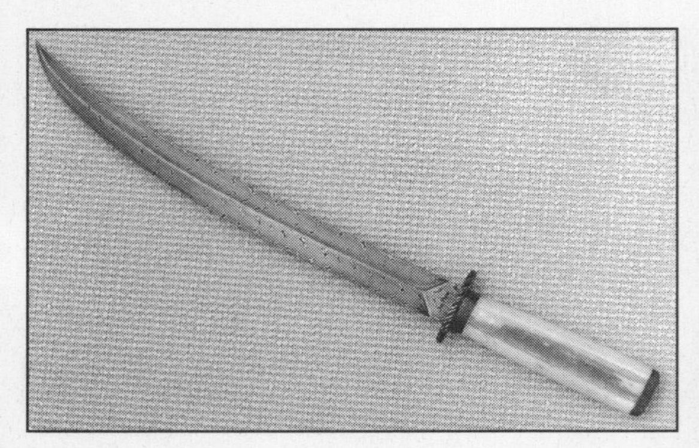

▲*Jim Fister:* Swordlike in every detail, this slim dagger in Turkish Damascus, iron and walrus ivory goes 16 inches overall.

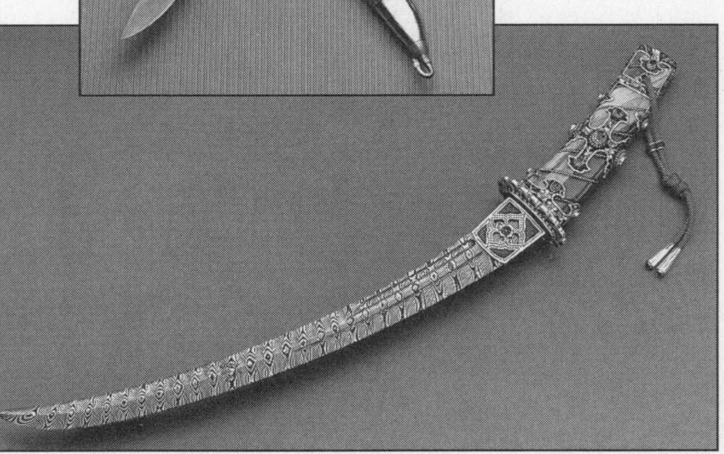

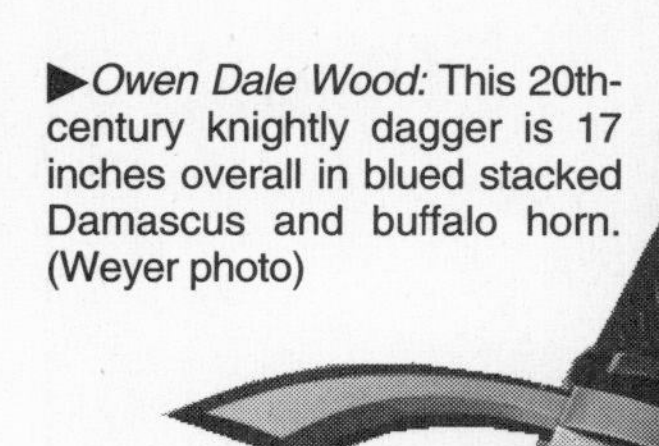

▶*Owen Dale Wood:* This 20th-century knightly dagger is 17 inches overall in blued stacked Damascus and buffalo horn. (Weyer photo)

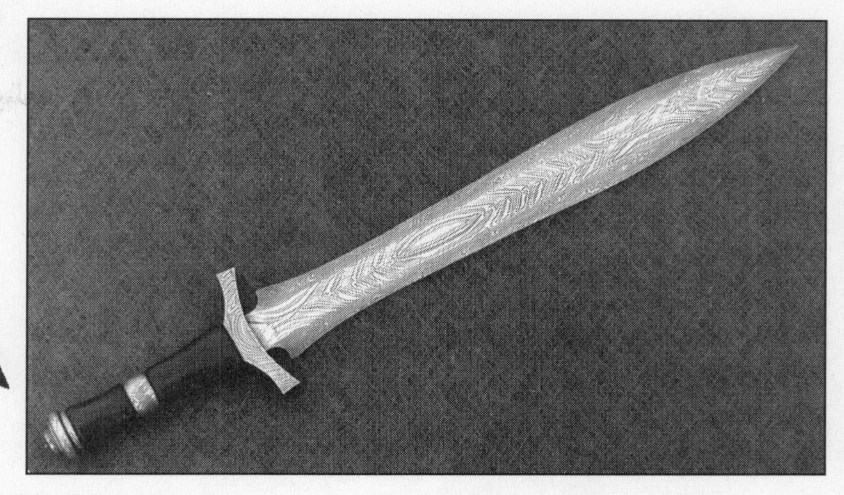

◀*Steven J. Rapp:* A 20-inch hunting sword in a Joseph Rodgers style is 440C and ivory, mostly. (Weyer photo)

▲*Kevin R. Cashen:* Just about two feet of gladius here, in appropriately patterned Damascus and horn.

▼*Wally Hayes:* This big-looking Scots dirk, in composite Damascus with carved purple heart grip, has an amethyst pommel-set. (Weyer photo)

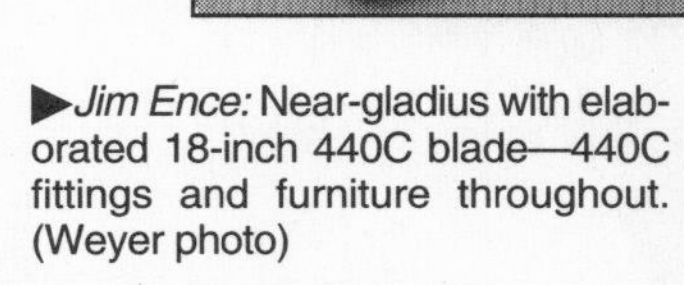

▶*Jim Ence:* Near-gladius with elaborated 18-inch 440C blade—440C fittings and furniture throughout. (Weyer photo)

▼*Thomas J. Griffin:* This knightly left-hand dagger with parrying quillon and wire wrap is about the right size.

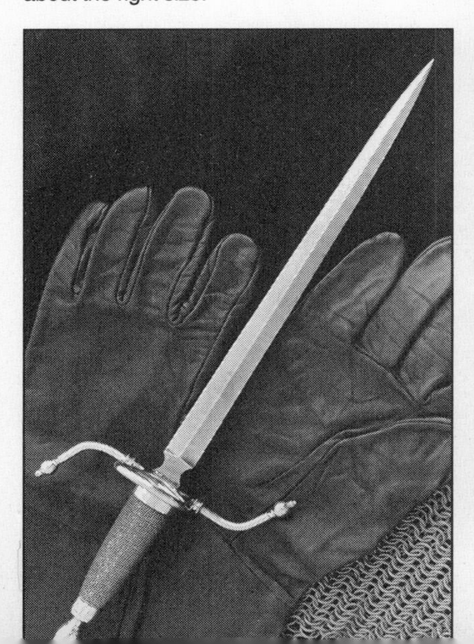

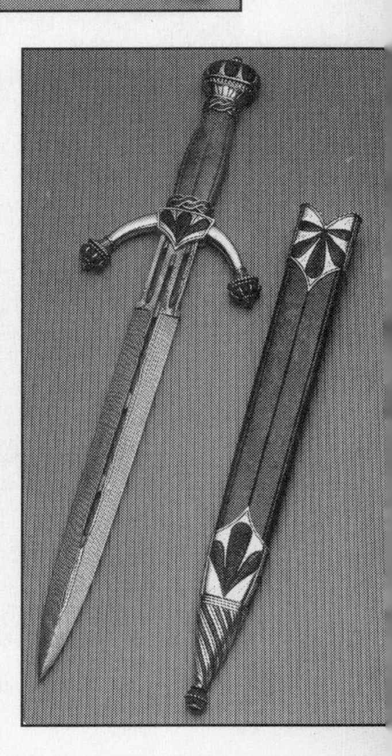

▶*Paul M. Jarvis:* The 64-layer Damascus provides texture and pattern—the rest is sea cow bone and bronze silver at 20 inches overall. (Weyer photo)

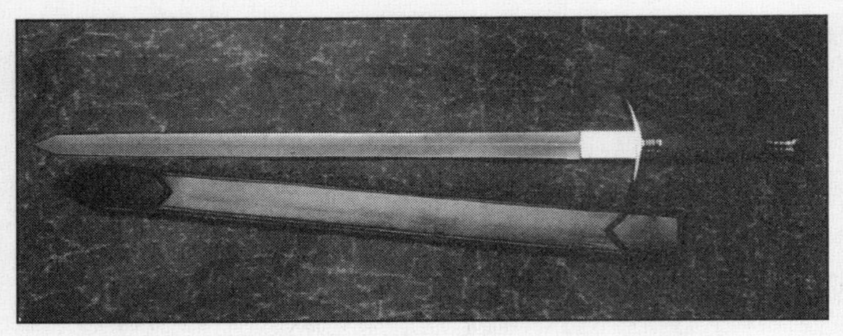

▲*Leonardo Williams Gonzalez:* Very straightforward knightly broadsword—the compleat 12th-century gent's tool. (Walters photo)

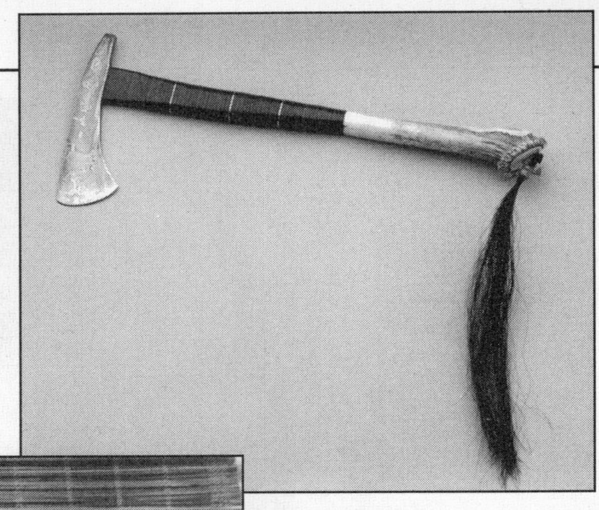

▲*Tim Scholl:* A North American fighting axe in Damascus with a composite bone/leather handle.

◀*Wally Hayes:* Short sword in typical layout; grip is silk-wrapped rayskin.

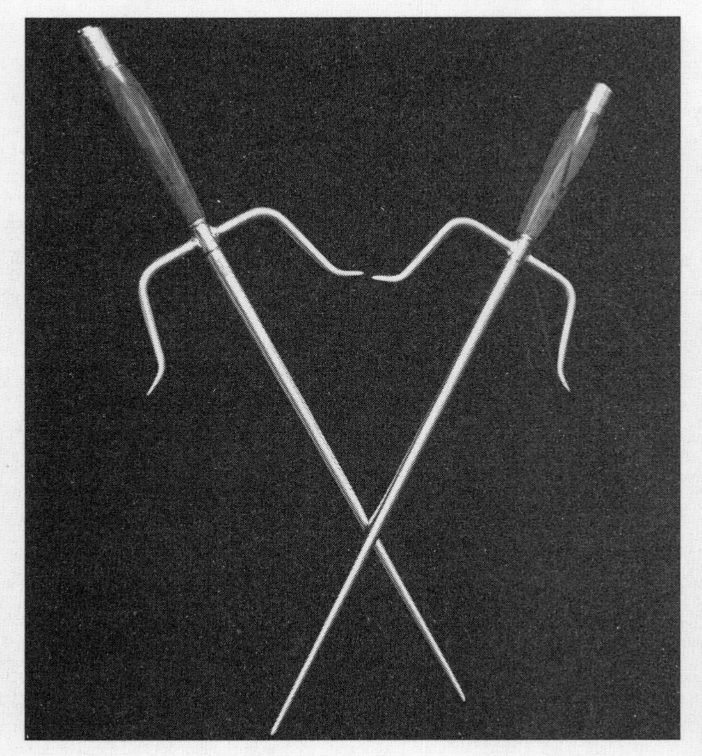

▲*Jerry Gerus:* Not built to match, these two swordplay defenses are balanced individually.

◀*Pat Crawford:* A selection of gents' walking sticks with 10-inch blades—you just pull and there it is.

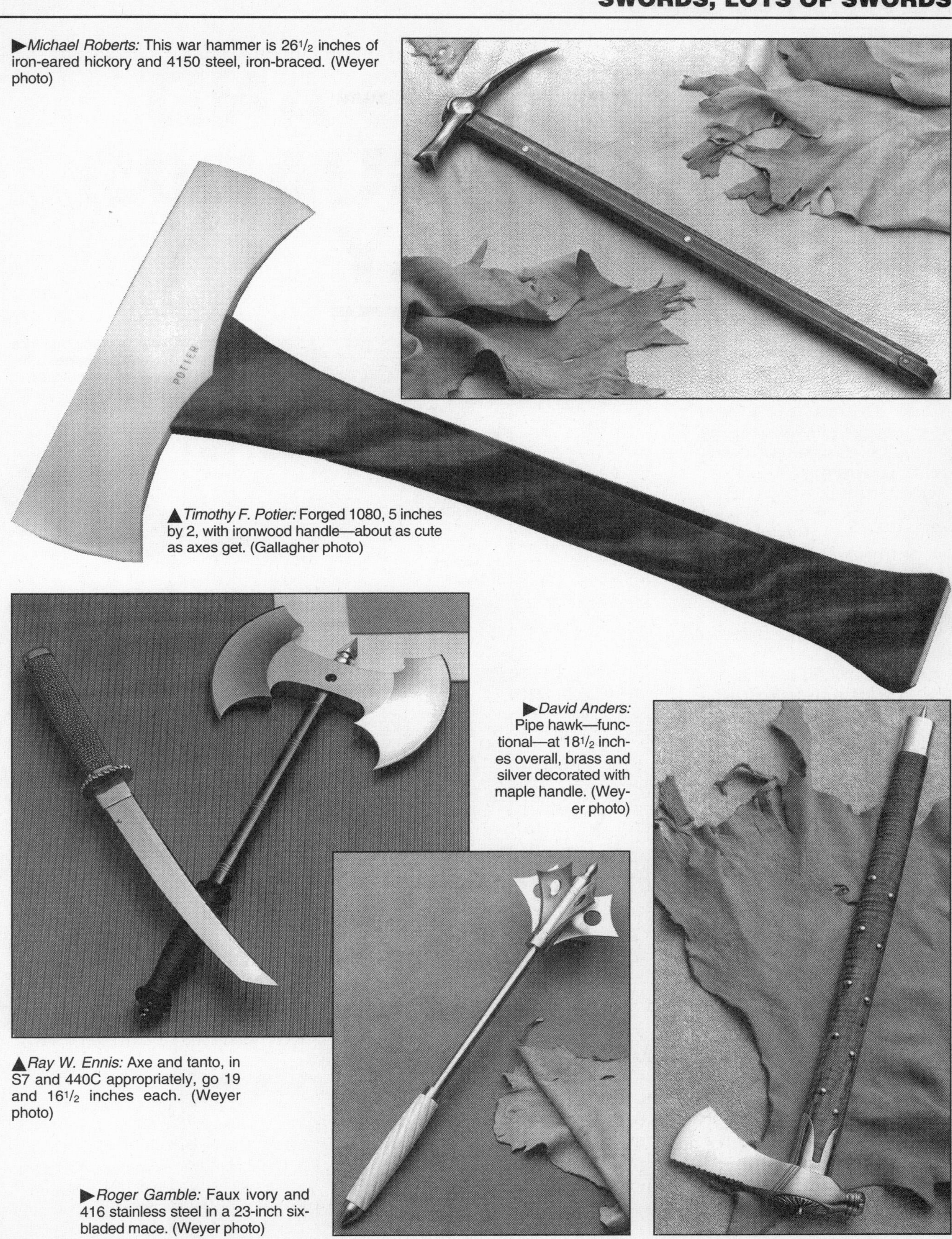

▶*Michael Roberts:* This war hammer is $26\frac{1}{2}$ inches of iron-eared hickory and 4150 steel, iron-braced. (Weyer photo)

▲*Timothy F. Potier:* Forged 1080, 5 inches by 2, with ironwood handle—about as cute as axes get. (Gallagher photo)

▶*David Anders:* Pipe hawk—functional—at $18\frac{1}{2}$ inches overall, brass and silver decorated with maple handle. (Weyer photo)

▲*Ray W. Ennis:* Axe and tanto, in S7 and 440C appropriately, go 19 and $16\frac{1}{2}$ inches each. (Weyer photo)

▶*Roger Gamble:* Faux ivory and 416 stainless steel in a 23-inch six-bladed mace. (Weyer photo)

SUB-HILTS AND KNUCKLEGUARDS TODAY

FOR TWO RELATIVELY simple ideas—retaining control for sub-hilts and hand protection for knuckleguards—there seem to be several ways to go. Like musicians at play, knifemakers elaborate these two themes in many ways.

It's the customers' idea. Hardly anybody but people likes these knife features. All the experts say the sub-hilt interferes with handling and that D-guards, knuckle guards, whatever, interfere with that and everything else as well.

However, the expert is voting with his knowledge, his sincerity, his appreciation of fact and his experience. He gets out-voted in a New York minute by the customer who is balloting with dollars—often lots of dollars.

The modern progenitor of the sub-hilt was, I believe, R.W. Loveless, and who pulled his sub-hilt chain I don't know. More than most, you could get your fingers in and out of Loveless sub-hilts with some celerity. The second hilt was far enough from the first, and gracefully shaped for entrances and exits.

In part, it's exiting that the sub-hilt is for—it gives the user something to haul on to get the knife from, say, a recalcitrant ribcage. Ooops, did I say something naughty?

Well, I was there when another famous custom cutler named Moran redesigned his S-23 fighter. A customer had returned from Vietnam without a knife because he just couldn't, at the moment of which we speak, take a few seconds to pry his knife loose from his late opponent. He wanted another Moran, but it had to let him tug on it, so Moran provided a hooked pommel.

◀*Roger M. Green:* Loveless-shaped 6-inch fighter in 440C, stag and 416. Note the relieved inner faces. (Gallagher photo)

▶*Anthony Brett Schaller:* This big boy has fully worked hilt surfaces and Micarta grips. (Weyer photo)

▶*Rick Browne:* A little different set of gripping and hilting arrangements behind an 8-inch blade. (Weyer photo)

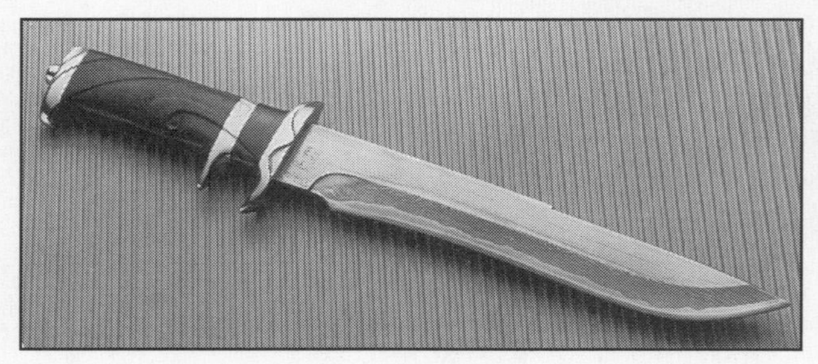

◀*Wally Hayes:* Sculpted *san-mai* blade, handle and guard, but again a little tight forefinger spot. (Weyer photo)

In certain sorts of unrealistic knife play, the sub-hilt confers some advantage of control. However, those are excessivley fine points (sorry) for this reporter to consider.

The knuckleguard, however, is much less equivocal. There's no doubt about the simple splendor of the bash-and-slash potential to a fellow in a complex melee, folks yelling and swinging and bouncing off each

◀*Al Eaton:* Now we're into a trigger guard design—the forefinger better get in there on the draw. (Weyer photo)

◀*Michael K. Manabe:* Besides the triple temper lines and the cute little choil cutouts, we're looking at a pretty tight sub-hilt setup. (Weyer photo)

▲*Scottie H. White:* It maybe isn't a sub-hilt, but rather a snappy choil cutout, but the effect is the same. (Weyer photo)

▶*Mudd Sharrigan:* A certain insouciance here. As it should be, the guard is steel so it won't fold back. (Weyer photo)

▲*Dan Keyes:* This is called the Underwater Tactical, and the function of the forefinger ring is retention, pure and simple. (Weyer photo)

▲*Zaza Revishvili:* Pendray blade and, no doubt, guard in Wootz steel; classic Russian filigree otherwise. (Weyer photo)

other. If you got that problem, the knuckleguard is part of a solution.

The ultimate expressions of this idea were basket hilts and full-cup swords and naval cutlasses. They worked, and they carried fine because they were not close aboard the person.

On a knife? Well, the best way to handle the matter would be to have a simple knife for most stuff and have a trusted servant deliver your knuckle-guarded beauty just before the melee starts.

Those jaundiced viewpoints notwithstanding, a lot of knives so-equipped are pretty slick. So look at a few here and enjoy.

Ken Warner

▶*Robert J. McDonald:* Seriously massive Bowie with birdseye grip and iron S-guard. (Gallagher photo)

▲*Grant Fraser:* Nasty sharply pointed fighter with somewhat slim brass guard. (Weyer photo)

▲*Harvey J. Dean:* Walrus ivory and engraved sterling silver and—oh, yes—an 11-inch Damascus blade. (Weyer photo)

▼*Sava Damlovac:* Big fighter with big spooned finger guard for that close-in crunch. (Weyer photo)

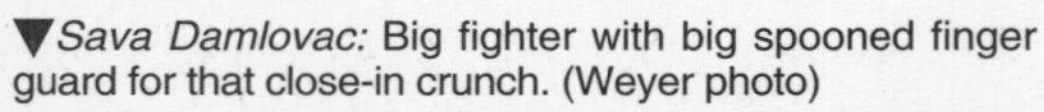

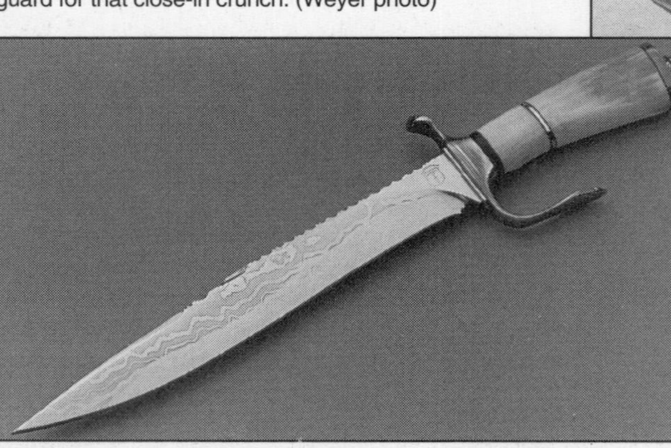

▲*Ken Hoy:* This improbably guarded Persian dagger has *two* flared finger guards. (Weyer photo)

▼*Gary D. Anderson:* Not-so-big (overall 13 inches) D-guarded fighter with file-worked mild steel fittings and a copper acorn. (Weyer photo)

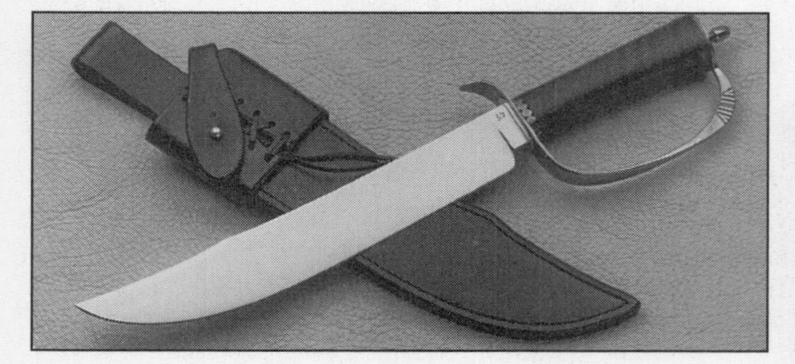

▲*Rich McDonald:* Big no-nonsense Bowie in 5160 and oak, with a mild steel D-guard. (Weyer photo)

FANCY DAGGERS

THERE ARE ONLY three or four patterns the knifemaker bent on display chooses, and the dagger is high on that list. A dagger, if you just got here, is a mostly symmetrical, generally two-edged knife, small or large, with, for the most part, only social utility.

Yes, there *are* working daggers. In the meat industry, they are called stickers. They are called that because they are designed to stick butchered animals—that is, reach in and cut blood vessels efficiently so the carcass bleeds out.

That, in essence and perhaps a little gross, is what the whole idea of the dagger is about. It is a tool to let the hot blood out and the cold air in.

All sorts of interesting people have carried daggers—kings and queens, pimps and whores, soldiers and bandits, cooks and bakers—you know. For this reporter, the most interesting were 19th-century American hunters who—a lot of them, anyway—carried small daggers sheathed on their hunting bags and bag straps. Powder and ball was expensive, and a fellow with a little manual dexterity and a good short dagger could do the *coup de grace* by hand, as it were.

Actually, it may surprise the reader to know this reporter has tried that on groundhogs, big hogs and deer here, and even kudu and others in Africa. It really isn't all that difficult.

But that's not what these daggers, the ones you see here, are into. These are bragging stuff—for the owner, for the maker. As well might be.

Ken Warner

◀*Hank Ishihara:* Etched ATS-34 blade on a knife called Devil's Dagger—pretty elaborate. (Weyer photo)

▼*Joe D. Huddleston:* Celtic motifs in silver here with a leaf-shaped blade and a decorated sheath—about 8 inches of blade.

▼*Al Scott:* Ivory handled 13½-inch dagger with heavy Mideast lineage. (Weyer photo)

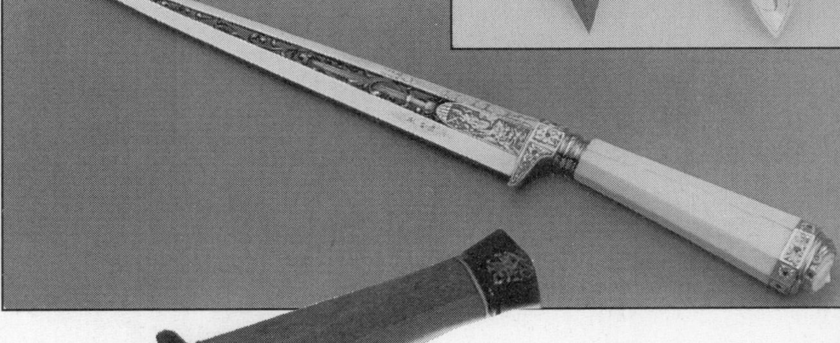

◀*Don Fogg:* This textured Damascus dagger is a slim sort of Viking pattern—copper, gold and bloodwood.

◀*Larry Fuegen:* This is art nouveau, he says—gold, frogskin, Damascus steel and carved fossil ivory. (Weyer photo)

▶*Zaza Revishvili:* Gil Hibben blade in a rich silver filigree setting. (Weyer photo)

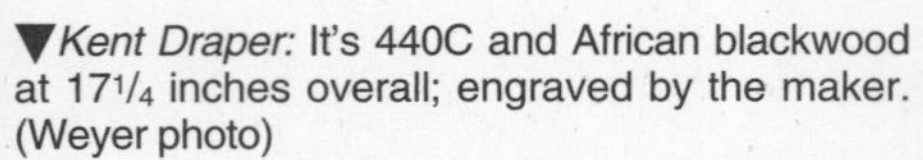

▼*Kent Draper:* It's 440C and African blackwood at $17\frac{1}{4}$ inches overall; engraved by the maker. (Weyer photo)

▼*Paul M. Jarvis:* Considerable texture in an elaborate dagger of European shape and Japanese style. (Weyer photo)

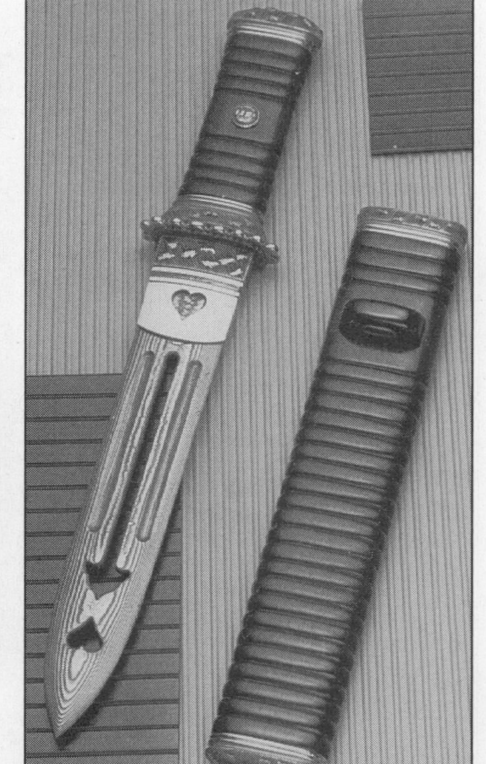

▲*Buster Warenski:* Julie-engraved flying dagger goes a big $27\frac{1}{4}$ inches overall—more of a sword, actually. (Weyer photo)

▲*Douglas Casteel:* Big 440C dagger, fitted in 416 and 17 inches overall with blast jade handle. (Weyer photo)

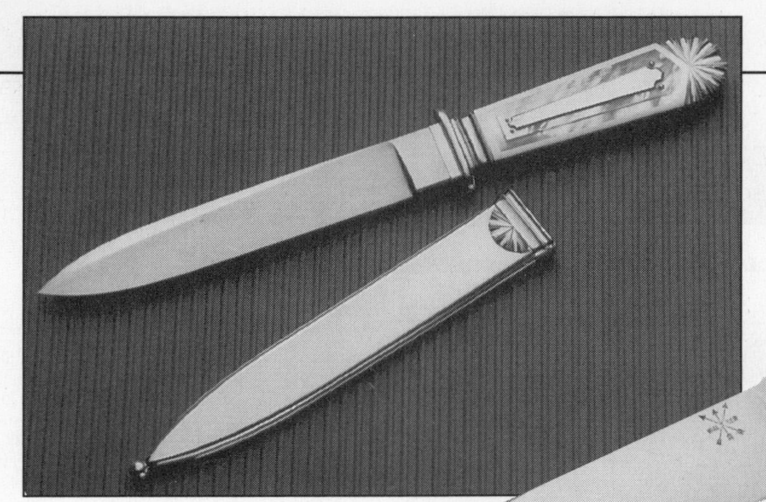

◀*Wolfgang Loerchner:* San Francisco styling, newly interpreted with an interframe, filework and plating—11½ inches overall. (Weyer photo)

◀*Jim Walker:* Pretty close replication of a famous Michael Price knife in 5160 steel—12 inches overall. (Weyer photo)

◀*Herman J. Schneider:* The classic stuff in heavy fullered blades and fluted grips. (Weyer photo)

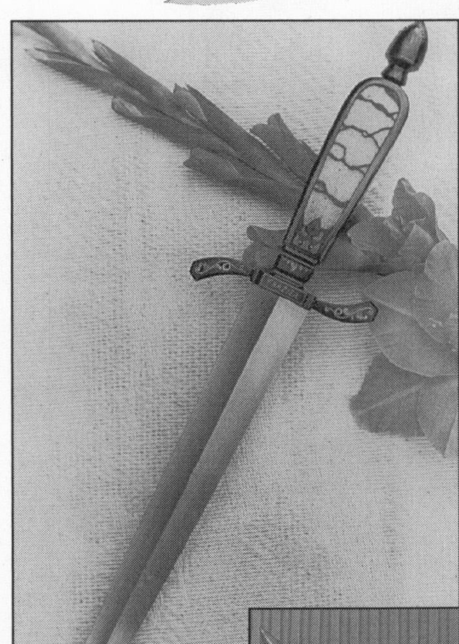

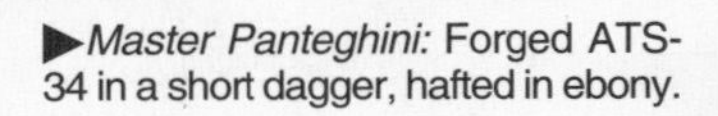

▶*Master Panteghini:* Forged ATS-34 in a short dagger, hafted in ebony.

▼*Richard DiMarzo:* Curved double-edged 5½-inch blade in Damascus teamed with curved walrus ivory. (Weyer photo)

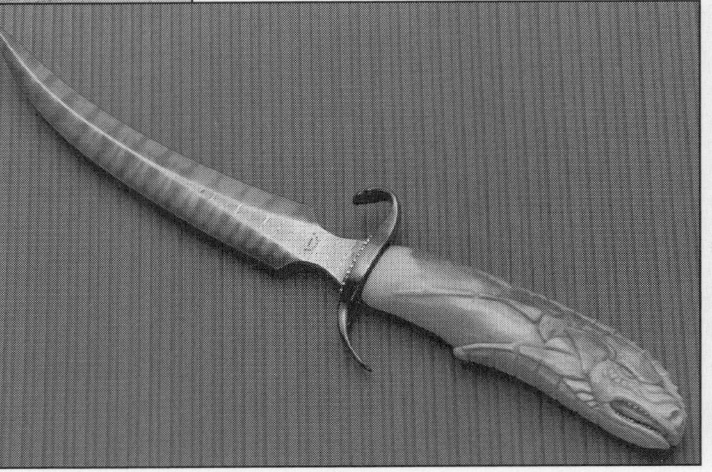

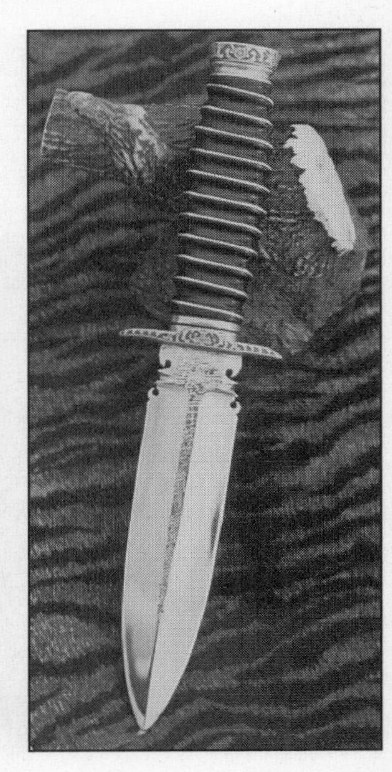

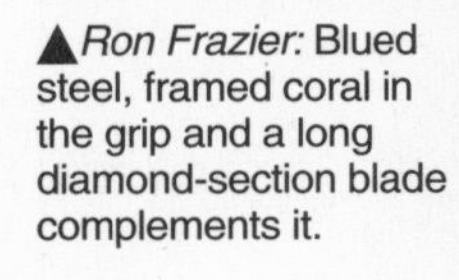

▲*Ron Frazier:* Blued steel, framed coral in the grip and a long diamond-section blade complements it.

MORE DAGGERS

WHEN ALL ELSE fails, the daggers will sell. They're simple-looking, but not easy to make, mostly because the typical blade has four major surfaces, and they meet in long lines where it's easy to see the mistakes, but people like them.

Still, the dagger is somehow just a little more serious than the average knife. It's the double edges and the obvious bias toward penetration that does it. Mostly.

There is also a lot of history in the shape. All those knightly forebears, you know, as well as all those peasants everyone else descended from. They all required the same service of a knife.

The unreal "reality quotient" creates a certain number of plain and simple daggers every year. It's not clear whether the buyers want to carry them or to own them just in case. It's probably the latter.

They sell, though. That means probably nobody likes them but people. And you. And me.

Ken Warner

◀*Steven J. Rapp:* Workaday dress dagger; 6 inches of 440C, with ebony and leather and blued steel. (Weyer photo)

▲*Charles F. Ochs:* He makes these serious tools, forged from 52100 at 7 inches with blackwood grip, for serious people. (Weyer photo)

▲*Wolfgang Dell:* A 19th-century design at 6½ inches in stainless steel and ebony.

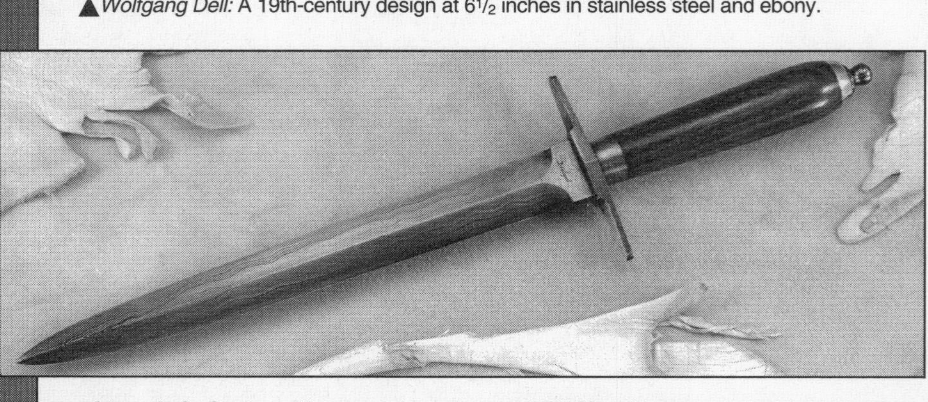

◀*Joseph G. Cordova:* Massive 8½- and 9-inch daggers, called "Gladiator" in 440C. (Weyer photo)

▲*Bill Dietzel:* Long and slim in nickel Damascus and *lignum vitae*—solid. (Gallagher photo)

◀*J.D. Smith:* The medieval stylist at work in somber, rich detail—11¼ inches overall. (Weyer photo)

▼*Ed Halligan:* Nearly 9 inches of slim Damascus with a gold nugget forged-in about an inch from the handle—neat knife. (Weyer photo)

▶*Scottie H. White:* All stainless and fossil ivory and big—17 inches overall—unornamented Baroque. (Weyer photo)

▼*Bruce James Hartmann:* A whimsical exercise in 15¾ inches of shiny, but right pretty. (Weyer photo)

◀*Dean Piesner:* A World War II shape and size, but classic, thus neither Fairbairn's nor Sykes's. (Gallagher photo)

▶*Bob Kramer:* This classic twisted-grip quillon dagger, 14½ inches overall, is bigger than it looks. (Gallagher photo)

TRENDS

MINIATURES AS SMALL AS CAN BE

IN FINANCIAL AFFAIRS, they say, bad money drives out good. Presumably, that means well-backed currencies disappear quickly when weaker currencies are about. Or something like that.

This does not seem to be the way it works in the supply of miniature knives. It seems quite the opposite; i.e., faced with really good ones, the mediocre disappear.

Since, for some knifemakers, the miniature itch is hard to scratch, the mediocre only go away long enough—most of the time—for their makers to learn to do better. And then those guys are back.

We are left with splendid little knives in all the categories—elegant, expensive, plain, workmanlike—and in all the patterns—folders and Bowies and swords and daggers—there are. You can, if your wallet holds out, have a hell of a broad-gauged knife show in your attache case, given a scrap or two of velveteen.

One fellow took the whole thing to the inevitable extreme. It was at the Blade Show. In one place, and indeed in one case, he went from a 12-inch knife in six 50-percent steps to one you had to peer at through a built-in lens to see. It was maybe 3/8-inch long, but made just like the big guy.

That's still the touchstone for the miniature collector. They have to be made like the big guys. And a lot are, as you can see for yourself.

Ken Warner

◀*Daniel E. Osterman:* A pair of bad-boy Bowies and just a simple thimble, which if it weren't there who would know?

▼*Frank J. Dilluvio:* Turquoise and stainless steel in a style the maker provides in big knives, too.

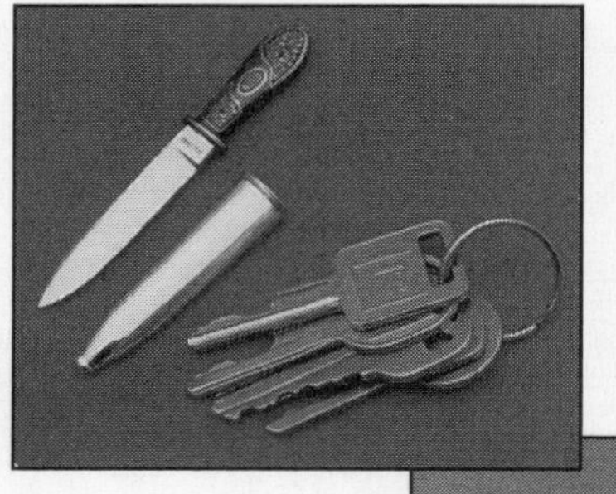

▲*Charles L. Weiss:* The maker says the tough part of this engraved dagger was making the giant keys.

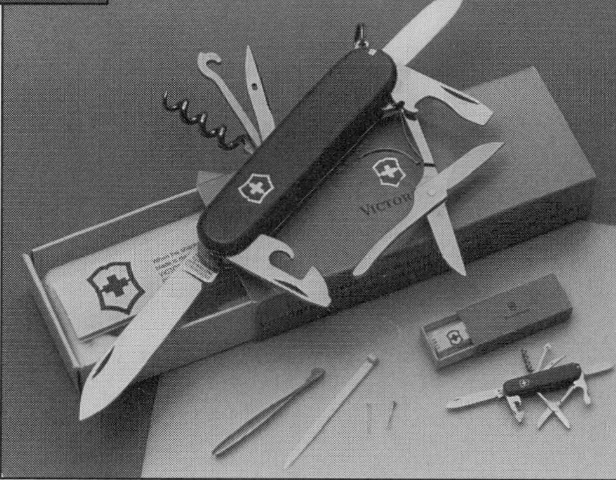

▶*Yvon Vachon:* Two versions of a Victorinox Climber, its box and its instructions. Vachon made the inch-long one. (Weyer photo)

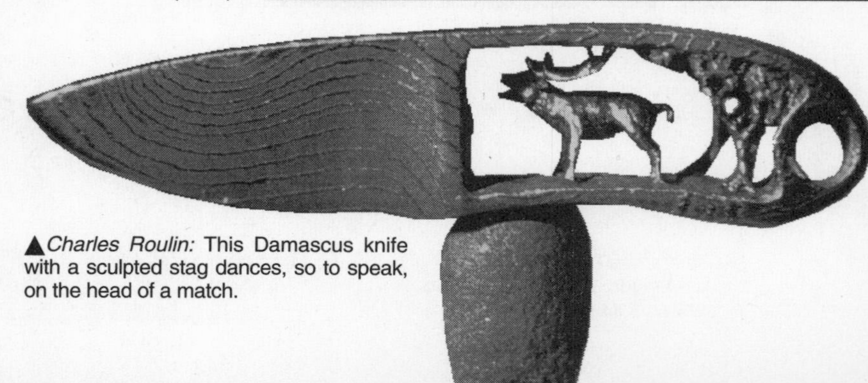

▲*Charles Roulin:* This Damascus knife with a sculpted stag dances, so to speak, on the head of a match.

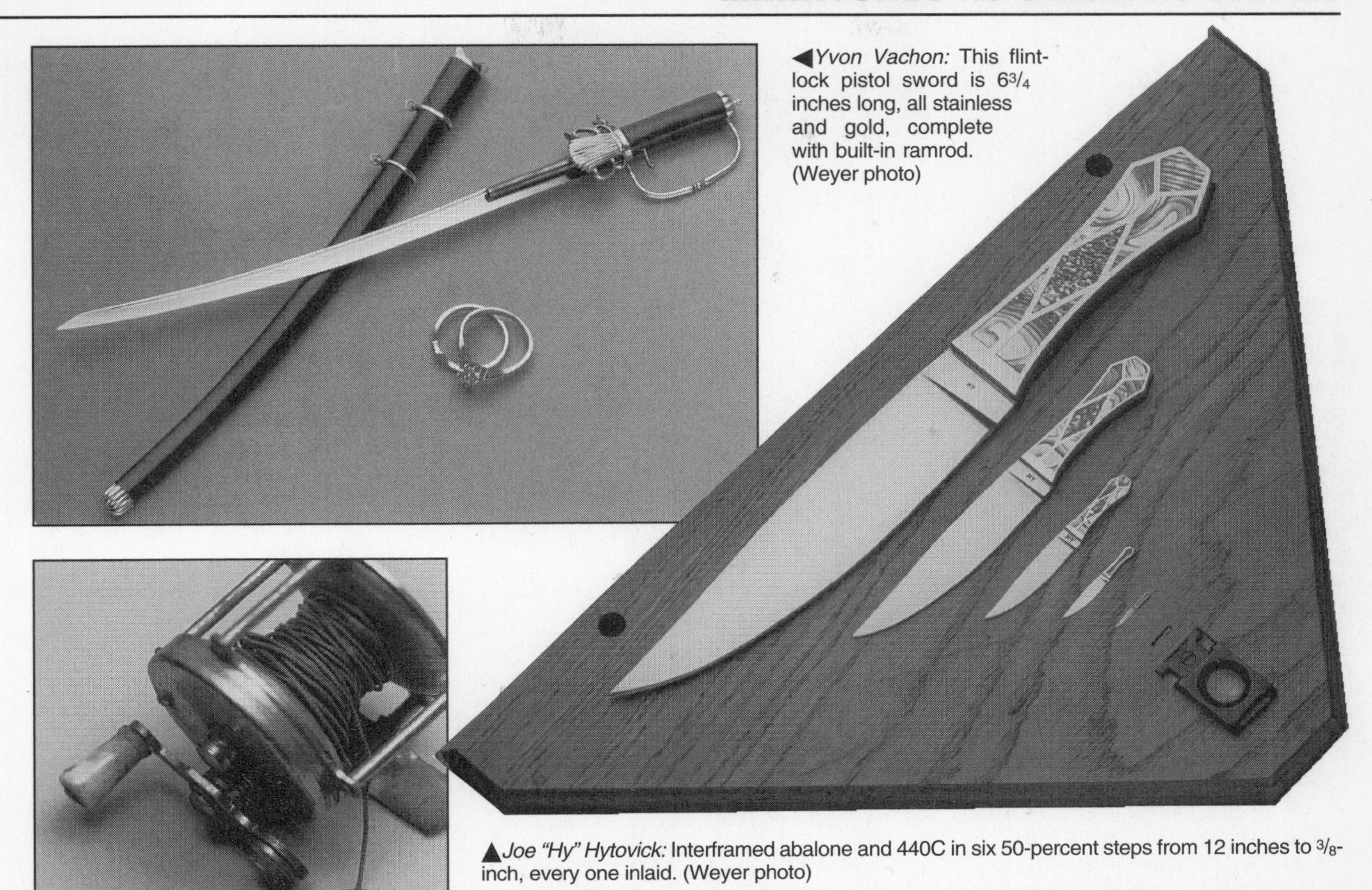

◀*Yvon Vachon:* This flintlock pistol sword is $6\frac{3}{4}$ inches long, all stainless and gold, complete with built-in ramrod. (Weyer photo)

▲*Joe "Hy" Hytovick:* Interframed abalone and 440C in six 50-percent steps from 12 inches to $\frac{3}{8}$-inch, every one inlaid. (Weyer photo)

▲*Earl Witsaman:* In honor of the poet of the hammer, here's a $2\frac{1}{2}$-inch Ed Fowler hunter. (Weyer photo)

▶*Eugene W. Shadley:* The white spot is an aspirin; the knife is a $1\frac{1}{8}$-inch folder.

▲*Ralph Boos:* Two-hander for a small barbarian, with a turned grip and a clawed pearl pommel.

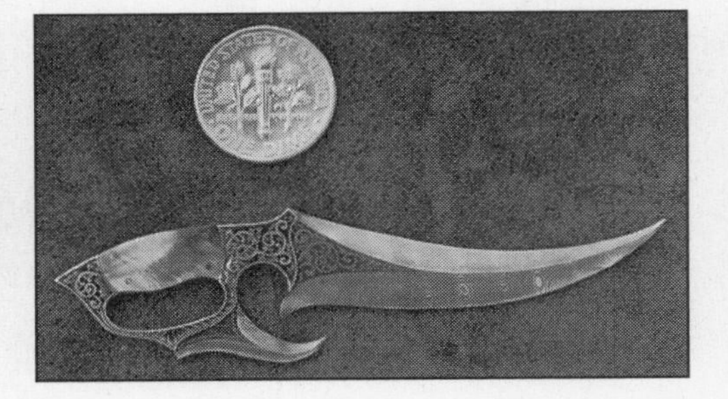

◀*James D. Whitehead:* A romantic fighter in Thomas Damascus, 18-karat gold and black pearl—a prize-winner just under 3 inches long.

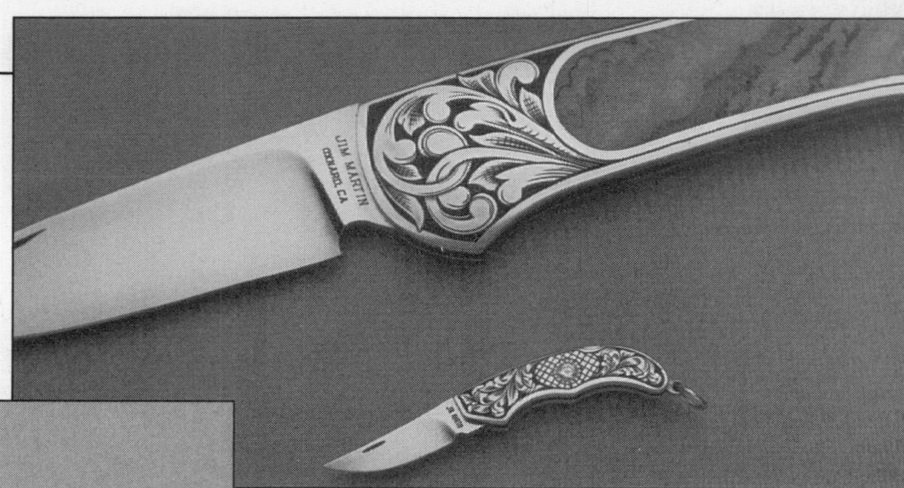

▶*Jim Martin:* Big ones or little ones—all off the same bench in deluxe style. (Chan photo)

▼*Mike Yurko:* A heavy-duty fighter, just about an index finger long in 440C and ironwood.

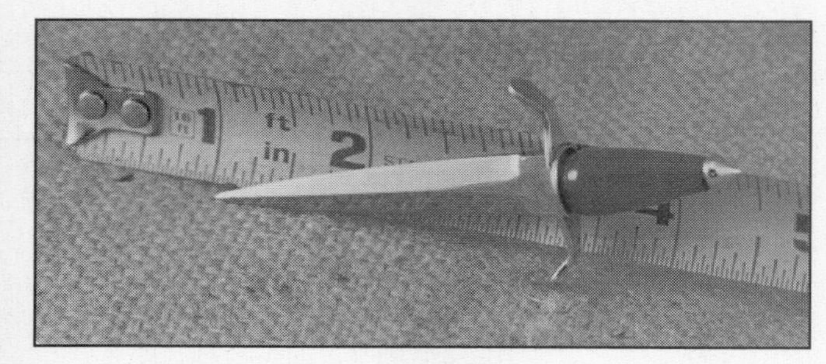

▲*Larry Mensch:* A parrying dagger in ATS-34 for a very small duelist who has a big little hand.

▶*James D. Whitehead:* All out here at 4[1]/[8] inches overall. That's a ten-piece demountable handle.

▼*D.F. "Doc" Gundersen:* Ready for small wars in northern places—you see a sword, a shield, an axe and a dime.

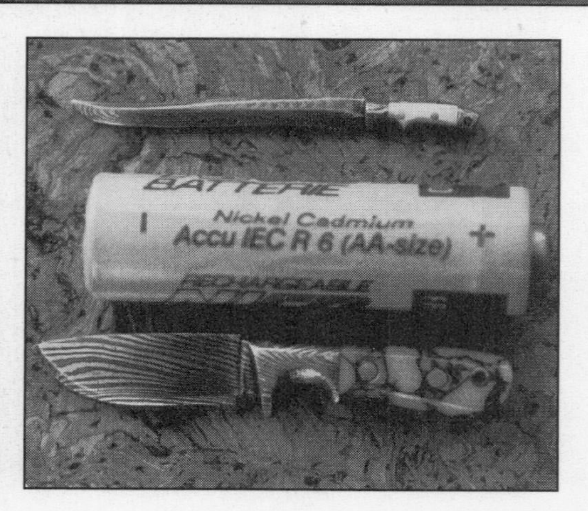

◀*Guenter Boehlke:* Look closely—you see one battery and two knives; one is, indeed, a tiny yataghan of sorts.

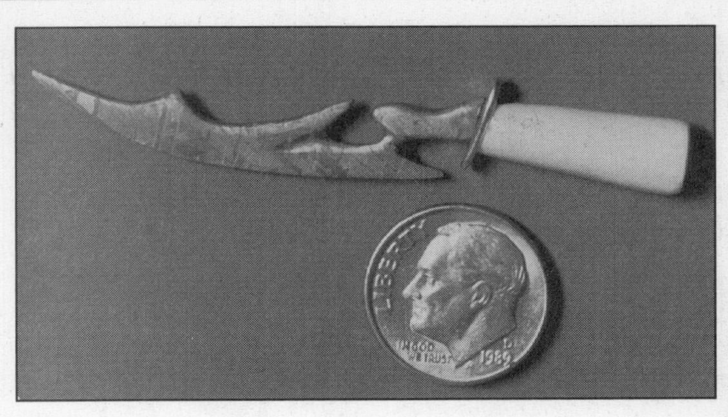

▲*Ron Wilson:* A fantasy in meteorite iron and mastodon ivory—the guard is gold.

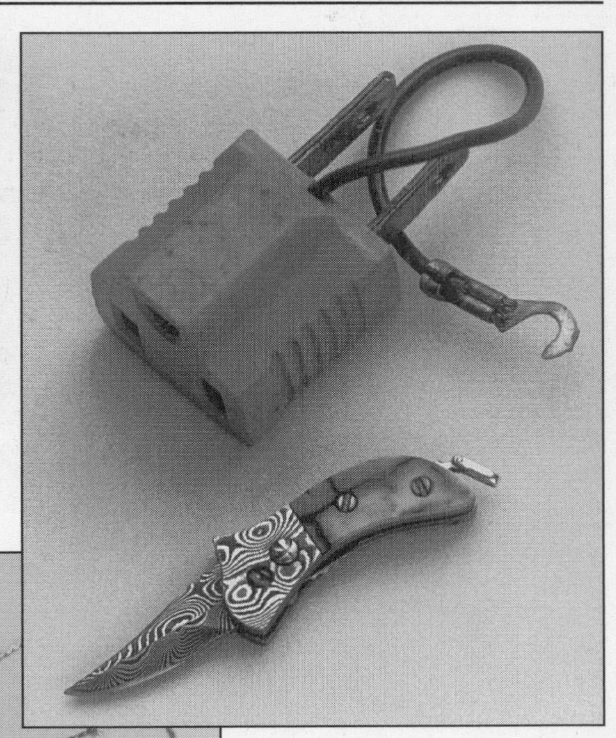

▶*Darrel Ralph:* It had to happen—a $1\frac{7}{8}$-inch automatic folder in Damascus and fossil ivory. (Weyer photo)

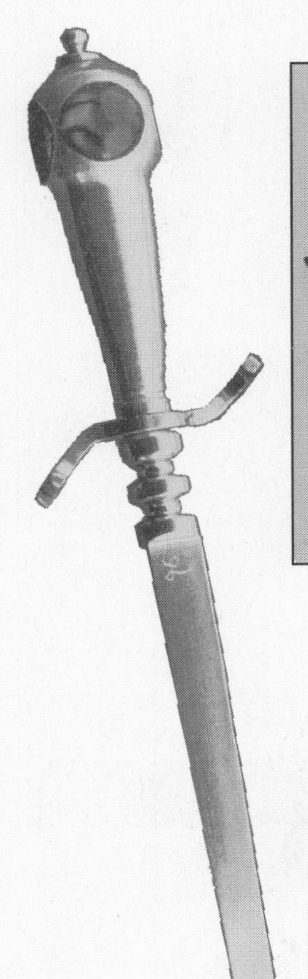

◀*Terry L. Kranning:* Meteorite iron and pearl and brass in the real meaning of "necklace knife"—$1\frac{7}{8}$ inches.

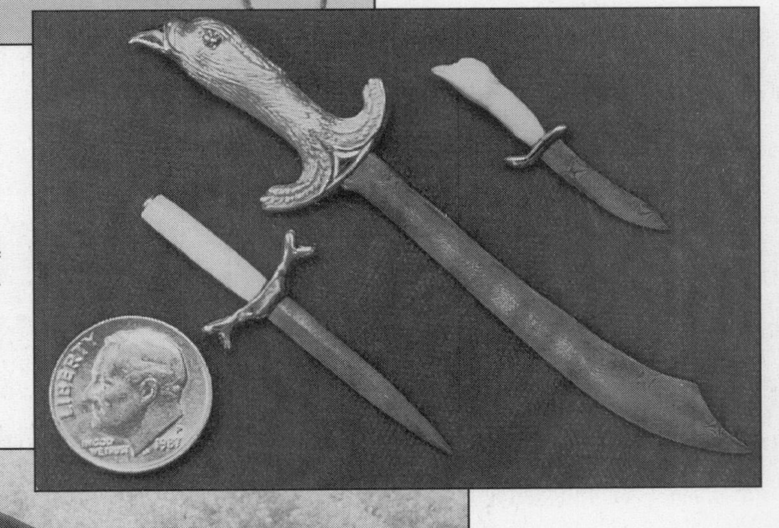

▶*Ron Wilson:* Pretty small stuff in Thomas Damascus and 18-karat gold—even diamonds.

▲*Henry C. Loos:* The 18-karat guard and pommel, a red stone and a $1\frac{3}{4}$-inch O1 blade—cute stuff.

◀*Everett Scofield:* The carved lady is helmeted; the curved blade is sharp.

TRENDS

THE TANTO FAMILY

HERE WE ARE going to try, briefly, to discuss the tanto's patterns and development without getting very far into the Japaneseness of it. Discussing *the originals* at that level takes more scholarly aptitudes and dedication than are presently available amongst our editorial staff.

No, we're going to begin with what should be obvious. We will then move on to what is even plainer to see.

So, the genuine Japanese tanto was a slim, easy-to-carry, user-friendly fighting man's knife. Its very basic design adapted well to the modes of Japanese swordplay and self-defense; it was large enough to do real damage and real service; it was small enough to conceal if you're wearing robes.

The tanto was as simple as its profile, and often plain. Its simplicity of line encouraged the rich use of subtle embellishment. Its size invited gaudy decoration as well, and we see both. In use, fanciness didn't matter, of course.

For the artisans of a world bereft of samurai, the tanto *idea* became absolutely splendid. You could start with that idea and go nearly anywhere. And that happened: Not only did the un-Japanese "develop" the tanto as, among others, hunting knives and folding knives, they also awarded it untanto features, some with a tenuous connection to Japanese culture.

The result, for a decade and more, has been interesting. Horrifying to some; exhilarating to others; but always interesting.

Thus, we saw knives of all sizes—with both chisel-edged and center-edged blades, fitted with an angular point with its separate edge—and called tantos. Indeed, that blade style is now called the "tanto" blade. Scholars mumbling about "eel-skinning blades" could save their breath.

There were also tantos with Loveless-style hafting, with guards, with full-tang construction. None of those were usual in the old tanto style. However, thanks to all those things, it was found a stout and very simple blade would do a lot of cutting well.

And now we have people who

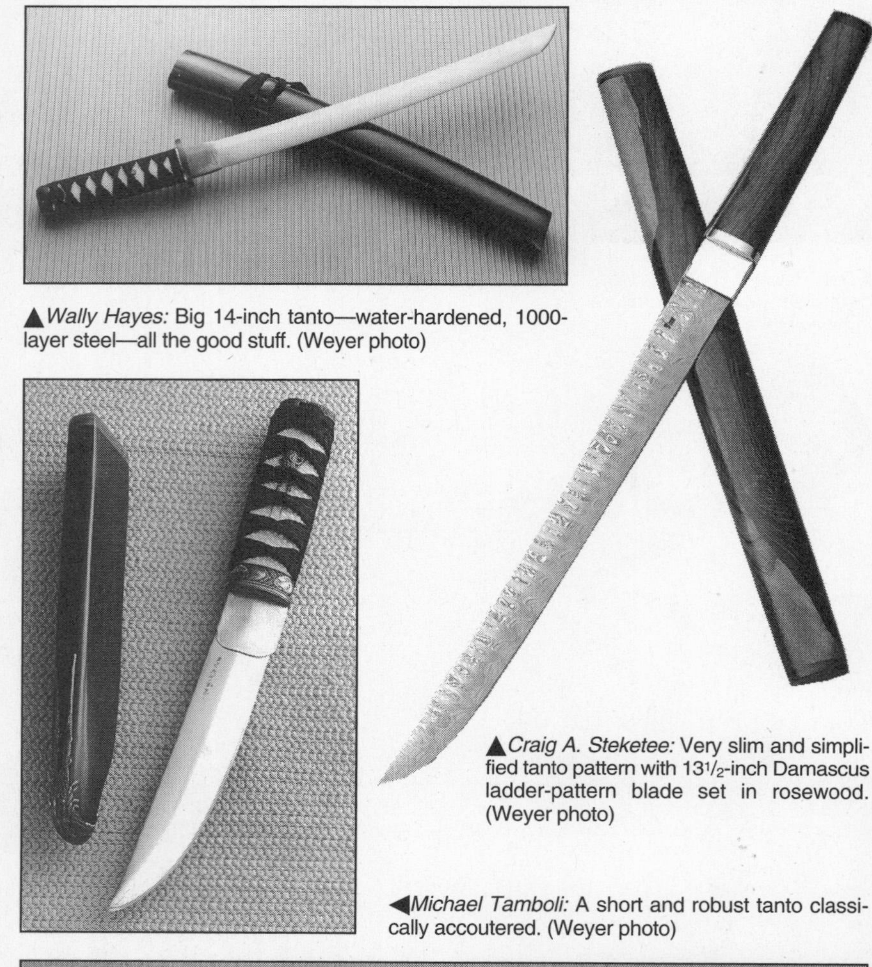

▲*Wally Hayes:* Big 14-inch tanto—water-hardened, 1000-layer steel—all the good stuff. (Weyer photo)

▲*Craig A. Steketee:* Very slim and simplified tanto pattern with 13½-inch Damascus ladder-pattern blade set in rosewood. (Weyer photo)

◀*Michael Tamboli:* A short and robust tanto classically accoutered. (Weyer photo)

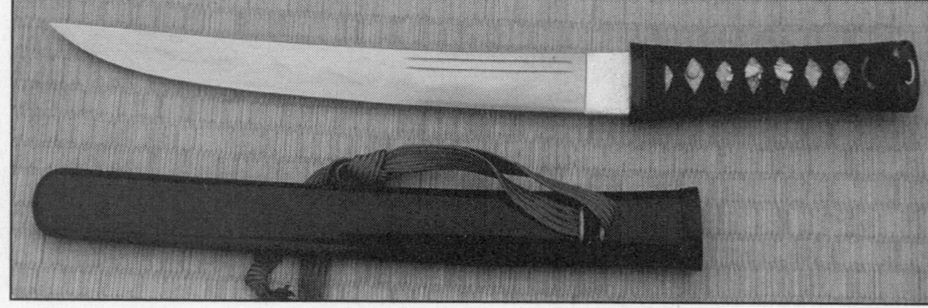

▲*Michael Bell:* The original concept in pure form—a comfortable, simple all-purpose knife.

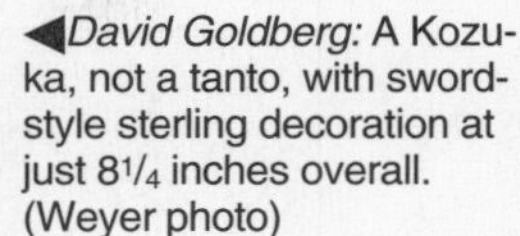

▲*Don Polzien:* The tanto idea, the shape, with new furniture and new blade grind.

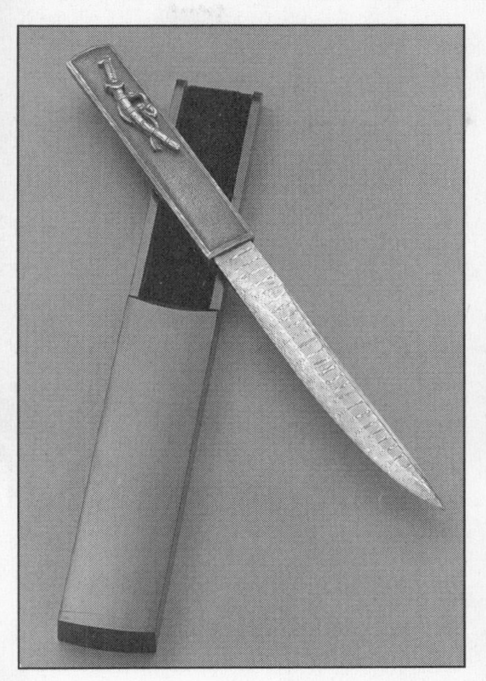

◀*David Goldberg:* A Kozuka, not a tanto, with sword-style sterling decoration at just 8¼ inches overall. (Weyer photo)

▼*Don Polzien:* Very nicely accoutered chisel-pointed Damascus blade, very geometrically ground.

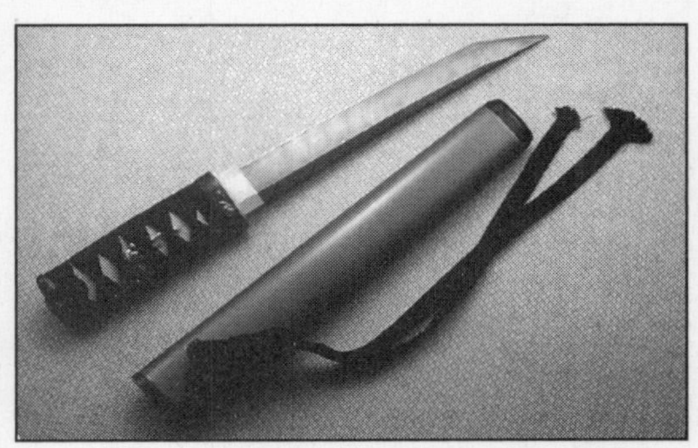

▶*David Goldberg:* Small tanto, with clay temper line, deluxe fittings, for a 1000-layer blade. (Weyer photo)

◀*Wally Hayes:* Short tanto, sword-furnitured, water-hardened, fitted in steel and copper. (Weyer photo)

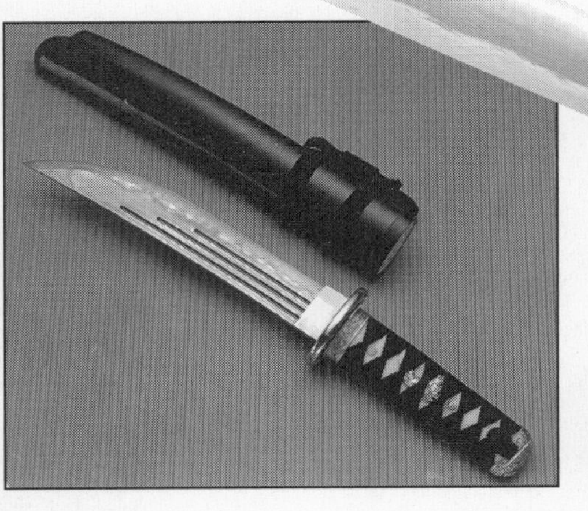

◀*Don Polzien:* Chisel-edged 9¼-inch blade with three stiffening grooves, partially sword-mounted. (Weyer photo)

◀*David Goldberg:* Chain Damascus, steel in a double-edged ken, traditionally dressed. (Weyer photo)

work pretty near the original *ideal*, some superlatively so; we have many who use the profile and the idea in a very tactical sense, providing the variety and versatility of a simple blade and easy shape; there are those who can't give up that angular up-front treatment. There remain those who work in a softly American easy-handling shape. And more—even folders.

We even have grown to where a fellow can sell a knife with a simple blade like an old tanto had. There's a fair sampling right here. Enjoy—every one is a knife.

Ken Warner

◀*James S. Piorek:* Big tanto with selected cultural details and a non-traditional construction.

▲*Stephen R. Burrows:* Pinned together, tang-signed, rosewood and a quarter-pound of sterling—complex detail in a simple knife. (Gallagher photo)

▲*James S. Piorek:* Compact tactical tanto shape set up for fast response—an all-purpose knife.

▲*Steve Stuart:* Short tantos, chisel or center edges, chopped out of files in full tang-pattern. (Weyer photo)

▲*Randall J. Martin:* Short chisel-edged-and-pointed wrapped tanto, set up in a magnetic sheath. (Weyer photo)

▲*Randall J. Martin:* Robust short chisel-edged tanto with carbon-fiber wrapping under the cord wrap. (Weyer photo)

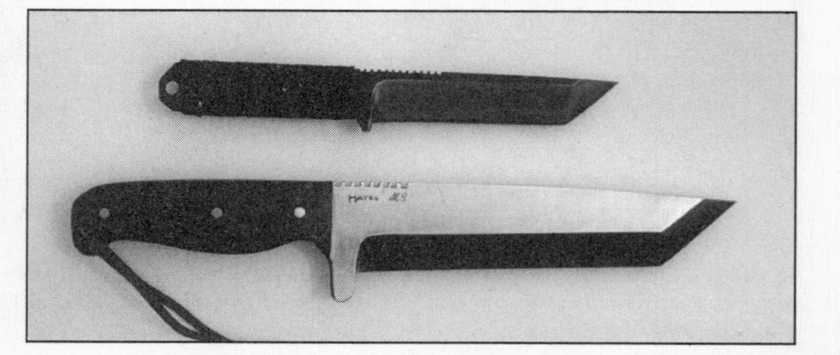

▶*Wally Hayes:* The tanto idea with North American grips and chisel edges.

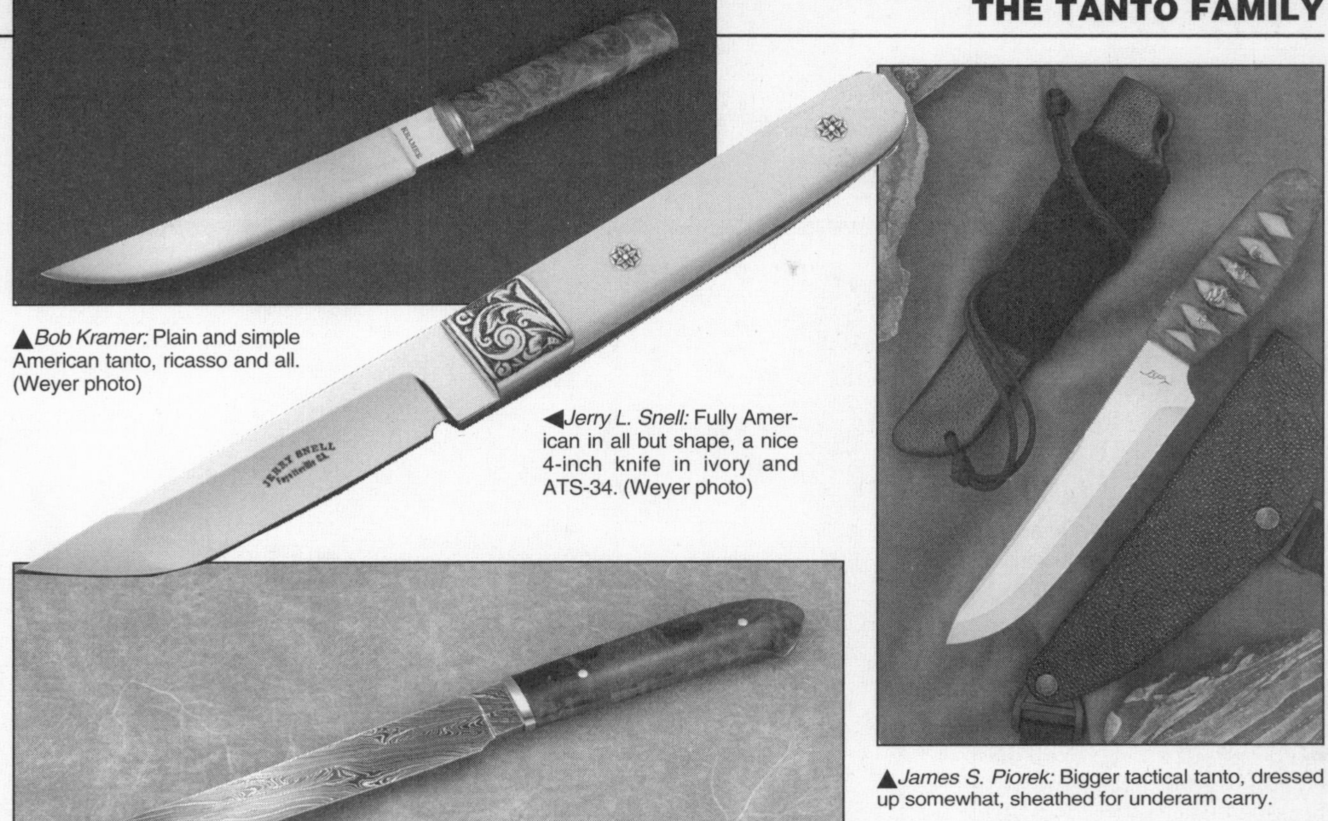

▲*Bob Kramer:* Plain and simple American tanto, ricasso and all. (Weyer photo)

◀*Jerry L. Snell:* Fully American in all but shape, a nice 4-inch knife in ivory and ATS-34. (Weyer photo)

▲*James S. Piorek:* Bigger tactical tanto, dressed up somewhat, sheathed for underarm carry.

◀*Jarrel D. Lambert:* American tanto, full 500-layer Damascus, double-pinned in ironwood and nickel silver. (Gallagher photo)

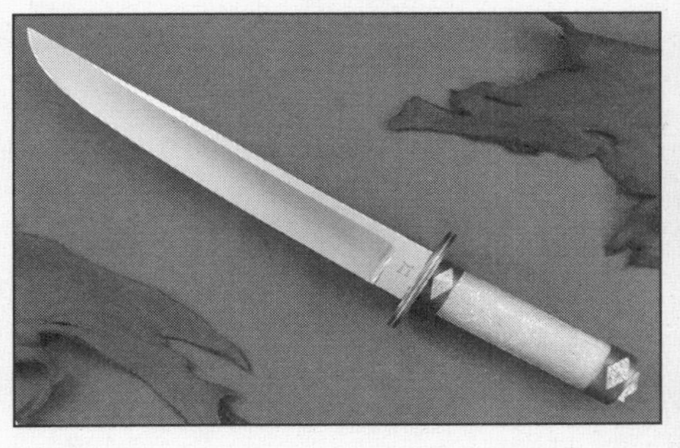

▲*Joel Ellefson:* Very American—ricasso and hollow-grind in stainless with gold trim.

▲*Jean Yves Bourbeau:* American tanto, full of borrowed culture but still an easy-handling all-purpose knife. (Weyer photo)

◀*Don Laughlin:* Seriously changed—full tang, bolstered and pommeled—but still a tanto. (Weyer photo)

TRENDS

THE LOCKING FOLDER

TO BE SURE, some folders lock closed as well, and some don't lock at all, but the main game is the one-blade knife, that blade securely locked open when in play.

Actually, that's a pretty big game even for commercial pocketknife makers. All the traditional pocketknives and pen knives are there and in big numbers, still. But those companies and other, newer companies sell a *lot* of single-blade locking folders.

There is not such a variety in locking mechanisms as one would think. The plain old top-lock, whether toward the front, at the middle or elsewhere, is still the biggest overall. The liner-lock is hanging in, and other tricks arrive in the trade with some frequency. The price spread in folders, from Pakistani Buck-mimics at $3-$5 to $3000-$5000 one-offs by top makers, is enormous. Neither handmades nor benchmades get under $100, and the selection doesn't really broaden until you get to $200

We get ordinary folders here, from pocketable pals to hunting sizes. We got some pretty aggressive patterns and some upscale ones. And then some high-dollar knives. We put the slip-joint knives elsewhere.

Ken Warner

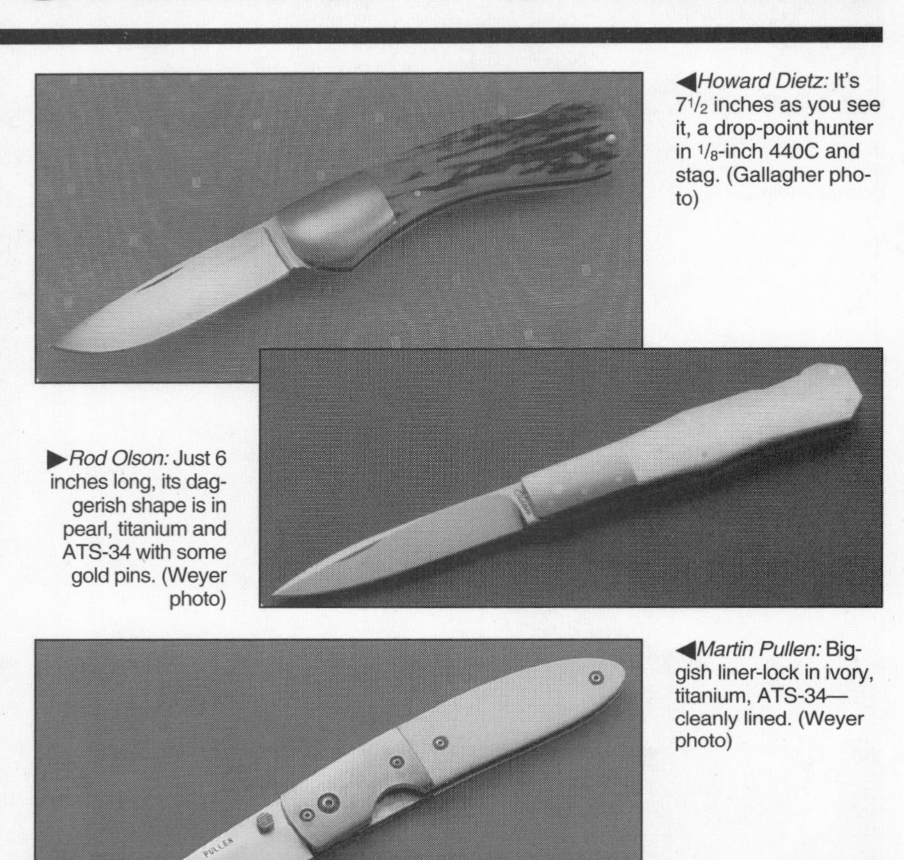

◀*Howard Dietz:* It's 7½ inches as you see it, a drop-point hunter in 1/8-inch 440C and stag. (Gallagher photo)

▶*Rod Olson:* Just 6 inches long, its daggerish shape is in pearl, titanium and ATS-34 with some gold pins. (Weyer photo)

◀*Martin Pullen:* Biggish liner-lock in ivory, titanium, ATS-34—cleanly lined. (Weyer photo)

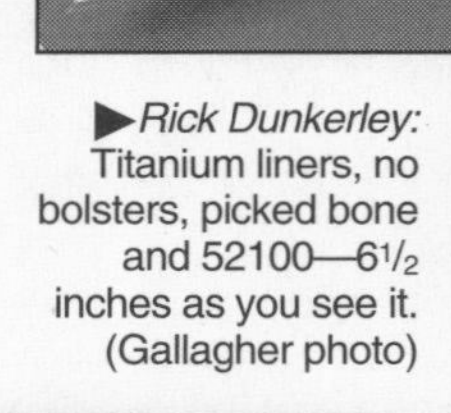

▶*Rick Dunkerley:* Titanium liners, no bolsters, picked bone and 52100—6½ inches as you see it. (Gallagher photo)

◀*S. Russell Sutton:* Cozy package, back-locker, with a robust blade in a stainless case and a big inlay.

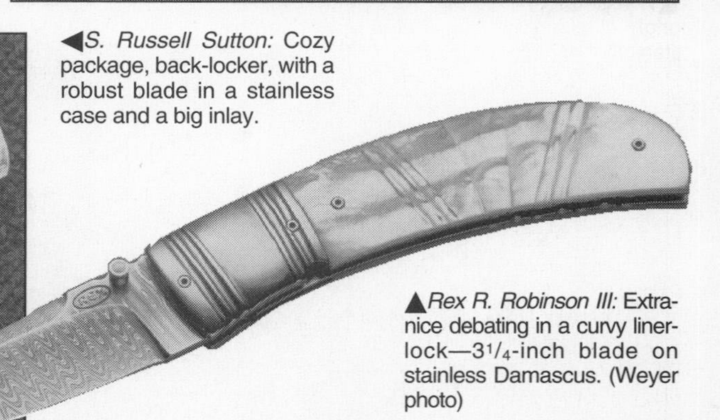

▲*Rex R. Robinson III:* Extra-nice debating in a curvy liner-lock—3¼-inch blade on stainless Damascus. (Weyer photo)

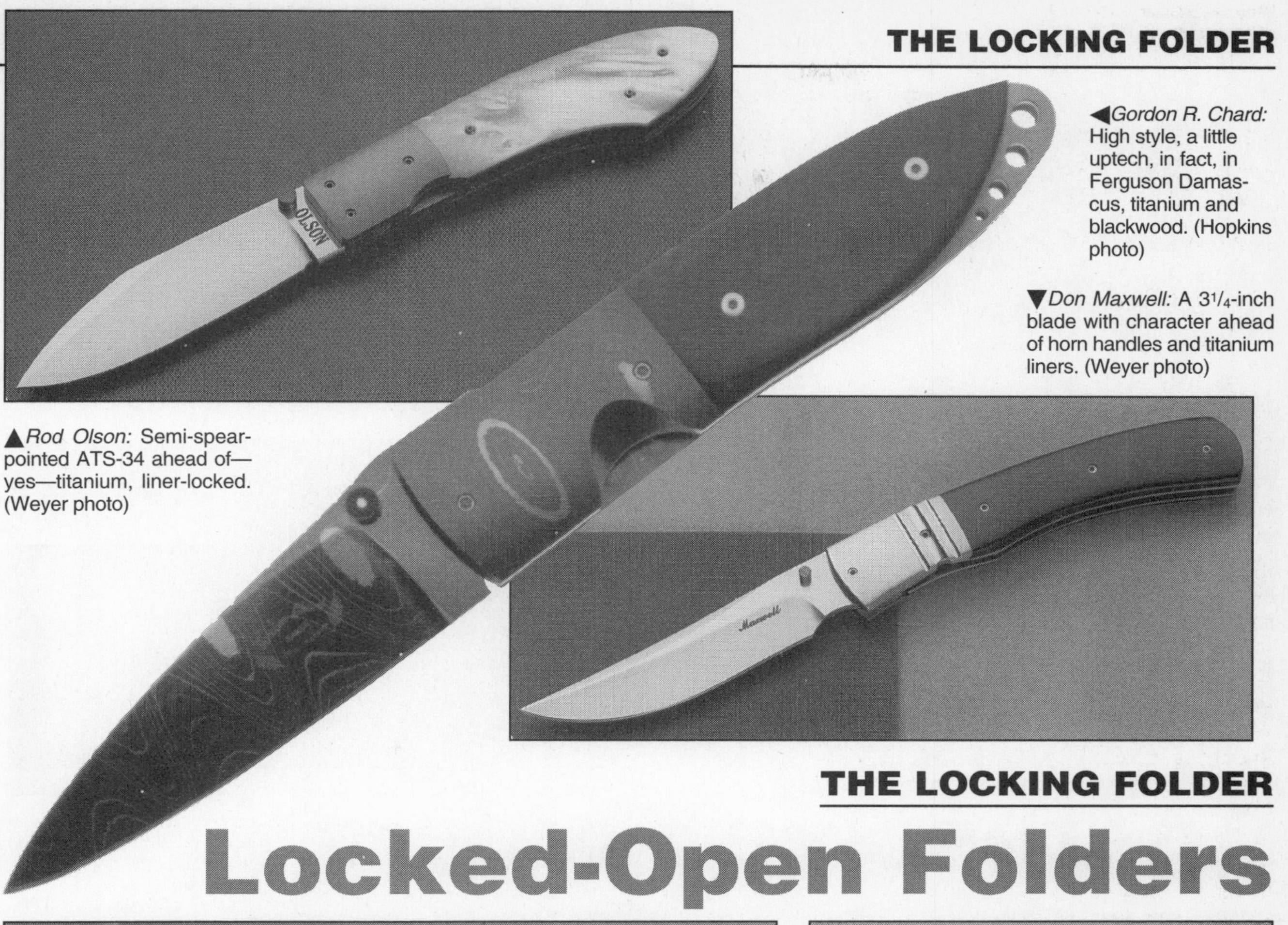

◀*Gordon R. Chard:* High style, a little uptech, in fact, in Ferguson Damascus, titanium and blackwood. (Hopkins photo)

▼*Don Maxwell:* A 3¼-inch blade with character ahead of horn handles and titanium liners. (Weyer photo)

▲*Rod Olson:* Semi-spear-pointed ATS-34 ahead of—yes—titanium, liner-locked. (Weyer photo)

THE LOCKING FOLDER

Locked-Open Folders

▲*Weldon G. Whitley:* Slick as a new minute in bright colors—the kind you get by anodizing titanium. (Gallagher photo)

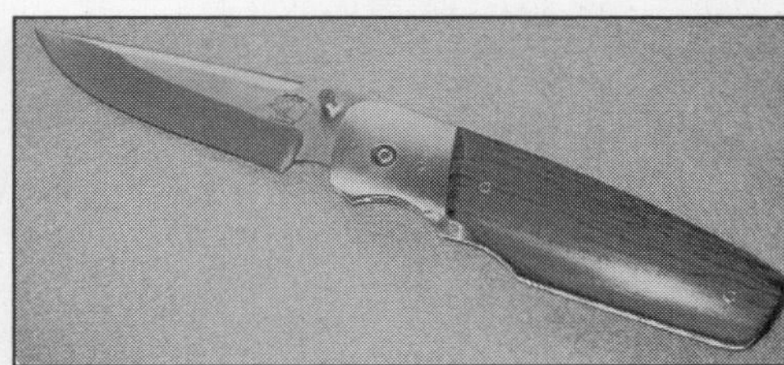

▲*Roger Gamble:* Workaday liner-lock in clean wood and stainless steel—a nice handle for a small tool.

▶*Melvin G. Fassio:* Modest little guy, modestly engraved, with maybe a little oosic—a nice companion.

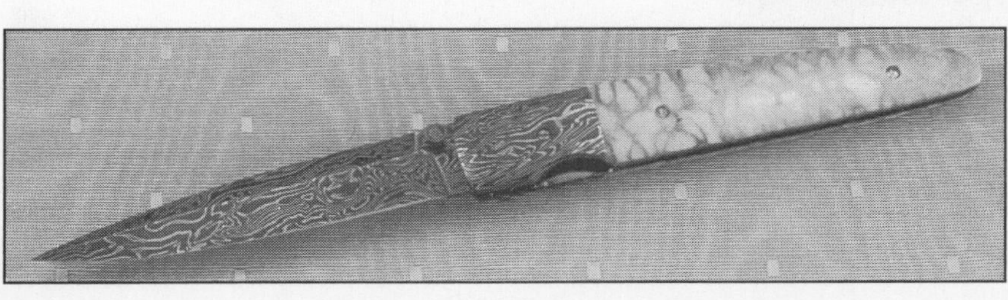

◀*Barry Gallagher:* Nothing fancy but the choice of materials: tiger coral and nickel Damascus.

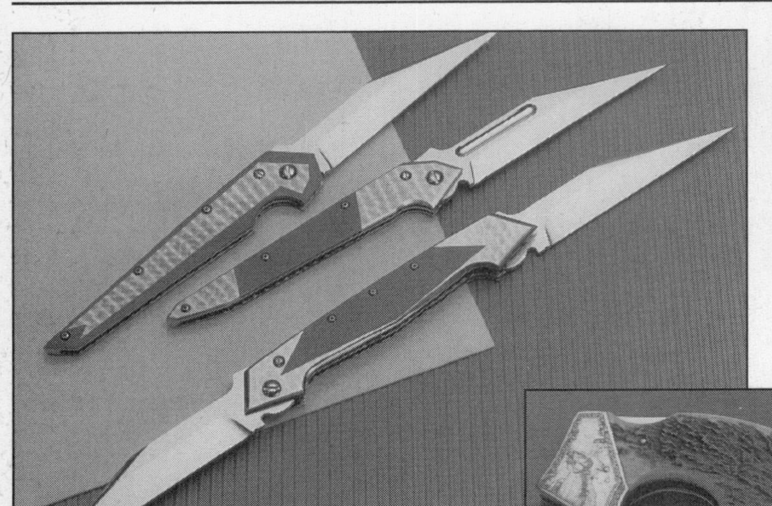

▲*Steven E. Hill:* Genuine 19th-century Bowieness—9 1/4 inches long and liner-locked. (Weyer photo)

▲*Romas Banaitis:* With Scott Richter—some very aggressive attitudes and a lot of size. (Weyer photo)

▲*Melvin M. Pardue:* Right pushy, this one—it's engraved with the Four Horsemen and goes 14 inches long as you see it. (Weyer photo)

THE LOCKING FOLDER

Aggressive Folders

▶*Howard F. Clark:* Folding stiletto of Italo-classic mien, probably made better.

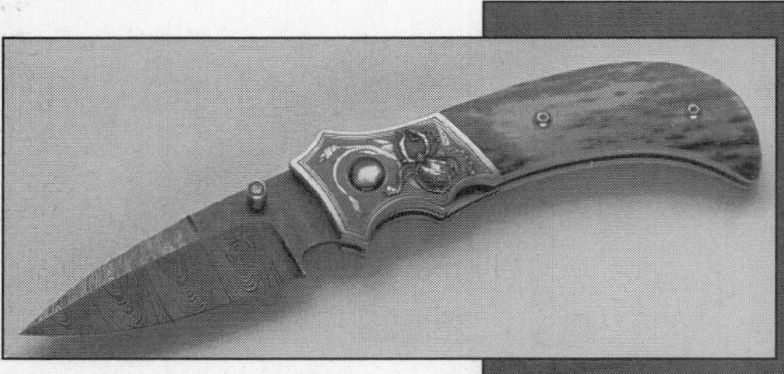

▲*Jot Singh Khalsa:* A deluxe liner-lock folder that has not fallen far from the Kirpan tree. (Weyer photo)

▶*Charles A. West:* It's a folding boot dagger and no mistake—only one sharp edge, of course.

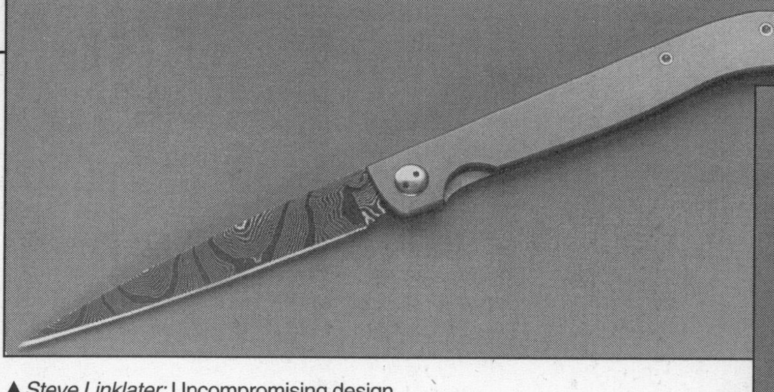

▲*Steve Linklater:* Uncompromising design in solid titanium and stainless Norris Damascus—$7^{7}/_{8}$ inches long. (Weyer photo)

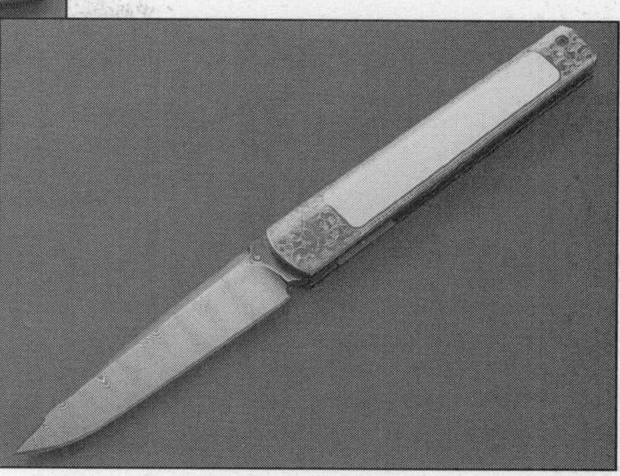

▶*J.A. Harkins:* Business-like big guy with nifty trim, like ivory and Shaw engraving. (Weyer photo)

▲*James F. Downs:* Red bone, aluminum and 440C in a hefty-looking liner-lock. (Lear photo)

THE LOCKING FOLDER

Aggressive Folders

▶*John A. Kubasek:* Says it's a two-finger fighter—titanium with overlaid stag and 9 inches overall. (Weyer photo)

▼*Ronald M. Lui:* Pretty pointed, but it looks tough. ATS-34 and such, of course. (Weyer photo)

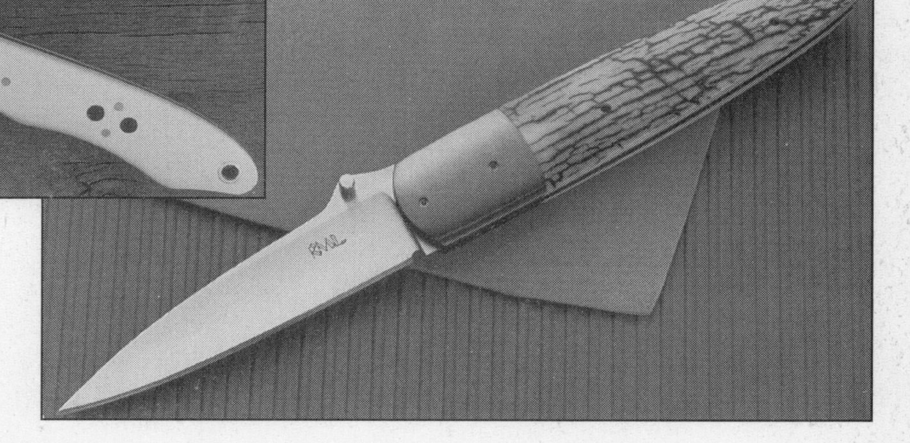

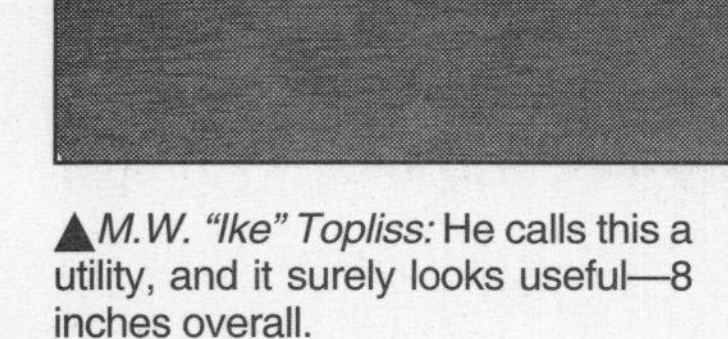

▲*M.W. "Ike" Topliss:* He calls this a utility, and it surely looks useful—8 inches overall.

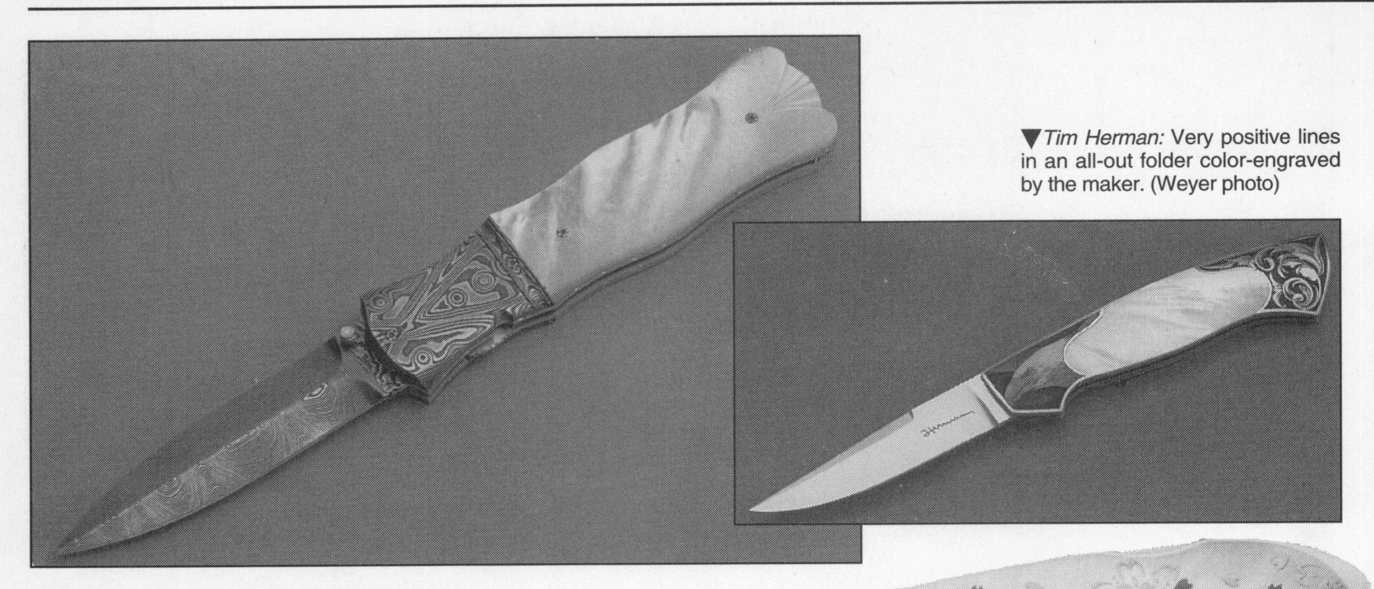

▼*Tim Herman:* Very positive lines in an all-out folder color-engraved by the maker. (Weyer photo)

▲*Jim Turecek:* Compact and delicately solid, its name is "Last Ice"; its overall length is 7 inches. (Weyer photo)

▲*Shun Fujikawa:* Just 5 1/2 inches as you see it, the mother of pearl embellished with copper and gold. (Weyer photo)

THE LOCKING FOLDER

Upscale Folders

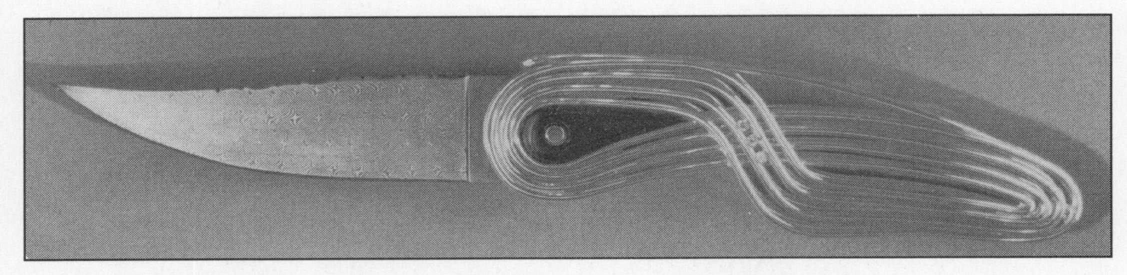

▶*Arthur Soppera:* Rados Damascus blade and shining silver wire with blue titanium creates "Marabou."

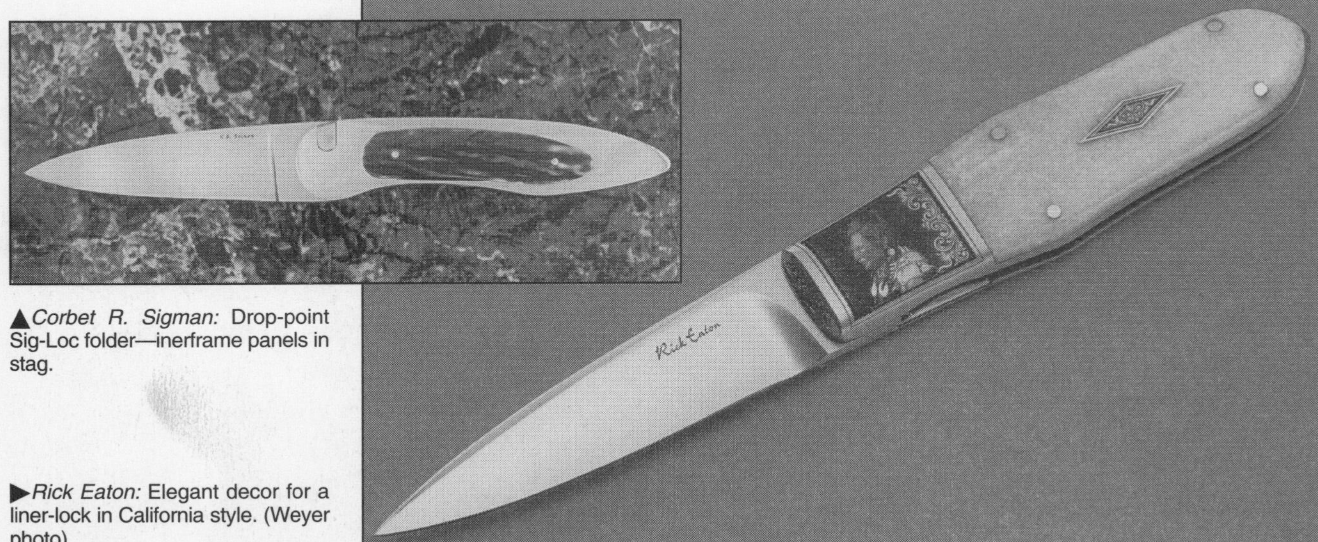

▲*Corbet R. Sigman:* Drop-point Sig-Loc folder—inerframe panels in stag.

▶*Rick Eaton:* Elegant decor for a liner-lock in California style. (Weyer photo)

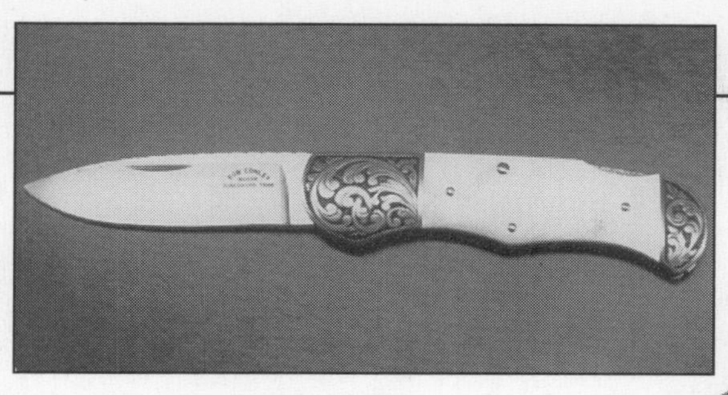

▶*Bob Conley:* Ivory and full scroll for a nice presentation.

▼*Phil Boguszewski:* Fully exploited Damascus patterning, with the bolster extension that changes the configuration visually. (Weyer photo)

◀*Richard Spinale:* The good old stuff, handsomely styled and crafted.

THE LOCKING FOLDER

Upscale Folders

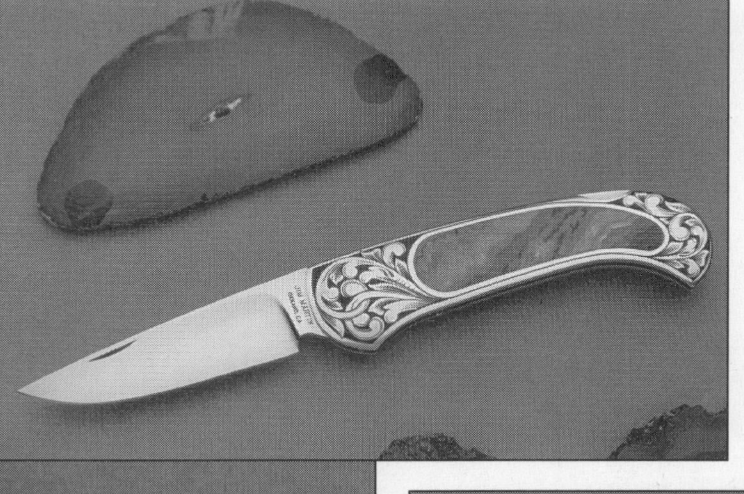

◀*Jim Martin:* Serious scroll all around an interframe holding polished agate—all by maker at $6^1/_2$ inches overall. (Chan photo)

▼*Wally Hayes:* Worked bolster, grooved blade—quite handsome. (Weyer photo)

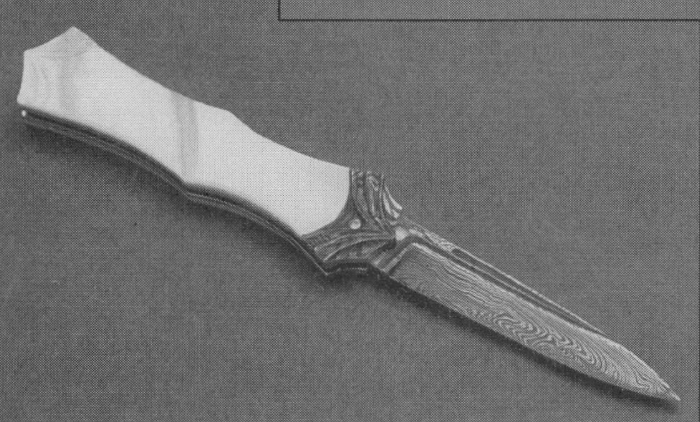

▼*Phil Boguszewski:* Pearl and 415 and 440C stainless and delicacy: $10^1/_2$ inches of obsession. (Weyer photo)

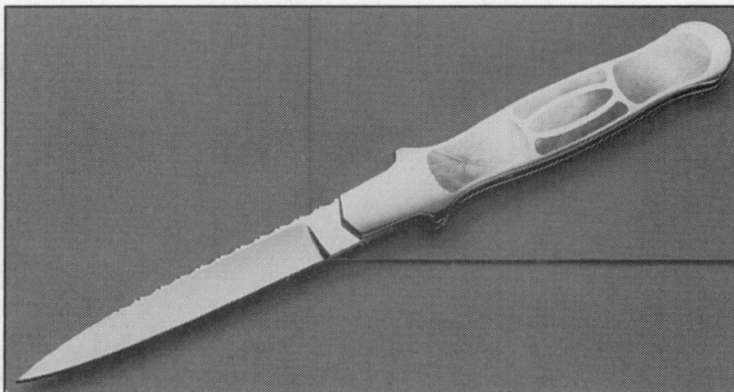

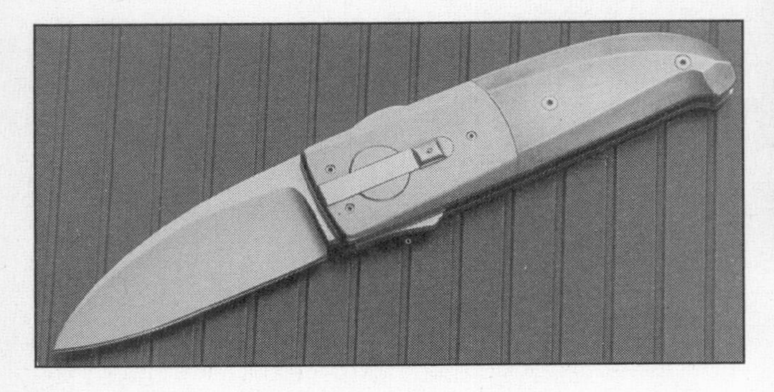

◀▲ *Michael L. Walker:* The Crescent has the famous "zipper" blade and titanium handles; other knife has the "D2 lock" with beryllium copper grips. It's uptech stuff. (Weyer photos)

▼*Larry Fuegen:* Called the Revival folder, it carries carved mammoth ivory, blued steel bolsters, gold fittings—just under 7 inches. (Weyer photo)

▶*Dellana Warren:* Neoclassic dagger—composite blade, gold and garnet trim. (Weyer photo)

THE LOCKING FOLDER

High-Dollar Folders

▶*Dellana Warren:* Her own Damascus, sterling bolsters with gold, rubies—a heavy production. (Petrocelli photo)

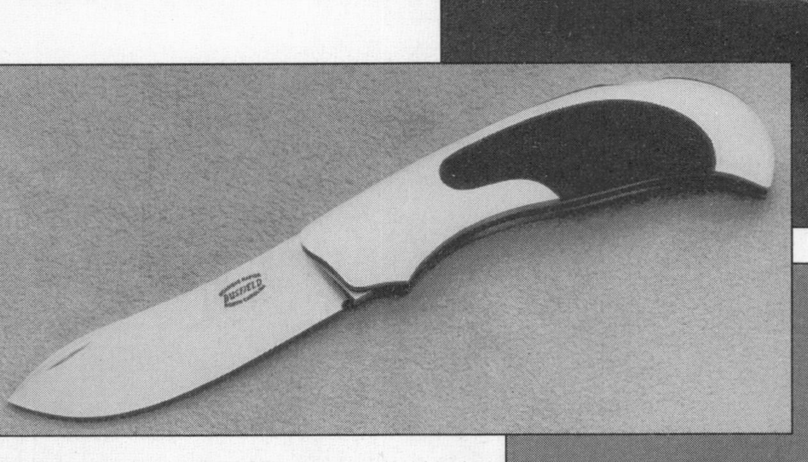

▲▶*John Busfield:* A few days amongst the black jade in two sculpted knife forms. They are not large. (Weyer and Busfield photos)

IT'S AUTOMATIC TIME

THERE ISN'T MUCH to say. It's like figuring out how to praise Elvis or say something naughty about lawyers—it's all been said.

Whether it's the triumph of greed over good sense, mechanical fascination over money management, or simple market rules, the automatic knife—the switchblade—is omnipresent in the world of knives. From $29 smuggled Chinese knives (or Italian or whatever) to $4000 handcrafted works of art made in America, we got 'em.

So go shopping here first. This is the high end. And some of them are splendid.

Ken Warner

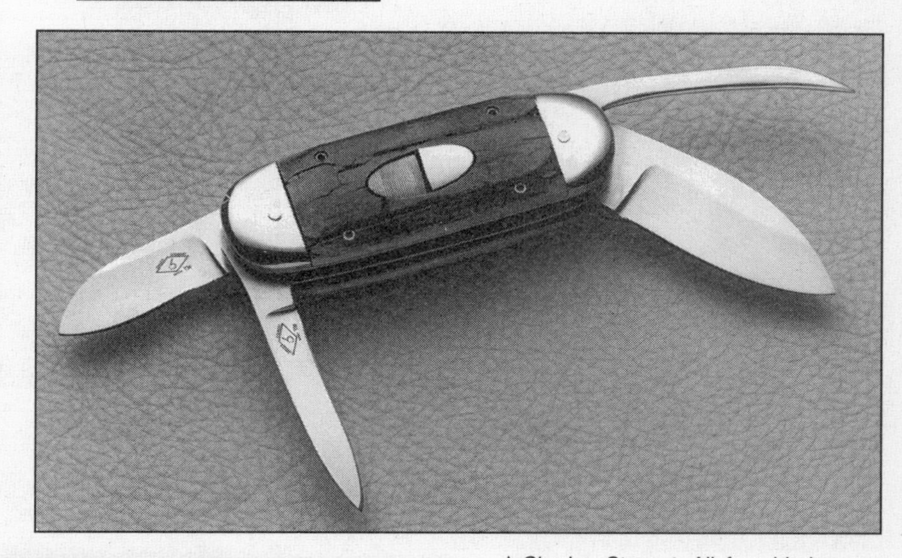

▲*Charles Stewart:* All four blades pop (one at a time, of course)! It's 4¼ inches closed; the long blades go 3 inches; and it's all ATS-34, stainless and mastodon ivory. (Weyer photo)

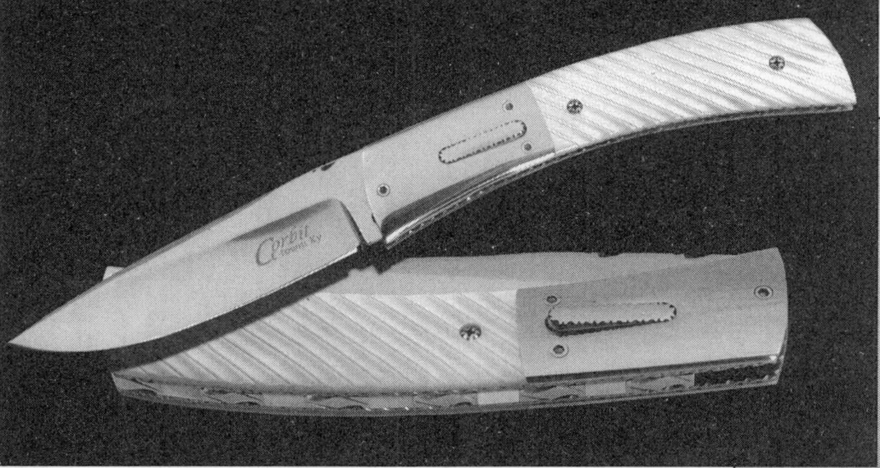

▲*Gerald E. and Philip E. Corbit:* Handsome file-worked gold-lip pearl with a release in the bolster—right-handed, of course.

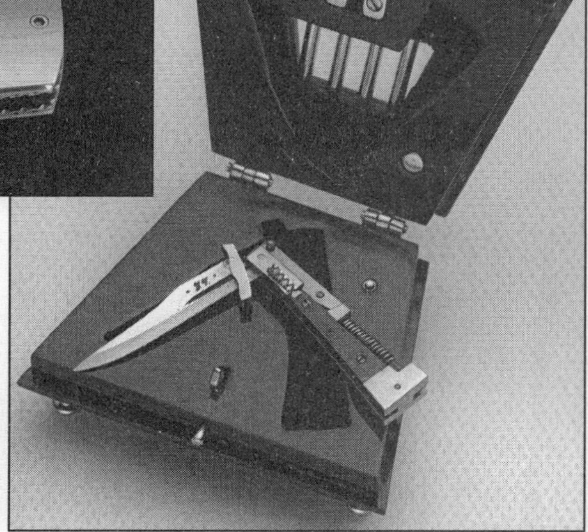

▶*Yvon Vachon:* Everything's on view, assembled with screws; the box lid is button-released, too. (Weyer photo)

▶*Darrel Ralph:* The negative and positive patterns are nice; so's the inside mirror polish. (Weyer photo)

▼*Shane Sloan:* Pretty stag, 4$^{1}/_{2}$ inches long closed—it's coil-spring driven.

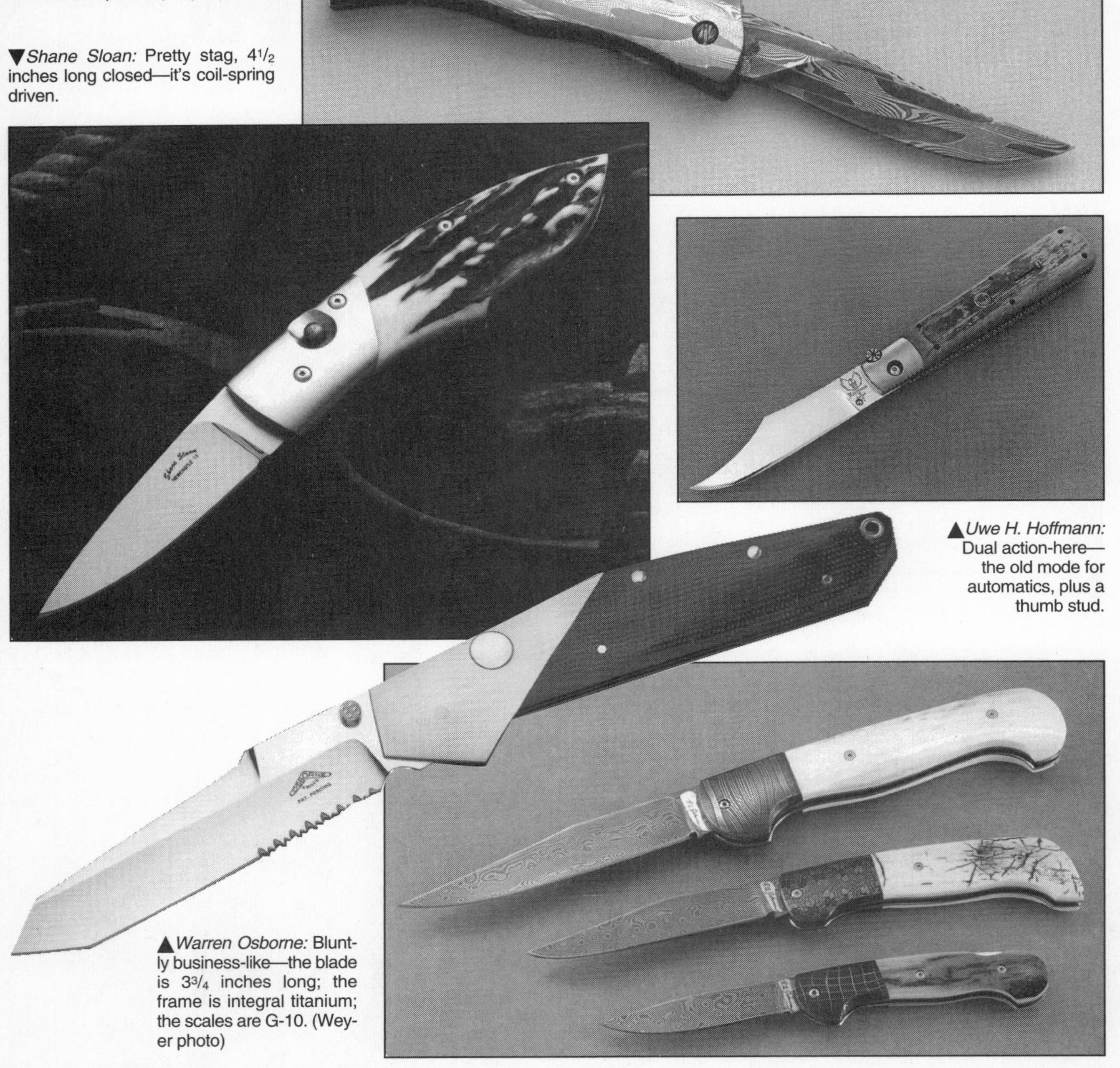

▲*Uwe H. Hoffmann:* Dual action-here—the old mode for automatics, plus a thumb stud.

▲*Warren Osborne:* Bluntly business-like—the blade is 3$^{3}/_{4}$ inches long; the frame is integral titanium; the scales are G-10. (Weyer photo)

▲*R.B. Johnson:* Scale release automatics in three sizes and four Damascus patterns. (Gallagher photo)

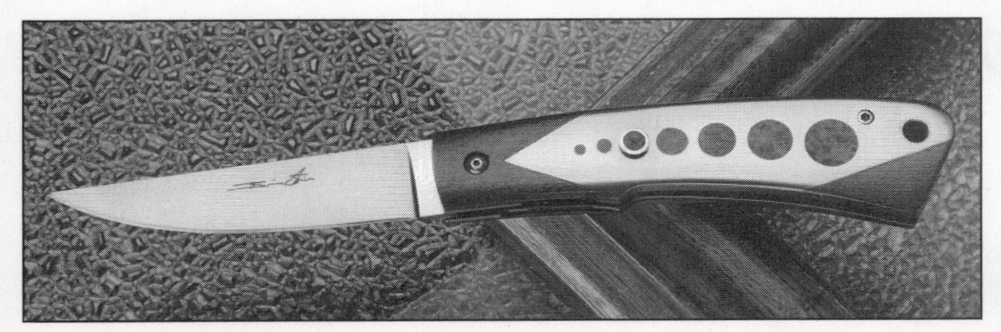

◀*Brian Tighe:* The release is the third rock on this one—an all-titanium case with walnut inlays!

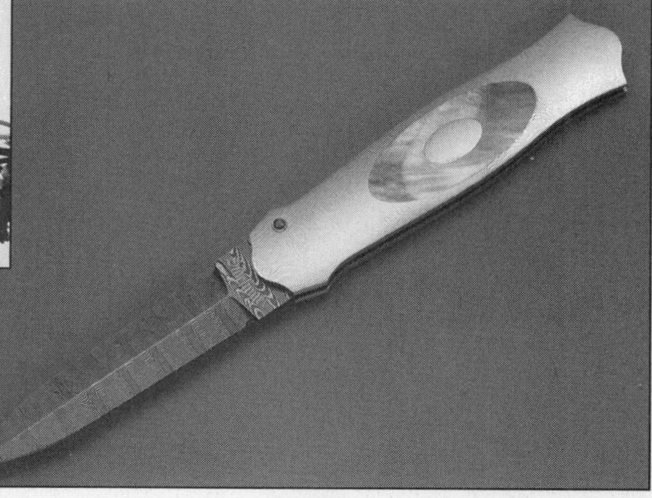

▲*Shane Sloan:* A $5 gold piece is the button; the frame is 416 steel—cute.

▶*Robert Sidelinger:* The button is that little ruby, the handle is pearl-inlaid mokume and the blade is stainless. (Weyer photo)

▲*C.M. Dake:* Complex Damascus arrangement in a small double-action knife—6½ inches open. (Weyer photo)

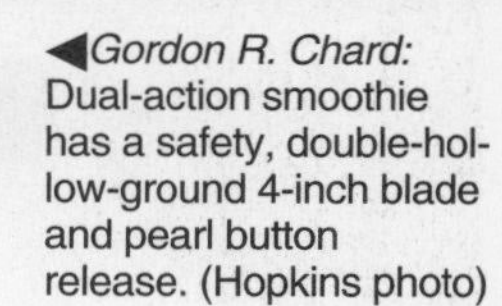

◀*Gordon R. Chard:* Dual-action smoothie has a safety, double-hollow-ground 4-inch blade and pearl button release. (Hopkins photo)

▲*Thomas Ferrara:* It goes 8½ inches open, a large knife in ATS-34 and Micarta. (Weyer photo)

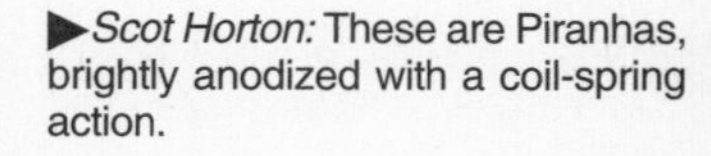

▶*Scot Horton:* These are Piranhas, brightly anodized with a coil-spring action.

◀*Joseph Szilaski:* Bear jaw and bronze for a heavy-bladed automatic.

▼*Joseph Szilaski:* A Buck 101-shaped automatic in Damascus—liner-locked open.

◀*Jack Levin:* This big folder—10 inches as you see it—has a button release for either hand. (Weyer photo)

▼*George "Steve" Copeland:* Sportsman's Canoe—both blades automatic—has 3- and 4-inch models with several frame options.

▲*J.D. Smith:* Its name is Sin and Tears; it's built in fossil walrus, nickel silver and Damascus. (Weyer photo)

▶*Ralph J. Selvidio:* Big knife—blade is 5 inches—set up in Damascus and pearl. (Weyer photo)

◀▼*William James McHenry:* Different strokes for different knives—two slim autos, all Damascus, but with different locks.

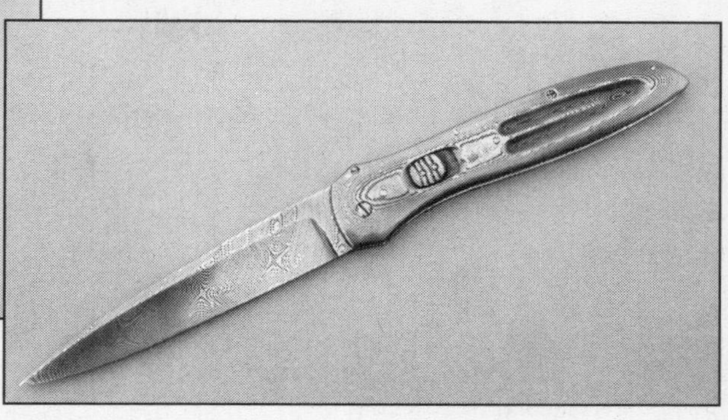

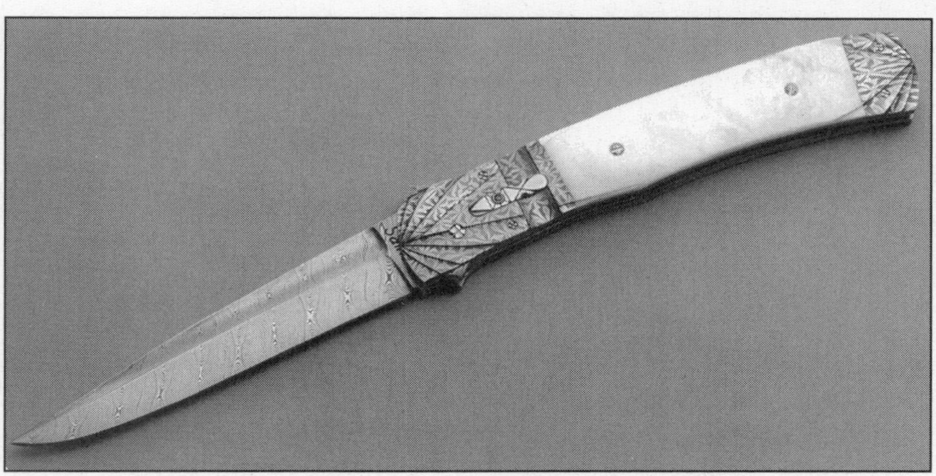

◀*R. Bill Saindon:* This one goes 10½ inches in twist Damascus and mother of pearl—all carved and filed. (Weyer photo)

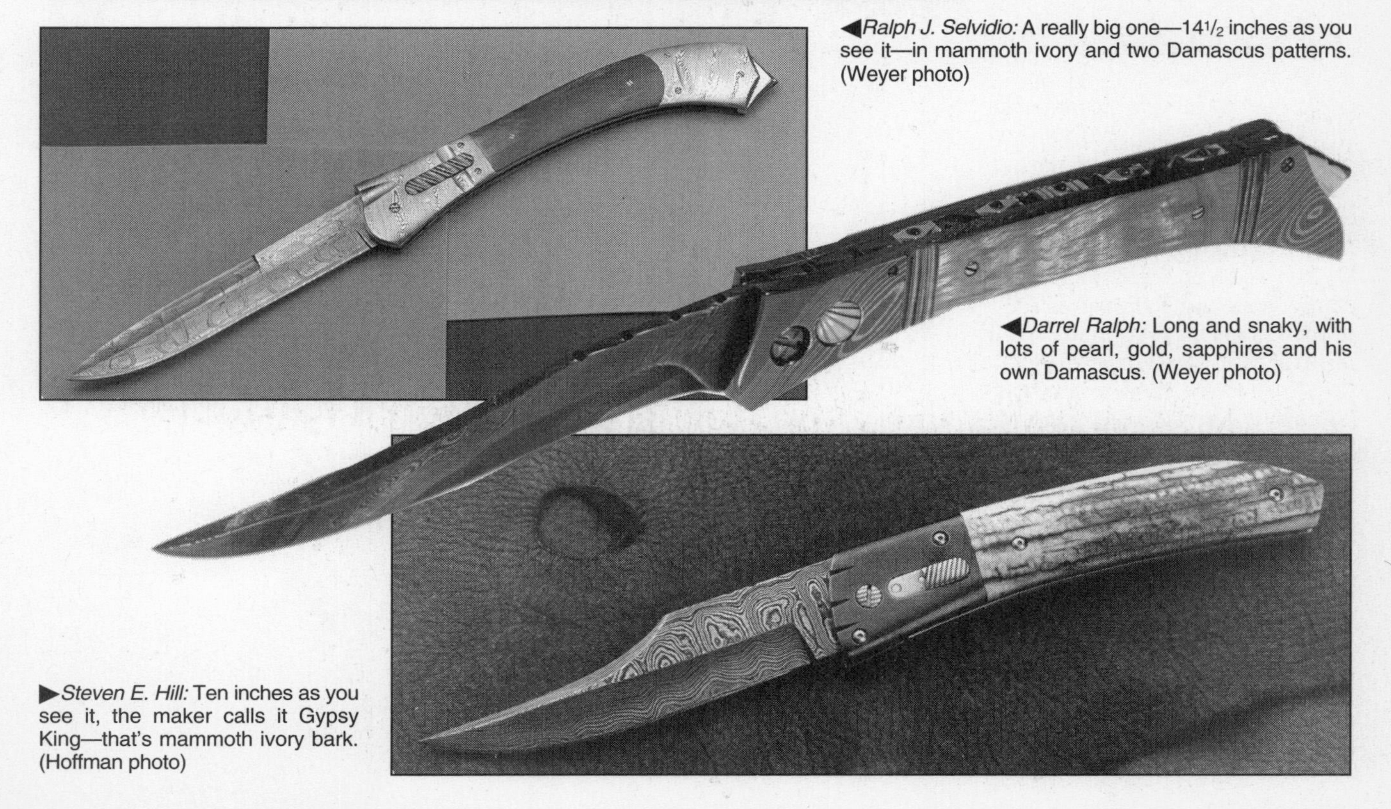

◀*Ralph J. Selvidio:* A really big one—14½ inches as you see it—in mammoth ivory and two Damascus patterns. (Weyer photo)

◀*Darrel Ralph:* Long and snaky, with lots of pearl, gold, sapphires and his own Damascus. (Weyer photo)

▶*Steven E. Hill:* Ten inches as you see it, the maker calls it Gypsy King—that's mammoth ivory bark. (Hoffman photo)

SIMPLE, NOT CRUDE

A KNIFE—ANY knife—is a cutting edge, with or without point, plus a handle. That goes for all of them.

Some, of course, are more elaborate. Indeed, you wouldn't have to look far from here to find some genuiunely extravagant knives. They have their place, of course, but there's a lot more simple ones.

The simple knife—just a handle and a blade—is in wide use. Printers and people who do flooring and people in mills—from flour mills to knitting mills—all use knives all day. Their knives are part of the workplace equipment, not personal, and they are, one and all, as simple and cheap as will do the job. They are seldom good-looking.

In restaurant kitchens and in households, simple knives are somewhat niftier. Some are very much so; some not so.

So, there are a lot of simple and crude knives at work in the world today.

And then there are the simple knives we're showing you here. None has any more pieces than the web-ripping, paper-cutting knife a printer picks up and throws down a couple dozen times a shift. Apart from those essentials, however, they are a world apart.

It's often hard to tell if a given simple knife just happened as its form was shaped to its function or if the maker planned it from the git-go. If you get to see a dozen or so by the same guy, and they're all that way, then you know.

Still, if it happens just once, it's worth looking at. That's what we're doing here.

Ken Warner

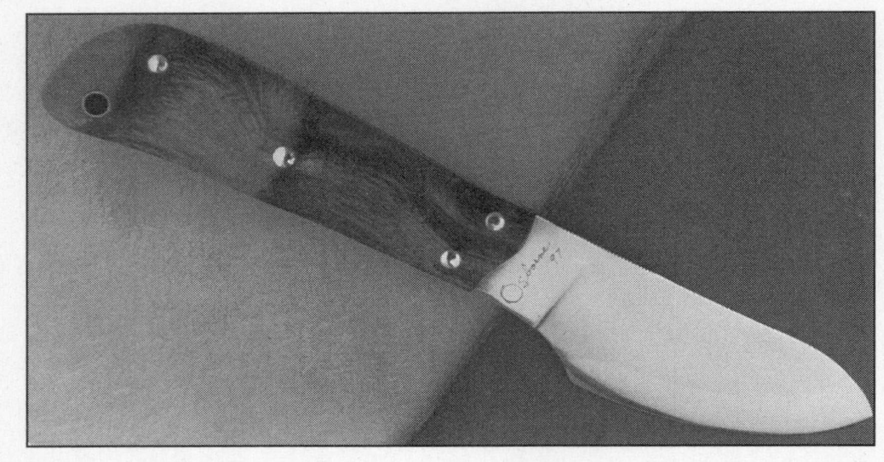

▲*Michael Osborne:* Forged 5160 and pinned ironwood in a $3^1/_2$-inch semi-skinner.

▼*Alfredo Kehiayan:* Apart from the six-faceted blade, this leaf-shaped dagger is simplicity itself.

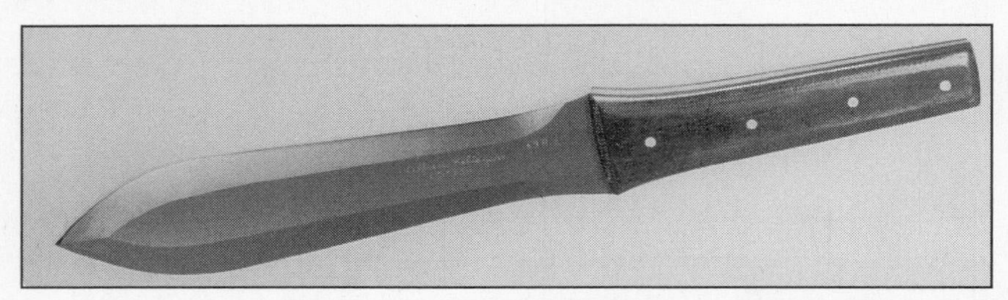

▲*Wayne Watanabe:* Eleven-sided wood, antique brass and an O1 blade. The other knife ain't complex, either.

▶*Ricky Fowler:* A 5-inch O1 blade with amber stag—lots bigger than it looks here.

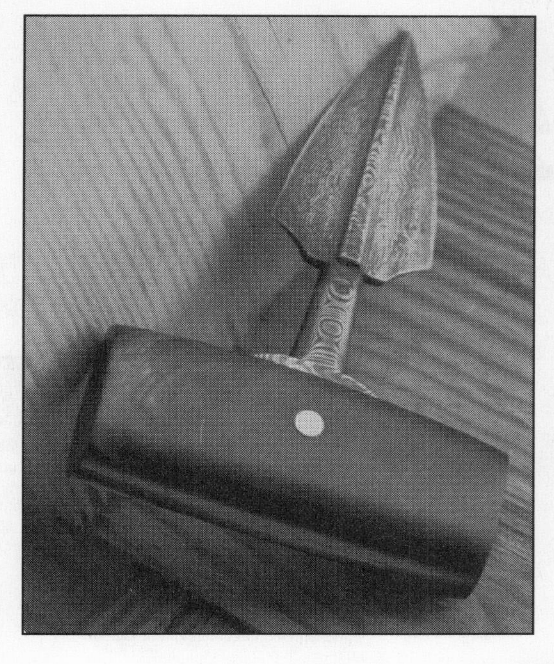

◀*Stephen R. Burrows:* Cleanly and simply cut arrowhead-style push dagger in ironwood and Damascus.

▲*Geoff Hague:* Hollow-ground ATS-34 at $3^1/_2$ inches, with ironwood pinned with stainless.

▲▼*Wayne Watanabe:* How to do simple: one ATS-34 blade and a length of cord.

▲*Mel Anderson:* Big 7-inch clip-point in carbon steel and canvas Micarta.

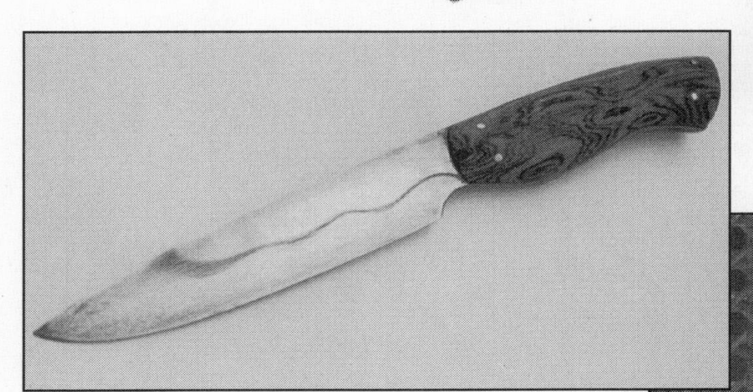

▲*Terry L. Kranning:* Camp knife with wave temper line in 1095 and brass-pinned cocobolo.

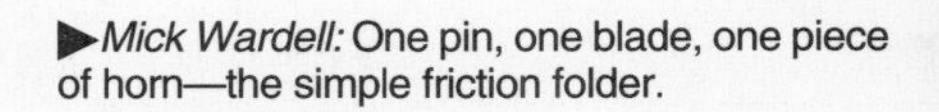

▶*Mick Wardell:* One pin, one blade, one piece of horn—the simple friction folder.

TRENDS

THE TACTICAL IDEA

FACT IS, EVERY knife has a tactical potential. I know a fellow who, when dining out in a strange city, almost always leaves the restaurant with one of its cheap Chinese steak knives sort of up his sleeve. He subsequently drops it in the first trash basket *inside* his hotel.

Why in the world would he do that? Because guns are *so* inconvenient in air travel is why.

Does that make steak knives tactical? No. It only makes that one steak knife so (though, for the length of the walk or the taxi ride, that knife is *very* tactical). Tactical in the U.S. market means something else.

It's a design idea and a style and a pattern format and a finish option, all at once. The design idea is, of course, "Just in case, what should you have?" Style and pattern are, by and large, fighter/defense oriented, whether fixed blade or folding. And the finish option is the tough look—not casually shiny yet with a lot of black.

Obviously, "What should you have?" swiftly becomes a question of opinion, but can be answered simply. It's "Whatever it takes and not a bit more." There's a large-sized compromise extending from 12 inches of all-out fighter to a lockblade folder with a 3-inch blade, not forgetting the automatic folder.

In a way, the tactical knife is a duty knife for folks who are—probably perpetually—off-duty. All the same shapes and sizes are available shiny, with high-end handle material, but those are not—obviously—tactical. They're too—well—shiny.

The knives you see here are almost all benchmade or handmade. There is a full panoply of factory knives in this category. Indeed, several nicely prosperous factories have their entire product line *based* on the tactical idea.

Actually, if you have to ask, you probably won't understand. It will help to look at these pictures.

◀▲*Schultz, Richard A.:* The current real deal for a SEAL, in titanium, with sheath; the other is for a grunt.

◀*Tom Watson:* G10 and ATS-34 with $3^5/_8$-inch barrel—a slightly hooked dagger.

▼*Bud Nealy:* The nouvelle vogue in the concealment tactical—a bonanza of shapes and sizes, all slick. (Weyer photo)

◀*Wilbur G. Stegner:* One piece of ATS-34 in a classic boot shape—blade is 4 inches. (Deckner photo)

◀▲*Robert J. McDonald:* All the mechanics the same in two different folding fighters. (Weyer photo and Gallagher photo)

◀*W.R. Clark:* Black Hawk, a fast-opening drop-point in ATS-34 and titanium for man-sized comfort. (Gallagher photo)

▼*W.R. Clark:* Chisel-tantoed in G10, titanium and GS-10—the PDK Special. (Gallagher photo)

▶*H.J. Viele:* The baron of deadly style did this with a 3⁵/₈-inch blade in ATS-34, titanium and G10—what else? (Weyer photo)

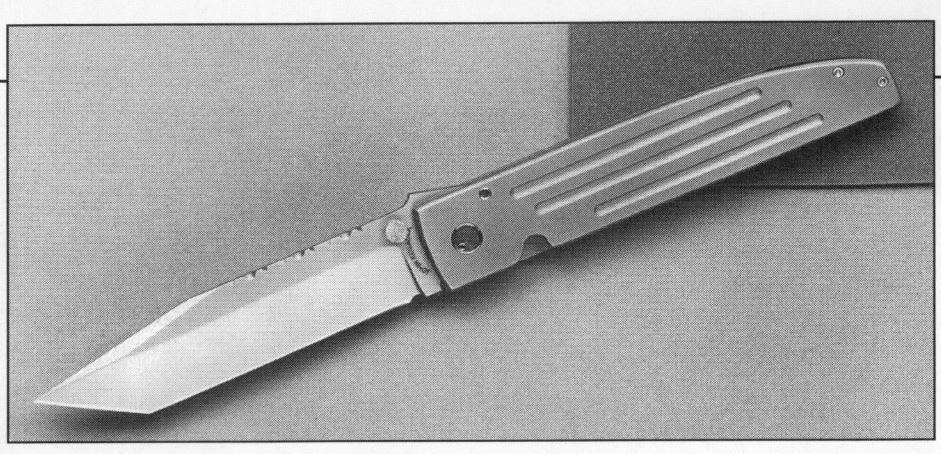

▲*John A. Kubasek:* All the usual stuff, but in a space-worthy shape—the tanto-point blade is 4 inches. (Weyer photo)

◀*Tim Britton:* Bead-blasted all over in stainless and green canvas Micarta—a big 'un and a li'l 'un.

◀*Wm. R. "Bill" Herndon:* One of the big guys, 12 inches overall, in surfaced Micarta and ATS-34. (Weyer photo)

▲*Bill Levengood:* No-nonsense slick fighter, dagger-bladed in Swedish steel and Micarta. Blade is 3½ inches. (Weyer photo)

◀*John A. Kubasek:* Titanium body and ATS-34 blade, with stainless hardware—8¾ inches overall—a big claw. (Weyer photo)

▶*Marcus McElhannon:* Nice handle styling with 154CM and G10, just over 8 inches.

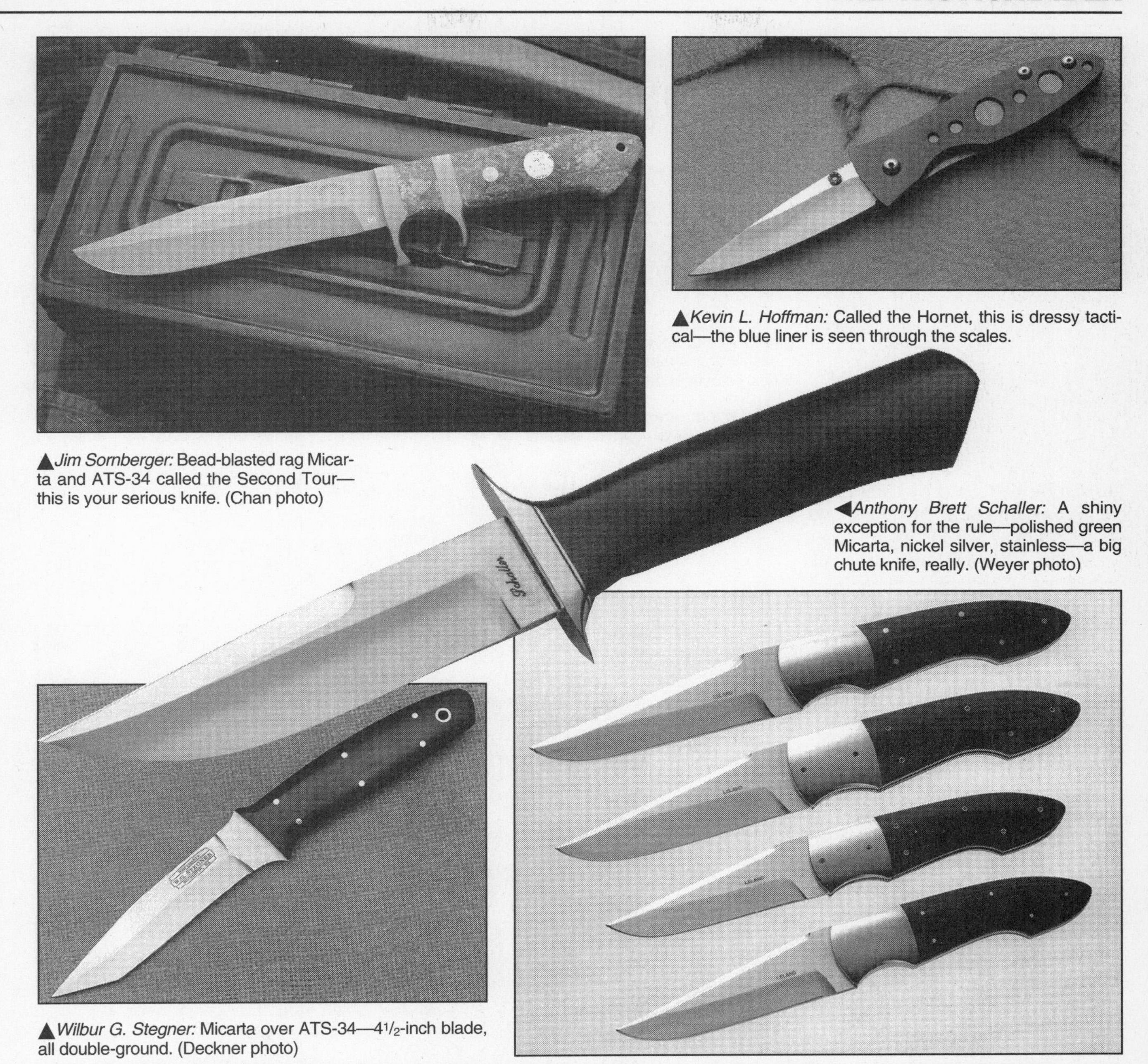

▲*Kevin L. Hoffman:* Called the Hornet, this is dressy tactical—the blue liner is seen through the scales.

▲*Jim Sornberger:* Bead-blasted rag Micarta and ATS-34 called the Second Tour—this is your serious knife. (Chan photo)

◀*Anthony Brett Schaller:* A shiny exception for the rule—polished green Micarta, nickel silver, stainless—a big chute knife, really. (Weyer photo)

▲*Wilbur G. Stegner:* Micarta over ATS-34—4½-inch blade, all double-ground. (Deckner photo)

▲*Steve Leland:* A real stunt—four, actually—in ATS-34 and Micarta. At top and bottom are straight knives; the middle two are folders. (Weyer photo)

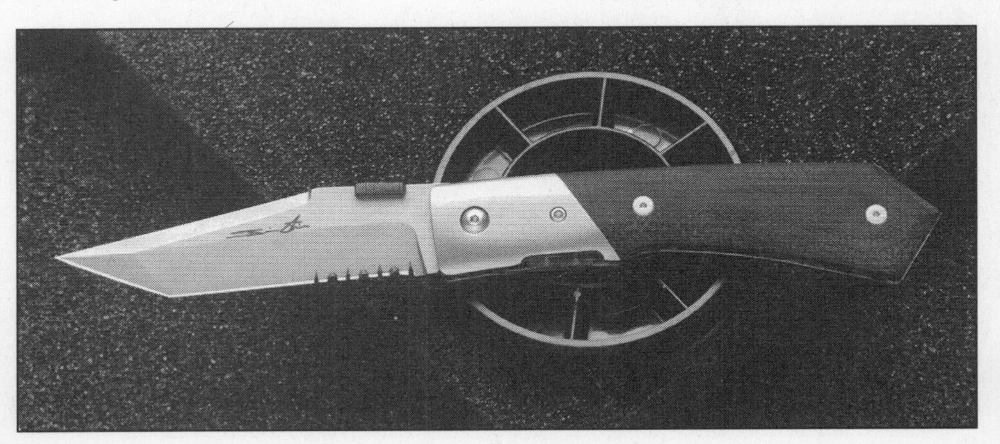

◀*Brian Tighe:* Just 4⅜ inches closed, this is not your big tactical folder, but it looks tough.

THE PURE LINE

IT WASN'T WHEN W.D. Randall Jr. emulated William Scagel that this trend started; it was when later knifemakers chose Randall knives as models that the perfect line—actually, lots of them—became reality. Randall put his own stamp on the Scagel line; the next guys just made knives like Randall's.

The next big name, and big wave of knives like his, was R.W. Loveless, who himself once made knives a lot like Randall's. His slick designs went across the tables of knife shows like wildfire.

Much more slowly, a much smaller number of knifesmiths chose W.F. Moran's route to knife design. George Herron and Jim Schmidt are two other guys with "schools."

There was a time a fellow like this writer could come close to figuring where a fellow was from by looking at the knives he made. It's not nearly so true now.

But believers in the pure line are there. They're hewing to it pretty close, and there are new names. It's kind of fun.

Normally, the pure line gets changed—Europeans tend to put a big lanyard slot in the pommel of otherwise-Loveless patterns, for example—but sometimes not.

See for yourself.

Ken Warner

▲*James R. Lucie:* As clean a copy of a real Scagel as deer antler will permit in forged 5160.

◀*Mark Lubrich:* A Scagel cover knife replicated in the round and in 5160 steel.

▲▼*Tom Downing:* It's Loveless all the way here—full height hollows, double hollows, sub-hilts, sexy handle line—all of it. (Weyer photo)

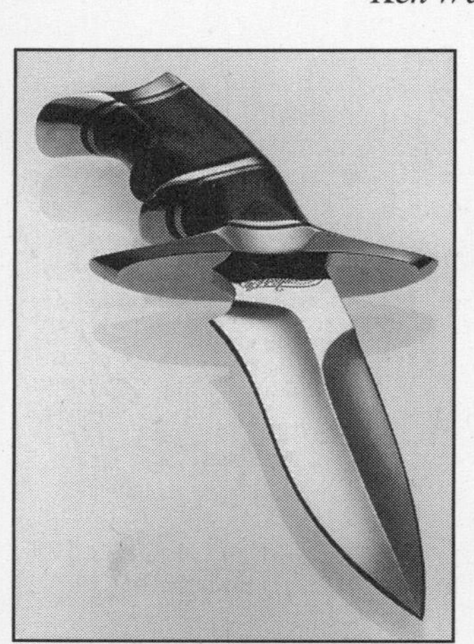

◀*Bill Luckett:* Obviously, we're looking at the Rod Chappell influence here, maybe with a little extra flair—and flare, too. (Weyer photo)

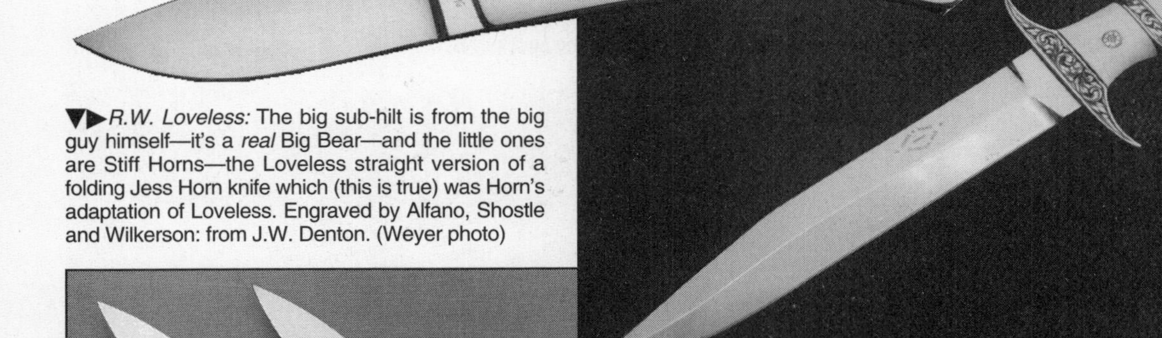

◀*Ettore Bertuzzi:* This year, the Italian copyist has chosen to honor Ron Lake and did a series like these—they're ATS-34 and nickel silver with lapis lazuli and turquoise.

▼▶*R.W. Loveless:* The big sub-hilt is from the big guy himself—it's a *real* Big Bear—and the little ones are Stiff Horns—the Loveless straight version of a folding Jess Horn knife which (this is true) was Horn's adaptation of Loveless. Engraved by Alfano, Shostle and Wilkerson: from J.W. Denton. (Weyer photo)

▲*Steven J. Rapp:* This craftsman can do anything he wants in metal, and often does, and here he's done the decades-ago Rod Chappel. (Weyer photo)

▶*James R. Lucie:* This big hunter—and its sheath, too—are line-for-line stuff.

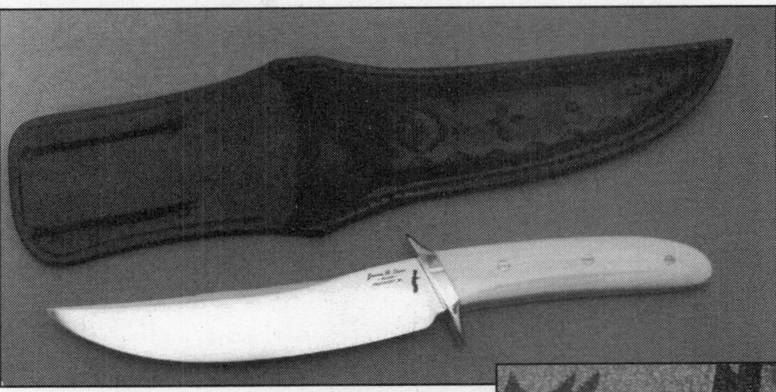

◀▲*Audra (Sharp) Draper:* Neighbor and apprentice to the poet of 52100, Ed Fowler, the lady makes 'em like he does—in every detail, as with the sheephorn knife here—or not, as in the other knife which is only close.

THE THEORETICAL FIGHTER

THESE AREN'T SOLDIERS' knives, nor assassins' daggers, but rather idealized versions of the mid-19th-century Bowie. They are, for the most part, theoretical sidearms.

It's interesting, that theoretical part. No one would willingly or knowingly go anywhere near a knife fight without a gun or a police officer or both. The theory is, *if* you had to, one of these would be a good tool—not the best, mind you, but built to do it and a lot easier to carry than, say, a 24-inch baton.

It's at this point that the discussion waxes hotter. You can get into single-guard, cross-guard, no-guard arguments; slashing versus stabbing can get a lot of attention; the minutiae of blade profile, steel recipe; the *finish* of various parts—all are worth debate.

It's all good fun. There *are* or *have been* reasons for the differences. We are not, after all, Scandinavian or Japanese. Those folks had all this decided for them centuries ago.

Nope. We're into fighter variety. One size does not fit all. Nor one shape either. Right now, we're showing a fair sampling of the knives they're making these days for the theoretical fight.

Ken Warner

▲*Nestor Lorenzo Rho:* The traditional gaucho-style knife in useful stainless steel at 56 Rc. The composite handle is stag, ivory, ebony and bronze. (Hence photo)

◀*Max A. Berger:* A set of fighters in 440C and ironwood—each to suit, presumably, a style or a situation. (Chan photo)

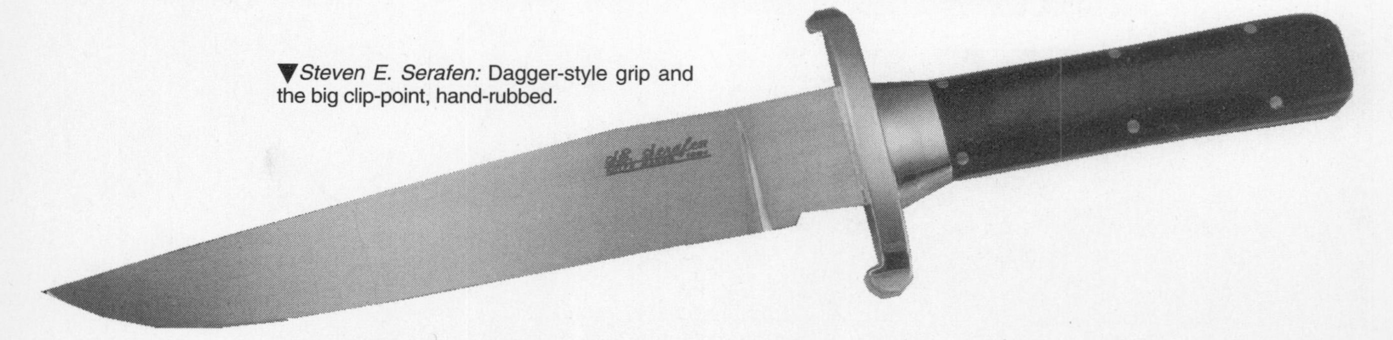

▼*Steven E. Serafen:* Dagger-style grip and the big clip-point, hand-rubbed.

▼*Wayne Hensley:* Not steak knives—they're over a foot long, with Collins engraving, in 440C. (Weyer photo)

▲*Vance Francis:* It's 15 inches overall, in ATS-34 and ironwood, with a fencing tilt, plus a dressy sheath. (Weyer photo)

▲*Douglas and Dianna Casteel:* Meier Damascus and *lapis lazuli* handles, trimmed in blued steel—big stuff. (Weyer photo)

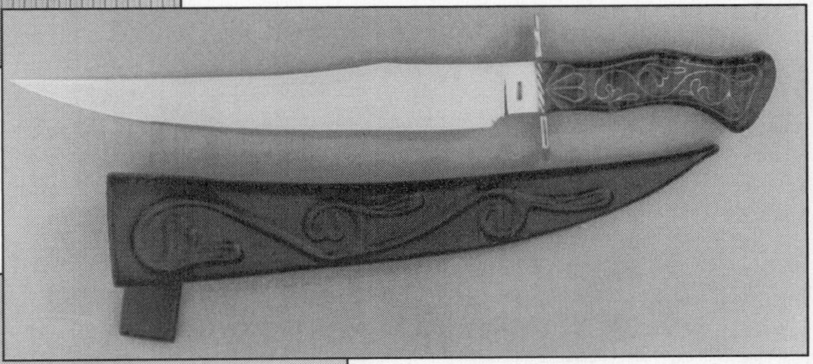

▲*Wm. F. Moran, Jr.:* This is the S-24, the evolved, longer, slimmer fighter design—the blade is 12 inches. (Holter photo)

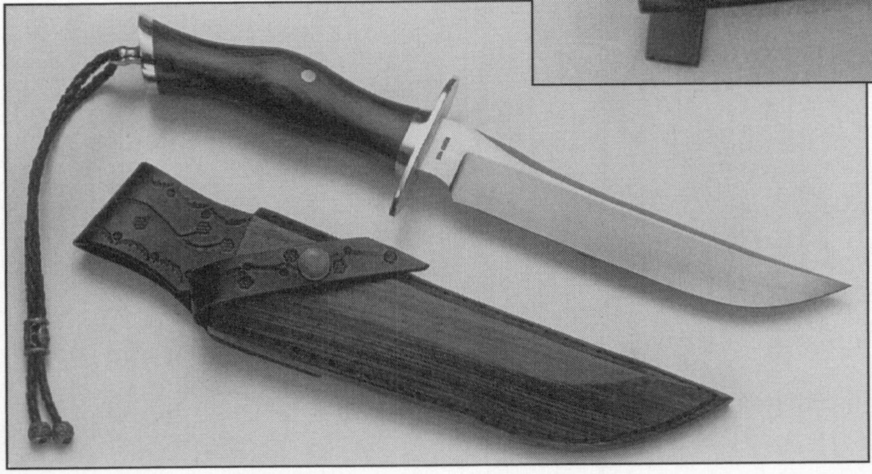

◀*Scott Richter:* Fencer grip and a very stout blade grind in ABS steel—just under 14 inches overall. (Weyer photo)

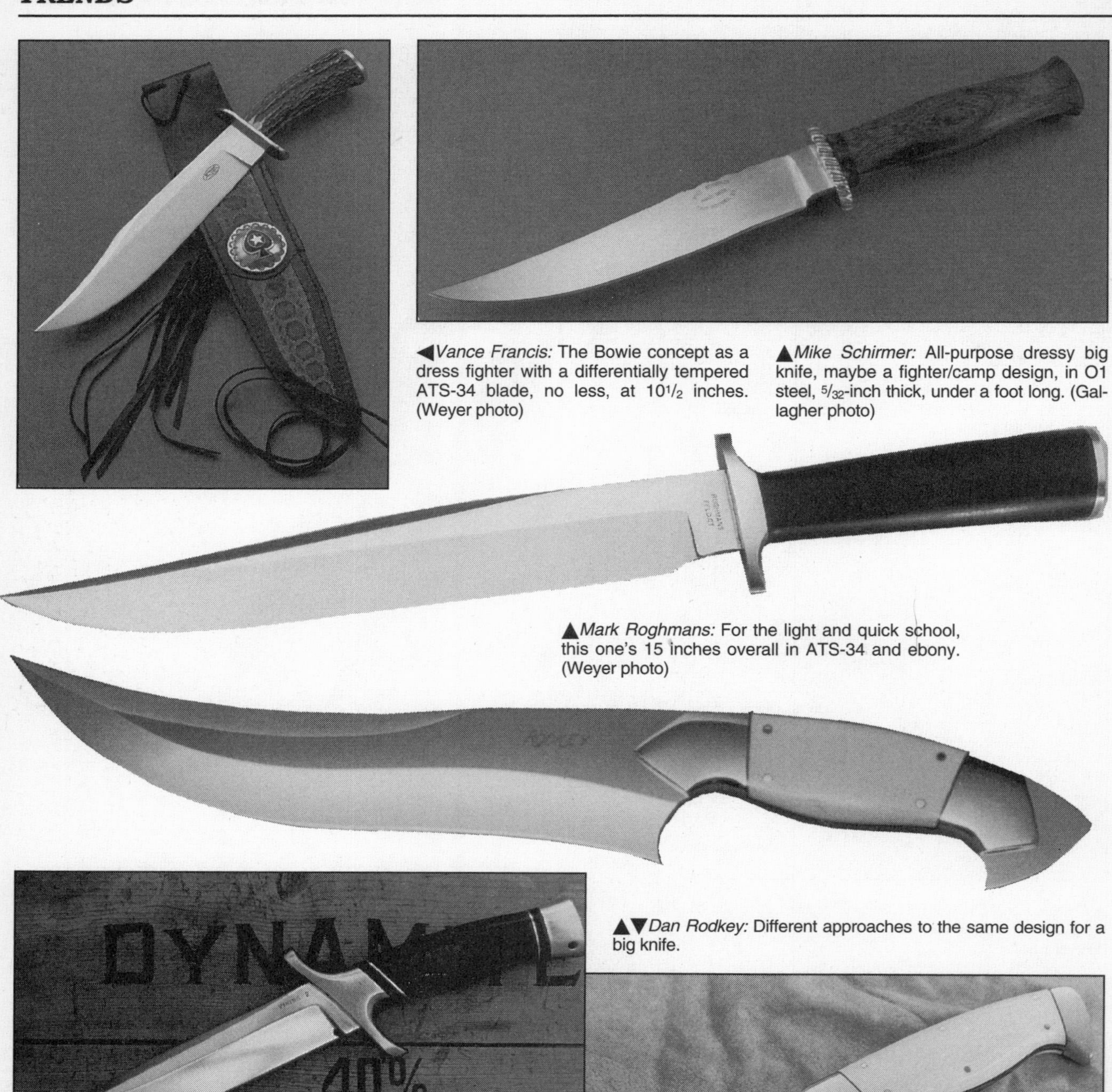

◀*Vance Francis:* The Bowie concept as a dress fighter with a differentially tempered ATS-34 blade, no less, at 10 1/2 inches. (Weyer photo)

▲*Mike Schirmer:* All-purpose dressy big knife, maybe a fighter/camp design, in O1 steel, 5/32-inch thick, under a foot long. (Gallagher photo)

▲*Mark Roghmans:* For the light and quick school, this one's 15 inches overall in ATS-34 and ebony. (Weyer photo)

▲▼*Dan Rodkey:* Different approaches to the same design for a big knife.

▲*James Thorlief Eriksen:* Big Micarta grip for an 8-inch blade—set up for a martial arts approach.

◀*Gus A. Montaño:* Broad-bladed dress fighter in stag, brass and 1095. (Weyer photo)

▲*William Dean Ellis:* Short—under 6 inches—stout blade in ATS-34 coupled with a complex grip.

▲*Colin J. Cox:* A heavy center spine inspires confidence; the knife has a $6^{1}/_{2}$-inch 440C blade.

◀*Jim Walker:* A $6^{1}/_{2}$-inch 5160 clip-blade and burl ash grip—delicate filework. (Weyer photo)

▼*Jed Darby:* A dramatic nickel Damascus blade, nearly 7 inches long, surmounts a dark oosic grip. (Weyer photo)

▲*Ken Markley:* Forged from $^{1}/_{4}$-inch 1095 and balanced with sambar stag, it looks quick. (Gallagher photo)

▲*Colin J. Cox:* Called The Sting, it's a boot-sized heavy-duty knife.

▶*James E. Hand M.D.:* Chute knife with big pinned double guard.

▲*James D. Ragsdale:* A broad dagger-style blade is one solution in the fighter problem—it's just under 15 inches overall. (Weyer photo)

▲*Ludwig Fruhmann:* Gold-pinned pearl in a full integral chute knife in CPM-T-440V steel.

▲*Rick Browne:* A chute knife with the European pommel style—under 10 inches overall. (Weyer photo)

◀*Dusty Moulton:* Called Falcon, it's ATS-34 and ivory—Jere Davidson engraved. (Weyer photo)

THE SLIP-JOINT FOLDER

IF YOU'D PREDICTED, in any but the general "here's hoping" way this reporter did, that there could be seven pages of slip-joint folder pictures in this edition, well, you'd have been all by yourself. It's a marvel.

Yet, here they are, everything from springless friction "penny knives" to five-bladed sowbelly folders. And they are slick.

Back when there was Bob Enders and a couple of others, the knowledgeable J. Bruce Voyles told his readers the new handmade folders were "Sheffield quality" in stainless steels. And that's about it.

Except you can add in a certain verve, an elan. So some of the patterns are pefectly recognizable, but that maker's very own. Bob Cargill's Cripple Creek patterns had some of that.

There's not much more to say. They walk and talk and shine like new-minted. They ain't cheap, either, and the full trend to upscaling hasn't even started.

We divide them here just like a factory catalog: one blade, two blades, more blades. Enjoy.

Ken Warner

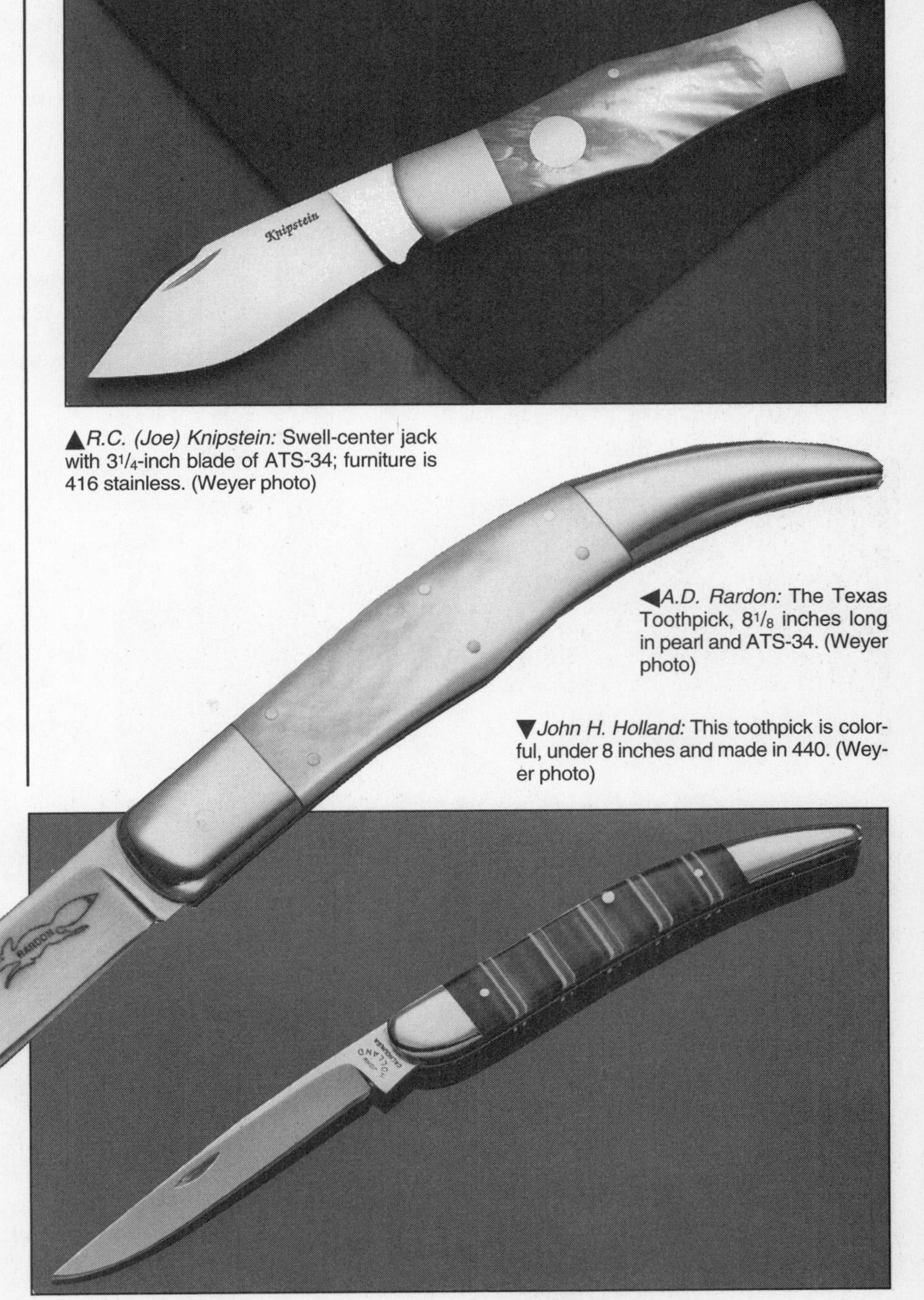

▲*R.C. (Joe) Knipstein:* Swell-center jack with $3^{1}/_{4}$-inch blade of ATS-34; furniture is 416 stainless. (Weyer photo)

◀*A.D. Rardon:* The Texas Toothpick, $8^{1}/_{8}$ inches long in pearl and ATS-34. (Weyer photo)

▼*John H. Holland:* This toothpick is colorful, under 8 inches and made in 440. (Weyer photo)

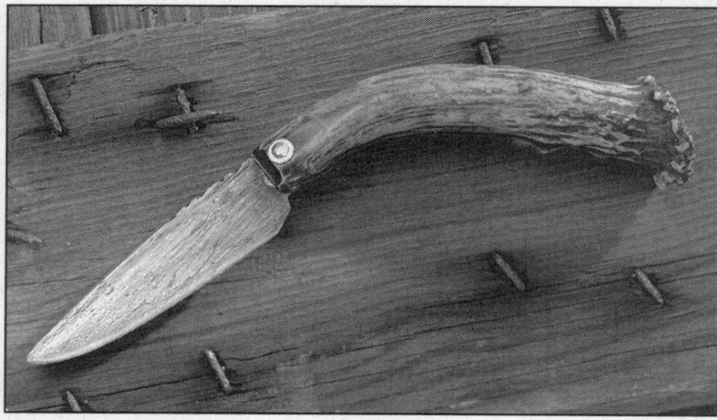

◀*Richard Plunkett:* Three ways to play the jackknife game. The wiggly one is called humpbacked.

▲*Joe Click:* This folder does not click, of course, but it really looks right. (Weyer photo)

▼*Chuck Patrick:* The maker did it all and got it $7\frac{1}{2}$ inches long, which is about right.

THE SLIP-JOINT FOLDER

One Blade Only

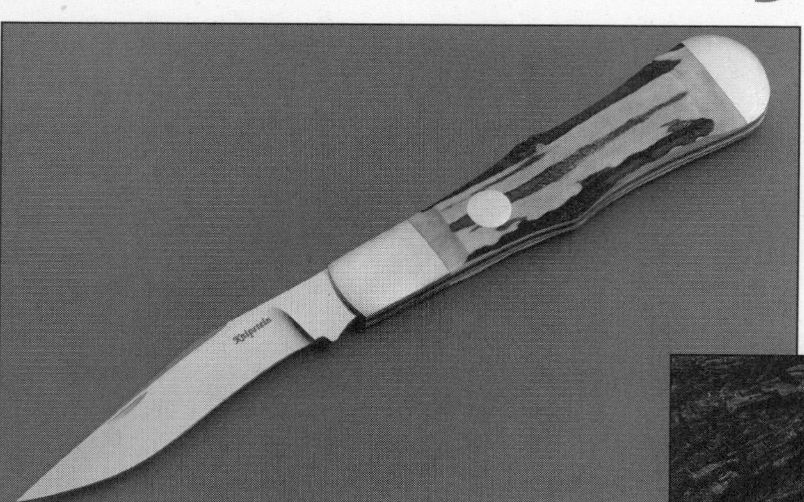

◀*R.C. (Joe) Knipstein:* Big jack in stag and stainless goes $9\frac{3}{4}$ inches as you see it. (Weyer photo)

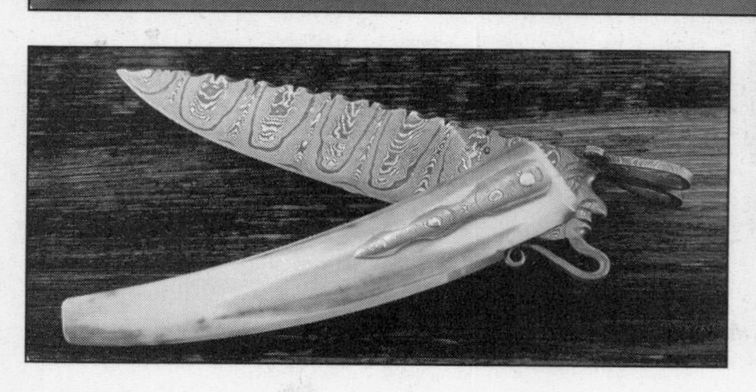

◀*Wade Colter:* Upscale friction folder in ladder-pattern Damascus and a walrus tip—a neat face there. (Gallagher photo)

▲*Shane Sloan:* A big lightweight with 7075 aluminum frame and ATS-34 blade, 5 inches closed.

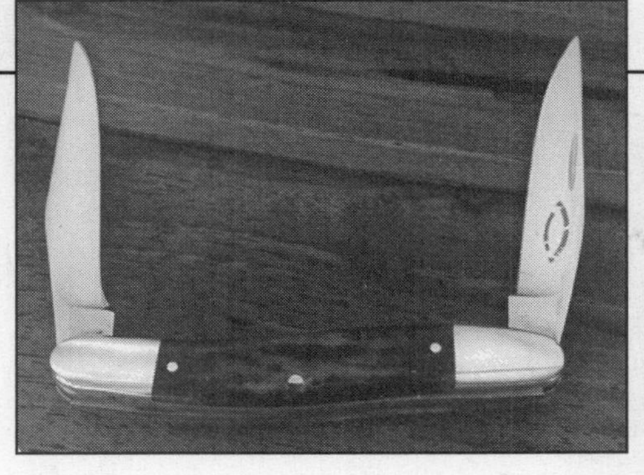

▲*Beryl Driskill:* Just $2^{3}/_{4}$ inches long—ATS-34 and nickel silver and bone.

▲*Harold E. Brown:* A trapper and a two-blade jack—blades in the 3-inch area. (Weyer photo)

◀*R.C. (Joe) Knipstein:* The sunfish with a taper and maybe an attitude. (Weyer photo)

THE SLIP-JOINT FOLDER

Two Blades Each

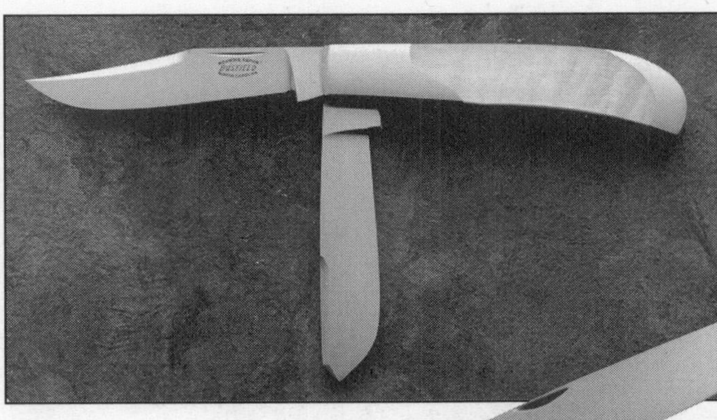

◀*John Busfield:* Semi-interframed trapper in 416 and gold pearl. (Weyer photo)

▲*Shane Sloan:* Not all that usual coke-bottle trapper in ATS-34 and nickel silver.

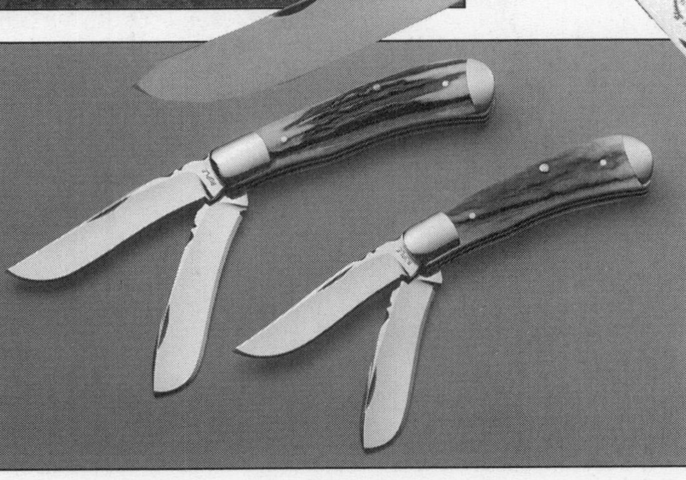

▶*William Ruple:* Trappers in two sizes—stag and ATS-34 and 416 stainless. (Weyer photo)

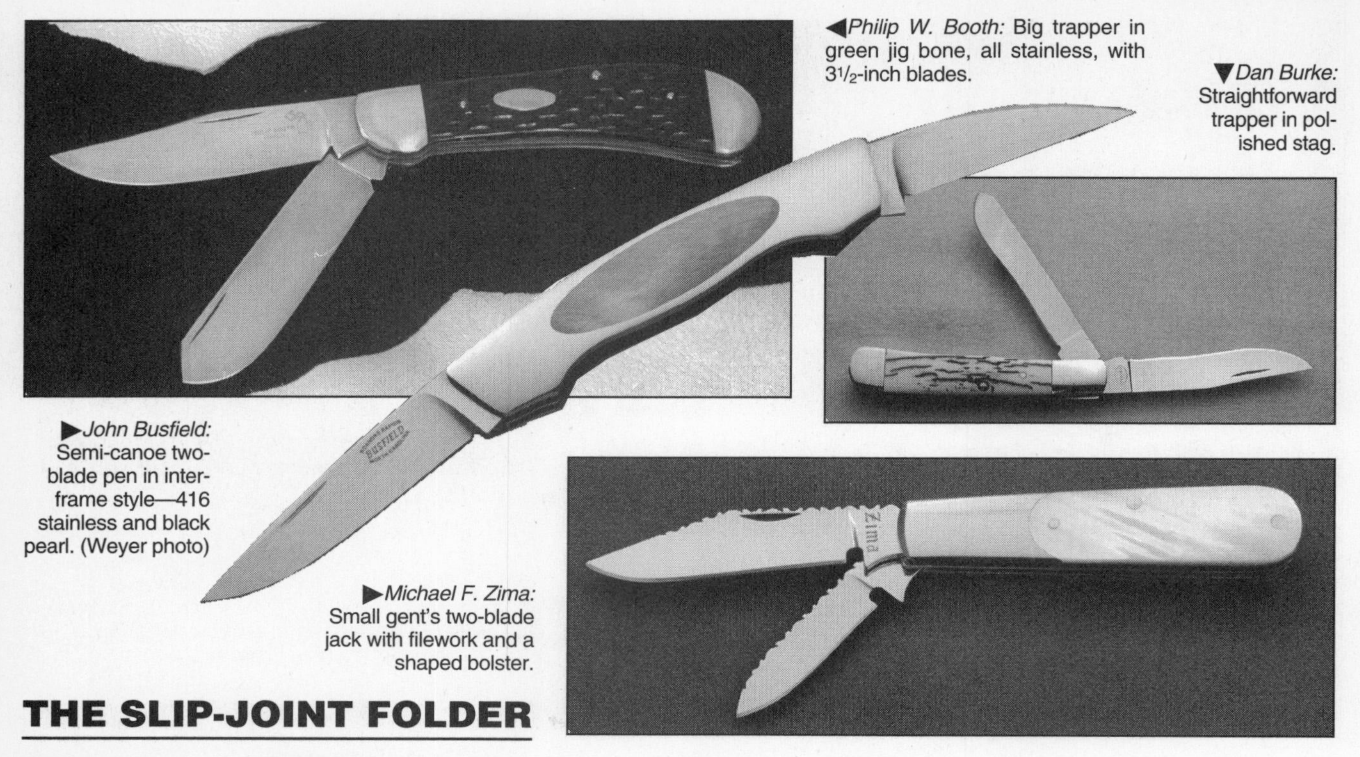

◀*Philip W. Booth:* Big trapper in green jig bone, all stainless, with $3^1/_2$-inch blades.

▼*Dan Burke:* Straightforward trapper in polished stag.

▶*John Busfield:* Semi-canoe two-blade pen in inter-frame style—416 stainless and black pearl. (Weyer photo)

▶*Michael F. Zima:* Small gent's two-blade jack with filework and a shaped bolster.

THE SLIP-JOINT FOLDER

Two Blades Each

▶*Weldon G. Whitley:* Bigger than it looks—4 inches closed—with pearl and a jazzy bolster. (Gallagher photo)

▼*R.C. (Joe) Knipstein:* A pair of 3-inch blades with pearl and 416 stainless. (Weyer photo)

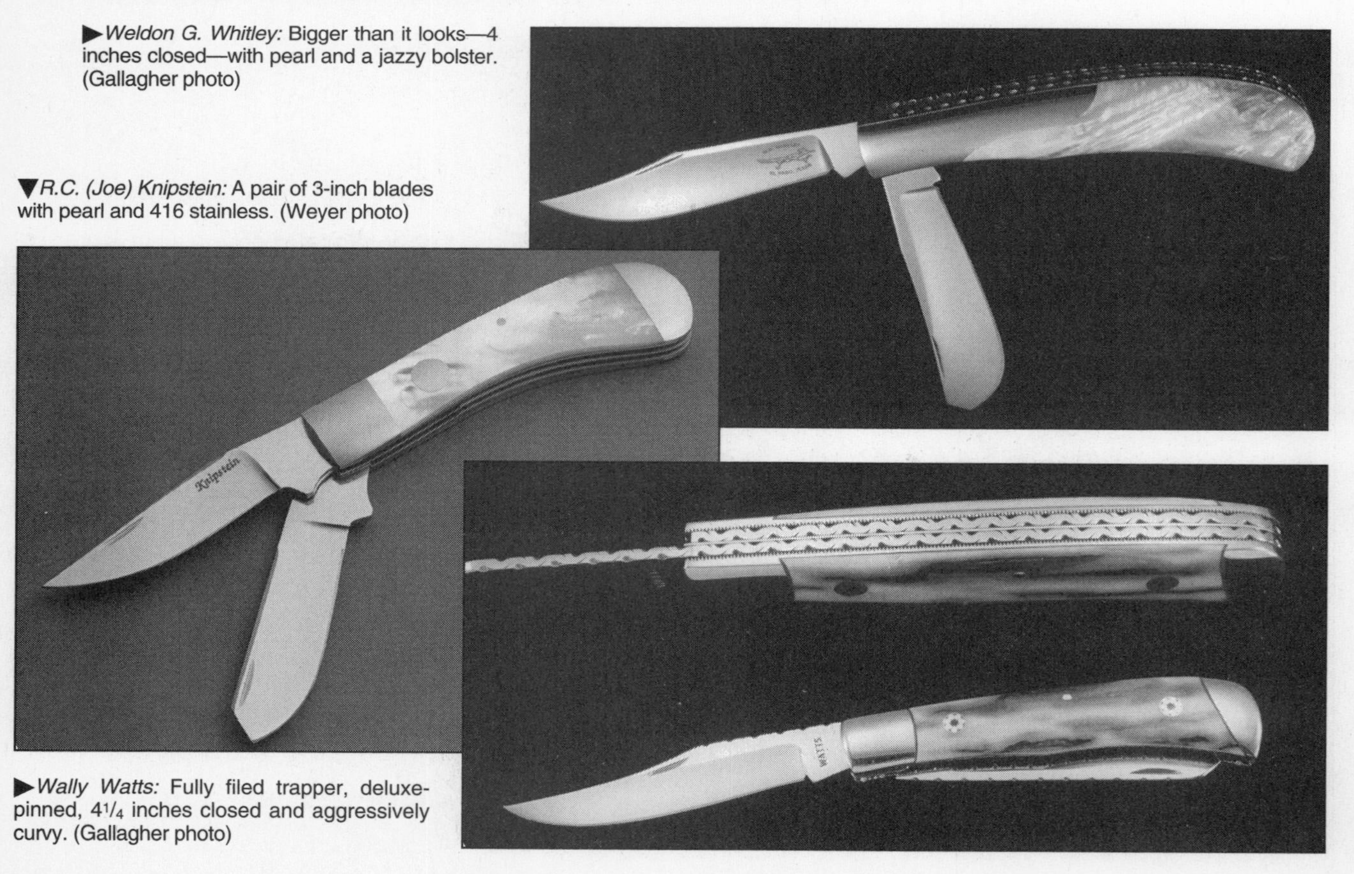

▶*Wally Watts:* Fully filed trapper, deluxe-pinned, $4^1/_4$ inches closed and aggressively curvy. (Gallagher photo)

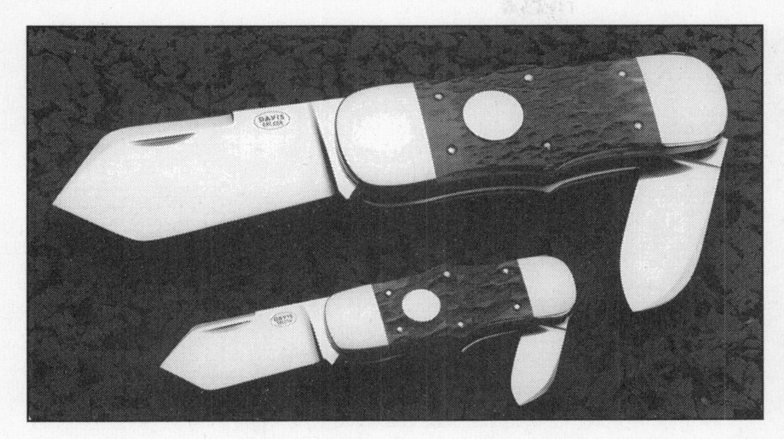

▲*Terry Davis:* Big and little sunfish—swell-centered—and finished pretty swell, too.

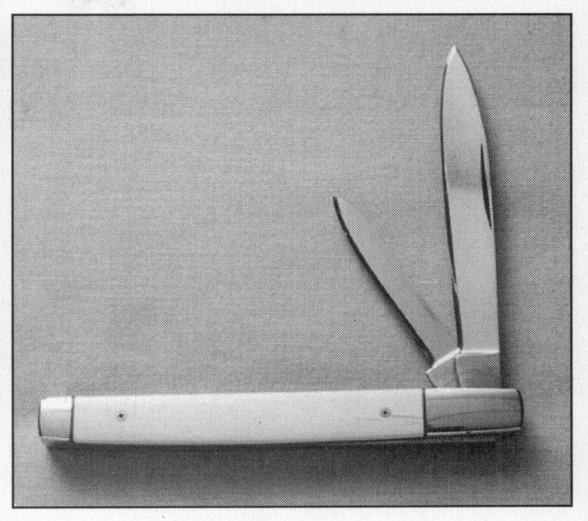

▶*Dan Burke:* The doctor, very plain, in ivory with red liners.

◀*Cecil Terry Barrett:* West Damascus in a short trapper with dove-tailed scales. (Weyer photo)

THE SLIP-JOINT FOLDER

Two Blades Each

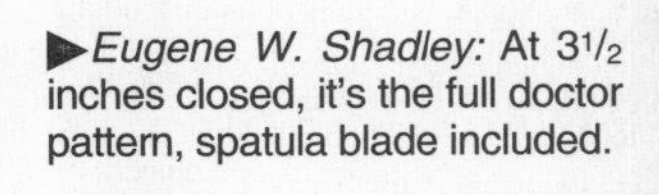

▶*Eugene W. Shadley:* At 3 1/2 inches closed, it's the full doctor pattern, spatula blade included.

▼*Philip W. Booth:* Rich patterning in blue mastodon and a special Thomas Damascus.

▲*Peter Martin:* It's Turkish twist Damascus, titanium liners, nickel silver bolsters and gold pins.

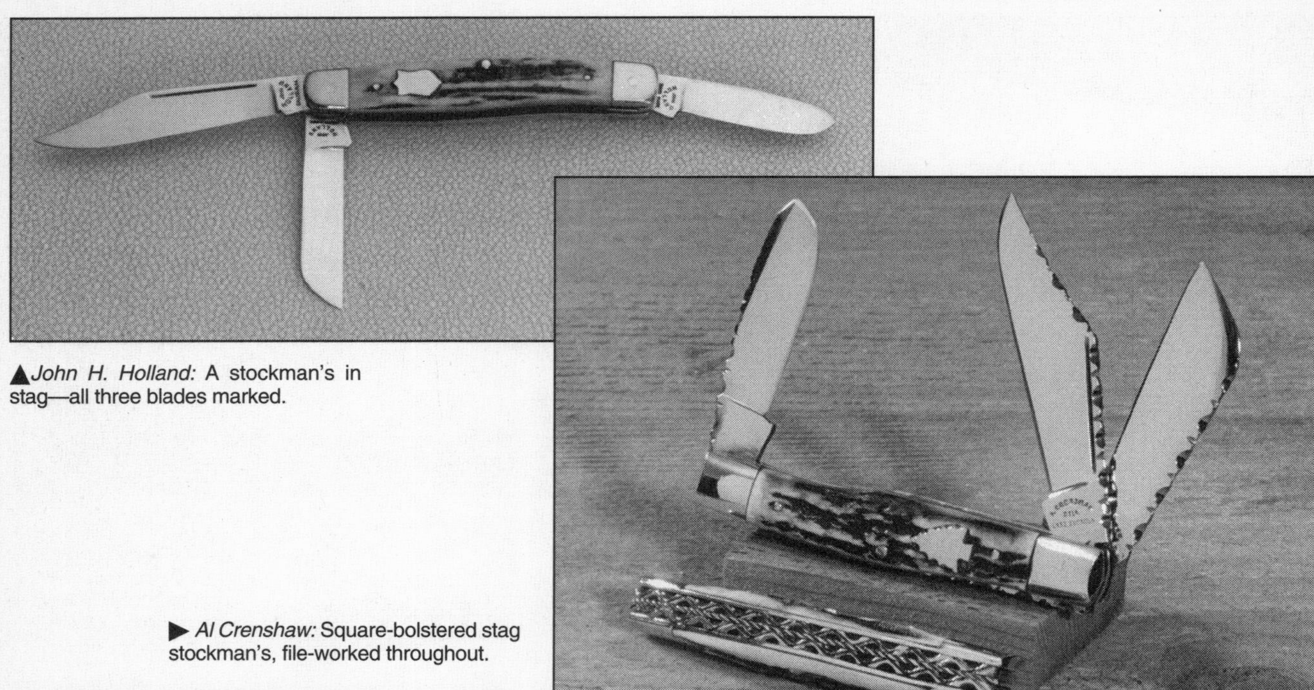

▲*John H. Holland:* A stockman's in stag—all three blades marked.

▶ *Al Crenshaw:* Square-bolstered stag stockman's, file-worked throughout.

THE SLIP-JOINT FOLDER

Three Blades and More

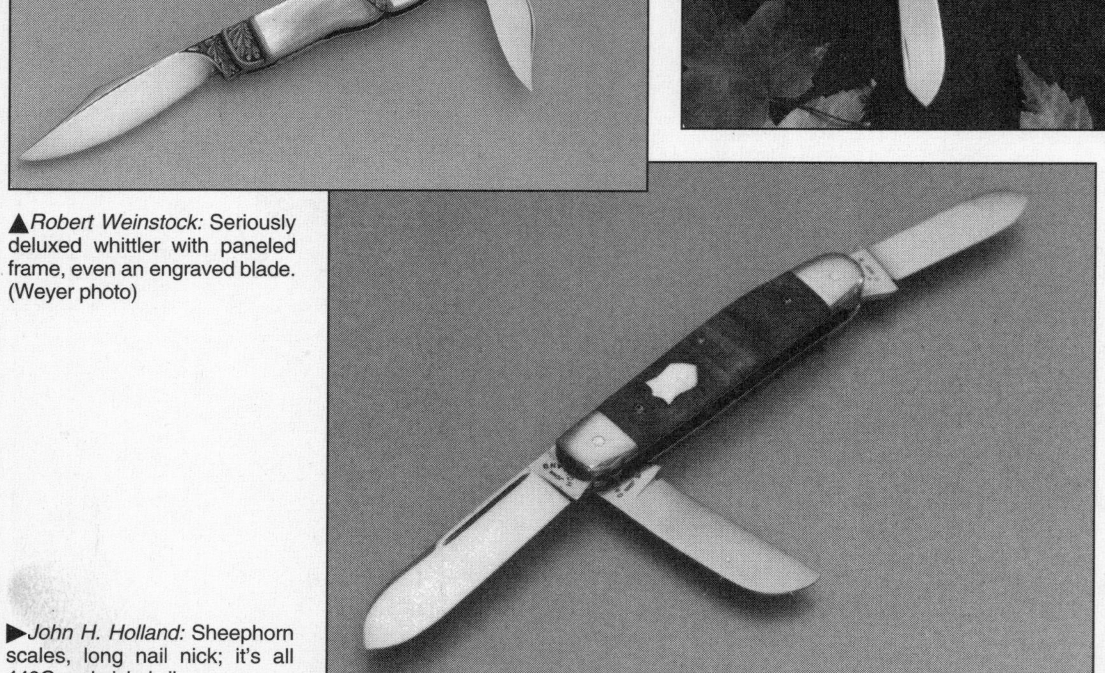

▲*Robert Weinstock:* Seriously deluxed whittler with paneled frame, even an engraved blade. (Weyer photo)

▲*Philip W. Booth:* Sowbelly stockman's pattern, all nice and curvy in ATS-34 and ivory.

▶*John H. Holland:* Sheephorn scales, long nail nick; it's all 440C and nickel silver.

◀*Reese Bose:* Antique—1930s brown bone in a stainless frame with ATS-34 blades. (Weyer photo)

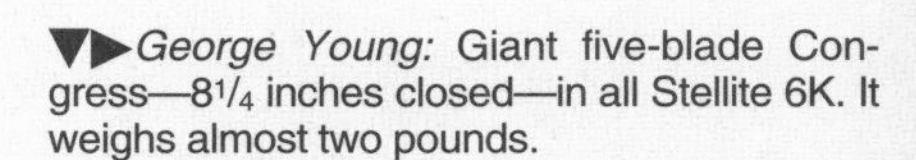

▼▶*George Young:* Giant five-blade Congress—8¼ inches closed—in all Stellite 6K. It weighs almost two pounds.

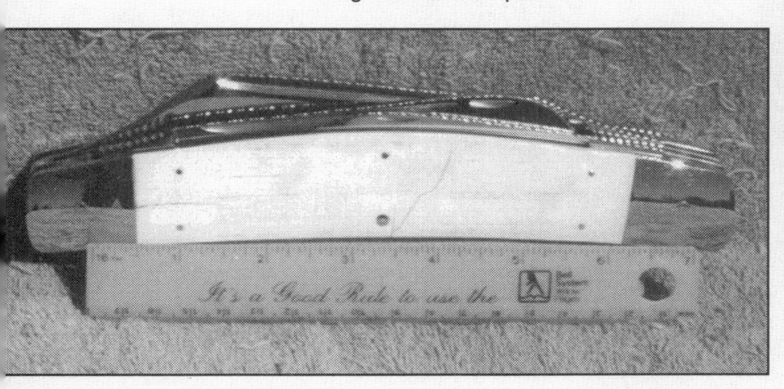

THE SLIP-JOINT FOLDER

Three Blades and More

▶*Terry Davis:* At 3¼ inches closed, this is a pretty big Wharnecliffe whittler—with a gold shield.

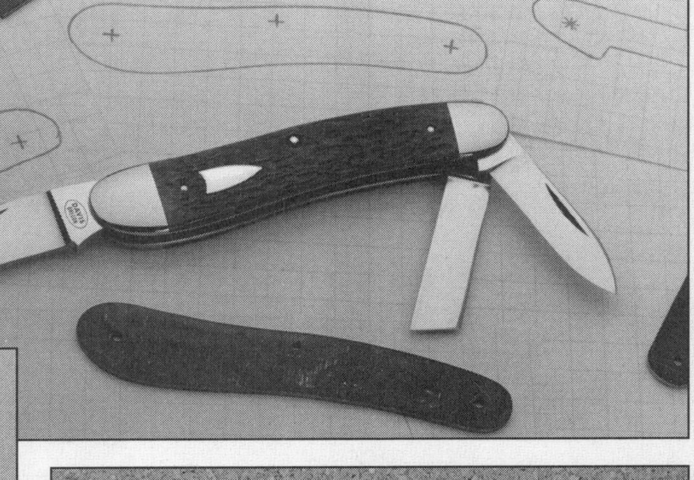

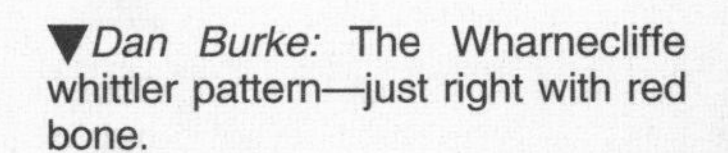

▼*Dan Burke:* The Wharnecliffe whittler pattern—just right with red bone.

▶*Rick Nowland:* Mokume bolsters, pink pearl, twist Damascus blades—an all-out five-blade sowbelly. (Gallagher photo)

TRENDS

CAMP KNIVES NOW

THIS WHOLE GENRE was invented as a cooperation between W.F. Moran Jr. and an unknown 19th-century catalogist who made up the name "Rio Grande Camp Knife." All you see here are developments from Moran's successive interpretations of that old knife *and* other people's interpretations of Moran's interpretations.

That includes this writer, who prevailed upon Moran in the long ago to make him a 10-inch Rio Grande knife. In search of the undamageable, we just about found it.

Moran, mind you, used to go to the woods—in the '50s and '60s—with big knives, so he didn't start from scratch. And for a good bit of the time, he made himself a new knife every year for a special trip, along through the '70s and '80s.

A lot of people began to make knives for that kind of trip, and here we are. They're built for sharp and for tough and for general utility, and a good one will skin and chop with either a butcher knife or a hatchet.

Ken Warner

◀*Wesley A. Whipple:* It goes 16 inches overall in 5160 and maple—very wieldy looking.

▼*Ed A. Fowler:* Built to order in the ordained style, you can count on it—that blade's 52100.

▲*Bob Kramer:* More 5160 in a 10-inch blade and a lot of snakewood in the grip. (Gallagher photo)

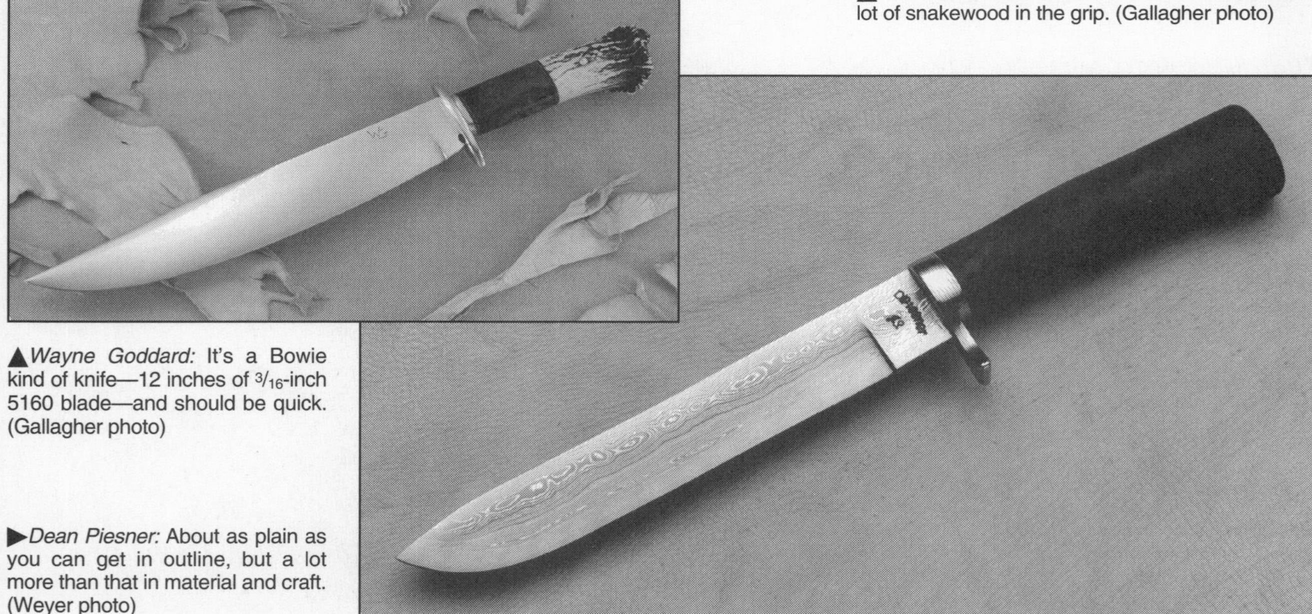

▲*Wayne Goddard:* It's a Bowie kind of knife—12 inches of $^{3}/_{16}$-inch 5160 blade—and should be quick. (Gallagher photo)

▶*Dean Piesner:* About as plain as you can get in outline, but a lot more than that in material and craft. (Weyer photo)

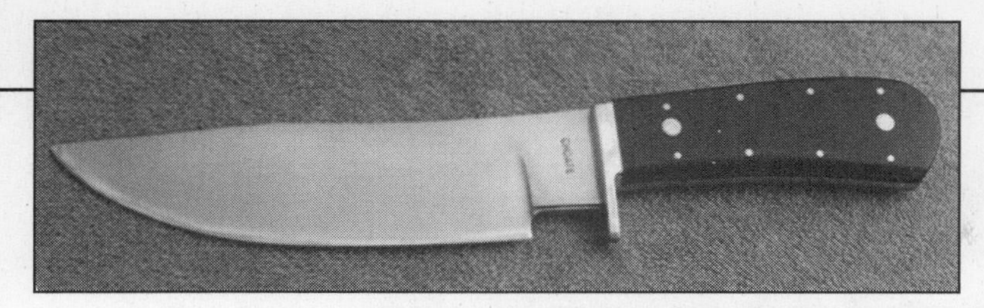

◀*Milton Choate:* Somewhat short and more than somewhat stout, it's $1/4$-inch 5160 forged $1\,3/4$ inches wide.

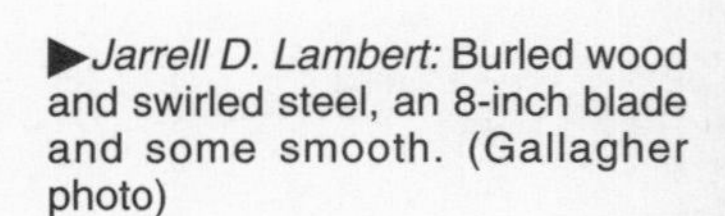

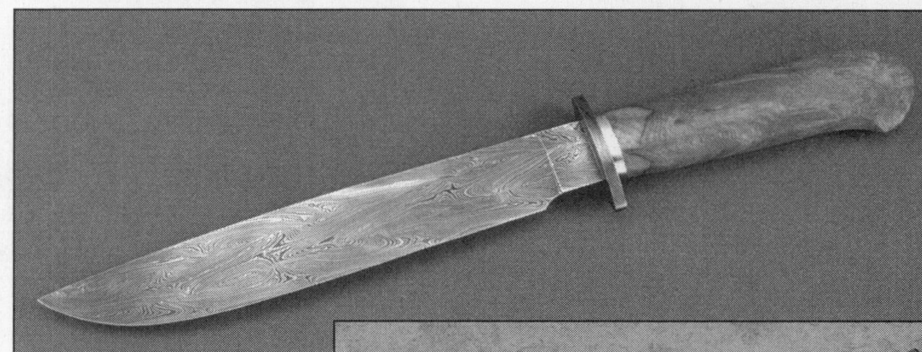

▶*Jarrell D. Lambert:* Burled wood and swirled steel, an 8-inch blade and some smooth. (Gallagher photo)

▶*Tim Britton:* A do-everything style, a sort of tactical camp knife. (Weyer photo)

▲*Danny Thayer:* Sheath by Kenny Rowe, spalted Madrone and—yes—5160 at 16 inches overall. (Weyer photo)

◀*Rich McDonald:* Every big knife was a camp knife back yonder, and this backwoodsy specimen forged from a file is no exception. (Weyer photo)

▼*Steven E. Serafen:* Robust single-edged and heavy-tanged all-around knife.

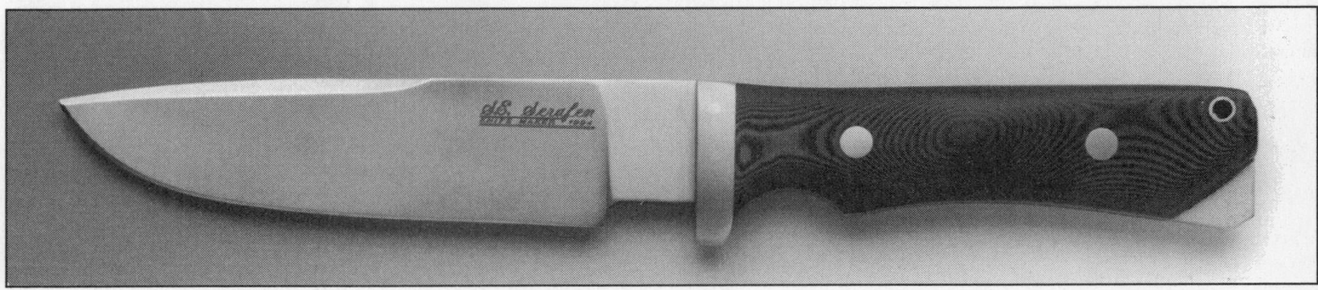

TRENDS

THE HUNTER'S KNIFE

ALL THE TACTICALS, and fighters, and Bowies, and folders aside, this is where it starts. The production of all-purpose belt knives for the outdoor sportsman was and is the basis of the interest in handmade knives.

Of course there are knifemakers who never make hunters. Virgil England says he'll pump gas before he'll do another 4-inch drop-point, unless, of course, it is a cavalry soldier's uniform requirement in another galaxy. There are lots of makers who now specialize in knives to use in another part of the forest.

There are even a few who have *never* made a hunter. They are few on the ground.

And there are lots of hunting knives on that ground. We won't try here to break them down by type, but you can see about all the kinds there are. Enjoy.

Ken Warner

▲*Charles F. Ochs:* Big knife—5 1/2-inch blade forged of 52100—in stag, 11 inches overall. (Weyer photo)

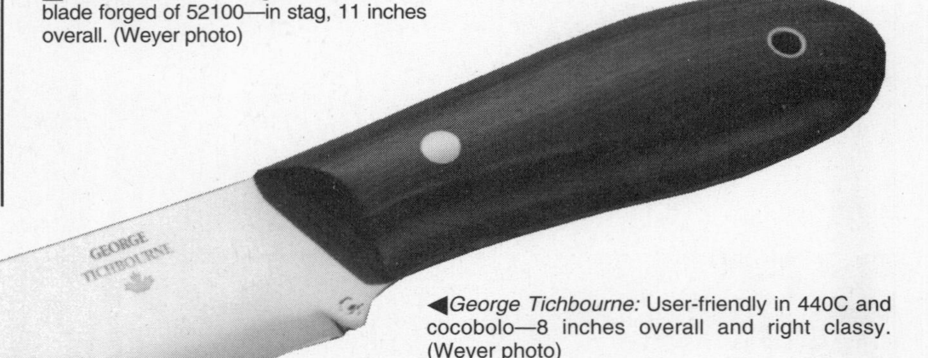

◀*George Tichbourne:* User-friendly in 440C and cocobolo—8 inches overall and right classy. (Weyer photo)

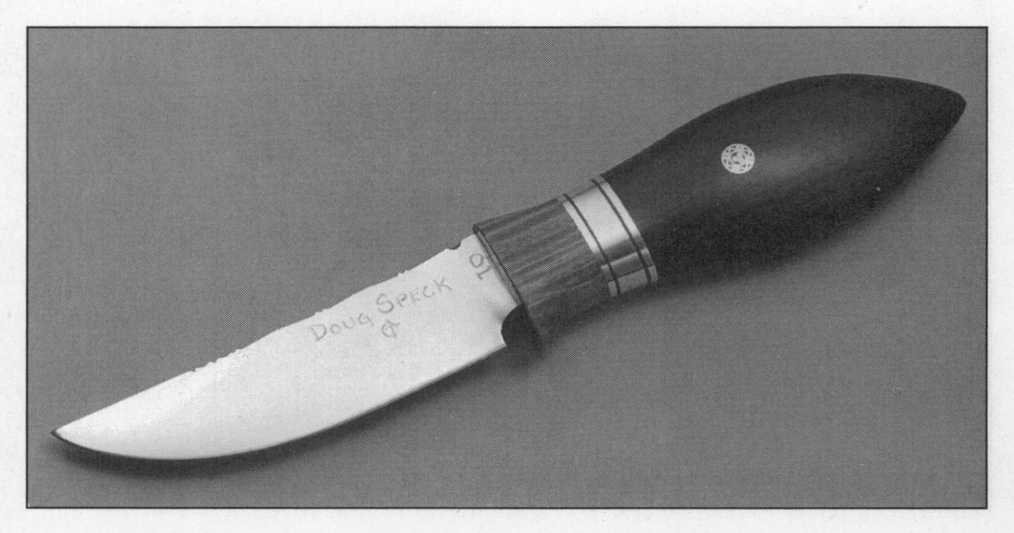

▶*Doug Speck:* His Model 2—almost 9 inches—in O1 steel, with pinned stub tang and comfy grip. (Weyer photo)

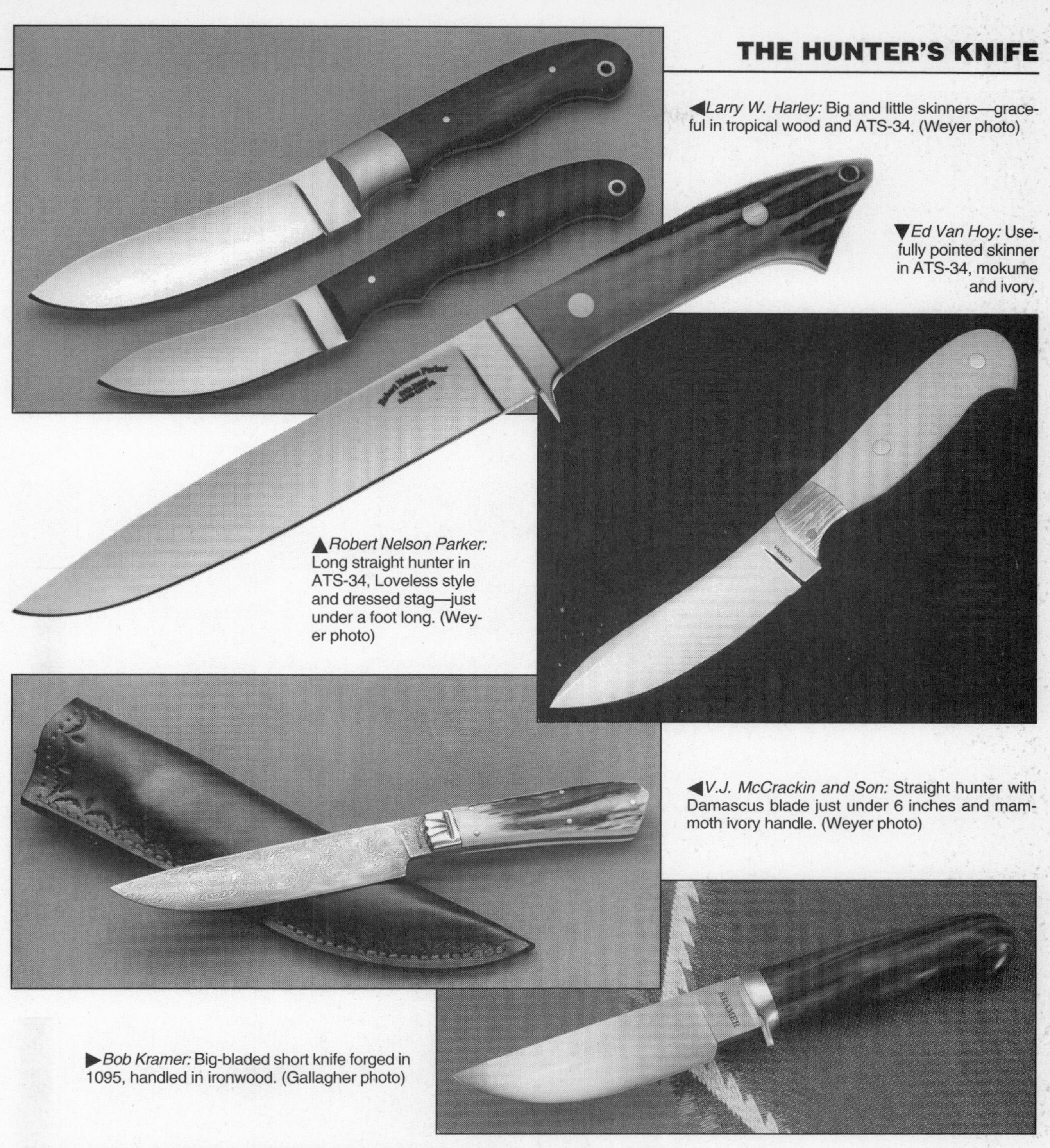

◀*Larry W. Harley:* Big and little skinners—graceful in tropical wood and ATS-34. (Weyer photo)

▼*Ed Van Hoy:* Usefully pointed skinner in ATS-34, mokume and ivory.

▲*Robert Nelson Parker:* Long straight hunter in ATS-34, Loveless style and dressed stag—just under a foot long. (Weyer photo)

◀*V.J. McCrackin and Son:* Straight hunter with Damascus blade just under 6 inches and mammoth ivory handle. (Weyer photo)

▶*Bob Kramer:* Big-bladed short knife forged in 1095, handled in ironwood. (Gallagher photo)

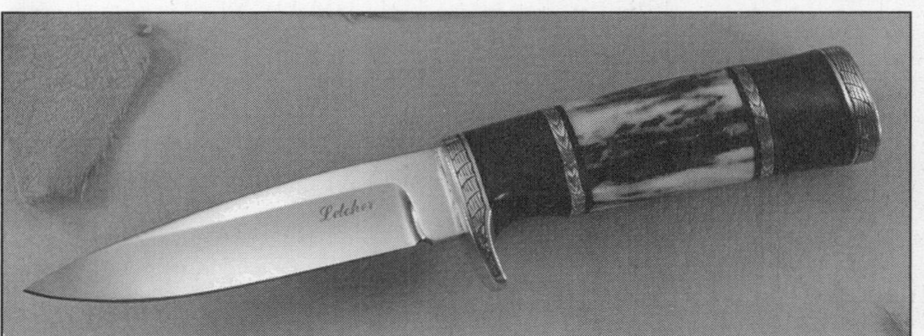

◀*Billy Letcher:* Four-inch 440C straight blade ahead of a compound handle, engraved by the maker. (Gallagher photo)

▼*Paul S. Goertz:* Simple hunter, carefully pinned and nicely setup with burled wood.

▲*Corbin Newcomb:* Paddle-bladed Damascus skinner with nicely compressed cutting edge.

▼*Eric E. McFarlin:* Idiosyncratic sharp-pointed skinner, sheephorn-gripped.

▼*W.J. "Jerry" McDonald:* Finger-grooved and upswept in mildly "retro" styling. (Weyer photo)

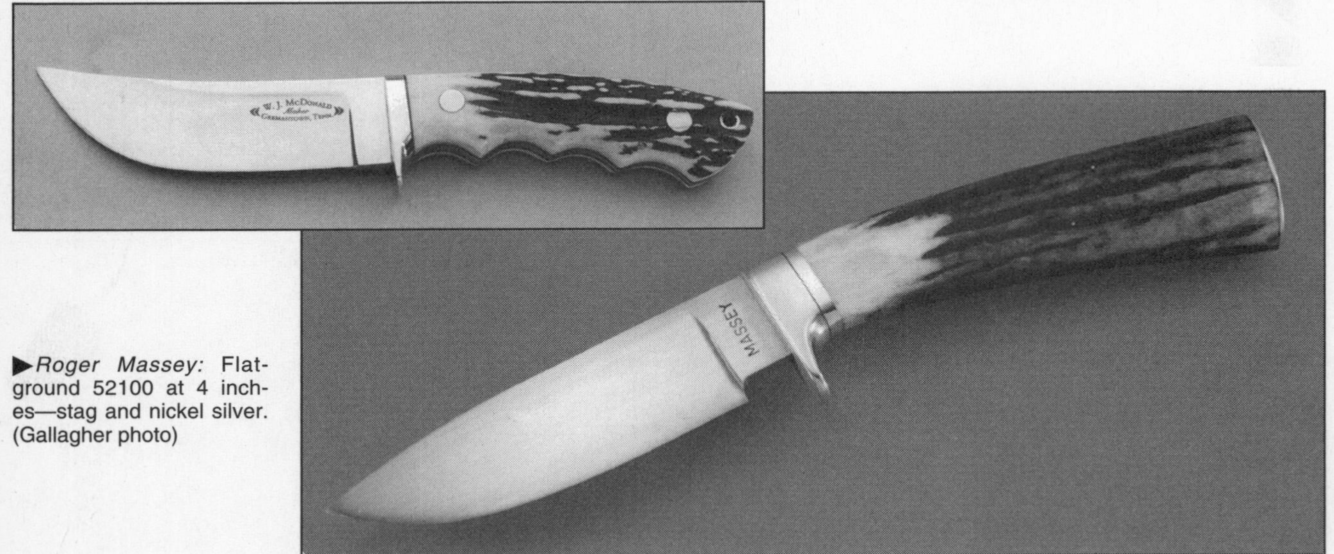

▶*Roger Massey:* Flat-ground 52100 at 4 inches—stag and nickel silver. (Gallagher photo)

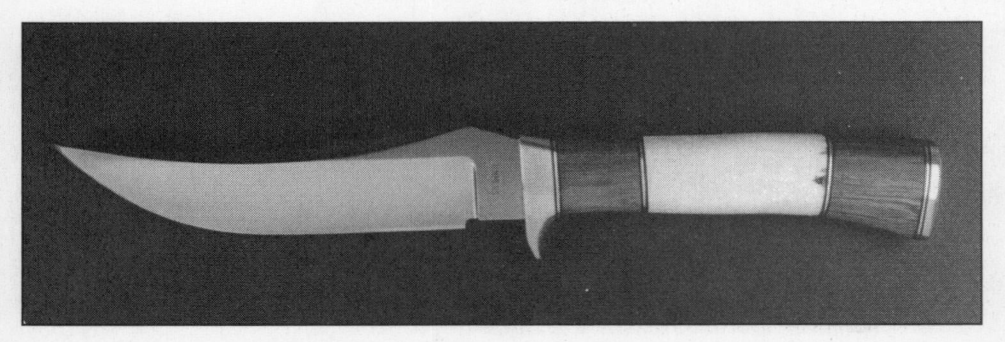

◀*Arthur L. Summers:* Composite handle on a 440C 5-inch straight hunter with buffalo skinner outline.

▲*Glenn A. Long:* Just 7 inches overall, built stout in 440V and stag. (Weyer photo)

▲*Stu Bold:* Nifty pair, finger-grooved and handsomely ground in 440C—a lot of personal style. (Weyer photo)

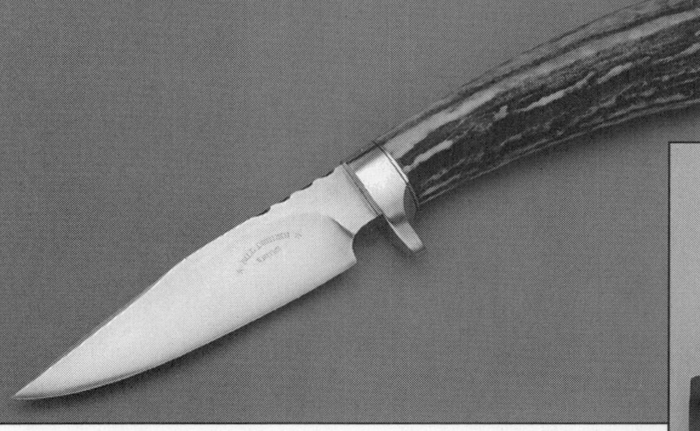

▲*William Behnke:* Forged of W1, this sharply pointed blade is 4$\frac{1}{4}$ inches—grip is stag, of course. (Weyer photo)

▼*Bob Dozier:* Small hunters in several point styles, set up in horizontal Kydex sheathes. (Weyer photo)

▲*George Cousino:* Neat old-time components and '90s profile in a deeply hollow-ground 4-inch blade. (Weyer photo)

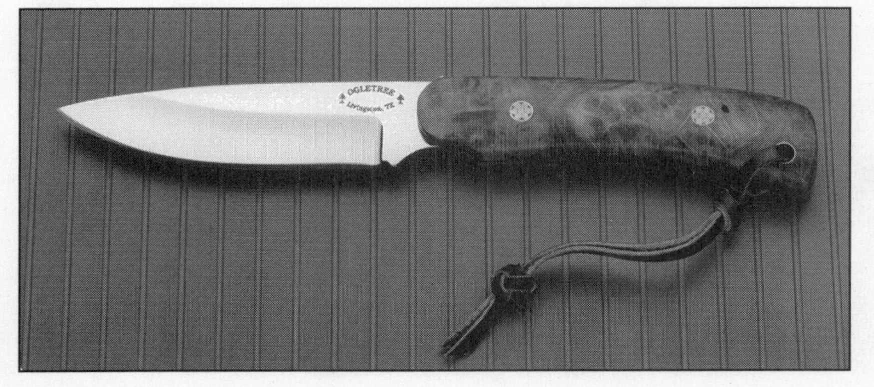

◀*Ben R. Ogletree Jr.:* Simple straight 4-incher in ATS-34 with stabilized buckeye grip. (Weyer photo)

▲*John D. Dennehy:* Reminiscent styling in a trailing-point hunter just about the right size.

▲*Bruce A. Fuller:* Nearly 6 inches of 1084, flat-ground, teamed with smooth mesquite. (Weyer photo)

◀*Tom R. Lewis:* Big straight blade—6 inches of ATS-34—with linen Micarta grip.

▲*Philip C. Wilson:* Nice skinner and a slick signature with 4 1/2-inch CPM-440V blade. (Gallagher photo)

▶*Eric E. McFarlin:* Large trailing-point heavy-duty hunter with a nifty stag pommel.

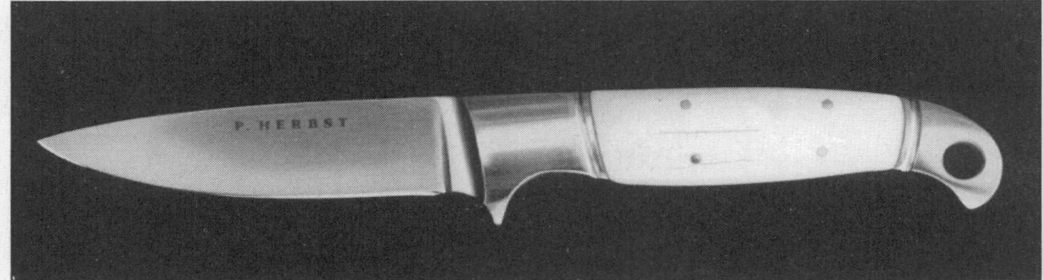

◀*Peter Herbst:* Just 3 inches of CPM-T-440V—all integral blade, bolster, guard and birdshead pommel.

TRENDS

THE DISPLAYED KNIFE

NOT VERY MANY knifemakers prepare displays for their knives. There are big exceptions, naturally, but in the main, it's owners who do the displaying.

Still, it isn't too difficult to find examples. I've had a Gene Baskett knife on the sort of stand he furnishes sitting on a half-dozen desks over the years. And he's still doing it.

Some, as you see before you, work very well and make the knife, perhaps, more than it is. In a sense, all knives are sculpture—that is, they are three-dimensional—and that seems even truer when set up properly.

We have your elaborate background and we have your simple rack—either does the job. Of course, if you don't want to draw attention to your knives—well, I'm sure there's other stuff around to look at.

A special stand makes any given knife a lot more noticeable. That's what it's for.

Ken Warner

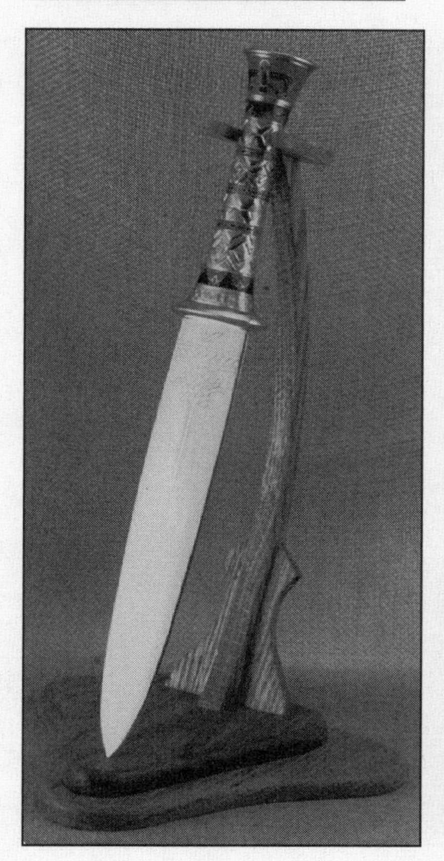

▲*Larry Mensch:* A simple wood stand gives this brazen King Tut dagger replica full display.

▲*Mel Anderson:* A piece of apple tree and a slim straight dagger hang together nicely—the unit is about 15 inches tall.

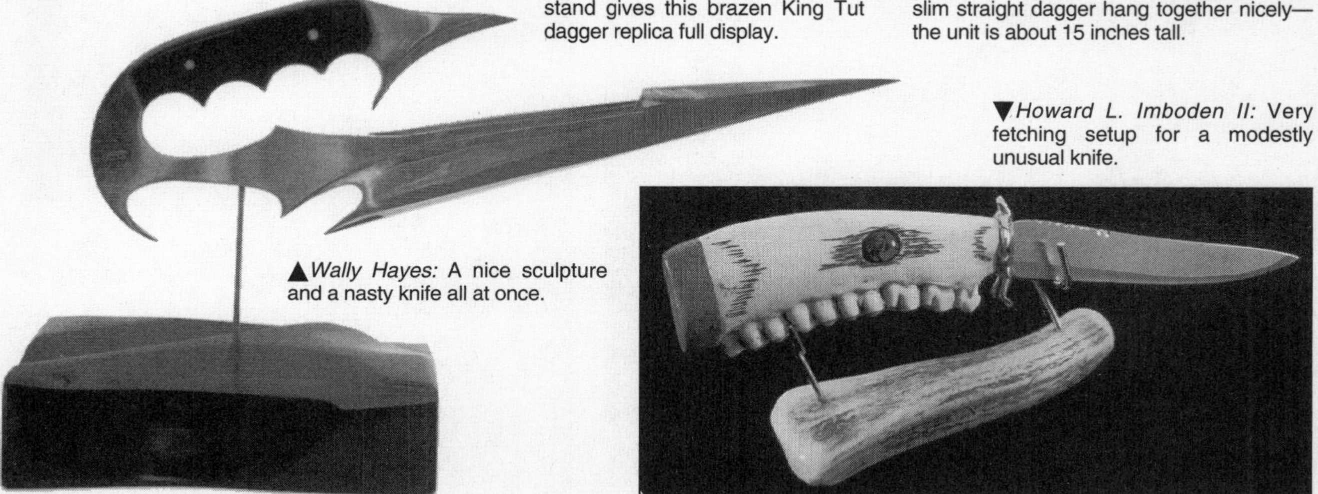

▲*Wally Hayes:* A nice sculpture and a nasty knife all at once.

▼*Howard L. Imboden II:* Very fetching setup for a modestly unusual knife.

▲*Jim Turecek:* A sort of waterless aquarium here with a very fishy knife. (Weyer photo)

▶*Bracey R. Ledford:* A dragon carved in mammoth ivory with rubies and gold. (Weyer photo)

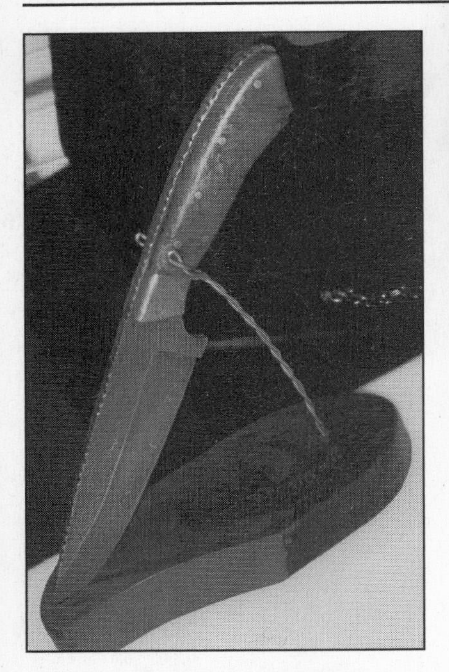

▲*Vernon Red:* A simple twisted coral stand shows off this blade.

▶*J.W. McFarlin:* A ramshorn throne for a most expressive dagger. (Weyer photo)

▲*Jay Fisher:* Desert Wind is its name, and it looks just like one.

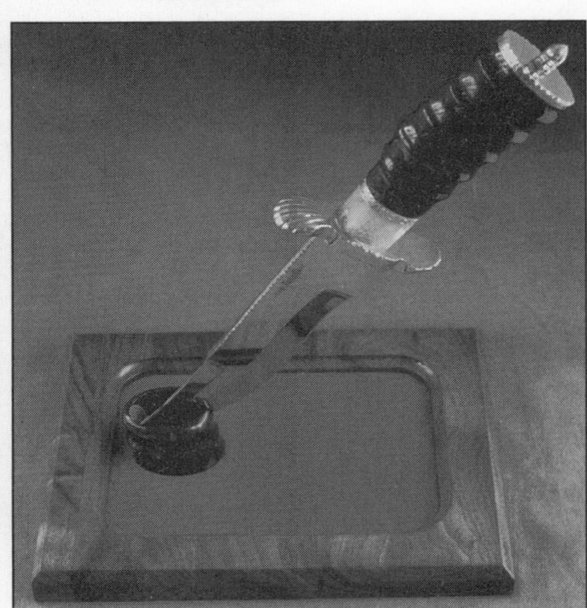

▶*John D'Andrea:* Pretty aggressive stance for desktop looking.

◀*Garvin Dickerson:* This dagger hangs on pegs set in a polished upright rod—quite impressive. (Reiners photo)

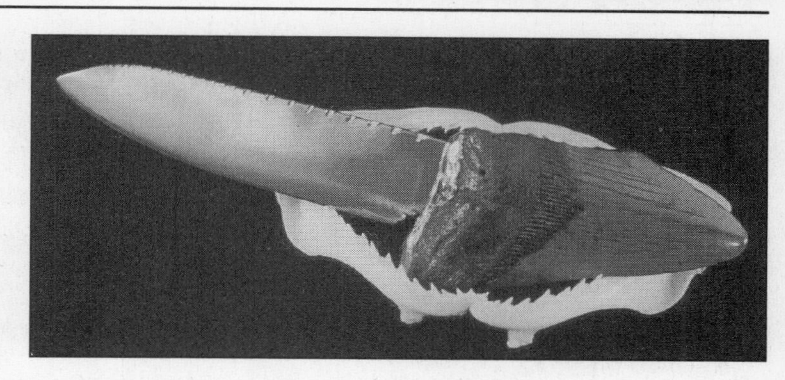

▶*Howard L. Imboden II:* White shark tooth with a 4-inch steel blade set in a cast bronze guard, the whole cradled in a shark jaw.

◀*Larry Fuegen:* Barbarossa he calls it—carved stag with gold and silver and sapphires and agates and ivory. (Weyer photo)

▼*Larry Downing:* French-fitted box for a really strange knife in nickel Damascus with a blue-green ivory handle.

▶*Mario Eiras Garcia:* Horseman's knife for a Brazilian frontier desk.

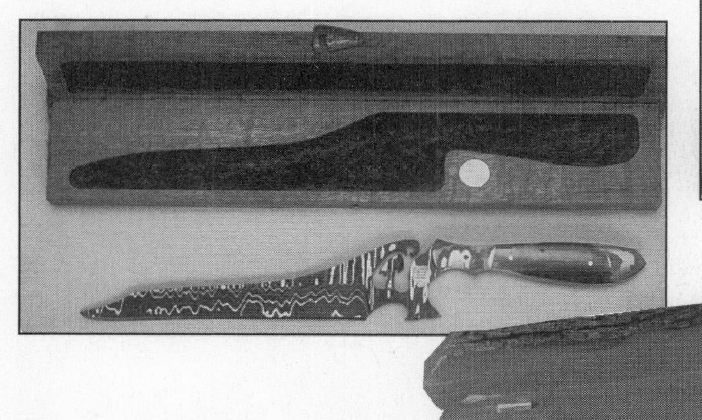

▶*Alfredo Kehiayan:* The box is nearly as striking as the knife, which is how the maker plans it.

STYLE IN KNIVES

WE HAVE INTERESTING knives and high-dollar knives and elegant knives—a nice selection of each—laid out elsewhere in this book. In each of those categories, there are knives with style, but that's not why they're there. Style is different.

Actually, there are a couple of sorts of style in knives. The first is a distinction of expression—a graceful, if you will, way to do something; the second is the particular manner or technique used to provide a pattern or shape. Sometimes both are in a single knife, but for our purposes, either will do.

Seems obvious, then, that sometimes we have styles that affect the knives being made and sold, just as Paris styles affect K-Mart. And there are the notable presentations of individuals.

Style is not, thus, universally a good thing. There are styles that don't work well, for instance, and even ugly ones. That, however, is something to discuss later and elsewhere.

Ken Warner

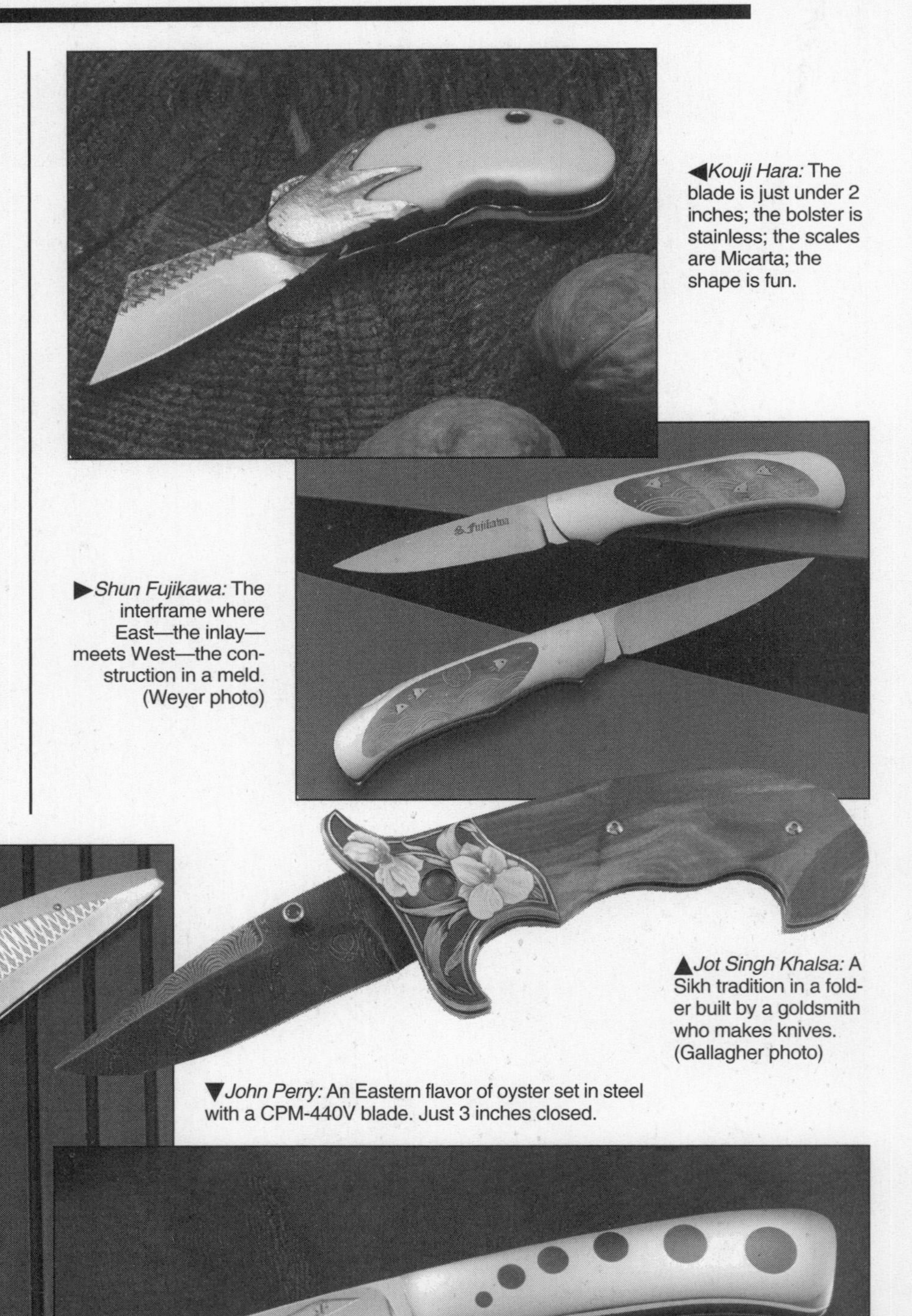

◀*Kouji Hara:* The blade is just under 2 inches; the bolster is stainless; the scales are Micarta; the shape is fun.

▶*Shun Fujikawa:* The interframe where East—the inlay—meets West—the construction in a meld. (Weyer photo)

▲*Jot Singh Khalsa:* A Sikh tradition in a folder built by a goldsmith who makes knives. (Gallagher photo)

▼*John Perry:* An Eastern flavor of oyster set in steel with a CPM-440V blade. Just 3 inches closed.

▲*Michael L. Walker:* Perhaps working as completely in his own style as anyone ever, Walker's Lockers dance to their own drum. (Weyer photo)

◀*Scott Richter:* Aggressive center-point belt knife, bigger ($5^1/_2$-inch blade) than it looks, well-sheathed. (Weyer photo)

◀*J.D. Smith:* This time in a backwoods mode, the aggressive functionality clearly shows. (Weyer photo)

▼*Peter Martin:* San mai blade at 3 inches has deep fuller; the slabs are coral, the pins gold—slick.

▲*Loyd A. McConnell Jr.:* Little liner-locked pocket guys—titanium-nitrided ATS-34, just over 4 inches open. (Weyer photo)

▶*Wayne Goddard:* The knifesmith exemplar as stylist? Yep—look at the lines, the decoration. (Gallagher photo)

◀*Gert van den Elsen:* Just a line here—the bottom line of the handle—and another there—the plunge line—and you got style.

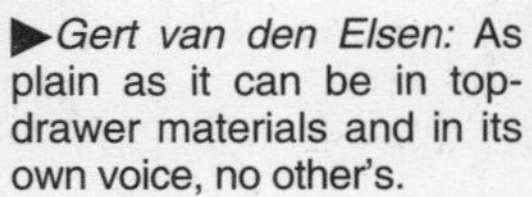

▶*Gert van den Elsen:* As plain as it can be in top-drawer materials and in its own voice, no other's.

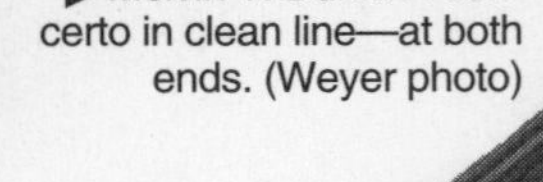

▶*Melvin T. Dunn:* A concerto in clean line—at both ends. (Weyer photo)

▲*Reinhard Tschager:* Clearly, this fellow knows exactly how he wants his knives to look. (Weyer photo)

▼*Michael Osborne:* In the trimmings and forthright profile of W.F. Moran—it's 9¼ inches overall.

▼*Marilyn (Jimmy) Lile:* Absolutely in the footsteps of Bo Randall, and handsome.

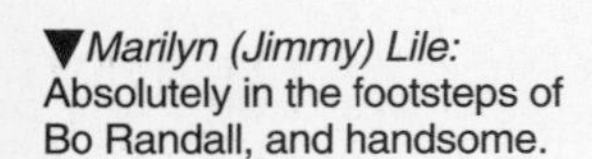

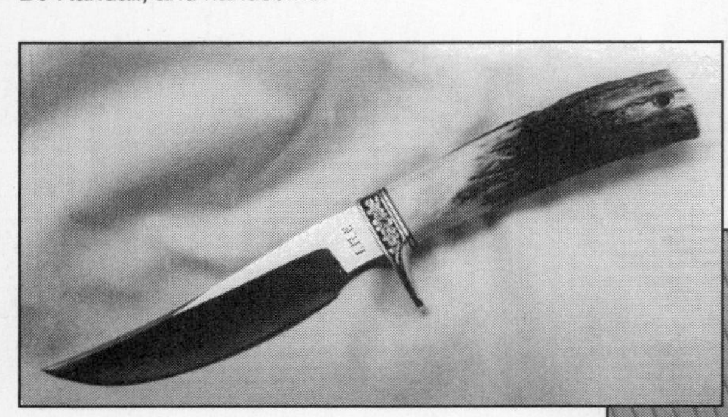

▶*Joseph F. Keeslar:* In the style of Saskatchewan, he says, and that's probably so—they're about a foot long. (Weyer photo)

▼*Tom Downing:* The West Coast style of R.W. Loveless in a narrow semi-skinner—delicious.

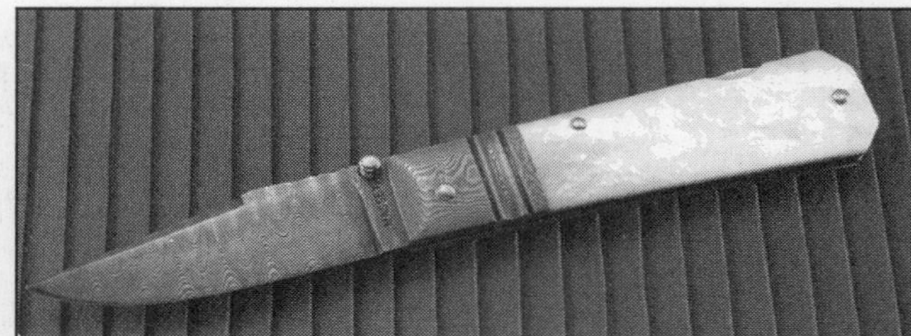

▲*Roger Massey:* New England school? After James Schmidt? Yep, and very nicely accomplished. (Gallagher photo)

STATE OF THE ART

Here's where we show you new kinds of knife stuff and also review how they are doing with the old kinds of knife stuff. Every year there are new tricks with steel, with style, with materials no one ever thought of as knife stuff.

And every year they do the old stunts—the engraving, the scrim, the Damascus patterns—better and better. So we have to have fresh looks.

Sometimes we get technical material we have to look at. We're keeping track of the bog iron right now, for instance. And it has come to us that all these knives have to be carried, and we take a long look at that.

The problem with the State of the Art is that it just is. You can't manipulate it very much. So we don't. What you see is what we get.

Ken Warner

STATE OF THE ART

NOT THE SAME OLD GRIND ANYMORE

MAKING A STEEL knife blade, any type of blade, involves four basic steps. These are shaping, grinding, heat-treating and finishing. Heat-treating (hardening and tempering) often precedes grinding, especially on smaller blades.

The shaping step involves cutting the metal for the blade from raw stock—usually bar, rod or strip. Shaping can also involve forging or hammering, although this step is not needed on most modern production knives. Blades can be cut out by hand, using a shear or a saw. They can be—and usually are—stamped out of uniformly dimensioned strip steel using precision-made steel dies. There are other processes including laser-cutting. Blades can be cut out using a wire EDM (electrical discharge machine), although this tool is more often used to make stamping dies, which are then used to shape blades.

The blanks produced by blade shaping operations look like blades in profile, but they are essentially useless. These blanks must be tapered down to a fine edge, which, after it is hardened and finished, will actually be able to cut things.

To taper these blade blanks efficiently, it is necessary to cut some metal away, using materials that are harder than the steel. These materials are rocks and minerals (remember the childhood game of Rock-Paper-Scissors?). Originally, only natural grindstones were used, but today these largely have been replaced by more uniform and predictable synthetics.

The basic operation of grinding dates back to antiquity. Even stone knife blades often had their edges ground on harder stones, after having first been shaped by flaking or knapping.

The use of grinding wheels to taper the edges of metal blades dates back at least to the Middle Ages. Whether millers or cutlers first used round rocks turning on axles I do not know, though I would be inclined to bet on the millers, since there were a lot more of them.

From the dawn of this rotating rock technology right up to the beginning of the present century, blade grinding was essentially a hand operation. Many improvements were made in the grinding wheels themselves, in the methods of mounting them, and above all in the technology of powering them—starting with man power and dog power, advancing to water power, then to steam

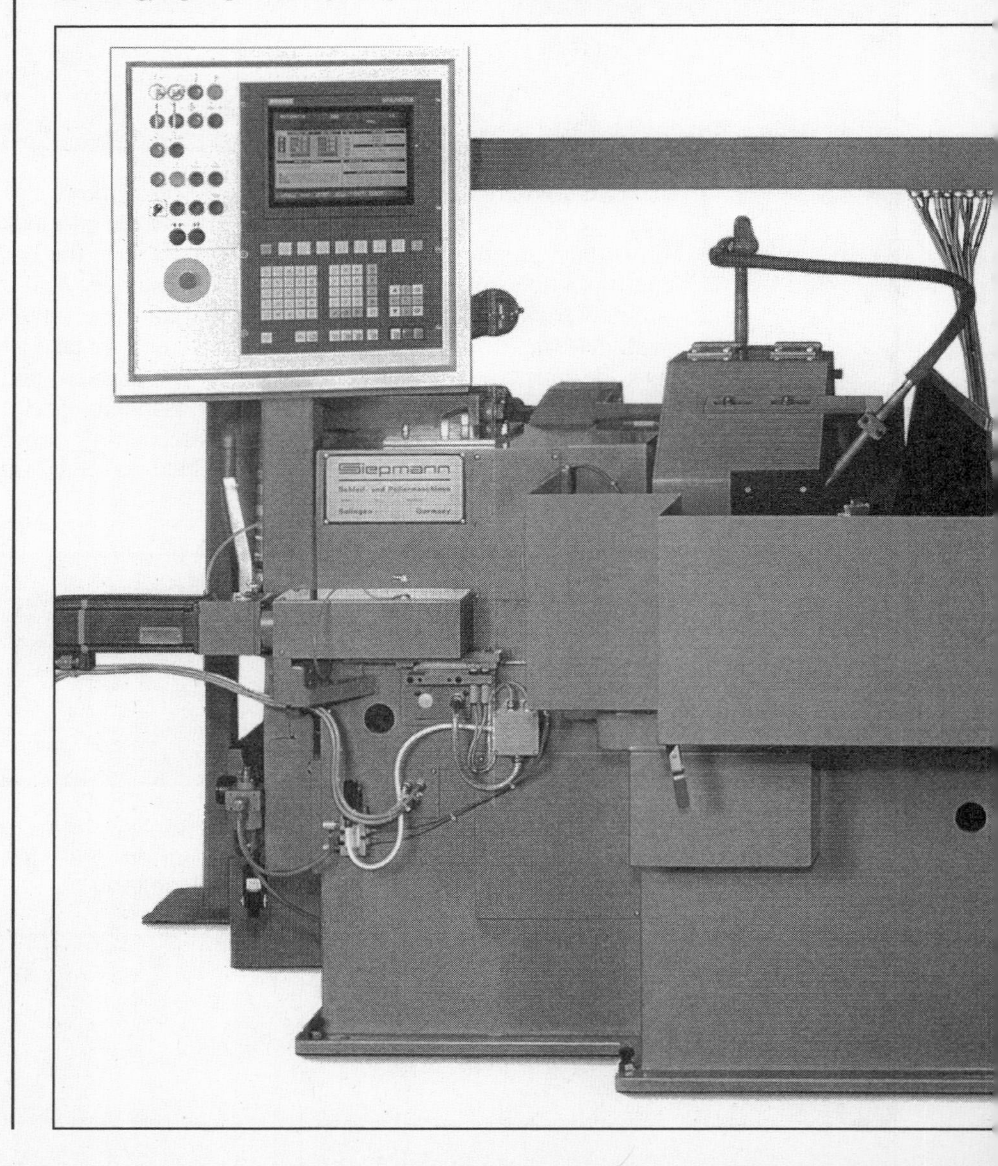

power, and finally to electric power. But out on the shop floor or down in the grinding hull (as wet filthy grinding rooms were called in Sheffield), it remained one wheel, one man and one blade at a time, right up until 1903.

All through the 19th century, countless attempts were made to mechanize grinding. Other metal working processes had adapted readily to mechanical operation and automatic control—drilling, boring, shaping, milling, turning, threading and so on. But grinding was different. There were just too many variables involved, and the fundamental cutting implement—the abrasive wheel—was too inconsistent for any scheme of automatic grinding to actually save labor. Even those early grinding machines which did work (sort of) fell down when it came to making a blade symmetrical, grinding it the same on both sides so that the cutting edge would come out in the middle.

This all changed in 1903 when the Hemming brothers of New Haven, Connecticut, introduced their automatic double-sided grinding machine. A Hemming machine is not actually double-sided, but a pair of the machines set up as mirror images will produce blades just as symmetrical as the most skilled hand grinder. Hemming machines rely essentially on the principle of the Blanchard gunstock lathe, in that they copy a handmade master part. Add to this, of course, the complex machinery needed to dress and advance the grinding wheel as it wore down.

When I started visiting American knife factories more than twenty years ago, Hemming machines (many of them dating back to 1903) were still in general use. They were usually set up in fours (two pairs), because it took the full attention of an operator to load and unload blade blanks into four machines. Where blades were large and cycle times long, an operator might handle eight or more machines. Each machine would grind one side of one blade consistently and repeatably. Each machine required a full set of masters and fixtures for every different blade shape that it might be required to grind. The operators did not need to know how to hand grind, although most of them did, but they did have to know a great deal about setting up, adjusting and maintaining their batteries of complex machines.

That was then...

Nowadays, one would be hard pressed to find a single pair of Hemming machines still running in any of the larger American knife factories. The machines did not wear out; indeed, most of them were sold to Third World cutlery firms. Instead, they were rendered obsolete by new technology. They are so thoroughly obsolete that even countries with nearly unlimited cheap labor, such as Pakistan and Brazil, are now beginning to replace their second-hand Hemmings (some are by now third- or fourth-hand). The big computer-controlled grinding machines that have supplanted the mechanical Hemmings are almost as different from those 1903 clockwork contraptions as those in their day were different from early man's hard flat rock in the creek bed.

The cutting edge of grinding technology now mainly comes from Germany. Go into a high-volume knife factory anywhere in the world today and you will see German automatic grinding machines (also German polishing machines, but that is another story). Even the Swiss use them. Even the Japanese.

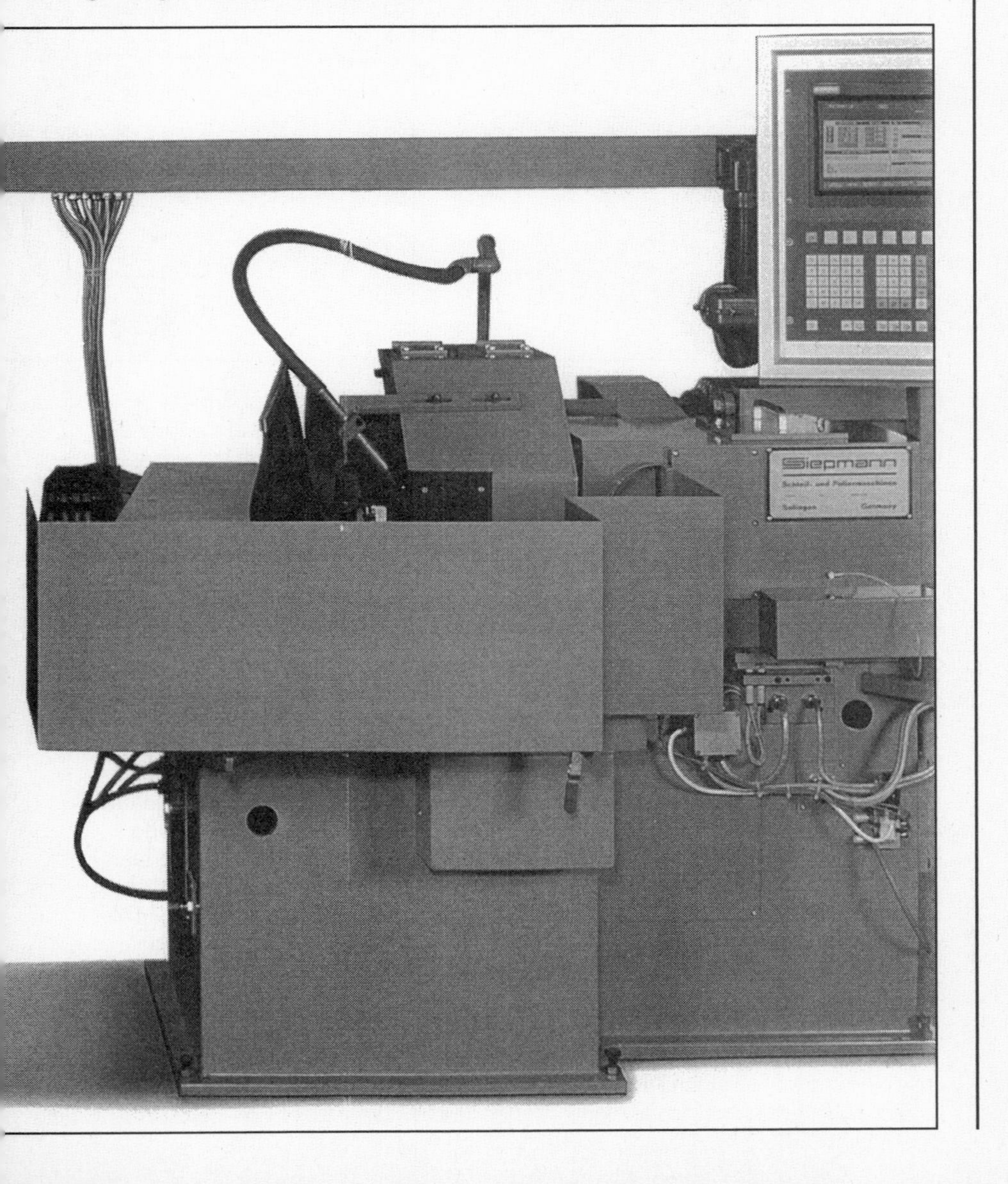

Siepmann's CNC technology in an all-out production grinder—nearly all-purpose, but big bucks.

Everything about the new grinding machines is revolutionary.

The blade blanks are fed into them from big magazines, rather than one at a time. Those machines that are mirror-image pairs move each workpiece from one side to the other automatically. Many of the new machines are truly double-sided, so they can grind an entire blade in one pass. The new machines' hollow cylindrical grinding wheels are self-dressing, and because they cut "on the bias" (at 45 degrees to the workpiece), they maintain a constant effective diameter and rotation speed until they are completely worn out. This essential innovation did away with nearly all of the complex self-adjusting mechanisms needed inside the Hemming machines.

The latest generation of German automatic grinding machines, introduced in the past two years or so, are all computer numerically controlled (CNC). This way, one machine can taper a variety of different sized and shaped blades merely by loading different programs and then swapping out workpiece holders. These holders are precisely aligned by steel dowels, so they only need to be adjusted once. The previous generation of hydraulically and mechanically controlled equipment is still in production and remains cost-effective for volume production of standardized blades. The two big names in automatic blade grinding today are Berger and Siepmann.

Emil Siepmann (1858-1938) began E. Siepmann & Co. as a kitchen and table cutlery firm in Solingen 112 years ago, in 1885. Emil's younger brother, Max, received formal training as a machine tool builder and then joined the family firm. According to one source, E. Siepmann & Co. also dealt in abrasives and grinding equipment, as well as doing contract blade grinding for other firms.

In 1906, three years after the Hemmings (who also manufactured knives), Emil Siepmann Jr. (second son of the founder, then age sixteen), together with his uncle Max, the engineer, developed Europe's first successful blade grinding machine. Meanwhile, Emil Siepmann Sr. had developed the special precision grinding wheels required for these machines

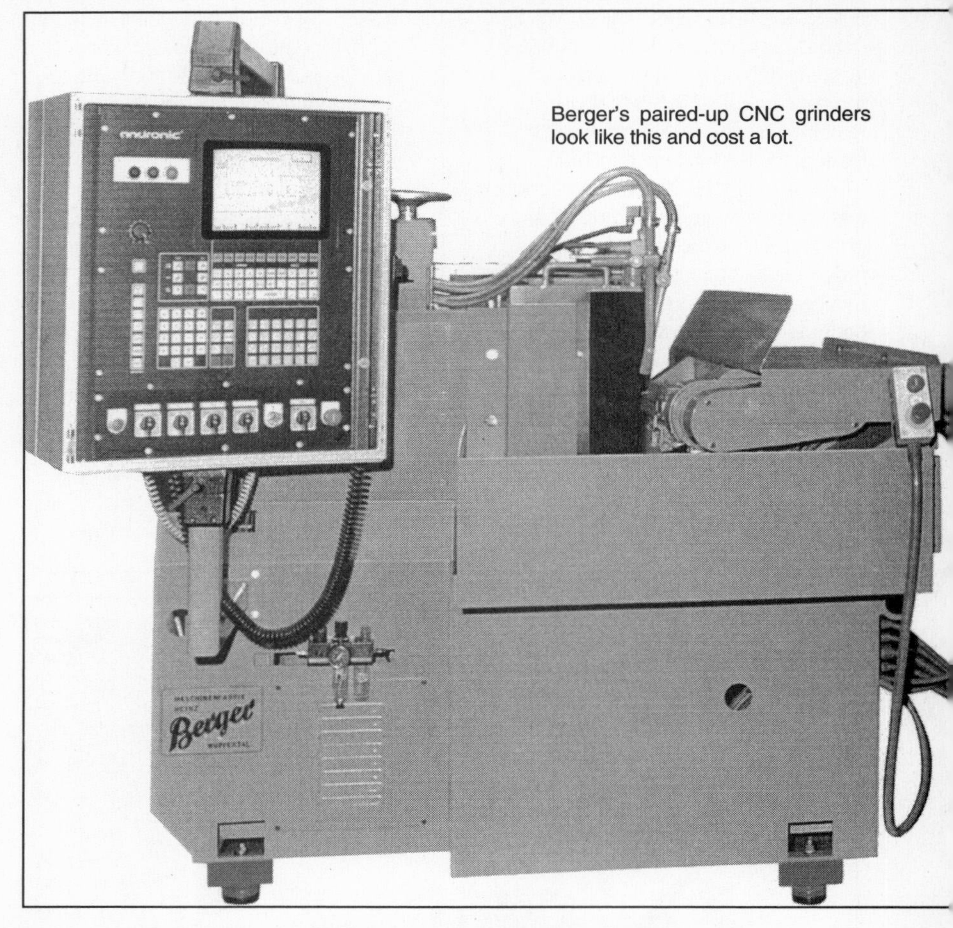

Berger's paired-up CNC grinders look like this and cost a lot.

(the binder for the abrasive particles was magnesite: magnesium oxychloride). In 1910, E. Siepmann & Co. made their first grinding machine sales in Sheffield. In the following years, the firm added glazing machines, twin-roll buffing machines, and (in 1928) scissor grinding machines. Later, these were followed by specialized hand tool and flatware grinding machines.

Siepmann got out of the knifemaking business in 1929 and thereafter concentrated entirely on machine building. In the 1960s, the firm introduced fully automated production lines for flatware knives, forks and spoons; by 1980, these lines were microprocessor controlled. In 1987, Siepmann introduced the world's first CNC (computer numerical controlled) blade grinding machine. Cutlery production in Solingen was declining in the 1970s, so Siepmann then aggressively expanded its export business so that now its machines are known around the world.

Heinz Berger Maschinenfabrik is located in Wuppertal, Germany, a modern industrial city in the Ruhr district that is more than twice as large as Solingen. Berger began in business in the late 1940s and has grown steadily since then.

Both of these German firms are represented by long-established American agencies. American Siepmann Corp. is located in Rochester, New York, while Berger is represented by Interamco, Inc., of Flint, Michigan. In addition to their primary grinding machinery lines and to their contract grinding services, both American firms also represent major lines of blade blanking, blade polishing, blade marking, handle moulding and knife testing machines, along with other knifemaking equipment and supplies suitable for large-scale manufacturing (not for home-workshop knifemaking, unless your hobby has a multi-million-dollar budget).

The flagships of Siepmann's line are the step sizes of GM-CNC com-

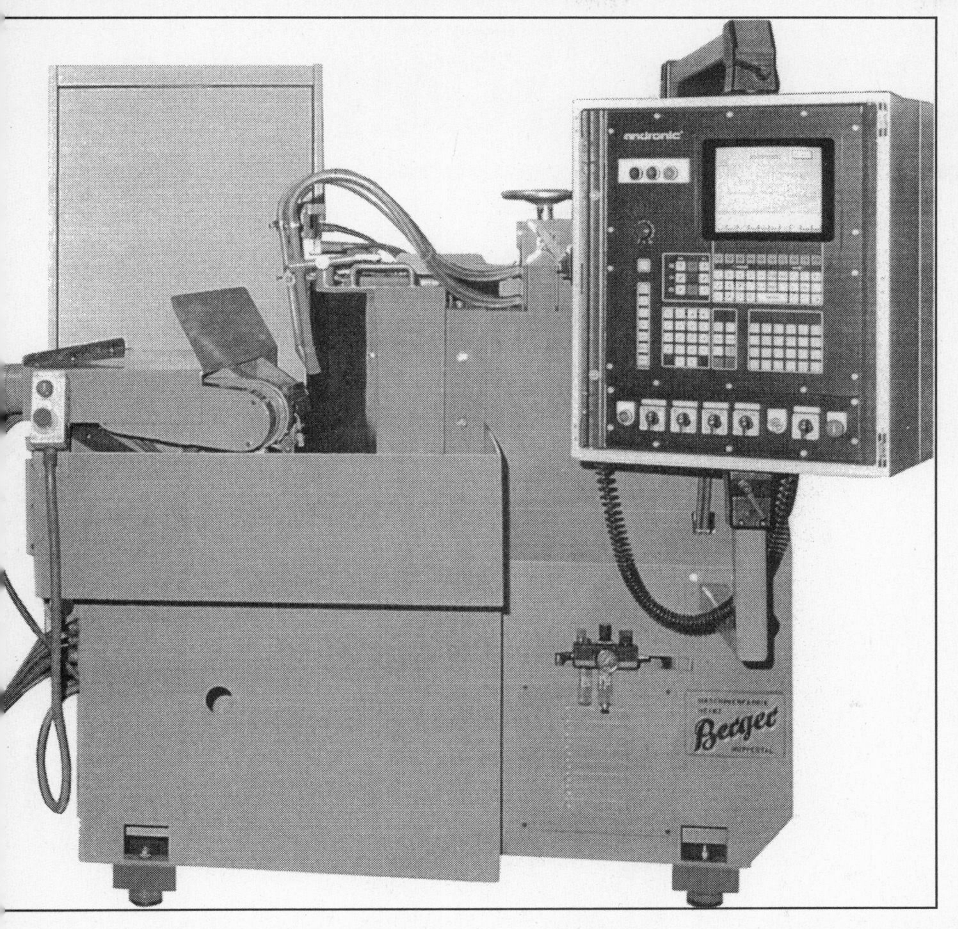

puter-controlled grinding machines. Each GM-CNC is actually a mirror pair of machines, like the old Hemmings, although that is where the resemblance ends. The two sides of each machine can be independently programmed for grinding asymmetrical blades (for example pruning shears). Each side of a machine can be programmed to grind up to five different surfaces on a workpiece, with the piece lifted and repositioned by the same robot arm that loads and unloads the machine, or rotated into position by the firm's patented rotating workpiece block. These various blade surfaces can either be flat or complexly curved (for example, the front of the bolster on a chef knife).

The flagship of Berger's line is the 4-axis BG-CNC. Like the Siepmanns and the old Hemmings, these big machines also work in pairs. The menu-driven software built into the computer controllers makes it easy to create and modify new blade designs.

Most inexpensive household, industrial and food-processing knives have hollow-ground blades, as do some premium lines of household, sport and pocketknives. When you consider that grinding wheels are round, you will understand why hollow-grinding is a relatively straightforward process to automate. That in turn explains why inexpensive blades are usually hollow-ground.

Two features in particular set hollow-grinding apart from more complex conventional grinding. First, a blade can be hollow-ground in one straight pass. Second, on a properly set up machine, both sides of each blade can be ground on that one pass.

In this specialized area of single-pass hollow-grinding, Berger and Siepmann compete with each other head to head. Berger's entries in this market are three, the HS2S, the HS1S and the HS1. Siepmann offers the HS2-CNC and the HS3-CNC. The Berger machines can be fed from stacked magazines or from rotating carousels, and can even be fed by hand, for short runs.

The Siepmann machines offer a choice of stackable- or chain-type magazines. Both offer pneumatic blade sensing, using high-pressure air streams, while the Berger can be fitted with mechanical sensing as an alternative.

An entirely different sort of machine that Berger offers is the DRS 1 CNC rotary-table surface grinder. Surface grinders are designed for grinding true flat surfaces. With its computer numerically controlled fixtures, the DRS 1 can grind even the most complexly shaped cutter that requires one truly flat surface (for example meat grinder and hair clipper blades).

Another Berger specialty is their back or profile grinder Model KB. A large number of blades can be clamped together and have their backs ground all at once in this machine. Berger also makes automatic Scotch-Brite and satin finishing machines for knife blades and blade backs.

Siepmann offers a variety of specialized grinding machines, too. One of particular interest is its WS-CNC serration and profile grinding machine. This machine can rapidly add full, partial or complex serrations to any type of cutting edge, as well as profiling the back of the blade. Berger introduced its own new serrating machine late in 1995.

Another Siepmann specialty is the BSM-2-CNC 4-axis grinding machine for extremely curved surfaces. This machine can do the especially complex grinding required on such items as nail nippers and surgical instruments.

Perhaps most impressive of all, at least in sheer power, is the Siepmann GM-5-CNC. This big heavy-duty cutlery grinder is used for large forged chef knives and hunting knives, as well as for swords and martial arts weapons.

So as we can see, the latest in high technology—and accompanying high cost—has entered the traditional world of knifemaking, and has done so in a big way. Knives today may be better than ever, but the way that their blades are ground will never be the same.

Bernard R. Levine

INTERESTING KNIVES

▲*Tim Zowada:* Look again at the forged stirrup binding the grip material—very showy. (Weyer photo)

▲*Bill Fiorini:* This is called Stag In Winter, and that's a snowstorm on the blade. (Weyer photo)

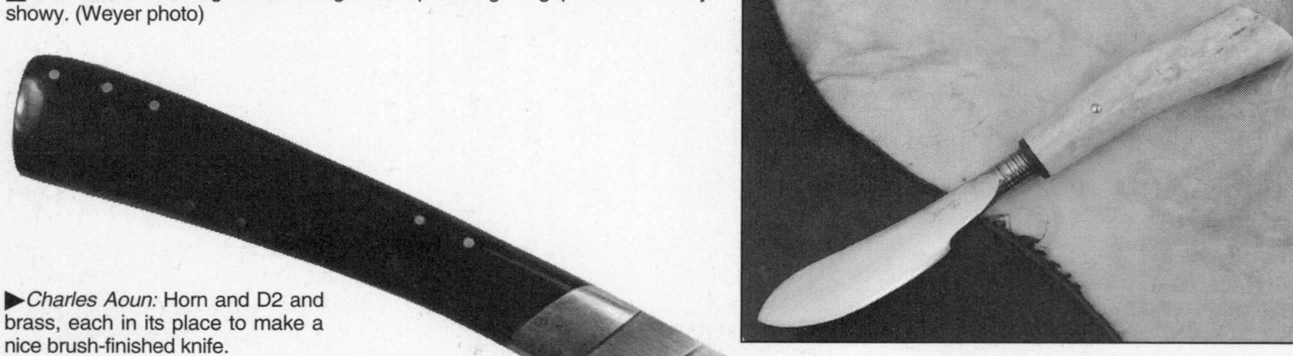

▶*Charles Aoun:* Horn and D2 and brass, each in its place to make a nice brush-finished knife.

▲*Michael Osborne:* Forged from round 1095, it's bigger than it looks—over 10 inches as you see it.

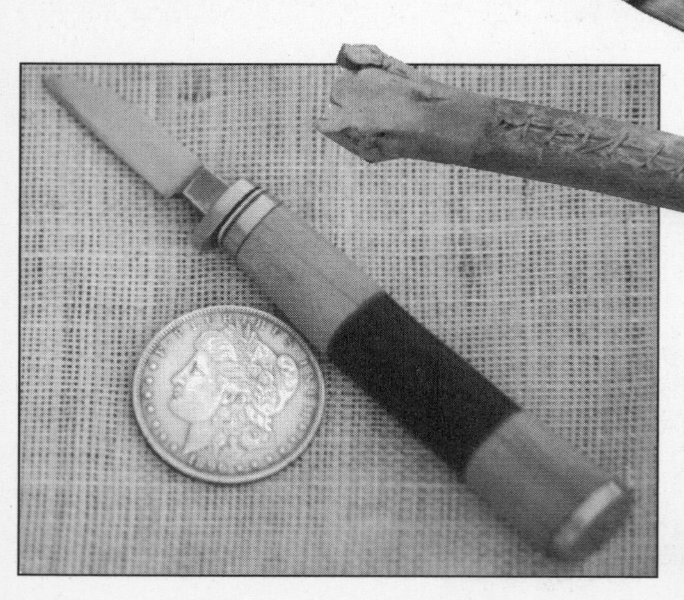

▲*Bill Randall:* Neo-Tribal Belt Knife, he calls it—all antiqued to look as if it was there, once, long ago.

◀*D.F. "Doc" Gundersen:* Small carver, fully detailed and cord-wrapped for purchase meat.

◀*Kouji Hara:* Called Higonokami, it's an all-metal folder with a most artistic blade finish—almost 7 inches long as shown.

▼*Mick Sears:* The sgian dubh as a dangler—it had to happen.

▲*A.D. Rardon:* The knife looks 19th century; the scrim is a map of Lewis and Clark's trip. (Weyer photo)

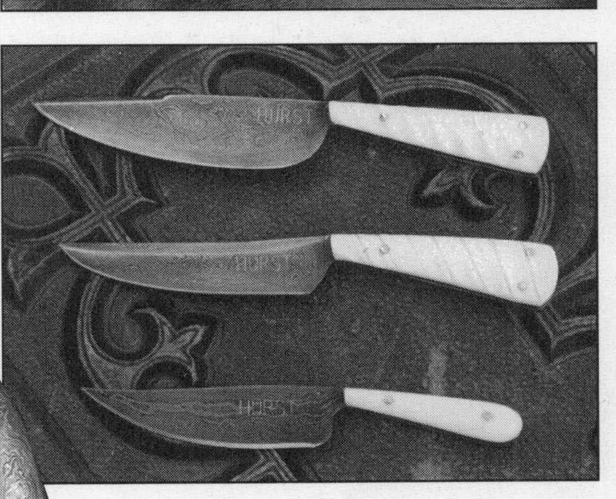

▲*Jeff Hurst:* French-looking, right? Whatever, they're handsome things.

▼*Mario Eiras Garcia:* Looks crude and is big, but all the edges, points and lines are straight—the editor checked 'em.

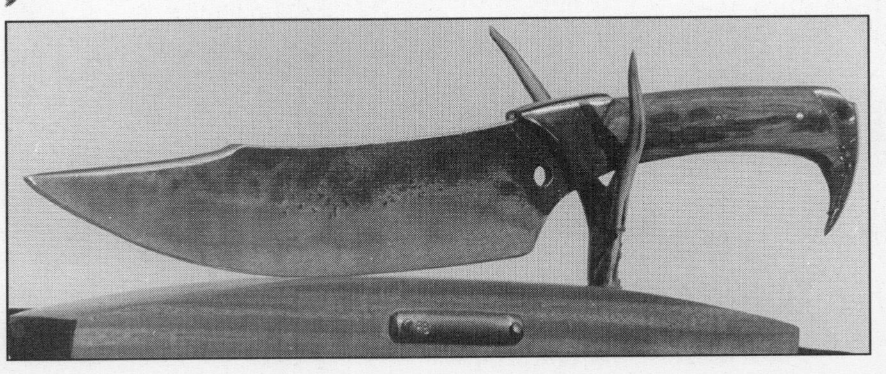

◀*Thijs Van de Manakker:* An Indonesian pattern, elegantly shaped the old way. (Hartjens photo)

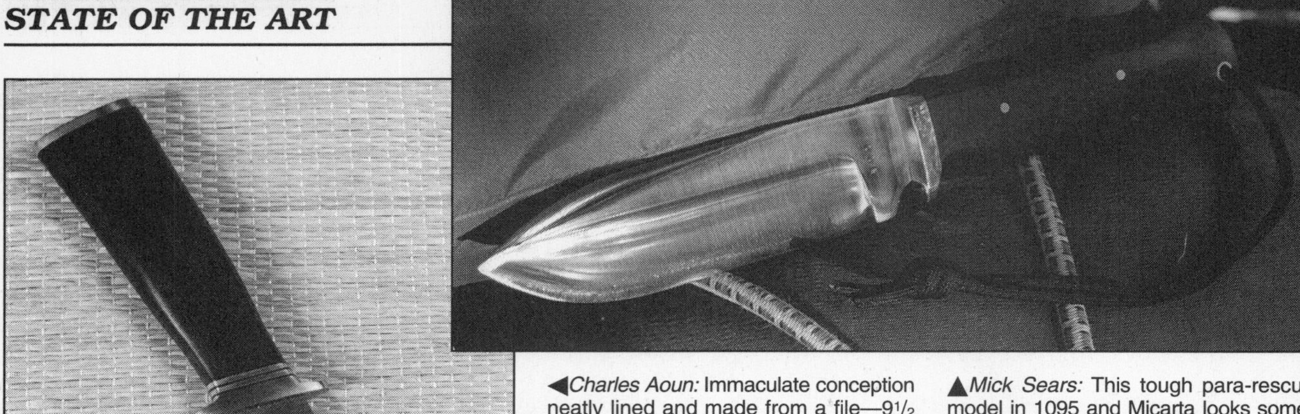

◀*Charles Aoun:* Immaculate conception neatly lined and made from a file—9½ inches as seen.

▲*Mick Sears:* This tough para-rescue model in 1095 and Micarta looks something like a Cattaraugus 225Q.

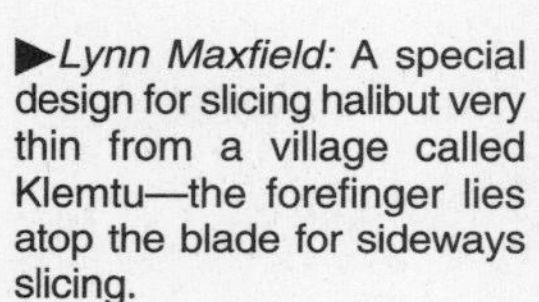

▶*Lynn Maxfield:* A special design for slicing halibut very thin from a village called Klemtu—the forefinger lies atop the blade for sideways slicing.

◀*Robin Golding:* Only an ambitious fellow would design a new diving knife—this is Golding's.

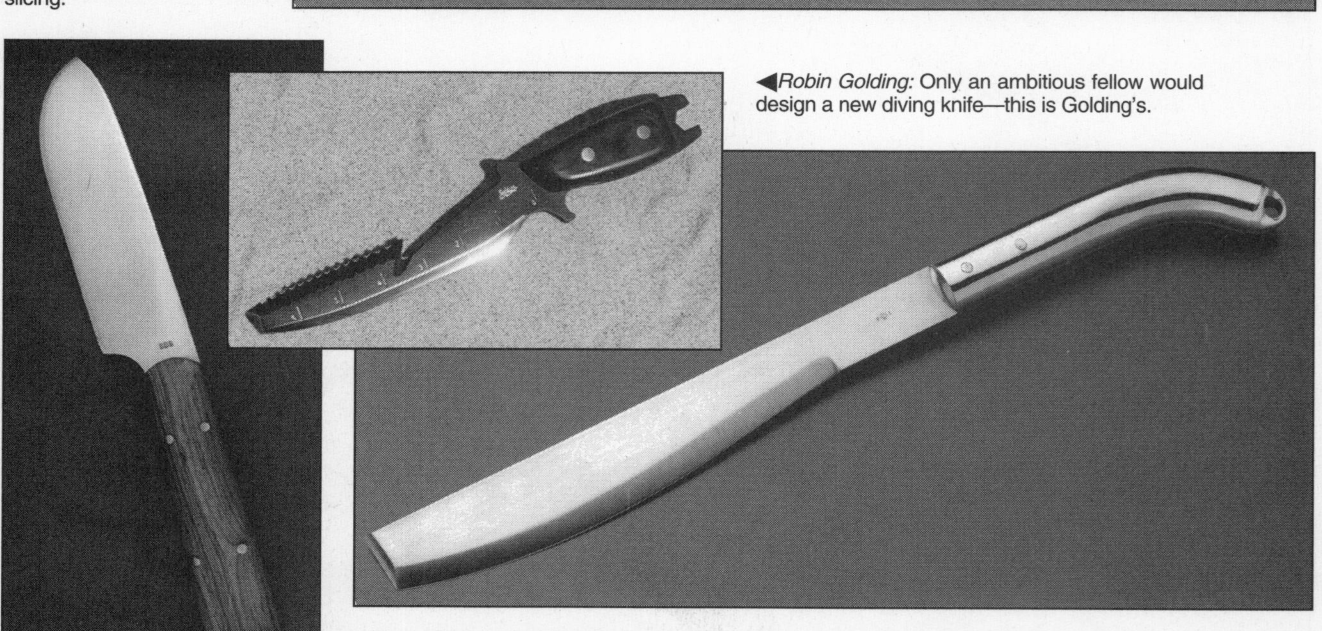

◀*Basel Boatwright:* Cleanly forged in 5160, just 8 inches overall and pinned with ten-penny nails. (Osborne photo)

▲*Paolo Scordia:* It's 19 inches long in 5/32-inch 440C, brass-gripped, chisel-ground and ready for whatever.

◀▲*Bruce James Hartmann:* A fighter, he says. Obviously, with a definite difference, but in regular 440C. (Weyer photo)

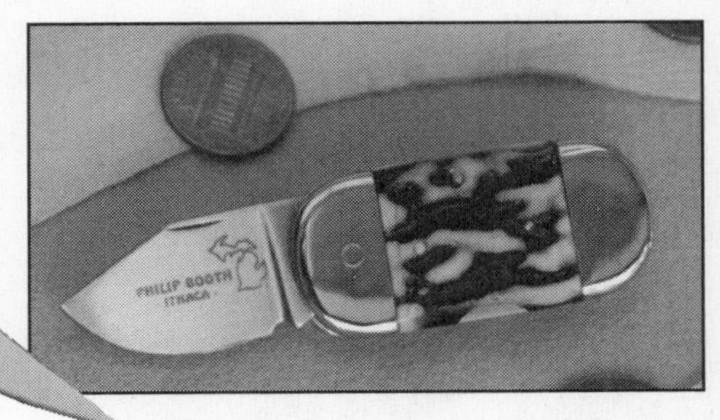

◀▼*Kevin L. Hoffman:* Seriously clever chess piece as liner-lock dagger; looks good open or shut.

▲*Philip W. Booth:* He calls them "minnows" because they're baby sunfish with $1\frac{1}{8}$-inch blades.

▼*Nestor Lorenzo Rho:* Ebullience for the pampas—$5\frac{1}{2}$ inches of stainless and a complex handle construction. (Herce photo)

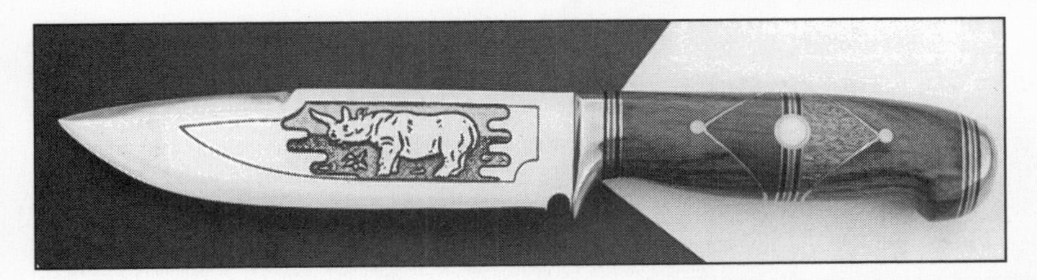

▼*Steven Rapp:* Called Rapp-tor, it is a 9-inch moderne barong in 440C, with four hollow grinds per side. (Weyer photo)

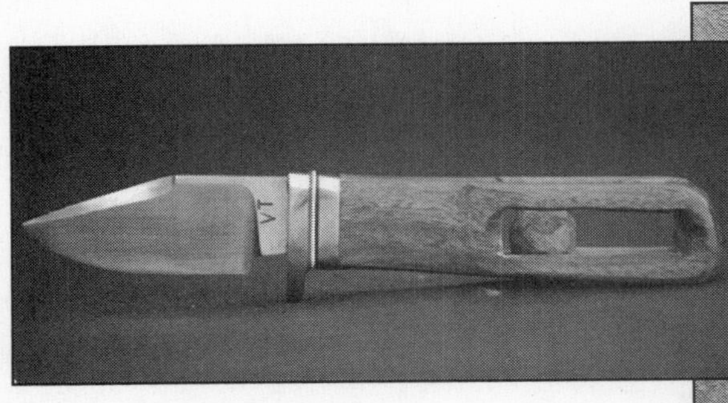

▲*D.F. "Doc" Gundersen:* Whimsical twiddle knife, doubtlessly built by and for whittlers.

STUDY OF STEEL AND SHAPE AND STUFF

◀*Steve Stuart:* These are 7-inch blades, the steel old rasps, reground and rehardened. (Weyer photo)

▲*FARID:* It looks bigger, but this all-purpose chisel-ground knife is 12 inches overall—high style for a brute.

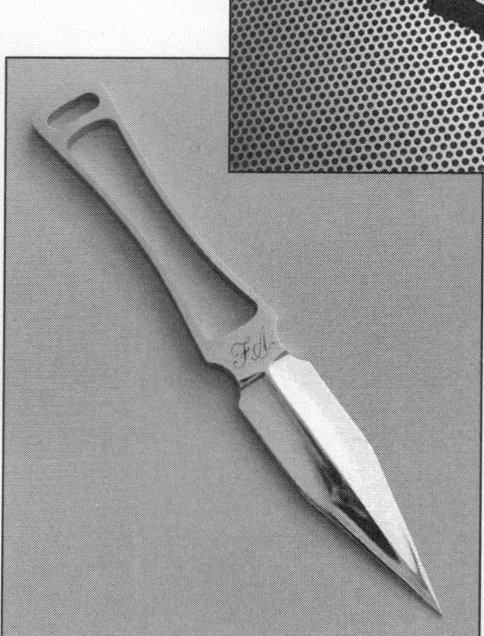

▶*Frans Van Eldik:* Seriously skeletonized, this Dutch boot knife has a penetrator point.

▼*Mark McCoun:* Full integrals in 440C—all hand-ground (no mill), which is a switch.

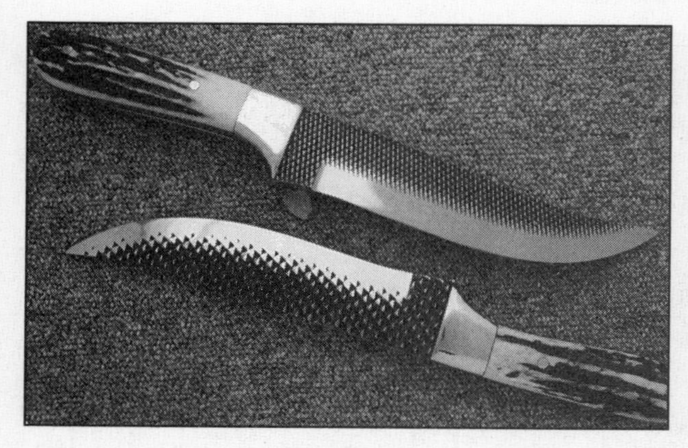

▲*Ron Hembrook:* Another elegant way to reuse big files—dramatic blades.

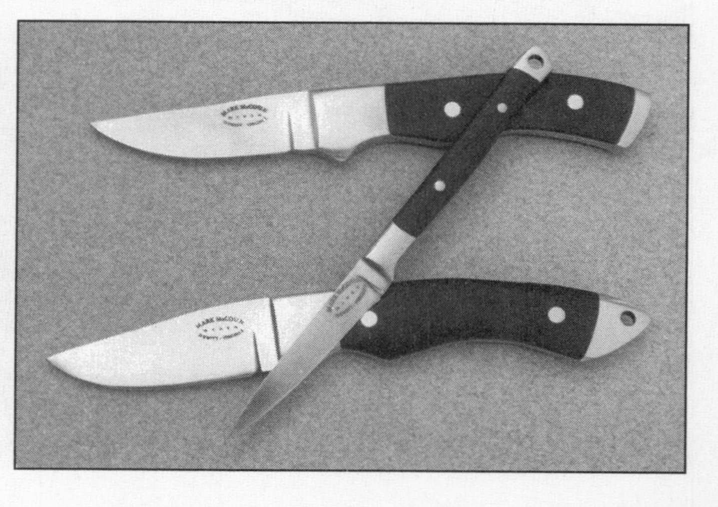

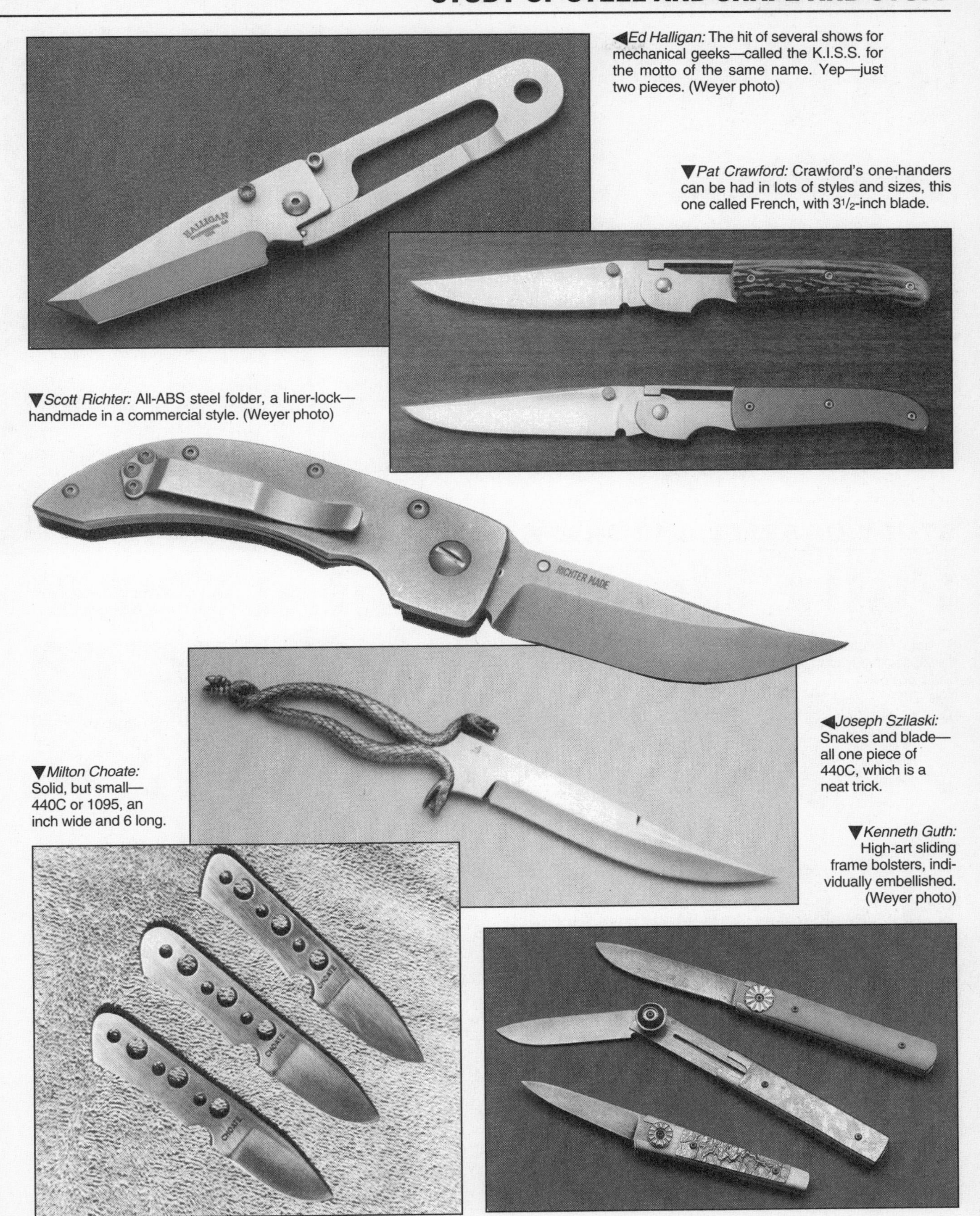

◀*Ed Halligan:* The hit of several shows for mechanical geeks—called the K.I.S.S. for the motto of the same name. Yep—just two pieces. (Weyer photo)

▼*Pat Crawford:* Crawford's one-handers can be had in lots of styles and sizes, this one called French, with $3\frac{1}{2}$-inch blade.

▼*Scott Richter:* All-ABS steel folder, a liner-lock—handmade in a commercial style. (Weyer photo)

◀*Joseph Szilaski:* Snakes and blade—all one piece of 440C, which is a neat trick.

▼*Milton Choate:* Solid, but small—440C or 1095, an inch wide and 6 long.

▼*Kenneth Guth:* High-art sliding frame bolsters, individually embellished. (Weyer photo)

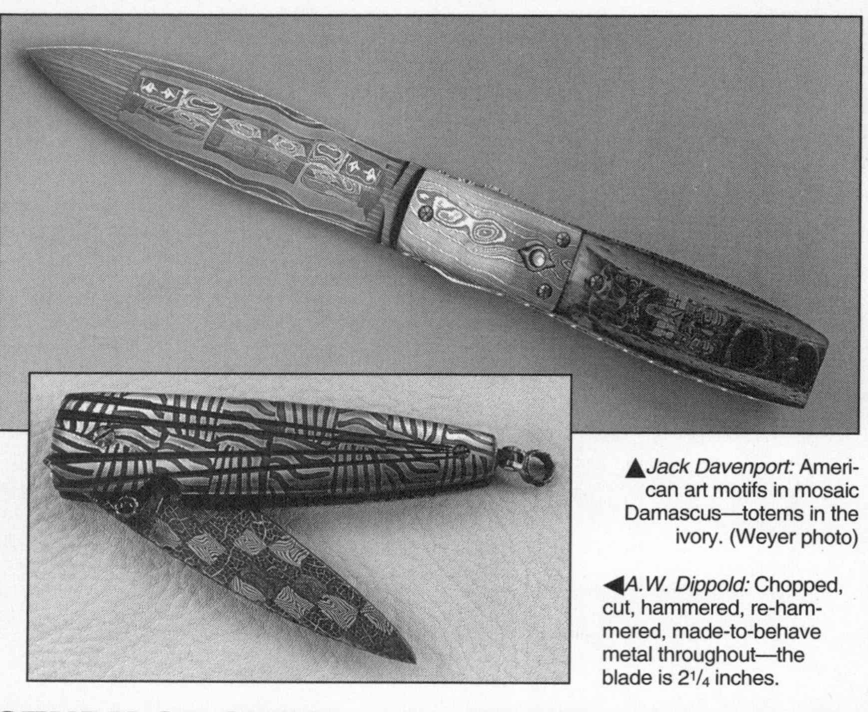

▲*Jack Davenport:* American art motifs in mosaic Damascus—totems in the ivory. (Weyer photo)

◀*A.W. Dippold:* Chopped, cut, hammered, re-hammered, made-to-behave metal throughout—the blade is 2 1/4 inches.

▲*Hank Knickmeyer:* A cornucopia of patterns in the blades of Pease knives. (Weyer photo)

STUDY OF STEEL AND SHAPE AND STUFF

Fully Worked Metal

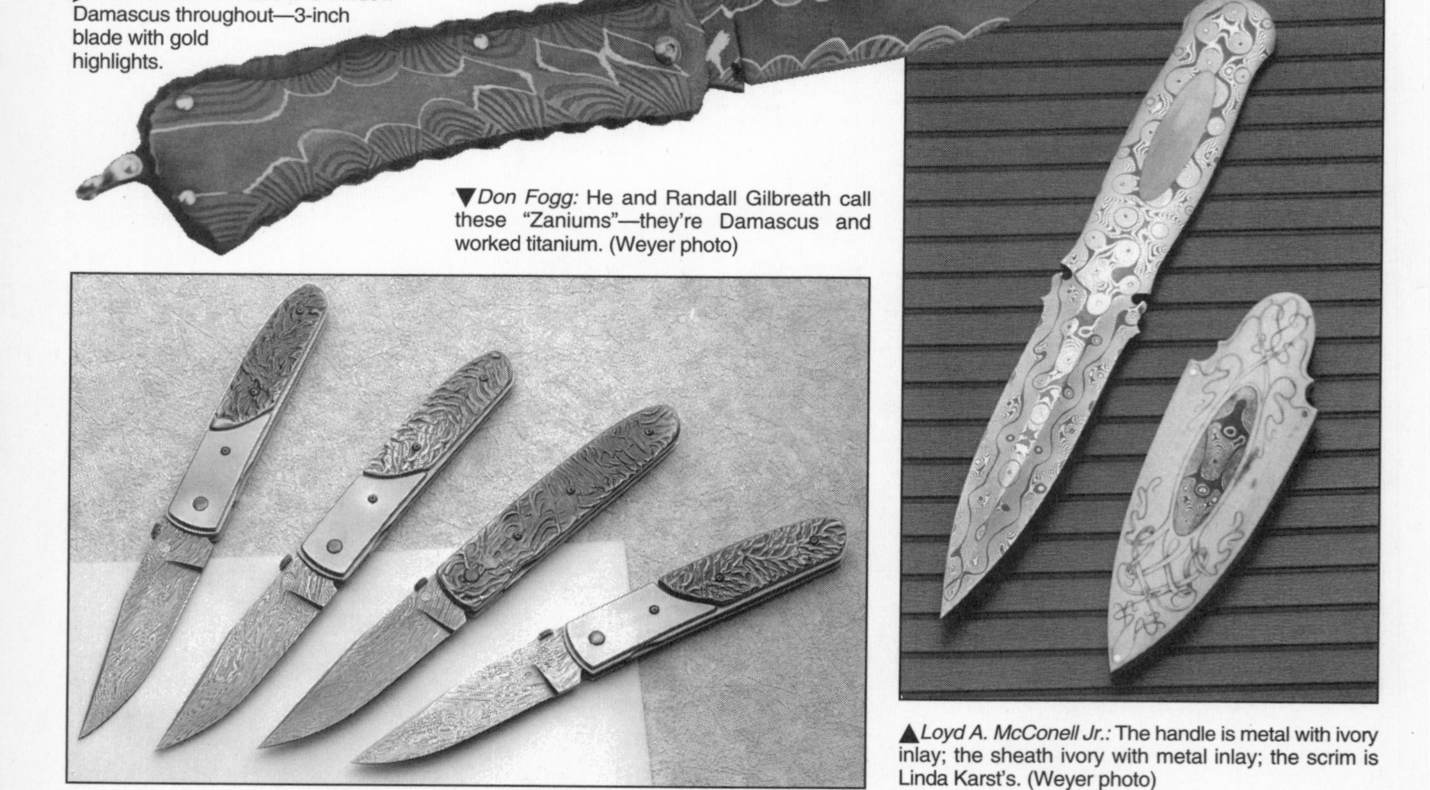

▶*Peter Martin:* Mosaic and window Damascus throughout—3-inch blade with gold highlights.

▼*Don Fogg:* He and Randall Gilbreath call these "Zaniums"—they're Damascus and worked titanium. (Weyer photo)

▲*Loyd A. McConell Jr.:* The handle is metal with ivory inlay; the sheath ivory with metal inlay; the scrim is Linda Karst's. (Weyer photo)

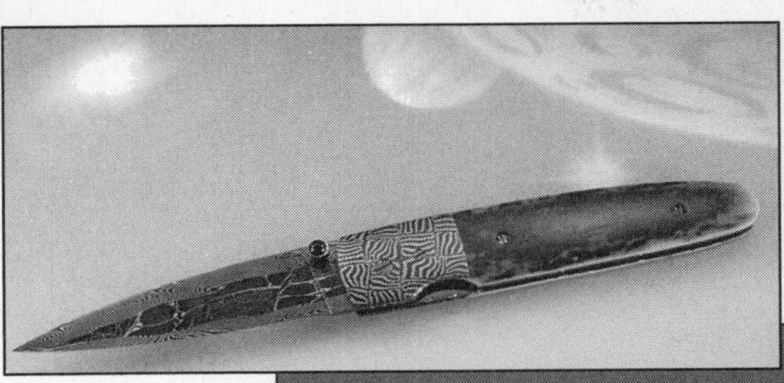

▲*Barry Gallagher:* Mosaic and twist composite blade with blue ivory—4 inches closed.

▲*Bill Fiorini:* Small flower mosaic square with a gold touchmark in a $4\frac{3}{4}$-inch blade. (Gallagher photo)

◀*Bill Fiorini:* Mammoth ivory with Skiles silver grapes; 6-inch blade in checkerboard and parquet mosaic. (Gallagher photo)

▲*Ralph A. Turnbull:* Meier Calico Rose Damascus in the blade—dramatic. (Gallagher photo)

STUDY OF STEEL AND SHAPE AND STUFF

Fully Worked Metal

◀*Barry Gallagher:* More Calico Rose in the blade; Taylor "Sunburst" in the bolster.

▲*Shane Taylor:* Wolf-track mosaic blade with ladder edges; scenic mosaic bolster—$6\frac{5}{8}$ inches overall. (Gallagher photo)

◀*Hyrum Hunter:* Mosaic stripes in one; a heart in the other; twist edges all around. (Weyer photo)

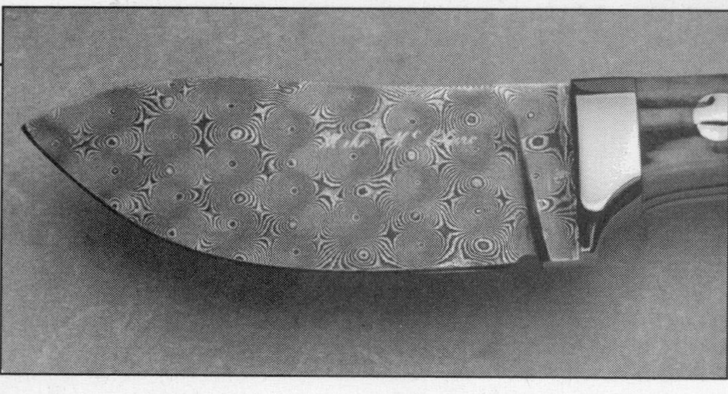

◀*Michael McClure:* Serious complexity on patterning overlays in very simple blades—bar stock by Thomas.

▲*Michael McClure:* Small skinner—big pattern effect. (Chan photo)

◀*Reinhard Tschager:* It's all one piece, visually, but the blade is the more intense.

STUDY OF STEEL AND SHAPE AND STUFF

Intensely Patterned Blades

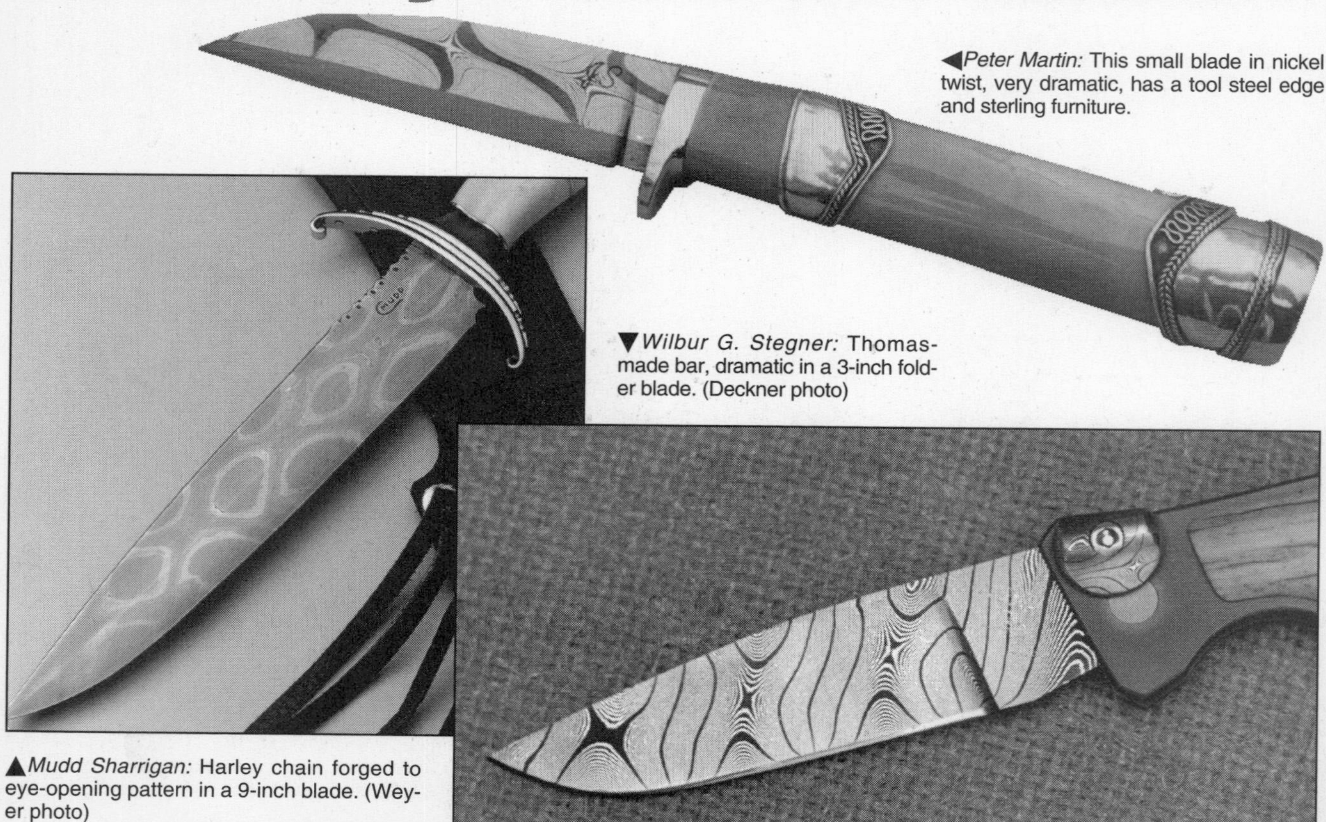

◀*Peter Martin:* This small blade in nickel twist, very dramatic, has a tool steel edge and sterling furniture.

▼*Wilbur G. Stegner:* Thomas-made bar, dramatic in a 3-inch folder blade. (Deckner photo)

▲*Mudd Sharrigan:* Harley chain forged to eye-opening pattern in a 9-inch blade. (Weyer photo)

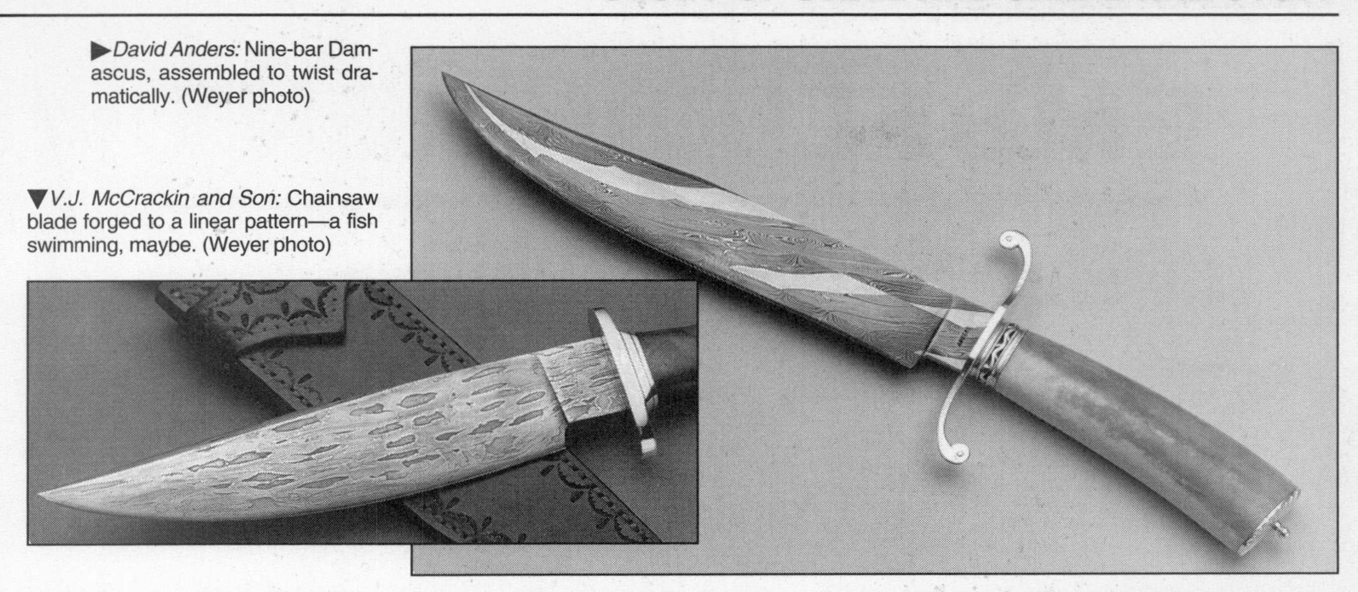

▶*David Anders:* Nine-bar Damascus, assembled to twist dramatically. (Weyer photo)

▼*V.J. McCrackin and Son:* Chainsaw blade forged to a linear pattern—a fish swimming, maybe. (Weyer photo)

Still More Bog Iron

▲*Thijs Van de Manakker:* Crooked Roman knife of the 100 BC type, all bog iron, 7 1/2 inches overall. (Hartjens photo)

▶*Thijs Van de Manakker:* Straight Roman kitchen knife—iron with steel core and 13 inches overall—replicating an AD 50 style. (Hartjens photo)

▲*Günter Bürger:* Knives of the Iron Age, made now in Germany of primitive metal.

◀*Günter Bürger:* Stone Age tools, replicated in Germany today by a smith who wanted to know.

EMBELLISHMENT

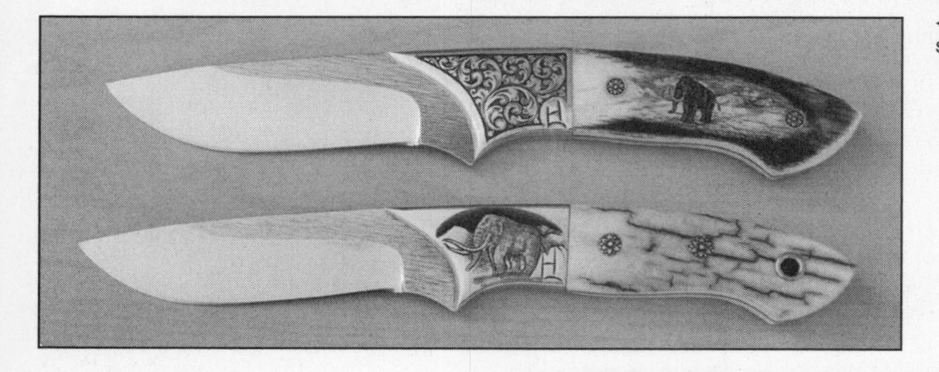

◀*Vladimir Vancura:* Engraving and scrimshaw on a Heinz Leber pair.

▼*Ben Shostle:* A gold quail flushes on a Beryl Driskill knife.

▼*Chris Meyer:* Coyote greets the moon on a Pease folder. (Weyer photo)

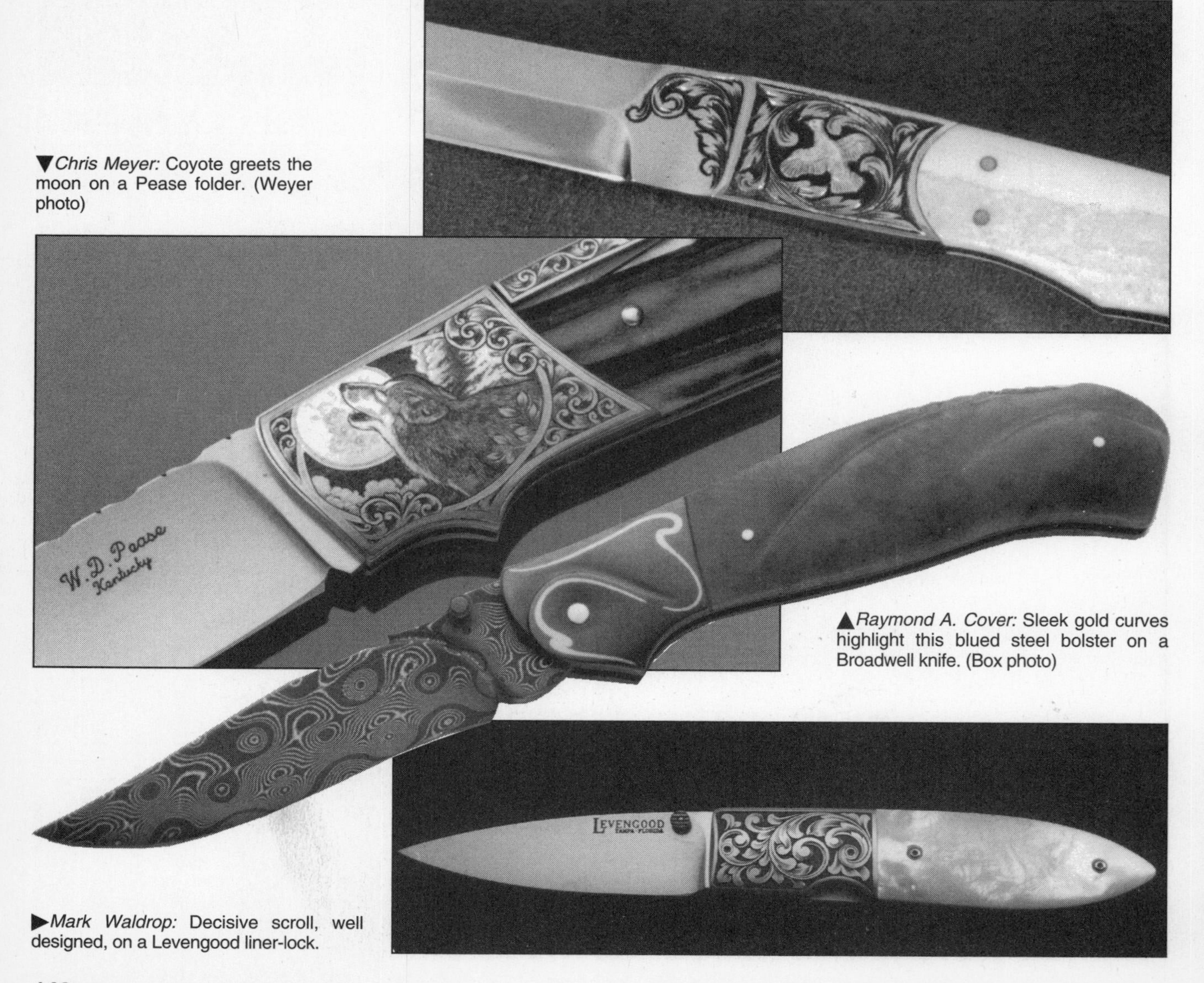

▲*Raymond A. Cover:* Sleek gold curves highlight this blued steel bolster on a Broadwell knife. (Box photo)

▶*Mark Waldrop:* Decisive scroll, well designed, on a Levengood liner-lock.

◀*Lisa Tomlin:* Elephant in gold on an ivory and ATS-34 Pendleton knife. (Weyer photo)

▼*Billy Letcher:* He did the whole thing—brass and ATS-34. (Gallagher photo)

▼*C.A. Pennington:* A gold kiwi pecks along in a tight space.

EMBELLISHMENT

Engraving

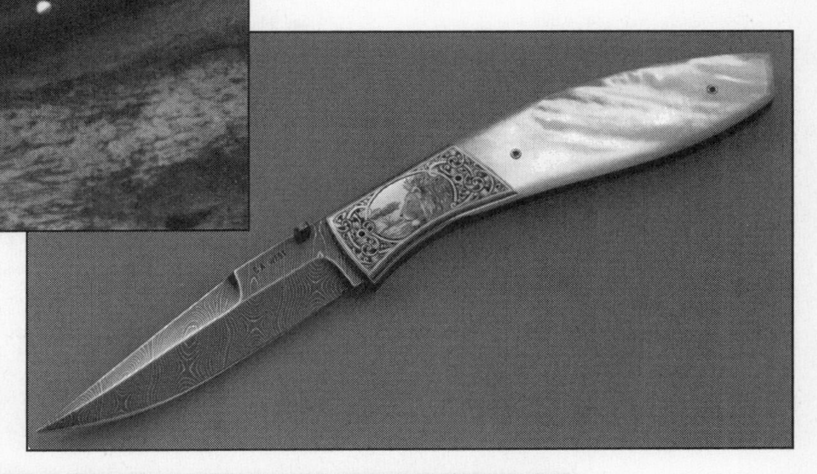

▶*Chris Meyer:* Charles A. West's big bolster frames a detailed lion. (Weyer photo)

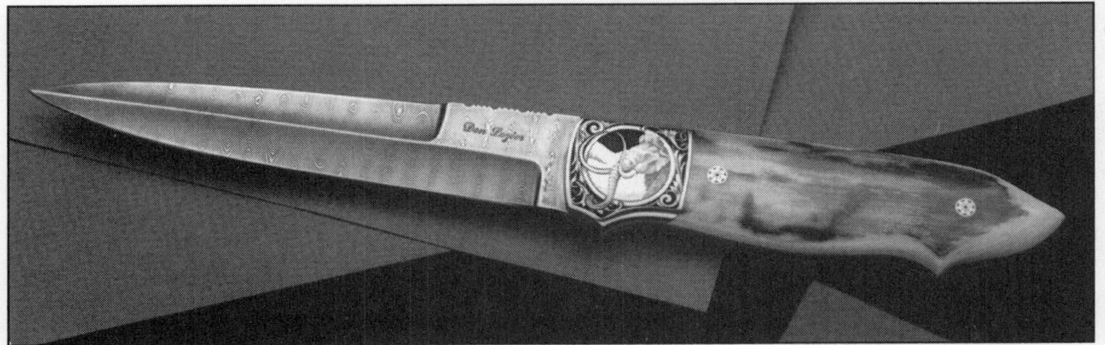

◀*Lisa Tomlin:* A mammoth marches over the stainless steel bolster of a Lozier knife. (Weyer photo)

▲*Harald Schlott:* Deep-cut scroll in brass on a Bernd Joehnk knife.

◀*Bruce Shaw:* Stars and stripes on a McConnell knife.

EMBELLISHMENT

Engraving

◀*Barry Lee Hands:* Elegant floral scroll on a Hill skinner. (Bilal photo)

▶*Geoff Hague:* Gold scroll flares on personal knife.

◀*Bruce Shaw:* Totemic style—buffalo skull and geometrics on a big Bardsley knife.

◀*Daniel Matagne:* Liege engraver does a Van Eldik fighter proud all over.

◀*Julie Warenski:* Seriously full coverage of a Price-style knife and sheath by Steven J. Rapp. (Weyer photo)

▼*Scott Allred:* Full coverage on a 3½-inch Perry folder—416 stainless frame here. (Gallagher photo)

▲*Harald Schlott:* Lady bugs in color on a gold blossom—the knife by Rinkes.

EMBELLISHMENT

Engraving

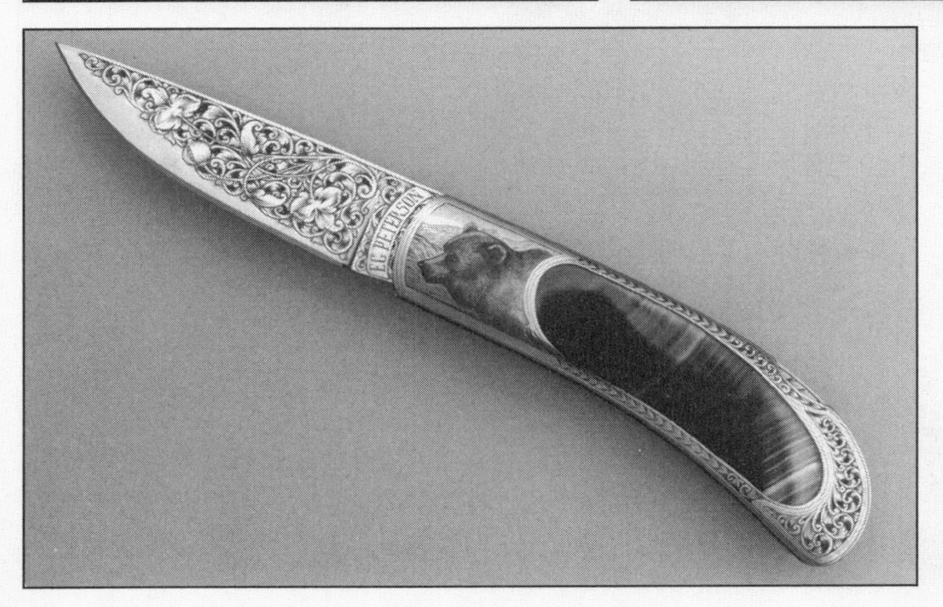

◀*Eldon G. Peterson:* He does it all and then engraves it all.

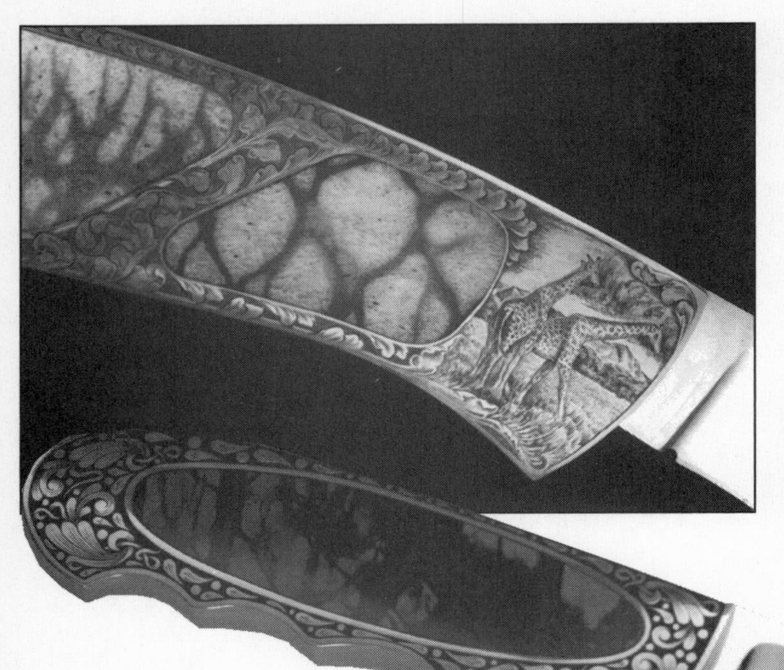

◀*Jim Blair:* Barrett-Smythe commission—gawky giraffes on a Charles Stewart knife.

▶*Ron P. Nott:* All brass, painted and engraved, in Egyptian motif.

◀*Pat Holder:* Full interframe coverage around a marble inlay on a D'Alton Holder knife. (Weyer photo)

EMBELLISHMENT

Engraving

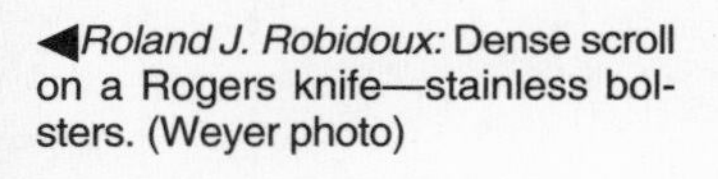

◀*Roland J. Robidoux:* Dense scroll on a Rogers knife—stainless bolsters. (Weyer photo)

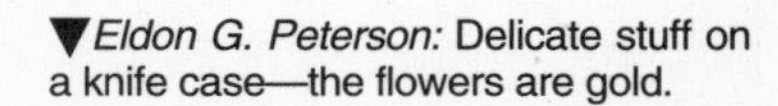

▼*Eldon G. Peterson:* Delicate stuff on a knife case—the flowers are gold.

◀*Matthew Lerch:* Business-like interframe folder neatly embellished.

▲*Bruce Shaw:* Big coverage, deep-cut, on a Parker hunter's axe.

▲*Ray Lee:* Dressing up a Buck Gent in American scroll.

EMBELLISHMENT

Engraving

▲*Judson Brennan:* Delicate gold and silver inlays on a delicate Damascus knife. (Weyer photo)

▼*Dwight L. Towell:* The knife, the engraving, the wood inlays—all by himself. (S. Towell photo)

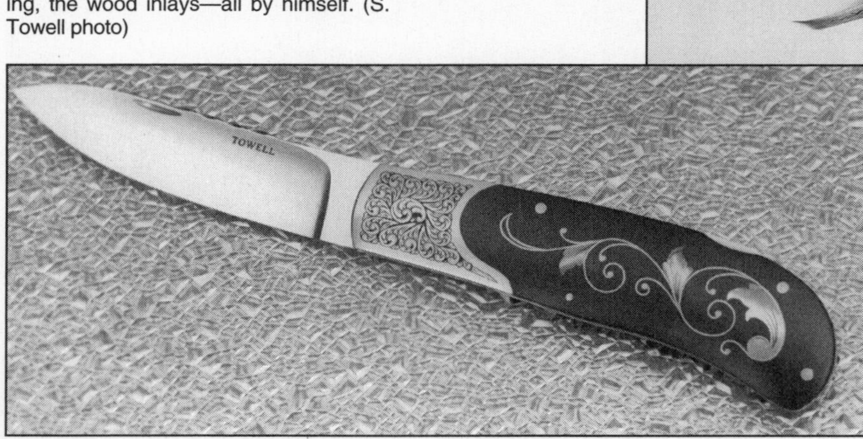

▲*Ron Smith:* There's a snake in the scroll of this Luckett Grizzly.

◀*Francesco Pachi:* Knifemaker scrimmed his own wolf with inlaid amber eyes.

▼*Tim Scholl:* An old pet will live a long time on a knife pommel.

EMBELLISHMENT

Scrimshaw

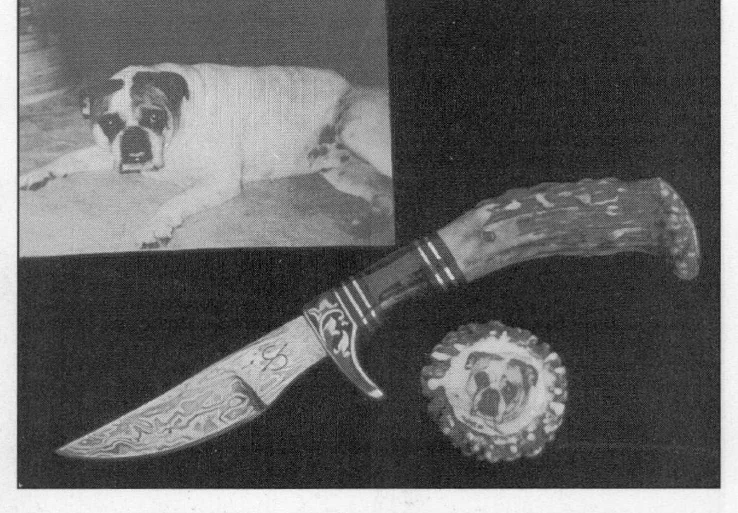

▲*Fred Ciamaritaro:* A very focused lion group in black and white.

◀*Juanita Rae Conover:* A prehistoric pachyderm ambles across a handle slab.

▲*Juanita Rae Conover:* Playing fox cubs in black and white.

▲*Linda K. Karst:* A cheetah lounges while the local giraffes socialize.

◀*Fred Ciamaritaro:* Looks like some real classy terriers here.

EMBELLISHMENT

Scrimshaw

▲▼*Juanita Rae Conover:* Raccoons in tangles and black and white.

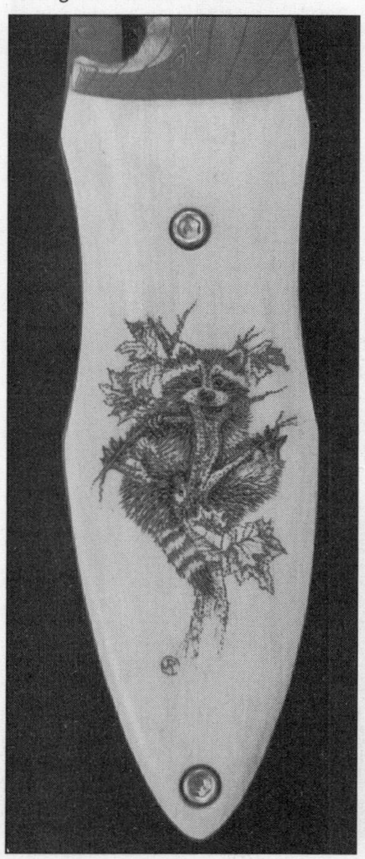

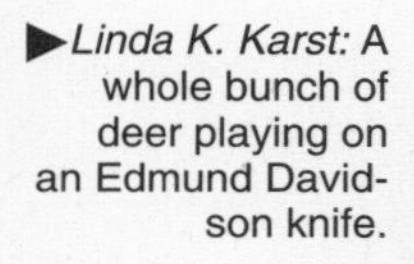

▶*Linda K. Karst:* A whole bunch of deer playing on an Edmund Davidson knife.

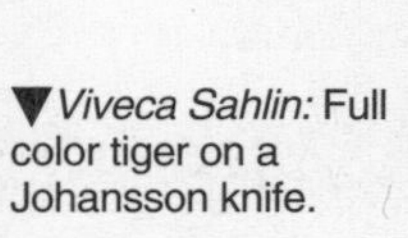

▼*Viveca Sahlin:* Full color tiger on a Johansson knife.

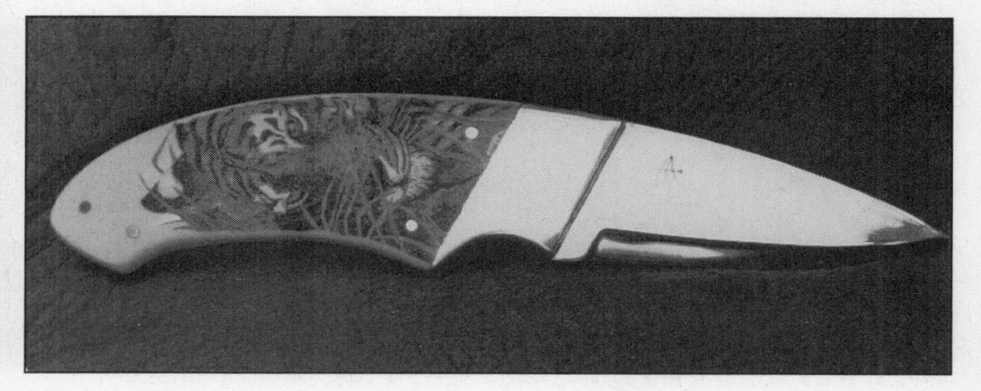

▼*Charles V. Rece:* Righteously arrogant fellow, this bull.

▲*Viveca Sahlin:* Tigers on a Momcilovic knife—in color.

▶*Susan Davenport:* Cheetah in repose on a C.H. Morris folder.

EMBELLISHMENTS

Scrimshaw

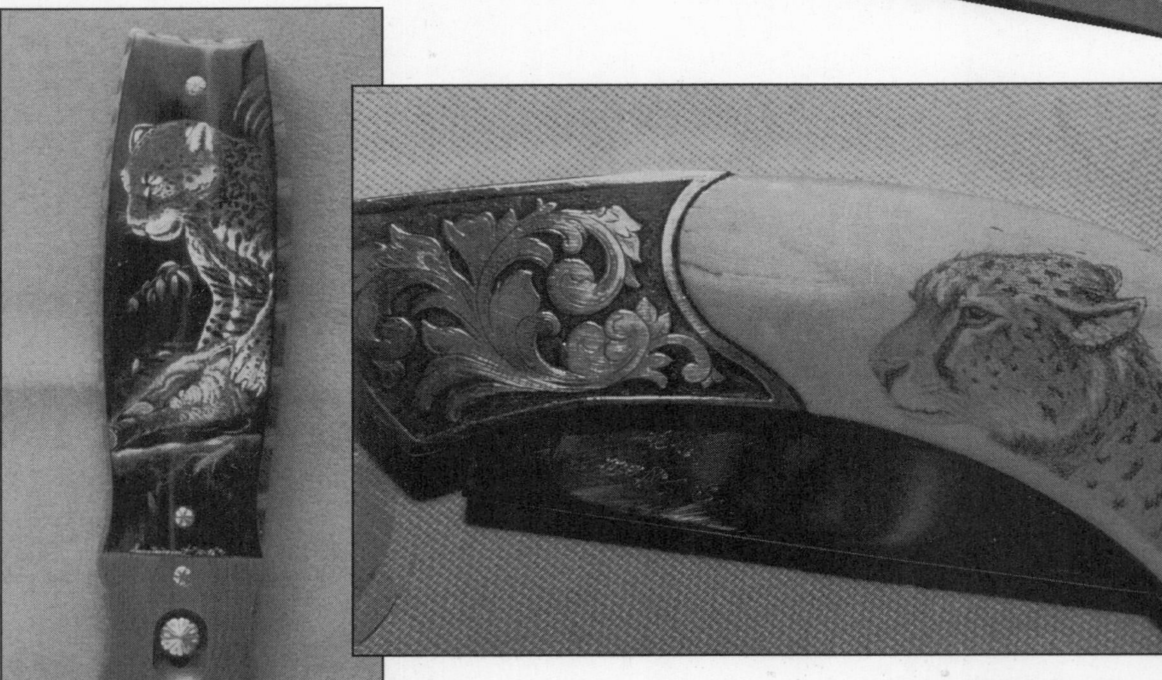

▲*Roni Dietrich:* Cheetah on a Ron Nott knife.

◀*Susan Davenport:* Leopard on a kill, scrimmed into dark fossil ivory.

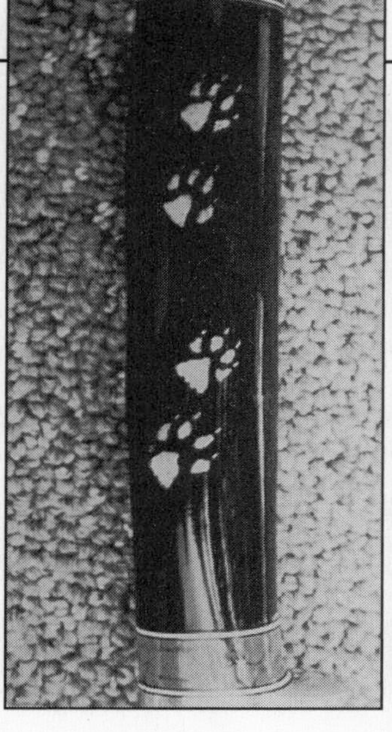

▲*Dunno Hughes:* A wolf and his tracks in white on black.

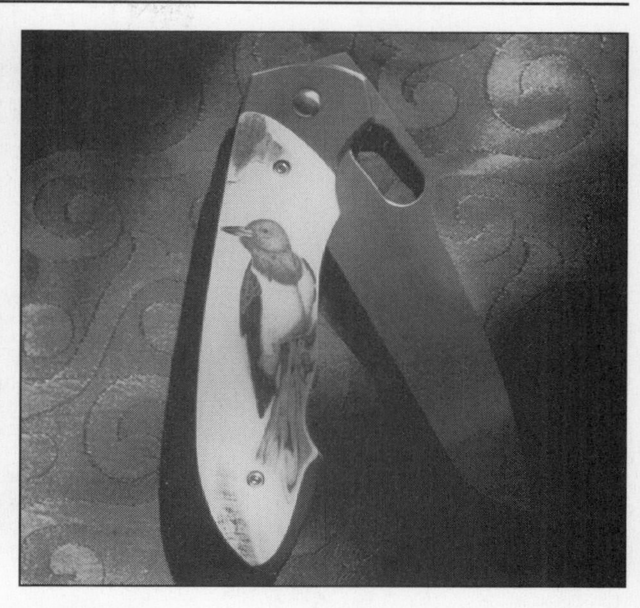

▲*Susan Davenport:* Woodpecker in color perched on a folder handle—neat design.

▼*Inna Pankova-Clark:* Tiger eyes on the ivory panels of a Tom Black skinner. (Weyer photo)

EMBELLISHMENT

Scrimshaw

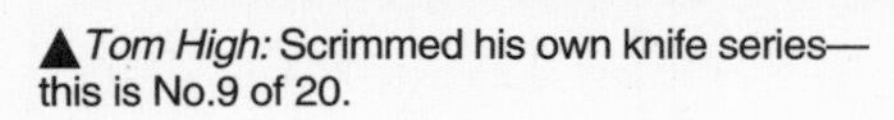

▲*Tom High:* Scrimmed his own knife series—this is No.9 of 20.

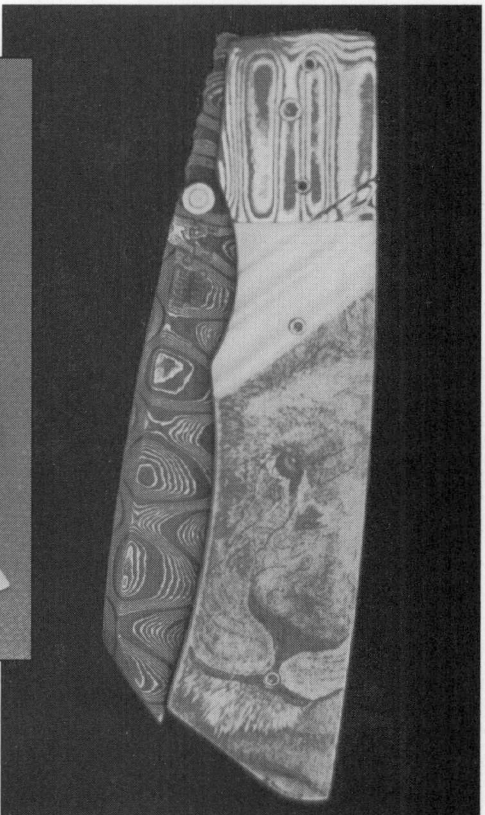

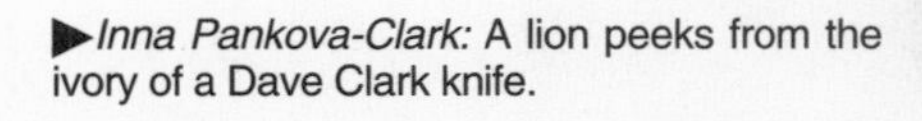

▶*Inna Pankova-Clark:* A lion peeks from the ivory of a Dave Clark knife.

◀*Pam Krogman:* Carved scrim of a laughing man on a Gunn knife.

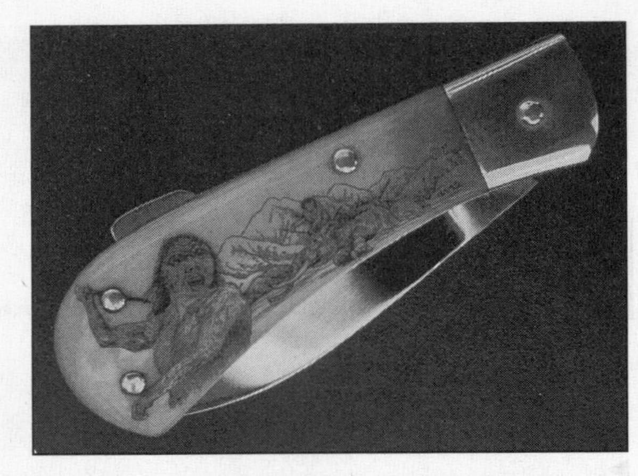

▶*Diane Iiams:* Prehistoric men on a kill and in a snit on a Koutsopoulos folder.

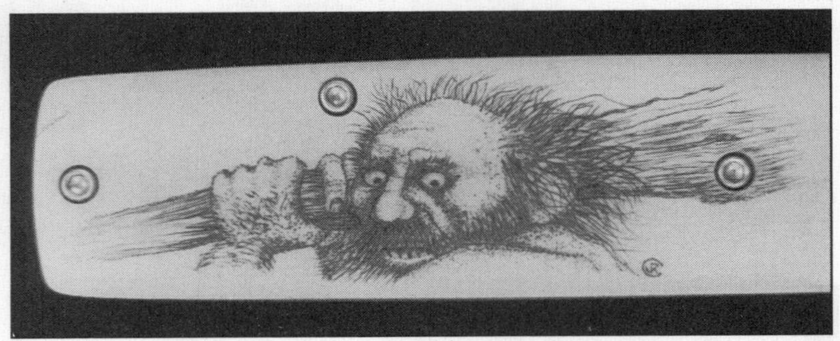

▲*Juanita Rae Conover:* Excited fellow with a club on a knife handle.

EMBELLISHMENT

Scrimshaw

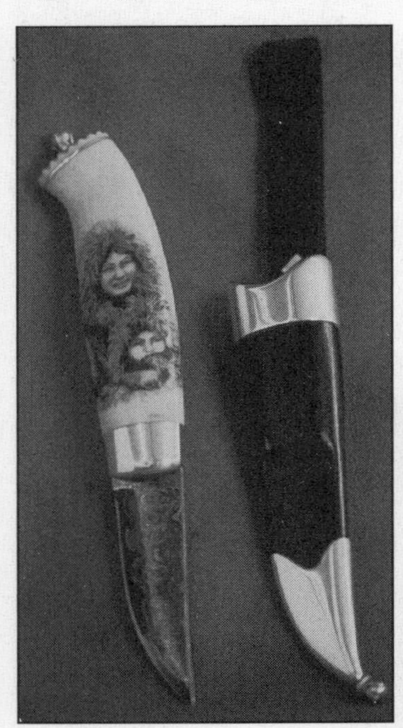

▲*Viveca Sahlin:* A happy couple in a very cold place on a Leif Reieksen knife.

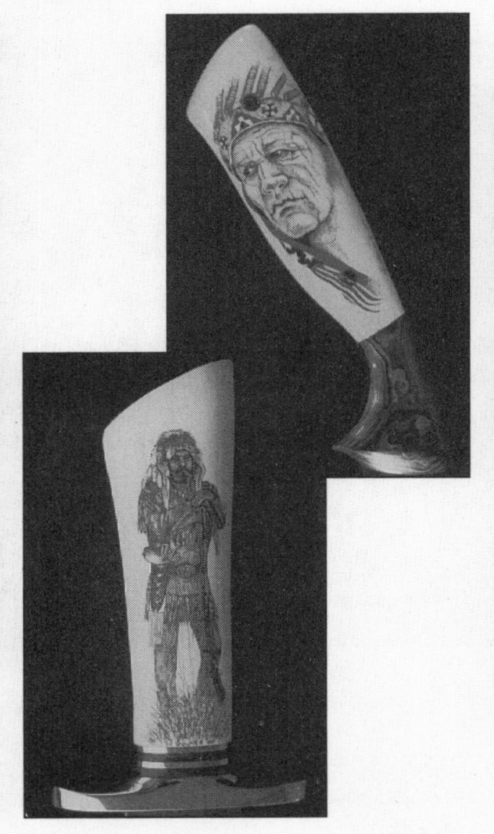

▶*Karen Walker:* George Walker scrimmed on a George Walker knife.

◀*Susan Davenport:* Portrait in color of a native American.

▲*Tom Black:* Northwest Territory motifs on a knife.

◀*Juanita Rae Conover:* Cave paintings on a knife handle.

▶*Gary (Garbo) Williams:* An Italian film star on a knife handle.

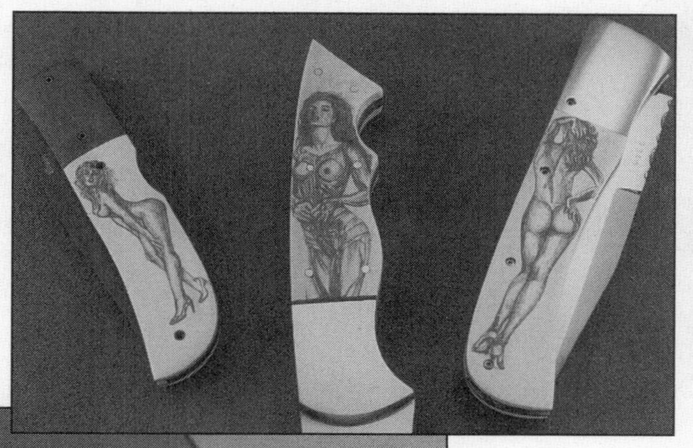

▶*Lynn Benade:* Girls, girls, girls—all on Scottie H. White knives. (Gallagher photo)

EMBELLISHMENT

Scrimshaw

▲*C.J. Cai:* Improbably arranged lady on the ivory Micarta of a Lui knife. (Weyer photo)

▶*Mary Mueller:* Woman in a quandary on a Friedly knife. (Weyer photo)

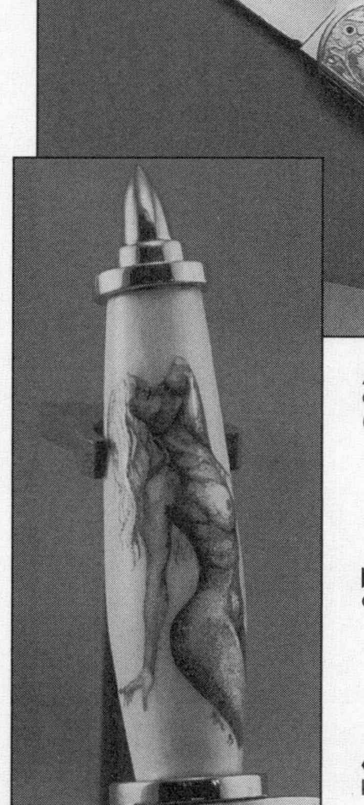

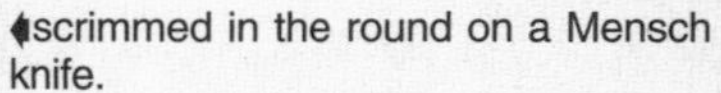

◀scrimmed in the round on a Mensch knife.

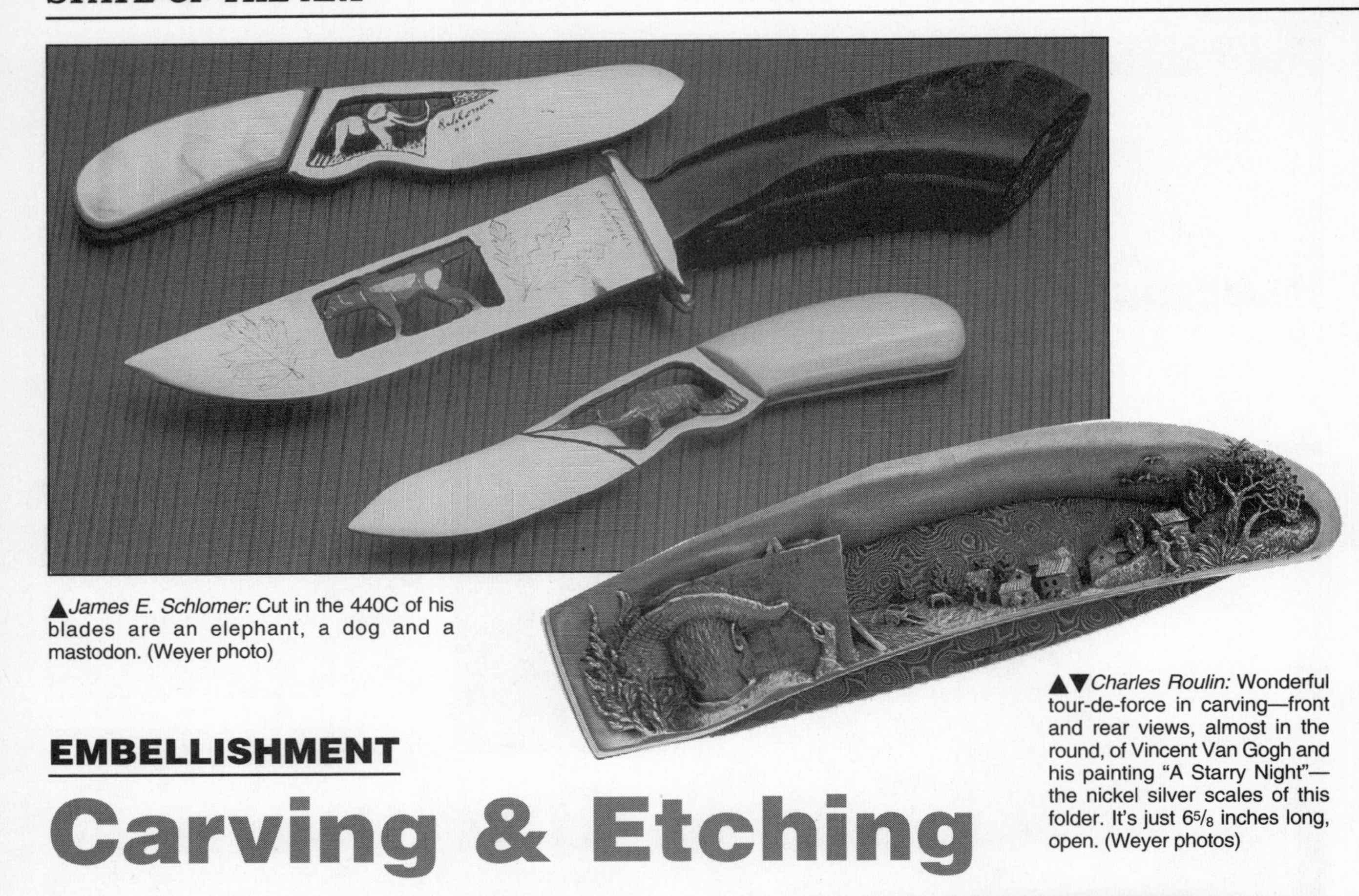

▲*James E. Schlomer:* Cut in the 440C of his blades are an elephant, a dog and a mastodon. (Weyer photo)

▲▼*Charles Roulin:* Wonderful tour-de-force in carving—front and rear views, almost in the round, of Vincent Van Gogh and his painting "A Starry Night"—the nickel silver scales of this folder. It's just $6^{5}/_{8}$ inches long, open. (Weyer photos)

EMBELLISHMENT

Carving & Etching

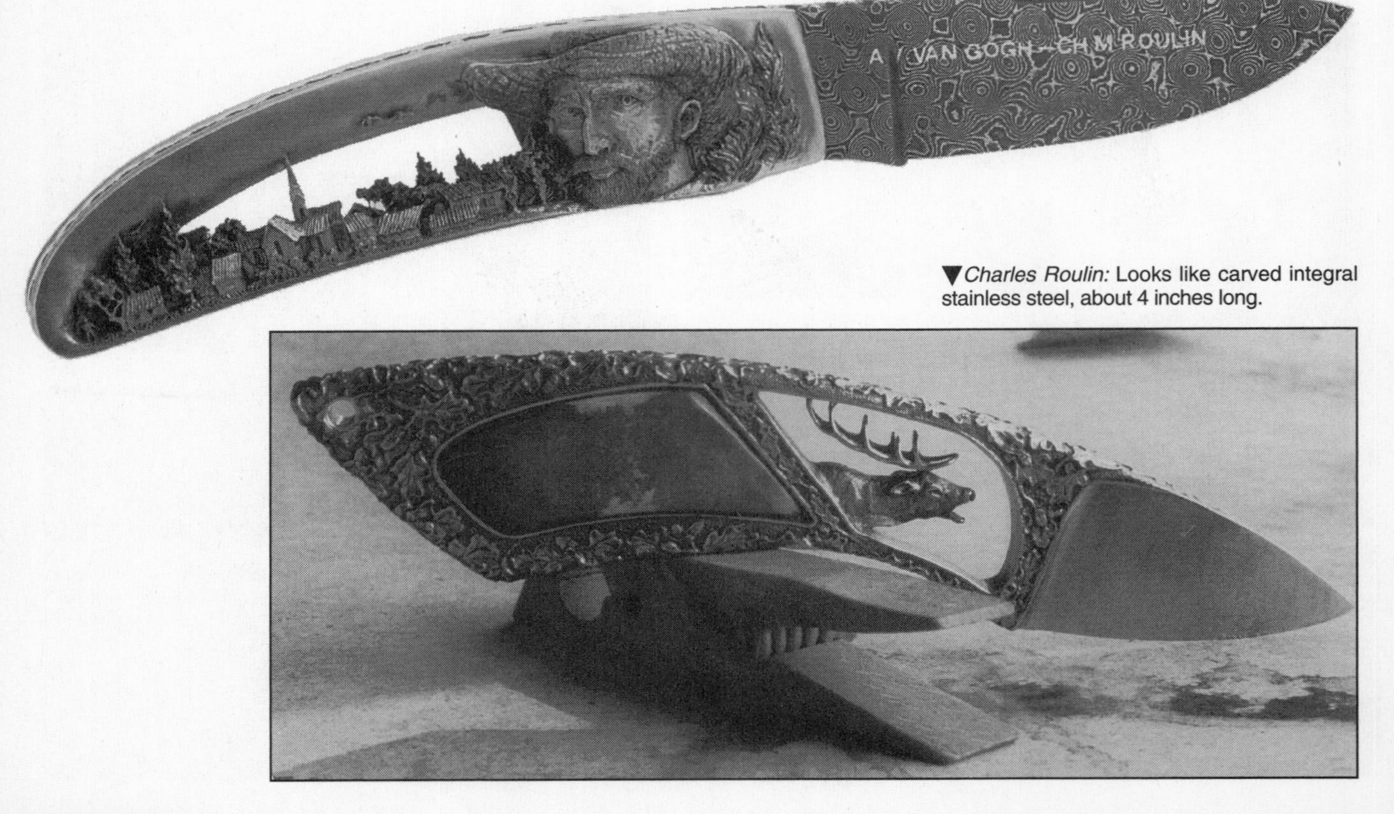

▼*Charles Roulin:* Looks like carved integral stainless steel, about 4 inches long.

▶*Ray Lee:* The Indian incarnate on the crown of an Edmund Davidson Bowie.

▼*Harald Schlott:* Engraved in metal, carved in ivory, the Cape buffalo in their world.

▲*Árpád Bojtos:* Two more fully worked celebrations of the hunt, this time the lion and a falconer. (Weyer photo)

EMBELLISHMENT

Carving & Etching

▲*Paul G. Grussenmeyer:* Kirin with an opal eye on one side, shishi with rubies the other—carved in mammoth ivory. (Weyer photo)

◀*Mel Anderson:* A barbarian woman, knife in hand, carved into the grip of a barbarous knife. (Weyer photo)

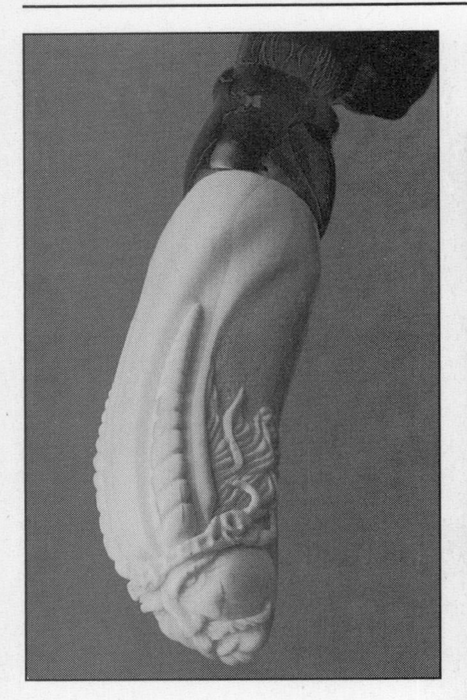

◀*Richard DiMarzo:* Carved warthog tusk becomes a scarred and mustached man or godling. (Weyer photo)

▼*Helmut Poskocil:* A lot of silver pommel cap on a not-very-big hunter. (Weyer photo)

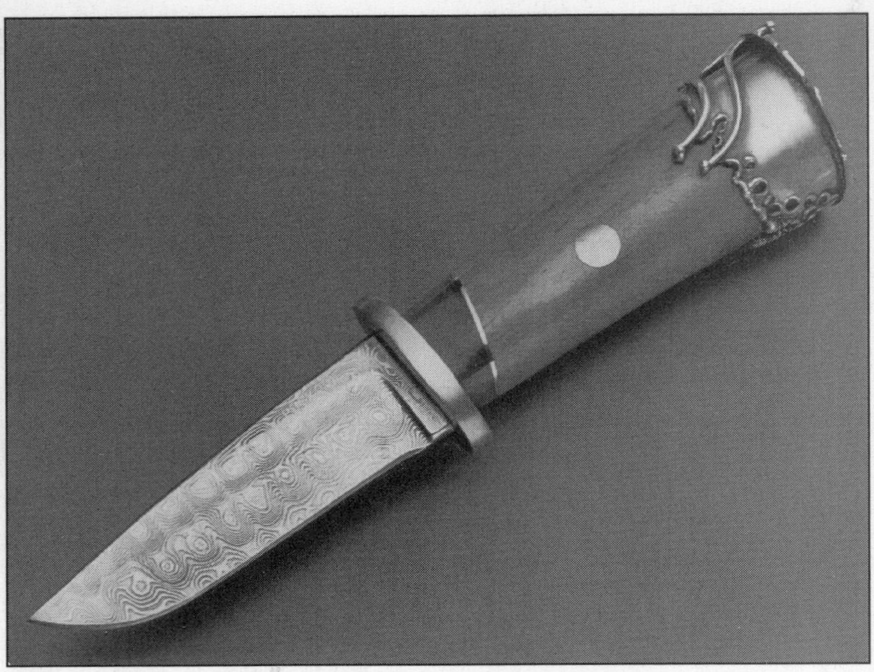

EMBELLISHMENT

Carving & Etching

▶*Laurent Doussot:* Lushly carved pearl and Damascus make a handsome folder case. (Weyer photo)

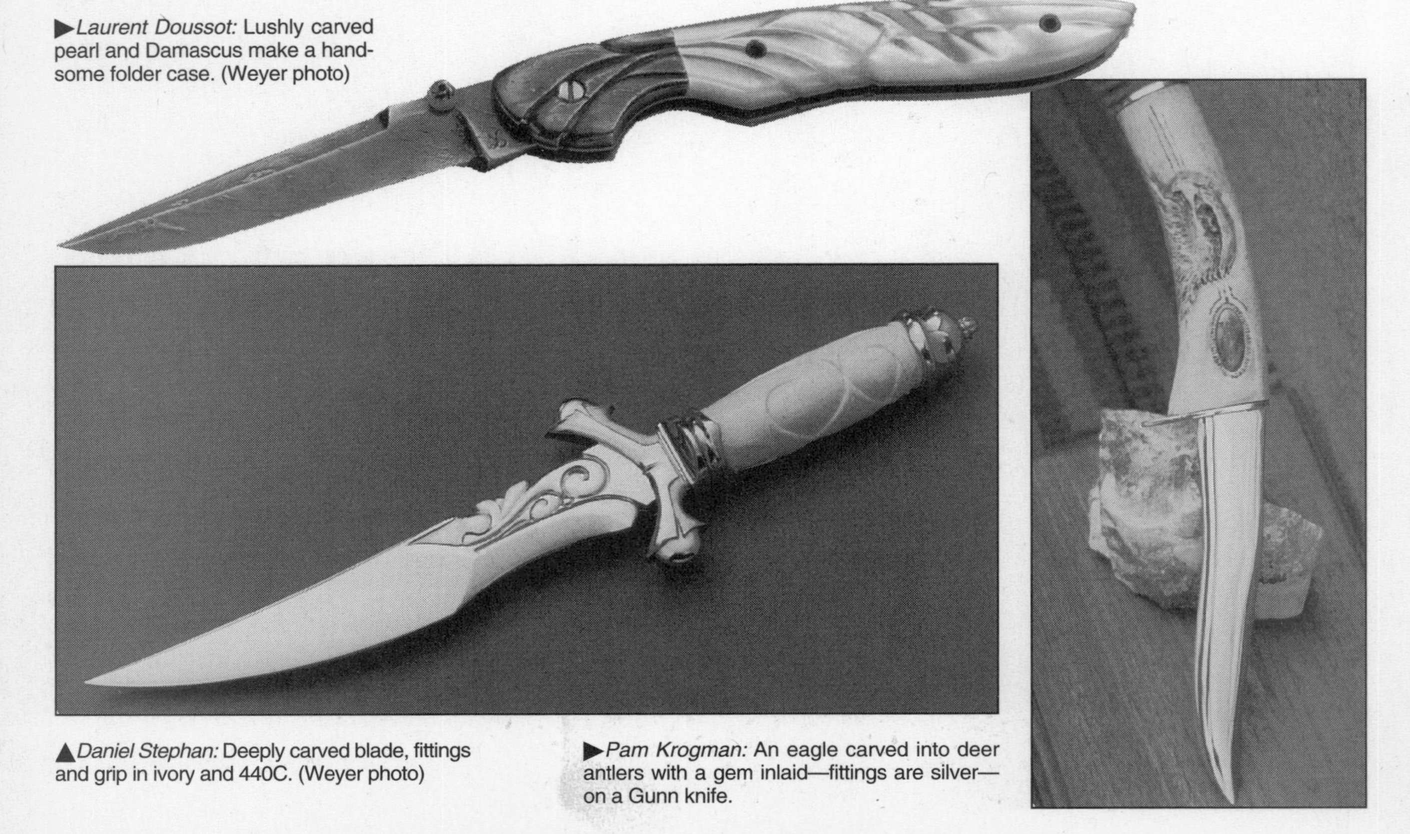

▲*Daniel Stephan:* Deeply carved blade, fittings and grip in ivory and 440C. (Weyer photo)

▶*Pam Krogman:* An eagle carved into deer antlers with a gem inlaid—fittings are silver—on a Gunn knife.

▲*Ray Lee:* Bronze guard and pommel castings—before they're carved.

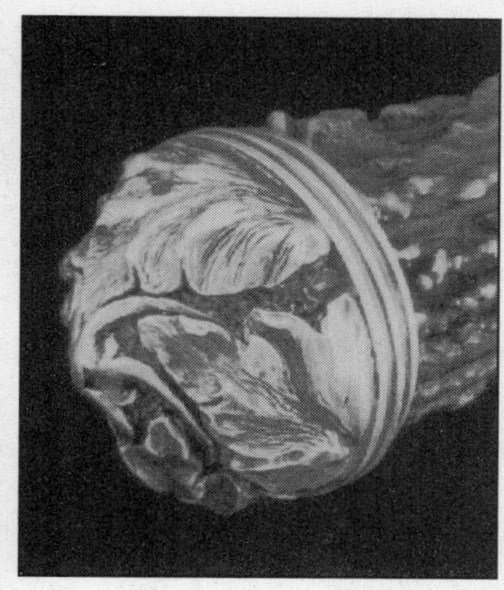

◀*Kirsten Skiles:* Silver pommel for a Fiorini quillon dagger. (Gallagher photo)

◀*Frank Crain:* A monster handle carved in linen Micarta and an etched temper line—a brave show. (Gallagher photo)

EMBELLISHMENT

Carving & Etching

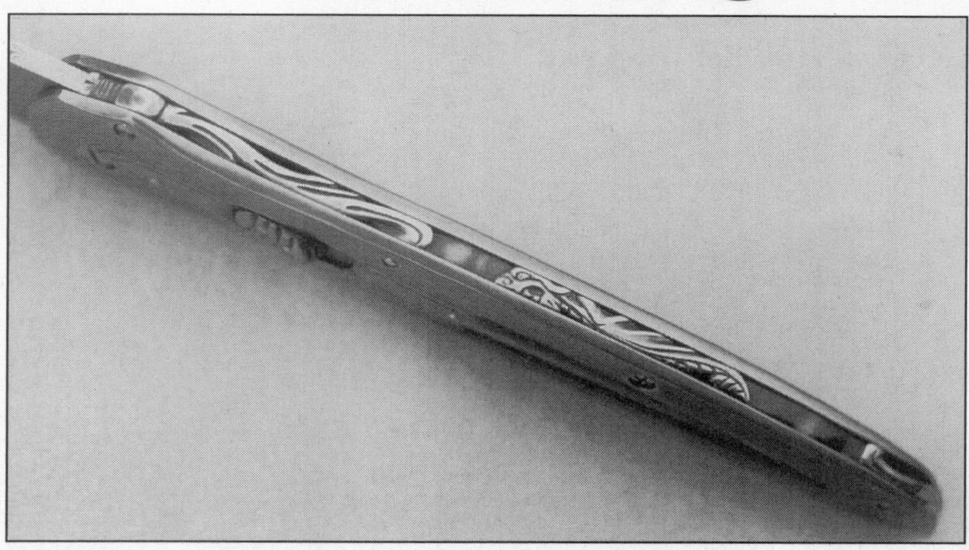

◀*William James McHenry:* File-work as carving in the springs and things of an automatic folder.

▼*Arthur Soppera:* Silver leaves and amethyst violets—improbably, they're a case for a button lock folder.

LEATHERWORK—IT'S BETTER THAN IT WAS

OF COURSE IT is—better, that is. An awful lot of the work you see here is accomplished by leatherwork specialists rather than by knifemakers, as has been the trend.

Not too long ago, these leather guys weren't doing knife leather (or Kydex or wood or nickel silver, either). In that time, the really good sheaths were made by knifemakers, those fellows who believed the sheath important and who had the personal skills to design and execute good leather stuff.

You know the corollary, of course: In that time, there were a lot of pretty bad sheaths sold with some pretty good knives. The makers who didn't like leatherworking didn't even have to say so—you could see it in the sheaths.

But enough of that. In the here and the now, we have great leather, great carrying and delivery systems, and a lot of good-looking complementary artifacts to go with the knives.

You need not take this reporter's word for it. You just have to look close, right here.

Ken Warner

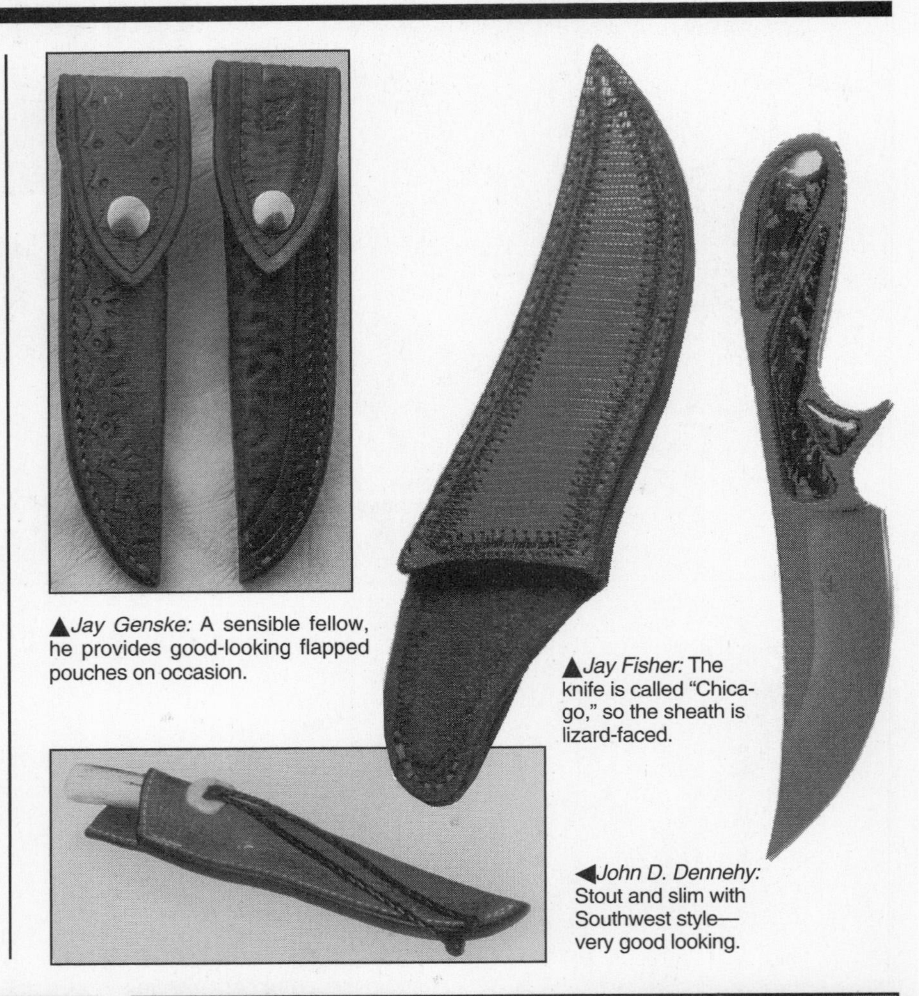

▲*Jay Genske:* A sensible fellow, he provides good-looking flapped pouches on occasion.

▲*Jay Fisher:* The knife is called "Chicago," so the sheath is lizard-faced.

◀*John D. Dennehy:* Stout and slim with Southwest style—very good looking.

◀*Karen Shook:* A styled and antiqued frontier sheath for a styled and antiqued Winkler knife. (Weyer photo)

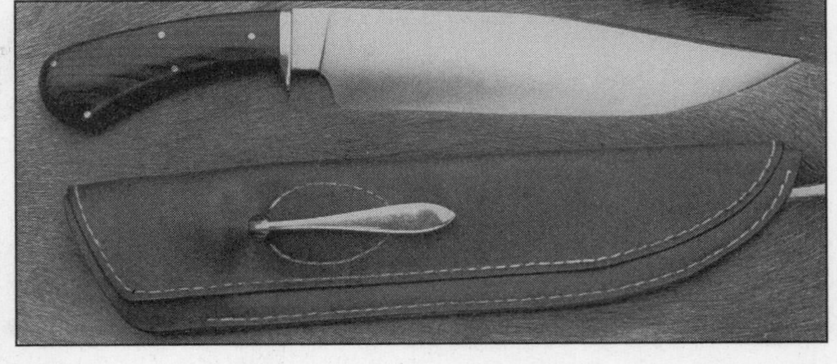

▲*David Congdon:* Belt-hooked inside-the-pants (or sash?) pouch for a big knife.

▲*Uwe H. Hoffmann:* For this small hunter, a lined flapped pouch seems very right.

▲*Mauro Ameri:* The fine Italian leather touch in a tilted belt sheath for a tough-looking belt knife.

▶*George Cubic:* A slim pouch overlaid in emu leg leather for an Ellis fighter.

LEATHERWORK—IT'S BETTER THAN IT WAS

Pouches...All Kinds

▼▶*Robert G. Schrap:* Plain or semi-fancy, a fitted pouch is always good.

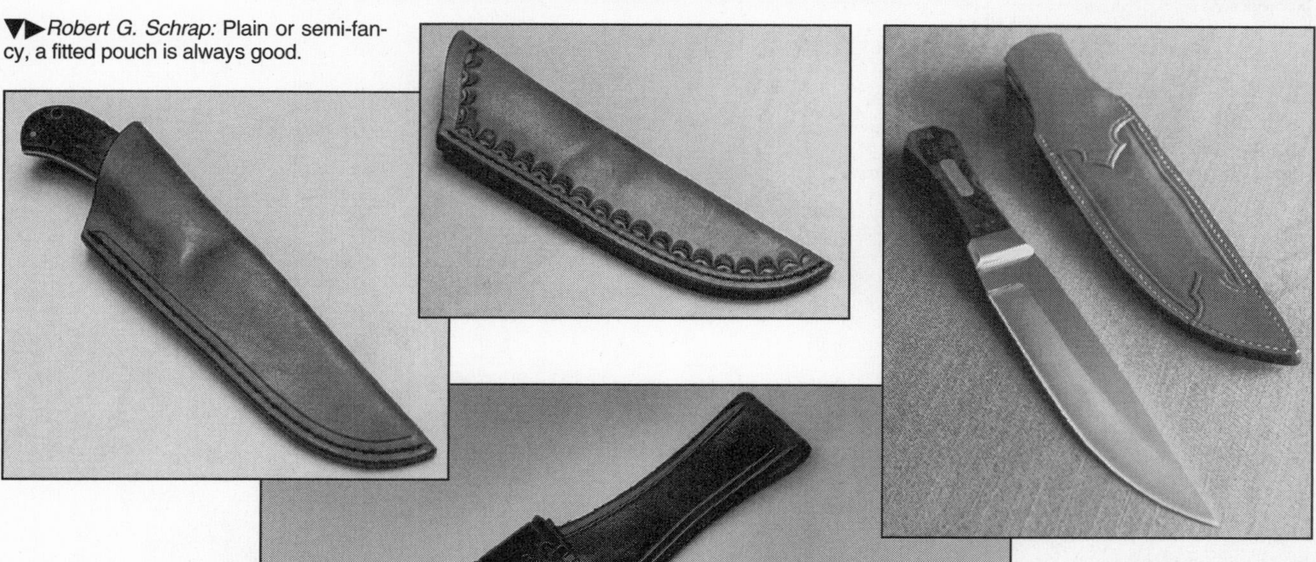

▲*Maker Unknown:* Splendid and elegant stitched sheath for a handsome Rose-style Bowie.

▶*Jim Jackson:* Green malachite and deep green leather made as a labor of love for a gift.

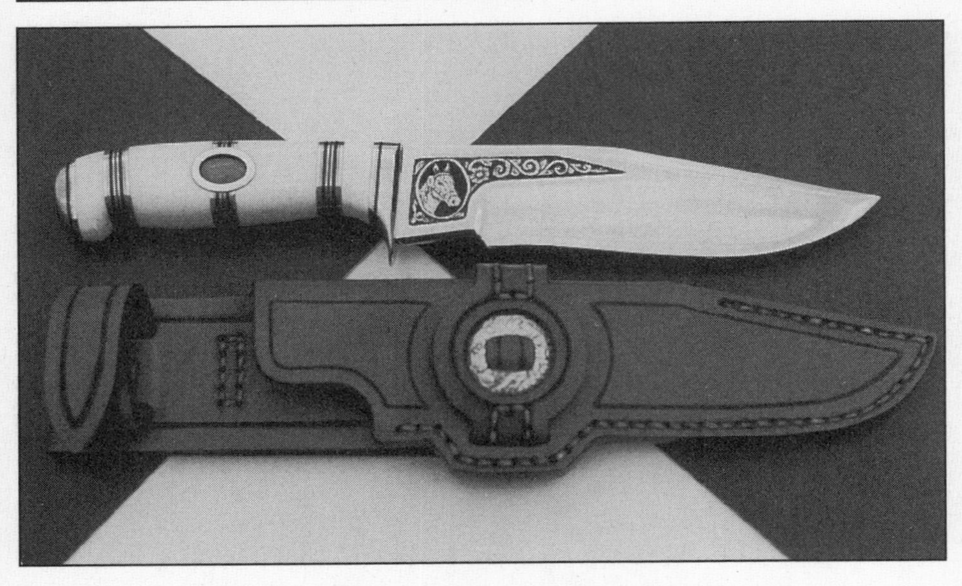

▲*Nestor-Lorenzo Rho:* The knife's ivory, bronze and turquoise are set off by a handsome, mannered sheath style. (Kerce photo)

▶*George Cubic:* Frank Gamble's knife looks good in an old-timey pattern, laid over with lizard.

LEATHERWORK—IT'S BETTER THAN IT WAS

Dress-Up Leather

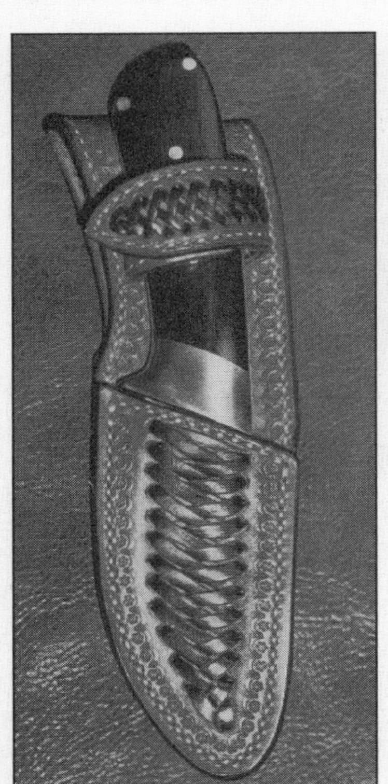

▲*George Cubic:* Not overlays, but a slick lacing trick here—on the body and the retainer.

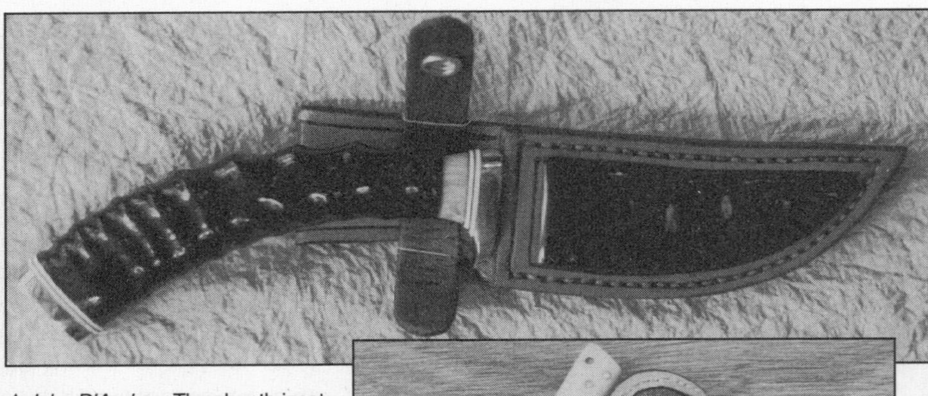

▲*John D'Andrea:* The sheath inset matches the impala knife grip.

▶*Kenny Rowe:* That's ostrich leather overlaying a strap pouch—the right texture.

▶*Kenny Rowe:* The pin-lock sheath's uncluttered pouch gives tooling a nice space. Bowie by Jerry Fisk.

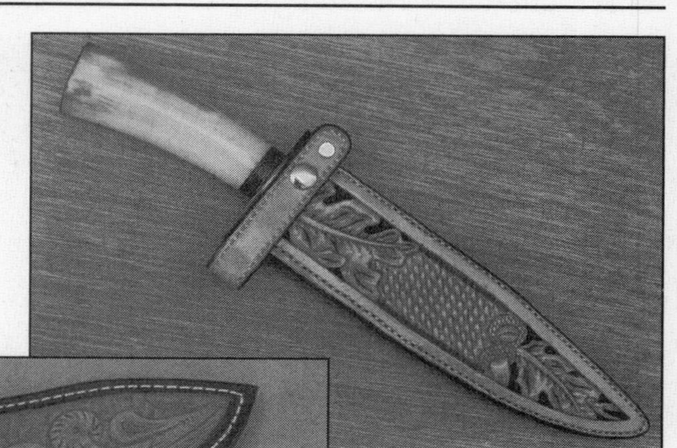

▲*Kenny Rowe:* A tooled initial and the full oak leaf for a high-ride cross-draw sheath to carry a Jim Walker knife.

◀*Dennis DesJardins:* Dramatic carving matched to a nice piece of cocobolo. (Gallagher photo)

LEATHERWORK—IT'S BETTER THAN IT WAS

Tooled Leather

◀*Russ Kommer:* Full tooling for an all-out semi-skinner—ATS-34 and mammoth ivory. (Wood photo)

▼*Martin Morrissey:* Traditional oak leaves in handsome symmetrical leather for a dagger.

◀*George Cubic:* Full basket stamping for an old Ka-Bar that probably deserves it.

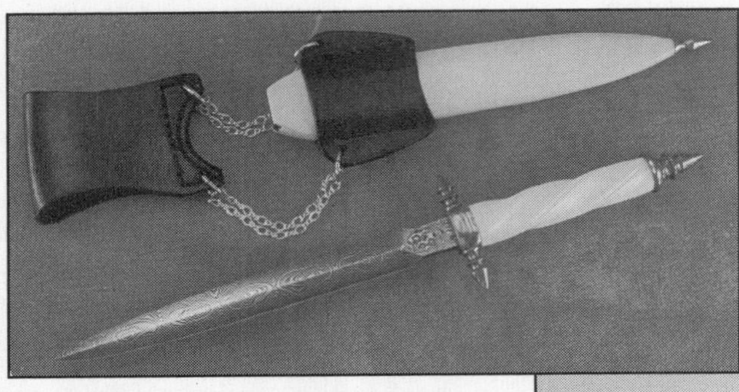

▶▼*Wendell Fox:* Forged blades and ivory grips fixed up with faux ivory sheaths very appropriately. (Gallagher photos)

▼*Harold Corby:* The big knife with all-out leather over wood, engraved by Tanya VanHoy.

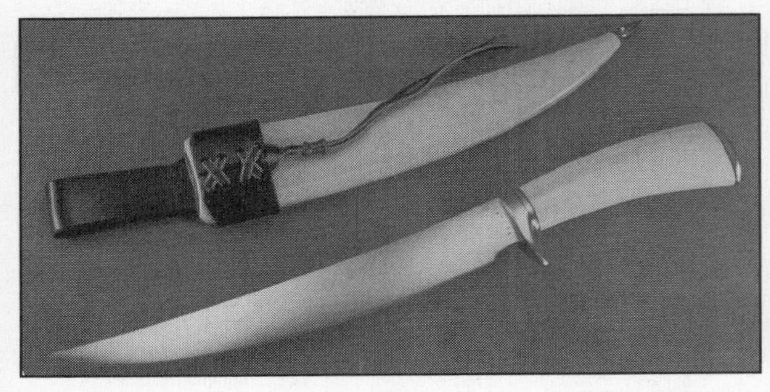

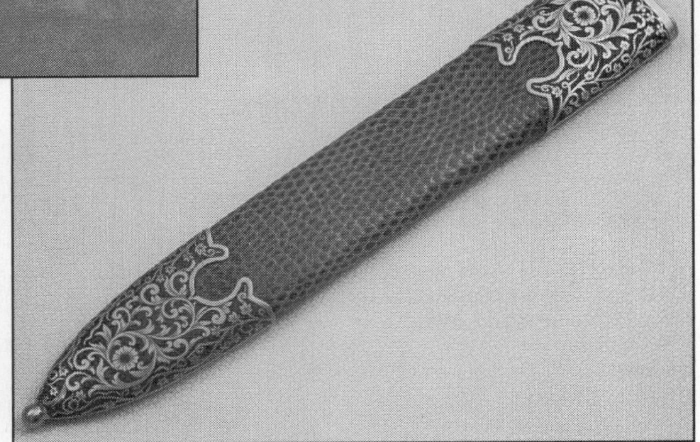

LEATHERWORK—IT'S BETTER THAN IT WAS

Special Stuff

▲*Wm. F. Moran, Jr.:* Moulded leather over wood for a Green River butcher knife. (Holter photo)

▲*Wolfgang Dell:* Sterling sheath and black leather inlay complements nickel silver and ivory grip.

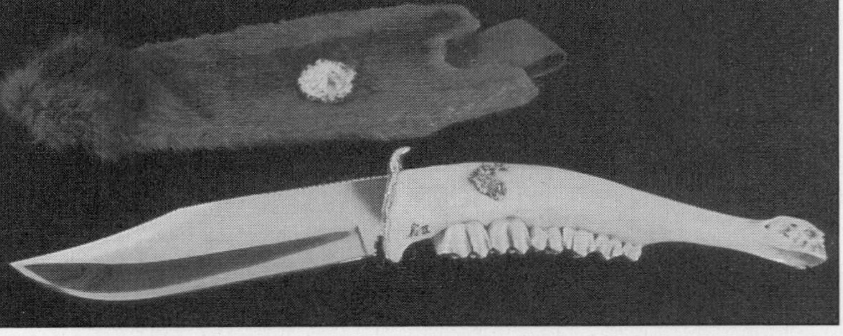

◀*Howard L. Imboden II:* An elk jaw grip and a furry deer hide sheath with carvings.

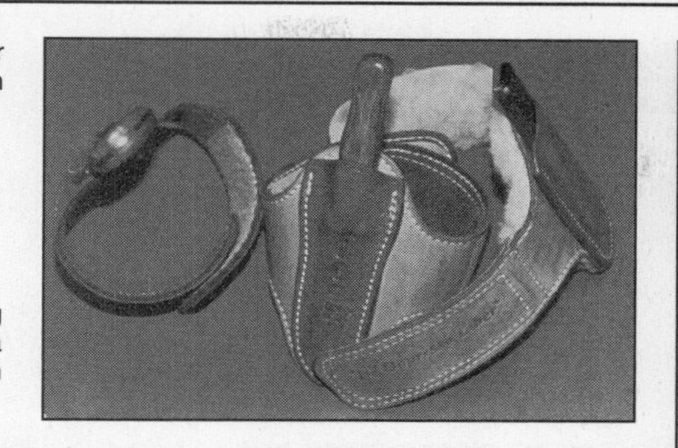

▶*John D. Dennehy:* A pair of ankle sheaths for smallish boot knives and folders.

▼*F.Terry Callahan:* Making the most of the thong as a design element in a sheath for a big knife.

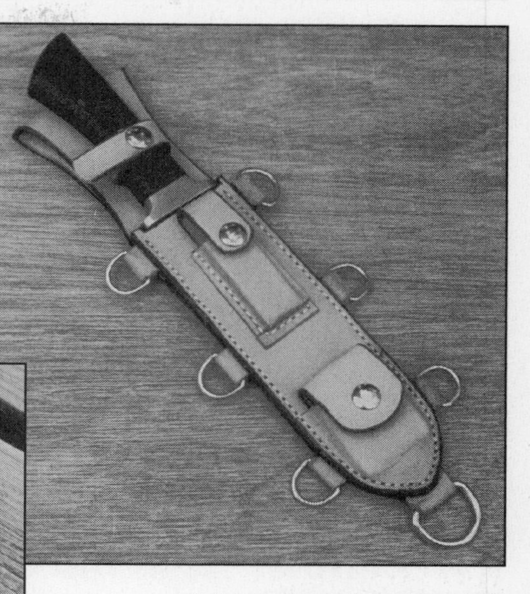

▲*Kenny Rowe:* Drop loop, both compass and stone pouches, and seven tie-down rings.

LEATHERWORK—IT'S BETTER THAN IT WAS

Special Functions

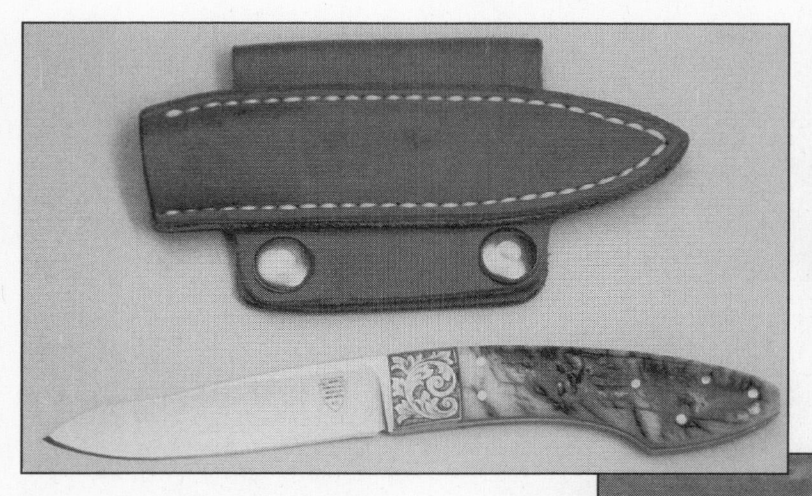

▲*Larry Downing:* A sideways pouch, set up to snap on the belt—a slick knife.

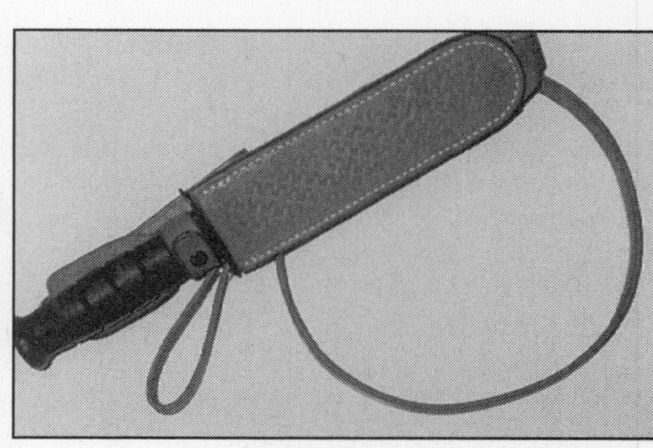

▲*John D. Dennehy:* A Ka-Bar in a serious sheath, seriously thonged.

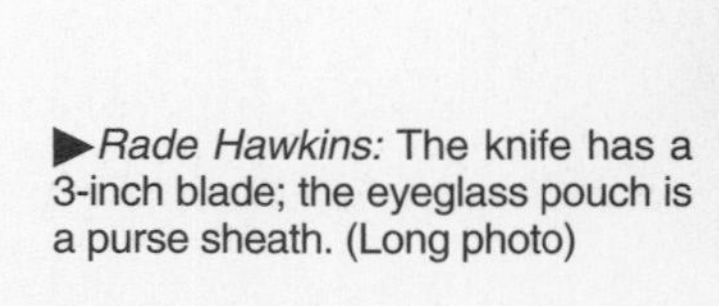

▶*Rade Hawkins:* The knife has a 3-inch blade; the eyeglass pouch is a purse sheath. (Long photo)

◀*Paolo Scordia:* A stylish sheath and a Kydex-wrapped grip.

▶*James S. Piorek:* Blade-Rigger dazzle camouflage on a wrap grip and Kydex sheath—you can see it, but what is it?

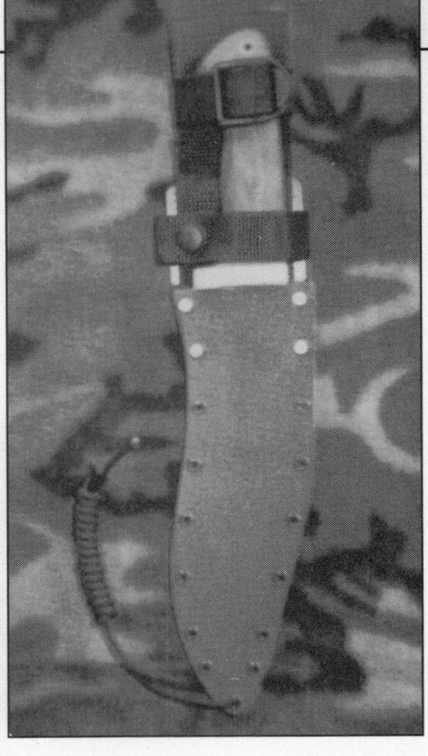

▲*Scott Hendryx:* All-out riveted Kydex built-to-order for your knife.

LEATHERWORK—IT'S BETTER THAN IT WAS

Kydex

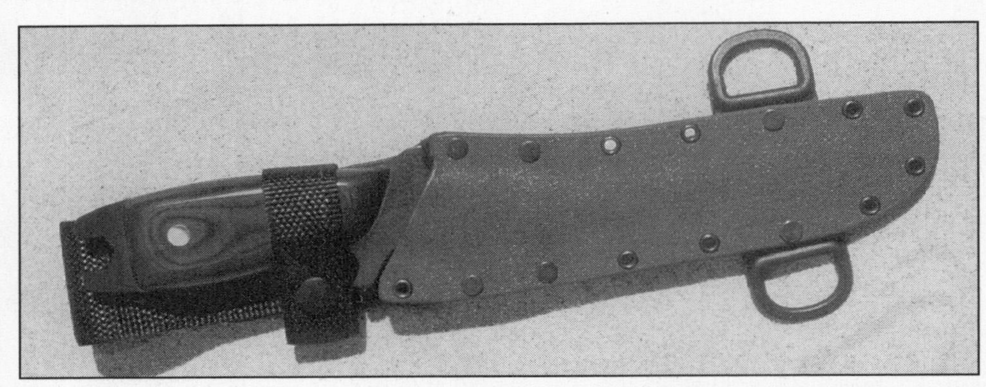

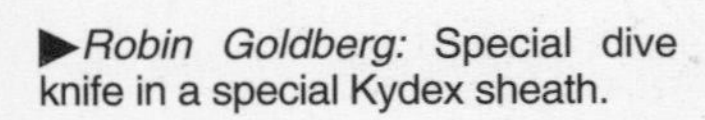

▶*Robin Goldberg:* Special dive knife in a special Kydex sheath.

◀▲*James S. Piorek:* This is a Blade Rigger "Aikuchi" with what's called a Courier Harness—multiple-choice carrier included.

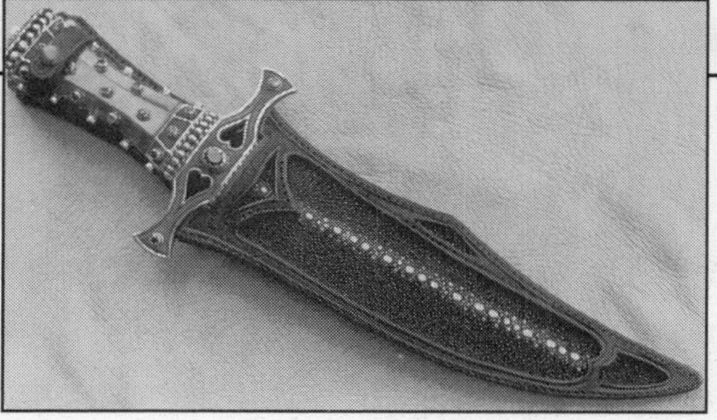

▲*Chris Kravitt:* Complex rayskin inlays for a complex Jarvis dagger from Tree Stump Leather.

▲*Charles Aoun:* An inlay complements the ivory and sterling silver of the knife in a nice pouch.

◀*Peter Martin:* A diamondback and an elephant contributed here.

LEATHERWORK—IT'S BETTER THAN IT WAS

Inlays In Plenty

▲*Kenny Rowe:* Gator back inlay in a concealment sheath for a Gaston Bowie.

▲*Robert G. Schrap:* Cowhide and a gator panel fit a classy folder pouch.

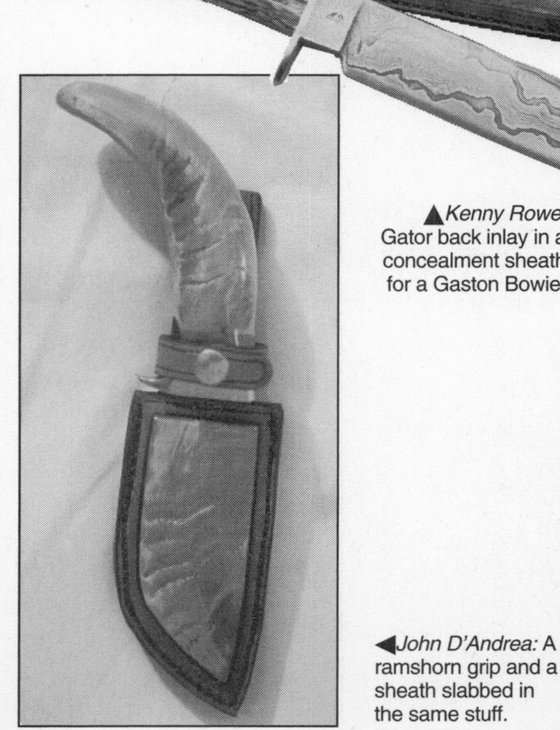

◀*John D'Andrea:* A ramshorn grip and a sheath slabbed in the same stuff.

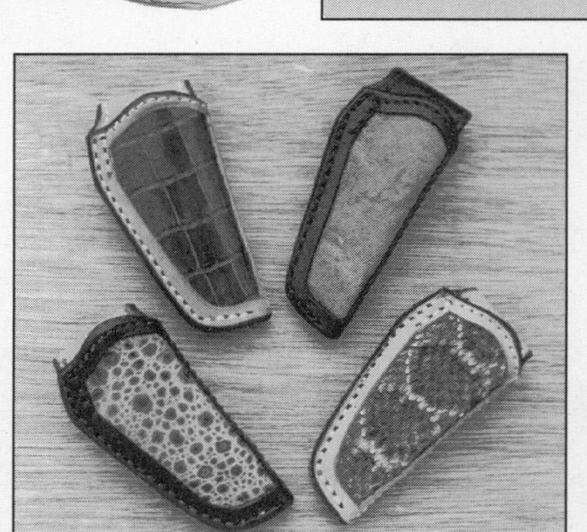

◀*Kenny Rowe:* For Fisk pocketknives, we have gator, elephant, frog and diamondback inlays.

MISCELLANY

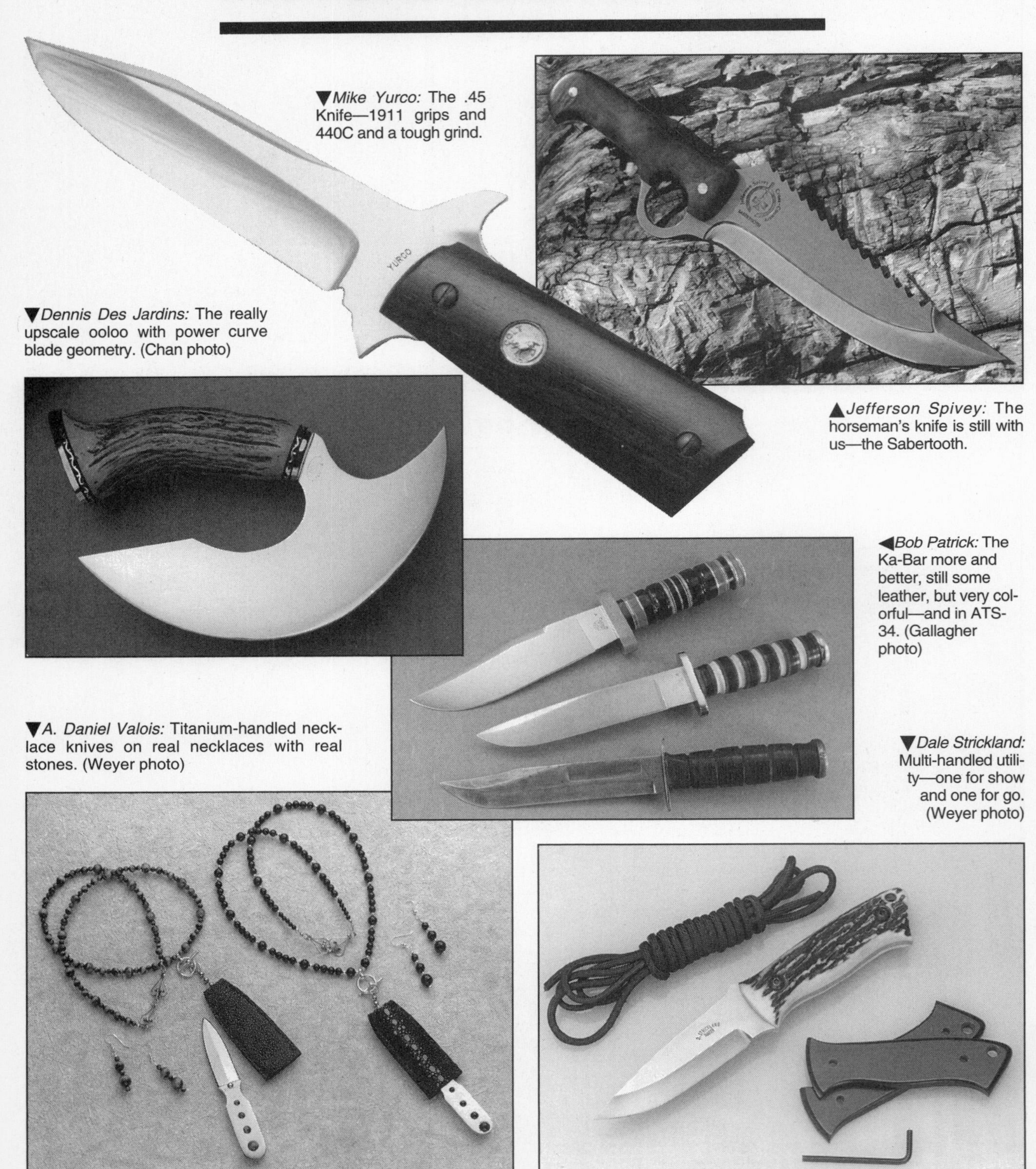

▼*Mike Yurco:* The .45 Knife—1911 grips and 440C and a tough grind.

▲*Jefferson Spivey:* The horseman's knife is still with us—the Sabertooth.

▼*Dennis Des Jardins:* The really upscale ooloo with power curve blade geometry. (Chan photo)

◀*Bob Patrick:* The Ka-Bar more and better, still some leather, but very colorful—and in ATS-34. (Gallagher photo)

▼*A. Daniel Valois:* Titanium-handled necklace knives on real necklaces with real stones. (Weyer photo)

▼*Dale Strickland:* Multi-handled utility—one for show and one for go. (Weyer photo)

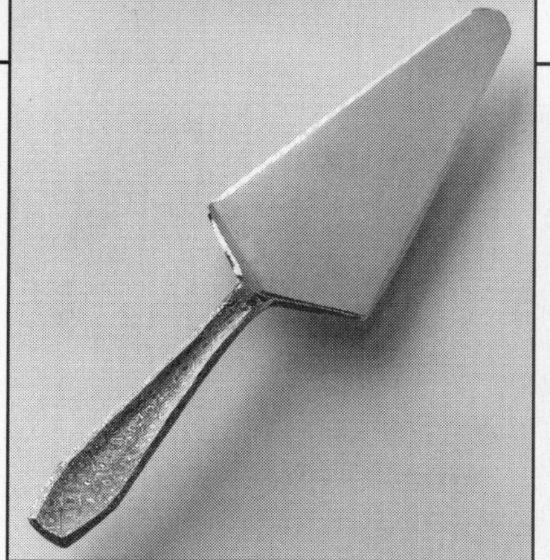

▲*Phillip Baldwin:* A foot-long cake knife in sterling and sterling/copper mokume. (Schreiber photo)

▲*Daniel E. Piergallini:* Yep. It's the state of Florida in 440C, pearl and such—800 miles, tip to tip. (Weyer photo)

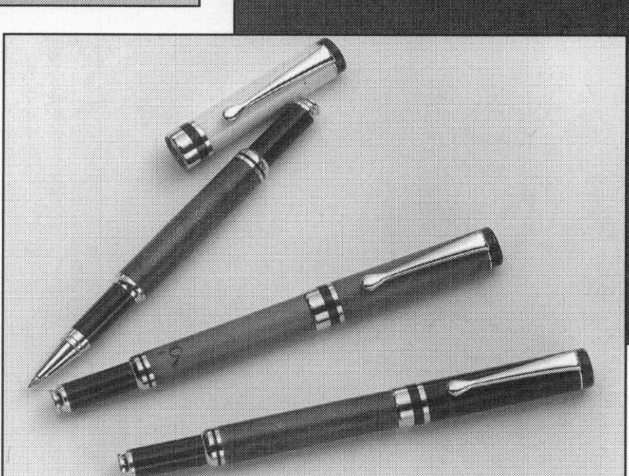

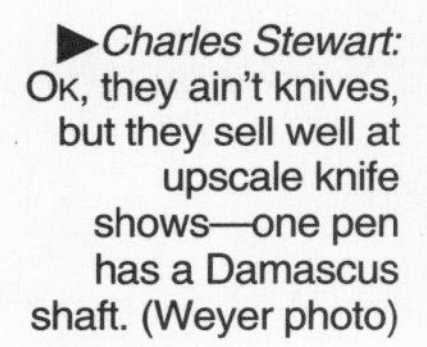

►*Charles Stewart:* Oκ, they ain't knives, but they sell well at upscale knife shows—one pen has a Damascus shaft. (Weyer photo)

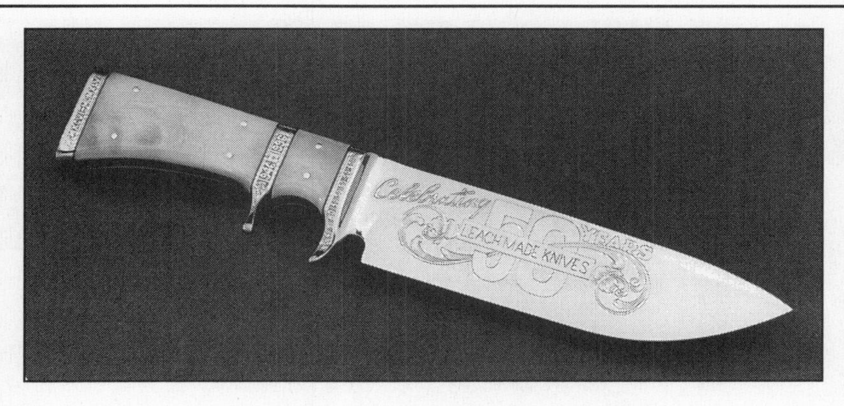

▲▼Last year these two knives appeared with some inadvertently sloppy language. For the record: *Mike J. Leach's* sub-hilt knife above celebrated his 50th year as a knifemaker; and *Glenn Marshall's* slim hunter commemorated his 70th year in knifemaking.

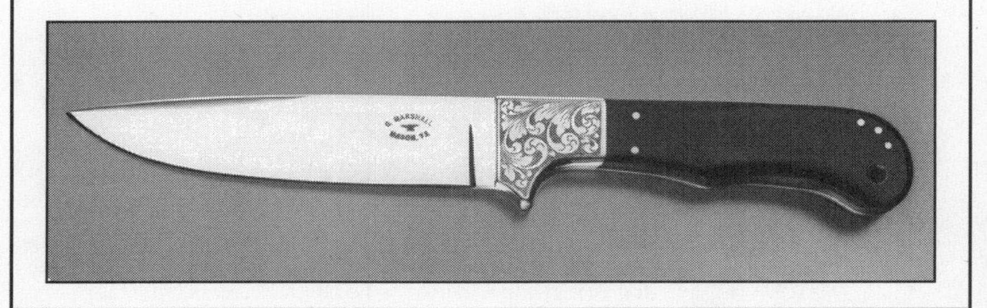

►*Joseph G. Cordova:* The Harley letter-opener given to Jim Weyer by the ABS. (Weyer photo)

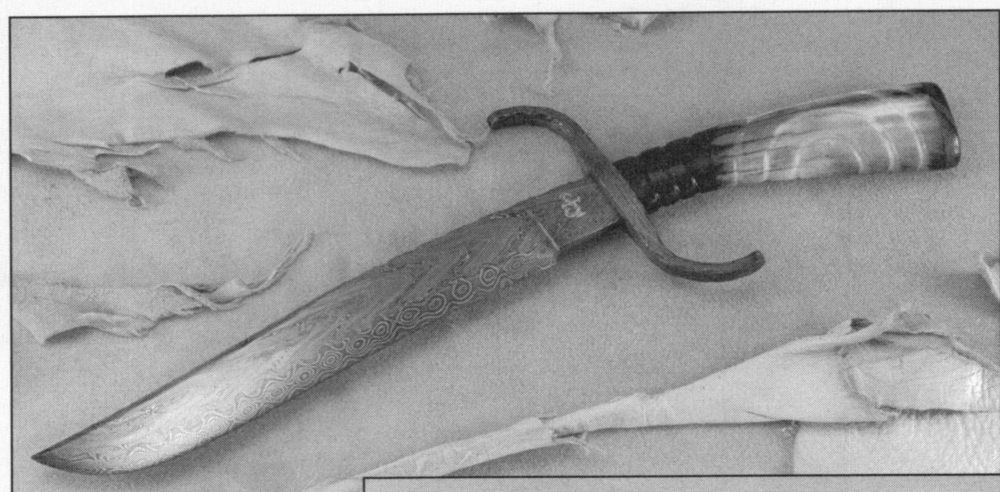

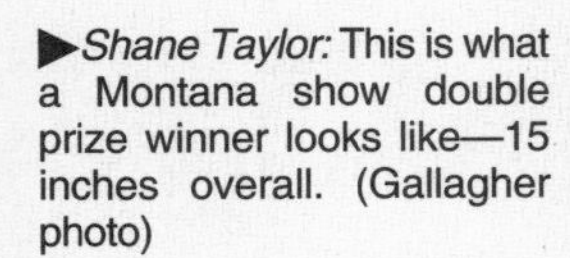

▶*Shane Taylor:* This is what a Montana show double prize winner looks like—15 inches overall. (Gallagher photo)

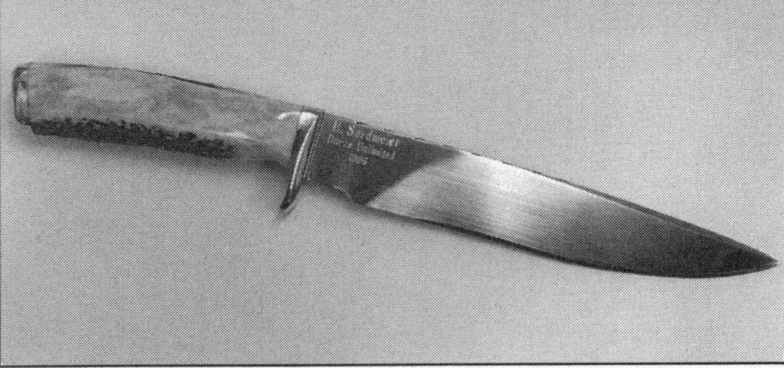

▲*Harlan Suedmeier:* One for DU—auctioned at big bucks for his Nebraska chapter.

▲*Bob Sims:* Give the governor a folder: get his name (Bush) on one side, your name on the other. It helps if it's a slick-looking knife. (Weyer photo)

▲*Richard M. Caudell:* Prototype for five 75th anniversary knives for the Illinois State Police.

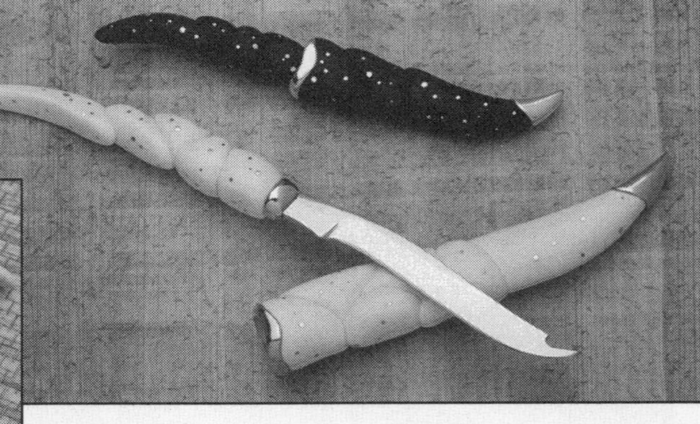

◀▲*Dolores Hayes:* When the plain ones were finished, the custom said, "Now jazz 'em up." The result included sterling fittings and pins in one and gold in the other. (Fitzgerald photos)

FACTORY TRENDS

We used to say commercial production knives tended toward the tried and true. That is not going to be factual for much longer.

We've got companies in major production of automatic knives for which they've found a legal law enforcement market; we've got sports knives from overseas that are very handcrafted, and some very, very high-tech.

There are companies turning to military-style knives —a wider range than ever, it would appear—and other companies shunning phosphate coatings and the dark look.

We only talk about the new ones—or ones we think you don't know about—here, but there will be nifty pictures to look at anyway.

Ken Warner

FACTORY TRENDS

NEW KNIVES IN PRODUCTION

▲*Camillus Cutlery Co.:* Right down the fairway—a robust black lock-back with clip blade and pocket clip.

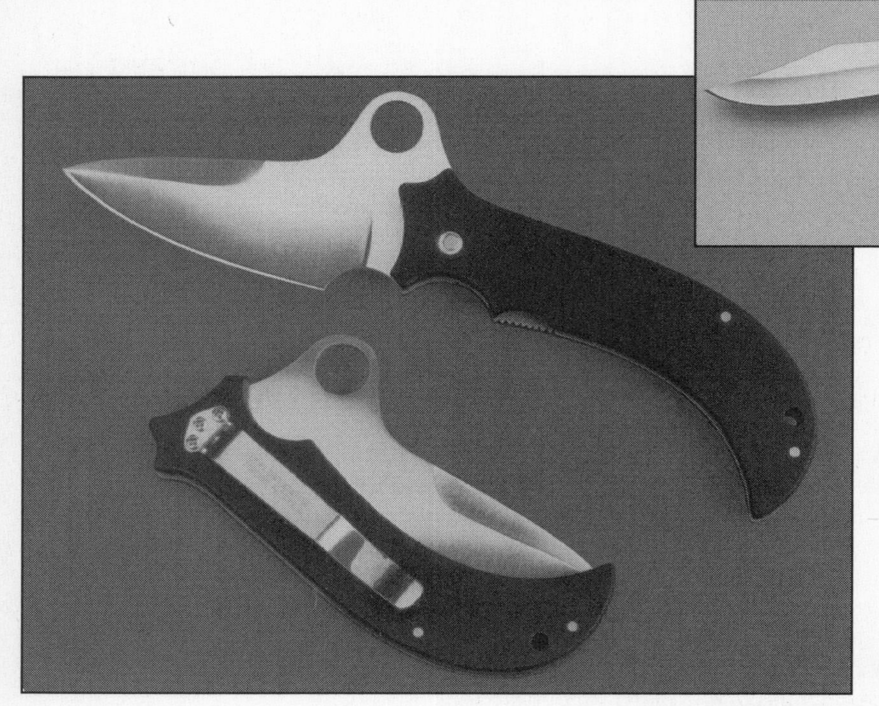

◀*Spyderco, Inc.:* Jot Singh Khalsa's turn in the box, with his Kirpan flavor all folded up.

▼*Klotzli (Messer Klotzli):* Swiss-made in a Wimpff design, it's G10 and 440C and absolutely current.

▼*SOG Specialty Knives & Tools, Inc.:* The Mini-Gent certainly looks like one—as handsome closed as folding knives get.

▲*Atlantic Bladesmiths:* All-out John Kubasek liner-lock—three blade shapes, lots of choices.

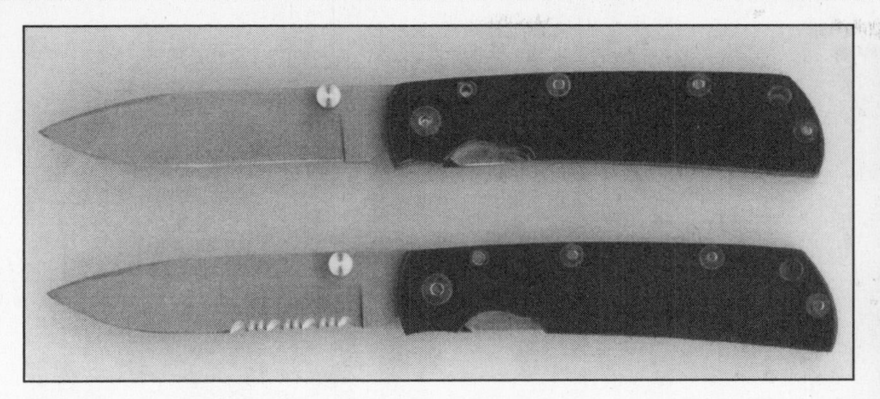

▲*Brunton Co./Lakota:* Plain vanilla and tough-looking, there's a pocket clip, of course. Micarta and stainless, it is.

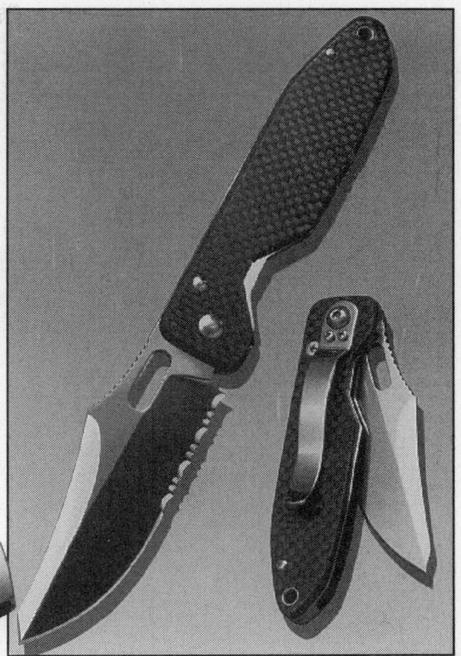

▶*SOG Specialty Knives & Tools, Inc.:* The Jet Edge folder, a la mode in liner-locking—and a very, very tough point.

NEW KNIVES IN PRODUCTION

Folders

▲▼*Barry B. Wood, Michael L. Irie:* The Wood-patent folder, in the slick form its makers call the Classic. (Weyer photo)

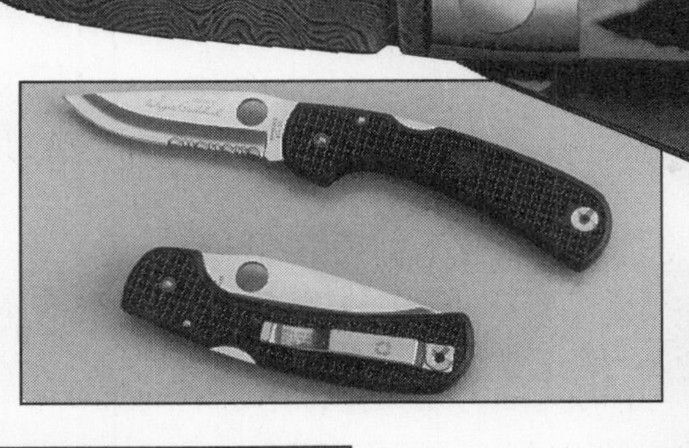

▶*Spyderco, Inc.:* A big hit and a good-size knife, this is the Wayne Goddard lightweight.

▼*Moki:* Little guys, immaculately made with all the features, they're the Zephyr and the Elite. From Spyderco, Inc.

▼*Imperial Schrade Corp.:* It's the Journeyman, an Uncle Henry at $2\frac{3}{4}$ inches, meant for the suit pocket.

▼*Camillus Cutlery Co.:* Soque's Lev-R-Lok is now in big-time factory production, as quick-opening as ever.

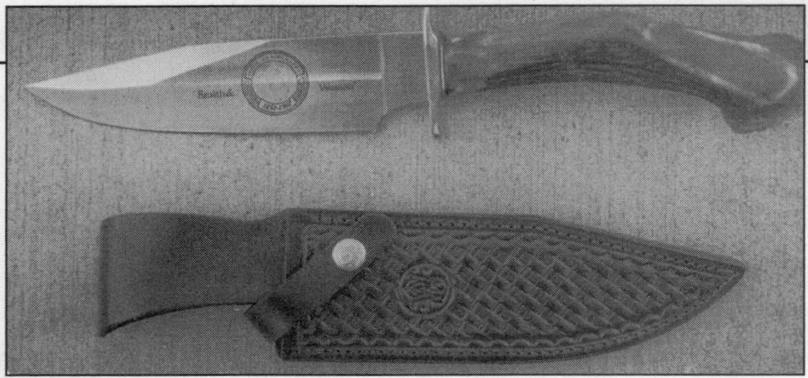

▲*Smith & Wesson Knives:* By *Taylor Cutlery*, an anniversary knife for S&W's 145th year.

▶*Camillus Cutlery Co.:* The old Western boot dagger, newly styled and sheathed entirely up-to-date.

◀*Boker USA,Inc.:* The Colonel's knife—the Applegate-Fairbairn—again, this time built in Germany, and in a serrated option as well.

NEW KNIVES IN PRODUCTION

Straight Knives

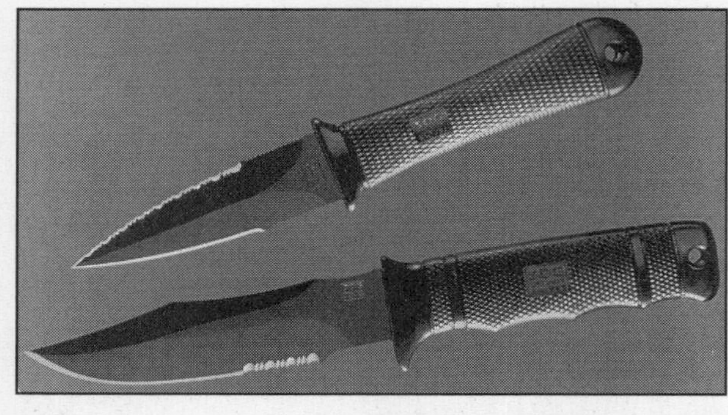

▲*SOG Specialty Knives & Tools, Inc.:* It's the SEAL Pup and the Mini-Pentagon, neat as can be and clear winners in the name contest.

▼*Imperial Schrade Corp.:* The STC, patterned and sheathed for all-around outdoor utility.

▶*Randall Made Knives:* New grinds, new handle mixes, same handmade quality—for special dealers.

◀*Barteaux Machetes, Inc.:* At lengths from 6 to 10 inches, there are now Mini Machetes, described as "chop cut knives."

◀*Busse Combat Knife Co.:* Strongly built simple knives, built for the fellow with a real need.

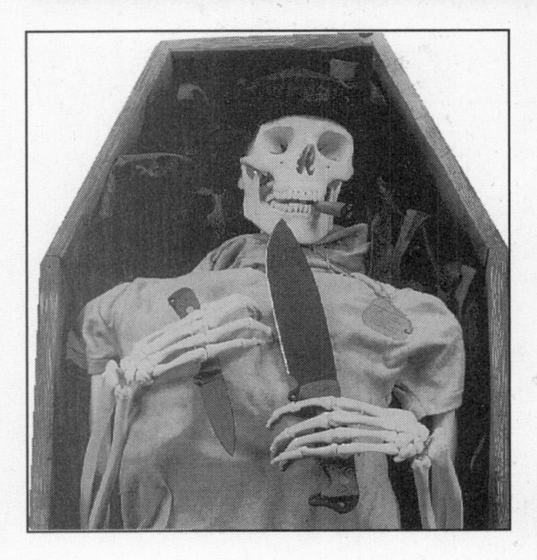

▶*Cold Steel, Inc.:* Variations on a most successful theme, these are Oyabuns, at $7\frac{1}{2}$ and 9 inches.

NEW KNIVES IN PRODUCTION

Straight Knives

▼*Camillus Cutlery Co.:* With a Western blade stamp, this is good-looking and about as simple as a knife can be.

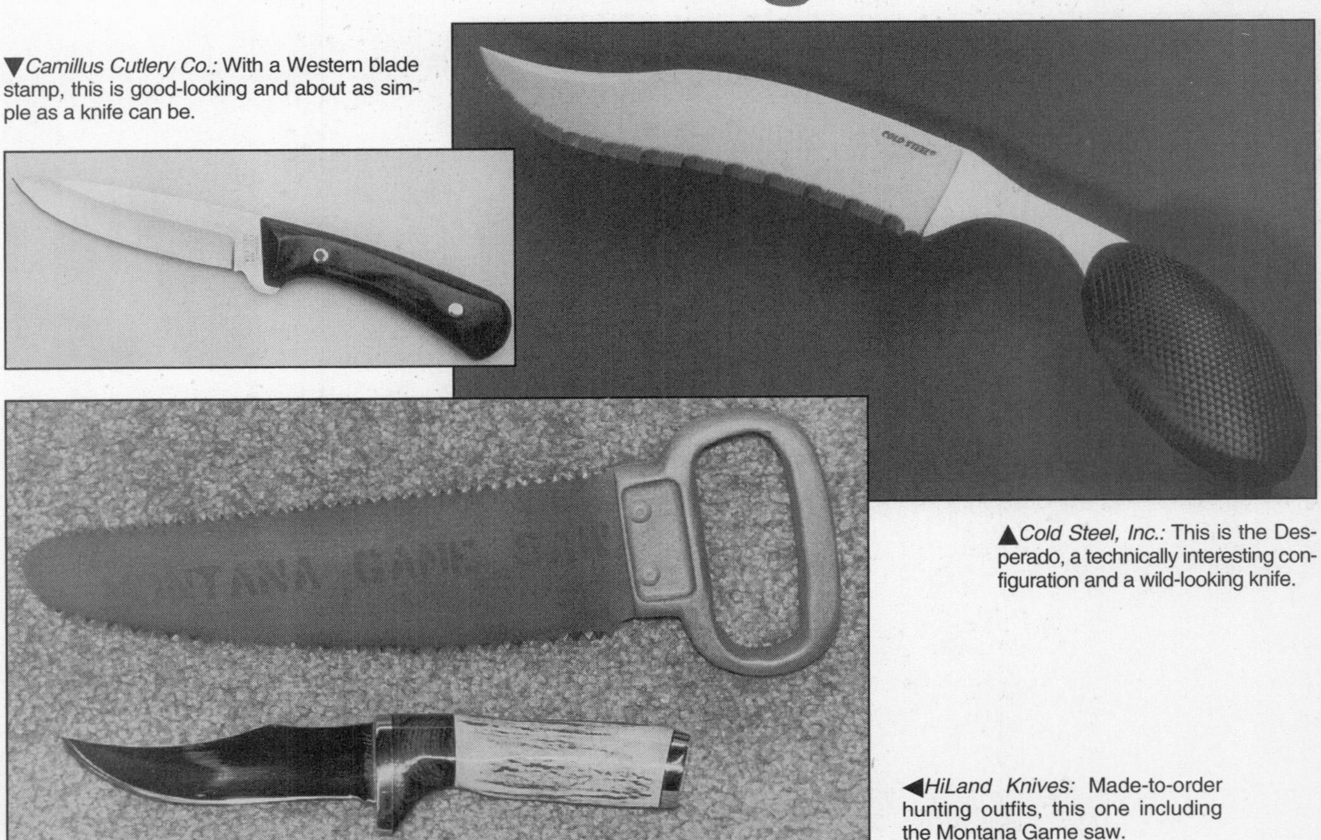

▲*Cold Steel, Inc.:* This is the Desperado, a technically interesting configuration and a wild-looking knife.

◀*HiLand Knives:* Made-to-order hunting outfits, this one including the Montana Game saw.

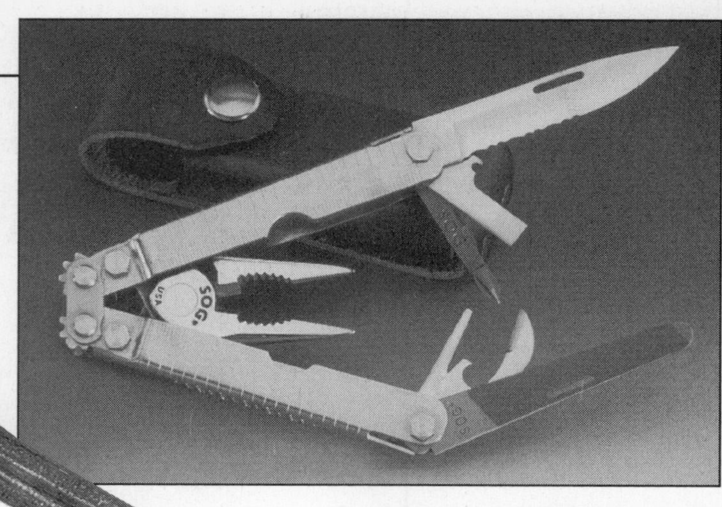

▶*Museum Replicas Ltd.:* A Viking sword called Aettartangi, 36 inches long in Damascus, with bone and copper and brass furniture.

▲*SOG Specialty Knives & Tools, Inc.:* The Power Plier, only pocket-sized this time, with six fold-out blades and a lot of functions.

▼*Atlanta Cutlery Corp.:* A replicated Persian Kard in Damascus and camel bone, 12$^{1}/_{2}$ inches overall and handsome.

NEW KNIVES IN PRODUCTION

Swords and Other Tools

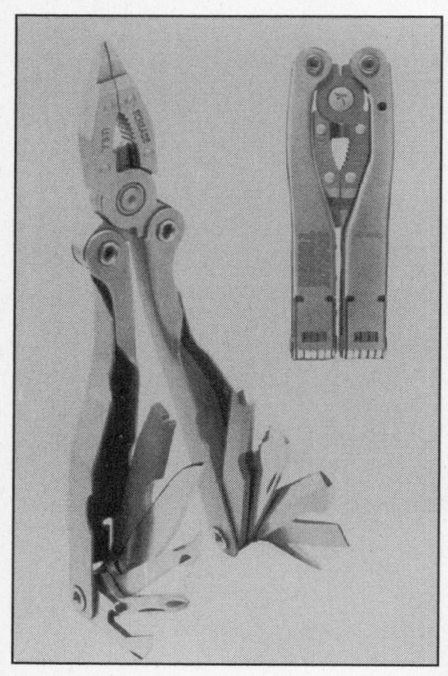

▲*Imperial Schrade Corp.:* They call it the Tough Tool—4$^{3}/_{4}$ inches and 8 ounces of stainless and twenty-one functions. The blades come out sideways.

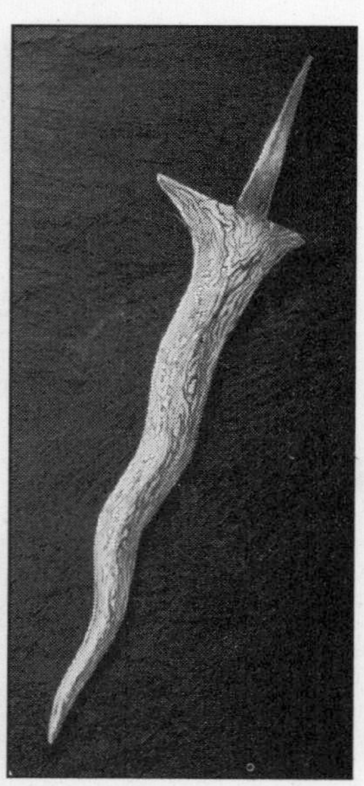

▲*Atlanta Cutlery Corp.:* Give in to your long-term wish to build a Japanese Kris with this 12-inch blade.

◀*Diamond Machining Technology Inc. (DMT):* New configurations for the old task and in four grits.

DIRECTORY

The only reason a maker or a source in the United States is not listed somewhere in this section is that we didn't hear of him or it, or something went wrong. This is intended to be a complete directory for knife owners. If you know of someone who should be in this Directory and isn't, please write and tell us. If you are that someone, please write. We'll definitely appreciate it.

This is not a catalog, so there will be incomplete entries, though not many. And with probably 1000 or more entries, it will have omissions. Very often, that will be the result of error on the part of the omitted. We tried to give everyone a chance.

The Directory is divided into different lists. The biggest is a compilation of short profiles of custom knifemakers, followed by a state-by-state list of those same knifemakers, and membership lists of professional knifemaker associations. In the knife photo index, we list all the photos of handmade knives in this edition, as well as the last five editions.

Then we list specialty cutlers; general cutlers; importers and foreign cutlers; sources for knifemaking supplies; mail-order houses that specialize in knives; and knife services, which include scrimshanders, engravers, leatherworkers and several other categories. Finally, we list major organizations and publications. Those seem the most useful categories. We hope they work for you.

Ken Warner

custom knifemakers

a

ABBOTT, WILLIAM M., Box 102A, RR #2, Chandlerville, IL 62627/217-458-2325
Specialties: High-grade edged weapons. **Patterns:** Locking folders, Bowies, working straight knives, kitchen cutlery, minis. **Technical:** Grinds D2, ATS-34, 440C and commercial Damascus. Heat-treats; Rockwell tests. Prefers natural handle materials. **Prices:** $100 to $1,000. **Remarks:** Part-time maker; first knife sold in 1984. **Mark:** Name.

ABERNATHY, PAUL J., 3033 Park St., Eureka, CA 95501/707-442-3593
Specialties: Period pieces and traditional straight knives of his design and in standard patterns. **Patterns:** Miniature daggers, fighters and swords. **Technical:** Forges and files SS, brass and sterling silver. **Prices:** $100 to $250; some to $500. **Remarks:** Part-time maker. Doing business as Abernathy's Miniatures. **Mark:** Stylized initials.

ABERNATHY'S MINIATURES (See Abernathy, Paul J.)

A CUT ABOVE (See Hartsfield, Phill)

ADAMS, LES, 6413 NW 200 St., Hialeah, FL 33015/305-625-1699
Specialties: Working straight knives of his design. **Patterns:** Fighters, hunters and fillet knives. **Technical:** Grinds ATS-34, 440C and D2. Offers scrimshawed handles. **Prices:** $100 to $200; some to $290. **Remarks:** Part-time maker; first knife sold in 1989. **Mark:** First initial, last name, Custom Knives.

ADAMS, WILLIAM D., 9318 Cole Creek Dr., Houston, TX 77040/713-855-5643; FAX: 713-855-5638
Specialties: Hunter scalpels and utility knives of his design. **Patterns:** Hunters and utility/camp knives. **Technical:** Grinds 1095, 440C and 440V. Uses stabilized wood and other stabilized materials. **Prices:** $100 to $200. **Remarks:** Part-time maker; first knife sold in 1994. **Mark:** Last name in script.

AIDA, YOSHIHITO, 26-7, Narimasu 2-chome, Itabashi-ku, Tokyo 175, JAPAN/81-3-3939-0052; FAX: 81-3-3939-0058
Specialties: High-tech working straight knives and folders of his design. **Patterns:** Bowies, lockbacks, hunters, fighters, fishing knives, boots. **Technical:** Grinds CV-134, ATS-34; buys Damascus; works in traditional Japanese fashion for some handles and sheaths. **Prices:** $400 to $900; some higher. **Remarks:** Full-time maker; first knife sold in 1978. **Mark:** Initial logo and Riverside West.

ALASKA KNIFE & SERVICE CO.
(See Trujillo, Thomas A., Adam or Miranda)

ALASKA KNIFEMAKER (See Shore, John I.)

ALASKAN MAID (See Kubaiko, Hank)

ALBERICCI, EMILIO, 19, via Masone, 24100, Bergamo, ITALY/01139-35-215120
Specialties: Folders and Bowies. **Patterns:** Collector knives. **Technical:** Uses stock removal with extreme lavoration accuracy; offers exotic and high-tech materials. **Prices:** Not currently selling. **Remarks:** Part-time maker. **Mark:** None.

ALDERMAN, ROBERT, 3388 Jewel Lake Rd., Sagle, ID 83860/208-263-5996
Specialties: Classic and traditional working straight knives in standard patterns or to customer specs and his design; period pieces. **Patterns:** Bowies, fighters, hunters and utility/camp knives. **Technical:** Casts, forges and grinds 1084; forges and grinds L6 and O1. Prefers an old appearance. **Prices:** $100 to $350; some to $700. **Remarks:** Full-time maker; first knife sold in 1975. Doing business as Trackers Forge. **Mark:** Deer track.

ALEXANDER, DARREL, Box 381, Ten Sleep, WY 82442/307-366-2699
Specialties: Traditional working straight knives. **Patterns:** Hunters, boots and fishing knives. **Technical:** Grinds D2, 440C, ATS-34 and 154CM. **Prices:** $75 to $120; some to $250. **Remarks:** Full-time maker; first knife sold in 1983. **Mark:** Name, city, state.

ALLEN, JOE, 120 W. Glendale St., Princeton, IN 47670/812-386-7276
Specialties: Hunting and outdoor knives. **Patterns:** Bowies, working hunters, daggers and skinners. **Technical:** Grinds 440C and ATS-34. **Prices:** $125 to $400. **Remarks:** Part-time maker; first knife sold in 1976. **Mark:** Full name, year, city, state.

ALLEN, MIKE "WHISKERS," 12745 Fontenot Acres Rd., Malakoff, TX 75148/903-489-1026
Specialties: Working and collector-quality lockbacks and automatic folders to customer specs. **Patterns:** Hunters, tantos, Bowies, swords and miniatures. **Technical:** Forges Damascus to shape; grinds 440C and ATS-34. Engraves. **Prices:** Start at $125. **Remarks:** Full-time maker; first knife sold in 1984. **Mark:** Whiskers and serial number.

ALLRED AND SONS (See Allred, Elvan)

ALLRED, ELVAN, 2403 Lansing Blvd., Wichita Falls, TX 76309/817-691-9563
Specialties: Fancy, high-art straight knives and folders of his design. **Patterns:** Fighters, hunters and locking folders. **Technical:** Grinds ATS-34, 440C and D2. Most knives are engraved; many have custom-fitted cases or sheaths. **Prices:** $250 to $750; some to $1,500. **Remarks:** Full-time maker; first knife sold in 1992. Doing business as Allred and Sons. **Mark:** First initial, last name, city, state.

ALPINE MOUNTAIN KNIVES (See Copeland, George "Steve")

ALSTAR (See Amoureux, A.W.)

ALVERSON, TIM (R.V.), 1158 Maple St., Klamath Falls, OR 97601/541-884-9119; FAX: 541-884-9119
Specialties: Fancy working knives to customer specs; other types on request. **Patterns:** Bowies, daggers, folders and miniatures. **Technical:** Grinds 440C, ATS-34; buys some Damascus. **Prices:** Start at $175. **Remarks:** Full-time maker; first knife sold in 1981. **Mark:** R.V.A. around rosebud.

AMERI, MAURO, Via Ridello No. 20, Trensasco, St. Olcese, 16121 Genova, ITALY/010-8363035
Specialties: Working and using knives of his design. **Patterns:** Hunters, Bowies and utility/camp knives. **Technical:** Grinds 440C, ATS-34 and 154CM. Handles in wood or Micarta; offers sheaths. **Prices:** $200 to $1,200. **Remarks:** Spare-time maker; first knife sold in 1982. **Mark:** Last name, city.

AMES FORGE (See Ames, Mickey L.)

AMES, MICKEY L., P.O. Box 549, 528 Spruce, Lebo, KS 66856/316-256-6222
Specialties: Traditional working and using straight knives of his design and to customer specs. **Patterns:** Bowies, hunters and utility/camp knives. **Technical:** Forges 5160, 1084, 1095 and makes own Damascus. Filework; silver wire inlay. **Prices:** Start at $100. **Remarks:** Part-time maker; first knife sold in 1990. Doing business as Ames Forge. **Mark:** Last name.

AMOR JR., MIGUEL, 485-H Judie Lane, Lancaster, PA 17603/717-290-0875
Specialties: Working and fancy straight knives in standard patterns; some to customer specs. **Patterns:** Bowies, hunters, fighters and tantos. **Technical:** Grinds 440C, ATS-34, carbon steel and commercial Damascus; forges some in high carbon steels. **Prices:** $125 to $500; some to $1,500 and higher. **Remarks:** Part-time maker; first knife sold in 1983. **Mark:** Last name. On collectors' pieces: last name, city, state.

AMOUREUX, A.W., 3210 Woodland Pk. Dr., Anchorage, AK 99517/907-248-4442
Specialties: Heavy-duty working straight knives. **Patterns:** Bowies, fighters, camp knives and hunters for Alaska use. **Technical:** Grinds 440C, ATS-34 and 154CM. **Prices:** $80 to $2,000. **Remarks:** Part-time maker; first knife sold in 1974. **Mark:** ALSTAR.

ANDERS, DAVID, 157 Barnes Dr., Center Ridge, AR 72027/501-893-2294
Specialties: Working straight knives of his design. **Patterns:** Bowies, fighters and hunters. **Technical:** Forges 5160, 1080 and Damascus. **Prices:** $175 to $2,500. **Remarks:** Part-time maker; first knife sold in 1988. Doing business as Dutton Mountain Forge. **Mark:** Last name/MS.

ANDERSEN, HENRIK LEFOLII, Jagtvej 8, Groenholt, 3480 Fredensborg, DENMARK/0011-45-48483026
Specialties: Hunters and matched pairs for the serious hunter. **Patterns:** Working folders for bowhunters. **Technical:** Grinds A2; uses materials native to Scandinavia. **Prices:** Start at $250. **Remarks:** Part-time maker; first knife sold in 1985. **Mark:** Initials with arrow.

ANDERSON, EDWIN, c/o Glen Cove Sport Shop, 189 Forest Ave., Glen Cove, NY 11542/516-676-7120
Specialties: Hunters, fighters, boot knives and folders. **Patterns:** Standard patterns or customer designs. **Technical:** Grinds Stellite 6K, ATS-34, and 440C. Offers integral patterns. **Prices:** $200 to $500; some to $1,500. **Remarks:** Full-time gunsmith, part-time knifemaker; first knife sold in 1977. **Mark:** Name over state.

ANDERSON, GARY D., RD 2, Box 2399C, Spring Grove, PA 17362-9802/717-229-2665
Specialties: Art-quality blades, folders and working knives. **Patterns:** Traditional and classic designs; customer patterns welcome. **Technical:** Forges Damascus and carbon steels. Offers silver inlay, mokume, filework, checkering. **Prices:** $250 to $750; some higher. **Remarks:** Full-time maker; first knife sold in 1985. **Mark:** GAND, MS.

ANDERSON, MEL, 1718 Lee Lane, Cedaredge, CO 81413/970-856-6465; FAX: 970-856-6465
Specialties: Full-size, miniature and one-of-a-kind straight knives and folders of his design. **Patterns:** Bowies, daggers, fighters, hunters and pressure folders. **Technical:** Grinds 440C, 5160, D2, 1095 and Damascus; offers antler, ivory and wood carved handles. **Prices:** Start at $145. **Remarks:** Full-time maker; first knife sold in 1987. **Mark:** Scratchy Hand.

ANDERSON, MICHAEL D., 2227 Spanish Trail, Arlington, TX 76013/817-274-3398
Specialties: Working and using straight knives of his design. **Patterns:** Hunters, Bowies, utility/camp knives and some fighters. **Technical:** Grinds D2, O1. All knives are individually ground using true North American Indian flaking styles. **Prices:** $175 to $350; some to $800. **Remarks:** Part-time maker; first knife sold in 1985. Doing business as Flint Steel Knives. **Mark:** Stylized initials.

ANDERSON, VIRGIL W., 16318 SE Taggart, Portland, OR 97236/503-761-4053
Specialties: Working straight knives of his design; fancy knives. **Patterns:** Bowies, boots, hunters and push knives. **Technical:** Grinds D2, 154CM and F8 Silvanite. **Prices:** $100 to $250; some to $500. **Remarks:** Part-time maker; first knife sold in 1984. **Mark:** Last name.

ANDRESS KNIVES (See Andress, Ronnie)

ANDRESS, RONNIE, 415 Audubon Dr. N., Satsuma, AL 36572/334-675-7604
Specialties: Working straight knives in standard patterns. **Patterns:** Boots, Bowies, hunters, friction folders and camp knives. **Technical:** Forges 1095, 5160, O1 and his own Damascus. Offers filework and inlays. **Prices:** $125 to $500. **Remarks:** Part-time maker; first knife sold in 1983. Doing business as Andress Knives. **Mark:** Last name, J.S.

ANDREWS, DON, N. 5155 Ezy St., Coeur D'Alene, ID 83814/208-765-8844
Specialties: Plain and fancy folders and straight knives. **Technical:** Grinds D2, 440C, ATS-34; does lost wax casting for guards and pommels. **Prices:** Moderate to upscale. **Remarks:** Full-time maker; first knife sold in 1983. **Mark:** Name.

ANDREWS, ERIC, 132 Halbert St.., Grand Ledge, MI 48837/517-627-7304
Specialties: Traditional working and using straight knives of his design. **Patterns:** Full-tang hunters, skinners and utility knives. **Technical:** Forges carbon steel; heat-treats. All knives come with sheath; most handles are of wood. **Prices:** $80 to $160. **Remarks:** Part-time maker; first knife sold in 1990. Doing business as The Tinkers Bench.

ANGEL SWORD (See Watson, Daniel)

ANKROM, W.E., 14 Marquette Dr., Cody, WY 82414/307-587-3017
Specialties: Straight working knives and folders of his design. **Patterns:** Hunters, fighters, boots; lockbacks and liner locks. **Technical:** Grinds ATS-34 and commercial Damascus. **Prices:** Start at $300. **Remarks:** Full-time maker; first knife sold in 1975. **Mark:** Name, city, state.

ANTHONY, THOMAS (See Trujillo, Thomas A.)

ANTONIO JR., WILLIAM J., 14540 Stirrup Lane, Golts, MD 21635/410-755-6789
Specialties: Fancy working straight knives of his design. **Patterns:** Hunting, survival and fishing knives. **Technical:** Grinds D2, 440C and 154CM; offers stainless Damascus. **Prices:** $125 to $395; some to $900. **Remarks:** Part-time maker; first knife sold in 1978. **Mark:** Last name, city, state.

ANVIL HEAD FORGE (See Leone, Nick)

ANVILS EDGE, THE (See Smith, Raymond L.)

ANZA KNIVES (See Davis, Charlie)

AOUN, CHARLES, 570 Massachusetts Ave., Boston, MA 02118/617-247-2431; FAX: 617-247-2431
Specialties: Classic and fancy straight knives of his design. **Patterns:** Fighters, hunters and personal knives. **Technical:** Grinds W2, 1095, ATS-34 and Damascus. Uses natural handle materials; embellishes with silver and semi-precious stones. **Prices:** Start at $290. **Remarks:** Part-time maker; first knife sold in 1995. Doing business as Galeb Knives. **Mark:** "G" stamped on ricasso or choil.

APPLETON, RAY, Box 321, Byers, CO 80103/303-822-5866
Specialties: One-of-a-kind folding knives. **Patterns:** Unique multi-locks and high-tech patterns. **Technical:** All parts machined or ground; likes D2. **Prices:** Start at $500. **Remarks:** Spare-time maker; first knife sold in 1986. **Mark:** Initials connected in arrowhead, date.

ARC MOUNTAIN FORGE (See Dearing, John)

ARNOLD, JOE, 47 Patience Cres., London, Ont., CANADA N6E 2K7/519-686-2623; FAX: 519-649-6553
Specialties: Traditional working and using straight knives of his design and to customer specs. **Patterns:** Fighters, hunters and Bowies. **Technical:** Grinds 440C, ATS-34 and 5160. **Prices:** $75 to $500; some to $2,500. **Remarks:** Part-time maker; first knife sold in 1988. **Mark:** Last name, country.

ARROW FORGE (See Harless, Walt)

ARROWOOD, DALE, 556 Lassetter Rd., Sharpsburg, GA 30277/404-253-9672
Specialties: Fancy and traditional straight knives of his design and to customer specs. **Patterns:** Bowies, fighters and hunters. **Technical:** Grinds ATS-34 and 440C; forges high-carbon steel. Engraves and scrimshaws. **Prices:** $125 to $200; some to $245. **Remarks:** Part-time maker; first knife sold in 1989. **Mark:** Anvil with an arrow through it; Old English "Arrowood Knives."

ART OF ISHI (See Cook, Mike A.)

ASHBY, DOUGLAS, 10123 Deermont, Dallas, TX 75243/214-238-7531
Specialties: Traditional and fancy straight knives of his design or to customer specs. **Patterns:** Hunters, fighters and utility/camp knives. **Technical:** Grinds 440C, ATS-34 and commercial Damascus. **Prices:** $75 to $200; some to $500. **Remarks:** Part-time maker; first knife sold in 1990. **Mark:** Name, city.

ASHLEY FORGE (See Bartrug, Hugh E.)

ASHWORTH, BOYD, 3135 Barrett Ct., Powder Springs, GA 30073/770-943-4963
Specialties: Fancy Damascus locking folders. **Patterns:** Fighters, hunters and gents. **Technical:** Forges own Damascus; offers filework; uses exotic handle materials. **Prices:** $500 to $2,500. **Remarks:** Part-time maker; first knife sold in 1993. **Mark:** Last name.

ATHENS FORGE (See Fannin, David A.)

ATHERN FORGE (See Sanders, A.A.)

ATKINSON, DICK, General Delivery, Wausau, FL 32463/904-638-8524
Specialties: Working straight knives and folders of his design; some fancy. **Patterns:** Hunters, fighters, boots; locking folders in interframes. **Technical:** Grinds A2, 440C and 154CM. Likes filework. **Prices:** $85 to $300; some exceptional knives. **Remarks:** Full-time maker; first knife sold in 1977. **Mark:** Name, city, state.

AYARRAGARAY, CRISTIAN L., Buenos Aires 250, (3100) Parana-Entre Rios, ARGENTINA/043-231753
Specialties: Traditional working straight knives of his design. **Patterns:** Fishing and hunting knives. **Technical:** Grinds and forges carbon steel. Uses native Argentine woods and deer antler. **Prices:** $150 to $250; some to $400. **Remarks:** Full-time maker; first knife sold in 1980. **Mark:** Last name, signature.

b

BABCOCK, RAYMOND G., Rt. 1, Box 328A, Vincent, OH 45784/614-678-2688
Specialties: Fancy working straight knives and some folders of his design or to customer specs. **Patterns:** Hunters and Bowies. **Technical:** Grinds L6. **Prices:** $95 to $450. **Remarks:** Full-time maker; first knife sold in 1973. **Mark:** First initial, last name.

BACHE-WIIG, TOM, N-5966 Eivindvik, NORWAY/4757784290; FAX: 4757784122
Specialties: High-art and working knives of his design. **Patterns:** Hunters, utility knives, hatchets, axes and art knives. **Technical:** Grinds Uddeholm Elmax, powder metallurgy tool stainless steel. Handles made of rear burls of Nordic woods stabilized with vacuum/high-pressure technique. **Prices:** $430 to $900; some to $2,300. **Remarks:** Part-time maker; first knife sold 1988. **Mark:** Etched name and eagle head.

BAILEY, JOSEPH D., 3213 Jonesboro Dr., Nashville, TN 37214/615-889-3172
Specialties: Working and using straight knives; collector pieces. **Patterns:** Bowies, hunters, fillet knives and personal knives. **Technical:** 440C, ATS-34, Damascus and wire Damascus. Offers scrimshaw. **Prices:** $65 to $175; some to $500. **Remarks:** Part-time maker; first knife sold in 1988. **Mark:** First and middle initials, last name—Custom Made.

BAILEY, KIRBY C., 2055 F.M. 2790 W., Lytle, TX 78052/210-772-3376
Specialties: Automatic folders and miniatures. **Patterns:** Hunting folders and double-bladed lockbacks; uses all his own patterns. **Technical:** Grinds ATS-34, 440C and O1 tool steel. Offers filework on liners, backlocks and blades. Handles made with natural materials. Scrimshaws, engraves and heat-treats. **Prices:** $185 to $650; large fighters to $800; miniatures $35 to $75. **Remarks:** Full-time maker; first knife sold 1959. Doing business as Hand Made Knives. **Mark:** Initials with serial number.

BAKER, HERB, 326 S. Hamilton St., Eden, NC 27288/910-627-0338; FAX: 910-823-8988

BAKER, RAY, P.O. Box 303, Sapulpa, OK 74067/918-224-8013
Specialties: High-tech working straight knives. **Patterns:** Hunters, fighters, Bowies, skinners and boots of his design and to customer specs. **Technical:** Grinds 440C, 1095 spring steel or customer request; heat-treats. Custom-made scabbards for any knife. **Prices:** $40 to $300; some to $1,000. **Remarks:** Full-time maker; first first knife sold in 1981. **Mark:** First initial, last name.

BAKER, VANCE, 574 Co. Rd., 675, Riceville, TN 37370/423-745-9157
Specialties: Traditional working straight knives of his design and to customer specs. Prefers drop-point hunters and small Bowies. **Patterns:** Hunters, utility and kitchen knives. **Technical:** Forges Damascus, cable, L6 and 5160. **Prices:** $100 to $250; some to $500. **Remarks:** Part-time maker; first knife sold in 1985. **Mark:** Initials connected.

BAKER, WILD BILL, Box 361, Boiceville, NY 12412/914-657-8646
Specialties: Primitive knives, buckskinners. **Patterns:** Skinners, camp knives and Bowies. **Technical:** Works with L6, files and rasps. **Prices:** $100 to $350. **Remarks:** Part-time maker; first knife sold in 1989. **Mark:** Oak leaf.

BALBACH, MARKUS, Friedrichstrasse 2, 35789 Weilmunster-Laubuseschbach/Ts., GERMANY/06475-8911; FAX: 912986
Specialties: High-art knives and working/using straight knives and folders of his design and to customer specs. **Patterns:** Hunters and daggers. **Technical:** Forges and grinds Damascus steel. **Prices:** $250 to $600; some to $2,000. **Remarks:** Full-time maker; first knife sold in 1984. Doing business as Kunst-und Damastschmiede M. Balbach. **Mark:** Initials stamped inside the handle.

BALDWIN, PHILLIP, P.O. Box 563, Snohomish, WA 98290/425-334-5569
Specialties: One-of-a-kind elegant table cutlery; exotics. **Patterns:** Elegant or exotic knives. Likes the challenge of axes, spears and specialty tools. **Technical:** Forges W2, W1 and his own pattern welded steel and mokume-gane. **Prices:** Start at $1,000. **Remarks:** Full-time maker; first knife sold in 1973. **Mark:** Last initial marked with chisel.

BALDY MOUNTAIN FORGE (See Dunkerley, Rick)

BALL CUSTOM KNIVES (See Ball, Ken)

BALL, KEN, 127 Sundown Manor, Mooresville, IN 46158/317-834-4803
Specialties: Classic working/using straight knives of his design and to customer specs. **Patterns:** Hunters and utility/camp knives. **Technical:** Flat-grinds ATS-34. Offers filework. **Prices:** $150 to $400. **Remarks:** Part-time maker; first knife sold in 1994. Doing business as Ball Custom Knives. **Mark:** Last name.

BALL, ROBERT, 809 W. 7th Ave., Port Angeles, WA 98362/360-457-0315
Specialties: Classic straight knives; working/using knives of all designs. **Patterns:** Bowies, hunters and fillets. **Technical:** Grinds ATS-34. Uses local Olympic hardwoods, stabilized woods, horn and antler. **Prices:** $225 to $1,700. **Remarks:** Part-time maker; first knife sold in 1990. Doing business as Olympic Knives. **Mark:** First initial, last name.

BALLESTRA, SANTINO, via D. Tempesta 11/17, 18039 Ventimiglia (IM), ITALY/0184-215228
Specialties: Using and collecting straight knives. **Patterns:** Hunting, fighting, skinners, Bowies, medieval daggers and knives. **Technical:** Forges ATS-34, D2, O2, 1060 and his own Damascus. Uses ivory and silver. **Prices:** $500 to $2,000; some higher. **Remarks:** Full-time maker; first knife sold in 1979. **Mark:** First initial, last name.

BALLEW, DALE, P.O. Box 1277, Bowling Green, VA 22427/804-633-5701
Specialties: Miniatures only to customer specs. **Patterns:** Bowies, daggers and fighters. **Technical:** Files 440C stainless; uses ivory, abalone, exotic woods and some precious stones. **Prices:** $100 to $800. **Remarks:** Part-time maker; first knife sold in 1988. **Mark:** Initials and last name.

BAM FORGE (See Milford, Brian A.)

BANAITIS, ROMAS, 516 East 2nd Street, So. Boston, MA 02127/617-464-4193
Specialties: Fantasy straight knives and folders of his design. **Patterns:** Daggers, fighters and locking folders. **Technical:** Forges and grinds O1, cable and motorcycle chain. Carves handles and fittings. **Prices:** $300 to $1,000. **Remarks:** Part-time maker; first knife sold in 1996. Doing business as Centipede Arms. **Mark:** First initial in center of centipede.

BANDIT BLADES (See Roberts, George A.)

BANKS, DAVID L., 99 Blackfoot Ave., #3, Riverton, WY 82501/307-856-3154
Specialties: Heavy-duty working straight knives. **Patterns:** Hunters, Bowies and camp knives. **Technical:** Forges 5160 and 52100. Handles made of horn, antlers and exotic wood. Hand-stitched harness leather sheaths. **Prices:** $200 to $500; some higher. **Remarks:** Part-time maker. **Mark:** Initials connected.

BARBEE, JIM, RR 1, Box B, Ft. Stockton, TX 79735/915-336-2882
Specialties: Texas-type hunter's knives. **Patterns:** Solid using patterns. **Technical:** Grinds 440C; likes stag, Micarta and ivory. **Prices:** $125 to $200; some to $500. **Remarks:** Full-time maker and heat-treater. First knife sold in the '60s. **Mark:** Name, city.

BARBER, ROBERT E., 1828 Franklin Dr., Charlottesville, VA 22911-8513/804-295-4036
Specialties: Working straight knives and trapper pocketknives, some fancy with filework. **Patterns:** Hunters, skinners, combat knives/fighters and Bowies. **Technical:** Grinds ATS-34, 440C, D2 and A2. **Prices:** $35 to $800. **Remarks:** Part-time maker; first knife sold in 1984. **Mark:** Initials within rebel hat logo.

BARDSLEY, NORMAN P., 197 Cottage St., Pawtucket, RI 02860/401-725-9132
Specialties: Working and fantasy knives. **Patterns:** Fighters, tantos, boots in renaissance and fantasy fashion; upscale display and presentation pieces. **Technical:** Grinds 440C, ATS-34, O1 and Damascus. Uses exotic hides for sheaths. **Prices:** $100 to $15,000. **Remarks:** Full-time maker. **Mark:** Last name in script with logo.

BARE KNIVES (See Stevens, Barry B.)

BAREFOOT, JOE W., 117 Oakbrook Dr., Liberty, SC 29657
Specialties: Working straight knives of his design. **Patterns:** Hunters, fighters and boots; tantos and survival knives. **Technical:** Grinds D2, 440C and ATS-34. Mirror finishes. Uses ivory and stag on customer request only. **Prices:** $50 to $160; some to $500. **Remarks:** Part-time maker; first knife sold in 1980. **Mark:** Bare footprint.

BARKER, ROBERT G., 2311 Branch Rd., Bishop, GA 30621/706-769-7827
Specialties: Traditional working/using straight knives of his design. **Patterns:** Bowies, hunters and utility knives. **Technical:** Forges to shape high-carbon 5160, cable and chain. Differentially heat-treats. **Prices:** $200 to $500; some to $1,000. **Remarks:** Spare-time maker; first knife sold in 1987. **Mark:** Last name.

BARLOW, KEN, 3800 Rohner St., Fortuna, CA 95540/707-725-3106
Specialties: Working straight knives and folders, some fancy. **Patterns:** Hunters, Bowies, skinners and locking folders. **Technical:** Grinds ATS-34, 440C and D2. Heat-treats, engraves and scrimshaws. Prefers mirror finishes and hollow-grinds. **Prices:** $100 to $250; some higher. **Remarks:** Part-time maker; first knife sold in 1980. **Mark:** Stylized initials.

BARNES, AUBREY G., 11341 Rock Hill Road, Hagerstown, MD 21740/301-791-1647
Specialties: Classic working and using knives of his design, to customer specs and in standard patterns. **Patterns:** Bowies, hunters, fighters, daggers and utility/camping knives. **Technical:** Forges 5160, 1085, 06 and Damascus. Silver-wire inlays. **Prices:** $300 to $2,500. **Remarks:** Full-time maker; first knife sold in 1992. Doing business as Falling Waters Forge. **Mark:** First and middle initials, last name, M.S.

BARNES CUSTOM KNIVES, JIM (See Barnes, Jim)

BARNES, GARY L., 305 Church St., Box 138, New Windsor, MD 21776/410-635-6243; FAX: 410-635-6243
Specialties: Color anodized aluminum button-lock folders. **Patterns:** Folders only. **Technical:** Mostly forges his own Damascus; uses exotic handle materials; creates unique locking mechanisms. Most knives are embellished. **Prices:** Start at $250. **Remarks:** Full-time maker. First knife sold in 1976. **Mark:** Name or an ornate last initial with a dagger.

BARNES, JACK, P.O. Box 1315, Whitefish, MT 59937-1315/406-862-6078

BARNES, JIM, 2909 Forest Trail, San Angelo, TX 76904/915-944-2239
Specialties: Traditional and working straight, folders and automatic knives of all designs. **Patterns:** Automatics, hunters and locking folders. **Technical:** Grinds ATS-34, 440C and D2; heat-treats. All folders have filework. Offers hand-tooled sheaths with basket weave. Engraves some knife bolsters. **Prices:** $95 to $350; some to $1,000. **Remarks:** Full-time maker; first knife sold in 1984. Doing business as Jim Barnes Custom Knives. **Mark:** Logo with name, city, state.

BARNETT, VAN, 168 Riverbend Blvd., Saint Albans, WV 25177/304-727-5512
Specialties: Investor-grade one-of-a-kind daggers and fighters. **Patterns:** Folders, miniatures and hunters. **Technical:** Grinds 440C, D2, Damascus and ATS-34; carves; engraves. **Prices:** Start at $200. **Remarks:** Full-time maker; first knife sold in 1981. **Mark:** First and middle initials, last name.

BARNGROVER, JERRY, RR #4, Box 1230, Afton, OK 74331/918-257-5076

BARR, A.T., P.O. Box 828, Nicholasville, KY 40340-0828/606-885-1042; WEB: http://www.customknives.com
Specialties: Working and collector-grade liner lock folders and sheath knives. **Patterns:** Liner lock folders, hunters and fighters. **Technical:** Flat-grinds ATS-34, 440V, D2, A2 and O1; hand-rubbed satin or bead blasted finish. **Prices:** Start at $225. **Remarks:** Part-time maker; first knife sold in 1979. **Mark:** Full name, city and state.

BARR CUSTOM KNIVES (See Quarton, Barr)

BARRETT, CECIL TERRY, 2514 Linda Lane, Colorado Springs, CO 80909/719-473-8325
Specialties: Working and using straight knives and folders of his design, to customer specs and in standard patterns. **Patterns:** Bowies, hunters, kitchen knives, locking folders and slip-joint folders. **Technical:** Grinds 440C, D2 and ATS-34. Wood and leather sheaths. **Prices:** $65 to $500; some to $750. **Remarks:** Full-time maker. **Mark:** Stamped middle name.

BARRETT, R.W., P.O. Box 304, Madison, AL 35758-0304/205-539-3439
Specialties: Traditional and fancy straight knives. Makes standard patterns and one-of-a-kinds. **Patterns:** Hunters, fighters, skinners and art knives. **Technical:** Grinds 440C, ATS-34 and O1. Scrimshaws and offers photography. **Prices:** $150 to $250; some to $500. **Remarks:** Spare-time maker; first knife sold in 1989. **Mark:** First and middle initials, last name, city, state.

BARRETT-SMYTHE (See Howard, Durvyn M.)

BARRON, BRIAN, 123 12th Ave., San Mateo, CA 94402/415-341-2683
Specialties: Traditional straight knives. **Patterns:** Daggers, hunters and swords. **Technical:** Grinds 440C, ATS-34 and 1095. Sculpts bolsters using an S-curve. **Prices:** $130 to $270; some to $1,500. **Remarks:** Part-time maker; first knife sold in 1993. **Mark:** Diamond Drag "Barron."

BARRY, JAMES J., P.O. Box 1571, West Palm Beach, FL 33402/561-832-4197
Specialties: High-art working straight knives of his design. **Patterns:** Hunters, daggers and fishing knives. **Technical:** Grinds 440C only. Prefers exotic materials for handles. Most knives embellished with filework, carving and scrimshaw. Many pieces designed to stand unassisted. **Prices:** $100 to $500; some to $5,000. **Remarks:** Part-time maker; first knife sold in 1975. **Mark:** Branded initials.

BARTLOW, JOHN, 111 Orchard Rd., Box 568, Norris, TN 37828/423-494-9421
Specialties: Working straight knives, some fancy. **Patterns:** Working hunters, skinners, capers, bird and trout knives, saltwater fillets. **Technical:** Grinds 440C and ATS-34; uses Tim Zowada and Jerry Rados Damascus. **Prices:** $150 to $1,500. **Remarks:** Part-time maker; first knife sold in 1979. Field-tests knives. **Mark:** Last name.

BARTRUG, HUGH E., 2701 34th St. N., #142, St. Petersburg, FL 33713/813-323-1136
Specialties: Inlaid straight knives and exotic folders; high-art knives and period pieces. **Patterns:** Hunters, Bowies and daggers; traditional patterns. **Technical:** Diffuses mokume. Forges 100 percent nickel, wrought iron, mosiac Damascus, shokeedo and O1 tool steel; grinds. **Prices:** $210 to $2,500; some to $5,000. **Remarks:** Retired maker; first knife sold in 1980. **Mark:** Ashley Forge or name.

BASKETT, LEE GENE, 427 Sutzer Ck. Rd., Eastview, KY 42732/502-862-5019
Specialties: Fancy working knives and fantasy pieces, often set up in desk stands. **Patterns:** Fighters, Bowies and survival knives; locking folders, butterflies and traditional styles. **Technical:** Grinds O1, 440C; buys Damascus. Filework provided on most knives. **Prices:** Start at $95. **Remarks:** Part-time maker; first knife sold in 1980. **Mark:** Last name.

BATCHELOR, RITCHIE, 308 Honeysuckle Trail, Salley, SC 29137/803-564-3247
Specialties: Traditional working/using straight knives and folders of his design and to customer specs. **Patterns:** Hunters, locking folders and utility/camp knives. **Technical:** ATS-34, 440C and O1. Prefers tapered tang, mirror, satin and bead blasted blade finish. **Prices:** $50 to $150; some to $250. **Remarks:** Part-time maker; first knife sold in 1994. **Mark:** Last name in script on left side of blade. First 100 knives sold are marked with Cody.

BATSON, JAMES, 176 Brentwood, Madison, AL 35758/205-971-6860
Specialties: Forged Damascus blades and fittings in collectible period pieces. **Patterns:** Integral art knives, Bowies, folders, American-styled blades and miniatures. **Technical:** Forges 52100, 5160 and his Damascus. **Prices:** $150 to $1,800; some to $4,500. **Remarks:** Full-time maker; first knife sold in 1978. **Mark:** Name, bladesmith with horse's head.

BATSON, RICHARD G., 6591 Waterford Rd., Rixeyville, VA 22737/540-937-5932
Specialties: Military, utility and fighting knives in working and presentation grade. **Patterns:** Daggers, combat and utility knives. **Technical:** Grinds O1, 1095 and 440C. Etches and scrimshaws; offers polished, Parkerized finishes. **Prices:** $175 to $350; some to $900. **Remarks:** Full-time maker. First knife sold in 1958. **Mark:** Bat in circle, hand-signed and serial numbered.

BATTS, KEITH, Rt. 1, Box 266E, Hooks, TX 75561/903-832-1140
Specialties: Working straight knives of his design or to customer specs. **Patterns:** Bowies, hunters, skinners, camp knives and others. **Technical:** Forges 5160 and his Damascus; offers filework. **Prices:** $245 to $895. **Remarks:** Part-time maker; first knife sold in 1988. **Mark:** Last name.

BAUCHOP HANDMADE KNIVES, ROBERT (See Bauchop, Robert)

BAUCHOP, PETER, Germiston, SOUTH AFRICA. c/o Beck's Cutlery Specialties, 748-F E. Chatham St., Cary, NC 27511/919-460-0203
Specialties: Working straight knives and period pieces. **Patterns:** Fighters, swords and survival knives. **Technical:** Grinds O1, D2, G3, 440C and ATS-34. Scrimshaws. **Prices:** $100 to $350; some to $1,500. **Remarks:** Full-time maker; first knife sold in 1980. **Mark:** Bow and axe (BOW-CHOP).

BAUCHOP, ROBERT, P.O. Box 9821, Elsburg 1407, SOUTH AFRICA/011-824-1300; FAX: 011-824-2662
Specialties: Fantasy knives; working and using knives of his design and to customer specs. **Patterns:** Hunters, swords, utility/camp knives, diver's knives and large swords. **Technical:** Grinds Sandvick 12C27, D2, 440C. Uses South African hardwoods—red ivory, wild olive, African blackwood, etc.—on handles. **Prices:** $200 to $800; some to $2,000. **Remarks:** Full-time maker; first knife sold in 1986. Doing business as Robert Bauchop Handmade Knives. **Mark:** Viking helmet with Bauchop (bow and chopper) crest.

BAYOU CUSTOM CUTLERY (See Dake, C.M.)

BEAM, JOHN R., 1310 Foothills Rd., Kalispell, MT 59901/406-755-2593
Specialties: Classic, high-art and working straight knives of his design. **Patterns:** Bowies and hunters. **Technical:** Grinds 440C, Damascus and scrap. **Prices:** $175 to $600; some to $3,000. **Remarks:** Part-time maker; first knife sold in 1996. Doing business as Beam's Knives. **Mark:** Beam's Knives.

BEAM'S KNIVES (See Beam, John R.)

BEAR KNIVES (See Goode, Bear)

BEAR RUN KNIFE (See Thill, Jim)

BEAR'S CUTLERY (See Jensen Jr., Carl A.)

BEATTY, GORDON H., 121 Petty Rd., Seneca, SC 29672/864-882-6278
Specialties: Working straight knives, some fancy. **Patterns:** Traditional patterns, mini-skinners and letter openers. **Technical:** Grinds 440C, D2 and ATS-34; makes knives one at a time. **Prices:** $45 to $200; some to $450. **Remarks:** Part-time maker; first knife sold in 1982. **Mark:** Name.

BEAUCHAMP, GAETAN, 125, de la Rivière, Stoneham, PQ. CANADA G0A 4P0/418-848-1914; FAX: 418-848-6859
Specialties: Working knives and folders of his design and to customer specs. **Patterns:** Hunters, fighters, fantasy knives. **Technical:** Grinds ATS-34, 440C, Damascus. Scrimshaws on ivory; specializes in buffalo horn and black backgrounds. Offers a variety of handle materials. **Prices:** Start at $125. **Remarks:** Full-time maker; first knife sold in 1992. **Mark:** Signature etched on blade.

BEAVER, D. "BUTCH" AND JUDY, 48835 N. 25 Ave. Phoenix, AZ 85027/602-465-7831; FAX: 602-465-7077
Specialties: Straight knives, daggers and "see-thru" titanium art folders. **Patterns:** No models or standard designs; prefer custom orders. **Technical:** Grind 440C and ATS-34. Most knives are embellished. **Prices:** $135 to $800; some much higher. **Remarks:** Full-time makers. First D. Beaver knife sold in 1979; first J. Beaver knife sold in 1984. **Mark:** Name, city, state with desert scene.

BEAVER, JUDY (See Beaver, D. "Butch" and Judy)

BECKER, FRANZ, AM Kreuzberg 2, 84533 Marktl/Inn, GERMANY/08678-8020
Specialties: Stainless steel knives in working sizes. **Patterns:** Semi- and full-integral knives; interframe folders. **Technical:** Grinds stainless steels; likes natural handle materials. **Prices:** $200 to $2,000. **Mark:** Name, country.

BECKETT KNIVES, NORM (See Beckett, Norman L.)

BECKETT, NORMAN L., 1501 N. Chaco Ave., Farmington, NM 87401/505-325-4468
Specialties: Fancy, traditional and working straight knives of his design. **Patterns:** Bowies, fighters and hunters. **Technical:** Grinds ATS-34, 440C and Damascus. File works blades; hollow and flat grinds. Prefers mirror finishes. Uses exotic handle material and stabilized woods. Hand-tooled or inlaid sheaths. **Prices:** $150 to $900; some to $2,500 and up. **Remarks:** Full-time maker; first knife sold in 1993. Doing business as Norm Beckett Knives. **Mark:** First and last name, maker, city and state.

BEERS, RAY, 8 Manorbrook Rd., Monkton, MD 21111 (summer)/410-472-2229; FAX: 410-472-9136
Specialties: Working straight knives, some fancy. **Patterns:** All fighters and tantos are popular. **Technical:** Grinds all steels; many patterns have a palm hunter handle. **Prices:** $100 to $5,000. **Remarks:** Full-time maker; first knife sold in 1976. **Mark:** Initials connected.

BEERS, RAY, 2501 Lakefront Dr., Lake Wales, FL 33853 (winter)/941-696-3036; FAX: 941-696-9421

BEHNKE, WILLIAM, P.O. Box 174, Lake City, MI 49651/616-839-3342
Specialties: Hunters, belt knives and folders. **Patterns:** Traditional styling in moderate-sized straight and folding knives. **Technical:** Forges his own Damascus, cable, saw chain and 5160; likes brass and natural materials. **Prices:** $100 to $1,500. **Remarks:** Part-time maker. **Mark:** Name.

BELL, DONALD, 2 Division St., Bedford, Nova Scotia, B4A 1Y8 CANADA/902-835-2623
Specialties: Fancy knives; working/using straight knives and folders of his design. **Patterns:** Hunters, locking folders, jewelry knives. **Technical:** Grinds Damascus and ATS-34; forges and grinds O1; pierces and carves blades. **Prices:** $150 to $650; some to $1,200. **Remarks:** Spare-time maker; first knife sold in 1993. **Mark:** Bell symbol with first initial inside.

BELL, MICHAEL, Rt. 1, Box 1220, Coquille, OR 97423/541-396-3605; E-Mail: bell@harborside.com
Specialties: Full line of traditional Japanese swords. **Patterns:** Tantos and Katanas in various styles. **Technical:** Uses own special steel; all blades forge-welded. **Prices:** $750 to $10,000. **Remarks:** Full-time maker; first knife sold in 1972. Served apprenticeship with Japanese swordmaker. Doing business as Dragonfly Forge. **Mark:** Kuni Mitsu or Dragonfly.

BENJAMIN JR., GEORGE, 3001 Foxy Lane, Kissimmee, FL 34746/407-846-7259
Specialties: Fighters in various styles to include Persian, Moro and military. **Patterns:** Daggers, skinners and one-of-a-kind grinds. **Technical:** Forges O1, D2, A2, 5160 and Damascus. Favors Pakkawood, Micarta, and mirror or Parkerized finishes. Makes unique para-military leather sheaths. **Prices:** $150 to $600; some to $1,200. **Remarks:** Doing business as The Leather Box. **Mark:** Southern Pride Knives.

BENNETT, PETER, P.O. Box 143, Engadine N.S.W. 2233, AUSTRALIA/02-520-4975 (home), 02-528-8219 (work)
Specialties: Fancy and embellished working and using straight knives to customer specs and in standard patterns. **Patterns:** Fighters, hunters, bird/trout and fillet knives. **Technical:** Grinds 440C, ATS-34 and Damascus. Uses rare Australian desert timbers for handles. **Prices:** $90 to $500; some to $1,500. **Remarks:** Full-time maker; first knife sold in 1985. **Mark:** First and middle initials, last name; country.

BENSON, DON, 2505 Jackson St., #112, Escalon, CA 95320/209-838-7921
Specialties: Working straight knives of his design. **Patterns:** Axes, Bowies, tantos and hunters. **Technical:** Grinds 440C. **Prices:** $100 to $150; some to $400. **Remarks:** Spare-time maker; first knife sold in 1980. **Mark:** Name.

BER, DAVE, 2230 Miller Rd., San Juan Island, WA 98250/206-378-7230
Specialties: Working straight knives for the sportsman; camp knives. Welcomes customer designs. **Patterns:** Hunters, Bowies, kitchen and fishing knives. **Technical:** Forges and grinds saw blade steel, welded wire Damascus, O1, L6 and 440C. **Prices:** $100 to $200; some to $500. **Remarks:** Full-time maker; first knife sold in 1985. Doing business as Cloudy Mt. Iron Works. **Mark:** Name.

BERGER, MAX A., 5716 John Richard Ct., Carmichael, CA 95608/916-972-9229
Specialties: Fantasy and working/using straight knives of his design. **Patterns:** Fighters, hunters and utility/camp knives. **Technical:** Grinds ATS-34 and 440C. Offers fileworks and combinations of mirror polish and satin finish blades. **Prices:** $200 to $600; some to $2,500. **Remarks:** Part-time maker; first knife sold in 1992. **Mark:** Last name.

BERTHOLUS, BERNARD 4, Rue du Petit Four, 06600 Antibes, FRANCE/04 93 34 18 12
Specialties: Traditional working and using straight knives of his design. **Patterns:** Bowies, daggers and hunters. **Technical:** Forges ATS-34, 440, D2 and carbon steels. **Prices:** $120 to $150; some to $400. **Remarks:** Full-time maker; first knife sold in 1990. **Mark:** City and last name.

BERTUZZI, ETTORE, Via Partigiani 3, 24068 Seriate (Bergamo) ITALY/035-294262; FAX: 035-294262
Specialties: Classic straight knives and folders of his design, to customer specs and in standard patterns. **Patterns:** Bowies, hunters and locking folders. **Technical:** Grinds ATS-34, D2 and O1. **Prices:** $200 to $300. **Remarks:** Part-time maker; first knife sold in 1993. **Mark:** Name and year etched on ricasso in script.

BESEDICK, FRANK E., RR 2, Box 802, Ruffsdale, PA 15679/412-696-3312
Specialties: Traditional working and using straight knives of his design. **Patterns:** Hunters, utility/camp knives and miniatures; buckskinner blades and tomahawks. **Technical:** Forges and grinds 5160, O1 and Damascus. Offers filework and scrimshaw. **Prices:** $75 to $300; some to $750. **Remarks:** Part-time maker; first knife sold in 1990. **Mark:** Name or initials.

BETHKE, LORA, 13420 Lincoln St., Grand Haven, MI 49417/616-842-8268; FAX: 616-865-3170
Specialties: Classic and traditional straight knives of his design. **Patterns:** Boots, Bowies and hunters. **Technical:** Forges 5160. **Prices:** Start at $175. **Remarks:** Part-time maker; first knife sold in 1997. **Mark:** Full name.

BEUKES, TINUS, 83 Henry St., Risiville, Vereeniging 1939, Republic of South Africa/016-232053
Specialties: Working straight knives. **Patterns:** Hunters, skinners and kitchen knives. **Technical:** Grinds D2, 440C and Damascus. **Prices:** $80 to $180. **Remarks:** Part-time maker; first knife sold in 1993. **Mark:** Full name, city, logo.

BEVERLY II, LARRY H., P.O. Box 741, Spotsylvania, VA 22553/540-898-3951
Specialties: Working straight knives, slip-joints and liner locks. Welcomes customer designs. **Patterns:** Bowies, hunters, guardless fighters and miniatures. **Technical:** Grinds 440C, A2 and O1. **Prices:** $65 to $400. **Remarks:** Part-time maker; first knife sold in 1986. **Mark:** Initials or last name in script.

BEZUIDENHOUT, BUZZ, 30 Surlingham Ave., Malvern, Queensburgh, Natal 4093, SOUTH AFRICA/031-444098; 031-3631259
Specialties: Traditional working and using straight knives of his design and to customer specs. **Patterns:** Boots, hunters, kitchen knives and utility/camp knives. **Technical:** Grinds 12C27, 440C and ATS-34. Uses local hardwoods, horn—kudu, impala, buffalo—giraffe bone and ivory for handles. **Prices:** $150 to $200; some to $1,500. **Remarks:** Spare-time maker; first knife sold in 1988. **Mark:** First name with a bee emblem.

BIG JOE'S CUSTOM KNIVES (See Hintz, Gerald M.)

BIGHORN KNIFEWORKS (See Padilla, Gary)

BILLY'S BLACKSMITH SHOP (See Watson, Billy)

BILLY'S BLADES (See Ellis, William Dean)

BLACK, EARL, 3466 S. 700 East, Salt Lake City, UT 84106/801-466-8395
Specialties: High-art straight knives and folders; period pieces. **Patterns:** Boots, Bowies and daggers; lockers and gents. **Technical:** Grinds 440C and 154CM. Buys some Damascus. Scrimshaws and engraves. **Prices:** $200 to $1,800; some to $2,500 and higher. **Remarks:** Full-time maker; first knife sold in 1980. **Mark:** Name, city, state.

BLACK, SCOTT, 570 Malcom Rd., Covington, GA 30209
Specialties: Working/using folders of his design. **Patterns:** Daggers, hunters, utility/camp knives and friction folders. **Technical:** Forges pattern welded, cable, 1095, O1 and 5160. **Prices:** $100 to $500. **Remarks:** Part-time maker; first knife sold in 1992. Doing business as Copperhead Forge. **Mark:** Hot mark on blade, copperhead snake.

BLACK, TOM, 921 Grecian NW, Albuquerque, NM 87107/505-344-2549
Specialties: Working knives to fancy straight knives of his design. **Patterns:** Drop-point skinners, folders, using knives, Bowies and daggers. **Technical:** Grinds 440C, 154CM, ATS-34, A2, D2 and Damascus. Offers engraving and scrimshaw. **Prices:** $185 to $1,250; some over $7,500. **Remarks:** Full-time maker; first knife sold in 1970. **Mark:** Name, city, state.

BLACK FOREST BLADES (See Neering, Walt and Repke, Mike)

BLACK OAK BLADES (See Sjostrand, Kevin)

BLACKTON, ANDREW E., 12521 Fifth Isle, Bayonet Point, FL 34667/813-869-1406
Specialties: Straight and folding knives, some fancy. **Patterns:** Hunters, Bowies and daggers. **Technical:** Grinds D2, 440C and 154CM.Offers some embellishment. **Prices:** $125 to $450; some to $2,000. **Remarks:** Full-time maker. **Mark:** Last name in script.

BLADE LAIR, THE (See Mortenson, Ed)

BLADE RIGGER (See Piorek, James S.)

BLADECATCHER KNIVES (See Huddleston, Joe D.)

BLADESMITH'S INC. (See Kramer, Bob)

BLANCHARD, G.R. (Gary), 3025 Las Vegas Blvd., #120, Las Vegas, NV 89109/702-733-8333; FAX: 702-732-0333.
Specialties: Fancy and high-art straight knives of his design. **Patterns:** Boots, daggers and locking folders. **Technical:** Grinds 440C and ATS-34, O1 blueable. Engraves knives. **Prices:** $400 to $15,000; some to $18,000 or more. **Remarks:** Full-time maker; first knife sold in 1989. **Mark:** First and middle initials, last name.

BLASINGAME, ROBERT, 2906 Swanson Lane, Kilgore, TX 75662/903-983-3546
Specialties: Classic working and using straight knives and folders of his design and to customer specs. **Patterns:** Bowies, daggers, fighters and hunters; one-of-a-kind historic reproductions. **Technical:** Hand-forges P.W. Damascus, cable Damascus and chain Damascus. **Prices:** $150 to $1,000; some to $2,000. **Remarks:** Full-time maker; first knife sold in 1968. **Mark:** Large knives—last name over anvil; folders—initials.

BLAUM, ROY, 319 N. Columbia St., Covington, LA 70433/504-893-1060
Specialties: Working straight knives and folders of his design; lightweight easy-open folders. **Patterns:** Hunters, boots, fishing and woodcarving/whittling knives. **Technical:** Grinds A2, D2, O1, 154CM and ATS-34. Offers leatherwork. **Prices:** $40 to $800; some higher. **Remarks:** Full-time maker; first knife sold in 1976. **Mark:** Engraved signature or etched logo.

BLOMBERG, GREGG, Rt. 1, Box 1762, Lopez, WA 98261/206-468-2103
Specialties: Edged tools for carvers and sculptors. **Patterns:** Crooked knives; straight utilities; adzes. **Technical:** Forges and grinds W2, D2, 1095 and ATS-34. **Prices:** Straight knives average $160. **Remarks:** Full-time maker; first knife sold in 1978. Doing business as Kestrel Tool. **Mark:** Kestrel with flying falcon logo.

BLOOMER, ALAN T., RR 1, Box 108, Maquon, IL 61458/309-875-3583
Specialties: Working and using straight knives and folders of his design. **Patterns:** Lock-back folders and Damascus straight knives and folders. **Technical:** Grinds 440C, D2 and A2. Does own leatherwork. **Prices:** $85 to $450. **Remarks:** Part-time maker; first knife sold in 1986. **Mark:** Last name stamp.

BLUM, CHUCK, 743 S. Brea Blvd., #10, Brea, CA 92621/714-529-0484
Specialties: Art and investment daggers and Bowies. **Technical:** Flatgrinds; hollow-grinds 440C, ATS-34 on working knives. **Prices:** $125 to $8,500. **Remarks:** Part-time maker; first knife sold in 1985. **Mark:** First and middle initials and last name with sailboat logo.

BLUM, KENNETH, Rt. 6, Box 6033, Brenham, TX 77833/409-836-9577
Specialties: Traditional working straight knives of his design. **Patterns:** Camp knives, Hunters and Bowies. **Technical:** Forges 5160; grinds 440C and D2. Uses exotic woods and Micarta for handles. **Prices:** $150 to $300. **Remarks:** Part-time maker; first knife sold in 1978. **Mark:** Last name on ricasso.

BOARDMAN, GUY, 39 Mountain Ridge R., New Germany, 3619 SOUTH AFRICA/031-726-921
Specialties: American and South African styles. **Patterns:** Bowies, American and South African hunters, plus more. **Technical:** Grinds Bohler steels, some ATS-34. **Prices:** $100 to $600. **Remarks:** Part-time maker; first knife sold in 1986. **Mark:** Name, city, country.

BOATRIGHT, BASEL, 11 Timber Point, New Braunfels, TX 78132/210-609-0807
Specialties: Working and using knives of his design. **Patterns:** Hunters, skinners and utility/camp knives. **Technical:** Grinds and hand-tempers 5160. **Prices:** $75 to $300. **Remarks:** Part-time maker. **Mark:** Stamped BBB.

BOB-SKY KNIVES (See Hajovsky, Robert J.)

BOCHMAN, BRUCE, 183 Howard Place, Grants Pass, OR 97526/503-471-1985
Specialties: Working straight knives in standard patterns. **Patterns:** Bowies, hunters, fishing and bird knives. **Technical:** 440C; mirror or satin finish. **Prices:** $140 to $250; some to $750. **Remarks:** Part-time maker; first knife sold in 1977. **Mark:** Custom blades by B. Bochman.

BODEN, HARRY, Via Gellia Mill, Bonsall, Matlock, Derbyshire DE4 2AJ, ENGLAND/0629-825176
Specialties: Traditional working straight knives and folders of his design. **Patterns:** Hunters, locking folders and utility/camp knives. **Technical:** Grinds Sandvik 12C27, D2 and O1. **Prices:** £70 to £150; some to £300. **Remarks:** Full-time maker; first knife sold in 1986. **Mark:** Full name.

BODNER, GERALD "JERRY," 4102 Spyglass Ct., Louisville, KY 40229/502-968-5946
Specialties: Fantasy straight knives in standard patterns. **Patterns:** Bowies, fighters, hunters and micro-miniature knives. **Technical:** Grinds Damascus, 440C and D2. Offers filework. **Prices:** $35 to $180. **Remarks:** Part-time maker; first knife sold in 1993. **Mark:** Last name in script and JAB in oval above knives.

BODOLAY, ANTAL, Rua Wilson Soares Fernandes, #31, Planalto, Belo Horizonte, MG-31730-700, BRAZIL/031-494-1885
Specialties: Working folders and fixed blades of his design or to customer specs; some art daggers and period pieces. **Patterns:** Daggers, hunters, locking folders, utility knives and Khukris. **Technical:** Grinds D6, high carbon steels and 420 stainless. Forges files on request. **Prices:** $30 to $350. **Remarks:** Full-time maker; first knife sold in 1965. **Mark:** Last name in script.

BOEHLKE, GUENTER, Parkstrasse 2, 56412 Grossholbach, GERMANY/02602-5440
Specialties: Classic working/using straight knives of his design. **Patterns:** Hunters, utility/camp knives and ancient remakes. **Technical:** Grinds Damascus, CPM-T-440V and 440C. Inlays gemstones and ivory. **Prices:** $220 to $700; some to $2,000. **Remarks:** Spare-time maker; first knife sold in 1985. **Mark:** Name, address and bow and arrow.

BOGUSZEWSKI, PHIL, P.O. Box 99329, Tacoma, WA 98499/253-581-7096
Specialties: Working folders—some fancy—mostly of his design. **Patterns:** Folders, slip-joints and lockers; also makes anodized titanium frame folders. **Technical:** Grinds 440C; offers filework. **Prices:** $300 to $1,500. **Remarks:** Full-time maker; first knife sold in 1979. **Mark:** Name, city and state.

BOHRMANN, BRUCE, 29 Portland St., Yarmouth, ME 04096/207-846-3385
Specialties: Straight using sport knives. **Patterns:** Hunters, fishing, camp and steak knives. **Technical:** Grinds 154CM; likes wood handles. **Prices:** $350 to $450. **Remarks:** Full-time maker; first knife sold in 1976. **Mark:** Name, city and state.

BOJTOS, ÁRPÁD, Dobsinskeho 10, 98403 Lucenec, Slovakia, 98403/0042-863-23214
Specialties: Fantasy and high-art knives. **Patterns:** Daggers, fighters and hunters. **Technical:** Grinds ATS-34. Carves on steel, handle materials and sheaths. **Prices:** $2,000 to $5,000; some to $8,000. **Remarks:** Full-time maker; first knife sold in 1990. **Mark:** Stylized initials.

BOLD, STU, 63 D'Andrea Tr., Sarnia, Ont., N7S 6H3, CANADA/519-383-7610; E-MAIL: sbold@sar.hookup.net
Specialties: Traditional working/using straight knives in standard patterns and to customer specs. **Patterns:** Boots, Bowies and hunters. **Technical:** Grinds ATS-34, 440C and Damascus; mozaic pins. Offers scrimshaw and hand-tooled leather sheaths. **Prices:** $140 to $500; some to $2,000. **Remarks:** Part-time maker; first knife sold in 1983. **Mark:** Name, city, province.

BOLEWARE, DAVID, P.O. Box 96, Carson, MS 39427/601-943-5372
Specialties: Traditional and working/using straight knives of his design, to customer specs and in standard patterns. **Patterns:** Bowies, hunters and utility/camp knives. **Technical:** Grinds ATS-34, 440C and Damascus. **Prices:** $85 to $350; some to $600. **Remarks:** Part-time maker; first knife sold in 1989. **Mark:** First and last name, city, state.

BOLTON, CHARLES B., P.O. Box 6, Jonesburg, MO 63351/314-488-5785
Specialties: Working straight knives in standard patterns. **Patterns:** Hunters, skinners, boots and fighters. **Technical:** Grinds 440C and ATS-34. **Prices:** $100 to $300; some to $600. **Remarks:** Full-time maker; first knife sold in 1973. **Mark:** Last name.

BONASSI, FRANCO, Via Superiore 14, Pordenone 33170 ITALY/434-550821
Specialties: Fancy and working one-of-a-kind straight knives of his design. **Patterns:** Hunters, skinners, utility and liner locks. **Technical:** Grinds CPM, ATS-34, 154CM and commercial Damascus. Uses only titanium foreguards and pommels. **Prices:** Start at $250. **Remarks:** Spare-time maker; first knife sold in 1988. **Mark:** FRANK.

BOOCO, GORDON, 175 Ash St., P.O. Box 174, Hayden, CO 81639/303-276-3195
Specialties: Fancy working straight knives of his design and to customer specs. **Patterns:** Hunters and Bowies. **Technical:** Grinds 440C, D2 and A2. Heat-treats. **Prices:** $150 to $350; some $600 and higher. **Remarks:** Part-time maker; first knife sold in 1984. **Mark:** Last name with push dagger artwork.

BOOS, RALPH, 5107 40 Ave., Edmonton, Alberta, CANADA T6L 1B3/403-463-7094
Specialties: Classic, fancy and fantasy miniature knives and swords of his design or to customer specs. **Patterns:** Bowies, daggers and swords. **Technical:** Hand files O1, stainless and Damascus. Engraves and carves. Does heat bluing and acid etching. **Prices:** $125 to $350; some to $1,000. **Remarks:** Part-time maker; first knife sold in 1982. **Mark:** First and last initials back to back.

BOOTH, PHILIP W., 301 S. Jeffery Ave., Ithaca, MI 48847/517-875-2844
Specialties: Classic multi-blade folders and straight knives; some fancy. **Patterns:** Fighters, hunters, slip-joint folders, stockman and muskrat knives. **Technical:** Grinds 440C, ATS-34, 1095 and commercial Damascus. Uses only natural materials. **Prices:** $100 to $500. **Remarks:** Part-time maker; first knife sold in 1991. **Mark:** Last name or name with city and map logo.

BORGER, WOLF, Benzstrasse 8, 76676 Graben-Neudorf, GERMANY/07255-72303; FAX: 07255-72304; E-MAIL: Wolf.Borger@t-online.de
Specialties: High-tech working and using straight knives and folders, many with corkscrews or other tools, of his design. **Patterns:** Hunters, Bowies and folders with various locking systems. **Technical:** Grinds 440C, ATS-34 and CPM. Uses stainless Damascus. **Prices:** $250 to $900; some to $1,500. **Remarks:** Full-time maker; first knife sold in 1975. **Mark:** Howling wolf and name; first name on Damascus blades.

BOSE, REESE, 9014 S. Co. Rd. 550W, Lewis, IN 47858/812-495-6372
Specialties: Traditional working and using knives in standard patterns and multi-blade folders. **Patterns:** Multi-blade slip-joints. **Technical:** Grinds commercial Damascus, ATS-34 and D2. **Prices:** $200 to $700. **Remarks:** Full-time maker; first knife sold in 1992. **Mark:** First initial, last name.

BOSE, TONY, 7252 N. County Rd., 300 E., Shelburn, IN 47879-9778/812-397-5114
Specialties: Traditional working and using knives in standard patterns; multi-blade folders. **Patterns:** Multi-blade slip-joints. **Technical:** Grinds commercial Damascus, ATS-34 and D2. **Prices:** $400 to $1200. **Remarks:** Full-time maker; first knife sold in 1975. **Mark:** First initial, last name, city, state.

BOSSAERTS, CARL, Rua Albert Einstein, 906, 14051-110 Ribeirao Preto, S.P. BRAZIL/016 633 7063

Specialties: Working and using straight knives of his design, to customer specs and in standard patterns. **Patterns:** Hunters, fighters and utility/camp knives. **Technical:** Grinds ATS-34, 440V and 440C; does filework. **Prices:** 60 to $400. **Remarks:** Part-time maker; first knife sold in 1992. **Mark:** Initials joined together.

BOSWORTH, DEAN, 329 Mahogany Dr., Key Largo, FL 33037/305-451-1564
Specialties: Working/using straight knives of his design. **Patterns:** Fighters, hunters and utility/camp knives. **Technical:** Grinds 440C, ATS-34 and D2; some stock removal. Offers hand-rubbed satin finish; most sheaths are wet formed and hand stitched. **Prices:** $225 to $375; some to $500. **Remarks:** Part-time maker; first knife sold in 1985. **Mark:** BOZ stamped in block letters.

BOURBEAU, JEAN YVES, 15 Rue Remillard, Notre Dame, Ile Perrot, Quebec J7V 8M9 CANADA/514-453-1069
Specialties: Fancy/embellished and fantasy folders of his design. **Patterns:** Bowies, fighters and locking folders. **Technical:** Grinds 440C, ATS-34 and Damascus. Carves precious wood for handles. **Prices:** $150 to $1,000. **Remarks:** Part-time maker; first knife sold in 1994. **Mark:** Interlaced initials.

BOUSE, D. MICHAEL, 1010 Victoria Pl., Waldorf, MD 20602/301-843-0449
Specialties: Traditional and working/using straight knives of his design. **Patterns:** Daggers, fighters and hunters. **Technical:** Forges 5160 and Damascus; grinds D2; differential hardened blades; decorative handle pins. **Prices:** $125 to $350. **Remarks:** Spare-time maker; first knife sold in 1992. Doing business as Michael's Handmade Knives. **Mark:** Etched last name.

BOWEN, TILTON, Rt. 1, Box 225A, Baker, WV 26801/304-897-6159
Specialties: Straight, stout working knives. **Patterns:** Hunters, fighters and boots; also offers buckskinner and throwing knives. **Technical:** Grinds D2 and 4140. **Prices:** $60 to $275. **Remarks:** Full-time maker; first knife sold in 1982-1983. Sells wholesale to dealers. **Mark:** Initials and BOWEN BLADES, WV.

BOYD, FRANCIS, 1811 Prince St., Berkeley, CA 94703/510-841-7210
Specialties: Folders and kitchen knives; Japanese swords. **Patterns:** Push-button sturdy locking folders; San Francisco-style chef's knives. **Technical:** Forges and grinds; mostly uses high-carbon steels. **Prices:** Moderate to heavy. **Remarks:** Designer. **Mark:** Name.

BOYE, DAVID, P.O. Box 1238, Dolan Springs, AZ 86441/520-767-4273
Specialties: Hunting and kitchen knives. Forerunner in the use of dendritic steel for blades. **Patterns:** Boye Basics sheath knives, lockback folders, kitchen knives and hunting knives. **Technical:** Casts blades in stainless 440C. **Prices:** From $79 to $500. **Remarks:** Full-time maker; author of *Step-by-Step Knifemaking*; sells at craft shows. **Mark:** Name.

BOYER BLADES (See Boyer, Mark)

BOYER, MARK, 10515 Woodinville Dr., #17, Bothell, WA 98011/206-487-9370; WEB: http://www.eskimo.com/tender/boyerblades.html
Specialties: High-tech and working/using straight knives of his design. **Patterns:** Fighters and utility/camp knives. **Technical:** Grinds 1095 and D2. Offers Kydex sheaths; heat-treats. **Prices:** $45 to $120. **Remarks:** Part-time maker; first knife sold in 1994. Doing business as Boyer Blades. **Mark:** Eagle holding two swords with name.

BRACK, DOUGLAS D., 119 Camino Ruiz, #71, Camirillo, CA 93012/805-987-0490
Specialties: Working straight knives of his design. **Patterns:** Heavy-duty skinners, fighters and boots. **Technical:** Grinds 440C, ATS-34 and 5160; forges cable. **Prices:** $90 to $180; some to $300. **Remarks:** Part-time maker; first knife sold in 1984. **Mark:** "tat."

BRADBURN, GARY, 1714 Park Pl., Wichita, KS 67203/316-269-4273
Specialties: Straight knives of his design and to customer specs. **Patterns:** Bowies, fighters, hunters and miniatures. **Technical:** Forges 5160 and his own Damascus; grinds D2. **Prices:** $50 to $350; some to $800. **Remarks:** Full-time maker; first knife sold 1991. **Mark:** Last name or last initial inside a shamrock.

BRADLEY, DENNIS, 2410 Bradley Acres Rd., Blairsville, GA 30512/706-745-4364
Specialties: Working straight knives and folders, some high-art. **Patterns:** Hunters, boots and daggers; slip-joints and two-blades. **Technical:** Grinds ATS-34, D2, 440C and commercial Damascus. **Prices:** $100 to $500; some to $2,000. **Remarks:** Part-time maker; first knife sold in 1973. **Mark:** BRADLEY KNIVES in double heart logo.

BRADLEY, JOHN, P.O. Box 37, Pomona Park, FL 32181/904-649-4739
Specialties: Fixed-blade using knives. **Patterns:** Skinners, camp knives, fillet knives and Bowies. **Technical:** All knives forged and heat-treated by hand. Uses 52100, 1095 and own Damascus. **Prices:** $50 to $500; some higher. **Remarks:** Full-time maker; first knife sold in 1988. **Mark:** Last name.

BRANDSEY, EDWARD P., 1207 Portage Lane, Woodstock, IL 60098/815-337-6010
Specialties: Working straight knives; period pieces and art knives. **Patterns:** Hunters, fighters, Bowies and daggers, some buckskinner styles. **Technical:** Grinds ATS-34, 440C and O1. **Prices:** $125 to $250; some to $2,500. **Remarks:** Part-time maker; first knife sold in 1973. **Mark:** Initials connected.

BRANNAN, RALPH, RR1, Box 343, West Frankfort, IL 62896/618-627-2450
Specialties: Working straight knives of his design. **Patterns:** Traditional using skinners, hunters and utility knives. **Technical:** Grinds 1095, 440C and commercial Damascus. Offers filework. **Prices:** $75 to $150; some to $250. **Remarks:** Part-time maker; first knife sold in 1976. **Mark:** Initials.

BRANTON, ROBERT, 4976 Seewee Rd., Awendaw, SC 29429/803-928-3624
Specialties: Working straight knives of his design or to customer specs; throwing knives. **Patterns:** Hunters, fighters and some miniatures. **Technical:** Grinds ATS-34, A2 and 1050; forges 5160, O1. Offers hollow- or convex-grinds. **Prices:** $25 to $400. **Remarks:** Part-time maker; first knife sold in 1985. Doing business as Pro-Flyte, Inc. **Mark:** Last name; or first and last name, city, state.

BRAY JR., W. LOWELL, 6931 Manor Beach Rd., New Port Richey, FL 34652
Specialties: Traditional working and using straight knives of his design. **Patterns:** Hunters, kitchen knives and utility knives. **Technical:** Grinds 440C; forges high carbon. **Prices:** $50 to $300. **Remarks:** Spare-time maker; first knife sold in 1992. **Mark:** Lowell Bray Knives in shield.

BRAYTON, JIM, 713 Park St., Burkburnett, TX 76354/817-569-4726
Specialties: Working knives and period pieces, some fancy. **Patterns:** Bowies, hunters, fighters. **Technical:** Grinds ATS-34, delivers it at 60 Rc. **Prices:** $55 to $500; some higher. **Remarks:** Full-time maker; first knife sold in 1970. **Mark:** Initials or name.

BREND, WALTER J., Rt. 7, Box 224, Walterboro, SC 29488/803-538-8256; FAX: 803-538-8416
Specialties: Art and working knives. **Patterns:** Combat knives, survival knives, liner locks and Bowies. **Technical:** ATS-34. **Prices:** $425 to $1,100; some to $3,500. **Remarks:** Full-time maker; first knife sold in 1980. **Mark:** Confederate flag.

BRENNAN, JUDSON, P.O. Box 1165, Delta Junction, AK 99737/907-895-5153
Specialties: Period pieces. **Patterns:** All kinds of Bowies, rifle knives, daggers. **Technical:** Forges miscellaneous steels. **Prices:** Upscale, good value. **Remarks:** Muzzle-loading gunsmith; first knife sold in 1978. **Mark:** Name.

BRESHEARS, CLINT, 1261 Keats, Manhattan Beach, CA 90266/310-372-0739
Specialties: Working straight knives and folders. **Patterns:** Hunters, Bowies and survival knives. Folders are mostly hunters. **Technical:** Grinds 440C, 154CM and ATS-34; prefers mirror finishes. **Prices:** $125 to $200; some to $500. **Remarks:** Part-time maker; first knife sold in 1978. **Mark:** First name.

BREUER, LONNIE, P.O. Box 877384, Wasilla, AK 99687-7384
Specialties: Fancy working straight knives. **Patterns:** Hunters, camp knives and axes, folders and Bowies. **Technical:** Grinds 440C, AEB-L and D2; likes wire inlay, scrimshaw, decorative filing. **Prices:** $60 to $150; some to $300. **Remarks:** Part-time maker; first knife sold in 1977. **Mark:** Signature.

BRIAR KNIVES (See Ralph, Darrel)

BRIDGES, JUSTIN W., Box 974, Fish Hatchery Rd., Dubois, WY 82513/307-455-2769
Specialties: Working and using straight knives and folders in standard patterns. **Patterns:** Hunters, gent's knives and locking folders. **Technical:** Grinds 440C, 154CM and buys Damascus. **Prices:** $250 to $1,000; some to $3,000. **Remarks:** Full-time maker; first knife sold in 1988. Doing business as Wind River Knives. **Mark:** WRK connected; sometimes a circle with name, city and state.

BRIDWELL, RICHARD A., Rt. 2, Milford Ch. Rd., Taylors, SC 29687/803-895-1715
Specialties: Working straight knives and folders. **Patterns:** Boot and fishing knives, fighters and hunters. **Technical:** Grinds stainless steels and D2. **Prices:** $85 to $165; some to $600. **Remarks:** Part-time maker; first knife sold in 1974. **Mark:** Last name logo.

BRIGHTWELL, MARK, 21104 Creekside Dr., Leander, TX 78641/512-267-4110
Specialties: Fancy and plain folders of his design. **Patterns:** Fighters, hunters and gents, some traditional. **Technical:** Hollow- or flat- grinds ATS-34, D2, custom Damascus; elaborate filework; heat-treats. Extensive choice of natural handle materials; no synthetics. **Prices:** $300 to $1,500. **Remarks:** Full-time maker. **Mark:** Last name.

BRIGNARDELLO, E.D., 71 Village Woods Dr., Crete, IL 60401/708-672-6687
Specialties: Working straight knives; some display pieces. **Patterns:** Hunters, fighters, boots and Bowies; some push knives. **Technical:** Grinds 440C, 154CM and ATS-34; likes mirror finishes. **Prices:** $130 to $250; some to $500. **Remarks:** Part-time maker; first knife sold in 1978. **Mark:** Name and city.

BRITTON, TIM, 2100 Wolf Lane, Kinston, NC 28501/919-523-8631; FAX: 919-523-8631
Specialties: Small and simple working knives, sgian dubhs and toggle lock folders to customer specs. **Technical:** Forges and grinds stainless steel. **Prices:** Upscale. **Remarks:** Veteran knifemaker. **Mark:** Etched signature.

BROADWELL, DAVID, P.O. Box 4314, Wichita Falls, TX 76308/817-692-1727
Specialties: Sculpted high-art straight and folding knives. **Patterns:** Daggers, sub-hilted fighters, folders, sculpted art knives and some Bowies. **Technical:** Grinds mostly Damascus; carves; prefers natural handle materials, including stone. Some embellishment. **Prices:** $300 to $3,000; some higher. **Remarks:** Full-time maker; first knife sold in 1982. **Mark:** Stylized emblem bisecting "B" with last name below.

BROCK, KENNETH L., P.O. Box 375, 207 N. Skinner Rd., Allenspark, CO 80510/303-747-2547
Specialties: Full-tang working knives and button-lock folders of his design. **Patterns:** Hunters, miniatures and minis. **Technical:** Flat-grinds D2 and 440C; makes own sheaths; heat-treats. **Prices:** $50 to $500. **Remarks:** Part-time maker; first knife sold in 1978. **Mark:** Last name, city, state and serial number.

BRONK'S KNIFEWORKS (See Brunckhorst, Lyle)

BROOKER, DENNIS, Rt. 1, Box 12A, Derby, IA 50068/515-533-2103
Specialties: Fancy straight knives and folders of his design. **Patterns:** Hunters, folders and boots. **Technical:** Forges and grinds. Full-time engraver and designer; instruction available. **Prices:** Moderate to upscale. **Remarks:** Part-time maker. Takes no orders; sells only completed work. **Mark:** Name.

BROOKS, MICHAEL, 3717 B 30th St., Lubbock, TX 79410/806-793-1635
Specialties: Working straight knives of his design or to customer specs. **Patterns:** Tantos, swords, Bowies, hunters, skinners and boots. **Technical:** Grinds 440C, D2 and ATS-34; offers wide variety of handle materials. **Prices:** $40 to $800. **Remarks:** Part-time maker; first knife sold in 1985. **Mark:** Initials.

BROOKS, STEVE R., Box 105, Big Timber, MT 59011/406-932-5114
Specialties: Working straight knives and folders; period pieces. **Patterns:** Hunters, Bowies and camp knives; folding lockers; axes, tomahawks and buckskinner knives; swords and stilettos. **Technical:** Forges O1, Damascus and mosaic Damascus. Some knives come embellished. **Prices:** $150 to $2,000. **Remarks:** Full-time maker; first knife sold in 1982. **Mark:** Lazy initials.

BROOME, THOMAS A., 1212 E. Aliak Ave., Kenai, AK 99611-8205
Specialties: Traditional working straight knives and folders. **Patterns:** Full range of straight knives and a few folders. **Technical:** Grinds D2, 440C, 440V, ATS-34 and BG42. **Prices:** $75 to $175; some to $2,000. **Remarks:** Full-time maker; first knife sold in 1979. Doing business as Thom's Custom Knives. **Mark:** Full name, city, state in logo.

BROTHERS, ROBERT L., 989 Philpott Rd., Colville, WA 99114/509-684-8922
Specialties: Traditional working and using straight knives and folders of his design and to customer specs. **Patterns:** Bowies, fighters and hunters. **Technical:** Grinds D2; forges Damascus. Makes own Damascus from saw steel wire rope and chain; part-time goldsmith and stonesetter. **Prices:** $100 to $400; some higher. **Remarks:** Part-time maker; first knife sold in 1986. **Mark:** Initials and year made.

BROUGHTON, DON R., 4690 Edwardsville-Galena Rd., Floyd Knobs, IN 47119/812-923-9222
Specialties: Period pieces and antique finish. **Patterns:** Bowies, tomahawks, rifleman's knives, patch knives and belt knives. **Technical:** Forges 1095, 5160, 52100 and own Damascus. Uses antique finish. **Prices:** $150 to $750; some to $1,500. **Remarks:** Full-time maker; first knife sold in 1987. **Mark:** Tomahawk head, M.S.

BROWER, MAX, 2016 Story St., Boone, IA 50036/515-432-2938
Specialties: Working/using straight knives. **Patterns:** Bowies, hunters and boots. **Technical:** Grinds 440C. **Prices:** Start at $125. **Remarks:** Spare-time maker; first knife sold in 1981. **Mark:** Last name.

BROWN CUSTOM KNIVES, TROY (See Brown, Troy L.)

BROWN, DAVID B., 3209 N. 60th St., Omaha, NE 68104/402-345-8302
Specialties: Working straight knives and folders; some fancy. **Patterns:** Hunters, tantos and Bowies; lockers and butterflies. **Technical:** Forges and grinds W2, 440C and his own Damascus. Etches. **Prices:** $85 to $750; some to $2,000. **Remarks:** Spare-time maker; first knife sold in 1979. **Mark:** First and middle initials, last name.

BROWN, HAROLD E., 3654 NW Hwy. 72, Arcadia, FL 34266/941-494-7514
Specialties: Fancy and exotic working knives. **Patterns:** Hunters, folders and fillet knives. **Technical:** Grinds D2, 440C and ATS-34. Embellishment available. **Prices:** $100 to $750; some to $1,000. **Remarks:** Full-time maker; first knife sold in 1976. **Mark:** Name and city with logo.

BROWN, JIM, 1097 Fernleigh Cove, Little Rock, AR 72210

BROWN, PETER, 10 Island View St., Emerald Beach 2456, AUSTRALIA/02-809-0265
Specialties: Heavy-duty working knives. **Patterns:** Swords, fighters, tantos, hunting and fishing knives. **Technical:** Grinds 440C, 420 and ATS-34; makes his own Damascus steel. Heat-treats; scrimshaws. **Prices:** $135 to $500; some to $800. **Remarks:** Spare-time maker; first knife sold in 1978. **Mark:** Interlacing initials.

BROWN, ROB E., P.O. Box 15107, Emerald Hill, 6011 Port Elizabeth, SOUTH AFRICA/27-41-361086; FAX: 27-41-411731
Specialties: Contemporary-designed straight knives and period pieces. **Patterns:** Utility knives, hunters, boots, fighters and daggers. **Technical:** Grinds 440C, D2, ATS-34 and commercial Damascus. Knives mostly mirror finished; African handle materials. **Prices:** $150 to $1,500. **Remarks:** Full-time maker; first knife sold in 1985. **Mark:** Name and country.

BROWN, TED, 7621 Firestone Blvd., Suite 104, Downey, CA 90241/213-869-9945
Specialties: Working straight knives in standard patterns. **Patterns:** Hunters, Bowies, fishing knives. **Technical:** Grinds stainless steel; some integral work. **Prices:** $100 to $350; some to $500. **Remarks:** Part-time maker; first knife sold in 1982. **Mark:** Name, address in snake logo.

BROWN, TOM, Suite 106, 5710-K High Point Rd., Greensboro, NC 27407/910-656-4955
Specialties: Classic and working straight knives of his design and in standard patterns. **Patterns:** Daggers, double edge fighters, hunters and folders. **Technical:** Grinds ATS-34 and 440C. Custom Kydex and Cordura sheaths offered. **Prices:** $165 to $550. **Remarks:** Part-time maker; first knife sold in 1991. **Mark:** Brown Knives.

BROWN, TROY L., HC 73 Box 526, Park Hill, OK 74451/918-457-4128 **Specialties:** Working and using straight knives and folders. **Patterns:** Bowies, hunters and locking folders. **Technical:** Grinds 440C and D2; forges 5160. Prefers stag, wood and Micarta for handles. Offers engraved bolsters and guards. **Prices:** $75 to $500. **Remarks:** Full-time maker; first knife sold in 1994. Doing business as Troy Brown Custom Knives. **Mark:** First and last name.

BROWNE, RICK, 980 West 13th St., Upland, CA 91786/909-985-1728 **Specialties:** High-tech integral working straight knives of his design. **Patterns:** Hunters, fighters and daggers. No heavy-duty knives. **Technical:** Grinds D2, 440C and ATS-34. **Prices:** Start at $200. **Remarks:** Part-time maker; first knife sold in 1975. **Mark:** Name, city, state.

BROZ KNIVES (See Meloy, Sean)

BRUMAGEN, JERRY (See Fannin, David A. and Brumagen, Jerry)

BRUNCKHORST, LYLE, Country Village, Suite B, 23716 Bothell-Everett Hwy., Bothell, WA 98021/425-402-3484; WEB: http://www.net-tech.com/bronks/bronks.htm
Specialties: Traditional working and using straight knives and folders of his design. **Patterns:** Bowies, hunters and locking folders. **Technical:** Grinds ATS-34; forges 5160 and his own Damascus. Irredescent RR spike knives. Offers scrimshaw, inlays and animal carvings in horn handles. **Prices:** $225 to $750; some to $3,750. **Remarks:** Full-time maker; first knife sold in 1976. Doing business as Bronk's Knifeworks. **Mark:** Bucking horse.

BRUNETTA, DAVID, P.O. Box 4972, Laguna Beach, CA 92652/714-497-9611; FAX: 714-497-6036
Specialties: One-of-a-kind art and fantasy knives. **Patterns:** Bowies, camp/hunting, folders, fighters. **Technical:** Makes his own Damascus; likes to forge; edge tempers. **Prices:** $500 to $5000; some higher. **Mark:** Circle DB logo with last name straight or curved.

BUCHMAN, BILL, 63312 South Rd., Bend, OR 97701/503-382-8851 **Specialties:** Working straight knives. **Patterns:** Hunters, Bowies, fighters, kitchen cutlery, carving sets and boots. Makes some saddlemaker knives. **Technical:** Forges 440C and Sandvik 15N20. Prefers 440C for saltwater. **Prices:** $95 to $400. **Remarks:** Part-time maker; first knife sold in 1982. **Mark:** Initials or last name.

BUCHNER, BILL, P.O. Box 73, Idleyld Park, OR 97447/541-498-2247 **Specialties:** Working straight knives, kitchen knives and high-art knives of his design. **Technical:** Uses W1, L6 and his own Damascus. Invented "spectrum metal" for letter openers, folder handles and jewelry. Likes sculpturing and carving in Damascus. **Prices:** $40 to $3,000; some higher. **Remarks:** Full-time maker; first knife sold in 1978. **Mark:** Signature.

BUCHOLZ, MARK A., 9197 West Parkview Terrace Loop, Eagle River, AK 99577/907-694-1037
Specialties: Liner lock folders. **Patterns:** Hunters and fighters. **Technical:** Grinds ATS-34. **Prices:** Upscale. **Remarks:** Full-time maker; first knife sold in 1976. **Mark:** Name, city and state in buffalo skull logo or signature.

BUCKBEE, DONALD M., 243 South Jackson Trail, Grayling, MI 49738/517-348-1386
Specialties: Working straight knives, some fancy, in standard patterns; concentrating on kitchen knives. **Patterns:** Kitchen knives, hunters, Bowies. **Technical:** Grinds D2, 440C, ATS-34. Makes ultra-lights in hunter patterns. **Prices:** $100 to $250; some to $350. **Remarks:** Part-time maker; first knife sold in 1984. **Mark:** Antlered bee—a buck bee.

BUCKNER, JIMMIE H., P.O. Box 162, Putney, GA 31782/912-436-4182 **Specialties:** High-tech working straight knives and locking folders of his design or to customer specs. **Patterns:** Hunters, fighters and camp knives. **Technical:** Forges O1, 1095 and his Damascus; heat-treats. **Prices:** $100 to $300; some to $900. **Remarks:** Full-time maker; first knife sold in 1980. **Mark:** Last name over spade.

BUEBENDORF, ROBERT E., 108 Lazybrooke Rd., Monroe, CT 06468/203-452-1769
Specialties: Traditional and fancy straight knives of his design. **Patterns:** Hand-makes and embellishes belt buckle knives. **Technical:** Forges and grinds 440C, O1, W2, 1095, his own Damascus and 154CM. **Prices:** $200 to $500. **Remarks:** Full-time maker; first knife sold in 1978. **Mark:** First and middle initials, last name and MAKER.

BUGDEN, JOHN, Rt. #6, Box 7, Murray, KY 42071/502-753-0305 **Specialties:** Working straight knives; period pieces. **Patterns:** Hunters, boots and survival knives. **Technical:** Grinds O1, 440C; buys Damascus. Offers filework. **Prices:** $125 to $500. **Remarks:** Full-time maker; first knife sold in 1975. **Mark:** Initials.

BULLARD, BILL, Rt. 5, Box 35, Andalusia, AL 36420/205-222-9003 **Specialties:** Traditional working and using straight knives and folders of his design. **Patterns:** Hunters, slip-joint folders and utility/camp knives. **Technical:** Forges Damascus, cable and carbon steels. Offers filework. **Prices:** $100 to $500; some to $1,500. **Remarks:** Part-time maker; first knife sold in 1974. Doing business as Five Runs Forge. **Mark:** Last name stamped on ricasso.

BULLARD CUSTOM KNIVES (See Bullard, Randall)

BULLARD, RANDALL, 7 Mesa Dr., Canyon, TX 79015/806-655-0590 **Specialties:** Working/using straight knives and folders of his design or to customer specs. **Patterns:** Hunters, locking folders and slip-joint folders. **Technical:** Grinds O1, ATS-34 and 440C. Does file work. **Prices:** $125 to $300; some to $500. **Remarks:** Part-time maker; first knife sold in 1993. Doing business as Bullard Custom Knives. **Mark:** First and middle initials, last name, maker, city and state.

BULLARD, TOM, Rt. 1, Box 127-B, Comfort, TX 78013/210-995-2003 **Specialties:** Traditional, classic, working and using straight knives and folders to customer specs; armadillo tail handles on sheath knives. **Patterns:** Bowies, hunters, locking folders and slip-joint folders. **Technical:** Grinds O1, ATS-34, 440C and commercial Damascus. Offers filework on blades, tangs and liners. Armadillo tail handle material. **Prices:** $150 to $500. **Remarks:** Full-time maker; first knife sold in 1966. **Mark:** Full name, maker, city and state.

BURDEN, JAMES, 405 Kelly St., Burkburnett, TX 76354

BURGER, FRED, P.O. Munster 4278, Kwa-Zulu Natal, SOUTH AFRICA/03930-92316
Specialties: Straight knives of his design. **Patterns:** Bowies, fighters and gentlemen's sword canes. **Technical:** Grinds ATS-34 and 440C. **Prices:** $200 to $400; some to $1,000. **Remarks:** Full-time maker; first knife sold in 1987. **Mark:** Last name in an oval pierced by a dagger.

BÜRGER, GÜNTER, Horststr. 55, 44581 Castrop-Rauxel, GERMANY/02305-77145; FAX:02305-77145

BURGER, PON, 12 Glenwood Ave., Woodlands, Bulawayo, Zimbabwe, AFRICA/75514
Specialties: Collectors items. **Patterns:** Fighters, locking folders of traditional styles, buckles. **Technical:** Scrimshaws 440C blade. Uses polished buffalo horn with brass fittings. Cased in buffalo hide book. **Prices:** Start at $1,000. **Remarks:** Full-time maker; first knife sold in 1973. Doing business as Burger Products. **Mark:** Last name.

BURGER PRODUCTS (See Burger, Pon)

BURKE, DAN, 22001 Ole Barn Rd., Edmond, OK 73034/405-341-3406 **Specialties:** Traditional folders of his design and in standard patterns. **Patterns:** Slip-joint folders and traditional folders. **Technical:** Grinds D2 and ATS-34. Prefers natural handle materials; heat-treats. **Prices:** $200 to $400. **Remarks:** Full-time maker; first knife sold in 1976. **Mark:** First initial and last name.

BURNS, DAVE, P.O. Box 1040, Boynton Beach, FL 33425/561-734-4509 **Specialties:** Period pieces and buckskinners of his design or to customer specs. **Patterns:** Traditional Bowies, hunters, guthooks, fighting and boot knives. **Technical:** Forges and grinds O1, 1095 and 5160; traditional slow rust blue (black) finnish. Prefers to use natural handle materials; offers filework. **Prices:** $75 to $500. **Remarks:** Part-time maker; first knife sold in 1980. Doing business as OL Blue Knives, Inc. **Mark:** Stamped OL Blue.

BURROWS, STEPHEN R., 3532 Michigan, Kansas City, MO 64109/816-921-1573
Specialties: Fantasy straight knives of his design, to customer specs and in standard patterns; period pieces. **Patterns:** Fantasy, bird and trout knives, daggers, fighters and hunters. **Technical:** Forges 5160 and 1090 high-carbon steel, O1 and his Damascus. Offers casting and lost wax bronzing of crossguards and pommels. **Prices:** $100 to $600; some to $2,000. **Remarks:** Full-time maker; first knife sold in 1983. Doing business as Gypsy Silk. **Mark:** Etched name.

BUSFIELD, JOHN, 153 Devonshire Circle, Roanoke Rapids, NC 27870/919-537-3949; FAX: 919-537-8704
Specialties: Investor-grade folders; high-grade working straight knives. **Patterns:** Original price-style and trailing-point interframe and sculpted-frame folders, drop-point hunters and semi-skinners. **Technical:** Grinds 154CM and ATS-34. Offers interframes, gold frames and inlays; uses jade, agate and lapis. **Prices:** $650 to $2,000. **Remarks:** Full-time maker; first knife sold in 1979. **Mark:** Last name and address.

BUSSE, JERRY, 11651 Co. Rd. 12, Wauseon, OH 43567/419-923-6471
Specialties: Working straight knives. **Patterns:** Heavy combat knives and camp knives. **Technical:** Grinds D2, A2, ATS-34 and 440C; hollow-grinds most blades. **Prices:** $1,100 to $3,500. **Remarks:** Full-time maker; first knife sold in 1983. **Mark:** Last name in logo.

BUZZARD'S KNOB FORGE (See Hurst, Jeff)

"BY GEORGE" (See Englebretson, George)

BYBEE, BARRY J., 795 Lock Rd. E., Cadiz, KY 42211-8615
Specialties: Working straight knives of his design. **Patterns:** Hunters, fighters, boot knives, tantos and Bowies. **Technical:** Grinds ATS-34, 440C. Likes stag and Micarta for handle materials. **Prices:** $125 to $200; some to $1,000. **Remarks:** Part-time maker; first knife sold in 1968. **Mark:** Arrowhead logo with name, city and state.

BYRD, DON E., Rt. 3, Box 223-A, Roanoke, TX 76262/817-430-1986
Specialties: Classic and working straight knives in standard patterns. **Patterns:** Fighters, hunters and utility knives. **Technical:** Grinds ATS-34, D2 and 440C. **Prices:** $125 to $275; some to $500. **Remarks:** Part-time maker; first knife sold in 1983. **Mark:** Last name.

C

CABIN CREEK FORGE (See Markley, Ken)

CACTUS CUSTOM KNIVES (See McConnell Jr., Loyd A.)

CACTUS FORGE (See Guignard, Gib)

CADILLAC BLACKSMITHING (See Pogreba, Larry)

CAFFREY, EDWARD J., 2608 Central Ave. West, Great Falls, MT 59404/406-727-9102
Specialties: Working/using knives and collector pieces; will accept customer designs. **Patterns:** Hunters, fighters, camp/utility, folders, hawks and hatchets. **Technical:** Forges 5160, 52100, his Damascus, cable and chain Damascus. Offers a special effect steel using various steels and nickel forge welding. **Prices:** Start at $125. **Remarks:** Part-time maker; first knife sold in 1989. **Mark:** Last name or engraved initials.

CALDWELL, BILL, 255 Rebecca, West Monroe, LA 71292/318-323-3025
Specialties: Straight knives and folders with machined bolsters and liners. **Patterns:** Fighters, Bowies, survival knives, tomahawks, razors and push knives. **Technical:** Owns and operates a very large, well-equipped blacksmith and bladesmith shop extant with six large forges and eight power hammers. **Prices:** $400 to $3,500; some to $10,000. **Remarks:** Full-time maker and self-styled blacksmith; first knife sold in 1962. **Mark:** Wild Bill & Sons.

CALLAHAN, ERRETT, 2 Fredonia, Lynchburg, VA 24503
Specialties: Obsidian knives. **Patterns:** Modern styles and Stone Age replicas. **Technical:** Flakes and knaps to order. **Prices:** $100 to $2,100. **Remarks:** Part-time maker; first flint blades sold in 1974. **Mark:** Blade—engraved name, year and arrow; handle—signed edition, year and unit number.

CALLAHAN, F. TERRY, P.O. Box 880, Boerne, TX 78006/210-981-8274; FAX: 210-981-8274
Specialties: Custom hand-forged edged knives, collectible and functional. **Patterns:** Bowies, folders, daggers, hunters, camp knives and swords. **Technical:** Forges 5160, 1095 and his own Damascus. Offers filework and handmade sheaths. **Prices:** $125 to $2,000. **Remarks:** First knife sold in 1990. **Mark:** Initials inside a keystone symbol.

CAMERON HANDMADE KNIVES (See Cameron, Ron G.)

CAMERON, RON G., P.O. Box 183, Logandale, NV 89021/702-398-3356
Specialties: Fancy and embellished working/using straight knives and folders of his design. **Patterns:** Bowies, hunters and utility/camp knives. **Technical:** Grinds ATS-34, 440C and Devin Thomas Damascus. Does filework, fancy pins, mokume fittings. Uses exotic hardwoods, stag and Micarta for handles. **Prices:** $100 to $300; some to $600. **Remarks:** Part-time maker; first knife sold in 1994. Doing business as Cameron Handmade Knives. **Mark:** Last name, town, state or last name.

CAMP, JEFF, 9987 Hwy. 146-W, Ruston, LA 71270/318-255-7796
Specialties: Fancy working and using straight knives of his design and to customer specs. **Patterns:** Bowies, hunters, utility/camp knives and folders. **Technical:** Forges 5168, L6 and his Damascus. Offers filework; makes mokume. **Prices:** $260 to $1,000. **Remarks:** Part-time maker; first knife sold in 1991. **Mark:** Initials in script and JS.

CAMPBELL, DICK, 20000 Silver Ranch Rd., Conifer, CO 80433/303-697-0150
Specialties: Fancy working straight knives and folders; period pieces. **Patterns:** Bowies, fighters, miniatures and titanium folders. **Technical:** Grinds 440C; uses titanium. Prefers natural materials. **Prices:** $130 to $750; some to $1,200. **Remarks:** Part-time maker; first knife sold in 1975. **Mark:** Name.

CANDRELLA, JOE, 1219 Barness Dr., Warminster, PA 18974/215-675-0143
Specialties: Working straight knives, some fancy. **Patterns:** Daggers, boots, Bowies. **Technical:** Grinds 440C and 154CM. **Prices:** $100 to $200; some to $1,000. **Remarks:** Part-time maker; first knife sold in 1985. Does business as Franjo. **Mark:** FRANJO with knife as J.

CANNADY, DANIEL L., Box 301, Allendale, SC 29810/803-584-2813
Specialties: Working straight knives and folders in standard patterns. **Patterns:** Drop-point hunters, Bowies, skinners, fishing knives with concave grind, steak knives and kitchen cutlery. **Technical:** Grinds D2, 440C and ATS-34. **Prices:** $65 to $325; some to $500. **Remarks:** Full-time maker; first knife sold in 1980. **Mark:** Last name.

CANNON, RAYMOND W., 894 Lupine Ct., Homer, AK 99603/907-235-7779
Specialties: Fancy working knives, folders and swords of his design or to customer specs; many one-of-a-kind pieces. **Patterns:** Bowies, daggers and skinners. **Technical:** Forges and grinds O1, A6, 52100, 5160, his combinations for his own Damascus. **Prices:** Start at $180. **Remarks:** First knife sold in 1984. **Mark:** Last name, first name, "Wes."

CANTER, RONALD E., 96 Bon Air Circle, Jackson, TN 38305/901-668-1780
Specialties: Traditional working knives to customer specs. **Patterns:** Beavertail skinners, Bowies, hand axes and folding lockers. **Technical:** Grinds A1, 440C and 154CM. **Prices:** $65 to $250; some $500 and higher. **Remarks:** Spare-time maker; first knife sold in 1973. **Mark:** Three last initials intertwined.

CAPDEPON KNIVES (See Capdepon, Randy)

CAPDEPON, RANDY, 553 Joli Rd., Carencro, LA 70520/318-896-4113; FAX: 318-896-8753
Specialties: Straight knives and folders of his design. **Patterns:** Hunters and locking folders. **Technical:** Grinds ATS-34, 440C and D2. **Prices:** $200 to $600. **Remarks:** Part-time maker; first knife made in 1992. Doing business as Capdepon Knives. **Mark:** Last name.

CAPDEPON, ROBERT, 829 Vatican Rd., Carencro, LA 70520/318-896-8753; FAX: 318-896-8753
Specialties: Traditional straight knives and folders of his design. **Patterns:** Boots, hunters and locking folders. **Technical:** Grinds ATS-34, 440C and D2. Hand-rubbed finish on blades. Likes natural horn materials for handles, including ivory. Offers engraving. **Prices:** $250 to $750. **Remarks:** Full-time maker; first knife made in 1992. **Mark:** Last name.

CAREY JR., CHARLES W., 1003 Minter Rd., Griffin, GA 30223/770-228-8994
Specialties: Working and using knives of his design and to customer specs; period pieces. **Patterns:** Fighters, hunters, utility/camp knives and forged-to-shape miniatures. **Technical:** Forges 5160, old files and cable. Offers filework; ages some of his knives. **Prices:** $35 to $400. **Remarks:** Part-time maker; first knife sold in 1991. **Mark:** Knife logo.

CARGILL, BOB, RR 1, Box 383, Ocoee, TN 37361/615-338-8418; FAX: 615-338-2086
Specialties: Unique multi-blade folders of his design. **Patterns:** Adaptations of traditional pocketknives in many styles. **Technical:** Grinds 1095, 440, ATS-34 and Damascus. **Prices:** Start at $500; some to $10,000. **Remarks:** Full-time maker; first knife sold in 1974. **Mark:** Cargill Knives.

CARGILL KNIVES (See Cargill, Bob)

CARISOLO (See Maestri, Peter A.)

CARLISLE CUTLERY (See Carlisle, Frank)

CARLISLE, FRANK, 5930 Hereford, Detroit, MI 48224/313-882-8349
Specialties: Fancy/embellished and fantasy folders of his design. **Patterns:** Hunters, locking folders and swords. **Technical:** Grinds Damascus and stainless. **Prices:** $80 to $300. **Remarks:** Full-time maker; first knife sold in 1993. Doing business as Carlisle Cutlery. **Mark:** Last name.

CARLSSON, MARC BJORN, Pileatraede 42, 1112 Copenhagen K, DENMARK/+45 46 35 97 24; FAX: +45 33 91 17 99
Specialties: High-tech knives and folders. **Patterns:** Skinners, tantos, swords, folders and art knives. **Technical:** Grinds ATS-34, Elmax and D2. **Prices:** Start at $250. **Remarks:** Professional jeweler and knifemaker. Doing business as Metal Point. **Mark:** First name in runic letters within Viking ship.

CAROLINA CUSTOM KNIVES
(See Daniel, Travis E.; McNabb, Tommy)

CARSON, HAROLD J. "KIT," 1076 Brizendine Lane, Vine Grove, KY 40175/502-877-6300; FAX: 502-877-6338; E-MAIL: CarsonKnives@kvnet.org; WEB: http://www.kvnet.org/knives
Specialties: Military fixed blades and folders; art pieces. **Patterns:** Fighters, D handles, daggers, combat folders and Crosslock styles. **Technical:** Grinds 440C, ATS-34, D2, O1 and Damascus. **Prices:** $250 to $750; some to $5,000. **Remarks:** Full-time maker; first knife sold in 1973. **Mark:** Name stamped or engraved.

CARTER, FRED, 5219 Deer Creek Rd., Wichita Falls, TX 76302/817-723-4020
Specialties: High-art investor-class straight knives; some working hunters and fighters. **Patterns:** Classic daggers, Bowies; interframe, stainless and blued steel folders with gold inlay. **Technical:** Grinds a variety of steels. Uses no glue or solder. Engraves and inlays. **Prices:** Generally upscale. **Remarks:** Full-time maker. **Mark:** Signature in oval logo.

CASHEN, KEVIN R., 5615 Tyler St., Hubbardston, MI 48845/517-981-6780
Specialties: Traditional working straight knives of his design or to customer specs. **Patterns:** Hunters, skinners, Bowies, fighters, tantos and utilty/camp knives. **Technical:** Forges 1095, 5160 and his own O1/L6 Damascus and mokume; does Japanese temper lines. **Prices:** $90 to $1,500; some to $3,000. **Remarks:** Full-time maker; first knife sold in 1985. Doing business as Matherton Forge. **Mark:** Old English initials and mastersmith stamp.

CASHION, MARY JANE, P.O. Box 8392, Ennis, TX 75120/214-797-5819
Specialties: Traditional working and using straight knives and folders of her design. **Patterns:** Hunters, locking folders and slip-joint folders. **Technical:** Grinds 440C, D2 and Donald Raymond Damascus. Makes sheaths. **Prices:** $150 to $400; some to $600. **Remarks:** Full-time maker; first knife sold in 1989. Doing business as M.J.C. Knives. **Mark:** Initials or name.

CASTEEL, DIANNA, P.O. Box 63, Monteagle, TN 37356/615-723-0851; FAX: 615-723-1856
Specialties: Small, delicate daggers and miniatures; most knives one-of-a-kind. **Patterns:** Daggers, boot knives, fighters and miniatures. **Technical:** Grinds 440C; makes her own Damascus. **Prices:** Start at $350; miniatures start at $250. **Remarks:** Full-time maker. **Mark:** Di in script.

CASTEEL, DOUGLAS, P.O. Box 63, Monteagle, TN 37356/615-723-0851; FAX: 615-723-1856
Specialties: One-of-a-kind collector-class period pieces. **Patterns:** Daggers, Bowies, swords and folders. **Technical:** Grinds 440C; makes his own Damascus. Offers gold and silver castings. **Prices:** Upscale. **Remarks:** Full-time maker; first knife sold in 1982. **Mark:** Last name.

CASTLE KNIVES (See Courtois, Bryan)

CAUDELL, RICHARD M., P.O. Box 602, Lawrenceville, IL/618-943-5278
Specialties: Classic working/using straight knives in standard patterns. **Patterns:** Boots, fighters, combat fighters and utility/camp knives. **Technical:** Hollow-grinds 440C, ATS-34 and A2. **Prices:** $115 to $600; some to $1,200. **Remarks:** First knife sold in 1994. Doing business as Caudell's Custom Knives. **Mark:** Last name.

CAUDELL'S CUSTOM KNIVES (See Caudell, Richard M.)

CENTIPEDE ARMS (See Banaitis, Romas)

CENTOFANTE, FRANK and TONY, P.O. Box 928, Madisonville, TN 37354-0928/423-442-5767
Specialties: Fancy working folders. **Patterns:** Lockers and liner locks. **Technical:** Grinds ATS-34; hand-rubbed satin finish on blades. **Prices:** $300 to $900. **Remarks:** Full-time maker; first knife sold in 1968. **Mark:** Name, city, state.

CENTOFANTE, TONY (See Centofante, Frank and Tony)

CHAFFEE, JEFF L., Washington St., P.O. Box 1, Morris, IN 47033/812-934-6350
Specialties: Traditional working/using straight knives and utility folders of his design or to customer specs. **Patterns:** Hunters, Bowies, fighters, folders and kitchen knives. **Technical:** Grinds commercial Damascus, 440C, ATS-34, D2 and O1. Prefers natural handle materials. **Prices:** $50 to $1,000. **Remarks:** Part-time maker; first knife sold in 1988. **Mark:** First and middle initials and last name or last name only.

CHAMBERLAIN, CHARLES R., P.O. Box 156, Barren Springs, VA 24313-0156/703-381-5137

CHAMBERLAIN, JOHN B., 1621 Angela St., Wenatchee, WA 98801/509-663-6720
Specialties: Fancy working and using straight knives mainly to customer specs, though starting to make some standard patterns. **Patterns:** Hunters, Bowies and daggers. **Technical:** Grinds D2, ATS-34, M2, M4 and L6. **Prices:** $60 to $190; some to $2,500. **Remarks:** Full-time maker; first knife sold in 1943. **Mark:** Name, city, state.

CHAMBERLAIN, JON A., 15 S. Lombard, E. Wenatchee, WA 98802/509-884-6591
Specialties: Working and kitchen knives to customer specs; exotics on special order. **Patterns:** Over 100 patterns in stock. **Technical:** Prefers ATS-34, D2, L6 and Damascus. **Prices:** Start at $50. **Remarks:** First knife sold in 1986. Doing business as Johnny Custom Knifemakers. **Mark:** Name in oval with city and state enclosing.

CHAMBERLIN, JOHN A., 11535 Our Rd., Anchorage, AK 99516/907-346-1524; FAX: 907-562-4583; E-MAIL: historyh@alaska.net
Specialties: Art and working knives. **Patterns:** Daggers and hunters; some folders. **Technical:** Grinds ATS-34, 440C, A2, D2 and Damascus. Uses Alaskan handle materials such as oosic, jade, whale jawbone, fossil ivory. **Prices:** Start at $100. **Remarks:** Full-time maker; first knife sold in 1984. **Mark:** Name over English shield and dagger.

CHAMBLIN, JOEL, 296 New Hebron Church Rd., Concord, GA 30206/770-884-9055
Specialties: Traditional folders. **Patterns:** Multiblades, utility and fancy locking folders. **Technical:** Grinds ATS-34 and commercial Damascus. Offers filework. **Prices:** Start at $250. **Remarks:** Full-time maker; first knife sold in 1989. **Mark:** Last name.

CHAMPAGNE, PAUL, 48 Brightman Rd., Mechanicville, NY 12118/518-664-4179
Specialties: Rugged, ornate straight knives in the Japanese tradition. **Patterns:** Katanas, wakizashis, tantos and some European daggers. **Technical:** Forges and hand-finishes carbon steels and his own Damascus. Makes Tamahagane for use in traditional blades; uses traditional heat-treating techniques. **Prices:** Start at $750. **Remarks:** Has passed all traditional Japanese cutting tests. Doing business as Twilight Forge. **Mark:** Three diamonds over a stylized crown.

CHAMPION, ROBERT, P.O. Box 19427, Amarillo, TX 79114/806-359-0446
Specialties: Traditional working straight knives and folders. **Patterns:** Hunters, locking and slip-joint folders; some sub-hilt fighters. **Technical:**

Grinds A2, 440C, D2. **Prices:** $100 to $600. **Remarks:** Part-time maker; first knife sold in 1979. **Mark:** Last name with dagger logo, city and state.

CHAPO, WILLIAM G., 45 Wildridge Rd., Wilton, CT 06897/203-544-9424
Specialties: Classic straight knives and folders of his design and to customer specs; period pieces. **Patterns:** Boots, Bowies and locking folders. **Technical:** Forges stainless Damascus. Offers filework. **Prices:** $350 to $950; some to $2,200. **Remarks:** Full-time maker; first knife sold in 1989. **Mark:** First and middle initials, last name, city, state.

CHARD, GORDON R., 104 S. Holiday Lane, Iola, KS 66749/316-365-2311
Specialties: High-tech locking folders. **Patterns:** Titanium sidelock folders, push-button locking folders, interframe lockbacks and some art knives. **Technical:** Flat- and hollow-grinds mostly ATS-34, some Damascus; hand-finishes blades. **Prices:** $135 to $2,500. **Remarks:** Full-time maker; first knife sold in 1983. **Mark:** Name, city and state in wheat logo.

CHASE, ALEX, 101 S. Sheridan Ave., DeLand, FL 32720/904-734-9918
Specialties: Classic and traditional straight knives of his design and to customer specs. **Patterns:** Fighters and hunters. **Technical:** Forges O1 and L6 Damascus, 52100 and 5160. Uses fossil walrus ivory tips, exotic hardwoods; embellishes with small stones and exotic skins. **Prices:** $150 to $1,000; some to $3,500. **Remarks:** Part-time maker; first knife sold in 1990. Doing business as Confederate Forge. **Mark:** Stylized initials.

CHASE, JOHN E., P.O. Drawer H, Aledo, TX 76008/817-441-8331
Specialties: Straight high-tech working knives in standard patterns or to customer specs. **Patterns:** Hunters, fighters, daggers and Bowies. **Technical:** Grinds D2, 440C; offers mostly satin finishes. **Prices:** Start at $165. **Remarks:** Part-time maker; first knife sold in 1974. **Mark:** Last name in logo.

CHASTAIN, WADE, Rt. 2, Box 137-A, Horse Shoe, NC 28742/704-891-4803
Specialties: Fancy fantasy and high-art straight knives of his design; period pieces. Known for unique mounts. **Patterns:** Bowies, daggers and fighters. **Technical:** Grinds 440C, ATS-34 and O1. Engraves; offers jeweling. **Prices:** $400 to $1,200; some to $2,000. **Remarks:** Full-time maker; first knife sold in 1984. Doing business as The Iron Master. **Mark:** Engraved last name.

CHAUVIN, JOHN, 200 Anna St., Scott, LA 70583/318-237-6138; FAX: 318-237-8079
Specialties: Traditional working and using straight knives of his design, to customer specs and in standard patterns. **Patterns:** Bowies, fighters and hunters. **Technical:** Grinds ATS-34, 440C and O1 high carbon. Offers heat-treating. Uses ivory, stag, oosic and stabilized Louisiana swamp maple for handle materials. Makes sheaths using alligator and ostrich. **Prices:** $125 to $200; Bowies start at $500. **Remarks:** Part-time maker; first knife sold in 1995. **Mark:** Full name, city, state.

CHEATHAM, BILL, P.O. Box 636, Laveen, AZ 85339/602-237-2786
Specialties: Working straight knives and folders. **Patterns:** Hunters, fighters, boots and axes; locking folders. **Technical:** Grinds 440C. **Prices:** $150 to $350; exceptional knives to $600. **Remarks:** Full-time maker; first knife sold in 1976. **Mark:** Name, city, state.

CHELQUIST, CLIFF, P.O. Box 91, Arroyo Grande, CA 93421/805-489-8095
Specialties: Highly polished sportsman's knives. **Patterns:** Bird knives to Bowies. **Technical:** Grinds D2 and ATS-34. **Prices:** $75 to $150; some to $400. **Remarks:** Spare-time maker; first knife sold in 1983. **Mark:** Last initial.

CHEROKEE KNIVES (See Chapman, Mike)

CHOATE, MILTON, 660 S. 7th Ave., Yuma, AZ 85364/520-329-1817
Specialties: Classic working and using straight knives of his design, to customer specs and in standard patterns. **Patterns:** Bowies, hunters and utility/camp knives. **Technical:** Grinds 440C; grinds and forges 1095 and 5160. Does filework on top and guards on request. **Prices:** $70 to $200. **Remarks:** Part-time maker; first knife made in 1990. **Mark:** Last name or last name above city.

CHURCHMAN, T.W., 7402 Tall Cedar, San Antonio, TX 78249/210-690-8641
Specialties: Fancy and traditional straight knives and bird/trout knives of his design and to customer specs. **Patterns:** Bird/trout knives, Bowies, daggers, fighters and boot knives. **Technical:** Grinds 440C and D2. Offers fancy filework, lined sheaths, exotic and stabilized woods, and twisted silver wire on fluted handles. **Prices:** $75 to $300; some to $1,500. **Remarks:** Part-time maker; first knife sold in 1981. Doing business as Custom Knives Churchman Made. **Mark:** Last name, dagger.

CISCO (See Syslo, Chuck)

CLAIBORNE, RON, 2918 Ellistown Rd., Knox, TN 37924/615-524-2054
Specialties: Working and using straight knives; period pieces. **Patterns:** Hunters, Bowies and daggers. **Technical:** Forges his own Damascus; grinds 440C, O1, W2 and 1095. Prefers bone and natural handle materials; some exotic woods. **Prices:** $125 to $300; some to $900. **Remarks:** Part-time maker; first knife sold in 1979. Doing business as Thunder Mountain Forge Claiborne Knives. **Mark:** Last name.

CLARK, DAVE, P.O. Box 597, Andrews, NC 28901/704-321-2230
Specialties: Folders to customer specs. **Patterns:** Locking folders. **Technical:** Grinds 440C, D2 and stainless Damascus. **Prices:** $400 to $1,500. **Remarks:** Full-time maker; first knife sold in 1988. **Mark:** Name.

CLARK, D.E. (LUCKY), 126 Woodland St., Mineral Point, PA 15942/814-322-4725
Specialties: Working straight knives and folders to customer specs. **Patterns:** Customer designs. **Technical:** Grinds D2, 440C, 154CM. **Prices:** $100 to $200; some higher. **Remarks:** Part-time maker; first knife sold in 1975. **Mark:** Name on one side; "Lucky" on other.

CLARK, HOWARD F., 115 35th Pl., Runnells, IA 50237/515-966-2126
Specialties: Damascus knives of all kinds; folders and straight knives. **Patterns:** Most anything. **Technical:** Forges 1086, L6, 52100 and his own all tool steel Damascus; bar stock; forged blanks. **Prices:** $500 to $3,000. **Remarks:** Full-time maker; first knife sold in 1979. Doing business as Morgan Valley Forge. **Mark:** Block letters and serial number on folders; anvil/initials logo on straight knives.

CLARK, ROGER, Rt. 1, Box 538, Rockdale, TX 76567/512-446-3388
Specialties: Traditional working and using straight knives of his design or to customer specs. **Patterns:** Hunters, Bowies and camp knives; primitive styles for blackpowder hunters. **Technical:** Forges 1084, O1 and Damascus. Sheaths are extra. **Prices:** Primitive styles start at $100; shiny blades start at $150; Damascus start at $250. **Remarks:** Full-time maker; first knife sold in 1989. **Mark:** First initial, last name.

CLARK, W.R., 13009 Los Nietos Rd., Bldg. G., Santa Fe Springs, CA 90670/310-906-0233; FAX: 310-906-0233

CLAY CUSTOM KNIVES, RICHARD (See Clay, Richard S.)

CLAY, J.D., 5050 Hall Rd., Greenup, KY 41144/606-473-6769
Specialties: Collector-grade working straight knives and locking folders. **Patterns:** Practical hunters and locking folders. **Technical:** Grinds 440C and ATS-34. **Prices:** Start at $120. **Remarks:** Full-time maker; first knife sold in 1972. **Mark:** Name in script on blade, sometimes medallion.

CLAY, RICHARD S., 1042 E. Cedar, Winchester, IN 47394/317-584-4017
Specialties: Traditional working and using straight knives of his design. **Patterns:** Bowies and hunters. **Technical:** Grinds 440C and ATS-34. Does filework. Gold inlay in handle material; exotic skin overlays on sheaths. **Prices:** $95 to $300; some to $400. **Remarks:** Part-time maker; first knife sold in 1988. Doing business as Richard Clay Custom Knives. **Mark:** Last name.

CLAY, WAYNE, Box 474B, Pelham, TN 37366/615-467-3472; FAX: 615-467-3076
Specialties: Working straight knives and folders in standard patterns. **Patterns:** Hunters, fighters and kitchen knives; gents and hunter patterns. **Technical:** Grinds 154CM and ATS-34. **Prices:** $125 to $250; some to $1,000. **Remarks:** Full-time maker; first knife sold in 1978. **Mark:** Name.

CLICK CUSTOM KNIVES (See Click, Joe)

CLICK, JOE, U-344 Rd. 2, Liberty Center, OH 43532/419-875-6199; FAX: 419-875-5736
Specialties: Fancy/embellished and traditional working/using straight knives of his design, to customer specs and in standard patterns. **Patterns:** Bowies, hunters and utility/camp knives. **Technical:** Grinds and forges A2, D2, 5160 and Damascus. Does fancy filework; triple temper. Uses ivory for handle material. **Prices:** $75 to $300; some to $700. **Remarks:** Doing business as Click Custom Knives. **Mark:** Full name.

CLOUDY MT. IRON WORKS (See Ber, Dave)

COATS, ELDON, P.O. Box 201, Bonanza, OR 97623/503-545-6960
Specialties: Plain to fancy working knives of his design or to customer specs. Will work with collectors. **Patterns:** Hunters, skinners, fighters, survival knives, Bowies, boots, fillet knives, axes and miniatures. **Technical:** Flat-grinds mostly by hand 440C, D2, 5160. Uses exotic hardwoods, Micarta and ivory for handles. Bead blasts; uses commercial heat-treater. Makes own sheaths. Scrimshaws and engraves. **Prices:** $50 to $250; miniatures start at $35; collector pieces to $1,200. **Remarks:** Full-time maker; first knife sold in 1987. **Mark:** Name, with dagger in "T."

COBB, LOWELL D., 823 Julia St., Daytona Beach, FL 32114/904-252-3514
Specialties: Working straight knives of his design or to customer specs. **Patterns:** Fighters, hunters, skinners, fillet knives and Bowies. **Technical:** Grinds 440C; embellishments available. **Prices:** $100 to $500. **Remarks:** Part-time maker; first knife sold in 1986. **Mark:** Name.

COFER, RON, 188 Ozora Road, Loganville, GA 30249-2159
Specialties: Fancy working and using straight knives of his design. **Patterns:** Hunters, Bowies and fighters. **Technical:** Grinds 440C and ATS-34. Heat-treats. Some knives have carved stag handles or scrimshaw. Makes leather sheath for each knife and walnut and deer antler display stands for art knives. **Prices:** $125 to $250; some to $600. **Remarks:** Spare-time maker; first knife sold in 1991. **Mark:** Name, serial number.

COFFMAN, DANNY, 505 Angel Dr. S., Jacksonville, AL 36265/205-435-5848
Specialties: Straight knives and folders of his design. **Patterns:** Hunters, locking and slip-joint folders. **Technical:** Grinds Damascus, 440C and D2. Offers filework and engraving. **Prices:** $100 to $400; some to $800. **Remarks:** Spare-time maker; first knife sold in 1992. Doing business as Customs by Coffman. **Mark:** Last name stamped or engraved.

COHEN, N.J. (NORM), 2408 Sugarcone Rd., Baltimore, MD 21209/410-484-3841
Specialties: Working class knives. **Patterns:** Hunters, skinners, bird knives, push daggers, boots, kitchen and practical customer designs. **Technical:** Stock removal 440C, ATS-34. Uses Micarta, Corian. Some woods in handles. **Prices:** $50 to $250. **Remarks:** Part-time maker; first knife sold in 1982. **Mark:** Etched initials or NJC MAKER.

COHEN, TERRY A., P.O. Box 406, Laytonville, CA 95454
Specialties: Working straight knives and folders. **Patterns:** Bowies to boot knives and locking folders; mini-boot knives. **Technical:** Grinds stainless; hand rubs; tries for good balance. **Prices:** $85 to $150; some to $325. **Remarks:** Part-time maker; first knife sold in 1983. **Mark:** TERRY KNIVES, city and state.

COIL, JIMMIE J., 2936 Asbury Pl., Owensboro, KY 42302/502-684-7827
Specialties: Traditional working and using straight knives of his design. **Patterns:** Hunters, Bowies and fighters. **Technical:** Grinds 440C, ATS-34 and D2. Blades are flat-ground with brush finish; most have tapered tang. Offers filework. **Prices:** $65 to $250; some to $750. **Remarks:** Spare-time maker; first knife sold in 1974. **Mark:** Name.

COLD SPRINGS FORGE (See Solomon, Marvin)

COLE, WELBORN I., 3284 Inman Dr. NE, Atlanta, GA 30319/404-261-3977
Specialties: Traditional straight knives of his design. **Patterns:** Hunters. **Technical:** Grinds 440C, ATS-34 and D2. Good wood scales. **Prices:** NA. **Remarks:** Full-time maker; first knife sold in 1983. **Mark:** Script initials.

COLEMAN, KEITH E., 13 Jardin Rd., Los Lunas, NM 87031/505-864-0024
Specialties: Affordable collector-grade straight knives and folders; some fancy. **Patterns:** Fighters, tantos, combat folders, gents folders and boots. **Technical:** Grinds ATS-34 and Damascus. Prefers specialty woods; offers filework. **Prices:** $150 to $700; some to $1,500. **Remarks:** Full-time maker; first knife sold in 1980. **Mark:** Name, city and state.

COLLETT, JERRY D., 2124 U.S. Highway 90 W. Castroville, TX 78009-5413
Specialties: Traditional-style folders. **Patterns:** Mainly slip-joint folders. **Technical:** 440C, ATS-34, D2 and O1. Extensive filework offered as standard. **Prices:** $175 to $500. **Remarks:** Full-time maker; first knife sold in 1989. **Mark:** Initials or last name.

COLLINS, A.J., 9651 Elon Ave., Arleta, CA 91331/818-762-7728
Specialties: Working dress knives of his design. **Patterns:** Street survival knives, swords, axes. **Technical:** Grinds O1, 440C, 154CM. **Prices:** Start at $100. **Remarks:** Full-time maker; first knife sold in 1972. Doing business as Kustom Krafted Knives—KKK. **Mark:** Name.

COLLINS, HAROLD, 503 First St., West Union, OH 45693/513-544-2982
Specialties: Traditional using straight knives and folders of his design or to customer specs. **Patterns:** Hunters, Bowies and locking folders. **Technical:** Forges and grinds 440C, ATS-34, D2, O1 and 5160. Flat-grinds standard; filework available. **Prices:** $75 to $300. **Remarks:** Full-time maker; first knife sold in 1989. **Mark:** First initial, last name, Maker.

COLLINS, LYNN M., 138 Berkley Dr., Elyria, OH 44035/216-366-7101
Specialties: Working straight knives. **Patterns:** Field knives, boots and fighters. **Technical:** Grinds D2, 154CM and 440C. **Prices:** Start at $150. **Remarks:** Spare-time maker; first knife sold in 1980. **Mark:** Initials, asterisks.

COLTER, WADE, P.O. Box 2340, Colstrip, MT 59323/406-748-4573
Specialties: Fancy and embellished straight knives, folders and swords of his design; historical and period pieces. **Patterns:** Bowies, swords and folders. **Technical:** Hand forges 52100 ball bearing steel and L6, 1090, cable and chain Damascus. Carves and makes sheaths. **Prices:** $100 to $2,500. **Remarks:** Part-time maker; first knife sold in 1990. Doing business as "Colter's Hell" Forge. **Mark:** Initials on left side ricasso.

"COLTER'S HELL" FORGE (See Colter, Wade)

COMPTON, WILLIAM E., 106 N. Sequoia Ct., Sterling, VA 20164/703-430-2129
Specialties: Working straight knives of his design or to customer specs; some fancy knives. **Patterns:** Hunters, camp knives, Bowies and some kitchen knives. **Technical:** Grinds ATS-34, 440C, D2 and O1. **Prices:** $65 to $300; some to $700. **Remarks:** Part-time maker; first knife sold in 1994. Doing business as Comptons Custom Knives. **Mark:** Last name, left side of blade.

COMPTON'S CUSTOM KNIVES (See Compton, William E.)

CONABLE, MATT, P.O. Box 1329, 26 North Rd. One West, Chino Valley, AZ 86323/520-636-2402.

CONFEDERATE FORGE (See Chase, Alex)

CONKEY, TOM, 9122 Keyser Rd., Nokesville, VA 22123/703-791-3867
Specialties: Classic straight knives and folders of his design and to customer specs. **Patterns:** Boots, hunters and locking folders. **Technical:** Grinds ATS-34, O1 and commercial Damascus. Lockbacks have jeweled scales and locking bars with dovetailed bolsters. Folders utilize unique 2-piece bushing of his design and manufacture. Sheaths are handmade. Presentation boxes made upon request. **Prices:** $100 to $500. **Remarks:** Part-time maker; first knife sold in 1991. Collaborates with Dan Thomas. **Mark:** Last name with "handcrafted" underneath.

CONKLIN, GEORGE L., Box 902, Ft. Benton, MT 59442/406-622-3268; FAX: 406-622-3410; E-MAIL: 7bbqrus@3rivers.net
Specialties: Designer and manufacturer of the "Brisket Breaker." **Patterns:** Hunters, utility/camp knives and hatchets. **Technical:** Grinds 440C, ATS-34, D2, 1095, 154CM and 5160. Offers some forging and heat-treats for others. Offers some jeweling. **Prices:** $65 to $200; some to $1,000. **Remarks:** Full-time maker. Doing business as Rocky Mountain Knives. **Mark:** Last name in script.

CONKLIN MEADOWS FORGE (See Little, Gary M.)

CONLEY, BOB, 1013 Creasy Rd., Jonesboro, TN 37659/423-753-3302
Specialties: Working straight knives and folders. **Patterns:** Lockers, two-blades, gents, hunters, traditional styles, straight hunters. **Technical:** Grinds 440C, 154CM and ATS-34. Engraves. **Prices:** $250 to $450; some to $600. **Remarks:** Full-time maker; first knife sold in 1979. **Mark:** Full name, city, state.

CONN JR., C.T., 206 Highland Ave., Attalla, AL 35954/205-538-7688
Specialties: Working folders, some fancy. **Patterns:** Full range of folding knives. **Technical:** Grinds O2, 440C and 154CM. **Prices:** $125 to $300; some to $600. **Remarks:** Part-time maker; first knife sold in 1982. **Mark:** Name.

CONNELL, STEVE, 601 Green Blvd., Adamsville, AL 35005-1849/205-674-0440
Specialties: Working and using straight knives, some one-of-a-kind.

Patterns: Hunters, fighters, Bowies and daggers. **Technical:** Uses 440C, ATS-34, Damascus. Satin finishes. **Prices:** $75 to $500; some to $600. **Remarks:** Part-time maker; first knife sold in 1987. **Mark:** Last name in block lettering.

CONNOLLY, JAMES, 2486 Oro-Quincy Hwy., Oroville, CA 95966/916-534-5363
Specialties: Classic working and using knives of his design. **Patterns:** Boots, Bowies and daggers. **Technical:** Grinds ATS-34; forges 5160; forges and grinds O1. **Prices:** $100 to $500; some to $1,500. **Remarks:** Full-time maker; first knife sold in 1980. Doing business as Gold Rush Designs. **Mark:** First initial, last name, Handmade.

CONNOR, MICHAEL, Box 502, Winters, TX 79567/915-754-5602
Specialties: High-art straight knives and folders. **Patterns:** Hunters to camp knives to traditional locking folders. **Technical:** Forges 5160, O1 and his own Damascus. **Prices:** $275 to $3,000. **Remarks:** Part-time maker; first knife sold in 1974. **Mark:** Last name, M.S.

CONTI, JEFFREY D., 4629 Feigley Rd. W., Port Orchard, WA 98366/206-405-0075
Specialties: Working straight knives. **Patterns:** Fighters and survival knives; hunters, camp knives and fishing knives. **Technical:** Grinds D2, 154CM and O1. Engraves. **Prices:** Start at $80. **Remarks:** Part-time maker; first knife sold in 1980. **Mark:** Initials, year, steel type, name and number of knife.

COOGAN, ROBERT, 1560 Craft Center Dr., Smithville, TN 37166/615-597-6801
Specialties: One-of-a-kind knives. **Patterns:** Unique items like ooloo-style Appalachian herb knives. **Technical:** Forges; his Damascus is made from nickel steel and W1. **Prices:** Start at $100. **Remarks:** Part-time maker; first knife sold in 1979. **Mark:** Initials.

COOK, JAMES R., 3611 Hwy. 26 W., Nashville, AR 71852/501-845-5173
Specialties: Working straight knives and folders of his design or to customer specs. **Patterns:** Bowies, hunters and camp knives. **Technical:** Forges 5160, O1 and Damascus from O1 and 1018. **Prices:** $195 to $5,500. **Remarks:** Part-time maker; first knife sold in 1986. **Mark:** First and middle initials, last name.

COOK, LOUISE, 475 Robinson Ln., Ozark, IL 62972/618-777-2932
Specialties: Working and using straight knives of her design and to customer specs; period pieces. **Patterns:** Bowies, hunters and utility/camp knives. **Technical:** Forges 5160. Filework; pin work; silver wire inlay. **Prices:** Start at $50/inch. **Remarks:** Part-time maker; first knife sold in 1990. Doing business as Panther Creek Forge. **Mark:** First name and journeyman stamp on one side; panther head on the other.

COOK, MIKE, Rt. 1, Box 104, Ozark, IL 62972/618-777-2932
Specialties: Traditional working and using straight knives of his design and to customer specs. **Patterns:** Bowies, hunters and utility/camp knives. **Technical:** Forges 5160. Filework; pin work. **Prices:** Start at $50/inch. **Remarks:** Spare-time maker; first knife sold in 1991. **Mark:** First initial, last name and journeyman stamp on one side; panther head on the other.

COOK, MIKE A., 10927 Shilton Rd., Portland, MI 48875/517-647-2518
Specialties: Fancy/embellished and period pieces of his design. **Patterns:** Daggers, fighters and hunters. **Technical:** Stone bladed knives in agate, obsidian and jasper. Scrimshaws; opal inlays. **Prices:** $60 to $300; some to $800. **Remarks:** Part-time maker; first knife sold in 1988. Doing business as Art of Ishi. **Mark:** Initials and year.

COOMBS JR., LAMONT, RFD #1, Box 1412, Bucksport, ME 04416/207-469-3057
Specialties: Classic fancy and embellished straight knives; traditional working and using straight knives. Knives of his design and to customer specs. **Patterns:** Hunters, folders and utility/camp knives. **Technical:** Hollow- and flat-grinds ATS-34, 440C, A2, D2 and O1; grinds Damascus from other makers. **Prices:** With sheaths—$65 to $500; some to $1,500. **Remarks:** Part-time maker; first knife sold in 1988. **Mark:** Last name on banner, handmade underneath.

COON, RAYMOND C., 21135 SE Tillstrom Rd., Gresham, OR 97080/503-658-2252; E-MAIL: jeramo@teleport.com
Specialties: Working straight knives in standard patterns. **Patterns:** Hunters, Bowies, boots and axes. **Technical:** Forges high carbon steel and Damascus; grinds stainless. **Prices:** Start at $100. **Remarks:** Part-time maker; first knife sold in 1995. **Mark:** First initial, last name.

COPELAND, GEORGE "STEVE," 220 Pat Carr Lane, Alpine, TN 38543/615-823-5214
Specialties: Traditional and fancy working straight knives and folders. **Patterns:** Friction folders, Congress two- and four-blade folders, button locks and one- and two-blade automatics. **Technical:** Stock removal of 440C, ATS-34 and A2; heat-treats. **Prices:** $180 to $950; some higher. **Remarks:** Full-time maker; first knife sold in 1979. Doing business as Alpine Mountain Knives. **Mark:** G.S. Copeland (HANDMADE); some with four-leaf clover stamp.

COPPERHEAD FORGE (See Black, Scott)

CORBIN KNIVES (See Newcomb, Corbin)

CORBIN CUSTOM KNIVES (See Corbit, Gerald E and Philip E.)

CORBIT, GERALD E. AND PHILIP E., 1701 St. John Rd., Elizabethtown, KY 42701/502-765-7728
Specialties: Fancy and working liner lock folders and automatic knives. **Patterns:** Automatics and liner lock folders. **Technical:** Grinds 440C, ATS-34 and commercial Damascus. Heat-treats; offers scrimshaw, engraving and filework on blades and liners. Finishes include polished, satin and bead blasted. **Prices:** $200 to $2,000. **Remarks:** Part-time makers; first knife sold in 1991. Doing business as Corbit Custom Knives. **Mark:** Last name in script, town and state.

CORBIT, PHILIP E. (See Corbit, Gerald E. and Philip E.)

CORBY, HAROLD, 218 Brandonwood Dr., Johnson City, TN 37604/615-926-9781
Specialties: Large fighters and Bowies; self-protection knives; art knives. **Patterns:** Sub-hilt fighters and hunters. **Technical:** Grinds 154CM, ATS-34 and 440C. **Prices:** $200 to $6,000. **Remarks:** Full-time maker; first knife sold in 1969. Doing business as Knives by Corby. **Mark:** Last name.

CORDOVA, JOSEPH G., P.O. Box 977, Peralta, NM 87042/505-869-3912
Specialties: One-of-a-kind designs, some to customer specs. **Patterns:** Fighter called the 'Gladiator,' hunters, boots and cutlery. **Technical:** Forges 1095, 5160; grinds ATS-34, 440C and 154CM. **Prices:** Moderate to upscale. **Remarks:** Full-time maker; first knife sold in 1953. **Mark:** Cordova made.

CORKEN KNIVES (See Johnson, Kenneth R.)

CORKUM, STEVE, 5301 Buckeystown Pike, Box 103-127, Frederick, MD 21704/301-631-8329; FAX: 301-631-5609
Specialties: Traditional working and using straight knives of his design. **Patterns:** Bowies, fighters and swords. **Technical:** Grinds 1050, 1095 and 1084. Japanese clay treating on blades prior to heat treating; traditional Japanese handle wrappings and scabbard carving. **Prices:** $125 to $2,200; some to $3,500. **Remarks:** Full-time maker; first knife sold in 1996. Doing business as Hawk Knives. **Mark:** Outline of a hawk.

CORRADO, JIM, 2915 Cavitt Creek Rd., Glide, OR 97443/503-496-3951; FAX: 503-496-3595
Specialties: High-tech, high-art folding knives. **Patterns:** Makes early European single and multi-blade designs. **Technical:** Forges mostly L6 and his own Damascus. Uses natural handle material; stag, pearl, ivory, and imitation tortoise shell. **Prices:** Start at $250. **Remarks:** Full-time maker; first knife sold in 1974. **Mark:** Name, date and state with shield logo.

CORWIN, DON, 5064 Eber Rd., Monclova, OH 43542/419-877-5210
Specialties: Traditional-style knives to customer specs. **Patterns:** One- to five-blade folders, slip-joints, lockers and miniatures. **Technical:** Grinds 440C, ATS-34, 154CM and Damascus; makes own mokume. **Prices:** $200 to $600. **Remarks:** Part-time maker; first knife sold in 1987. **Mark:** Last name in arrowhead logo and year.

COSBY, E. BLANTON, 2954 Pierpont Ave., Columbus, GA 31904/706-323-0327
Specialties: Traditional working and using straight knives and folders of his design or to customer specs. **Patterns:** Hunters, Bowies, boots and switchblades. **Technical:** Grinds 440C, 12C27, ATS-34 and commercial Damascus. **Prices:** $125 to $350; some to $700. **Remarks:** Full-time maker; first knife sold in 1988. **Mark:** Engraved initials and year.

COSGROVE, CHARLES G., 2112 Briarwood Dr., Amarillo, TX 79124/806-352-0334

Specialties: Traditional fixed or locking blade working knives. **Patterns:** Hunters, Bowies and locking folders. **Technical:** Stock removal using 440C, ATS-34 and D2; heat-treats. Makes heavy, hand-stitched sheaths. **Prices:** $250 to $2,500. **Remarks:** Full-time maker; first knife sold in 1968. No longer accepting customer designs. **Mark:** First initial, last name, or full name over city and state.

COSTA, SCOTT, Rt. 2, Box 503, Spicewood, TX 78669/210-693-3431
Specialties: Working straight knives. **Patterns:** Hunters, skinners, axes, trophy sets, custom boxed steak sets, carving sets and bar sets. **Technical:** Grinds D2, ATS-34, 440 and Damascus. Heat-treats. **Prices:** $225 to $2,000. **Remarks:** Full-time maker; first knife sold in 1985. **Mark:** Initials connected.

CÔTÉ, YVES, 1A-788 Philippe, Ste-Foy (Quebec), CANADA G1V 2R1/418-683-3285
Specialties: Classic and fancy straight knives. **Patterns:** Bowies, daggers, swords and miniatures. **Technical:** Grinds ATS-34 and Damascus. Full-time scrimshander and carver. **Prices:** $50 to $700. **Remarks:** Full-time maker; first knife sold in 1991. **Mark:** First name.

COTTRILL, JAMES I., 1776 Ransburg Ave., Columbus, OH 43223/614-274-0020
Specialties: Working straight knives of his design. **Patterns:** Caters to the boating and hunting crowd; cutlery. **Technical:** Grinds O1, D2 and 440C. Likes filework. **Prices:** $95 to $250; some to $500. **Remarks:** Full-time maker; first knife sold in 1977. **Mark:** Name, city, state, in oval logo.

COUGHLIN, MICHAEL M., #65 West Street, New Milford, CT 06776/860-350-6511
Specialties: Edged weapons, fighters, folders and special weapons. **Patterns:** Bowies, fighters, tomahawks, utility/camp knives, concealment knives, duty knives for police/fire rescue and swords. **Technical:** Grinds O1, D2, ATS-34 and Damascus. Offers filework. **Prices:** $300 to $750. **Remarks:** Part-time maker; first knife sold in 1985. **Mark:** Last name and model.

COURTNEY, ELDON, 2718 Bullinger, Wichita, KS 67204/316-838-4053
Specialties: Working straight knives of his design. **Patterns:** Hunters, fighters and one-of-a-kinds. **Technical:** Grinds and tempers L6, 440C and spring steel. **Prices:** $100 to $500; some to $1,500. **Remarks:** Full-time maker; first knife sold in 1977. **Mark:** Full name, city and state.

COURTOIS, BRYAN, 3 Lawn Avenue, Saco, ME 04072
Specialties: Working straight knives; prefers customer designs, no standard patterns. **Patterns:** Functional hunters; everyday knives. **Technical:** Grinds S7, O1, 440C or customer request. Hollow-grinds with a variety of finishes. Specializes in granite handles and custom skeleton knives. **Prices:** Start at $75. **Remarks:** Part-time maker; first knife sold in 1988. Doing business as Castle Knives. **Mark:** A rook chess piece machined into blade using electrical discharge process.

COUSINO, GEORGE, 7818 Norfolk, Onsted, MI 49265/517-467-4911
Specialties: Working straight knives. **Patterns:** Hunters, Bowies, buckskinners, folders and daggers. **Technical:** Grinds D2, 440C. **Prices:** $85 to $125; some to $600. **Remarks:** Part-time maker; first knife sold in 1981. **Mark:** Last name.

COVER, RAYMOND A., Rt. 1, Box 194, Mineral Point, MO 63660/314-749-3783
Specialties: High-tech working straight knives and folders in standard patterns. **Patterns:** Bowies and boots; two-bladed folders. **Technical:** Grinds D2, 440C and 154CM. **Prices:** $135 to $250; some to $400. **Remarks:** Part-time maker; first knife sold in 1974. **Mark:** Name.

COWLES, DON, 1026 Lawndale Dr., Royal Oak, MI 48067/810-541-4619
Specialties: Traditional and working/using straight knives of his design. **Patterns:** Hunters, kitchen knives and utility/camp knives. **Technical:** Grinds O1, 440C and ATS-34. Scrimshaws; pearl inlays in some handles. **Prices:** $75 to $400; some to $750. **Remarks:** Part-time maker; first knife sold in 1994. **Mark:** Full name, city and state with oak leaf.

COX CALL (See Cox, Sam)

COX, COLIN J., 107 N. Oxford Dr., Raymore, MO 64083/816-322-1977
Specialties: Working straight knives and folders of his design; period pieces. **Patterns:** Hunters, fighters and survival knives. Folders, two-blades, gents and hunters. **Technical:** Grinds D2, 440C, 154CM and ATS-34. **Prices:** $125 to $750; some to $4,000. **Remarks:** Full-time maker; first knife sold in 1981. **Mark:** Full name, city and state.

COX, SAM, 1756 Love Springs Rd., Gaffney, SC 29341/864-489-1892; FAX: 864-489-0403
Specialties: Classic high-art working straight knives of his design. Duck knives copyrighted. **Patterns:** Diverse. **Technical:** Grinds 440C, ATS-34 and Damascus. **Prices:** $200 to $1,400. **Remarks:** Full-time maker; first knife sold in 1983. **Mark:** Cox Call and name.

C.P. KNIFEMAKER (See Pienaar, Conrad)

CRAFT III, JOHN M., Lockett Springs Ranch, P.O. Box 682, Williams, AZ 86046/602-635-2190
Specialties: High-art straight knives to customer specs; period pieces. **Patterns:** Daggers, swords and utility/camp knives. **Technical:** Forges his own Damascus; 440C and ATS-34 by stock removal. **Prices:** $95 to $450; some to $2,500. **Remarks:** Full-time maker; first knife sold in 1985. **Mark:** Runic "M" in pommel or near butt.

CRAFT, RICHARD C., 3045 Longwood Dr., Jackson, MS 39212/601-373-4046
Specialties: Fancy working knives. **Patterns:** Offers chopping knife and block for kitchen, bird knives and steak knives with presentation case. **Technical:** Grinds O1, L6 and 440C. Cases made of cherry or mahogany. **Prices:** $65 to $275; some to $600. **Remarks:** Full-time maker; first knife sold in 1985. **Mark:** Last name.

CRAIG KNIVES (See Craig, Roger L.)

CRAIG, ROGER L., 1327 Lane, Topeka, KS 66604/913-233-3845
Specialties: Fantasy and working/using knives of his design. **Patterns:** Fighters, hunters and locking folders. **Technical:** Grinds O1 tool steel and 5160. Offers filework and cowhide sheaths colored to match the knives. **Prices:** $80 to $175; some to $450. **Remarks:** Part-time maker; first knife sold in 1991. Doing business as Craig Knives. **Mark:** Last name, sometimes with a coyote.

CRAIN, FRANK, 1127 W. Dalke, Spokane, WA 99205/509-325-1596

CRAIN, JACK W., 400 Walden Rd., Weatherford, TX 76087/817-599-6414
Specialties: Fantasy and period knives; combat and survival knives. **Patterns:** One-of-a-kind art or fantasy daggers, swords and Bowies; survival knives. **Technical:** Forges Damascus; grinds stainless steel. Carves. **Prices:** $350 to $2,500; some to $20,000. **Remarks:** Full-time maker; first knife sold in 1969. Designer and maker of the knives seen in the films *Executive Decision*, *Demolition Man*, *Predator I and II*, *Commando*, *Die Hard I and II*, *Road House*, *Ford Fairlane* and *Action Jackson*, and television shows *War of the Worlds*, *Air Wolf*, *Kung Fu: The Legend Cont.* and *Tales of the Crypt*. **Mark:** Annual change of registered trademark—stylized crane.

CRAWFORD, PAT, 205 N. Center, West Memphis, AR 72301/501-735-4632
Specialties: High-tech working straight knives—self-defense and combat types—and folders. **Patterns:** Folding patent locks, interframes, fighters and boots. **Technical:** Grinds 440C, ATS-34, D2 and 154CM. **Prices:** $125 to $2,000. **Remarks:** Full-time maker; first knife sold in 1973. **Mark:** Last name.

CRAWLEY, BRUCE R., 16 Binbrook Dr., Croydon 3136, VIC, AUSTRALIA
Specialties: Folders. **Patterns:** Hunters, lockback folders and Bowies. **Technical:** Grinds 440C, ATS-34 and commercial Damascus. Offers filework and mirror polish. **Prices:** $160 to $850. **Remarks:** Part-time maker; first knife sold in 1990. **Mark:** Initials.

CREATIONS YVON VACHON (See Vachon, Yvon)

CRENSHAW KNIVES, A. (See Crenshaw, Al)

CRENSHAW, AL, Rt. 1 Box 717, Eufaula, OK 74432/918-452-2128
Specialties: Folders of his design and in standard patterns. **Patterns:** Hunters, locking folders and slip-joint folders. **Technical:** Grinds 440C, D2 and ATS-34. Does filework on backsprings and blades; offers scrimshaw on some handles. **Prices:** $175 to $300. **Remarks:** Full-time maker; first knife sold in 1981. Doing business as A. Crenshaw Knives. **Mark:** First initial, last name, Lake Efaula, state stamped; first initial last name in rainbow; Lake Efaula across bottom with Okla. in middle.

CRISP, HAROLD, 3885 Bow St. NE, Cleveland, TN 37312/615-476-8240
Specialties: Fancy working straight knives and folders. **Patterns:** Hunters, Bowies, tomahawks and miniatures. Locking folders, interframes and traditional-style knives. **Technical:** Grinds O1, D2 and 440C; forges. **Prices:** $85 to $250; some to $800. **Remarks:** Part-time maker; first knife sold in 1972. **Mark:** Initials or name.

CROCKFORD, JACK, 1859 Harts Mill Rd., Chamblee, GA 30341/770-457-4680
Specialties: Lockback folders. **Patterns:** Hunters, fishing and camp knives, traditional folders. **Technical:** Grinds A2, D2, ATS-34 and 440C. Engraves and scrimshaws. **Prices:** Start at $175. **Remarks:** Part-time maker; first knife sold in 1975. **Mark:** Name.

CROSS, JOHN M., Rt. 1, Box 351, Bryceville, FL 32009/904-266-9092
Specialties: Traditional working and using straight knives of his design. **Patterns:** Hunters, Bowies, utility/camp knives. **Technical:** Forges his own Damascus, O1 and 1095. Prefers natural handle materials, especially buffalo bone. **Prices:** $150 to $350; some up to $750. **Remarks:** Full-time maker; first knife sold in 1985. **Mark:** A cross.

CROSS, ROBERT, RMB 200B, Manilla Rd., Tamworth 2340 NSW, AUSTRALIA/067-618385

CROWDER, ROBERT, Box 1374, Thompson Falls, MT 59873/406-827-4754
Specialties: Traditional working knives to customer specs. **Patterns:** Hunters, Bowies, fighters and fillets. **Technical:** Grinds ATS-34, 154CM, 440C, Vascowear and commercial Damascus. **Prices:** $160 to $250; some to $2,500. **Remarks:** Part-time maker; first knife sold in 1985. **Mark:** First initial, last name.

CROWELL, JAMES L., H.C. 74, Box 368, Mtn. View, AR 72560/501-269-4215
Specialties: Fancy period pieces and working knives to customer specs. **Patterns:** Hunters to daggers, war hammers to tantos; locking folders and slip-joints. **Technical:** Forges W2, O1, 5160, 1095 and his own Damascus. **Prices:** $295 to $2,500; some to $6,000. **Remarks:** Part-time maker; first knife sold in 1980. **Mark:** A shooting star.

CULPEPPER, JOHN, 2102 Spencer Ave., Monroe, LA 71201/318-323-3636
Specialties: Working straight knives. **Patterns:** Hunters, Bowies and camp knives in heavy-duty patterns. **Technical:** Grinds O1, D2 and 440C; hollow-grinds. **Prices:** $75 to $200; some to $300. **Remarks:** Part-time maker; first knife sold in 1970. Doing business as Pepper Knives. **Mark:** Pepper.

CULVER, STEVE, 1604 Willow, Valley Falls, KS 66088/913-945-3553
Specialties: Period pieces and working straight knives. **Patterns:** Hunters, Bowies, daggers. **Technical:** Forges his own Damascus, O1 and 5160. Fancy filework available. **Prices:** $100 to $500; some to $1,000. **Remarks:** Full-time maker; first knife sold in 1989. **Mark:** Last name, J.S.

CUMMING, R.J., American Embassy Tunis, U.S. Dept. of State, Washington D.C., 20521-6360/Int'l. direct dial 216-1-741-314
Specialties: Custom designs. **Patterns:** Hunters, fighters, Bowies and one-of-a-kind straight knives. Diver's tool knife. **Technical:** Grinds D2, 440C and 154CM. **Prices:** $175 to $550; some to $2,000. **Remarks:** Part-time maker; first knife sold in 1978. **Mark:** Last name.

CUSTOM CUTLERY (See Boeckman, R. Von)

CUSTOM KNIFE (See Parker, J.E.)

CUSTOM KNIVES (See Morris, C.H.)

CUSTOM KNIVES BY STEVE DAVIS (See Davis, Steve)

CUSTOM KNIVES CHURCHMAN MADE (See Churchman, T.W.)

CUSTOM TOICH (See Toich, Nevio)

CUSTOMS BY COFFMAN (See Coffman, Danny)

CUTCHIN, ROY D., 960 Hwy. 169 S., Seale, AL 36875/334-855-3080
Specialties: Fancy and working folders and small straight knives of his design, to customer specs and in standard patterns. **Patterns:** Liner lock folders. **Technical:** Grinds ATS-34; uses anodized titanium. Offers filework. **Prices:** Start at $250. **Remarks:** Part-time maker. **Mark:** First initial, last name, city and state.

CUTE, THOMAS, State Rt. 90-7071, Cortland, NY 13045/607-749-4055
Specialties: Working straight knives. **Patterns:** Hunters, Bowies and fighters. **Technical:** Grinds O1, 440C and ATS-34. **Prices:** $100 to $1,000. **Remarks:** Full-time maker; first knife sold in 1974. **Mark:** Full name.

CYPRESS BEND CUSTOM KNIVES (See Ellerbe, W.B.)

d

DACONCEICAO, JOHN M., 138 Perryville Rd., Rehoboth, MA 02769/508-252-9686
Specialties: One-of-a-kind straight knives of his design and to customer specs. **Patterns:** Boots, fighters and folders. **Technical:** Grinds O1, 1095 and commercial Damascus. All knives come with leather sheath; cross-draw and shoulder harnesses available. **Prices:** $90 to $200; some to $500. **Remarks:** Part-time maker; first knife sold in 1993. **Mark:** JMD Blades.

DAHL, CHRIS W., Rt. 4, Box 558, Lake Geneva, WI 53147/414-248-2464
Specialties: Period pieces and high-art display knives. **Patterns:** Daggers, fighters and hunters. **Technical:** Grinds 440C and stainless steel Damascus. Works exclusively with gemstone handles on all daggers. **Prices:** $500 to $5,000; some to $10,000. **Remarks:** Full-time maker. **Mark:** Full name—maker.

DAILEY, G.E., 577 Lincoln St., Seekonk, MA 02771/508-336-5088
Specialties: One-of-a-kind exotic designed edged weapons. **Patterns:** Folders, daggers and swords. **Technical:** Reforges and grinds Damascus; prefers hollow-grinding. Engraves, carves, inlays and scrimshaws; offers filework. **Prices:** Start at $800. **Remarks:** Full-time maker. First knife sold in 1982. **Mark:** Last name or stylized initialed logo.

DAKE, C.M., 19759 Chef Menteur Hwy., New Orleans, LA 70129-9602/504-254-0357; FAX: 504-254-9501
Specialties: Fancy working folders. **Patterns:** Front-lock lockbacks, button-lock folders. **Technical:** Grinds ATS-34 and 440C. **Prices:** $200 to $850; some higher. **Remarks:** Full-time maker; first knife sold in 1988. Doing business as Bayou Custom Cutlery. **Mark:** Last name.

DAMLOVAC, SAVA, 10292 Bradbury Dr., Indianapolis, IN 42631/317-839-4952
Specialties: Working knives, fantasy and period pieces of his design. **Patterns:** Bowies and hunters. **Technical:** Uses Damascus, 440C, ATS-34 and other steels. Offers filework; uses exotic woods and fossilized ivory for handles. **Prices:** $75 to $1,000; some higher. **Remarks:** Full-time maker; first knife sold in 1993. **Mark:** First name on top of bowie knife inside a shield with city and state on outside of shield.

D'ANDREA, JOHN, 77 Pinecrest Terr., Wayne, NJ 07470/201-839-4559
Specialties: Fancy working straight knives and folders with filework and distinctive leatherwork. **Patterns:** Hunters, fighters, daggers, folders and an occasional sword. **Technical:** Grinds ATS-34, 154CM, 440C and D2. **Prices:** $180 to $600; some to $1,000. **Remarks:** Part-time maker; first knife sold in 1986. **Mark:** First name, last initial imposed on samurai sword.

D'ANGELO, LAURENCE, 14703 NE 17th Ave., Vancouver, WA 98686/360-573-0546
Specialties: Straight knives of his design. **Patterns:** Bowies, hunters and locking folders. **Technical:** Grinds D2, ATS-34 and 440C. Handmakes all sheaths. **Prices:** $100 to $200. **Remarks:** Full-time maker; first knife sold in 1987. **Mark:** Football logo—first and middle initials, last name, city, state, Maker.

DANIEL, TRAVIS E., 4015 Brownsboro Rd., Winston-Salem, NC 27106/919-759-0640
Specialties: Traditional working straight knives of his design or to customer specs. **Patterns:** Hunters, fighters and utility/camp knives. **Technical:** Forges and grinds ATS-34 and his own Damascus. **Prices:** $90 to $1,250; some to $2,000. **Remarks:** Full-time maker; first knife sold in 1976. **Mark:** Carolina Custom Knives.

DANIELS, ALEX, 1416 County Rd. 415, Town Creek, AL 35672/205-685-0943
Specialties: Working and using straight knives and folders; period pieces. **Patterns:** Hunters, reproduction Bowies, fishing knives, locking folders and traditional slip-joints. **Technical:** Grinds 440C and ATS-34. **Prices:** $150 to $1,000. **Remarks:** Full-time maker; first knife sold in 1963. **Mark:** First and middle initials, last name, city and state.

DARBY, JED, 7878 E. Co. Rd. 50 N., Greensburg, IN 47240/812-663-2696
Specialties: Traditional working/using straight knives of his design and to customer specs. **Patterns:** Bowies, hunters and utility/camp knives. **Technical:** Grinds 440C, ATS-34 and Damascus. **Prices:** $70 to $550; some to $1,000. **Remarks:** Full-time maker; first knife sold in 1992. Doing business as Darby Knives. **Mark:** Last name and year.

DARBY KNIVES (See Darby, Jed)

DARBY, RICK, 4026 Shelbourne, Youngstown, OH 44511/216-793-3805
Specialties: Working straight knives. **Patterns:** Boots, fighters and hunters with mirror finish. **Technical:** Grinds 440C and CPM440V. **Prices:** $90 to $300. **Remarks:** Part-time maker; first knife sold in 1974. **Mark:** First and middle initials, last name.

DAVENPORT, JACK, 36842 W. Center Ave., Dade City, FL 33525/352-521-4088
Specialties: Titanium linerlock, button-lock and release. **Patterns:** Boots and double-ground fighters. **Technical:** Grinds ATS-34, 12C27 SS and Damascus; liquid nitrogen quench; heat-treats. **Prices:** $250 to $5,000. **Remarks:** Full-time maker; first knife sold in 1986. **Mark:** Last name.

DAVIDSON, EDMUND, Rt. 1, Box 319, Goshen, VA 24439/540-997-5651
Specialties: Working straight knives; many integral patterns and upgraded models. **Patterns:** Heavy-duty skinners and camp knives. **Technical:** Grinds A2, ATS-34, BG-42, S7, 440C, CPM-T-440V. **Prices:** $75 to $1,500. **Remarks:** Full-time maker; first knife sold in 1986. **Mark:** Name in deerhead or motorcycle logo.

DAVIS, BARRY L., 4262 U.S. 20, Castleton, NY 12033/518-477-5036
Specialties: Collector-quality and Damascus interframe folders. **Patterns:** Traditional gentlemen's folders. **Technical:** Makes Damascus; uses only natural handle materials. **Prices:** $1,000 to $2,500; some to $6,000. **Remarks:** Part-time maker; first knife sold in 1980. **Mark:** Initials.

DAVIS, CHARLIE, P.O. Box 710806, Santee, CA 92072/619-561-9445
Specialties: Fancy and embellished working straight knives of his design. **Patterns:** Hunters, camp and utility knives. **Technical:** Grinds high-carbon files. **Prices:** $20 to $80; some to $150. **Remarks:** Full-time maker; first knife sold in 1980. **Mark:** ANZA U.S.A.

DAVIS, DIXIE, Rt. 3, Clinton, SC 29325/803-833-4964
Specialties: Working straight knives; fantasy pieces. **Patterns:** Hunters, fighters and boots. **Technical:** Grinds 440C, 154CM and ATS-34 with mirror finish. **Prices:** $85 to $140; some to $200. **Remarks:** Part-time maker; first knife sold in 1981. **Mark:** First name.

DAVIS, DON, 8415 Coyote Run, Loveland, CO 80537-9665/970-669-9016; FAX: 970-669-8072
Specialties: Working straight knives in standard patterns or to customer specs. **Patterns:** Hunters, utility knives, skinners and survival knives. **Technical:** Grinds 440C, ATS-34. **Prices:** $75 to $250. **Remarks:** Full-time maker; first knife sold in 1985. **Mark:** Signature, city and state.

DAVIS, GREG, 90 E. Main, Redmond, UT 84652

DAVIS, JESSE W., 7398A Hwy. 3, Sarah, MS 38665/601-382-7332
Specialties: Working straight knives and folders in standard patterns and to customer specs. **Patterns:** Tantos, Bowies, locking folders, hunters and miniatures. **Technical:** Grinds O1, A2, D2, 440C and commercial Damascus. **Prices:** $125 to $300. **Remarks:** Part-time maker; first knife sold in 1977. **Mark:** Name or initials.

DAVIS, JOHN, 235 Lampe Road, Selah, WA 98942/509-697-3845; FAX: 509-697-8087
Specialties: Working and using straight knives of his own design, to customer specs and in standard patterns. **Patterns:** Boots, hunters, kitchen and utility/camp knives. **Technical:** Grinds ATS-34, 440C and commercial Damascus. Embellishes with stabilized wood, mokume and nickel-silver. **Prices:** $100 to $250; some to $500. **Remarks:** Part-time maker; first knife sold in 1996. **Mark:** Full name, city, state.

DAVIS, K.M. "TWIG," P.O. Box 267, Monroe, WA 98272/206-794-7274
Specialties: Fancy working straight knives. **Patterns:** Hunters, boots, fishing knives, Bowies and daggers. **Technical:** Grinds ATS-34, D2, 440C. **Prices:** $150 to $450; some to $600. **Remarks:** Part-time maker; first knife sold in 1979. **Mark:** Twig.

DAVIS, STEVE, 3370 Chatsworth Way, Powder Springs, GA 30073/770-427-5740
Specialties: Traditional fancy folders and automatics of his design and to customer specs. **Patterns:** Automatics, locking folders and slip-joint folders. **Technical:** Grinds ATS-34, 440C and Damascus. Offers filework; prefers hand-rubbed finishes and natural handle materials. Uses pearl, ivory, stag and exotic woods. **Prices:** $150 to $500; some to $1,200. **Remarks:** Part-time maker; first knife sold in 1988. Doing business as Custom Knives by Steve Davis. **Mark:** Name engraved on blade. Snapdragon engraved on blades of automatics.

DAVIS, TERRY, Box 111, Sumpter, OR 97877/541-894-2307
Specialties: Traditional and contemporary folders. **Patterns:** Multiblade folders, whittlers and interframe multiblades; sunfish patterns. **Technical:** Flat-grinds ATS-34. **Prices:** $400 to $1,000; some higher. **Remarks:** Full-time maker; first knife sold in 1985. **Mark:** Name in logo.

DAVIS, VERNON M., 1006 Lewis St., Waco, TX 76705/817-799-7671
Specialties: Presentation-grade straight knives. **Patterns:** Bowies, daggers, boots, fighers, hunters and utility knives. **Technical:** Hollow-grinds 440C, ATS-34 and D2. Grinds an aesthetic grind line near choil. **Prices:** $125 to $550; some to $5,000. **Remarks:** Part-time maker; first knife sold in 1980. **Mark:** Last name and city inside outline of state.

DAVIS, W.C., 19300 S. School Rd., Raymore, MO 64083/816-331-4491
Specialties: Fancy working straight knives and folders. **Patterns:** Folding lockers and slip-joints; straight hunters, fighters and Bowies. **Technical:** Grinds 440C, A2, ATS-34. **Prices:** $100 to $300; some to $1,000. **Remarks:** Full-time maker; first knife sold in 1972. **Mark:** Name.

DAWKINS, DUDLEY L., 221 NW Broadmoor Ave., Topeka, KS 66606-1254

DAWSON, BARRY, 10A Town Plaza, Suite 303, Durango, CO 81301
Specialties: Samurai swords, combat knives, collector daggers, folding knives and hunting knives. **Patterns:** Offers over 60 different models. **Technical:** Grinds 440C; heat-treats. **Prices:** $75 to $1,500; some to $5,000. **Remarks:** Full-time maker; first knife sold in 1975. **Mark:** Last name, USA in print or last name in script.

DAYNIA FORGE (See Saindon, R. Bill)

DE CARVALHO, HENRIQUE M.
(See Neto Jr., Nelson and de Carvalho, Henrique M.)

DEAN, HARVEY J., Rt. 2, Box 137, Rockdale, TX 76567/512-446-3111; FAX: 512-446-5060
Specialties: Collectible, functional knives. **Patterns:** Bowies, hunters, folders, daggers, swords, battle axes, camp and combat knives. **Technical:** Forges 1095, O1 and his Damascus. **Prices:** $195 to $4,000. **Remarks:** Full-time maker; first knife sold in 1981. **Mark:** Last name and MS.

DEARING, JOHN, 1569 Flucom Rd., DeSoto, MO 63020/314-586-1772
Specialties: Traditional working and using straight knives of his design; period pieces and fancy/embellished straight knives. **Patterns:** Hunters, Bowies, fighters, skinners, utility/camp knives and buckskinner blades. **Technical:** Forges and grinds 5160, 154CM and his own Damascus. Prefers natural handle materials. **Prices:** $85 to $350. **Remarks:** Part-time maker; first knife sold in 1985. Doing business as Arc Mountain Forge. **Mark:** Initials stylized into a deer hoofprint.

DeBRAGA, JOSE C., 1519 Du Grand Bourg, Val Belair, Queb. G3J 1K4, CANADA/418-847-7855
Specialties: Art knives, fantasy pieces and working knives of his design or to customer specs. **Patterns:** Knives with sculptured or carved handles, from miniatures to full-size working knives. **Technical:** Grinds and hand-files 440C and ATS-34. A variety of steels and handle materials available. Offers lost wax casting. **Prices:** Start at $300. **Remarks:** Full-time maker; wax modeler, sculptor and knifemaker; first knife sold in 1984. **Mark:** Initials in stylized script and serial number.

DEER (See Laughlin, Don)

DEER CREEK FORGE (See Quarton, Barr)

DEES, JAY, Rt. 1, Box 17C, Collins, MS 39428/601-765-1846
Specialties: Traditional working/using straight knives of his design and to customer specs. **Patterns:** Bowies, skinners, hatchets, hunters and utility/camp knives. **Technical:** Grinds ATS-34, 440C and CPM440V. **Prices:** $75 to $200; some to $500. **Remarks:** Spare-time maker; first knife sold in 1995. **Mark:** Full name, city and state.

DEFEO, ROBERT A., 403 Lost Trail Dr., Henderson, NV 89014/702-434-3717
Specialties: Working straight knives and period pieces. **Patterns:** Hunters, fighters, daggers and Bowies. **Technical:** Grinds D2, 440C and ATS-34. **Prices:** $150 to $500; some higher. **Remarks:** Part-time maker; first knife sold in 1982. **Mark:** Last name.

DEFREEST, WILLIAM G., P.O. Box 573, Barnwell, SC 29812/803-259-7883
Specialties: Working straight knives and folders. **Patterns:** Fighters, hunters and boots; locking folders and slip-joints. **Technical:** Grinds 440C, 154CM and ATS-34; clean lines and mirror finishes. **Prices:** $100 to $700. **Remarks:** Full-time maker; first knife sold in 1974. **Mark:** GORDON.

DeGRAEVE, RICHARD, 329 Valencia St., Sebastian, FL 32958/407-589-9005
Specialties: Working straight knives of his design or to customer specs. **Patterns:** Hunters and skinners with or without gut hooks, fillets, fighters, folders, skeleton knives, mini and art knives. **Technical:** Forges and grinds 440C, ATS-34, O1, high carbon steels; scrimshaws; enjoys filework. **Prices:** $55 to $400. **Remarks:** Full-time maker; first knife sold in 1985. **Mark:** Rich

DELL, WOLFGANG, Am Alten Berg 9, D-73277 Owen-Teck, GERMANY/49-7021-81802
Specialties: Fancy high-art straight of his design and to customer specs. **Patterns:** Fighters, hunters and utility/camp knives. **Technical:** Grinds ATS-34, 440B and 440C. Offers high gloss finish and engraving. **Prices:** $500 to $1,000; some to $1,600. **Remarks:** Full-time maker; first knife sold in 1992. **Mark:** Hopi hand of peace.

DELLANA (See Warren, Dellana)

DeLONG, DICK, 17561 E. Ohio Circle, Aurora, CO 80017/303-745-2652
Specialties: Fancy working knives and fantasy pieces. **Patterns:** Hunters and small skinners. **Technical:** Grinds and files O1, D2, 440C and Damascus. Offers cocobolo and osage orange for handles. **Prices:** Start at $50. **Remarks:** Part-time maker. **Mark:** Last name; some unmarked.

DEMPSEY, GORDON S., P.O. Box 7497, N. Kenai, AK 99635/907-776-8425
Specialties: Working straight knives. **Patterns:** Hunters. **Technical:** Forges O1, pattern welded Damascus and carbon steel. **Prices:** $80 to $250. **Remarks:** Part-time maker; first knife sold in 1974. **Mark:** Name.

DENNEHY, DAN, P.O. Box 2F, Del Norte, CO 81132/719-657-2545
Specialties: Working knives, fighting and military knives, throwing knives. **Patterns:** Full range of straight knives, tomahawks, buckle knives. **Technical:** Forges and grinds A2, O1 and D2. **Prices:** $50 to $110. **Remarks:** Full-time maker; first knife sold in 1942. **Mark:** First name and last initial, city, state and shamrock.

DENNEHY, JOHN D., P.O. Box 431, 3926 Hayes, Wellington, CO 80549/970-568-9055
Specialties: Leatherworkers' knives to presentation Bowies. **Patterns:** Bowies, fighters, hunters, utilities, throwers. **Technical:** Uses 440C and O1; heat treats. **Remarks:** Part-time maker; first knife sold in 1989. Doing business as John-D Custom Leatherworks and Handmade Knives. **Mark:** John-D and shamrock.

DENT, DOUGLAS M., 1208 Chestnut St., S. Charleston, WV 25309/304-768-3308
Specialties: Straight and folding sportsman's knives. **Patterns:** Hunters, boots and Bowies, interframe folders. **Technical:** Forges and grinds D2, 440C, 154CM and plain tool steels. **Prices:** $70 to $300; exceptional knives to $800. **Remarks:** Part-time maker; first knife sold in 1969. **Mark:** Last name.

DERINGER, CHRISTOPH, 1559 St. Louis, #4, Sherbrooke, Quebec CANADA J1H 4P7/819-565-4260
Specialties: Traditional working/using straight knives and folders of his design and to customer specs. **Patterns:** Boots, hunters, folders, art knives, kitchen knives and utility/camp knives. **Technical:** Forges 5160, O1 and Damascus. Offers a variety of filework. **Prices:** Start at $250. **Remarks:** Full-time maker; first knife sold in 1989. **Mark:** Last name stamped/engraved.

DERR, HERBERT, P.O. Box 972, Clendenin, WV 25045

DES JARDINS, DENNIS, P.O. Box 1103, Plains, MT 59859/406-826-3981
Specialties: Classic working/using straight knives of his design and to customer specs. **Patterns:** Boots, hunters and utility/camp knives. **Technical:** Forges 5160 and L6, 5160, 203E and 1095 Damascus; fancy file work on all knives. **Prices:** $100 to $500; some to $1,000. **Remarks:** Full-time maker; first knife was sold in 1985. **Mark:** Initials, city and state.

DETMER, PHILLIP, 14140 Bluff Rd., Breese, IL 62230/618-526-4834
Specialties: Working knives. **Patterns:** Bowies, daggers and hunters. **Technical:** Grinds ATS-34 and D2. **Prices:** $60 to $400. **Remarks:** Part-time maker; first knife sold in 1977. **Mark:** Last name with dagger.

DeYONG, CLARENCE, 4140 Cripple Creek Way, Kennesaw, GA 30144-2165/770-928-8051
Specialties: Working and using straight knives of his design and to customer specs. **Patterns:** Hunters, fighters and boots. **Technical:** Grinds 440C, D2, ATS-34. Son Brian does scrimshaw, filework. **Prices:** $75 to $150; some to $400. **Remarks:** Part-time maker; first knife sold in 1981. **Mark:** Last name and serial number.

D'HOLDER (See Holder, D'Alton)

DIAMOND DRAG "Barron" (See Barron, Brian)

DICKERSON, GAVIN, P.O. Box 7672, Petit, 1512, REPUBLIC OF SOUTH AFRICA/011-966-1988; FAX: 011-965-1176
Specialties: Straight knives of his design or to customer specs. **Patterns:** Hunters, skinners, fighters and Bowies. **Technical:** Hollow-grinds D2, 440C, ATS-34, 12C27 and Damascus upon request. Prefers natural handle materials; offers synthetic handle materials. **Prices:** $190 to $2,500. **Remarks:** Part-time maker; first knife sold in 1982. **Mark:** Initials.

DICKISON, SCOTT S., 185 Mill Lane, Portsmouth, RI 02871/401-683-7439
Specialties: Working and using straight knives and locking folders of his design. **Patterns:** Trout knives, fishing and hunting knives. **Technical:** Forges and grinds commercial Damascus and D2, O1. Uses natural handle materials. **Prices:** $350 to $600; some higher. **Remarks:** Part-time maker; first knife sold in 1989. **Mark:** Stylized initials.

DIETZ, HOWARD, 421 Range Rd., New Braunfels, TX 78132/830-885-4662

DIETZEL, BILL, P.O. Box 1613, Middleburg, FL 32068/904-282-1091
Specialties: Forged straight knives and folders. **Patterns:** His interpretations. **Technical:** Forges his Damascus and other steels. **Prices:** Middle ranges. **Remarks:** Likes natural materials; uses titanium in folder liners. **Mark:** Name.

DIGANGI, JOSEPH M., Box 225, Santa Cruz, NM 87567/505-753-6414
Specialties: Kitchen and table cutlery. **Patterns:** French chef's knives, carving sets, steak knife sets, some camp knives and hunters. Holds patents and trademarks for "System II" kitchen cutlery set. **Technical:** Grinds 440C; buys Damascus. **Prices:** $150 to $450; some to $1,000. **Remarks:** Full-time maker; first knife sold in 1983. **Mark:** Last name.

DILL, DAVE, 7404 NW 30th St., Bethany, OK 73008/405-789-0750
Specialties: Folders of his design. **Patterns:** Various patterns. **Technical:** Hand-grinds 440C, ATS-34 and D2. Offers engraving and filework on all folders. **Prices:** $275 to $600. **Remarks:** Part-time maker; first knife sold in 1987. **Mark:** First initial, last name.

DILL, ROBERT, 1812 Van Buren, Loveland, CO 80538/303-667-5144; FAX: 303-667-5144
Specialties: Fancy and working knives of his design. **Patterns:** Hunters, Bowies and fighters. **Technical:** Grinds 440C and D2. **Prices:** $100 to $800. **Remarks:** Full-time maker; first knife sold in 1984. **Mark:** Logo stamped into blade.

DILLON, EARL E., 8908 Stanwin Ave., Arleta, CA 91331
Specialties: Fancy straight knives and folders. **Patterns:** Contemporary interpretations. **Technical:** Grinds 440C and AEB. **Prices:** $250 to $350; some over $500. **Remarks:** Part-time maker; first knife sold in 1984. Collaborates with Chuck Stapel. **Mark:** STAPEL-DILLON.

DILLUVIO, FRANK J., 13611 Joyce Dr., Warren, MI 48093/810-775-1216
Specialties: Traditional working straight knives, some high-tech. **Patterns:** Hunters, Bowies, fishing knives, sub-hilts and miniatures. **Technical:** Grinds D2, 440C, CPM; works for precision fits—no solder. **Prices:** $95 to $450; some to $800. **Remarks:** Full-time maker; first knife sold in 1984. **Mark:** Name and state.

DI MARZO, RICHARD, 2357 Center Pl., Birmingham, AL 35205/205-252-3331

DINGMAN, SCOTT, 4298 Parkers Lake Rd., NE, Bemidji, MN 56601/218-751-6908

Specialties: Fancy working knives of his design. **Patterns:** Hunters, daggers, boots and camp knives. **Technical:** Forges O1, L6 and wire Damascus. Provides lost wax casting and hard cast bronze. Prefers exotic woods and high mirror finishes. **Prices:** $150 to $225; some to $500. **Remarks:** Full-time maker; first knife sold in 1983. **Mark:** Last name.

DION, GREG, 3032 S. Jackson St., Oxnard, CA 93033/805-483-1781 (evenings)
Specialties: Working straight knives, some fancy. Welcomes special orders. **Patterns:** Hunters, fighters, camp knives, Bowies and tantos. **Technical:** Grinds ATS-34, 154CM and 440C. **Prices:** $85 to $300; some to $600. **Remarks:** Part-time maker; first knife sold in 1985. **Mark:** Name.

DIPPOLD, A.W., RFD 3, Box 162A, Perryville, MO 63775/573-547-1119
Specialties: Fancy one-of-a-kind locking folders. **Patterns:** Locking folders. **Technical:** Forges and grinds mosaic and pattern welded Damascus. Offers filework on all folders. **Prices:** $500 to $2,500; some higher. **Remarks:** Full-time maker; first knife sold in 1980. **Mark:** Last name in logo inside of liner.

DIXON JR., IRA E., P.O. Box 2581, Ventura, CA 93002-2581/805-659-5867
Specialties: Working fixed blade knives of his design. **Patterns:** Fighters, hunters, boot knives, utility knives. **Technical:** Grinds 440C and ATS-34; forges 5160 and Damascus. **Prices:** $150 to $400. **Remarks:** Part-time maker; first knife sold in 1993. **Mark:** First name, Handmade.

DOC HAGEN (See Hagen, Phillip L.)

DOG KNIVES (See Dugger, Dave)

DOLAN, ROBERT L., 220—B Naalae Road, Kula, HI 96790/808-878-6406
Specialties: Working straight knives in standard patterns, his designs or to customer specs. **Patterns:** Fixed blades and potter's tools, ceramic saws. **Technical:** Grinds O1, D2, 440C and ATS-34. Heat-treats and engraves. **Prices:** Start at $75. **Remarks:** Full-time tool and knifemaker; first knife sold in 1985. **Mark:** Last name, USA.

DOMINY, CHUCK, P.O. Box 593, Colleyville, TX 76034/817-498-4527
Specialties: Titanium liner lock folders. **Patterns:** Hunters, utility/camp knives and liner lock folders. **Technical:** Grinds 440C and ATS-34. **Prices:** $60 to $1,800. **Remarks:** Full-time maker; first knife sold in 1976. **Mark:** Last name.

DONOVAN, PATRICK, 1770 Hudson Dr., San Jose, CA 95124/408-267-9825
Specialties: Working straight knives and folders; period pieces. **Patterns:** Hunters, boots and daggers; lockers and slip-joints. **Technical:** Grinds 440C. Embellishes. **Prices:** $75 to $475; some to $1,200. **Remarks:** Full-time maker; first knife sold in 1980. **Mark:** First name.

DOOLITTLE, MIKE, 13 Denise Ct., Novato, CA 94947/415-897-3246
Specialties: Working straight knives in standard patterns. **Patterns:** Hunters and fishing knives. **Technical:** Grinds 440C, 154CM and ATS-34. **Prices:** $125 to $200; some to $750. **Remarks:** Part-time maker; first knife sold in 1981. **Mark:** Name, city and state.

DOTSON, TRACY, 1280 Hwy. C-4A, Baker, FL 32531/850-537-2407
Specialties: Folding fighters and small folders. **Patterns:** Liner lock and lockback folders. **Technical:** Hollow-grinds ATS-34 and commercial Damascus. **Prices:** Start at $250. **Remarks:** Part-time maker; first knife sold in 1995. **Mark:** Last name.

DOUGLAS, JOHN J., Rt. 1, Box 379, Lynch Station, VA 24571/804-369-7196
Specialties: Fancy and traditional straight knives and folders of his design and to customer specs. **Patterns:** Locking folders, swords and sgian dubhs. **Technical:** Grinds 440C stainless, ATS-34 stainless and customer's choice. Offers newly designed non-pivot uni-lock folders. Prefers highly polished finish. **Prices:** $160 to $1,400. **Remarks:** Full-time maker; first knife sold in 1975. Doing business as Douglas Keltic. **Mark:** Stylized initial. Folders are numbered; customs are dated.

DOUGLAS KELTIC (See Douglas, John J.)

DOURSIN, GERARD, Chemin des Croutoules, F 84210 Pernes les Fontaines, FRANCE
Specialties: Period pieces. **Patterns:** Liner locks and daggers. **Technical:** Forges mosaic Damascus. **Prices:** $600 to $4,000. **Remarks:** First knife sold in 1983. **Mark:** First initial, last name and I stop the lion.

DOUSSOT, LAURENT, 6262 De La Roche, Montreal, Quebec, H2H 1W9, CANADA/516-270-6992; FAX: 516-722-1641
Specialties: Fancy and embellished folders and fantasy knives. **Patterns:** Fighters and locking folders. **Technical:** Grinds ATS-34 and commercial Damascus. Scale carvings on all knives; most bolsters are carved titanium. **Prices:** $350 to $3,000. **Remarks:** Part-time maker; first knife was sold in 1992. **Mark:** Stylized initials inside circle.

DOVE KNIVES (See Rollert, Steve)

DOWELL, T.M., 139 NW St. Helen's Pl., Bend, OR 97701/503-382-8924
Specialties: Integral construction in hunting knives and period pieces. Famous "Funny" folders. **Patterns:** Hunters to sword canes, Price-style daggers to axes. **Technical:** Forges 1060, 5160 and 1095. Grinds BG42, D2, 440C and 154CM. Makes his own bright Damascus. **Prices:** $185 to $1,050. **Remarks:** Full-time maker; first knife sold in 1967. **Mark:** Initials logo.

DOWNIE, JAMES T., RR #1, Port Franks, Ont. NOM 2LO, CANADA/519-243-2290
Specialties: Serviceable straight knives and folders; period pieces. **Patterns:** Hunters, Bowies, camp knives and miniatures. **Technical:** Grinds D2, 440C and ATS-34. **Prices:** $100 to $500; some higher. **Remarks:** Part-time maker; first knife sold in 1978. **Mark:** Signature of first and middle initials, last name.

DOWNING, LARRY, 12268 Hwy. 181N, Bremen, KY 42325/502-525-3523; FAX: 502-525-3372
Specialties: Working straight knives and folders. **Patterns:** From mini-knives to daggers, folding lockers to interframes. **Technical:** Forges and grinds 154CM, ATS-34 and his own Damascus. **Prices:** $150 to $750; some higher. **Remarks:** Part-time maker; first knife sold in 1979. **Mark:** Name in arrowhead.

DOWNING, TOM, 129 S. Bank St., Cortland, OH 44410/216-637-0623
Specialties: Working straight knives; period pieces. **Patterns:** Hunters, fighters and tantos. **Technical:** Grinds 440C, ATs-34 and CPM-T-440V. Prefers natural handle materials. **Prices:** $100 to $500. **Remarks:** Part-time maker; first knife sold in 1979. **Mark:** First and middle initials, last name.

DOWNS, JAMES F., 35 Sunset Rd., Londonderry, OH 45647/614-887-2099
Specialties: Working straight knives of his design or to customer specs. **Patterns:** Hunting and utility knives, some boots. **Technical:** Grinds 440C. Prefers stag, jigged bone, Micarta and stabilized woods. **Prices:** $68 to $900. **Remarks:** Part-time maker; first knife sold in 1981. **Mark:** Last name.

DOZIER, BOB, P.O. Box 1941, Springdale, AR 72765/501-756-0023; FAX: 501-756-9139
Specialties: Using knives. **Patterns:** Some fine collector-grade knives. **Technical:** Uses D2. Prefers Micarta handle material. **Prices:** $75 to $350. **Remarks:** Full-time maker; first knife sold in 1961. **Mark:** State, made, last name in a circle.

DRAGON STEEL (See Lewis, Mike)

DRAGONFLY FORGE (See Bell, Michael)

DRAPER, AUDRA (SHARP), 923 E. Jackson, Riverton, WY 82501 307-856-6807; 307-856-9815
Specialties: Using and individual straight knives. **Patterns:** Hunters, Bowies, bird, fishing and camp knives. **Technical:** Forges 52100, 5160 and occasionally Damascus; heat-treats. Prefers natural and exotic wood and horn handle material; makes personalized hand-stitched heavy-duty leather sheaths. **Prices:** Start at $125. **Remarks:** Full-time maker; first knife sold in 1995. **Mark:** First name.

DRAPER, BART, 6727 W. Crittender Lane, Phoenix, AZ 85033/602-846-0801
Specialties: Classic knives, traditional working knives, fantasy and high-art knives and period pieces. All straight knives of his design and to customer specs. **Patterns:** Boots, Bowies, daggers, fighters, hunters, kitchen knives and utility knives. **Technical:** Grinds ATS-34, 440C and CPM-T-440V. Heat-treats. **Prices:** $175 to $725; some to $3,500. **Remarks:** Part-time maker; first knife sold in 1966. **Mark:** First initial, last name and state.

DRAPER, KENT, 23461 Hwy. 36, Cheshire, OR 97419/503-998-2448
Specialties: Art knives, historical and period pieces of his design. **Pat-**

terns: Hunters, combat fighters, folding knives and swords. **Technical:** Grinds 440C and ATS-34. Heat-treats, engraves and inlays. **Prices:** $100 to $5,000; some esoteric pieces to $10,000. **Remarks:** First knife sold in 1973. **Mark:** First initial, last name, state.

DRISCOLL, MARK, 4115 Avoyer Pl., La Mesa, CA 91941/619-670-0695 **Specialties:** High-art, period pieces and working/using knives of his design or to customer specs; some fancy. **Patterns:** Boots, Bowies, fighters and hunters. **Technical:** Forges 52100, 5160 and his own Damascus; casts own mokume. Uses exotic hardwoods, ivory and horn; scrimshaws. **Prices:** $150 to $550; some to $1,500. **Remarks:** Part-time maker; first knife sold in 1986. Doing business as Mountain Man Knives. **Mark:** Double "M."

DRISKILL, BERYL, P.O. Box 187, Braggadocio, MO 63826/573-757-6262 **Specialties:** Fancy working knives. **Patterns:** Hunting knives, fighters, Bowies, boots, daggers and lockback folders. **Technical:** Grinds ATS-34. **Prices:** Start at $200. **Remarks:** Part-time maker; first knife sold in 1984. **Mark:** Name.

DR KNIVES (See Raymond, Donald)

DROST CUSTOM KNIVES (See Drost, Michael B.)

DROST, J ASON D., Rt.2 Box 49, French Creek, WV 26218/304-472-7901 **Specialties:** Working/using straight knives of his design. **Patterns:** Hunters and utility/camp knives. **Technical:** Grinds 154 CM and D2. **Prices:** $75 to $200. **Remarks:** Spare-time maker; first knife sold in 1995. **Mark:** First and middle initials, last name, maker, city and state.

DROST, MICHAEL B., Rt. 2, Box 49, French Creek, WV 26218/304-472-7901 **Specialties:** Working/using straight knives and folders of all designs. **Patterns:** Hunters, locking folders and utility/camp knives. **Technical:** Grinds ATS-34, D2 and CPM-T-440V. Offers dove-tailed bolsters and spacers, filework and scrimshaw. **Prices:** $125 to $400; some to $740. **Remarks:** Full-time maker; first knife sold in 1990. Doing business as Drost Custom Knives. **Mark:** Name, city and state.

DUBE, PAUL, P.O. Box 122, Chaska, MN 55318/612-361-0930; 800-668-2223
Specialties: Traditional working and using straight knives, high-art knives and period pieces of his design and to customer specs. **Patterns:** Fighters, Bowies, daggers, utility knives. **Technical:** Forges A2, 1050, 1095, S5, ATS-34; stock removal O1, S7 and Vascowear. **Prices:** $80 to $1,500; some to $6,000. **Remarks:** Full-time maker; first knife sold in 1988. Doing business as Troll Hammer Forge. **Mark:** Varies.

DUBLIN, DENNIS, 708 Stanley St., Box 986, Enderby, BC V0E 1V0, CANADA/604-838-6753
Specialties: Working straight knives and folders, plain or fancy. **Patterns:** Hunters and Bowies, locking hunters, combination knives/axes. **Technical:** Forges and grinds high carbon steels. **Prices:** $100 to $400; some higher. **Remarks:** Full-time maker; first knife sold in 1970. **Mark:** Name.

DUFF, BILL, P.O. Box 694, Virginia City, NV 89440/702-847-0566 **Specialties:** Working straight knives and folders. **Patterns:** Hunters and Bowies; locking folders and interframes. **Technical:** Grinds D2, 440C and 154CM. **Prices:** $175 to $3,500. **Remarks:** Part-time maker; first knife sold in 1976. **Mark:** Name, city, state and date.

DUFOUR, ARTHUR J., 8120 De Armoun Rd., Anchorage, AK 99516/907-345-1701
Specialties: Working straight knives from standard patterns. **Patterns:** Hunters, Bowies, camp and fishing knives—grinded thin and pointed. **Technical:** Grinds 440C, ATS-34, AEB-L. Tempers 57-58R; hollow-grinds. **Prices:** $135; some to $250. **Remarks:** Part-time maker; first knife sold in 1970. **Mark:** Prospector logo.

DUGAN, BRAD M., P.O. Box 501831, San Diego, CA 92150/619-752-4417 **Specialties:** Classic and traditional straight knives and folders of his design. **Patterns:** Bowies, fighters, hunters, locking folders and utility/camp knives. **Technical:** Grinds ATS-34; forges 5160, O1 and 1095. Makes his own Damascus and wood sheaths. **Prices:** $200 to $800; some to $1,500. **Remarks:** Part-time maker; first knife sold in 1982. **Mark:** Last name.

DUGGER, DAVE, 2504 West 51, Westwood, KS 66205/913-831-2382 **Specialties:** Working straight knives; fantasy pieces. **Patterns:** Hunters, boots and daggers in one-of-a-kind styles. **Technical:** Grinds D2, 440C and 154CM. **Prices:** $75 to $350; some to $1,200. **Remarks:** Part-time maker; first knife sold in 1979. Not currently accepting orders. Doing business as Dog Knives. **Mark:** DOG.

DUNGY HANDCRAFTED (See Dungy, Lawrence)

DUNGY, LAWRENCE, 8 Southmont Dr., Little Rock, AR 72209/501-568-2769
Specialties: Working straight knives and folders. **Patterns:** Bowies, skinners, hunters, boots, bird and trout knives. **Technical:** Grinds stainless and plain steels. **Prices:** $65 to $800. **Remarks:** Part-time maker; first knife sold in 1983. **Mark:** Dungy Handcrafted.

DUNKERLEY CUSTOM KNIVES (See Dunkerley, Rick)

DUNKERLEY, RICK, Box 111, Lincoln, MT 59639/406-362-3097 **Specialties:** Working/using knives and folders of his design. **Patterns:** Hunters, fighters and locking folders. **Technical:** Forges 52100, Damascus and mosaic Damascus. Prefers natural handle materials. **Prices:** $300 to $800; some to $2,000. **Remarks:** Full-time maker; first knife sold in 1984. Doing business as Dunkerley Custom Knives. **Mark:** Last name.

DUNN, CHARLES K., 17740 GA Hwy. 116, Shiloh, GA 31826/706-846-2666
Specialties: Fancy and working straight knives and folders of his design and to customer specs. **Patterns:** Bowies, hunters and locking folders. **Technical:** Grinds 440C and ATS-34. Engraves; filework offered. **Prices:** $75 to $300. **Remarks:** Part-time maker; first knife sold in 1988. **Mark:** First initial, last name, city, state.

DUNN, MELVIN T., 5830 NW Carlson Rd., Rossville, KS 66533/913-584-6856
Specialties: Traditional working straight knives and folders. **Patterns:** Locking folders, straight hunters, fishing and kitchen knives. **Technical:** Grinds D2, 440V, 440C and 154CM; likes latest materials; heat-treats. **Prices:** $60 to $500. **Remarks:** Full-time maker; first knife sold in 1972. **Mark:** Name in script.

DUNN, STEVE, 376 Biggerstaff Rd., Smiths Grove, KY 42171/502-563-9830 **Specialties:** Working and using straight knives of his design; period pieces. **Patterns:** Hunters, skinners, Bowies, fighters, camp knives, folders, swords and battle axes. **Technical:** Forges his Damascus, O1, 5160, L6 and 1095. **Prices:** Moderate to upscale. **Remarks:** Full-time maker; first knife sold in 1990. **Mark:** Last name and MS.

DURAN, JERRY T., P.O. Box 80692, Albuquerque, NM 87198-0692/505-873-4676
Specialties: Working straight knives, folders and art knives. **Patterns:** Hunters, skinners, bird and trout knives, fighters. **Technical:** Forges Damascus and carbon steel. **Prices:** $125 to $500; some higher. **Remarks:** Part-time maker; influenced by Joeseph G. Cordova. **Mark:** Initials in elk rack logo.

DURIO, FRED, 289 Gulino St., Opelousas, LA 70570/318-948-4831 **Specialties:** Working straight knives and folders; period pieces. **Patterns:** Bowies, camp knives, small hunters, folders, fancy period pieces, miniatures. **Technical:** Forges and grinds W2, 5160, 1095 and O1. Makes own Damascus and forge-welds cable Damascus. Offers filework and tapered tangs; prefers exotic and natural materials. **Prices:** $100 to $350; some to $1,000. **Remarks:** Part-time maker; first knife sold in 1986. **Mark:** Last name and J.S.

DUTCH CREEK FORGE & FOUNDRY (See Knickmeyer, Hank)

DUTTON MOUNTAIN FORGE (See Anders, David)

DUVALL, FRED, 10715 Hwy. 190, Benton, AR 72015/501-778-9360 **Specialties:** Working straight knives and folders. **Patterns:** Locking folders, slip joints, hunters, fighters and Bowies. **Technical:** Grinds D2 and CPM440V; forges 5160. **Prices:** $100 to $400; some to $800. **Remarks:** Part-time maker; first knife sold in 1973. **Mark:** Last name.

DUVALL, LARRY E., Rt. 3, Gallatin, MO 64640/816-663-2742 **Specialties:** Fancy working straight knives and folders. **Patterns:** Hunters to swords, minis to Bowies; locking folders. **Technical:** Grinds D2, 440C and 154CM. **Prices:** $150 to $350; some to $2,000. **Remarks:** Part-time maker; first knife sold in 1980. **Mark:** Name and address in logo.

DYESS, EDDIE, 1005 Hamilton, Roswell, NM 88201/505-623-5599
Specialties: Working and using straight knives in standard patterns. **Patterns:** Hunters and fighters. **Technical:** Grinds 440C, 154CM and D2 on request. **Prices:** $85 to $135; some to $250. **Remarks:** Spare-time maker; first knife sold in 1980. **Mark:** Last name.

DYRNOE, PER, Sydskraenten 10, Tulstrup, DK 3400 Hilleroed, DENMARK/+45 42287041
Specialties: Hand-crafted knives with zirconia ceramic blades. **Patterns:** Hunters, skinners, Norwegian-style tolleknives, most in animal-like ergonomic shapes. **Technical:** Handles of exotic hardwood, horn, fossile ivory, etc. Norwegian-style sheaths. **Prices:** Start at $500. **Remarks:** Part-time maker in cooperation with Hans J. Henriksen; first knife sold in 1993. **Mark:** Initial logo.

E&E EMPORIUM (See Edwards, Lynn)

EAKER, ALLEN L., 416 Clinton Ave., Dept KI, Paris, IL 61944/217-466-5160
Specialties: Traditional straight knives and folders of his design. **Patterns:** Hunters, locking folders and slip-joint folders. **Technical:** Grinds 440C; inlays. **Prices:** $125 to $325; some to $500. **Remarks:** Spare-time maker; first knife sold in 1994. **Mark:** Initials in tankard logo stamped on tang, serial number on back side.

EASLER, PAULA, P.O. Box 301-1025, Cross Anchor Rd., Woodruff, SC 29388/803-476-7830; FAX: 803-476-3940
Specialties: Traditional fancy and embellished straight knives of her design. **Patterns:** Miniatures only—hunters, fighters, tantos, razors and mini-replicas. **Technical:** Grinds ATS-34, commercial Damascus. Stainless steel pins and bolsters. Heat-treats blades, many have file-worked tapered tangs; hand-rubbed satin finish standard; natural handle materials and gems. **Prices:** $85 to $400; some to $1,000. **Remarks:** Spare-time maker; first knife sold in 1989. **Mark:** First initial, last name in block letters.

EASLER JR., RUSSELL O., P.O. Box 301, Woodruff, SC 29388/803-476-7830; FAX: 803-476-3940
Specialties: Working straight knives and folders. **Patterns:** Hunters, tantos and boots; locking folders and interframes. **Technical:** Grinds 440C, 154CM and ATS-34. **Prices:** $85 to $250; some to $600. **Remarks:** Part-time maker; first knife sold in 1973. **Mark:** Name or name with bear logo.

EATON, AL, P.O. Box 43, Clayton, CA 94517/510-672-5351
Specialties: One-of-a-kind high-art knives and fantasy knives of his design, full size and miniature. **Patterns:** Hunters, fighters, daggers. **Technical:** Grinds 440C, 154CM and ATS-34; ivory and metal carving. **Prices:** $125 to $3,000; some to $5,000. **Remarks:** Full-time maker; first knife sold in 1977. **Mark:** Full name, city and state.

EATON, RICK, P.O. Box 327, Strawberry Valley, CA 95981/916-675-1632
Specialties: Interframe folders and one hand opening sidelocks. **Patterns:** Bowies, daggers, fighters and folders. **Technical:** Grinds 154CM, ATS-34, 440C and other maker's Damascus. Offers high-quality hand engraving, Bulino and gold inlay. **Prices:** Upscale. **Remarks:** Full-time maker; first knife sold in 1982. **Mark:** Full name or full name and address.

ECK, LARRY A., P.O. Box 665, Terrebonne, OR 97760/503-548-7599
Specialties: Traditional working and using straight knives of his design, to customer specs and in standard patterns. **Patterns:** Boots, Bowies, fighters, hunters, fillets and tantos. **Technical:** Grinds ATS-34, D2, 440C and commercial Damascus. Prefers natural handle materials. Offers mirror and hand-rubbed finishes. **Prices:** $175 to $400; some to $750. **Remarks:** Part-time maker; first knife sold in 1991. **Mark:** First and middle initials, last name and state in logo.

ECKERSON, CHARLEY, 1117 Horseshoe Dr., Pueblo, CO 81001/719-543-3387
Specialties: Traditional working/using straight knives. **Patterns:** Skinners, hunters, fishing, Bowies, military and SWAT. **Technical:** Grinds 440C, ATS-34, A2 and D2. Prefers Micarta and stag. **Prices:** $125 to $400; some to $600. **Remarks:** Full-time maker; first knife sold in 1984. **Mark:** Last name.

EDGE, TOMMY, P.O. Box 156, Cash, AR 72421/501-477-5210
Specialties: Fancy/embellished working knives of his design. **Patterns:** Bowies, hunters and utility/camping knives. **Technical:** Grinds 440C, ATS-34 and D2. Makes own cable Damascus; offers filework. **Prices:** $70 to $250; some to $1,500. **Remarks:** Part-time maker; first knife sold in 1993. **Mark:** Stamped first initial, last name and stenciled name, city and state in oval shape.

EDGEWISE KNIVES (See Lott, David)

EDWARDS, FAIN E., 209 E. Mtn. Ave., Jacksonville, AL 36265/205-435-4994; FAX: 205-435-8499
Specialties: Classic and traditional knives, working/using knives and period pieces. **Patterns:** Bowies, daggers, hunters, kitchen knives, locking and slip-joint folders, swords and utility/camp knives. **Technical:** Forges Damascus and 5160. **Prices:** $500 to $2,500; some to $6,000. **Remarks:** Full-time maker; first knife sold in 1976. **Mark:** First and middle initials, last name, city and state with two bleeding hearts.

EDWARDS, LYNN, Rt. 2, Box 614, W. Columbia, TX 77486/409-345-4080; FAX: 409-345-3472
Specialties: Traditional working and using straight knives of his design and to customer specs. **Patterns:** Bowies, hunters and utility/camp knives. **Technical:** Forges 5168 and O1; forges and grinds D2. Triple-hardens on request; offers silver wire inlay, stone inlays and spacers, filework. **Prices:** $100 to $395; some to $800. **Remarks:** Part-time maker; first knife sold in 1988. Doing business as E&E Emporium. **Mark:** Last name in script.

EK, GARY WHITNEY, 1580 NE 125th St., North Miami, FL 33161/305-891-2283
Specialties: Working straight knives of his design and to customer specs; period pieces. **Patterns:** Bowies, fighters and special-effect knives and swords. **Technical:** Grinds D2, Sandvik 13C26; forges and grinds 43-40 Ni Crm Moly. Offers custom refinishing and sharpening. **Prices:** $150 to $450; some to $1,200. **Remarks:** Full-time maker; first knife sold in 1971. **Mark:** Name or EKNIVES, city.

EKLUND, MAIHKEL, Föne 1155, S-82041 Färila, SWEDEN/+46 651 24192
Specialties: Collector-grade working straight knives. **Patterns:** Hunters, Bowies and fighters. **Technical:** Grinds ATS-34, Uddeholm and Dama steel. Engraves and scrimshaws. **Prices:** $150 to $700. **Remarks:** Full-time maker; first knife sold in 1983. **Mark:** Initials or name.

EKNIVES WORKS (See Ek, Gary Whitney)

ELDRIDGE, ALLAN, 1424 Kansas Lane, Gallatin, TN 37066/615-452-6027
Specialties: Fancy classic straight knives in standard patterns. **Patterns:** Hunters, Bowies, fighters and miniatures. **Technical:** Grinds O1 and Damascus. Engraves, silver-wire inlays, pearl inlays, scrimshaws and offers filework. **Prices:** $50 to $500; some to $1,200. **Remarks:** Spare-time maker; first knife sold in 1965. **Mark:** Initials.

ELISHEWITZ, ALLEN, 17194 Preston Rd., Suite 123, #227, Dallas, TX 75248-1203/972-380-4304
Specialties: Collectible high-tech working straight knives and folders of his design. **Patterns:** Fighters, combat knives, skinners and utility/camp knives. **Technical:** Grinds ATS-34, D2, A2 and Vascowear. All designs drafted and field-tested. **Prices:** $300 to $500; some to $1,000. **Remarks:** Full-time maker; first knife sold in 1989. **Mark:** Last name with a Japanese crane.

ELK RACK, THE (See Peele, Bryan)

ELKINS, R. VAN, P.O. Box 156, Bonita, LA 71223/318-823-2124
Specialties: High-art Bowies, fighters, folders and period daggers; all one-of-a-kind pieces. **Patterns:** Welcomes customer designs. **Technical:** Forges his own Damascus in several patterns, O1 and 5160. **Prices:** $250 to $2,800. **Remarks:** First knife sold in 1984. **Mark:** Last name.

ELLEFSON, JOEL, P.O. Box 1016, 310 S. 1st St., Manhattan, MT 59741/406-284-3111
Specialties: Working straight knives, fancy daggers and one-of-a-kinds. **Patterns:** Hunters, daggers and some folders. **Technical:** Grinds A2, 440C and ATS-34. Makes own mokume in bronze, brass, silver and shibuishi; makes brass/steel blades. **Prices:** $75 to $500; some to $2,000. **Remarks:** Part-time maker; first knife sold in 1978. **Mark:** Stylized last initial.

ELLENBERG, WILLIAM C., 10 Asbury Ave., Melrose Park, PA 19027/215-635-1313; FAX: 215-635-1363
Specialties: Traditional working and using straight knives of his design. **Patterns:** Bowies, hunters and utility/camp knives. **Technical:** Flat-grinds 440C and ATS-34. Offers hardwood handles. Stitches leather sheaths with stainless steel wire. **Prices:** $150 to $250; some to $450. **Remarks:** Spare-time maker; first knife sold in 1990. **Mark:** None.

ELLERBE, W.B., 3871 Osceola Rd., Geneva, FL 32732/407-349-5818
Specialties: Period and primitive knives and sheaths. **Patterns:** Bowies to patch knives, some tomahawks. **Technical:** Grinds Sheffield O1 and files. **Prices:** Start at $35. **Remarks:** Full-time maker; first knife sold in 1971. Doing business as Cypress Bend Custom Knives. **Mark:** Last name or initials.

ELLIOTT, J.P., 4507 Kanawha Ave., Charleston, WV 25304/304-925-5045
Specialties: Classic and traditional straight knives and folders of his design and to customer specs. **Patterns:** Hunters, locking folders and Bowies. **Technical:** Grinds ATS-34, 154CM, O1, D2 and T-440-V. All guards silver-soldered; bolsters are pinned on straight knives, spot-welded on folders. **Prices:** $80 to $265; some to $1,000. **Remarks:** Full-time maker; first knife sold in 1972. **Mark:** First and middle initials, last name, knifemaker, city, state.

ELLIOTT, MARCUS, Pen Dinas, Wyddfydd Rd., Great Orme, Llandudno, Gwynedd, GREAT BRITAIN LL30 2QL/01492-872747
Specialties: Fancy working knives. **Patterns:** Boots and small hunters. **Technical:** Grinds O1, 440C and ATS-34. **Prices:** $160 to $250. **Remarks:** Spare-time maker; first knife sold in 1981. Makes only a few knives each year. **Mark:** Last name.

ELLIS, DAVID, 3505 Camino Del Rio S., #334, San Diego, CA 92108/619-285-1305 days; 760-632-7302 evenings
Specialties: Fighters and Bowies. **Patterns:** Utility knives. **Technical:** Forges and grinds 5160, O1, 1095; now working with pattern-welded Damascus. Most knives have hand-rubbed finish and single and double temper lines. Most knives are double or triple hardened and triple drawn. Prefers natural handle materials. **Prices:** $300 to $800; some to $2,000. **Remarks:** Part-time maker; first knife sold in 1988. **Mark:** Last name with dagger and rose below.

ELLIS, WILLIAM DEAN, 8875 N. Barton, Fresno, CA 93720/209-299-0303
Specialties: Classic and fancy knives of his design. **Patterns:** Boots, fighters and utility knives. **Technical:** Grinds ATS-34, D2 and Damascus. Offers tapered tangs and six patterns of filework; tooled multi-colored sheaths. **Prices:** $180 to $350; some to $1,300. **Remarks:** Part-time maker; first knife sold in 1991. Doing business as Billy's Blades. **Mark:** "B" in a five-point star next to "Billy," city and state within a rounded-corner rectangle.

EMBRETSEN, KAJ, P.O. Box 54, S-82821 Edsbyn, SWEDEN/46-271-21057; FAX: 46-271-22961
Specialties: High quality folders. **Patterns:** Scandinavian style knives. **Technical:** Forges Damascus. Uses only his blades; natural materials. **Prices:** Upscale. **Remarks:** Full-time maker. **Mark:** Name.

EMBRY, BRAD 4802 Bruton Road, Plant City, FL 33565/813-752-8143
Specialties: High-tech and high-art folders and automatics. **Patterns:** Bowies and locking folders. **Technical:** Grinds ATS-34, 440C and Sanvik 12C27; integral frame inlays. **Prices:** $300 to $750; some to $1,000. **Remarks:** Full-time maker; first knife sold in 1974. Doing business as Embry Custom Knives.

EMBRY CUSTOM KNIVES (See Embry, Brad)

EMERSON, ERNEST R., 4142 W. 173nd St., Torrance, CA 90504/310-542-3050
Specialties: High-tech folders and combat fighters. **Patterns:** Fighters, linerlock combat folders and SPECWAR combat knives. **Technical:** Grinds ATS-34 and D2. Makes folders with titanium fittings, liners and locks. Chisel grind specialist. **Prices:** $275 to $475; some to $3,000. **Remarks:** Full-time maker; first knife sold in 1983. **Mark:** Last name and Specwar knives.

ENCE, JIM, 145 S. 200 East, Richfield, UT 84701/801-896-6206
Specialties: High-art period pieces. **Patterns:** Daggers, art folders, fancy boot knives, fighters, Bowies and occasional hunters. **Technical:** Grinds 440C; makes his own and buys Damascus. **Prices:** $300 to $5,000; some higher. **Remarks:** Full-time maker; first knife sold in 1977. **Mark:** Name, city, state.

ENDERS, ROBERT, 3028 White Rd., Cement City, MI 49233/517-529-9667
Specialties: Pocketknives and working straight knives. **Patterns:** Traditional folders with natural materials. **Technical:** Grinds D2, O1, 440C and ATS-34. **Prices:** $200 to $3,000. **Remarks:** Full-time maker; first knife sold in 1981. **Mark:** Name in state map logo.

ENEBOE, JAMES, 2860 Rosendale Rd., Schenectady, NY/518-370-0101
Specialties: Fantasy high-art straight knives, folders and automatics of his design. **Patterns:** Daggers and locking folders. **Technical:** Forges high-carbon steel; grinds W2-203E pattern welded, 52100 and 203E. Offers filework, stone inlays and sterling silver handle material. **Prices:** $1,000 to $5,000. **Remarks:** Full-time maker. **Mark:** Last name.

ENGLAND, VIRGIL, 629 W. 15th Ave., Anchorage, AK 99501/907-274-9494
Specialties: Edged weapons and equipage, one-of-a-kind only. **Patterns:** Axes, swords, lances and body armor. **Technical:** Forges and grinds as pieces dictate. Offers stainless and Damascus. **Prices:** Upscale. **Remarks:** A veteran knifemaker. No commissions. **Mark:** Stylized initials.

ENGLE, WILLIAM, 16608 Oak Ridge Rd., Boonville, MO 65233/816-882-6277
Specialties: Traditional working and using straight knives of his design. **Patterns:** Hunters, Bowies and fighters. **Technical:** Grinds 440C, ATS-34 and 154 CM. **Prices:** $250 to $500; some higher. **Remarks:** Part-time maker; first knife sold in 1982. All knives come with certificate of authenticity. **Mark:** Last name in block lettering.

ENGLEBRETSON, GEORGE, 1209 NW 49th St., Oklahoma City, OK 73118/405-840-4784
Specialties: Working straight knives. **Patterns:** Hunters and Bowies. **Technical:** Grinds A2, D2, 440C and ATS-34. **Prices:** Start at $150. **Remarks:** Full-time maker; first knife sold in 1967. **Mark:** "By George," name and city.

ENGLISH, JIM, 14586 Olive Vista Dr., Jamul, CA 91935/619-669-0833
Specialties: Traditional working straight knives to customer specs. **Patterns:** Hunters, Bowies, fighters, tantos, daggers, boot and utility/camp knives. **Technical:** Grinds 440C, ATS-34, commercial Damascus and customer choice. **Prices:** $130 to $350. **Remarks:** Part-time maker; first knife sold in 1985. In addition to custom line, also does business as Mountain Home Knives. **Mark:** Double "A," Double "J" logo.

ENGNATH, BOB, 1217 B. Crescent Dr., Glendale, CA 91205/818-241-3629
Specialties: Replica antique tantos; complete knives and swords. **Patterns:** Traditional Japanese knives; some miniatures. Kit blades also offered. **Technical:** Makes soft-back/hard-edge blades with temper lines. **Prices:** $125 to $350; some to $600. **Remarks:** Full-time maker/grinder; first knife sold in 1972. **Mark:** KODAN in Japanese script.

ENNIS, RAY W., 509 S. 3rd St., Grand Forks, ND 58201/701-775-8216/800-410-7603
Specialties: Working straight knives and folders of his design or to customer specs. **Patterns:** Hunters, fighters and locking folders. **Technical:** Grinds ATS-34, D2 and O1. **Prices:** $100 to $2,000. **Remarks:** Full-time maker; first knife sold in 1973. **Mark:** Initials connected.

ENOS III, THOMAS M., 12302 State Rd. 535, Orlando, FL 32836/407-239-6205
Specialties: Heavy-duty working straight knives to customer specs; unusual designs. **Patterns:** Machetes, saltwater sport knives, carvers. **Technical:** Grinds 440C, D2, 154CM. **Prices:** $75 to $1,000. **Remarks:** Full-time maker; first knife sold in 1972. **Mark:** Name in knife logo and date, type of steel and serial number.

ERIKSEN, JAMES THORLIEF, 3830 Dividend Dr., Garland, TX 75042/972-494-3667; FAX: 972-235-4932
Specialties: Heavy-duty working and using straight knives and folders utilizing traditional, Viking original and customer specification patterns. Some high-tech and fancy/embellished knives available. **Patterns:** Bowies, hunters, skinners, boot and belt knives, utility/camp knives, fighters, daggers, locking folders, slip-joint folders and kitchen knives. **Technical:** Hollow-grinds 440C, D2, ASP-23, ATS-34, 154CM, Vascowear. **Prices:** $150 to $300; some to $600. **Remarks:** Full-time maker; first knife sold in 1985. Doing business as Viking Knives. **Mark:** VIKING or VIKING USA for export.

ERICKSON, CURT, 449 Washington Blvd., Ogden, UT 84404/801-782-1184
Specialties: Daggers and large knives of integral construction. **Patterns:** Period pieces; Bowies and hunting knives. **Technical:** Grinds 440C and commercial Damascus steel; sculpts and carves components. **Prices:** $240 to $1,500; some to $3,000. **Remarks:** Full-time maker; first knife sold in 1982. **Mark:** Name, state.

ERICKSON, L.M., P.O. Box 132, Liberty, UT 84310/801-745-2026
Specialties: Straight knives; period pieces. **Patterns:** Bowies, fighters, boots and hunters. **Technical:** Grinds 440C, 154CM and commercial Damascus. **Prices:** $200 to $900; some to $5,000. **Remarks:** Part-time maker; first knife sold in 1981. **Mark:** Name, city, state.

ERICKSON, WALTER E., 23883 Ada St., Warren, MI 48091/313-759-1105
Specialties: Unusual survival knives and high-tech working knives. **Patterns:** Butterflies, hunters, tantos. **Technical:** Grinds ATS-34 or customer choice. **Prices:** $150 to $500; some to $1,500. **Remarks:** Full-time maker; first knife sold in 1981. **Mark:** ERIC or last name.

ESSEGIAN, RICHARD, 7387 E. Tulare St., Fresno, CA 93727/309-255-5950
Specialties: Fancy working knives of his design; art knives. **Patterns:** Bowies and some small hunters. **Technical:** Grinds A2, D2, 440C and 154CM. Engraves and inlays. **Prices:** Start at $600. **Remarks:** Part-time maker; first knife sold in 1986. **Mark:** Last name, city and state.

ETZLER, JOHN, 11200 N. Island, Grafton, OH 44044/216-748-2460
Specialties: High-art and fantasy straight knives and folders of his design and to customer specs. **Patterns:** Fighters, hunters, swords and utility knives. **Technical:** Forges and grinds nickel Damascus and tool steel; grinds stainless steels. Prefers exotic, natural materials. **Prices:** $175 to $300; some to $6,000. **Remarks:** Full-time maker; first knife sold in 1992. **Mark:** Name or initials.

EVANS, GRACE (See Evans, Vincent K. and Grace)

EVANS, VINCENT K. and GRACE, HCR 1, Box 5221, Keaau, HI 96749/808-966-4831
Specialties: Working straight knives; period pieces; swords. **Patterns:** Scottish and central Asian patterns, Bowies and clip-point using knives. **Technical:** Forges 5160 and his own Damascus. **Prices:** $50 to $400; some to $3,000. **Remarks:** Full-time maker; first knife sold in 1983. **Mark:** Bronze-filled double last initial with fish logo.

EWING, JOHN H., 3276 Dutch Valley Rd., Clinton, TN 37716/615-457-5757
Specialties: Working straight knives. **Patterns:** Hunters. **Technical:** Grinds 440C and O1; prefers forging. **Prices:** $150 to $1,000. **Remarks:** Part-time maker; first knife sold in 1985. **Mark:** First initial, last name, Handmade.

EXOTIC BLADES (See Hesser, David)

f

FAGAN, JAMES A., 109 S. 17th Ave., Lake Worth, FL 33460

FALCON CREST FORGE (See Fowler, Charles R.)

FALLING WATERS FORGE (See Barnes, Aubrey G.)

FANNIN, DAVID A. and BRUMAGEN, JERRY, 2050 Idle Hour Center, #191, Lexington, KY 40502
Specialties: High-tech classic straight knives; period pieces; traditional working knives. **Patterns:** Hunters, fighters and swords. **Technical:** Draws wire from Damascus billets for wire Damascus. High-density, migrationless and hand-smelted Sagami school Damascus steel. Offers Hamon tempering; makes mokume. **Prices:** $200 to $1,200. **Remarks:** Full-time maker; first knife sold in 1985. Doing business as Athens Forge. **Mark:** None.

FARID, 8 Sidney Close, Tunbridge Wells, Kent, ENGLAND TN2 5QQ/01892-520345
Specialties: High-tech fighters and folders. **Patterns:** Fighters and integral locking folders. **Technical:** Grinds 440C, CPM-T-440V and tool steel D7. **Prices:** $275 to $1,200; some to $5,000. **Remarks:** Full-time maker; first knife sold in 1991. Accepts orders on Alpha-Beta alloy titanium integral locking folders only. **Mark:** First name and country.

FARR, DAN, 285 Glen Ellyn Way, Rochester, NY 14618

FARRIS, CAL, Box 41, Altoona, FL 32702/904-669-9427
Specialties: Embellished working and using straight knives of his design. **Patterns:** Bowies, hunters and utility/camp knives. **Technical:** Grinds 440C and ATS-34; forges his own Damascus. Inlays with natural materials; uses sterling silver. Offers filework and heavy spacer work. **Prices:** $175 to $600; some to $1,000. **Remarks:** Full-time maker; first knife sold in 1976. **Mark:** Last name.

FASSIO, MELVIN G., 4585 Twin Cr. Rd., Bonner, MT 59823/406-244-5208
Specialties: Working folders to customer specs. **Patterns:** Locking folders, hunters and traditional-style knives. **Technical:** Grinds 440C. **Prices:** $60 to $100; some to $200. **Remarks:** Part-time maker; first knife sold in 1975. **Mark:** Name and city, dove logo.

FAUCHEAUX, HOWARD J., P.O. Box 206, Loreauville, LA 70552/318-229-6467
Specialties: Working straight knives and folders; period pieces. Also a hatchet with caping knife in the handle. **Patterns:** Traditional locking folders, hunters, fighters and Bowies. **Technical:** Forges W2, 1095 and his own Damascus; stock removal D2. **Prices:** Start at $200. **Remarks:** Full-time maker; first knife sold in 1969. **Mark:** Last name.

FAULKNER, ALLAN, Rt. 11, Box 161, Jasper, AL 35501/205-387-0083
Specialties: Working and fancy straight knives; kitchen cutlery. **Patterns:** Pocketknives, traditional folders, miniatures, hunters, fighters and Bowies. **Technical:** Grinds D2, 440C and 154CM; prefers natural handle materials. **Prices:** $150 to $350; some to $1,500. **Remarks:** Part-time maker; first knife sold in 1978. **Mark:** Last name.

FAUST, JOACHIM, Kirchgasse 10, 95497 Goldkronach, GERMANY

FECAS, STEPHEN J., 1312 Shadow Lane, Anderson, SC 29625/803-287-4834
Specialties: Working straight knives in standard patterns; some period pieces. **Patterns:** Hunters to claws, folding slip-joints to buckskinners. **Technical:** Grinds D2, 440C and 154CM; most knives hand-finished to 600 grit. **Prices:** $140 to $400; some to $750. **Remarks:** Part-time maker; first knife sold in 1977. **Mark:** Last name.

FERDINAND, DON, P.O. Box 1564, Shady Cove, OR 97539-1564/503-560-3355
Specialties: One-of-a-kind working knives and period pieces; all tool steel Damascus. **Patterns:** Bowies, push knives and fishing knives. **Technical:** Forges high-carbon alloy steels—L6, D2; makes his own Damascus. Exotic handle materials offered. **Prices:** $100 to $500. **Remarks:** Full-time maker since 1980. Does business as Wyvern. **Mark:** Initials connected.

FERGUSON, JIM, 32131 Via Bande, Temecula, CA 92592/909-676-2634
Specialties: One-of-a-kind straight knives. **Patterns:** Bowies and daggers. **Technical:** Forges 1095 and 200 twisted nickel; makes commercial Damascus. **Prices:** $100 to $3,000. **Remarks:** Part-time maker; first knife sold in 1987. Doing business as Twisted Nickel Knives. **Mark:** First and last name over a push dagger.

FERGUSON, JIM, P.O. Box 764, San Angelo, TX 76902/915-651-6656
Specialties: Straight working knives and folders. **Patterns:** Working belt knives, hunters, Bowies and some folders. **Technical:** Grinds ATS-34, D2 and Vascowear. Flat-grinds hunting knives. **Prices:** $200 to $600; some to $1,000. **Remarks:** Full-time maker; first knife sold in 1987. **Mark:** First and middle initials, last name.

FERGUSON, LEE, Rt. 2, Box 109, Hindsville, AR 72738/501-443-0084
Specialties: Straight working knives and folders, some fancy. **Patterns:** Hunters, daggers, swords, locking folders and slip-joints. **Technical:** Grinds D2, 440C and ATS-34; heat-treats. **Prices:** $50 to $600; some to $4,000. **Remarks:** Part-time maker; first knife sold in 1977. **Mark:** Last name.

FERRARA, THOMAS, 122 Madison Dr., Naples, FL 33942/813-597-3363; FAX: 813-597-3363
Specialties: High-art, traditional and working straight knives and folders of all designs. **Patterns:** Boots, Bowies, daggers, fighters and hunters. **Technical:** Grinds 440C, D2 and ATS-34; heat-treats. **Prices:** $100 to $700; some to $1,300. **Remarks:** Part-time maker; first knife sold in 1983. **Mark:** Last name.

FIELDER, WILLIAM V., 8406 Knowland Circle, Richmond, VA 23229 23229/804-750-1198
Specialties: Fancy working straight knives and folders of his design. **Patterns:** Hunters, boots and daggers; locking folders, interframes and traditional-style knives. **Technical:** Forges W2, O1 and his own Damascus; likes wire inlay. **Prices:** $25 to $500; some to $1,000. **Remarks:** Full-time maker; first knife sold in 1982. **Mark:** Last name.

FIKES, JIMMY L., P.O. Box 3457, Jasper, AL 35502/205-387-9302; FAX: 205-221-1980
Specialties: High-art working knives; artifact knives; using knives with cord-wrapped handles; swords and combat weapons. **Patterns:** Axes to buckskinners, camp knives to miniatures, tantos to tomahawks; springless folders. **Technical:** Forges W2, O1 and his own Damascus. **Prices:** $135 to $3,000; exceptional knives to $7,000. **Remarks:** Full-time maker. **Mark:** Stylized initials.

FINCH KNIVES (See Finch, Ricky D.)

FINCH, RICKY D., HC 68 Box 311-C, West Liberty, KY 41472/606-743-7151
Specialties: Traditional working/using straight knives of his design or to customer specs. **Patterns:** Hunters, skinners and utility/camp knives. **Technical:** Grinds 440C and ATS-34 and others upon request. Hand-rubbed stain finish on blades; uses Micarta, Pakkawood, stag and natural and exotic woods on handles. Offers filework and hand-sewn, tooled sheaths. **Prices:** $40 to $125; some to $150. **Remarks:** Part-time maker; first knife made in 1994. Doing business as Finch Knives. **Mark:** Last name inside outline of state of Kentucky.

FINE CUSTOM KNIVES (See Nielson, Jeff V.)

FIORINI, BILL, P.O. Box 131, LaCrescent, MN 55947/507-895-2378
Specialties: Fancy working knives and lockbacks. **Patterns:** Hunters, boots, Japanese-style knives and kitchen/utility knives. **Technical:** Forges own Damascus. **Prices:** Full range. **Remarks:** Full-time metalsmith researching pattern materials. **Mark:** "W" over "F" with Japanese lettering.

FIRE FORGED KNIVES (See Lockett, Lowell C.)

FIREPOINT KNIVES (See Renner, Terry Lee)

FISCHER, CLYDE E., HCR 40, Box 133, Nixon, TX 78140-9400/512-582-1353
Specialties: Working knives for serious and professional hunters. **Patterns:** Heavy-duty hunters and survival blades; camp knives and buckskinner knives. **Technical:** Forges and grinds L6, O1 and his own Damascus. **Prices:** $100 to $250; some to $800. **Remarks:** Full-time maker; first knife sold in 1957. **Mark:** Fish.

FISHER, JAY, 104 S. Main St., P.O. Box 267, Magdalena, NM 87825
Specialties: High-art, ancient and exact working and using straight knives of his design. **Patterns:** Hunters, daggers and high-art sculptures. **Technical:** Grinds 440C, ATS-34 and D2. Prolific maker of stone-handled knives. **Prices:** $65 to $50,000; some higher. **Remarks:** Full-time maker; first knife sold in 1984. **Mark:** Very fine—JaFisher—Quality Custom Knives.

FISHER, THEO (TED), 8115 Modoc Lane, Montague, CA 96064/916-459-3804
Specialties: Moderately-priced working knives in carbon steel. **Patterns:** Hunters, fighters, kitchen and buckskinner knives. Damascus miniatures. **Technical:** Grinds ATS-34, L6 and 440C. **Prices:** $65 to $165; exceptional knives to $300. **Remarks:** First knife sold in 1981. **Mark:** Name in banner logo.

FISK, JERRY, 157 N. Park Ave. Lockesburg, AR 71846/870-289-3240; E-MAIL: jfisk@cswnet.com
Specialties: Edged weapons, collectible and functional. **Patterns:** Bowies, daggers, swords, hunters, camp knives and others. **Technical:** Forges carbon steels and his own pattern welded steels. **Prices:** $200 to $10,000. **Remarks:** Full-time maker; first knife sold in 1980. **Mark:** Name, MS.

FISTER, JIM, 5067 Fisherville Rd., Simpsonville, KY 40067/502-834-7841
Specialties: Working straight knives and period pieces. **Patterns:** Bowies, hunters, buckskinners, fighters, daggers and folders. **Technical:** Forges O1, 5160, 52100, his own wire and regular and exotic Damascus. **Prices:** $150 to $1,400; some to $2,000. **Remarks:** Part-time maker; first knife sold in 1982. **Mark:** Last name.

FITZGERALD, DENNIS M., 4219 Alverado Dr., Fort Wayne, IN 46816-2847/219-447-1081
Specialties: Straight working knives. **Patterns:** Skinners, fighters, camp and utility knives; period pieces. **Technical:** Forges W2, O1, billet and cable-wire Damascus. Likes integral guards, bolsters and pommels. **Prices:** $100 to $500. **Remarks:** Part-time maker; first knife sold in 1985. Doing business as The Ringing Circle. **Mark:** Name and circle logo.

FIVE RUNS FORGE (See Bullard, Bill)

FLECHTNER, CHRIS, 224 St. Camille, Fitchburg, MA 01420/508-342-4371

FLINT STEEL KNIVES (See Anderson, Michael D.)

FLOURNOY, JOE, 5750 Lisbon Rd., El Dorado, AR 71730/870-863-7208

FLYNN, BRUCE, 8139 W. County Rd. 650 S, Knightstown, IN 46148-9348/317-779-4034
Specialties: Working straight knives and folders. **Patterns:** Fighters, Bowies, daggers, skinners and hunters. **Technical:** Grinds 440C, 154CM and D2. **Prices:** Moderate. **Remarks:** Full-time maker. **Mark:** First and middle initials, last name.

FOGARIZZU, BOITEDDU, via Crispi, 6, 07016 Pattada, ITALY
Specialties: Traditional italian straight knives and folders. **Patterns:** Collectible folders. **Technical:** Forges and grinds 12C27, ATS-34 and his Damascus. **Prices:** $200 to $3,000. **Remarks:** Full-time maker; first knife sold in 1958. **Mark:** Full name and registered logo.

FOGG, DON, 40 Alma Road, Jasper, AL 35501-8813/205-483-0822; E-MAIL: dfogg@concentric.net
Specialties: Straight knives. **Patterns:** Bowies, stout hunters, daggers. **Technical:** Forges carbon steels, *san-mai* and Damascus; all natural materials. **Prices:** $150 to $5,000. **Remarks:** Full-time maker; first knife sold in 1976. Doing business as Kemal. **Mark:** 24K gold cherry blossom.

FOLEY, BARNEY, 3M Reler Lane, Somerset, NJ 08873/908-297-1880

FOLTS, ALAN C., 2792 Powhotan Rd., Clayton, NC 27520/919-550-9352

FORD, ALLEN, 3927 Plumcrest Rd., Smyrna, GA 30080/404-432-5061
Specialties: Art knives of his design. **Patterns:** Bowies, daggers and hunters. **Technical:** Hand finishes every knife. Scrimshaws. **Mark:** First initial, last name in script.

FORSTALL, AL, 346 Mapleleaf Dr., Slidell, LA 70458/504-646-0721
Specialties: Traditional working and using straight knives of his design or to customer specs. **Patterns:** Fighters, hunters and utility/camp knives. **Technical:** Grinds ATS-34, 440C, commercial Damascus and others upon request. **Prices:** $60 to $250. **Remarks:** Spare-time maker; first knife sold in 1991. **Mark:** The number 4 with "stall" around it.

FORTHOFER, PETE, 5535 Hwy. 93S, Whitefish, MT 59937/406-862-2674
Specialties: Interframes with checkered wood inlays; working straight knives. **Patterns:** Interframe folders and traditional-style knives; hunters, fighters and Bowies. **Technical:** Grinds D2, 440C, 154CM and ATS-34. **Prices:** $250 to $1,000; some to $1,500. **Remarks:** Part-time maker; full-time gunsmith. First knife sold in 1979. **Mark:** Name and logo.

FOSTER, AL, HC 73, Box 117, Dogpatch, AR 72648/501-446-5137
Specialties: Working straight knives and folders. **Patterns:** Hunting, fishing knives, folders, Bowies. **Technical:** Grinds 440C, ATS-34 and D2. **Prices:** $95 to $600. **Remarks:** Full-time maker; first knife sold in 1981. **Mark:** Scorpion logo and name.

FOSTER, R.L. (BOB), 745 Glendare Blvd., Mansfield, OH 44907

FOWLER, CHARLES R., Rt. 2, Box 1446 A, Ft. McCoy, FL 32134/904-467-3215
Specialties: Fancy high-art straight knives and traditional working straight knives of his design. **Patterns:** Boots, Bowies, daggers, fighters, hunters and utility knives. **Technical:** Forges L6, W2 and 5160. **Prices:** $300 to $1,200. **Remarks:** Part-time maker; first knife sold in 1986. Doing business as Falcon Crest Forge. **Mark:** Circle with falcon bust, name, bladesmith.

FOWLER CUSTOM KNIVES (See Fowler, Ricky)

FOWLER, ED A., Willow Bow Ranch, P.O. Box 1519, Riverton, WY 82501/307-856-9815
Specialties: Heavy-duty working and using straight knives. **Patterns:** Hunters, camp, bird and trout knives, Bowies. **Technical:** Forges 52100, chainsaw Damascus; multiple-quench heat-treats. Engraves all knives. All handles are domestic sheephorn, processed and aged for a minimum of four years. Makes heavy-duty, hand-stitched, waxed, harness leather pouch-type sheaths. **Prices:** $450 to $3,000. **Remarks:** Full-time maker; first knife sold in 1962. **Mark:** Initials connected.

FOWLER FORGE KNIFEWORKS (See Fowler, Jerry)

FOWLER, JERRY, 610 FM 1660 N., Hutto, TX 78634/512-846-2860; E-MAIL: fowler@inetport.com
Specialties: Using straight knives of his design. **Patterns:** A variety of hunting and camp knives, combat knives. Custom designs considered. **Technical:** Forges 5160, his own Damascus and cable Damascus. Makes sheaths. Prefers natural handle materials. **Prices:** Start at $150. **Remarks:** Part-time maker; first knife sold in 1986. Doing business as Fowler Forge Knifeworks. **Mark:** First initial, last name, date and J.S.

FOWLER, RICKY, Rt. 4, Box 83-B, Richton, MS 39476/601-989-2553
Specialties: Traditional working/using straight knives and folders of his design. **Patterns:** Skinners, fighters, folders, Tantos, Bowies and utility/camp knives. **Technical:** Grinds O1; forges Damascus. **Prices:** $85 to $250; some to $400. **Remarks:** Part-time maker; first knife sold in 1994. Doing business as Fowler Custom Knives. **Mark:** Last name, Custom Knives, city and state in oval.

FOX, JACK L., 7085 Canelo Hills Dr., Citrus Heights, CA 95610/916-723-8647
Specialties: Traditional working/using straight knives of all designs. **Patterns:** Hunters, utility/camp knives and bird/fish knives. **Technical:** Grinds ATS-34, 440C and D2. **Prices:** $125 to $225; some to $350. **Remarks:** Spare-time maker; first knife sold in 1985. Doing business as Fox Knives. **Mark:** Stylized fox head.

FOX KNIVES (See Fox, Jack L.)

FOX, PAUL, 4721 Rock Barn Road, Claremont, NC 28610/704-459-2000; FAX: 704-459-9200
Specialties: Unusual one-of-a-kinds of all-bolted construction; mostly folders. **Patterns:** High-tech folding fighters; straight daggers and fighters. **Technical:** Grinds O1, 154CM and commercial Damascus. **Prices:** $200 to $6,000. **Remarks:** Full-time maker; first knife sold in 1977. **Mark:** Signature.

FOX, WENDELL, 4080 S. 39th, Springfield, OR 97478/541-747-2126
Specialties: Large camping knives and friction folders of his design and to customer specs. **Patterns:** Hunters, locking folders, slip-joint folders and utility/camp knives. **Technical:** Forges high-carbon steel, cable, 52100, Damascus and his own timbers steel. All carbon cable blades are differentially tempered; all sheaths are wet-moulded. Offers fancy filework. **Prices:** Start at $200. **Remarks:** Full-time maker; first knife sold in 1952. **Mark:** Stamped name or logo.

FOX VALLEY FORGE (See Werth, George W.)

FOXWOOD FORGE (See Kilby, Keith)

FRALEY, DEREK, 430 South Ct., Dixon, CA 95620/916-678-0393
Specialties: Traditional working/using straight knives and folders of his design and in standard patterns. **Patterns:** Fighters, hunters, utility/camp knives. **Technical:** Grinds ATS-34. Offers hand-stitched sheaths. **Prices:** Start at $100. **Remarks:** Part-time maker; first knife sold in 1990. **Mark:** First and middle initials, last name over buffalo.

FRANCE, DAN, Box 218, Cawood, KY 40815/606-573-6104
Specialties: Traditional working and using straight knives of his design. **Patterns:** Hunters, Bowies and utility/camp knives. **Technical:** Forges and grinds O1, 5160 and L6. **Prices:** $35 to $125; some to $350. **Remarks:** Spare-time maker; first knife sold in 1985. **Mark:** First name.

FRANCIS, VANCE, 2612 Alpine Blvd., Alpine, CA 91901/619-445-0979
Specialties: Working straight knives. **Patterns:** Bowies and utility knives. **Technical:** Uses ATS-34, A2, D2 and Damascus; differentially tempers large blades. **Prices:** $175 to $600. **Remarks:** Part-time maker. **Mark:** First name, last name, city and state under feather in oval.

FRANJO (See Candrella, Joe)

FRANK KNIVES, H.H. (See Frank, Heinrich H.)

FRANK, HEINRICH H., 13868 NW Keleka Pl., Seal Rock, OR 97376/541-563-3041; FAX: 541-563-3041
Specialties: High-art investor-class folders, handmade and engraved. **Patterns:** Folding daggers, hunter-size folders and gents. **Technical:** Grinds 07 and O1. **Prices:** $4,800 to $16,000. **Remarks:** Full-time maker; first knife sold in 1965. Doing business as H.H. Frank Knives. **Mark:** Name, address and date.

FRANK'S CUSTOM KNIVES (See Dilluvio, Frank J.)

FRANK'S PLACE (See Niro, Frank)

FRANKLAND, ANDREW, P.O. Box 256, Wilderness 6560, SOUTH AFRICA/0441-877-0260; FAX: 0441-877-0260
Specialties: Classic working and using straight knives and folders of his design and to customer specs. **Patterns:** Daggers, fighters, hunters and utility/camp knives. **Technical:** Grinds 440C, D2 and ATS-34. All double-edge knives have broad spine. **Prices:** $250 to $400; some to $1,500. **Remarks:** Full-time maker; first knife sold in 1979. **Mark:** Last name surrounded by mountain, lake, forest scene.

FRANKLIN, MIKE, 9878 Big Run Road, Aberdeen, OH 45101/937-549-2598
Specialties: High-tech tactical folders. **Patterns:** Tactical folders. **Technical:** Grinds CPM-T-440V, 440-C, ATS-34; titanium liners and bolsters; carbon fiber scales. Uses radical grinds and severe serrations. **Prices:** $275 to $600. **Remarks:** Full-time maker; first knife sold in 1969. **Mark:** Stylized boar with HAWG.

FRANKS, JOEL, 6610 Quaker, Lubbock, TX 79413/806-792-7112
Specialties: Working straight knives and folders in standard patterns or to customer specs. **Patterns:** Belt knives, hunters, gut hook skinners, folders and utility knives. **Technical:** Grinds 440C, 440A and L6. Makes trophy and commemorative cases and racks to accompany his knives. Repairs and refinishes old knives. **Prices:** $35 to $300. **Remarks:** Part-time maker; first knife sold in 1973. **Mark:** Initials connected.

FRASER, GRANT, RR2 Foresters Falls, Ont., CANADA K0J 1V0/613-582-3582
Specialties: Fancy and working straight knives of his design and to customer specs. **Patterns:** Bowies, daggers and hunters. **Technical:** Forges and grinds O1 and 5160; grinds ATS-34. **Prices:** $125 to $255; some to $1,200. **Remarks:** Full-time maker; first knife sold in 1983. **Mark:** Initial tang stamp.

FRAZIER, RON, 2107 Urbine Rd., Powhatan, VA 23139/804-794-8561
Specialties: Classy working knives of his design; some high-art straight knives. **Patterns:** Wide assortment of straight knives, including miniatures and push knives. **Technical:** Grinds 440C; offers satin, mirror or sand finishes. **Prices:** $85 to $700; some to $3,000. **Remarks:** Full-time maker; first knife sold in 1976. **Mark:** Name in arch logo.

FRED KNIFEMAKER, R.W. (See Fred, Reed Wyle)

FRED, REED WYLE, 3149 X Street, Sacramento, CA 95817/916-739-0237
Specialties: Working/using straight knives of his design. **Patterns:** Hunters, kitchen and utility/camp knives. **Technical:** Forges any 10 series, old files and carbon steels. Offers initialing upon request; prefers natural handle materials. **Prices:** $20 to $125; some to $300. **Remarks:** Part-time maker; first knife sold in 1994. Doing business as R.W. Fred Knifemaker. **Mark:** Engraved first and last initials.

FREEMAN, JOHN, 160 Concession St., Cambridge, Ont. N1R 2H7 CANADA/519-740-2767; FAX: 519-740-2785; E-MAIL: freeman@golden.net
Specialties: Working straight knives. **Patterns:** Hunters, skinners, utilities, backpackers. **Technical:** Grinds A2, 440C and ATS-34. **Prices:** Start at $125. **Remarks:** Full-time maker; first knife sold in 1985. **Mark:** Full name, city, state, Handmade.

FREER CUSTOM KNIVES (See Freer, Ralph)

FREER, RALPH, P.O. Box 3482, Seal Beach, CA 90740/310-493-4925; FAX: 310-799-8844
Specialties: Art pieces and straight knives of his design. **Patterns:** Hunters, fighters and Bowies. **Technical:** Forges ATS-34, 440C, 5160,

1095 and O1; forges and makes own Damascus. **Prices:** $200 to $1,500. Offers custom filework. Works with natural materials, exotic woods and horn. **Remarks:** Part-time maker; first knife sold in 1991. Doing business as Freer Custom Knives. **Mark:** Last name.

FREILING, ALBERT J., 3700 Niner Rd., Finksburg, MD 21048/301-795-2880
Specialties: Working straight knives and folders; some period pieces. **Patterns:** Boots, Bowies, survival knives and tomahawks in 4130 and 440C; some locking folders and interframes; ball-bearing folders. **Technical:** Grinds O1, 440C and 154CM. **Prices:** $100 to $300; some to $500. **Remarks:** Part-time maker; first knife sold in 1966. **Mark:** Initials connected.

FREY JR., W. FREDERICK, 305 Walnut St., Milton, PA 17847/717-742-9576
Specialties: Working straight knives and folders, some fancy. **Patterns:** Wide range—boot knives to tomahawks. **Technical:** Grinds A2, O1 and D2; hand finishes only. **Prices:** $55 to $170; some to $600. **Remarks:** Spare-time maker; first knife sold in 1983. **Mark:** Last name in script.

FRIEDLY, DENNIS E., 12 Cottontail Ln., Cody, WY 82414/307-527-6811
Specialties: Fancy working straight knives and daggers. **Patterns:** Hunters, fighters, short swords, minis and miniatures; new line of full-tang hunters/boots. **Technical:** Grinds 440C, ATS-34 and commercial Damascus; prefers hidden tangs. **Prices:** $135 to $900; some to $2,500. **Remarks:** Full-time maker; first knife sold in 1972. **Mark:** Name, city, state.

FRITZ, JESSE, P.O. Box 241, Slaton, TX 79364/806-828-6190; FAX: 915-530-0508
Specialties: Working and using straight knives in standard patterns. **Patterns:** Hunters, utility/camp knives and skinners with gut hook. **Technical:** Grinds 440C, O1 and 1095. Flint-napped steel design, blued blades, filework and machine jeweling. Inlays handles with turquoise, coral and mother-of-pearl. Makes sheaths. **Prices:** $85 to $275; some to $500. **Mark:** Crossed half ovals: handmade on top, last name in middle, city and state on bottom.

FRIZZELL, TED, 14056 Low Gap Rd., West Fork, AR 72774/501-839-2516
Specialties: Swords, axes and self defense weapons. **Patterns:** Small skeleton knives to large swords. **Technical:** Grinds 5160 almost exclusively—1/4" to 1/2" bars—some O1 and A2 on request. All knives come with Kydex sheaths. **Prices:** $45 to $1,200. **Remarks:** Full-time maker; first knife sold in 1984. Doing business as Mineral Mountain Hatchet Works. Wholesale orders welcome. **Mark:** A circle with line in the middle; MM and HW within the circle.

FRONEFIELD, MIKE, P.O. Box 10268, Truckee, CA 95737/916-587-3003
Specialties: Working straight knives in standard patterns. **Patterns:** Fly knives to remove fly hooks from fish; utility knives; some swords. **Technical:** Forges and grinds cable Damascus, 440C and L6. Scrimshaws and engraves. Makes own sheaths. **Prices:** $50 to $150; some to $500. **Remarks:** Part-time maker; first knife sold in 1986. Doing business as Truckee Knifeworks. **Mark:** Name.

FRUHMANN, LUDWIG, Stegerwaldstr 8, 84489 Burghausen, GERMANY
Specialties: High-tech and working straight knives of his design. **Patterns:** Hunters, fighters and boots. **Technical:** Grinds ATS-34, CPM-T-440V and Schneider Damascus. Prefers natural handle materials. **Prices:** $200 to $1,500. **Remarks:** Spare-time maker; first knife sold in 1990. **Mark:** First initial and last name.

FUEGEN, LARRY, RR 1, Box 279, Wiscasset, ME 04578/207-882-6391; FAX: 207-882-7905; E-MAIL: fuegen@clinic.net
Specialties: High-art folders and classic and working straight knives. **Patterns:** Forged scroll folders, lockback folders and classic straight knives. **Technical:** Forges 5160, 1095 and his own Damascus. Works in exotic leather; offers elaborate filework and carving; likes natural handle materials. **Prices:** $400 to $5,200. **Remarks:** Full-time maker; first knife sold in 1975. **Mark:** Initials connected.

FUJIKAWA, SHUN, Sawa 1157 Kaizuka, Osaka 597, JAPAN/81-724-23-4032; FAX: 81-724-31-3145
Specialties: Folders of his design and to customer specs. **Patterns:** Locking folders. **Technical:** Grinds his own steel. **Prices:** $450 to $2,500; some to $3,000. **Remarks:** Part-time maker.

FUJISAKA, STANLEY, 45-004 Holowai St., Kaneohe, HI 96744/808-247-0017
Specialties: Fancy working straight knives and folders. **Patterns:** Hunters, boots, personal knives, daggers, collectible art knives. **Technical:** Grinds 440C, 154CM and ATS-34; clean lines, inlays. **Prices:** $150 to $1,200; some to $3,000. **Remarks:** Full-time maker; first knife sold in 1984. **Mark:** Name, city, state.

FUKUTA, TAK, 38-Umeagae-cho, Seki-City, Gifu-Pref, JAPAN/0575-22-0264
Specialties: Bench-made fancy straight knives and folders. **Patterns:** Sheffield-type folders, Bowies and fighters. **Technical:** Grinds commercial Damascus. **Prices:** Start at $300. **Remarks:** Full-time maker. **Mark:** Name in knife logo.

FULLCO FORGE (See Fuller, Bruce A.)

FULLER, BRUCE A., 1305 Airhart Dr., Baytown, TX 77520/713-427-1848
Specialties: One-of-a-kind working/using straight knives and folders of his designs. **Patterns:** Bowies, hunters, folders and utility/camp knives. **Technical:** Forges high-carbon steel and his own Damascus. Prefers El Solo Mesquite and natural materials. Offers filework. **Prices:** $200 to $500; some to $1,800. **Remarks:** Spare-time maker; first knife sold in 1991. Doing business as Fullco Forge. **Mark:** Fullco, M.S.

FULLER, JACK A., 7103 Stretch Ct., New Market, MD 21774/301-831-9749
Specialties: Straight working knives of his design and to customer specs. **Patterns:** Fighters, camp knives, hunters and art knives. **Technical:** Forges 5160, O1, W2 and his own Damascus. Offers leatherwork; scrimshaws. **Prices:** $300 to $750; some to $2,000. **Remarks:** Full-time maker; first knife sold in 1979. **Mark:** Fuller's Forge, MS.

FULLER, JOHN W., 6156 Ridge Way, Douglasville, GA 30135/770-942-1155
Specialties: Fancy working straight knives and folders in standard patterns. **Patterns:** Straight and folding hunters, gents, fighters. **Technical:** Grinds ATS-34, 440C and commercial Damascus. **Prices:** $75 to $300. **Remarks:** Part-time maker; first knife sold in 1978. **Mark:** Name, city, state.

FULLER'S FORGE (See Fuller, Jack A.)

FULTON, MICKEY, P.O. Box 1062, Willows, CA 95988/916-934-5780
Specialties: Working straight knives and folders of his design. **Patterns:** Hunters, Bowies, lockback folders and steak knife sets. **Technical:** Hand-filed, sanded, buffed ATS-34, 440C and A2. **Prices:** $65 to $600; some to $1,200. **Remarks:** Full-time maker; first knife sold in 1979. **Mark:** Signature.

g

GADDY, GARY LEE, 205 Ridgewood Lane, Washington, NC 27889/919-946-4359
Specialties: Working/using straight knives of his design; period pieces. **Patterns:** Bowies, hunters, utility/camp knives. **Technical:** Grinds ATS-34, D2 and O1. Offers filework. **Prices:** $100 to $225; some to $400. **Remarks:** Spare-time maker; first knife sold in 1991. **Mark:** Etched name and quarter moon logo.

GAETA, ANGELO, R. Saldanha Marinho, 1295, Centro, Jau, SP-17201-310, BRAZIL/0146-224543; FAX: 0146-224543
Specialties: Straight using knives to customer specs. **Patterns:** Hunters, kitchen and utility knives. **Technical:** Grinds D6, ATS-34 and 440C stainless. Titanium nitride golden finish upon request. **Prices:** $60 to $170. **Remarks:** Full-time maker; first knife sold in 1992. **Mark:** First initial, last name.

GAETA, ROBERTO, Rua Shikazu Myai 80, 05351 Sao Paulo, S.P., BRAZIL/11-268-4626; Av. Francisco Morato, 3680, 05520, Sao Paulo, S.P., BRAZIL (shop)
Specialties: Wide range of using knives. **Patterns:** Brazilian and North American hunting and fighting knives. **Technical:** Grinds stainless steel; likes natural handle materials. **Prices:** $100 to $250; some to $500. **Remarks:** Full-time maker; first knife sold in 1979. **Mark:** BOB'G.

GAINEY, HAL, 904 Bucklevel Rd., Greenwood, SC 29649/864-223-0225
Specialties: Traditional working and using straight knives and folders. **Patterns:** Hunters, slip-joint folders and utility/camp knives. **Technical:** Hollow-grinds ATS-34 and D2; makes sheaths. **Prices:** $95 to $145; some to $500. **Remarks:** Full-time maker; first knife sold in 1975. **Mark:** Eagle head and last name.

GALEB KNIVES (See Aoun, Charles)

GALLAGHER, BARRY, 714 8th Ave. N., Lewistown, MT 59457/406-538-7056
Specialties: Traditional working/using straight knives and folders of his design and to customer specs. **Patterns:** Folders, hunters, Bowies and fighters. **Technical:** Grinds ATS-34, 440C, 440V and D2; forges carbon steel and Damascus. **Prices:** $100 to $1,000; some to $2,500. **Remarks:** Full-time maker; first knife sold in 1993. Doing business as Gallagher Custom Knives. **Mark:** Last name.

GALLAGHER CUSTOM KNIVES (See Gallagher, Barry)

GAMBLE, FRANK, 3872 Dunbar Pl., Fremont, CA 94536/510-797-7970
Specialties: Fantasy and high-art straight knives and folders of his design. **Patterns:** Daggers, fighters, hunters and special locking folders. **Technical:** Grinds 440C and ATS-34; forges Damascus/cable Damascus. Inlays; offers jeweling. **Prices:** $150 to $10,000. **Remarks:** Full-time maker; first knife sold in 1976. **Mark:** First initial, last name.

GAMBLE KNIVES (See Gamble, Roger)

GAMBLE, ROGER, 2801 65 Way N., St. Petersburg, FL 33710/813-384-1470
Specialties: Traditional working/using straight knives and folders of his design. **Patterns:** Hunters and slip-joints. **Technical:** Grinds ATS-34 and Damascus. **Prices:** $100 to $600; some to $1,000. **Remarks:** Part-time maker; first knife sold in 1982. Doing business as Gamble Knives. **Mark:** First name in a fan of cards over last name.

GAME TRAIL KNIVES (See Watson, Bert)

GAND (See Anderson, Gary D.)

GANSTER, JEAN-PIERRE, 18, Rue du Vieil Hopital, F-67000 Strasbourg, FRANCE/(00333) 88 32 65 61; FAX: (00333) 88 32 52 79
Specialties: Fancy and high-art miniatures of his design and to customer specs. **Patterns:** Bowies, daggers, fighters, hunters, locking folders and miniatures. **Technical:** Forges and grinds stainless Damascus, ATS-34, gold and silver. **Prices:** $100 to $380; some to $2,500. **Remarks:** Part-time maker; first knife sold in 1972. **Mark:** Stylized first initials.

GARBE, BOB, 33176 Klein, Fraser, MI 48026/810-293-3664
Specialties: Folders and straight knives. **Patterns:** Hunters, locking folders and slip-joint folders. **Technical:** Grinds ATS-34. Offers filework. **Prices:** $100 to $1,000. **Remarks:** Full-time maker; first knife sold in 1991. **Mark:** Last name.

GARCIA, MARIO EIRAS, R. Edmundo Scanapieco, 300, Caxingui, Sao Paulo, SP-05516-070, BRAZIL/011-2124528
Specialties: Fantasy knives of his design; one-of-a-kind only. **Patterns:** Fighters, daggers, boots and two-bladed knives. **Technical:** Forges car leaf springs. Uses only natural handle material. **Prices:** $100 to $200. **Remarks:** Part-time maker; first knife sold in 1976. **Mark:** Two "B"s, one opposite the other.

GARCIA, TONY, 134 Gregory Place, West Palm Beach, FL 33405/561-582-1291; FAX: 561-585-9532
Specialties: Traditional working/using straight knives of his design and to customer specs. **Patterns:** Bowies, hunters, fillet and utility/camp knives. **Technical:** Grinds 440C, 440V and ATS-34. **Prices:** $125 to $250. **Remarks:** Part-time maker; first knife sold in 1992. **Mark:** Name, city, state; logo of fishing hook with arrow across it.

GARDNER, ROB, 387 Mustang Blvd., Port Aransas, TX 78373/48103/512-749-3597
Specialties: High-art working and using knives of his design and to customer specs. **Patterns:** Daggers, hunters and ethnic-patterned knives. **Technical:** Forges Damascus, L6 and 10-series steels. Engraves and inlays. Handles and fittings may be carved. **Prices:** $175 to $500; some to $2,500. **Remarks:** Spare-time maker; first knife sold in 1987. **Mark:** Engraved initials.

GARNER JR., WILLIAM O., 2803 East DeSoto St., Pensacola, FL 32503/904-438-2009
Specialties: Working straight knives, some fancy. **Patterns:** Hunters, Bowies, fighters, double-edged daggers, folders and fishing knives. **Technical:** Grinds 440C, 154CM and ATS-34, D2 and O1 steels. **Prices:** $85 to $500. **Remarks:** Full-time maker; first knife sold in 1985. **Mark:** First and last name in oval logo or last name.

GARSON, STEVEN, 1108 Pike St., Seattle, WA 98101/206-233-9893

GARTMAN, M.D., Rt. 4, Box 423G, Gatesville, TX 76528/817-865-6090
Specialties: Working straight knives and folders in standard patterns. **Patterns:** A variety of folders, some Bowies and miniatures. **Technical:** Uses ATS-34. **Prices:** $125 to $235. **Remarks:** Part-time maker; first knife sold in 1982. **Mark:** Last name.

GASTON, BERT, P.O. Box 9047, North Little Rock, AR 72119/501-372-4747
Specialties: Traditional working and using straight knives of his design. **Patterns:** Hunters, Bowies and fighters. **Technical:** Forges his Damascus, 5168 and L6. Only uses natural handle materials. **Prices:** $200 to $500; some to $1,500. **Remarks:** Part-time maker; first knife sold in 1989. **Mark:** Stylized last initial and M.S.

GASTON, RON, 330 Gaston Dr., Woodruff, SC 29388/803-433-0807; FAX: 803-433-9958
Specialties: Working period pieces. **Patterns:** Hunters, fighters, tantos, boots and a variety of other straight knives; single-blade slip-joint folders. **Technical:** Grinds ATS-34. Hand-rubbed satin finish is standard. **Prices:** $100 to $350; some to $1,000. **Remarks:** Full-time maker; first knife sold in 1980. **Mark:** Name.

GAUDETTE, LINDEN L., 5 Hitchcock Rd., Wilbraham, MA 01095/413-596-4896
Specialties: Traditional working knives in standard patterns. **Patterns:** Broad-bladed hunters, Bowies and camp knives; wood carver knives; locking folders. **Technical:** Grinds ATS-34, 440C and 154CM. **Prices:** $150 to $400; some higher. **Remarks:** Full-time maker; first knife sold in 1975. **Mark:** Last name in Gothic logo; used to be initials in circle.

GAULT, CLAY, Rt. 1, Box 287, Lexington, TX 78947/512-273-2873
Specialties: Classic straight and folding hunting knives and multi-blade folders of his design. **Patterns:** Folders and hunting knives. **Technical:** Grinds BX-NSM 174 steel, custom rolled from billets to his specifications. Uses exotic leathers for sheaths, and natural materials for the multi-blade folders. **Prices:** $275 to $525; some higher. **Remarks:** Full-time maker; first knife sold in 1970. **Mark:** Name or name with cattle brand.

G-E KNIVES (See Van Den Elsen, Gert)

GEISLER, GARY R., P.O. Box 294, Clarksville, OH 45113/513-383-4055
Specialties: Light and smooth working straight knives to customer specs. **Patterns:** Working knives. **Technical:** Grinds ATS-34, 440C and A2. Prefers mirror finishes. **Prices:** Start at $50. **Remarks:** Part-time maker; first knife sold in 1982. **Mark:** First and middle initials, last name and Maker in script.

GENGE, ROY E., P.O. Box 57, Eastlake, CO 80614/303-451-7991
Specialties: High-tech working knives. **Patterns:** Bowies, hatchets, hunters, survival knives, buckskinners, kukris and others. **Technical:** Forges and grinds L6, S7, W1, W2, O1, Vascowear, 154CM, ATS-34 and commercial Damascus. **Prices:** $100 to $1,200. **Remarks:** Part-time maker; first knife sold in 1968. **Mark:** Name, city, state.

GENOVESE, RICK, 116 Fawn Drive, Sedona, AZ 86336/520-282-2493
Specialties: Fancy and embellished folders of his design. **Patterns:** Locking folders. **Technical:** Grinds ATS-34 and J. Rados Damascus. All folders are interframes with inlays such as jade, lapis, dinosaur bone, charoite, etc. **Prices:** $800 to $1,500; some to $10,000. **Remarks:** Full-time maker; first knife sold in 1976. **Mark:** Last name.

GENSKE, JAY, 262 1/2 Elm St., Fond du Lac, WI 54935/414-921-6505
Specialties: Working/using knives and period pieces of his design and to customer specs. **Patterns:** Bowies, fighters, hunters. **Technical:** Grinds ATS-34 and 440C; forges and grinds Damascus and cable. Offers custom-tooled sheaths, scabbards and hand carved handles. **Prices:** $95 to $500; some to $1,000. **Remarks:** Full-time maker; first knife sold in 1985. Doing business as Genske Knives. **Mark:** Stamped or engraved last name.

GENSKE KNIVES (Genske, Jay)

GENTILE, AL, 101 Ticonderoga Dr., Warwick, RI 02889/401-737-4534

GEORGE CUSTOM KNIVES (See George, Les)

GEORGE, HARRY, 3137 Old Camp Long Rd., Aiken, SC 29801/803-649-1963; E-MAIL: hdkk-george@scescape.net
Specialties: Working straight knives of his design or to customer specs. **Patterns:** Hunters, skinners and utility knives. **Technical:** Grinds ATS-34. Prefers natural handle materials, hollow-grinds and mirror finishes. **Prices:** Start at $70. **Remarks:** Part-time maker; first knife sold in 1985. Trained under George Herron. Member SCAK. **Mark:** Name, city, state.

GEORGE, LES, 1703 Payne, Wichita, KS 67203/316-267-0736
Specialties: Classic, traditional and working/using straight knives of his design and to customer specs. **Patterns:** Fighters, hunters, swords and miniatures. **Technical:** Grinds D2; forges 5160 and Damascus. Uses mosaic handle pins and his own mokume-gane. **Prices:** $35 to $200; some to $800. **Remarks:** Part-time maker; first knife sold in 1992. Doing business as George Custom Knives. **Mark:** Last name or initials stacked.

GEORGE, TOM, P.O. Box 1298, Magalia, CA 95954/916-873-3306
Specialties: Working straight knives, display knives and folders of his design. **Patterns:** Hunters, Bowies, daggers and buckskinners and folders. **Technical:** Uses D2, 440C, ATS-34 and 154CM. **Prices:** $175 to $4,500. **Remarks:** First knife sold in 1981. No custom orders accepted. **Mark:** Name.

GEPNER, DON, 2615 E. Tecumseh, Norman, OK 73071/405-364-2750
Specialties: Traditional working and using straight knives of his design. **Patterns:** Bowies and daggers. **Technical:** Forges his Damascus, 1095 and 5160. **Prices:** $100 to $400; some to $1,000. **Remarks:** Spare-time maker; first knife sold in 1991. Has been forging since 1954; first edged weapon made at 9 years old. **Mark:** Last initial.

GERUS, GERRY, P.O. Box 2295, G.P.O. Cairns, Qld. 4870 AUSTRALIA/070-341451; 019 617935
Specialties: Fancy working and using straight knives of his design. **Patterns:** Hunters, Bowies and fighters. **Technical:** Uses 440C, ATS-34 and commercial Damascus. **Prices:** $275 to $600; some to $1,200. **Remarks:** Part-time maker; first knife sold in 1988. **Mark:** Last name; or last name, Hand Made, city, country.

GEVEDON, HANNERS (HANK), 1410 John Cash Rd., Crab Orchard, KY 40419-9770
Specialties: Traditional working and using straight knives. **Patterns:** Hunters, swords, utility and camp knives. **Technical:** Forges and grinds his own Damascus, 5160 and L6. Cast aluminum handles. **Prices:** $50 to $250; some to $400. **Remarks:** Part-time maker; first knife sold in 1983. **Mark:** Initials and LBF tang stamp.

G.H. KNIVES (See Hielscher, Guy)

GIAGU, SALVATORE AND DEROMA MARIA ROSARIA Via V. Emanuele 64, 07016 Pattada (SS), ITALY/079-755918; FAX: 079-755918
Specialties: Using and collecting traditional and new folders from Sardegna. **Patterns:** Folding, hunting, utility, skinners and kitchen knives. **Technical:** Forges ATS-34, 440, D2 and Damascus. **Prices:** $200 to $2,000; some higher. **Mark:** First initial, last name and name of town and muflon's head.

GIBSON, JAMES HOOT, RR1, Box 177F, Bunnell, FL 32110/904-437-4383
Patterns: Bowies, daggers and hunters. **Technical:** Grinds ATS-34, 440C and Damascus. **Prices:** $150 to $1,200; some to $2,500. **Remarks:** Part-time maker; first knife sold in 1965. Doing business as Hoot's Handmade Knives. **Mark:** Hoot.

GILBERT, CHANTAL, 1421 Cb du South, St. Romuald, Quebec G6W 2MX CANADA/418-839-8746

GILBREATH, RANDALL, 55 Crauswell Rd., Dora, AL 35062/205-648-3902
Specialties: Damascus folders and fighters. **Patterns:** Folders and fixed blades. **Technical:** Forges Damascus and stainless steel; stock removal. **Prices:** $300 to $1,500. **Remarks:** Part-time maker; first knife sold in 1979. **Mark:** Name in ribbon.

GILJEVIC, BRANKO, 35 Hayley Cresent, Queanbeyan 2620, N.S.W., AUSTRALIA/06-2977613
Specialties: Classic working straight knives and folders of his design. **Patterns:** Hunters, Bowies, skinners and locking folders. **Technical:** Grinds 440C. Offers acid etching, scrimshaw and leather carving. **Prices:** $150 to $1,500. **Remarks:** Part-time maker; first knife sold in 1987. Doing business as Sambar Custom Knives. **Mark:** Company name in logo.

GILPIN, DAVID, 902 Falling Star Ln., Alabaster, AL 35007/205-664-4777
Specialties: Classic, fancy and traditional knives of his design. **Patterns:** Japanese style swords. **Technical:** Grinds 440C, forges and grinds Damascus stainless, 1010, 1095 and 1084. Offers metal casting, electoplate and inlay. **Prices:** $500 to $5000; some to $12,000. **Remarks:** Full-time maker; first knife sold in 1994. **Mark:** First name in Japanese/Chinese characters.

GLASER, KEN, Rt. #1, Box 148, Purdy, MO 65734/417-442-3371
Specialties: Working straight knives in standard patterns. **Patterns:** Hunters, bird and trout knives, boots. **Technical:** Hollow-grinds O1, D2 and 440C. **Prices:** $75 to $125; some to $250. **Remarks:** Part-time maker; first knife sold in 1983. **Mark:** Initials.

GLOVER, RON, 6775 Socialville-Foster Rd., Mason, OH 45040/513-398-7857
Specialties: High-tech working straight knives and folders. **Patterns:** Hunters to Bowies; some interchangeable blade models; unique locking mechanisms. **Technical:** Grinds 440C, 154CM; buys Damascus. **Prices:** $70 to $500; some to $800. **Remarks:** Part-time maker; first knife sold in 1981. **Mark:** Name in script.

GODDARD, WAYNE, 473 Durham Ave., Eugene, OR 97404/541-689-8098
Specialties: Working/using straight knives and folders. **Patterns:** Hunters and folders. **Technical:** Works exclusively with wire Damascus and his own-pattern welded material. **Prices:** $250 to $4,000. **Remarks:** Full-time maker; first knife sold in 1963. Three-year backlog on orders. **Mark:** Blocked initials on forged blades; regular capital initials on stock removal.

GOERS, BRUCE, 3423 Royal Ct. S., Lakeland, FL 33813/941-646-0984
Specialties: Fancy working and using straight knives of his design and to customer specs. **Patterns:** Hunters, fighters, Bowies and fantasy knives. **Technical:** Grinds ATS-34, some Damascus. **Prices:** $195 to $600; some to $1,300. **Remarks:** Part-time maker; first knife sold in 1990. Doing business as Vulture Cutlery. **Mark:** Buzzard with initials.

GOERTZ, PAUL S., 201 Union Ave. SE, #207, Renton, WA 98059/425-228-9501
Specialties: Working straight knives of his design and to customer specs. **Patterns:** Hunters, skinners, camp, bird and fish knives, camp axes, some Bowies, fighters and boots. **Technical:** Grinds ATS-34, D2 and 440V. **Prices:** $75 to $500; some to $900. **Remarks:** Full-time maker; first knife sold in 1985. **Mark:** Signature.

GOFOURTH, JIM, 3776 Aliso Cyn. Rd., Santa Paula, CA 93060/805-659-3814
Specialties: Period pieces and working knives. **Patterns:** Bowies, locking folders, patent lockers and others. **Technical:** Grinds A2 and 154CM. **Prices:** Moderate. **Remarks:** Spare-time maker. **Mark:** Initials interconnected.

GOGUEN, SCOTT, 166 Goguen Rd., Newport, NC 28570/919-393-6013
Specialties: Classic and traditional straight knives; working/using knives of all designs. **Patterns:** Boots, Bowies, fighters, hunters, kitchen knives, utility/camp knives and swords. **Technical:** Forges 1095 and O1. Offers clay tempering and cord wrapped handles. **Prices:** $85 to $1,500. **Remarks:** Spare-time maker; first knife sold in 1988. **Mark:** Last name.

GOLD HILL KNIFE WORKS (See Scarrow, Wil)

GOLDBERG, DAVID, 1120 Blyth Ct., Blue Bell, PA 19422/215-654-7117
Specialties: Japanese style designs. **Patterns:** Kozuka to dai-sho. **Technical:** Forges his own Damascus; hand-rubbed finish. Uses traditional materials, carves fittings, handles and scabbards. **Remarks:** Full-time maker; first knife sold in 1987. **Mark:** Last name in English and Japanese.

GOLDENBERG, T.S., P.O. Box 238, Fairview, NC 28730
Specialties: Working straight knives and period pieces to customer specs. **Patterns:** Hunters, boots and Bowies. **Technical:** Grinds A2, O1 and 440C. **Prices:** $75 to $500; some to $700. **Remarks:** Part-time maker; first knife sold in 1975. **Mark:** Surname in mountain; some with TEDDYHAWK.

GOLDING, ROBIN, P.O. Box 267, Lathrop, CA 95330/209-982-0839
Specialties: Working straight knives of his design. **Patterns:** Survival knives, Bowie extractions, camp knives, dive knives and skinners. **Technical:** Grinds 440C, 154CM and ATS-34. **Prices:** $95 to $250; some to $500. **Remarks:** Full-time maker; first knife sold in 1985. Up to 1 1/2-year waiting period on orders. **Mark:** Signature of last name.

GOLD RUSH DESIGNS (See Connolly, James)

GOLTZ, WARREN L., 802 4th Ave. E., Ada, MN 56510/218-784-7721; E-MAIL: goltzfam@ada.polaristel.net
Specialties: Fancy working knives in standard patterns. **Patterns:** Hunters, Bowies and camp knives. **Technical:** Grinds 440C and ATS-34. **Prices:** $120 to $595; some to $950. **Remarks:** Part-time maker; first knife sold in 1984. **Mark:** Last name.

GONZALEZ, LEONARDO WILLIAMS, Ituzaingo 473, Maldonado, CP 20000, URUGUAY/(598.42)21617
Specialties: Classic high-art and fantasy straight knives; traditional working and using knives of his design, in standard patterns or to customer specs. **Patterns:** Hunters, Bowies, daggers, fighters, boots, swords and utility/camp knives. **Technical:** Forges and grinds 440C, 1095 and carbon steel. **Prices:** $100 to $900. **Remarks:** Full-time maker; first knife sold in 1985. **Mark:** Willy, whale, R.O.U.

GOO, TAI, 3225 N. Winstel Blvd., Tucson, AZ 85716/520-325-8095
Specialties: High-art, neo-tribal and fantasy knives. **Patterns:** Fighters, daggers, Bowies, buckskinners, edged fetishes and sculptures. **Technical:** Forges and grinds A6, 440C and his own Damascus with iron meteorites. **Prices:** $150 to $500; some to $10,000. **Remarks:** Full-time maker; first knife sold in 1978. **Mark:** Chiseled signature; mark in spacer and tang.

GOODE, BEAR, P.O. Box 6474, Navajo Dam, NM 87419/505-632-8184
Specialties: Working/using straight knives of his design and in standard patterns. **Patterns:** Bowies, hunters and utility/camp knives. **Technical:** Grinds 440C, ATS-34, 154-CM; forges and grinds 1095, 5160 and other steels on request; uses Damascus. **Prices:** $45 to $125; some to $350. **Remarks:** Part-time maker; first knife sold in 1993. Doing business as Bear Knives. **Mark:** First and last name with a three-toed paw print.

GORDON (See Defreest, William G.)

GORENFLO, JAMES T. (JT), 9145 Sullivan Rd., Baton Rouge, LA 70818/504-261-5868
Specialties: Traditional working and using straight knives of his design. **Patterns:** Bowies, hunters and utility/camp knives. **Technical:** Forges 5160, 1095, 52100 and his own Damascus. **Prices:** Start at $125. **Remarks:** Part-time maker; first knife sold in 1992. **Mark:** Last name or initials, J.S. on reverse.

GOSHAWK KNIVES (See Hollar, Bob)

GOTTAGE, DANTE, 43227 Brooks Drive, Clinton Twp., MI 48038-5323/810-286-7275
Specialties: Working knives of his design or to customer specs. **Patterns:** Large and small skinners, fighters, Bowies and fillet knives. **Technical:** Grinds O1, 440C and 154CM and ATS-34. **Prices:** $150 to $600. **Remarks:** Part-time maker; first knife sold in 1975. **Mark:** Full name in script letters.

GOTTAGE, JUDY, 43227 Brooks Drive., Clinton Twp., MI 48038-5323/810-286-7275
Specialties: Custom folders of her design or to customer specs. **Patterns:** Interframes or integral. **Technical:** Stock removal. **Prices:** $300 to $3,000. **Remarks:** Full-time maker; first knife sold in 1980. **Mark:** Full name, maker in script.

GOTTSCHALK, GREGORY J., 12 First St. (Ft. Pitt), Carnegie, PA 15106/412-279-6692
Specialties: Fancy working straight knives and folders to customer specs. **Patterns:** Hunters to tantos, locking folders to minis. **Technical:** Grinds 440C, 154CM, ATS-34. Now making own Damascus. Most knives have mirror finishes. **Prices:** Start at $75. **Remarks:** Part-time maker; first knife sold in 1977. **Mark:** Full name in crescent.

GOUKER, GARY B., P.O. Box 955, Sitka, AK 99835/907-747-3476
Specialties: Hunting knives for hard use. **Patterns:** Skinners, semi-skinners, and such. **Technical:** Likes natural materials, inlays, stainless steel. **Prices:** Moderate. **Remarks:** New Alaskan maker. **Mark:** Name.

GRAFFEO, ANTHONY I., 100 Riess Place, Chalmette, LA 70043/504-277-1428
Specialties: Traditional working and using straight knives of his design, to customer specs and in standard patterns. **Patterns:** Hunters, utility/camp knives and fishing knives. **Technical:** Hollow- and flat-grinds ATS-34, 440C and 154CM. Handle materials include Pakkawood, Micarta and sambar stag. **Prices:** $65 to $100; some to $250. **Remarks:** Part-time maker; first knife sold in 1991. Doing business as Knives by: Graf. **Mark:** First and middle initials, last name city, state, Maker.

GRAVELINE, ISABELLE (See Graveline, Pascal and Isabelle)

GRAVELINE, PASCAL and ISABELLE, Rue de a Gare, 63290 Ris, FRANCE/33 04 73 94 69 25; FAX: 33 04 73 94 69 25
Specialties: French replicas from the 17th, 18th and 19th centuries. **Patterns:** Traditional folders and multi-blade pocket knives; traveling knives, fruit knives and fork sets; puzzle knives and friend's knives; rivetless knives. **Technical:** Grind 12C27, ATS-34, Damascus and carbon steel. **Prices:** $200 to 1,500; some to $2,000. **Remarks:** Full-time makers; first knife sold in 1992. **Mark:** Last name over head of ram.

GRAY, BOB, 8206 N. Lucia Court, Spokane, WA 99208/509-468-3924
Specialties: Straight working knives of his own design or to customer specs. **Patterns:** Hunter, fillet and carving knives. **Technical:** Forges 5160, L6 and some 52100; grinds 440C. **Prices:** $100 to $600. **Remarks:** Part-time knife maker; first knife sold in 1991. Doing business as Hi-Land Knives. **Mark:** HI-L.

GREBE, GORDON S., P.O. Box 296, Anchor Point, AK 99556-0296/907-235-8242
Specialties: Working straight knives and folders, some fancy. **Patterns:** Tantos, Bowies, boot fighter sets, locking folders. **Technical:** Grinds stainless steels; likes 1/4-inch stock and glass-bead finishes. **Prices:** $75 to $250; some to $2,000. **Remarks:** Full-time maker; first knife sold in 1968. **Mark:** Initials in lightning logo.

GRECO, JOHN, 100 Mattie Jones Road, Greensburg, KY 42743
Specialties: One-of-a-kind limited edition knives. **Patterns:** Fighters, daggers, camp knives. **Technical:** Forges and stock removes carbon steel. **Prices:** Moderate. **Remarks:** Full-time maker; first knife sold in 1986. **Mark:** Last name.

GREEN, BILL, 706 Bradfield, Garland, TX 75042/214-272-4748
Specialties: High-art and working straight knives and folders of his design and to customer specs. **Patterns:** Bowies, hunters, kitchen knives and locking folders. **Technical:** Grinds ATS-34, D2 and 440V. Hand-tooled custom sheaths. **Prices:** $70 to $350; some to $750. **Remarks:** Part-time maker; first knife sold in 1990. **Mark:** Last name.

GREEN, ROGER M., 4640 Co. Rd. 1022, Joshua, TX 76058/817-641-5057
Specialties: 19th century period pieces. **Patterns:** Investor-grade Sheffield Bowies and dirks, fighters and hunters. **Technical:** Grinds 440C and tool steels; forges Damascus and occasionally carbon steel. Prefers flat grinds and hand-rubbed finishes. **Prices:** $350 to $3,500. **Remarks:** Full-time maker; first knife sold in 1984. **Mark:** First and middle initials, last name.

GREEN, WILLIAM (BILL), 46 Warren Rd., View Bank, Vic. 3084, AUSTRALIA/03-9459-1529
Specialties: Traditional high-tech straight knives and folders. **Patterns:** Japanese-influenced designs, hunters, Bowies, folders and miniatures. **Technical:** Forges O1, D2 and his own Damascus. Offers lost wax castings for bolsters and pommels. Likes natural handle materials, gems, silver and gold. **Prices:** $400 to $750; some to $1,200. **Remarks:** Full-time maker. **Mark:** Initials.

GREENE, CHRIS, 707 Cherry Lane, Shelby, NC 28150/704-434-5620

GREENE, DAVID, 570 Malcom Rd., Covington, GA 30209/770-784-0657
Specialties: Straight working/using knives. **Patterns:** Hunters. **Technical:** Forges mosaic and twist Damascus. Prefers stag and desert ironwood for handle material.

GREENFIELD, G.O., 2605 15th St., #522, Everett, WA 98201/206-259-1672; 206-239-1708
Specialties: High-tech and working straight knives and folders of his design. **Patterns:** Boots, daggers, hunters and one-of-a-kinds. **Technical:** Grinds ATS-34, D2, 440C and T-440V. Makes sheaths for each knife. **Prices:** $100 to $800; some to $10,000. **Remarks:** Part-time maker; first knife sold in 1978. **Mark:** Springfield®, serial number.

GREGORY, MICHAEL, 211 Calhoun Rd., Belton, SC 29627/803-338-8898
Specialties: Working straight knives and folders. **Patterns:** Hunters, tantos, locking folders and slip-joints, boots and fighters. **Technical:** Grinds 440C, 154CM and ATS-34; mirror finishes. **Prices:** $95 to $200; some to $1,000. **Remarks:** Part-time maker; first knife sold in 1980. **Mark:** Name, city in logo.

GREINER, RICHARD, 1073 E. County Rd. 32, Green Springs, OH 44836

GREISS, JOCKL, obere Muhlstr. 5, 73252 Gutenberg, GERMANY/07026-3224
Specialties: Classic and working/using straight knives of his design. **Patterns:** Bowies, daggers and hunters. **Technical:** Uses stainless Damascus, D2 and ATS-34. All knives are one-of-a-kind made by hand; no machines are used. **Prices:** $500 to $1500; some to $3000. **Remarks:** Full-time maker; first knife sold in 1984. **Mark:** An "X" with a long vertical line through it.

GRENIER, ROGER, 497 Chemin Paquette, Saint Jovite, P. Que. J0T 2H0, CANADA/819-425-8893
Specialties: Working straight knives. **Patterns:** Heavy-duty Bowies, fighters, hunters, swords and miniatures. **Technical:** Grinds O1, D2 and 440C. **Prices:** $70 to $225; some to $800. **Remarks:** Full-time maker; first knife sold in 1981. **Mark:** Last name on blade.

GREY, PIET, P.O. Box 1493, Silverton 0127, REPUBLIC OF SOUTH AFRICA/012-803-8206
Specialties: Fancy working and using straight knives of his design. **Patterns:** Fighters, hunters and utility/camp knives. **Technical:** Grinds ATS-34 and AEB-L; forges and grinds Damascus. Solderless fitting of guards. Engraves and scrimshaws. **Prices:** $125 to $750; some to $1,500. **Remarks:** Full-time maker; first knife sold in 1970. **Mark:** Last name.

GRIFFIN JR., HOWARD A., 14299 SW 31st Ct., Davie, FL 33330/305-474-5406
Specialties: Working straight knives and folders. **Patterns:** Hunters, Bowies, locking folders with his own push-button lock design. **Technical:** Grinds 440C. **Prices:** $100 to $200; some to $500. **Remarks:** Part-time maker; first knife sold in 1983. **Mark:** Initials.

GRIFFIN KNIVES (GRIFFIN, THOMAS J.)

GRIFFIN, MARK (See Griffin, Rendon and Mark)

GRIFFIN, RENDON and MARK, 9706 Cedardale, Houston, TX 77055/713-468-0436
Specialties: Working folders and automatics of their designs. **Patterns:** Standard lockers and slip-joints. **Technical:** Most blade steels; stock removal. **Prices:** Start at $350. **Remarks:** Part-time makers; Rendon's first knife sold in 1966; Mark's in 1974. **Mark:** Last name logo.

GRIFFIN, THOMAS J., 591 Quevli Ave., Windom, MN 56101/507-831-1089
Specialties: Period pieces and fantasy straight knives of his design. **Patterns:** Daggers and swords. **Technical:** Forges 1095, 52100 and L6. Most blades are his own Damascus; turned fittings and wire-wrapped grips. **Prices:** $250 to $800; some to $2,000. **Remarks:** Full-time maker; first knife sold in 1991. Doing business as Griffin Knives. **Mark:** Last name etched.

GRIGSBY, BEN, The Bluff Dweller House, P.O. Box 2096, 318 E. Main, Mt. View, AR 72560/501-269-3337
Specialties: Period pieces in steel or flint. **Patterns:** Arkansas toothpicks, Bowies and flint blades of late archaic period. **Technical:** Grinds O1, D2, 440C and knappes flint of Ozark Hills. **Prices:** $150 to $500; some to $1,500. **Remarks:** Full-time maker; first knife sold in 1976. Doing business as Ben Grigsby Edged Tools and Weapons. **Mark:** Initials with cache river arrowhead logo.

GRIGSBY EDGED TOOLS AND WEAPONS, BEN (See Grigsby, Ben)

GRINDSTONE, THE (See Grospitch, Ernie)

GROSPITCH, ERNIE, 18440 Amityville St., Orlando, FL 32820/407-568-5438
Specialties: Working knives of his design and in standard patterns. **Patterns:** Bowies, hunters and kitchen knives. **Technical:** Grinds ATS-34, 440V and 440C. Offers dovetailed bolsters and brass space between blade and bolster. Hand-stitched sheaths. **Prices:** $140 to $180; some to $300. **Remarks:** Part-time maker; first knife sold in 1989. Doing business as The Grindstone. **Mark:** First and last name, city, state.

GROSS, W.W., 325 Sherbrook Dr., High Point, NC 27260
Specialties: Working knives. **Patterns:** Hunters, boots, fighters. **Technical:** Grinds. **Prices:** Moderate. **Remarks:** Full-time maker. **Mark:** Name.

GROSSMAN, STEWART, 24 Water St., #419, Clinton, MA 01510/508-365-2291; 800-my sword
Specialties: Miniatures and full-size knives and swords. **Patterns:** One-of-a-kind miniatures—jewelry, replicas—and wire-wrapped figures. Full-size art, fantasy and combat knives, daggers and modular systems. **Technical:** Forges and grinds most metals and Damascus. Uses gems, crystals, electronics and motorized mechanisms. **Prices:** $20 to $300; some to $4,500 and higher. **Remarks:** Full-time maker; first knife sold in 1985. **Mark:** G1.

GRUBB, RICHARD E., 2759 Maplewood Dr., Columbus, OH 43231/614-882-1530
Specialties: Miniatures to Bowies. **Patterns:** Bowies, drop-point hunters, fighters, tantos and miniatures. **Technical:** Grinds 440C; likes filework; offers exotic woods, stag and Micarta, wire wrap. **Prices:** $50 to $500. **Remarks:** Part-time maker; first knife sold in 1989. **Mark:** Name.

GRUSSENMEYER, PAUL G., 101 S. White Horse Pike, Lindenwold, NJ 08021-2304/609-435-1500; FAX: 609-435-3786
Specialties: Assembling fancy and fantasy straight knives with his own carved handles. **Patterns:** Bowies, daggers, folders, swords, hunters and miniatures. **Technical:** Uses forged steel and Damascus, stock removal and knapped obsidian blades. **Prices:** $500 to $2,500; some to $12,000. **Remarks:** Part-time maker; first knife sold in 1991. **Mark:** First and last initial hooked together on handle.

GT KNIVES (See Tally, Grant C.)

GUESS, RAYMOND L., 7214 Salineville Rd. NE, Mechanicstown, OH 44651/330-738-2793
Specialties: Working straight knives and folders of his design or to customer specs. **Patterns:** Hunters, Bowies, fillet knives, steak and paring knife sets. **Technical:** Grinds 440C. Offers silver inlay work and mirror finishes. Custom-made leather sheath for each knife. **Prices:** $55 to $400; some to $700. **Remarks:** Spare-time maker; first knife sold in 1985. **Mark:** First initial, last name.

GUIGNARD, GIB, Box 3477, Quartzsite, AZ 85359/520-927-4831
Specialties: Traditional working/using straight knives of his design and in standard patterns. **Patterns:** Bowies, hunters, utility/camp knives and period pieces. **Technical:** Forges 5160, O1 and 1095; grinds 440C. Heat-treats. **Prices:** $50 to $275; some to $400. **Remarks:** Part-time maker; first knife sold in 1989. Doing business as Cactus Forge. **Mark:** Last name or G+.

GUN ROOM, THE (T.G.R.) (See Shostle, Ben)

GUNDERSEN, D.F. "DOC," 5811 South Siesta Lane, Tempe, AZ 85283
Specialties: Small and medium straight knives and lock-back folders. **Patterns:** Utility, hunters, fighters and sailors' knives. **Technical:** Forges 5160 and grinds 1095; other steels on request. Offers caricature carved handles. **Prices:** $75 to $250. **Remarks:** Full-time maker; first knife sold in 1988. Doing business as L&H Knife Works. **Mark:** L&H.

GUNN, NELSON L., 77 Blake Road, Epping, NH 03042/603-679-5119
Specialties: Classic and working/using straight knives of his design. **Patterns:** Bowies, fighters and hunters. **Technical:** Grinds O1 and 440C. Carved stag handles with turquoise inlays. **Prices:**$125 to $300; some to $700. **Remarks:** Part-time maker; first knife sold in 1996. Doing business as Nelson's Custom Knives. **Mark:** First and last initial.

GUNTER, BRAD, 13 Imnaha Road, Tijeras, NM 87059/505-281-8080

GURGANUS, CAROL, Star Rt., Box 50-A, Colerain, NC 27924/919-356-4831
Specialties: Working and using straight knives. **Patterns:** Fighters, hunters and kitchen knives. **Technical:** Grinds D2, ATS-34 and Damascus steel. Uses stag, sheephorn and exotic wood handles. **Prices:** $100 to $300. **Remarks:** Full-time maker; first knife sold in 1992. **Mark:** Female symbol, last name, city, state.

GURGANUS, MELVIN H., Star Rt., Box 50-A, Colerain, NC 27924/919-356-4831
Specialties: High-tech working folders. **Patterns:** Leaf-lock and back-lock designs, bolstered and interframe. **Technical:** D2 and 440C; makes mokume. Wife Carol scrimshaws. Heat-treats, carves and offers lost wax casting. **Prices:** $300 to $3,000. **Remarks:** Full-time maker; first knife sold in 1983. **Mark:** First initial, last name and maker.

GUTH, KENNETH, 8 S. Michigan, 32nd Floor, Chicago, IL 60603/312-346-1760
Specialties: One-of-a-kind ornate straight knives and folders. **Patterns:** Flemish, Japanese and African-styled knives. Also makes a few forged Damascus miniature knives with fossil ivory handles and 18K gold fittings and rivets. **Technical:** Forges and grinds high-carbon and 440C. Offers brass and steel laminations, goldsmithing. **Prices:** Upscale. **Remarks:** Full-time goldsmith and knifemaker. **Mark:** Last name.

GUTHRIE, GEORGE B., 1912 Puett Chapel Rd., Bassemer City, NC 28016/704-629-3031
Specialties: Working knives of his design or to customer specs. **Patterns:** Hunters, boots, fighters, locking folders and slip-joints in traditional styles. **Technical:** Grinds D2, 440C and 154CM. **Prices:** $105 to $300; some to $450. **Remarks:** Part-time maker; first knife sold in 1978. **Mark:** Name in state.

GWOZDZ, BOB, 71 Starr Ln., Attleboro, MA 02703/508-226-7475
Specialties: Fancy working straight knives. **Patterns:** Fighters, tantos and hunters. **Technical:** Grinds 440C. **Prices:** $150 to $400; some $500 and higher. **Remarks:** Part-time maker; first knife sold in 1983. Now attending law school. Will accept phone orders during summer months only. **Mark:** Name and serial number.

GYPSY SILK KNIVES (See Burrows, Stephen R.)

h

H&K ENTERPRISE (See Hunter, Hyrum)

HAGEN, PHILIP L., P.O. Box 58, Pelican Rapids, MN 56572/218-863-8503
Specialties: High-tech working straight knives and folders. **Patterns:** Defense-related straight knives; wide variety of folders. **Technical:** Forges and grinds 440C and his own Damascus; Uddeholm UHB. **Prices:** $100 to $800; some to $3,000. **Remarks:** Part-time maker; first knife sold in 1975. **Mark:** DOC HAGEN in shield, knife, banner logo; or DOC.

HAGGERTY, GEORGE S., P.O. Box 88, Jacksonville, VT 05342/802-368-7437
Specialties: Working straight knives and folders. **Patterns:** Hunters, claws, camp and fishing knives, locking folders and backpackers. **Technical:** Forges and grinds W2, 440C and 154CM. **Prices:** $85 to $300. **Remarks:** Part-time maker; first knife sold in 1981. **Mark:** Initials or last name.

HAGUE, GEOFF, The Malt House, Hollow Ln., Wilton, Marlborough, Wiltshire, SN8 3SR, ENGLAND/01672-870212
Specialties: Working knives to his design or to customer specs. **Patterns:** Hunters, skinners and fillet knives. **Technical:** Grinds ATS-34, D2, O1 and Damascus. **Prices:** Start at $160. **Remarks:** Full-time maker; first knife sold in 1992. **Mark:** Last name.

HAGWOOD, KELLIE, 9231 Ridgetown, San Antonio, TX 78250/210-521-8710
Specialties: Working straight knives and folders of his design or to customer specs. **Patterns:** Folders, fighters, Bowies, hunters and swords. **Technical:** Grinds 440C, ATS-34, D2 and Damascus; heat-treats. Makes leather sheaths. **Prices:** Start at $200. **Remarks:** Full-time maker; first knife sold in 1969. Exclusive maker for Texas Parks and Wildlife. Doing business as Longhorn Knife Works. **Mark:** Name, city, state in script.

HAJOVSKY, ROBERT J., P.O. Box 77, Scotland, TX 76379/817-541-2219
Specialties: Working straight knives; sub-hilted fighters. **Patterns:** Variety of straight knives. **Technical:** Grinds ATS-34 and others on request. **Prices:** $150 to $700. **Remarks:** Part-time maker; first knife sold in 1973. **Mark:** Bob-Sky Knives and name, city, state.

HALLIGAN, ED, 14 Meadow Way, Sharpsburg, GA 30277/770-251-7720; FAX: 770-251-7720
Specialties: Working straight knives and folders, some fancy. **Patterns:** Linerlocks, hunters, skinners, boots, fighters and swords. **Technical:** Grinds 440C and ATS-34; forges 5160; makes cable and pattern Damascus. **Prices:** $125 to $1,200. **Remarks:** Full-time maker; first knife sold in 1985. Doing business as Halligan Knives. **Mark:** Last name, city, state and USA.

HALLIGAN KNIVES (See Halligan, Ed)

HALPERN CUSTOM KNIVES, LES (See Halpern, Les)

HALPERN, LES, 14 Maxwell Rd., Monson, MA 01057/413-283-8627; FAX: 413-283-8627
Specialties: High-tech working and using knives. **Patterns:** Locking folders. **Technical:** Grinds O1, 440C and ATS-34; uses anodized titanium. **Prices:** $200 to $400. **Remarks:** Part-time maker; first knife sold in 1996. Doing business as Les Halpern Custom Knives. **Mark:** Full name, star of David, city, state.

HAMLET JR., JOHNNY, 300 Billington, Clute, TX 77531/409-265-6929
Specialties: Working straight knives and folders. **Patterns:** Hunters, fighters, fillet and kitchen knives, locking folders. Likes upswept knives and trailing-points. **Technical:** Grinds 440C, D2, ATS-34. Makes sheaths. **Prices:** $55 to $225; some to $500. **Remarks:** Part-time maker; first knife sold in 1988. **Mark:** Hamlet's Handmades in script.

HAMMERSMITH (See Smith, J.D.)

HAMMOND, JIM, P.O. Box 486, Arab, AL 35016/205-586-4151
Specialties: High-tech fighters and folders. **Patterns:** Proven-design fighters. **Technical:** Grinds 440C and ATS-34. **Prices:** $385 to $1,200; some to $8,500. **Remarks:** Full-time maker; first knife sold in 1977. **Mark:** Full name, city, state in shield logo.

HANCOCK, TIM, 10805 N. 83rd St., Scottsdale, AZ 85260/602-998-8849
Specialties: High-art and working straight knives and folders of his design and to customer specs. **Patterns:** Fighters, hunters, daggers, tantos, swords and locking folders. **Technical:** Forges Damascus and 52100; grinds ATS-34. Makes Damascus. Silver-wire inlays; offers carved fittings. **Prices:** $175 to $350; some to $5,000. **Remarks:** Full-time maker; first knife sold in 1988. **Mark:** Last name or heart.

HAND, BILL, P.O. Box 773, 1103 W. 7th St., Spearman, TX 79081/806-659-2967
Specialties: Traditional working and using straight knives of his design or to customer specs. **Patterns:** Hunters, Bowies and fighters. **Technical:** Forges 5160 and Damascus. **Prices:** Start at $125. **Remarks:** Spare-time maker; first knife sold in 1988. Current delivery time twelve to sixteen months. **Mark:** Stylized initials.

HAND M.D., JAMES E., 1001 Mockingbird Ln., Gloster, MS 39638/601-225-4197
Specialties: All types of straight knives. **Patterns:** Hunters, fighters, boots and collector knives. **Technical:** Grinds ATS-34 and commercial Damascus. All knives are handmade. **Prices:** $125 to $850; some to $1,200. **Remarks:** Full-time maker; first knife sold in 1985. **Mark:** Name and city.

HAND MADE KNIVES (See Bailey, Kirby C.)

HANDMADE KNIVES BY MARK LUBRICH (See Lubrich, Mark)

HANGAS & SONS (See Ruana Knife Works)

HANSEN, ROBERT W., 35701 University Ave. N.E., Cambridge, MN 55008/612-689-3242
Specialties: Working straight knives, folders and integrals.. **Patterns:** From hunters to minis, camp knives to miniatures; folding lockers and slip-joints in original styles. **Technical:** Grinds O1, 440C and 154CM; likes filework. **Prices:** $75 to $175; some to $550. **Remarks:** Part-time maker; first knife sold in 1983. **Mark:** Fish with last initial inside.

HANSON, TRAVIS, 651 Rangeline Rd., Mosinees, WI 54455/715-693-3940
Specialties: Straight knives of his design and in standard patterns. **Patterns:** Hunters and miniatures. **Technical:** Grinds D2, 440C and Damascus. Offers scrimshaw and filework. **Prices:** $50 to $300; some to $550. **Remarks:** First knife sold in 1993. **Mark:** Name in script.

HARA, KOUJI, 292-2, Ohsugi, Seki-City, Gifu-Pref., 501-32, JAPAN/0575-24-7569; FAX: 0575-24-7569
Specialties: High-tech and working straight knives of his design; some folders. **Patterns:** Hunters, locking folders and utility/camp knives. **Technical:** Grinds Cowry X, Cowry Y and ATS-34. Prefers high mirror polish; pearl handle inlay. **Prices:** $80 to $500; some to $1,000. **Remarks:** Full-time maker; first knife sold in 1980. Doing business as Knife House "Hara." **Mark:** First initial, last name in fish.

HARA, KOUJI, c/o Ryuichi Hara, P.O. Box 265, Vincennes, IN 47591

HARDY, SCOTT, 639 Myrtle Ave., Placerville, CA 95667/916-622-5780
Specialties: Traditional working and using straight knives of his design. **Patterns:** Bowies, hunters and utility knives. **Technical:** Forges O1 and W2. Offers mirror finish; differentially tempers. **Prices:** $76 to $350; some to $1,000. **Remarks:** Part-time maker; first knife sold in 1982. **Mark:** First initial, last name and Handmade with bird logo.

HARKINS, J.A., P.O. Box 218, Conner, MT 59827/406-821-1060
Specialties: One-of-a-kind modern art knives of his design. **Patterns:** Folders, fighters and swords. **Technical:** Grinds ATS-34 and Ferguson Damascus. Engraves; offers gem work. **Prices:** Start at $450. **Remarks:** Full-time maker and engraver; first knife sold in 1988. **Mark:** First and middle initials, last name.

HARLESS, WALT, P.O. Box 845, Stoneville, NC 27048-0845/910-573-9768; E-MAIL: starscrim@msn.com
Specialties: Traditional working straight knives. **Patterns:** Hunters, utility, combat and specialty knives; one-of-a-kind historical interpretations. **Technical:** Grinds ATS-34 and 440C. **Prices:** $90 to $350; some to $1,200. **Remarks:** Full-time maker; first knife sold in 1978. Doing business as Arrow Forge. **Mark:** "A" with arrow; name, city, state.

HARLEY, LARRY W., 348 Deerfield Dr., Bristol, TN 37620/423-878-5368 (shop); 540-466-6771 (home)
Specialties: Working knives; period pieces. **Patterns:** Full range of straight knives, tomahawks, razors, buckskinners and hog spears. **Technical:** Forges and grinds ATS-34, D2, 440, O1, L6 and his own Damascus. **Prices:** $65 to $6,500. **Remarks:** Full-time maker; first knife sold in 1983. Guides (knife only) wild boar hunts. Doing business as Lonesome Pine Knives. **Mark:** Name, city and state in pine logo.

HARMON, JAY, 462 Victoria Rd., Woodstock, GA 30189/770-928-2734
Specialties: Working straight knives and folders of his design or to customer specs; collector-grade pieces. **Patterns:** Bowies, daggers, fighters, boots, hunters and folders. **Technical:** Grinds 440C, 440V, ATS-34, D2 1095 and Damascus; heat-treats; makes own mokume. **Prices:** Start at $185. **Remarks:** Part-time maker; first knife sold in 1984. **Mark:** Last name.

HARMON, JOE, 8014 Fisher Dr., Jonesboro, GA 30236/770-471-0024
Specialties: High-tech and working folders of his design. **Patterns:** Liner lock and traditional folders. **Technical:** Grinds 12C27 Sandvik, ATS-34 and A2. Offers heat-treating, anodized-titanium and inlays; prefers natural handle materials. **Prices:** Start at $125. **Remarks:** Part-time maker; first knife sold in 1988. **Mark:** First name, middle initial, last name, city, state.

HARRIS, JAY, 991 Johnson St., Redwood City, CA 94061/415-366-6077
Specialties: Traditional high-tech straight knives and folders of his design. **Patterns:** Daggers, fighters and locking folders. **Technical:** Uses 440C, ATS-34 and CPM. **Prices:** $250 to $850. **Remarks:** Spare-time maker; first knife sold in 1980.

HARRIS, RALPH DEWEY, 2607 Bell Shoals Rd., Brandon, FL 33511/813-681-5293
Specialties: Collectible and working interframe locking folders. **Patterns:** Straight and folding hunters, fighters and pocketknives; backlocks, sidelocks, leverlocks and buttonlocks. **Technical:** Grinds 440C, ATS-34 and some commercial Damascus. Uses jeweled and color anodized titanium and 416SS for frames. **Prices:** $150 to $800; some to $1,000. **Remarks:** Full-time maker; first knife sold in 1978. **Mark:** Last name, or name and city.

HARSEY, WILLIAM H., 82710 N. Howe Ln., Creswell, OR 97426/503-895-4941
Specialties: High-tech kitchen and outdoor knives. **Patterns:** Folding hunters, trout and bird folders; straight hunters, camp knives and axes. **Technical:** Grinds; etches. **Prices:** $125 to $300; some to $1,500. Folders start at $350. **Remarks:** Full-time maker; first knife sold in 1979. **Mark:** Full name, state, U.S.A.

HART, BILL, 647 Cedar Dr., Pasadena, MD 21122/410-255-4981
Specialties: Fur-trade era working straight knives and folders. **Patterns:** Springback folders, skinners, Bowies and patch knives. **Technical:** Forges and stock removes 1095 and 5160 wire Damascus. **Prices:** $100 to $600. **Remarks:** Part-time maker; first knife sold in 1986. **Mark:** Name.

HARTMAN, ARLAN (LANNY), 340 Ruddiman, N. Muskegon, MI 49445/616-744-3635
Specialties: Working straight knives and folders. **Patterns:** Drop-point hunters, coil spring lockers, slip-joints. **Technical:** Flat-grinds D2, 440C and ATS-34. **Prices:** $150 to $250; some to $2,000. **Remarks:** Part-time maker; first knife sold in 1982. **Mark:** Last name.

HARTMANN, BRUCE JAMES, 961 Waterloo, Port Elgin, Ontario NOH 2C0, CANADA

HARTSFIELD, PHILL, P.O. Box 1637, Newport Beach, CA 92659-0637/714-722-9792; 714-636-7633
Specialties: Heavy-duty working and using straight knives. **Patterns:** Fighters, swords and survival knives, most in Japanese profile. **Technical:** Grinds A2 and M2. **Prices:** $350 to $20,000. **Remarks:** Full-time maker; first knife sold about 1966. Doing business as A Cut Above. **Mark:** Initials, chiseled character plus register mark.

HARVEST MOON FORGE (See Rua, Gary [Wolf])

HARVEY, MAX, 14 Bass Rd., Bull Creek, Perth, 6155, WESTERN AUSTRALIA/09-332-7585
Specialties: Daggers, Bowies, fighters and fantasy knives. **Patterns:** Hunters, Bowies, tantos and skinners. **Technical:** Hollow- and flat-grinds 440C, ATS-34, 154CM and Damascus. Offers gem work. **Prices:** $250 to $4,000. **Remarks:** Part-time maker; first knife sold in 1981. **Mark:** First and middle initials, last name.

HATCH, KEN, P.O. Box 82, Jensen, UT 84035
Specialties: Working knives; period pieces. **Patterns:** Buckskinners, tomahawks, period Bowies. **Technical:** Forges and grinds 1095, O1, W2, ATS-34. Prefers natural handle materials. **Prices:** $85 to $400. **Remarks:** Part-time maker; first knife sold in 1977. **Mark:** Name or dragonfly stamp.

HAWK, GAVIN, Box 401, Idaho City, ID 83631/208-392-4911

HAWK, GRANT, Box 401, Idaho City, ID 83631/208-392-4911

HAWK, JACK L., Rt. 1, Box 771, Ceres, VA 24318/703-624-3878, 703-624-3282
Specialties: Fancy and embellished working and using straight knives of his design or to customer specs. **Patterns:** Hunters, Bowies and daggers. **Technical:** Hollow-grinds 440C, ATS-34 and D2; likes bone and ivory handles. **Prices:** $75 to $1,200. **Remarks:** Full-time maker; first knife sold in 1982. **Mark:** Full name and initials.

HAWK, JOE, Rt. 1, Box 196, Ceres, VA 24318/703-624-3282
Specialties: Fancy working knives of his design or to customer specs. **Patterns:** Hunters, combat knives, Bowies and fighters. **Technical:** Grinds mostly ATS-34, 154CM and 440C. Scrimshaws, carves, engraves and silver inlays. **Prices:** $150 to $2,100. **Remarks:** Full-time maker; first knife sold in 1958. **Mark:** Name with tomahawk logo.

HAWK, JOEY K., Rt. 1, Box 196, Ceres, VA 24318/703-624-3282
Specialties: Working straight knives, some fancy. Welcomes customer designs. **Patterns:** Hunters, fighters, daggers, Bowies and miniatures. **Technical:** Grinds 440C or customer preference. Offers some knives with jeweling. **Prices:** $100 to $250; some to $500. **Remarks:** Part-time maker; first knife sold in 1983. **Mark:** First and middle initials, last name stamped.

HAWK KNIVES (See Corkum, Steve)

HAWKINS, RADE, 110 Buckeye Rd., Fayetteville, GA 30214/770-964-1177; FAX: 770-306-2877
Specialties: Exotic steels, custom designs, one-of-a-kind knives. **Patterns:** All styles. **Technical:** Grinds CPM10V, CPM440V, Vascomax C-350, Stelite K6 and Damascus. **Prices:** Start at $190. **Remarks:** Full-time maker; first knife sold in 1972. **Mark:** Full name, city, state; some last name only.

HAYES, DOLORES, P.O. Box 41405, Los Angeles, CA 90041/213-258-9923
Specialties: High-art working and using straight knives of her design. **Patterns:** Art knives and miniatures. **Technical:** Grinds 440C, stainless AEB, commercial Damascus and ATS-34. **Prices:** $50 to $500; some to $2,000. **Remarks:** Spare-time maker; first knife sold in 1978. **Mark:** Last name.

HAYES, WALLY, 1024 Queen St., Orleans, Ont., CANADA K4A-3N2/613-824-9520
Specialties: Classic and fancy straight knives and folders. **Patterns:** Daggers, Bowies, fighters, tantos. **Technical:** Forges own Damascus and O1; engraves. **Prices:** $250 to $1,500; some to $4,500. **Mark:** Last name, M.S. and serial number.

HAYNES, CHAP, RR #4, Tatamagouche, NS B0K 1V0, CANADA
Specialties: Ergonomic tools. **Patterns:** Hunters, Bowies, fixed blade, working knives, tomahawks, swords and miniatures. **Technical:** Forges carbon steel, meteorite and his own Damascus. **Prices:** Start at $400. **Remarks:** Part-time maker; first knife sold in 1985. **Mark:** Smith at anvil logo with HAYNES GREAT BLADES.

HAYNIE, CHARLES, 125 Cherry Lane, Toccoa, GA 30577/706-886-8665

HAYNIE'S HANDCRAFTED KNIVES (See Haynie, Charles)

HAYS, MARK, 1034 Terry Way, Carrollton, TX 75006/214-242-5197
Specialties: Working straight knives and folders. Patterns inspired by Randall & Stone. **Patterns:** Bowies, hunters and slip-joint folders. **Technical:** 440C stock removal. Repairs and restores Stone knives. **Prices:** Start at $150. **Remarks:** Part-time maker; first knife sold in 1984. **Mark:** First initial, last name, state and serial number.

HEASMAN, H.G., 28, St. Mary's Rd., Llandudno, N. Wales U.K., LL302UB/(UK)0492-876351
Specialties: Miniatures only. **Patterns:** Bowies, daggers and swords. **Technical:** Files from stock high-carbon and stainless steel. **Prices:** $400 to $600. **Remarks:** Part-time maker; first knife sold in 1975. Doing business as Reduced Reality. **Mark:** NA.

HEDRICK, DON, 131 Beechwood Hills, Newport News, VA 23608/804-877-8100
Specialties: Working straight knives; period pieces and fantasy knives. **Patterns:** Hunters, boots, Bowies and miniatures. **Technical:** Grinds 440C and commercial Damascus. **Prices:** $150 to $550; some to $1,200. **Remarks:** Part-time maker; first knife sold in 1982. **Mark:** First initial, last name in oval logo.

HEGWALD, J.L., 1106 Charles, Humboldt, KS 66748/316-473-3523
Specialties: Working straight knives, some fancy. **Patterns:** Makes Bowies, miniatures. **Technical:** Forges or grinds O1, L6, 440C; mixes materials in handles. **Prices:** $35 to $200; some higher. **Remarks:** Part-time maker; first knife sold in 1983. **Mark:** First and middle initials.

HEGWOOD, JOEL, Rt. 4, Box 229, Summerville, GA 30747/404-397-8187
Specialties: High-tech working knives of his design. **Patterns:** Hunters, boots and survival knives; locking folders, slip-joints and interframes. **Technical:** Grinds A2, O1 and D2; uses 7075 aluminum in lightweight folder frames. **Prices:** $65 to $125; some to $200. **Remarks:** Part-time maker; first knife sold in 1979. **Mark:** Last name.

HEHN, RICHARD KARL, Lehnmuehler Str. 1, D-6531 Doerrebach GERMANY/06724 3152
Specialties: High-tech working knives. **Patterns:** Hunters, fighters, Bowies and locking folders. **Technical:** Forges and grinds 440C, CPM and his own stainless Damascus; high-tech polishing for all steels; clean grinds; deluxe natural handles. **Prices:** $350 to $4,000; some to $9,000. **Remarks:** Full-time maker; first knife sold in 1963. **Mark:** Runic last initial in logo.

HEITLER, HENRY, P.O. Box 15025, Tampa, FL 33684-5025/813-933-1645
Specialties: Traditional working and using straight knives of his design and to customer specs. **Patterns:** Fighters, hunters, utility/camp knives and fillet knives. **Technical:** Flat-grinds ATS-34; offers tapered tangs. **Prices:** $135 to $450; some to $600. **Remarks:** Part-time maker; first knife sold in 1990. **Mark:** First initial, last name, city, state circling double "H"s.

HELTON, ROY, 5650 District Blvd., #128, Bakersfieldd, CA 93313/805-833-2795
Specialties: Tactical and fancy lockback and liner lock folders. **Patterns:** Lockback and liner lock folders. **Technical:** Grinds ATS-34; commercial A2 and Damascus. Likes filework; anodizes. Mosly Ti frames. Uses mostly natural handle materials. **Prices:** Start at $300. **Remarks:** Full-time maker; first knife sold in 1975. **Mark:** Name, city, state.

HEMBROOK, RON, P.O. Box 153, Neosho, WI 53059/414-625-3607
Specialties: Period pieces, art knives and working straight knives; enjoys customer designs. **Patterns:** Hunters, push daggers, miniatures, fighters, folders and Bowies. **Technical:** Grinds O1, 440C, D2 and ATS-34; uses Damascus. **Prices:** $95 to $325; some to $1,000. **Remarks:** Part-time maker; first knife sold in 1980. **Mark:** Last name and serial number.

HEMPHILL, JESSE, 896 Big Hill Rd., Berea, KY 40403
Specialties: Period pieces, folders and scagel reproductions. **Patterns:** Hawks, Bowies sets, fighters and utility knives. **Technical:** Forges his own Damascus, D2, 5160 and 52100. **Prices:** $50 to $300; some to $500. **Remarks:** Full-time maker; first knife sold in 1986. **Mark:** Initials or a turtle.

HENDRICKS, SAMUEL J., 2162 Van Buren Rd., Maurertown, VA 22644/703-436-3305
Specialties: Integral hunters and skinners of thin design. **Patterns:** Boots, hunters and locking folders. **Technical:** Grinds ATS-34, 440C and D2. Integral liners and bolsters of N-S and 7075 T6 aircraft aluminimum. Does leatherwork. **Prices:** $50 to $250; some to $500. **Remarks:** Full-time maker; first knife sold in 1992. **Mark:** First and middle initials, last name, city and state in football-style logo.

HENDRICKSON, E. JAY, 4204 Ballenger Creek Pike, Frederick, MD 21701/301-663-6923
Specialties: Classic collectors and working straight knives of his design. **Patterns:** Bowies, Kukri's, camp, hunters, and fighters. **Technical:** Forges 06, 1084, 5160, 52100, D2, L6 and W2; makes Damascus; offers silver wire inlay and Moran styles. **Prices:** $300 to $4,000. **Remarks:** Full-time maker; first knife sold in 1975. **Mark:** Last name, M.S.

HENDRIX, WAYNE, Rt.1, Box 111P, Allendale, SC 29810/803-584-3825
Specialties: Working/using knives of his design. **Patterns:** Hunters and fillet knives. **Technical:** Grinds ATS-34, D2 and 440C. **Prices:** $40 to $150. **Remarks:** Full-time maker; first knife sold in 1985. **Mark:** Last name.

HENNON, ROBERT, 940 Vincent Lane, Ft. Walton Beach, FL 32547/904-862-9734

HENRIKSEN, HANS J., Birkegaardsvej 24, DK 3200 Helsinge, DENMARK/FAX: 45 4879 4899
Specialties: Zirconia ceramic blades. **Patterns:** Customer designs. **Technical:** Slip-cast zirconia-water mix in plaster mould; offers hidden or full tang. **Prices:** White blades start at $10/cm; colored +50 percent. **Remarks:** Part-time maker; first ceramic blade sold in 1989. **Mark:** Initial logo.

HENRY & SON, PETER, 332 Nine Mile Ride, Wokingham, Berkshire RG11 3NJ, ENGLAND/01734-734475
Specialties: Period pieces. **Patterns:** Period pieces only—Scottish dirks, sgian dubhs and Bowies, moden hunters. **Technical:** Grinds O1. **Prices:** $67 to $247. **Remarks:** Full-time maker; first knife sold in 1974. **Mark:** P. Henry & Son.

HENSLEY, WAYNE, P.O. Box 904, Conyers, GA 30207/404-483-8938
Specialties: Period pieces and fancy working knives. **Patterns:** Boots to Bowies, locking folders to miniatures. Large variety of straight knives. **Technical:** Grinds D2, 440C, 154CM and commerical Damascus. **Prices:** $50 to $150; some to $800. **Remarks:** Part-time maker; first knife sold in 1974. **Mark:** Last name.

HERBST, PETER, Komotauer Strasse 26, 91207 Lauf a.d. Pegn., GERMANY/09123-13315; FAX: 09123-13379
Specialties: Working/using knives and folders of his design. **Patterns:** Hunters, fighters and daggers; interframe and integral. **Technical:** Grinds CPM-T-440V, UHB-Elmax, ATS-34 and stainless Damascus. **Prices:** $300 to $3,000; some to $8,000. **Remarks:** Full-time maker; first knife sold in 1981. **Mark:** First initial, last name.

HERMAN, TIM, 7721 Foster, Overland Park, KS 66204/913-649-3860; FAX: 913-649-0603
Specialties: Investment-grade folders of his design; interframes and bolster frames. **Patterns:** Boots, Bowies, daggers and push knives; high-quality folders and interframes. **Technical:** Grinds ATS-34 and A.J. Hubbard Damascus. Engraves and gold inlays with pearl, jade, lapis and Australian opal. **Prices:** $1,000 to $15,000. **Remarks:** Full-time maker; first knife sold in 1978. **Mark:** Etched signature.

HERMES, DANA E., 39594 Kona Ct., Fremont, CA 94538/415-490-0393
Specialties: Fancy and embellished classic straight knives of his design. **Patterns:** Hunters and Bowies. **Technical:** Grinds 440C and D2. **Prices:** $200 to $600; some to $1,000. **Remarks:** Spare-time maker; first knife sold in 1985. **Mark:** Last name.

HERNDON, WM. R. "BILL," 32520 Michigan St., Acton, CA 93510/ 805-269-5860; FAX: 805-269-4568
Specialties: Straight knives, plain and fancy. **Technical:** Carbon steel (white and blued), Damascus, stainless steels. **Prices:** Start at $120. **Remarks:** Full-time maker; first knife sold in 1981. **Mark:** Signature and/or helm logo.

HERRON, GEORGE, 474 Antonio Way, Springfield, SC 29146/803-258-3914
Specialties: High-tech working and using straight knives; some folders. **Patterns:** Hunters, fighters, boots in personal styles. **Technical:** Grinds 154CM, ATS-34. **Prices:** $75 to $500; some to $750. **Remarks:** Full-time maker; first knife sold in 1963. About a seven- to eight-year (or more) backlog; will not quote a delivery date. **Mark:** Last name in script.

HESSER, DAVID, P.O. Box 1079, Dripping Springs, TX 78620/512-894-0100
Specialties: High-art daggers and fantasy knives of his design; court weapons of the Renaissance. **Patterns:** Daggers, swords, axes, miniatures and sheath knives. **Technical:** Forges 1065, 1095, O1, D2 and recycled tool steel. Offers custom lapidary work and stone-setting, stone handles and custom hardwood scabbards. **Prices:** $95 to $500; some to $6,000. **Remarks:** Full-time maker; first knife sold in 1989. Doing business as Exotic Blades. **Mark:** Last name, year.

HETHCOAT, DON, Box 1764, Clovis, NM 88101/505-762-5721
Specialties: Working straight knives and folders. **Patterns:** Hunters, axes, fishing knives, Bowies, boots, locking and liner lock folders. **Technical:** Grinds ATS-34 and 440C. Forges some 5168 on Bowies; uses his own Damascus. **Prices:** $100 to $2,000. **Remarks:** Part-time maker; first knife sold in 1969. **Mark:** Last name and zip code on stock removal; last name on forged 5168 and Damascus.

HETMANSKI, THOMAS S., 494 Orchard Dr., Mansfield, OH 44903-9471/419-774-0165
Specialties: Working knives, replicas, military-style knives and miniatures. **Patterns:** Hunters, boots, miniatures and some folders. **Technical:** Grinds A2, 440C, ATS-34 and commercial Damascus. **Prices:** $150 to $400; some higher. **Remarks:** Part-time maker; first knife sold in 1982. **Mark:** Initials in monogram.

HI II ORIGINALS (See Imboden II, Howard L.)

HIBBEN, DARYL, P.O. Box 172, 1331 Dawkins Rd., LaGrange, KY 40031-0172/502-222-0983
Specialties: Working straight knives, some fancy to customer specs. **Patterns:** Hunters, fighters, Bowies, short sword, art and fantasy. **Technical:** Grinds 440C, ATS-34, 154CM, Damascus; prefers hollow-grinds. **Prices:** $175 to $3,000. **Remarks:** Full-time maker; first knife sold in 1979. **Mark:** Etched full name in script.

HIBBEN, GIL, P.O. Box 13, LaGrange, KY 40031/502-222-1397; FAX: 502-222-2676
Specialties: Working knives and fantasy pieces to customer specs. **Patterns:** Full range of straight knives, including swords, axes and miniatures; some locking folders. **Technical:** Grinds D2, 440C and 154CM. **Prices:** $300 to $2,000; some to $10,000. **Remarks:** Full-time maker; first knife sold in 1957. Maker and designer of *Rambo III* knife; made swords for movie *Marked for Death* and throwing knife for movie *Under Seige*; made belt buckle knife and knives for movie *Perfect Weapon*; made knives featured in movie *Star Trek the Next Generation*; designer for United Cutlery. **Mark:** Hibben Knives, city and state, or signature.

HIBBEN, JOLEEN, P.O. Box 172, LaGrange, KY 40031/502-222-0983
Specialties: Miniature straight knives of her design; period pieces. **Patterns:** Hunters, axes and fantasy knives. **Technical:** Grinds Damascus, 1095 tool steel and stainless 440C or ATS-34. Uses wood, ivory, bone, feathers and claws on/for handles. **Prices:** $60 to $200. **Remarks:** Spare-time maker; first knife sold in 1991. **Mark:** Initials or first name.

HIBBEN, WESTLEY G., 14101 Sunview Dr., Anchorage, AK 99515
Specialties: Working straight knives of his design or to customer specs. **Patterns:** Hunters, fighters, daggers, combat knives and some fantasy pieces. **Technical:** Grinds 440C mostly. Filework available. **Prices:** $200 to $400; some to $3,000. **Remarks:** Part-time maker; first knife sold in 1988. **Mark:** Signature.

HIELSCHER, GUY, HC34, P.O. Box 992, Alliance, NE 69301/308-762-4318
Specialties: Traditional and working straight knives of his design, to customer specs and in standard pattersn. **Patterns:** Bowies, fighters, skinners, daggers and hunters. **Technical:** Forges his own Damascus from O1 and 1018 steel. **Prices:** $150 to $225; some to $850. **Remarks:** Part-time maker; first knife sold in 1988. Doing business as G.H. Knives. **Mark:** Initials in arrowhead.

HIGH, TOM, 5474 S. 112.8 Rd., Alamosa, CO 81101/719-589-2108
Specialties: Hunters, some fancy. **Patterns:** Drop-points in several shapes; some semi-skinners. Knives designed by and for top outfitters and guides. **Technical:** Grinds ATS-34; likes hollow-grinds, mirror finishes; prefers scrimmable handles. **Prices:** $195 to $5,000. **Remarks:** Full-time maker; first knife sold in 1965. Three-year backlog on all ordered knives. **Mark:** Initials connected; arrow through last name on fancy knives.

HI-LAND KNIVES (See Gray, Bob)

HILKER, THOMAS N., P.O. Box 409, Williams, OR 97544/541-846-6461
Specialties: Traditional working straight knives and folders. **Patterns:** Folding skinner in two sizes, Bowies, fork and knife sets, camp knives and interchangeables. **Technical:** Grinds D2, 440C and ATS-34. Heat-treats. **Prices:** $50 to $350; some to $400. Doing business as Thunderbolt Artisans. Only limited production models available; not currently taking orders. **Remarks:** Full-time maker; first knife sold in 1983. **Mark:** Last name.

HILL, HOWARD E., 111 Mission Lane, Polson, MT 59860/406-883-3405
Specialties: All types of straight knives and folders in personal designs. **Patterns:** Bowies, daggers, skinners and lockback folders. **Technical:** Grinds 440C; uses micro and satin finish. **Prices:** $150 to $1,000. **Remarks:** Full-time maker; first knife sold in 1981. **Mark:** Persuader.

HILL, RICK, 20 Nassau, Maryville, IL 62062-5618/618-288-4370
Specialties: Working knives and period pieces to customer specs. **Patterns:** Hunters, locking folders, fighters and daggers. **Technical:** Grinds D2, 440C and 154CM; forges his own Damascus. **Prices:** $75 to $500; some to $3,000. **Remarks:** Part-time maker; first knife sold in 1983. **Mark:** Full name in hill shape logo.

HILL, STEVEN E., 7814 Toucan Dr., Orlando, FL 32822/407-277-3549
Specialties: Classic collectible and using grade liner lock folders; some exotic mechanisms. **Patterns:** Bowies, California daggers, fighters, hunters, and liner lock folders. **Technical:** Grinds 440C, D2, ATS-34 and Damascus. Prefers natural handle materials. **Prices:** $250 to $2,000; some higher. **Remarks:** Full-time maker; first knife sold in 1978. **Mark:** First initial, last name and handmade.

HINDERER, RICK, 5423 Kister Rd., Wooster, OH 44691/216-263-0962
Specialties: Working knives to one-of-a-kind Damascus straight knives and folders. **Patterns:** All. **Technical:** Grinds ATS-34 and D2; forges O1, W2 and his own nickel Damascus steel. **Prices:** $50 to $3,200. **Remarks:** Part-time maker; first knife sold in 1988. Doing business as Mustang Forge. **Mark:** Initials or first initial, last name.

HINK III, LES, 1599 Aptos Lane, Stockton, CA 95206/209-547-1292
Specialties: Working straight knives and traditional folders in standard patterns or to customer specs. **Patterns:** Hunting and utility/camp knives; others on request. **Technical:** Grinds carbon and stainless steels. **Prices:** $80 to $200; some higher. **Remarks:** Part-time maker; first knife sold in 1980. **Mark:** Last name, or last name 3.

HINSON and SON, R., 2419 Edgewood Rd., Columbus, GA 31906/706-327-6801
Specialties: Working straight knives and folders. **Patterns:** Locking folders, liner locks, combat knives and swords. **Technical:** Grinds 440C and commercial Damascus. **Prices:** $100 to $350; some to $1,500.

Remarks: Part-time maker; first knife sold in 1983. Son Bob is co-worker. **Mark:** HINSON, city and state.

HINTZ, GERALD M., 5402 Sahara Ct., Helena, MT 59602/406-458-5412
Specialties: Fancy, high-art, working/using knives of his design. **Patterns:** Bowies, hunters, daggers, fish fillet and utility/camp knives. **Technical:** Forges ATS-34, 440C and D2. Animal art in horn handles or in the blade. **Prices:** $75 to $400; some to $1,000. **Remarks:** Part-time maker; first knife sold in 1980. Doing business as Big Joe's Custom Knives. Will take custom orders. **Mark:** F.S. or W.S. with first and middle initials and last name.

HIRAM KNIVES (See Price, Joel Hiram)

HIRAYAMA, HARUMI, 4-5-13, Kitamachi, Warabi City, Saitama Pref., JAPAN 335/048-443-2248; FAX: 048-443-2248
Specialties: High-tech working knives of her design. **Patterns:** Locking folders, interframes, straight gents and slip-joints. **Technical:** Grinds 440C or equivalent; uses natural handle materials and gold. **Prices:** Start at $700. **Remarks:** Part-time maker; first knife sold in 1985. **Mark:** First initial, last name.

HITCHMOUGH, HOWARD, 95 Old Street Road, Peterborough, NH 03458-1637/603-924-4265
Specialties: High class folding knives. **Patterns:** Locking folders, pocketknives, liner locks, hunters and boots. **Technical:** Uses ATS-34, stainless Damascus and titanium. Prefers hand-rubbed finishes and natural handle materials. **Prices:** $250 to $1,500; some to $4,000. **Remarks:** Full-time maker; first knife sold in 1967. **Mark:** Last name.

HOCKENSMITH, DAN, P.O. Box E, Drake, CO 80515/970-669-5404
Specialties: Traditional working and using straight knives of his design. **Patterns:** Hunters, Bowies, folders and utility/camp knives. **Technical:** Uses his Damascus, 5160, carbon steel and wire cable. **Prices:** $150 to $600; some to $1,000. **Remarks:** Full-time maker; first knife sold in 1987. **Mark:** Stylized initials.

HODGE, J.B., 1100 Woodmont Ave. SE, Huntsville, AL 35801/205-536-8388
Specialties: Fancy working folders. **Patterns:** Slip-joints. **Technical:** Grinds 154CM and ATS-34. **Prices:** Start at $175. **Remarks:** Part-time maker; first knife sold in 1978. Not currently taking orders. **Mark:** Name, city and state.

HODGE III, JOHN, 422 S. 15th St., Palatka, FL 32177/904-328-3897
Specialties: Fancy straight knives and folders. **Patterns:** Various. **Technical:** Pattern-welded Damascus—"Southern-style." **Prices:** To $1,000. **Remarks:** Part-time maker; first knife sold in 1981. **Mark:** JH3 logo.

HODGSON, RICHARD J., 9081 Tahoe Lane, Boulder, CO 80301/303-666-9460
Specialties: Straight knives and folders in standard patterns. **Patterns:** High-tech knives in various patterns. **Technical:** Grinds 440C, AEB-L and CPM. **Prices:** $850 to $2,200. **Remarks:** Part-time maker. **Mark:** None.

HOEL, STEVE, P.O. Box 283, Pine, AZ 85544/602-476-4278
Specialties: Investor-class folders, straight knives and period pieces of his design. **Patterns:** Folding interframes—lockers and slip-joints; straight Bowies, boots and daggers. **Technical:** Grinds 154CM, ATS-34 and commercial Damascus. **Prices:** $600 to $1,200; some to $7,500. **Remarks:** Full-time maker. **Mark:** Initial logo with name and address.

HOFFMAN, KEVIN L., P.O. Box 5107, Winter Park, FL 32793/407-678-3124; FAX: 407-678-3124
Specialties: High-tech working knives. **Patterns:** Frame lock folders, fighters, concealment rigs. **Technical:** Grinds ATS-34, 440C and Damascus; titanium folders. Makes Kydex sheaths. **Prices:** $150 to $2,000. **Remarks:** Full-time maker; first knife sold in 1981. **Mark:** Initials.

HOFFMANN, UWE H., P.O. Box 60114, Vancouver, BC V5W 4B5 CANADA/604-572-7320 (after 5 p.m.)
Specialties: High-tech working knives, folders and fantasy knives of his design or to customer specs. **Patterns:** Hunters, fishing knives, combat and survival knives, folders and diver's knives. **Technical:** Grinds 440C, ATS-34, D2 and commercial Damascus. **Prices:** $95 to $900; some to $2,000 and higher. **Remarks:** Full-time maker; first knife sold in 1985. **Mark:** Hoffmann Handmade Knives.

HOLBROOK, H.L., Rt. #3, Box 585, Olive Hill, KY 41164/606-784-4127, days; 606-738-6542, evenings
Specialties: Traditional working/using straight knives and folders of his design, to customer specs and in standard patterns. **Patterns:** Hunters, locking folders and slip-joint folders. **Technical:** Grinds 440C, ATS-34 and D2. Blades have hand-rubbed satin finish. Uses exotic woods, stag and Micarta. Hand sewn sheath with each straight knife. **Prices:** $75 to $170; some to $250. **Remarks:** Part-time maker; first knife sold in 1983. Doing business as Holbrook knives. **Mark:** Name, city, state.

HOLBROOK KNIVES (See Holbrook, H.L.)

HOLDER, D'ALTON, 7148 W. Country Gables Dr., Peoria, AZ 85381/602-878-3064; FAX: 602-878-3964
Specialties: Deluxe working knives and high-art hunters. **Patterns:** Drop-point hunters, fighters, Bowies, miniatures and locking folders. **Technical:** Grinds 440C and 154CM; uses amber and other materials in combination on stick tangs. **Prices:** $150 to $350; some to $1,000. **Remarks:** Full-time maker; first knife sold in 1970. **Mark:** D'HOLDER, city and state.

HOLLAND, JOHN H., 143 Green Meadow Lane, Calhoun, GA 30701/706-629-9622
Specialties: Traditional and fancy working/using straight knives and folders of his design, to customer specs and in standard patterns. **Patterns:** Hunters, and slip-joint folders. **Technical:** Grinds 440V and 440C. Offers engraving. **Prices:** $200 to $500; some to $1,000. **Remarks:** Part-time maker; first knife sold in 1988. Doing business as Holland Knives. **Mark:** First and last name, city, state.

HOLLAND KNIVES (See Holland, John H.)

HOLLAR, BOB, 205 Riverfront Lane, Great Falls, MT 59404/406-965-2945
Specialties: Working/using straight knives and folders of his design and to customer specs; period pieces. **Patterns:** Fighters, hunters and locking folders. **Technical:** Forges 52100, 5160, 1095, nickel and his own Damascus. Differentially hardened blades; freeze-treats. Burled woods, stag and stabilized material for handles. **Prices:** $190 to $500; some to $1,200. **Remarks:** Full-time maker. Doing business as Goshawk Knives. **Mark:** Last name stamped on left; head and feet of goshawk etched on right.

HOLLETT, JEFF, 210 E. Washington St., Rockwall, TX 75087-3711/214-771-2014
Specialties: Classic, traditional, fantasy and working straight knives and folders of his design, to customer specs and in standard patterns; period pieces. **Patterns:** Bowies, fighters and hunters. **Technical:** Grinds ATS-34, 440C and D2. Heat-treats. **Prices:** $100 to $700; some to $1,000. **Remarks:** Full-time maker; first knife sold in 1989. **Mark:** Name, city, state, month and year.

HOLLOWAY, PAUL, 714 Burksdale Rd., Norfolk, VA 23518/804-588-7071
Specialties: Working straight knives and folders to customer specs. **Patterns:** Lockers and slip-joints; fighters and boots; fishing and push knives, from swords to miniatures. **Technical:** Grinds A2, D2, 154CM, 440C and ATS-34. **Prices:** $125 to $400; some to $1,200. **Remarks:** Part-time maker; first knife sold in 1981. **Mark:** Last name, or last name and city in logo.

HOLLY KNIVES (See Miller, Robert)

HOLMES, DOC (See Holmes, Robert)

HOLMES, ROBERT, 4423 Lake Larto Circle, Baton Rouge, LA 70816/504-291-4864
Specialties: Using straight knives and folders of his design or to customer specs. **Patterns:** Bowies, utility hunters, camp knives, skinners, slip-joint and lock-back folders. **Technical:** Forges 1065, 1095 and L6. Makes his own Damascus and cable Damascus. Offers clay tempering. **Prices:** $150 to $1,500. **Remarks:** Part-time maker; first knife sold in 1988. **Mark:** DOC HOLMES, or anvil logo with last initial inside.

HOLUM, MORTEN, Bolerskrenten 28, 0691 Oslo, NORWAY/011-47-22-27-69-96
Specialties: Working straight knives. **Patterns:** Traditional Norwegian knives, hunters, fighters, axes. **Technical:** Forges Damascus. Uses his own blades. **Prices:** $200 to $800; some to $1,500. **Remarks:** Part-time maker; first knife sold in 1986. **Mark:** Last name.

HOMER, GLEN, 927 Judy St., Bloomfield, NM 87413/505-632-9615
Specialties: Damascus skinners. **Patterns:** Bowies, skinners, camp

knives and folders. **Technical:** Forges 5160; will grind stainless on request; makes his own Damascus. **Prices:** $100 to $500. **Remarks:** Part-time maker; first knife sold in 1987. **Mark:** Name or initials.

HOOT'S HANDMADE KNIVES (See Gibson, James Hoot)

HORN, JESS, 87481 Rhodowood Dr., Florence, OR 97439/541-997-2593; FAX: 541-997-4550
Specialties: Investor-class working folders; period pieces; collectibles. **Patterns:** High-tech design and finish in folders; liner locks, traditional slip-joints and featherweight models. **Technical:** Grinds ATS-34, 154CM. **Prices:** Start at $600. **Remarks:** Full-time maker; first knife sold in 1968. **Mark:** Full name or last name.

HORSEHEAD CREEK KNIVES (Thomsen, Loyd W.)

HORTON, SCOT, P.O. Box 451, Buhl, ID 83316/208-543-4222
Specialties: Traditional working straight knives and folders. **Patterns:** Hunters, skinners and utility knives. **Technical:** Grinds ATS-34. Uses stag, abalone and exotic woods. **Prices:** $200 to $1,200. **Remarks:** Full-time maker; first knife sold in 1990. Doing business as Piranha Knife Co. **Mark:** Full name in arch underlined with arrow, city, state.

HOWARD, DURVYN M., 4220 McLain St. S., Hokes Bluff, AL 35903/205-492-5720
Specialties: Collectible upscale folders; multiple patents. **Patterns:** Fine gentlemen's folders. **Technical:** Uses natural and exotic materials, precious metals and gemstones. **Prices:** $5,000 to $20,000. **Remarks:** Full-time maker; now accepting orders—purchase through Barrett-Smythe Gallery, New York, NY, exclusive agent. **Mark:** Last name etched on tang; opposite side marked Barrett-Smythe.

HOWARD, SETH, P.O. Box 65051, Baton Rouge, LA 70896

HOWELL CO. (See Howell, Ted)

HOWELL KNIVES (See Howell, Robert L.)

HOWELL, LEN, 550 Lee Rd. 169, Opelika, AL 36804/334-749-1942
Specialties: Traditional and working knives of his design and to customer specs. **Patterns:** Bowies, buckskinner, hunters and utility/camp knives. **Technical:** Forges cable Damascus, 1085 and 5160; makes own Damascus. **Prices:** $100 to $175; some to $400. **Remarks:** Full-time maker; first knife sold in 1991. **Mark:** Stamped or engraved last name.

HOWELL, ROBERT L., Box 1617, Kilgore, TX 75663/903-986-4364
Specialties: Straight knives and folders of his design. **Patterns:** Hunters and locking folders. **Technical:** Grinds D2 and ATS-34; forges and grinds Damascus. **Prices:** $75 to $200; some to $2,500. **Remarks:** Part-time maker; first knife sold in 1978. Doing business as Howell Knives. **Mark:** Last name.

HOWELL, TED, 1294 Wilson Rd., Wetumpka, AL 36092/205-569-2281; FAX: 205-569-1764
Specialties: Working/using straight knives and folders of his design; period pieces. **Patterns:** Bowies, fighters, hunters. **Technical:** Forges 5160, 1085 and cable. Offers light engraving and scrimshaw; filework. **Prices:** $75 to $250; some to $450. **Remarks:** Part-time maker; first knife sold in 1991. Doing business as Howell Co. **Mark:** Last name, Slapout AL.

HOWLING WOLF FORGE (See O'Ceilaghan, Michael)

HOWSER, JOHN C., 54 Bell Ln., Frankfort, KY 40601/502-875-3678
Specialties: Practical working knives. **Patterns:** Hunters, fighters, locking folders, fillet knives, slip-joint folders, liner locks. **Technical:** Grinds D2 and ATS-34; hand-rubbed satin finish; natural materials. **Prices:** $85 to $350; some to $500. **Remarks:** Part-time maker; first knife sold in 1974. **Mark:** Signature or stamp.

HOY, KEN, 54744 Pinchot Dr., North Fork, CA 93643/209-877-7805

HRISOULAS, JIM, 330 S. Decatur Ave., Suite 109, Las Vegas, NV 89107/702-566-8551
Specialties: Working straight knives; period pieces. **Patterns:** Swords, daggers and sgian dubhs. **Technical:** Double-edged differential heat treating. **Prices:** $85 to $175; some to $600 and higher. **Remarks:** Full-time maker; first knife sold in 1973. Author of *The Complete Bladesmith*, *The Pattern Welded Blade* and *The Master Bladesmith*. Doing business as Salamander Armoury. **Mark:** 8R logo and sword and salamander.

HRS CUSTOM KNIVES (See Simmons, H.R.)

HUBBARD, ARTHUR J., 574 Cutlers Farm Road, Monroe, CT 06468/203-268-3998
Specialties: Working knives of his design or to customer specs. **Patterns:** Hunters, fighters, boots, wood carvers and liner lock folders. **Technical:** Makes precision engineered Damascus in all-stainless steel, Mokume of copper and stainless steel, copper, brass and nickel-silver, copper and brass. **Prices:** Start at $100. **Remarks:** Full-time maker; first knife sold in 1976. **Mark:** Name, city and state; first and middle initials, last name, stainless; P.E.D. stainless.

HUDDLESTON, JOE D., 14129 93rd Ave. SE, Yelm, WA 98597-9459/360-458-2361
Specialties: Period pieces, fancy straight knives of his design. **Patterns:** Daggers and Scottish dirks. **Technical:** Grinds ATS-34. Hand-carved knotwork handles, wooden or wood lined sheaths; uses gemstones and sterling silver mounts. **Prices:** $550 to $1,850; some to $5,000. **Remarks:** Full-time maker; first knife sold in 1993. Doing business as BladeCatcher Knives. **Mark:** BladeCatcher over a Spanish notch.

HUDSON, C. ROBBIN, 22280 Frazier Rd., Rock Hall, MD 21661/410-639-7273
Specialties: High-art working knives. **Patterns:** Hunters, Bowies, fighters and kitchen knives. **Technical:** Forges W2, nickle steel, pure nickle steel, composite and mosaic Damascus; makes knives one at a time. **Prices:** $300 to $700; some to $5,000. **Remarks:** Full-time maker; first knife sold in 1970. **Mark:** Last name and MS.

HUDSON, ROBERT, 3802 Black Cricket Ct., Humble, TX 77396/713-454-7207
Specialties: Working straight knives of his design. **Patterns:** Bowies, hunters, skinners, fighters and utility knives. **Technical:** Grinds D2, 440C, 154CM and commercial Damascus. **Prices:** $85 to $350; some to $1,500. **Remarks:** Part-time maker; first knife sold in 1980. **Mark:** Full name, handmade, city and state.

HUEY, STEVE, 27645 Snyder Rd., #38, Junction City, OR 97448/503-689-5010
Specialties: Working straight knives, some one-of-a-kind. **Patterns:** Hunters, fighters, fishing knives and kitchen cutlery. **Technical:** Hollow- or flat-grinds 1095, L6, 440C, D2 and ATS-34. **Prices:** $75 to $600. **Remarks:** Full-time maker; first knife sold in 1981. **Mark:** Last name in rectangle.

HUGHES, DAN, 13743 Persimmon Blvd., West Palm Beach, FL 33411
Specialties: Working straight knives to customer specs. **Patterns:** Hunters, fighters, fillet knives. **Technical:** Grinds 440C and ATS-34. **Prices:** $55 to $175; some to $300. **Remarks:** Part-time maker; first knife sold in 1984. **Mark:** Initials.

HUGHES, DARYLE, 10979 Leonard, Nunica, MI 49448/616-837-6623
Specialties: Working knives. **Patterns:** Buckskinners, hunters, camp knives, kitchen and fishing knives. **Technical:** Forges and grinds W2, O1 and D2. **Prices:** $40 to $100; some to $400. **Remarks:** Part-time maker; first knife sold in 1979. **Mark:** Name and city in logo.

HUGHES, ED, 280½ Holly Lane, Grand Junction, CO 81503/970-243-8547
Specialties: Working and art folders. **Patterns:** Folders. **Technical:** Grinds stainless steels. Engraves. **Prices:** $75 to $250; some to $600. **Remarks:** Full-time maker; first knife sold in 1978. **Mark:** Name or initials.

HUGHES, LAWRENCE, 207 W. Crestway, Plainview, TX 79072/806-293-5406
Specialties: Working and display knives. **Patterns:** Bowies, daggers, hunters, buckskinners. **Technical:** Grinds D2, 440C and 154CM. **Prices:** $125 to $300; some to $2,000. **Remarks:** Full-time maker; first knife sold in 1979. **Mark:** Name with buffalo skull in center.

HULL, MICHAEL J., 1330 Hermits Circle, Cottonwood, AZ 86326/520-634-2871
Specialties: Period pieces and working knives; will work to customer specs. **Patterns:** Hunters, fighters, Bowies, camp and Mediterranean knives, etc. **Technical:** Grinds 440C, ATS-34 and D2. **Prices:** $100 to $350; some to $700. **Remarks:** Full-time maker; first knife sold in 1983. **Mark:** Name, city, state.

HULSEY, HOYT, 5699 Pope Ave., Steele, AL 35987/205-538-6765
Specialties: Traditional working straight knives and folders of his

design. **Patterns:** Hunters and utility/camp knives. **Technical:** Grinds 440C, ATS-34, O1 and A2. **Prices:** $75 to $150. **Remarks:** Part-time maker; first knife sold in 1989. **Mark:** Full name, city and state.

HUME, DON, 3511 Camino De La Cumbre, Sherman Oaks, CA 91423/818-783-5486
Specialties: Medieval theme, straight blade working and collector designed pieces. **Patterns:** Hunters, daggers and Bowies. **Technical:** Grinds Damascus, 440C, 154CM with exotic handle material. **Prices:** $180 to $1600. **Remarks:** Part-time maker; first knife sold in 1987. **Mark:** Curved first and middle initials and last name; first of a series or one-of-a-kinds also marked with the Fiera Madonna.

HUMENICK, ROY, P.O. Box 55, Rescue, CA 95672
Specialties: Traditional working knives and multi-blade folders of his design. **Patterns:** Bowies, hunters, fighters and folders. **Technical:** Grinds ATS-34, works in Damascus. **Prices:** $200 to $600; some to $1,500. **Remarks:** First knife sold in 1984. **Mark:** Name or initials in logo.

HUMPHREYS, JOEL, Rt. 1, Box 179-B, Bowling Green, FL 33834/941-773-0439
Specialties: Traditional working/using straight knives and folders of his design and in standard patterns. **Patterns:** Hunters, folders and utility/camp knives. **Technical:** Grinds ATS-34, D2, 440C. All knives have tapered tangs, mitered bolster/handle joints, handles of horn or bone and hand-stitched fitted sheaths. **Prices:** $135 to $225; some to $350. **Remarks:** Part-time maker; first knife sold in 1990. Doing business as Sovereign Knives. **Mark:** First name or "H" pierced by arrow.

HUNTER, HYRUM, 285 N. 300 W., P.O. Box 179, Aurora, UT 84620/801-529-7244
Specialties: Working/using straight knives of his design and to customer specs. **Patterns:** Daggers, fighters and hunters. **Technical:** Forges and grinds O1, 5160, L6 A-36, mosaic and two piece Damascus. Uses mokume fittings; offers leaf pattern filework. **Prices:** $185 to $300; some to $500. **Remarks:** Part-time maker; first knife sold in 1990. **Mark:** First initial, last name, state in circle or initials and state in circle.

HURST, COLE, 1583 Tedford, E. Wenatchee, WA 98802/509-884-9206
Specialties: Fantasy, high-art and traditional straight knives. **Patterns:** Bowies, daggers and hunters. **Technical:** Blades are made of stone; handles are made of stone, wood or ivory and embellished with fancy woods, ivory or antlers. **Prices:** $100 to $300; some to $2,000. **Remarks:** Spare-time maker; first knife sold in 1985. **Mark:** Name and year.

HURST, JEFF, P.O. Box 247, Rutledge, TN 37861/615-828-5729
Specialties: Working straight knives and folders of his design. **Patterns:** Tomahawks, hunters, boots, folders and fighters. **Technical:** Forges W2, O1 and his own Damascus. Makes mokume. **Prices:** $175 to $350; some to $500. **Remarks:** Full-time maker; first knife sold in 1984. Doing business as Buzzard's Knob Forge. **Mark:** Last name; partnered knives are marked with Newman L. Smith, handle artisan, and SH in script.

HURT, WILLIAM R., 9222 Oak Tree Cir., Frederick, MD 21701/301-898-7143
Specialties: Traditional and working/using straight knives. **Patterns:** Bowies, hunters, fighters and utility knives. **Technical:** Forges 5160, O1 and 06; makes own Damascus. Offers silver wire inlay. **Prices:** $200 to $600; some higher. **Remarks:** Full-time maker; first knife sold in 1989. **Mark:** First and middle initials, last name.

HUSIAK, MYRON, P.O. Box 238, Altona 3018, Victoria, AUSTRALIA/03-315-6752
Specialties: Straight knives and folders of his design or to customer specs. **Patterns:** Hunters, fighters, lock-back folders, skinners and boots. **Technical:** Forges and grinds his own Damascus, 440C and ATS-34. **Prices:** $200 to $900. **Remarks:** Part-time maker; first knife sold in 1974. **Mark:** First initial, last name in logo and serial number.

HYDE, JIMMY, 5094 Stagecoach Rd., Ellenwood, GA 30049/404-968-1951; FAX: 404-209-1741
Specialties: Working straight knives of any design; period pieces. **Patterns:** Bowies, hunters and utility knives. **Technical:** Grinds 440C and 5160; forges O1. Makes his own Damascus and cable Damascus. **Prices:** $75 to $200; some to $400. **Remarks:** Part-time maker; first knife sold in 1978. **Mark:** First initial, last name.

HYTOVICK, JOE "HY," 14872 SW 111th St., Dunnellon, FL 34432/800-749-5339

i

IIAMS, RICHARD D., P.O. Box 963, Mills, WY 82644/307-265-2435 evenings
Specialties: Using straight knives and folders. **Patterns:** camp knives, drop-point hunters, lock-back folders and skinners. **Technical:** Pattern-welded DAmascus, 52100 and mild steel. Uses filework on folders. **Prices:** $85 to $300; some higher. **Remarks:** Part-time maker; first knife sold in 1981. **Mark:** First and middle initials, last name on blade.

IKOMA, FLAVIO YUJI, R. Manoel R. Teixeira, 108, Centro, Presidente Prudente, SP-19031-220, BRAZIL/0182-22-0115
Specialties: Straight knives and folders of all designs. **Patterns:** Fighters, hunters, Bowies, swords, folders, skinners, utility and defense knives. **Technical:** Grinds and forges D6, 440C, high-carbon steels and Damascus. **Prices:** $60 to $350; some to $3,300. **Remarks:** Full-time maker; first knife sold in 1991. **Mark:** Ikoma Knives beside eagle.

IKOMA KNIVES (See Ikoma, Flavio Yuji)

IMBODEN II, HOWARD L., 620 Deauville Dr., Dayton, OH 45429/513-439-1536
Specialties: One-of-a-kind hunting, flint, steel and art knives. **Technical:** Forges and grinds stainless, high-carbon and Damascus. Uses obsidian, cast sterling silver, 14K and 18K gold guards. Carves ivory animals and more. **Prices:** $65 to $25,000. **Remarks:** Full-time maker; first knife sold in 1986. Doing business as hi II Originals. **Mark:** First and last initials, II.

IMEL, BILLY MACE, 1616 Bundy Ave., New Castle, IN 47362/765-529-1651
Specialties: High-art working knives, period pieces and personal cutlery. **Patterns:** Daggers, fighters, hunters; locking folders and slip-joints with interframes. **Technical:** Grinds D2, 440C and 154CM. **Prices:** $200 to $2,000; some to $6,000. **Remarks:** Part-time maker; first knife sold in 1973. **Mark:** Name in monogram.

IRIE, MICHAEL L. (See Wood, Barry B. and Irie, Michael L.)

IRON MASTER, THE (See Chastain, Wade)

IRON MOUNTAIN FORGE WORKS (See Small, Ed)

ISHIHARA, HANK, 86-18 Motomachi, Sakura City, Chiba Pref. JAPAN/043-485-3208; FAX: 043-485-3208
Specialties: Fantasy working straight knives and folders of his design. **Patterns:** Boots, Bowies, daggers, fighters, hunters, fishing, locking folders and utility/camp knives. **Technical:** Grinds ATS-34, 440C, D2, 440V, CV-134, COS25 and Damascus. Engraves. **Prices:** $250 to $1,000; some to $10,000. **Remarks:** Full-time maker; first knife sold in 1987. **Mark:** HANK.

IVANOV, BLADIMIR (See Shushunov, Sergei)

j

JACKS, JIM, 344 S. Hollenbeck Ave., Covina, CA 91723-2513/818-331-5665
Specialties: Working straight knives in standard patterns. **Patterns:** Bowies, hunters, fighters, fishing and camp knives, miniatures. **Technical:** Grinds Stellite 6K, 440C and ATS-34. **Prices:** Start at $100. **Remarks:** Spare-time maker; first knife sold in 1980. **Mark:** Initials in diamond logo.

JACKSON, JIM, 10 Chantry Close, Windsor, Berkshire SL4 5EP, ENGLAND/0171-839-1283
Specialties: Working straight knives of his designs. **Patterns:** Large Bowies and hunters. **Technical:** Forges O1, 5160 and occasionally Damascus. Offers leatherwork. **Prices:** NA. **Remarks:** Part-time maker. **Mark:** Kentucky Dreamer around last initial, J.S..

JAGED (See Smith, Gregory H.)

JAMES & SON, PETER (See James, Peter)

JAMES, PETER, 2549 W. Golf Rd., #290, Hoffman Estates, IL 60194/708-310-9113; FAX: 708-885-1716

Specialties: Working/using straight knives of his design and in standard patterns. **Patterns:** Bowies, daggers and urban companion knives. **Technical:** Grinds 440C and soligen tool. Makes a variety of sheaths for urban companion series. **Prices:** $48 to $250. **Remarks:** Part-time maker; first knife sold in 1986. Doing business as Peter James & Sons. **Mark:** Initials overlapped.

JANIGA, MATTHEW A., 15950 Xenia St. NW, Andover, MN 55304/612-427-2510
Specialties: Period pieces, fantasy straight knives of his design. **Patterns:** Daggers, fighters and swords. **Technical:** Forges 5160, Damascus and 52100. Triple hardens, triple tempers and quenches blades. **Prices:** $150 to $750; some to $3,000. **Remarks:** Spare-time maker; first knife sold in 1991. **Mark:** Initials connected.

JARVIS, PAUL M., 30 Chalk St., Cambridge, MA 02139/617-491-2900
Specialties: High-art knives and period pieces of his design. **Patterns:** Japanese and Mid-Eastern knives. **Technical:** Grinds Myer Damascus, ATS-34, D2 and O1. Specializes in height-relief Japanese-style carving. Works with silver, gold and gems. **Prices:** $200 to $17,000. **Remarks:** Part-time maker; first knife sold in 1978.

JBL KNIVES (See Lincoln, James)

JEAN, GERRY, 25B Cliffside Dr., Manchester, CT 06040/203-649-6449
Specialties: Historic replicas. **Patterns:** Survival and camp knives. **Technical:** Grinds A2, 440C and 154CM. Handle slabs applied in unique tongue-and-groove method. **Prices:** $125 to $250; some to $1,000. **Remarks:** Spare-time maker; first knife sold in 1973. **Mark:** Initials and serial number.

JEFFRIES, ROBERT W., Route 1, Box 227, Red House, WV 25168/304-586-9780
Specialties: Straight knives and folders. **Patterns:** Hunters, skinners and folders. **Technical:** Uses 440C, ATS-34; makes his own Damascus. **Prices:** $50 to $150; some higher. **Remarks:** Part-time maker; first knife sold in 1988. **Mark:** NA.

J.E.M. KNIVES (See May, James E.)

JENSEN JR., CARL A., RR #3, Box 74, Blair, NE 68008/402-426-3353
Specialties: Working knives of his design; some customer designs. **Patterns:** Hunters, fighters, boots and Bowies. **Technical:** Grinds A2, D2, O1, 440C, 5160 and ATS-34; recycles old files, leaf springs; heat-treats. **Prices:** $35 to $350. **Remarks:** Part-time maker; first knife sold in 1980. **Mark:** Bear's Cutlery.

JENSEN, JOHN LEWIS, 138 Medway St., 2nd Floor, Providence, RI 02906/401-351-5838; FAX: 401-331-2460; WEB: http://www.magnus-design.com
Specialties: One-of-a-kind exotic and fantasy edged weapons of his design. **Patterns:** Daggers, fighters, swords, axes, war hammers and maces. **Technical:** Hollow-grinds; reforges commercial Damascus. **Prices:** $1,000 to $10,000. **Remarks:** Doing business as Magnus Design Studio. **Mark:** Logo.

JERNIGAN, STEVE, 3082 Tunnel Rd., Milton, FL 32571/904-994-0802; FAX: 904-994-0802
Specialties: Investor-class folders and various theme pieces. **Patterns:** Array of models and sizes in sideplate locking interframes and conventional liner construction. **Technical:** Grinds ATS-34, CPM-T-440V and Damascus. Inlays mokume in blades and sculpts marble cases. **Prices:** $650 to $1,800; some to $6,000. **Remarks:** Full-time maker; first knife sold in 1982. Takes orders for folders only. **Mark:** Last name.

JETTON, CAY, P.O. Box 315, Winnsboro, TX 75494/903-342-3317

JMD BLADES (See DaConceicao, John M.)

JOBIN, JACQUES, 46 St. Dominique, Levis Quebec, CANADA G6V 2M7/418-833-0283; FAX: 418-833-8378
Specialties: Fancy and working straight knives and folders; miniatures. **Patterns:** Minis, fantasy knives, fighters and some hunters. **Technical:** ATS-34, some Damascus and titanium. Likes native snakewood. Heat-treats. **Prices:** Start at $250. **Remarks:** Full-time maker; first knife sold in 1986. **Mark:** Signature on blade.

JOEHNK, BERND, Posadowskystrasse 22, 24148 Kiel, GERMANY/0431-7297705
Specialties: One-of-a-kind fancy/embellished and traditional straight knives of his design and to customer specs. **Patterns:** Daggers, fighters, hunters and letter openers. **Technical:** Grinds 440C, ATS-34, commercial Damascus and various stainless and corrosion-resistant steels. Likes filework. Leather sheaths. Offers engraving. **Prices:** Start at $300. **Remarks:** Spare-time maker; first knife sold in 1990. **Mark:** Full name and city.

JOHANSSON, ANDERS, Lövhagsgatan 39, S-724 71 Västerås, SWEDEN/+46 21 358778; FAX: +46 21 358778
Specialties: Scandinavian traditional and modern straight knives. **Patterns:** Hunters, fighters and utility knives. **Technical:** Grinds Uddeholm MARSS 500 and Sandvik 12C27. Prefers Scandinavian wood, reindeer, water buffalo and mammoth for handle material. **Prices:** Start at $100. **Remarks:** Spare-time maker; first knife sold in 1994. **Mark:** Stylized initials.

JOHNNY CUSTOM KNIFEMAKERS (See Chamberlain, Jon A.)

JOHNS, ROB, 1423 S. Second, Enid, OK 73701/405-242-2707
Specialties: Classic and fantasy straight knives of his design or to customer specs; fighters for use at Medieval fairs. **Patterns:** Bowies, daggers and swords. **Technical:** Forges and grinds 440C, D2 and 5160. Handles of nylon, walnut or wire-wrap. **Prices:** $150 to $350; some to $2,500. **Remarks:** Full-time maker; first knife sold in 1980. **Mark:** Medieval Customs, initials.

JOHNSON, C.E. "GENE," 5648 Redwood Ave., Portage, IN 46368/219-762-5461
Specialties: Lock-back folders and springers of his design or to customer specs. **Patterns:** Hunters, Bowies, survival lock-back folders. **Technical:** Grinds D2, 440C, A18, O1, Damascus; likes filework. **Prices:** $100 to $2,000. **Remarks:** Full-time maker; first knife sold in 1975. **Mark:** "Gene," city, state and serial number.

JOHNSON, DAVID L., P.O. Box 222, Talkeetna, AK 99676/907-733-2777
Specialties: Traditional working and using straight knives. **Patterns:** Bowies, fighters and hunters; outdoor knives. **Technical:** Grinds ATS-34, D2 and 440C. **Prices:** $100 to $200; some to $450. **Remarks:** Full-time maker; first knife sold in 1979. **Mark:** Name, city and state in banner.

JOHNSON, DURRELL CARMON, P.O. Box 594, Sparr, FL 32192/352-622-5498
Specialties: Old-fashioned working straight knives and folders of his design or to customer specs. **Patterns:** Bowies, hunters, fighters, daggers, camp knives and Damascus miniatures. **Technical:** Forges 5160, his own Damascus, W2, wrought iron, nickel and horseshoe rasps. Offers filework. **Prices:** $100 to $2,000. **Remarks:** Full-time maker and blacksmith; first knife sold in 1957. **Mark:** Middle name.

JOHNSON, GORDEN W., 5426 Sweetbriar, Houston, TX 77017/713-645-8990
Specialties: Working knives and period pieces. **Patterns:** Hunters, boots and Bowies. **Technical:** Flat-grinds 440C; most knives have narrow tang. **Prices:** $90 to $450. **Remarks:** Full-time maker; first knife sold in 1974. **Mark:** Name, city, state.

JOHNSON, HAROLD "HARRY" C., 1014 Lafayette Rd., Chickamauga, GA 30707
Specialties: Working straight knives. **Patterns:** Mostly hunters and large Bowies. **Technical:** Grinds popular steels. Offers heat treating, leatherwork, sheaths and cases; keeps large assortment of woods in stock. **Prices:** $125 to $2,000; some higher. **Remarks:** Part-time maker; first knife sold in 1973. **Mark:** First initial, last name, city, state in oval logo.

JOHNSON, KENNETH R., W3565 Lockington, Mindoro, WI 54644/608-857-3035
Specialties: Hunters, clip-points, special orders. **Patterns:** Hunters, utility/camp knives and kitchen knives. **Technical:** Grinds 440C, D2 and O1. Makes sheaths. **Prices:** $65 to $500. **Remarks:** Full-time maker; first knife sold in 1990. Doing business as Corken Knives. **Mark:** CORKEN.

JOHNSON, RANDY, 2575 E. Canal Dr., Turlock, CA 95380/209-632-5401
Specialties: Straight knives and folders. **Patterns:** Locking folders. **Technical:** Grinds Damascus. **Prices:** $200 to $300. **Remarks:** Spare-time maker; first knife sold in 1989. Doing business as Puedo Knifeworks. **Mark:** PUEDO

JOHNSON, R.B., Box 11, Clearwater, MN 55320/320-558-6128
Specialties: Automatic switch blades and lockbacks. **Patterns:** Traditional hunters and locking folders; liner locks with titanium. **Technical:** Grinds 440C, 154CM, 1095 steel and ATS-34; uses no plastic; prefers natural materials; offers mammoth ivory. **Prices:** $200 to $2,000. **Remarks:** Full-time maker; first knife sold in 1973. Now accepting orders. **Mark:** Signature.

JOHNSON, RUFFIN, 215 LaFonda Dr., Houston, TX 77060/713-448-4407
Specialties: Working straight knives and folders. **Patterns:** Hunters, fighters and locking folders. **Technical:** Grinds 440C and 154CM; hidden tangs and fancy handles. **Prices:** $200 to $400; some to $1,095. **Remarks:** Full-time maker; first knife sold in 1972. **Mark:** Wolf head logo and signature.

JOHNSON, RYAN M., 7320 Foster Hixson Cemetery Rd., Hixson, TN 37343/615-842-9323
Specialties: Working and using straight knives of his design and to customer specs. **Patterns:** Bowies, hunters and utiltiy/camp knives. **Technical:** Forges 5160, Damascus and files. **Prices:** $70 to $400; some to $800. **Remarks:** Full-time maker; first knife sold in 1986. **Mark:** Sledgehammer with halo.

JOHNSON, STEVEN R., 202 E. 200 N., P.O. Box 5, Manti, UT 84642/801-835-7941; FAX: 801-835-8052; WEB: http://www.hornnet.com/johnson; E-MAIL: srjohnson@sisna.com
Specialties: Investor-class working knives. **Patterns:** Hunters, fighters and boots in clean-lined contemporary patterns. **Technical:** Grinds ATS-34. **Prices:** $450 to $4,500. **Remarks:** Full-time maker; first knife sold in 1972. **Mark:** Name, city, state.

JOHNSON, W.C. "BILL," 1006 Clayton Ct., New Carlisle, OH 45344/513-845-1185
Specialties: Fancy working knives to order. **Patterns:** Hunters, fighters, tantos and push knives. **Technical:** Grinds 440C and ATS-34. **Prices:** $125 to $350; some higher. **Remarks:** Full-time maker; first knife sold in 1979. **Mark:** First and middle initials, last name.

JOKERST, CHARLES, 9312 Spaulding, Omaha, NE 68134/402-571-2536
Specialties: Working knives in standard patterns. **Patterns:** Hunters, fighters and pocketknives. **Technical:** Grinds 440C, ATS-34. **Prices:** $90 to $170. **Remarks:** Spare-time maker; first knife sold in 1984. **Mark:** Early work marked RCJ; current work marked with last name and city.

JONES, BARRY M. and PHILLIP G., 221 North Ave., Danville, VA 24540/804-793-5282
Specialties: Working and using straight knives and folders of their design and to customer specs; combat and self-defense knives. **Patterns:** Bowies, fighters, daggers, swords, hunters and lockback folders. **Technical:** Grinds 440C, ATS-34 and D2; flat-grinds only. All blades hand polished. **Prices:** $100 to $500, some higher. **Remarks:** Part-time makers; first knife sold in 1989. **Mark:** Jones Knives, city, state.

JONES, BOB, 6219 Aztec NE, Albuquerque, NM 87110/505-881-4472
Specialties: Fancy working knives of his design. **Patterns:** Mountainman/buckskinner-type knives; multi-blade folders, locking folders and slip-joints. **Technical:** Grinds A2, O1, 1095 and commercial Damascus; uses no stainless steel. Engraves. **Prices:** $100 to $500; some to $1,500. **Remarks:** Full-time maker; first knife sold in 1960. **Mark:** Initials on fixed blades; initials encircled on folders.

JONES, CHARLES ANTHONY, 36 Broadgate Close, Bellaire Barnstaple, No. Devon E31 4AL, ENGLAND/0271-75328
Specialties: Working straight knives. **Patterns:** Simple hunters, fighters and utility knives. **Technical:** Grinds 440C, O1 and D2; filework offered. Engraves. **Prices:** $100 to $500; engraving higher. **Remarks:** Spare-time maker; first knife sold in 1987. **Mark:** Tony engraved.

JONES, CURTIS J., 39909 176th St. E., Palmdale, CA 93591/805-264-2753
Specialties: Big Bowies, daggers, his own style of hunters. **Patterns:** Bowies, daggers, hunters, swords, boots and miniatures. **Technical:** Grinds 440C, ATS-34 and D2. Fitted guards only; does not solder. Heat-treats. Custom sheaths—hand-tooled and stitched. **Prices:** $125 to $1,500; some to $3,000. **Remarks:** Part-time maker; first knife sold in 1975. Not taking mail orders. **Mark:** Stylized initials on either side of three triangles interconnected.

JONES, ENOCH, 7278 Moss Ln., Warrenton, VA 20187/540-341-0292
Specialties: Fancy working straight knives. **Patterns:** Hunters, fighters, boots and Bowies. **Technical:** Forges and grinds O1, W2, 440C and Damascus. **Prices:** $100 to $350; some to $1,000. **Remarks:** Part-time maker; first knife sold in 1982. **Mark:** First name.

JONES, JOHN, 12 Schooner Circuit, Manly West, QLD 4179, AUSTRALIA/07-339-33390
Specialties: Straight knives and folders. **Patterns:** Working hunters, folding lockbacks, fancy daggers and miniatures. **Technical:** Grinds 440C, O1 and L6. **Prices:** $180 to $1200; some to $2,000. **Remarks:** Part-time maker; first knife sold in 1986. **Mark:** Jones Custom in script.

JONES, PHILLIP G. (See Jones, Barry M. and Phillip G.)

JORGENSEN, GERD, Ragnhildrod, N-3160 Stokke, NORWAY/(+47)33337347; FAX: (+47)33337347
Specialties: Traditional working/using straight knives of his design or in standard patterns. **Patterns:** Hunters, utility/camp knives and Scandinavian knives. **Technical:** Grinds ATS-34, Sandvik 12C27; forges UHB17VA. Sheaths are shaped with traditional pauting technique; uses natural materials. **Prices:** $150 to $300; some to $700. **Remarks:** Part-time maker; first knife sold in 1990. **Mark:** First name or initials.

J.P.M. KNIVES (See McMahon, John P.)

J&S KNIVES (See Kitsmiller, Jerry)

KACZOR, TOM, 375 Wharncliffe Rd. N., Upper London, Ont., CANADA N6G 1E4/519-645-7640

KAGAWA, KOICHI, 1556 Horiyamashita Hatano-Shi, Kanagawa, JAPAN
Specialties: Fancy high-tech straight knives and folders to customer specs. **Patterns:** Hunters, locking folders and slip-joints. **Technical:** Uses 440C and ATS-34. **Prices:** $500 to $2,000; some to $20,000. **Remarks:** Part-time maker; first knife sold in 1986. **Mark:** First initial, last name-YOKOHAMA.

KALFAYAN, EDWARD N., 410 Channing, Ferndale, MI 48220/248-548-4882
Specialties: Working straight knives and lockback folders; some art and fantasy pieces. **Patterns:** Bowies, toothpicks, fighters, daggers, swords and hunters. **Technical:** Grinds ATS-34, 440C, O1, 5160 and Damascus. **Prices:** $100 to $2,000. **Remarks:** Part-time maker; first knife sold in 1973. **Mark:** Last name.

KALUZA, WERNER, Lochnerstr. 32, 90441 Nurnberg, GERMANY/0911 666047
Specialties: Fancy high-art straight knives of his design. **Patterns:** Boots and ladies knives. **Technical:** Grinds ATS-34, CPM-T-440V and Schneider Damascus. Engraving available. **Prices:** NA. **Remarks:** Part-time maker. **Mark:** First initial and last name.

KANDA, MICHIO, 7-32-5 Shinzutumi-cho, Shinnanyo-shi, Yamaguchi 746 JAPAN/0834-62-1910; FAX: 011-81-83462-1910
Specialties: Fantasy knives of his design. **Patterns:** Animal knives. **Technical:** Grinds ATS-34. **Prices:** $300 to $3,000. **Remarks:** Full-time maker; first knife sold in 1985. Doing business as Shusui Kanda. **Mark:** Last name inside "M."

KAP FORGE (See Povisils, Karlis A.)

KARP, BOB P.O. Box 47304, Phoenix, AZ 85068

KATO, KIYOSHI, 4-6-4 Himonya Meguro-ku, Tokyo, 152 JAPAN
Specialties: Swords, Damascus knives, working knives and paper knives. **Patterns:** Traditional swords, hunters, Bowies and daggers. **Technical:** Forges his own Damascus and carbon steel. Grinds ATS-34. **Prices:** $260 to $700; some to $4,000. **Remarks:** Full-time maker. **Mark:** First initial, last name.

KAUFFMAN, DAVE, P.O. Box 9041, Helena, MT 59604/406-442-9328
Specialties: Mosaic Damascus folders and fancy straight hunters. **Patterns:** Fighters, Bowies and drop-point hunters. **Technical:** Uses ATS-34 and his own mosaic Damascus. **Prices:** $300 to $1,200. **Remarks:** Full-time maker; first knife sold in 1989. On the cover of Knives '94. **Mark:** First and last name, city and state.

KAUFMAN, SCOTT, 302 Green Meadows Cr., Anderson, SC 29624/864-231-9201
Specialties: Classic and working/using straight knives in standard patterns. **Patterns:** Fighters, hunters and utility/camp knives. **Technical:** Grinds ATS-34, 440C, O1. **Prices:** $100 to $500. **Remarks:** Part-time maker; first knife sold in 1987. **Mark:** Kaufman Knives with Bible in middle.

KAWASAKI, AKIHISA, 11-8-9 Chome Minamiamachi, Suzurandai Kita-Ku, Kobe JAPAN/078-593-0418; FAX: 078-593-0418
Specialties: Working/using knives of his design. **Patterns:** Hunters, kitchen and utility/camp knives. **Technical:** Forges and grinds Molybdenum Panadium. Grinds ATS-34 and stainless steel. Uses Chinese Quince wood, desert ironwood and cow leather. **Prices:** $300 to $800; some to $1,200. **Remarks:** Full-time maker. **Mark:** Last name, first name.

KAY, J. WALLACE, 332 Slab Bridge Rd., Liberty, SC 29657

KEESLAR, JOSEPH F., 391 Radio Rd., Almo, KY 42020/502-753-7919; FAX: 502-753-7919; E-MAIL: skeeslar@mursuky.campus.mci.net
Specialties: Classic Bowie reproductions and contemporary Bowies. **Patterns:** Period pieces, combat knives, hunters, daggers. **Technical:** Forges 5160 and his own Damascus. Decorative filework, engraving and custom leather sheaths available. **Prices:** $200 to $3,000. **Remarks:** Full-time maker; first knife sold in 1976. **Mark:** First and middle initials, last name in hammer, knife and anvil logo, M.S..

KEESLAR, STEVEN C., 115 Lane 216, Hamilton, IN 46742/219-488-3161; FAX: 219-488-3149
Specialties: Traditional working/using straight knives of his design and to customer specs. **Patterns:** Bowies, hunters, utility/camp knives. **Technical:** Forges 5160, files, 52100. **Prices:** $100 to $600; some to $1,500. **Remarks:** Part-time maker; first knife sold in 1976. **Mark:** First initial, last name.

KEETON, WILLIAM L., 6095 Rehoboth Rd. SE, Laconia, IN 47135/812-969-2836
Specialties: Plain and fancy working knives. **Patterns:** Hunters and fighters; locking folders and slip-joints. Names patterns after Kentucky Derby winners. **Technical:** Grinds D2, ATS-34, 440C, 440V and 154CM; mirror and satin finishes. **Prices:** $95 to $2,000. **Remarks:** Full-time maker; first knife sold in 1971. **Mark:** Logo of key.

KEHIAYAN, ALFREDO, Cuzco 1455, Ing. Maschwitz, CP 1623 Buenos Aires, ARGENTINA/0488-4-2212
Specialties: Functional straight knives. **Patterns:** Utility knives, skinners, hunters and boots. **Technical:** Forges and grinds SAE 52.100, SAE 6180, SAE 9260, SAE 5160, 440C and ATS-34, titanium with nitride. All blades mirror-polished; makes leather sheaths and wood cases. **Prices:** $150 to $800; some to $6,000. **Remarks:** Full-time maker; first knife sold in 1983. **Mark:** Name.

KEIDEL, GENE W. AND SCOTT J., 4661 105th Ave. SW, Dickinson, ND 58601
Specialties: Fancy/embellished and working/using straight knives of his design. **Patterns:** Bowies, hunters and miniatures. **Technical:** Grind 440C and O1 tool steel. Offer scrimshaw and filework. **Prices:** $95 to $500. **Remarks:** Full-time makers; first knife sold in 1990. Doing business as Keidel Knives. **Mark:** Last name.

KEIDEL KNIVES (See Keidel, Gene W. and Scott J.)

KEIDEL, SCOTT J. (See Keidel, Gene W. and Scott J.)

KELGIN KNIVES (See Largin, Ken)

KELLEY, GARY, 17485 SW Pheasant Lane, Aloha, OR 97006/503-848-9313
Specialties: Primitive knives and blades. **Patterns:** Fur trade era rifleman's knives, patch and throwing knives. **Technical:** Hand-forges and precision investment casts. **Prices:** $25 to $250. **Remarks:** Part-time maker. Staff photographer/writer for *Tactical Knives* magazine; does illustrative knife photography. Doing business as Reproduction Blades. **Mark:** Full name or initials.

KELLOGG, BRIAN R., Rt. 1, Box 357, New Market, VA 22844/703-740-4292
Specialties: Fancy and working straight knives of his design and to customer specs. **Patterns:** Fighters, hunters and utility/camp knives. **Technical:** Grinds 440C, D2 and A2. Offers filework and fancy pin and cable pin work. Prefers natural handle materials. **Prices:** $75 to $225; some to $350. **Remarks:** Part-time maker; first knife sold in 1983. **Mark:** Last name.

KELLY, LANCE, 1723 Willow Oak Dr., Edgewater, FL 32132/904-423-4933
Specialties: Investor-class straight knives and folders. **Patterns:** Kelly style in contemporary outlines. **Technical:** Grinds O1, D2 and 440C; engraves; inlays gold and silver. **Prices:** $600 to $3,500. **Remarks:** Full-time engraver and knifemaker; first knife sold in 1975. **Mark:** Last name.

KELSO, JIM, RD 1, Box 5300, Worcester, VT 05682/802-229-4254
Specialties: Fancy high-art straight knives and folders that mix Eastern and Western influences. Only uses own designs, but accepts suggestions for themes. **Patterns:** Daggers, swords and locking folders. **Technical:** Grinds only custom Damascus. Works with top Damascus bladesmiths. **Prices:** $3,000 to $8,000; some to $15,000. **Remarks:** Full-time maker; first knife sold in 1980. **Mark:** Stylized initials.

KEMAL (See Sayen, Murad)

KENNEDY JR., BILL, P.O. Box 850431, Yukon, OK 73085/405-354-9150
Specialties: Working straight knives. **Patterns:** Hunters, fighters, minis and fishing knives. **Technical:** Grinds D2, 440C and Damascus. **Prices:** $80 and higher. **Remarks:** Part-time maker; first knife sold in 1980. **Mark:** Last name and year made.

KENNEDY, JERRY, 2104 S.W.8A, Blue Springs, MO 64015/816-229-5468
Specialties: Traditional working and using knives. **Patterns:** Bowies, fighters, hunters and camp knives. **Technical:** Forges W2, 52100 and Damascus. Makes own Damascus with W2 and 203E. **Prices:** $125 to $750; some to $1,500. **Remarks:** Full-time maker; first knife sold in 1990. **Mark:** First initial, last name.

KENNEDY, KELLY S., 9894 A.W. University, Odessa, TX 79764/915-381-6165
Specialties: Traditional working and using straight knives of his design and to customer specs. **Patterns:** Bowies, hunters and utility/camp knives. **Technical:** Forges 5160, W2 and own Damascus. **Prices:** Moderate to upscale. **Remarks:** Full-time maker; first knife sold in 1991. Doing business as Noble House Armourers. **Mark:** Last name in script, J.S., A.B.S.

KENNELLEY, J.C., 1114 N. C St., Arkansas City, KS 67005/316-442-0848
Specialties: Working straight knives; some fantasy pieces. **Patterns:** Hunters, fighters, skinners and fillet knives. **Technical:** Grinds D2 and 440C. **Prices:** $75 to $200; some to $500. **Remarks:** Part-time maker; first knife sold in 1982. **Mark:** Name logo.

KENTUCKY DREAMER (See Jackson, Jim)

KERMIT'S KNIFE WORKS (See Laurent, Kermit)

KERSTEN, MICHAEL, Borkzeile 17, 13583 Berlin, GERMANY
Specialties: Working/using straight knives and folders of his design and to customer specs. **Patterns:** Fighters, locking folders and utility/camp knives. **Technical:** Grinds O1, D2, 440C, 440V and Damascus. Handle materials include brass, hardwood and bone. **Prices:** $250 to $1,000. **Remarks:** Spare-time maker; first knife sold in 1993. **Mark:** Last initial.

KESSLER, RALPH A., P.O. Box 357, 345 Sherwood Rd., Marietta, SC 29661/864-836-7944
Specialties: Traditional-style knives. **Patterns:** Folders, hunters, fighters, Bowies and kitchen knives. **Technical:** Grinds D2, O1, A2 and ATS-34. Forges 1090 and 1095. **Prices:** $100 to $500. **Remarks:** Part-time maker; first knife sold in 1982. **Mark:** Last name or initials with last name.

KESTREL TOOL (See Blomberg, Gregg)

KEYES, DAN, 6688 King St., Chino, CA 91710/909-628-8329

KHALSA, JOT SINGH, 368 Village St., Millis, MA 02054/508-376-8162; FAX: 508-376-8081
Specialties: Liner locks, straight knives and one-of-a-kind daggers of his design. **Patterns:** Classic with contemporary flair. Has line of knife jewelry sold through stores and dealers. **Technical:** Grinds ATS-34; forges his Damascus. Uses unusual natural handle material. Offers embellishment on daggers. **Prices:** Start at $225. **Remarks:** Full-time maker; first knife sold in 1978. **Mark:** An Adi Skakti symbol.

KHARLAMOV, YURI, Oboronnay 46/2, Tula, 300007 RUSSIA
Specialties: Classic, fancy and traditional knives of his design. **Patterns:** Daggers and hunters. **Technical:** Forges only Damascus with nickel. Uses natural handle materials; engraves on metal, carves on nut-tree; silver and pearl inlays. **Prices:** $600 to $2,380; some to $4,000. **Remarks:** Full-time maker; first knife sold in 1988. **Mark:** Initials.

KI, SHIVA, 5222 Ritterman Ave., Baton Rouge, LA 70805/504-356-7274
Specialties: Fancy working straight knives and folders to customer specs. **Patterns:** Emphasis on personal defense knives, martial arts weapons. **Technical:** Forges and grinds; makes own Damascus; prefers natural handle materials. **Prices:** $135 to $850; some to $1,800. **Remarks:** Full-time maker; first knife sold in 1981. **Mark:** Name with logo.

KIEFER, TONY, 112 Chateaugay Dr., Pataskala, OH 43062/614-927-6910
Specialties: Traditional working and using straight knives in standard patterns. **Patterns:** Bowies, fighters and hunters. **Technical:** Grinds 440C and D2; forges D2. Flat-grinds Bowies; hollow-grinds drop-point and trailing-point hunters. **Prices:** $95 to $140; some to $200. **Remarks:** Spare-time maker; first knife sold in 1988. **Mark:** Last name.

KILBY, KEITH, 402 Jackson Trail Rd., Jefferson, GA 30549/706-367-9997
Specialties: Works with all designs. **Patterns:** Mostly Bowies, camp knives and hunters of his design. **Technical:** Forges 52100, 5160, 1095, Damascus and mosaic Damascus. **Prices:** $100 to $3,500. **Remarks:** Part-time maker; first knife sold in 1974. Doing business as Foxwood Forge. **Mark:** Name or fox logo.

KIMSEY, KEVIN, 198 Cass White Rd. N.W., Cartersville, GA 30121/770-387-0779
Specialties: Classic and working straight knives of his design. **Patterns:** Fighters, hunters and utility knives. **Technical:** Grinds 440C, ATS-34 and D2 carbon. **Prices:** $100 to $400; some to $600. **Remarks:** Part-time maker; first knife sold in 1983. Doing business as Rafter KK Custom Knives. **Mark:** Rafter and stylized KK.

KING, BILL, 14830 Shaw Road, Tampa, FL 33625/813-961-3455
Specialties: Folders, lockbacks, liner locks and stud openers. **Patterns:** Wide varieties; folders and dive knives. **Technical:** Sandvik (12-C-27), ATS-34 and some Damascus; single and double grinds. Offers filework and jewel embellishment; nickel-silver Damacus and mokume bolsters. **Prices:** $135 to $425; some to $650. **Remarks:** Full-time maker; first knife sold in 1976. **Mark:** Last name in crown.

KING, FRED, P.O. Box 200342, Cartersville, GA 30120/404-382-8478
Specialties: Fancy and embellished working straight knives and folders. **Patterns:** Hunters, Bowies and fighters. **Technical:** Grinds ATS-34 and D2; forges 5160, L6, 52100, 203E and Damascus. Offers filework. **Prices:** $45 to $2,500. **Remarks:** Spare-time maker; first knife sold in 1984. **Mark:** Kings Edge.

KING JR., HARVEY G., 312 Walnut, Box 184, Eskridge, KS 66423-0184/913-449-2487
Specialties: Traditional working and using straight knives of his design and to customer specs. **Patterns:** Hunters, Bowies and fillet knives. **Technical:** Grinds O1, A2 and D2. Prefers natural handle materials; offers leatherwork. **Prices:** Start at $70. **Remarks:** Part-time maker; first knife sold in 1988. **Mark:** Name and serial number based on steel used, year made and number of knives made that year.

KING, RANDALL, 54 Mt. Carmel, #12, Asheville, NC 28806/704-254-7340
Specialties: Fancy and working straight knives of his design, to customer specs and in standard patterns; movie knives, prop knives and swords. **Patterns:** Fighters, hunters and locking folders. **Technical:** Grinds ATS-34, D2 and 440C. Prefers tapered tangs. Scrimshaws. Offers sheaths. **Prices:** $100 to $250; some to $500. **Remarks:** Part-time maker; first knife sold in 1987. **Mark:** First initial, last name, city and state.

KINGS EDGE (See King, Fred)

KINKADE, JACOB, 197 Rd. 154, Carpenter, WY 82054/307-649-2446
Specialties: Working/using knives of his design or to customer specs; some miniature swords, daggers and battle axes. **Patterns:** Hunters, daggers, boots; some miniatures. **Technical:** Grinds M2 and L6. Prefers natural handle material. **Prices:** Start at $30. **Remarks:** Part-time maker; first knife sold in 1990. **Mark:** Connected initials or none.

KINNIKIN, TODD, Eureka Forge, 8356 John McKeever Rd., House Springs, MO 63051/314-938-6248
Specialties: Mosaic Damascus. **Patterns:** Hunters, fighters, folders and automatics. **Technical:** Forges own mosaic Damascus with tool steel Damascus edge. Prefers natural, fossil and artifact handle materials. **Prices:** $400 to $2,400. **Remarks:** Full-time maker; first knife sold in 1994. **Mark:** Initials connected.

KIOUS, JOE, 1015 Ridge Pointe Rd., Kerrville, TX 78028/830-367-2277; FAX: 830-367-2286
Specialties: Investment-quality interframe folders. **Patterns:** Hunters, fighters, Bowies and miniatures; traditional folders. **Technical:** Grinds D2, 440C, CPM440V, 154CM and stainless Damascus. **Prices:** $175 to $1,000; some to $5,000. **Remarks:** Full-time maker; first knife sold in 1969. **Mark:** Last name, city and state.

KITSMILLER, JERRY, 67277 Las Vegas Dr., Montrose, CO 81401/970-249-4290
Specialties: Working straight knives in standard patterns. **Patterns:** Hunters, boots and locking folders. **Technical:** Grinds ATS-34 and 440C only. **Prices:** $75 to $200; some to $300. **Remarks:** Spare-time maker; first knife sold in 1984. **Mark:** J&S Knives.

KNEUBUHLER, W.K. (See Votaw, David P.)

KNICKMEYER, HANK, 6300 Crosscreek, Cedar Hill, MO 63016/314-285-3210
Specialties: Complex mosaic Damascus constructions. **Patterns:** Fixed blades, swords, folders and automatics. **Technical:** Mosaic Damascus with all tool steel Damascus edges. **Prices:** $500 to $2,000; some $3,000 and higher. **Remarks:** Part-time maker; first knife sold in 1989. Doing business as Dutch Creek Forge & Foundry. **Mark:** Initials connected.

KNIFE EMPORIUM (See Woodcock, Dennis "Woody")

KNIFE HOUSE "HARA" (See Hara, Kouji)

KNIFE STUDIO, THE (See Conable, Matt)

KNIFECRAFT (See Wise, Donald)

KNIP CUSTOM KNIVES (See Knipschield, Terry)

KNIPSCHIELD, TERRY, 808 12th Ave. NE, Rochester, MN 55906/507-288-7829
Specialties: Working straight and some folding knives in standard patterns. **Patterns:** Lockback and slip-joint knives. **Technical:** Grinds ATS-34. **Prices:** $55 to $350; some to $600. **Remarks:** Part-time maker; first knife sold in 1986. Doing business as Knip Custom Knives. **Mark:** KNIP in Old English with shield logo.

KNIPSTEIN, R.C. (JOE), 731 N. Fielder, Arlington, TX 76012/817-265-2021
Specialties: Traditional pattern folders along with custom designs. **Patterns:** Hunters, Bowies, folders, fighters, utility knives. **Technical:** Grinds 440C, D2, 154CM and ATS-34. Natural handle materials and full tangs are standard. **Prices:** Start at $200. **Remarks:** Part-time maker; first knife sold in 1989. **Mark:** Last name.

KNIVES BY CORBY (See Korby, Harold)

KNIVES BY: GRAF (See Graffeo, Anthony I.)

KNIVES BY TURCOTTE (See Turcotte, Larry)

KNOB HILL FORGE (See Pulliam, Morris C.)

KNOTT, STEVE, 206 Academy St., Clinton, SC 29325/803-833-6348
Specialties: Fantasy working straight knives and folders of his design or to customer specs. **Patterns:** Hunters and slip-joint folders; Bowies, daggers and fighters. **Technical:** Grinds 440C, ATS-34 and commercial Damascus. Offers filework, satin and mirror finishes; will do some bluing. **Prices:** $80 to $500. **Remarks:** Full-time maker; first knife sold in 1988. **Mark:** Last name.

KNUTH, JOSEPH E., 3307 Lookout Dr., Rockford, IL 61109/815-874-9597
Specialties: High-art working straight knives of his design or to customer specs. **Patterns:** Daggers, fighters and swords. **Technical:** Grinds 440C, ATS-34 and D2. **Prices:** $150 to $1,500; some to $15,000. **Remarks:** Full-time maker; first knife sold in 1989. **Mark:** Initials on bolster face.

KODAN (See Engnath, Bob)

KOJETIN, W., 20 Bapaume Rd., Delville, Germiston 1401 SOUTH AFRICA-011 825 6680
Specialties: High-art and working straight knives of all designs. **Patterns:** Daggers, hunters and his own Manhunter Bowie. **Technical:** Grinds D2 and ATS-34; forges and grinds 440B/C. Offers "wrap-around" pava and abalone handles, scrolled wood or ivory, stacked filework and setting of faceted semi-precious stones. **Prices:** $185 to $600; some to $11,000. **Remarks:** Spare-time maker; first knife sold in 1962. **Mark:** Billy K.

KOLITZ, ROBERT, W9342 Canary Rd., Beaver Dam, WI 53916/414-887-1287
Specialties: Working straight knives to customer specs. **Patterns:** Bowies, hunters, bird and trout knives, boots. **Technical:** Grinds O1, 440C; commercial Damascus. **Prices:** $50 to $100; some to $500. **Remarks:** Spare-time maker; first knife sold in 1979. **Mark:** Last initial.

KOMMER, RUSS, 9211 Abbott Loop Rd., Anchorage, AK 99507/907-346-3339
Specialties: Working straight knives with the outdoorsman in mind. **Patterns:** Hunters, semi-skinners, fighters and utility knives. **Technical:** Hollow-grinds ATS-34, 440C and 440V. **Prices:** $125 to $850; some to $1,200. **Remarks:** Part-time maker; first knife sold in 1995. **Mark:** Bear paw—full name, city and state or full name and state.

KOPP, TODD M., P.O. Box 3474, Apache Jct., AZ 85217/602-983-6143
Specialties: Classic and traditional straight knives. **Patterns:** Bowies, boots, daggers, fighters and hunters. **Technical:** Grinds M1, ATS-34 and 4160. Some engraving and filework. **Prices:** $125 to $400; some to $800. **Remarks:** Part-time maker; first knife sold in 1989. **Mark:** Name, city and state.

KOUTSOPOULOS, GEORGE, 41491 Biggs Rd., LaGrange, OH 44050/216-355-5013
Specialties: Heavy-duty working straight knives and folders. **Patterns:** Traditional hunters and skinners; lockbacks. **Technical:** Grinds 440C, 154CM, ATS-34. **Prices:** $75 to $275; some higher. **Remarks:** Spare-time maker; first knife sold in 1976. **Mark:** Initials in diamond logo.

KOVAL, MICHAEL T., 5819 Zarley St., New Albany, OH 43054/614-855-0777
Specialties: Working straight knives of his design; period pieces. **Patterns:** Bowies, boots and daggers. **Technical:** Grinds D2, 440C and 154CM. **Prices:** $95 to $195; some to $495. **Remarks:** Full-time knifemaker supply house; spare-time knifemaker. **Mark:** Last name.

KOVAR, EUGENE, 2626 W. 98th St., Evergreen Park, IL 60642/312-636-3724
Specialties: One-of-a-kind miniature knives only. **Patterns:** Fancy to fantasy miniature knives; knife pendants and tie tacks. **Technical:** Files and grinds nails, nickel-silver and sterling silver. **Prices:** $5 to $35; some to $100. **Remarks:** Spare-time maker; first knife sold in 1987. **Mark:** GK connected.

KRAFT, ELMER, 1358 Meadowlark Lane, Big Arm, MT 59910/406-849-5086; FAX: 406-883-3056
Specialties: Traditional working/using straight knives of all designs. **Patterns:** Fighters, hunters, utility/camp knives. **Technical:** Grinds 440C, D2. Custom makes sheaths. **Prices:** $125 to $350; some to $500. **Remarks:** Part-time maker; first knife sold in 1989. **Mark:** Kraft Knives.

KRAFT, STEVE, 315 S.E. 6th, Abilene, KS 67410/913-263-2198
Specialties: Motorcycle chain Damascus with foot peg handle. **Patterns:** Hunters, boot knives and fighters. **Technical:** Forges chain Damascus and stock removal; grinds ATS-34. **Prices:** $150 to $1,000. **Remarks:** Part-time maker; first knife sold in 1984. **Mark:** Last name.

KRAMER, BOB, 1028 1st Ave. S., Seattle, WA 98134/206-623-1088; FAX: 206-623-1088
Specialties: Traditional and working/using straight knives in standard patterns. **Patterns:** Bowies, daggers and kitchen knives. **Technical:** Forges 52100, 5160 and Damascus 1095 and L6. Triple quench, triple temper, nitro quench. **Prices:** $300 to $800; some to $3,000. **Remarks:** Full-time maker; first knife sold in 1992. Doing business as Bladesmith's Inc. **Mark:** Kramer M.S.

KRANNING, TERRY L., 1900 West Quinn, #153, Pocatello, ID 83202/208-237-9047
Specialties: Miniature and full-size fantasy and working knives of his design. **Patterns:** Miniatures and some mini straight knives including razors, tomahawks, hunters, Bowies and fighters. **Technical:** Grinds 1095, 440C, commercial Damascus and nickel-silver. Uses exotic materials like meteorite. **Prices:** $40 to $150. **Remarks:** Part-time maker; first knife sold in 1978. **Mark:** Last initial or full initials in eagle head logo.

KRAPP, DENNY, 1826 Windsor Oak Dr., Apopka, FL 32703/407-880-7115
Specialties: Fantasy and working straight knives of his design. **Patterns:** Hunters, fighters and utility/camp knives. **Technical:** Grinds ATS-34 and 440C. **Prices:** $85 to $300; some to $800. **Remarks:** Spare-time maker; first knife sold in 1988. **Mark:** Last name.

KRAUSE, ROY W., 22412 Corteville, St. Clair Shores, MI 48081/810-296-3995; FAX: 810-296-2663.
Specialties: Military and law enforcement/Japanese-style knives and swords. **Patterns:** Combat and back-up, Bowies, fighters, boot knives, daggers, tantos, wakazashis and katanas. **Technical:** Grinds ATS-34, A2, D2, 1045, O1 and commercial Damascus; differentially hardened Japanese-style blades. **Prices:** Moderate to upscale. **Remarks:** Full-time maker. **Mark:** Last name on traditional knives; initials in Japanese characters on Japanese-style knives.

KREIBICH, DONALD L., 6082 Boyd Ct., San Jose, CA 95123/408-225-8354
Specialties: Working straight knives in standard patterns. **Patterns:** Bowies, boots and daggers; camp and fishing knives. **Technical:** Grinds 440C, 154CM and ATS-34; likes integrals. **Prices:** $100 to $200; some to $500. **Remarks:** Part-time maker; first knife sold in 1980. **Mark:** First and middle initials, last name.

KREMZNER, RAYMOND L., P.O. Box 31, Stevenson, MD 21153/410-329-5226
Specialties: Working straight knives in standard patterns, some fancy. **Patterns:** Hunters, fighters, Bowies and camp knives. **Technical:** Forges 5160, 9260, W2 and his own Damascus. Offers wire inlay. **Prices:** $200 to $700; some higher. **Remarks:** Part-time maker; first knife sold in 1987. **Mark:** Last name, JS.

KRESSLER, D.F., AM Schlossberg 1, D-8063 Odelzhausen, GERMANY/08134-7758; FAX: 08134-7759
Specialties: High-tech working knives. **Patterns:** Hunters, fighters, daggers. **Technical:** Grinds new state-of-the-art steels; prefers natural handle materials. **Prices:** Upscale. **Mark:** Name in logo.

KRETSINGER JR., PHILIP W., 17536 Bakersville Rd., Boonsboro, MD 21713/301-432-6771
Specialties: Fancy and traditional period pieces. **Patterns:** Hunters, Bowies, camp knives, daggers, carvers, fighters. **Technical:** Forges W2, 5160 and his own Damascus. **Prices:** Start at $200. **Remarks:** Full-time knifemaker. **Mark:** Name.

KRUSE, MARTIN, P.O. Box 487, Reseda, CA 91335/818-713-0172
Specialties: Fighters and working straight knives. **Patterns:** Full line of straight knives, swords, fighters, axes, kitchen cutlery. **Technical:** Forges and grinds O1, 1095, 5160 and Damascus; differential tempering. **Prices:** $85 to $700; some to $2,000. **Remarks:** Full-time maker; first knife sold in 1964. **Mark:** Initials.

KUBAIKO, HANK, P.O. Box 2072, Palmer, AK 99645/907-746-4360
Specialties: Working straight knives and folders. **Patterns:** Bowies, fighters, fishing knives, kitchen cutlery, lockers, slip-joints, camp knives, axes and miniatures. Also makes American, European and traditional samurai swords and daggers. **Technical:** Grinds 440C, ATS-34 and D2; will use CPM-T-440V at extra cost. Worked under Joe Cordova. **Prices:** Moderate. **Remarks:** Full-time maker; first knife sold in 1982. Allow three months for sword order fulfillment. **Mark:** Alaskan Maid and name.

KUBASEK, JOHN A., 74 Northhampton St., Easthampton, MA 01027/413-527-7917
Specialties: Left- and right-handed liner lock folders of his design or to customer specs. **Patterns:** Fighters, tantos, drop points and survival knives. **Technical:** Grinds ATS-34 and Damascus. **Prices:** $175 to $750. **Remarks:** Part-time maker; first knife sold in 1985. **Mark:** Name and address etched.

KUNI MITSU (See Bell, Michael)

KUSTOM KRAFTED KNIVES—KKK (See Collins, A.J.)

l

L&H KNIFE WORKS (See Gundersen, D.F. "DOC")

LADD, JIM S., 1120 Helen, Deer Park, TX 77536/713-479-7286
Specialties: Working knives and period pieces. **Patterns:** Hunters, boots and Bowies plus other straight knives. **Technical:** Grinds D2, 440C and 154CM. **Prices:** $125 to $225; some to $550. **Remarks:** Part-time maker; first knife sold in 1965. Doing business as The Tinker. **Mark:** First and middle initials, last name.

LADD, JIMMIE LEE, 1120 Helen, Deer Park, TX 77536/713-479-7186
Specialties: Working straight knives. **Patterns:** Hunters, skinners and utility knives. **Technical:** Grinds 440C and D2. **Prices:** $75 to $225. **Remarks:** First knife sold in 1979. **Mark:** First and middle initials, last name.

LA GRANGE, FANIE, 22 Sturke Rd., Selborne, Bellville 7530, REPUBLIC OF SOUTH AFRICA/27-021-9134199; FAX: 27-021-9134199
Specialties: Fancy high-tech straight knives and folders of his design and to customer specs. **Patterns:** Daggers, hunters and locking folders. **Technical:** Grinds Sandvik 12C27 and ATS-34; forges and grinds Damascus. Engraves, enamels and anodizes bolsters. Uses rare and natural handle materials. **Prices:** $250 to $500; some higher. **Remarks:** Full-time maker; first knife sold in 1987. **Mark:** Name, town, country under Table Mountain.

LAGRANGE KNIFE (See Roghmans, Mark)

LAINSON, TONY, 114 Park Ave., Council Bluffs, IA 51503/712-322-5222
Specialties: Working straight knives, locking folders, straight razors, Bowies and tantos. **Technical:** Grinds ATS-34 and 440C. Prefers mirror finishes; handle materials include Micarta, Pakkawood and bone. **Prices:** $45 to $280; some to $450. **Remarks:** Part-time maker; first knife sold in 1987; not currently taking orders. **Mark:** Name and state.

LAKE, RON, 3360 Bendix Ave., Eugene, OR 97401/503-484-2683
Specialties: High-tech working knives; inventor of the modern interframe folder. **Patterns:** Hunters, boots, etc.; locking folders. **Technical:** Grinds 154CM and ATS-34. Patented interframe with special lock release tab. **Prices:** $2,200 to $3,000; some higher. **Remarks:** Full-time maker; first knife sold in 1966. **Mark:** Last name.

LALA, PAULO RICARDO P. AND LALA, ROBERTO P., R. Daniel Martins, 636, Centro, Presidente Prudente, SP-19031-260, BRAZIL/0182-210125
Specialties: Straight knives and folders of all designs to customer specs. **Patterns:** Bowies, daggers, fighters, hunters and utility knives. **Technical:** Grinds and forges D6, 440C, high-carbon steels and Damascus. **Prices:** $60 to $400; some higher. **Remarks:** Full-time makers; first knife sold in 1991. **Mark:** Sword carved on top of anvil under KORTH.

LALA, ROBERTO P.
(See Lala, Paulo Ricardo P. and Lala, Roberto P.)

LAMBERT, JARRELL D., 2321 FM 2982, Granado, TX 77962/512-771-3744
Specialties: Traditional working and using straight knives of his design and to customer specs. **Patterns:** Bowies, hunters, tantos and utility/camp knives. **Technical:** Grinds ATS-34; forges W2 and his own Damascus. Makes own sheaths. **Prices:** $80 to $600; some to $1,000. **Remarks:** Part-time maker; first knife sold in 1982. **Mark:** Etched first and middle initials, last name; or stamped last name.

LAMBERT, RONALD S., 24 Vermont St., Johnston, RI 02919/401-831-5427
Specialties: Traditional working and using straight knives of his design. **Patterns:** Boots, Bowies and hunters. **Technical:** Grinds O1 and 440C; forges 1070. Offers exotic wood handles; sheaths have exotic skin overlay. **Prices:** $100 to $500; some to $850. **Remarks:** Part-time maker; first knife sold in 1991. Doing business as RL Custom Knives. **Mark:** Initials; each knife is numbered.

LAMPREY, MIKE, 32 Pathfield, Great Torrington, Devon EX38 7BX ENGLAND/01805 622651
Specialties: High-tech locking folders of his design. **Patterns:** Sidelock folders. **Technical:** Grinds ATS-34, Dendritic 440C, PM stainless Damascus and Stellite 6K. Linerless handle shells in titanium. Belt clips in ATS-34. **Prices:** $300 to $750; some to $1,000. **Remarks:** Part-time maker; first knife sold in 1982. **Mark:** Signature and/or Celtic knot.

LAMPSON, FRANK G., 3215 E. Saddlebag Circle, P.O. Box 607, Rimrock, AZ 86335/520-567-7395; FAX: 520-567-7395
Specialties: Working folders; one-of-a-kinds. **Patterns:** Folders, hunters, utility knives, fillet knives and Bowies. **Technical:** Grinds ATS-34, 440C and 154CM. **Prices:** $100 to $750; some to $3,500. **Remarks:** Full-time maker; first knife sold in 1971. **Mark:** Name in fish logo.

LANCASTER, C.G., P.O. Box 26, Sasolburg, Free State, SOUTH AFRICA/016-762949
Specialties: High-tech working and using knives of his design and to customer specs. **Patterns:** Hunters, locking folders and utility/camp knives. **Technical:** Grinds Sandvik 12C27, 440C and D2. Offers anodized titanium bolsters. **Prices:** $450 to $750; some to $1,500. **Remarks:** Part-time maker; first knife sold in 1990. **Mark:** Etched logo.

LANCE, BILL, P.O. Box 4427, Eagle River, AK 99577/907-694-1487
Specialties: Ooloos and working straight knives; limited issue sets. **Patterns:** Several ooloo patterns, drop-point skinners. **Technical:** Uses ATS-34, Vascomax 350; ivory, horn and high-class wood handles. **Prices:** $85 to $300; art sets to $3,000. **Remarks:** First knife sold in 1981. **Mark:** Last name over a lance.

LANDERS, JOHN, 758 Welcome Rd., Newnan, GA 30263/404-253-5719
Specialties: High-art working straight knives and folders of his design. **Patterns:** Hunters, fighters and slip-joint folders. **Technical:** Grinds 440C, ATS-34, 154CM and commercial Damascus. **Prices:** $85 to $250; some to $500. **Remarks:** Part-time maker; first knife sold in 1989. **Mark:** Last name.

LANDRUM, LEONARD "LEN," 979 Gumpond-Beall Rd., Lumberton, MS 39455/601-796-4380
Specialties: Traditional working and using straight knives of his design and to customer specs. **Patterns:** Boots, Bowies, daggers, fighters, hunters, kitchen knives and utility/camp knives. **Technical:** Forges 52100, 5160 and pattern-welded steel; heat-treats. **Prices:** $100 to $500; some to $1,000. **Remarks:** Part-time maker; first knife sold in 1987. **Mark:** Handmade by Landrum.

LANE, BEN, 4802 Massie St., North Little Rock, AR 72218/501-753-8238
Specialties: Fancy straight knives of his design and to customer specs; period pieces. **Patterns:** Bowies, hunters, utility/camp knives. **Technical:** Grinds D2 and 154CM; forges and grinds 1095. Offers intricate handle work including inlays and spacers. **Prices:** $120 to $450; some to $5,000. **Remarks:** Part-time maker; first knife sold in 1989. **Mark:** Full name, city, state.

LANG, KURT, 4908 S. Wildwood Dr., McHenry, IL 60050/708-516-4649
Specialties: High-art working knives. **Patterns:** Bowies, utilitarian-type knives with rough finishes. **Technical:** Forges welded steel in European and Japanese styles. **Prices:** Moderate to upscale. **Remarks:** Part-time maker. **Mark:** "Crazy Eye" logo.

LANGE, DONALD G., Rt. 1, Box 66, Pelican Rapids, MN 56572
Specialties: High-quality Damascus hunters; welcomes customer designs. **Patterns:** Hunters, fighters and Bowies. **Technical:** Forges 5160, W2, L6 and his own Damascus. **Prices:** Moderate. **Remarks:** Full-time maker; first knife sold in 1969. **Mark:** Last name, M.S.

LANGLEY, GENE H., 1022 N. Price Rd., Florence, SC 29506/803-669-3150
Specialties: Working knives in standard patterns. **Patterns:** Hunters, boots, fighters, locking folders and slip-joints. **Technical:** Grinds 440C, 154CM and ATS-34. **Prices:** $125 to $450; some to $1000. **Remarks:** Full-time maker; first knife sold in 1979. **Mark:** Name or name, city and state.

LANGSTON, BENNIE E., 3233 Ridgecrest, Memphis, TN 38127/901-357-4559
Specialties: Traditional working straight knives and folders of his design. **Patterns:** Hunters, daggers and locking folders. **Technical:** Grinds 440C. Filework; mirror-finishes. **Prices:** $50 to $100; some to $200. **Remarks:** Part-time maker; first knife sold in 1970. **Mark:** Last name and outline of state.

LANKTON, SCOTT, 8065 Jackson Rd. R-11, Ann Arbor, MI 48103/313-426-3735
Specialties: Pattern welded swords, krisses and Viking period pieces. **Patterns:** One-of-a-kind. **Technical:** Forges W2, L6 nickel and other steels. **Prices:** $600 to $12,000. **Remarks:** Part-time bladesmith, full-time smith; first knife sold in 1976. **Mark:** Last name logo.

LAPEN, CHARLES, Box 529, W. Brookfield, MA 01585
Specialties: Fancy working straight knives. **Patterns:** camp knives, Japanese-style swords and wood working tools, hunters, Bowies and feudal European knives. **Technical:** Forges 1075, car spring and his own Damascus. Favors narrow and Japanese tangs. **Prices:** $200 to $400; some to $2,000. **Remarks:** Part-time maker; first knife sold in 1972. **Mark:** Last name.

LAPLANTE, BRETT, 110 Dove Creek, McKinney, TX 75069/972-837-4603
Specialties: Working straight knives and folders to customer specs. **Patterns:** Survival knives, Bowies, skinners, hunters. **Technical:** Grinds D2 and 440C. Heat-treats. **Prices:** $150 to $3,000. **Remarks:** Part-time maker; first knife sold in 1987. **Mark:** Last name in Canadian maple leaf logo.

LARGIN, KEN, 67 Arlington Dr., Batesville, IN 47006/812-934-5938
Specialties: Working knives in standard patterns. **Patterns:** Hunters, folders, miniatures and butterfly knives. **Technical:** Grinds 440-C, ATS-34; buys Damascus; offers filework. **Prices:** $99 to $250; some to $500. **Remarks:** Full-time maker; first knife sold in 1980. Doing business as KELGIN Knives. **Mark:** KELGIN or name.

LARRY'S KNIFE SHOP (See Mensch, Larry C.)

LARSON KNIVES (See Larson, Richard)

LARSON, RICHARD, 549 E. Hawkeye Ave., Turlock, CA 95380/209-668-1615
Specialties: Traditional working/using straight knives in standard patterns. **Patterns:** Bowies, hunters and utility/camp knives. **Technical:** Grinds ATS-34, 440C and 154CM. Engraves and scrimshaws holsters and handles. Hand-sews sheaths with tooling. **Prices:** $150 to $300; some to $1,000. **Remarks:** Part-time maker; first knife sold in 1986. Doing business as Larson Knives. **Mark:** Knife logo spelling last name.

LARY, ED, 651 Rangeline Rd., Mosinee, WI 54455/715-693-3940
Specialties: Entry level to embellished investment grade. **Patterns:** Hunters, interframe folders, fighters and one-of-a-kind. **Technical:** Grinds D2, 440C, ATS-34 and Damascus; prefers natural handle material. Does fancy filework and fabricated sheaths. **Prices:** Moderate to upscale. **Remarks:** First knife sold in 1974. **Mark:** Name in script.

LAUGHLIN, DON, 190 Laughlin Dr., Vidor, TX 77662/409-769-3390
Specialties: Straight knives and folders of his design. **Patterns:** Hunters, spring-back folders, drop points and trailing points. **Technical:** Grinds D2, 440C and 154CM; stock removal; makes his own Damascus. **Prices:** $175 to $250 for stock removal blades; $250 to $800 for Damascus blades. **Remarks:** Full-time maker; first knife sold in 1973. **Mark:** DEER or full name.

LAURENT, KERMIT, 1812 Acadia Dr., LaPlace, LA 70068/504-652-5629
Specialties: Traditional and working straight knives and folders of his design. **Patterns:** Bowies, hunters and utility knives. **Technical:** Forges his own patterned and wire Damascus and most tool steels. Specializes in altering cable patterns. Uses stabilized handle materials, especially select exotic woods. **Prices:** $100 to $500; some to $50,000. **Remarks:** Full-time maker; first knife sold in 1982. Doing business as Kermit's Knife Works. **Mark:** First name.

LAWLESS BLADES (See Lawless, Charles)

LAWLESS, CHARLES, 611 Haynes Rd. N.E., Arab, AL 35016/205-586-4862
Specialties: Classic and traditional straight knives of his design or to customer specs. **Patterns:** Bowies, fighters and hunters. **Technical:** Forges 5160, O1 and 1095. Uses tapered tangs, dovetailed bolsters and mortised handle frames. Mostly natural materials. **Prices:** $50 to $400; some to $1200. **Remarks:** Part-time maker; first knife sold in 1991. Doing business as Lawless Blades. **Mark:** Full name, bladesmith, city and state.

LAWRENCE, ALTON, 205 W. Stillwell, De Queen, AR 71832/501-642-7643
Specialties: Classic straight knives and folders to customer specs. **Patterns:** Bowies, hunters, folders and utility/camp knives. **Technical:** Forges 5160, 1095, 1084, Damascus and railroad spikes. **Prices:** Start at $100. **Remarks:** Part-time maker; first knife sold in 1988. **Mark:** Last name inside fish symbol.

LAY, L.J., 602 Mimosa Dr., Burkburnett, TX 76354/817-569-1329
Specialties: Working straight knives in standard patterns; some period pieces. **Patterns:** Drop-point hunters, Bowies and fighters. **Technical:** Grinds ATS-34 to mirror finish; likes Micarta handles. **Prices:** Moderate. **Remarks:** Full-time maker; first knife sold in 1985. **Mark:** Name or name with ram head and city.

LAY, R.J. (BOB), Box 2781, Vanderhoof, B.C. CANADA V0J 3A0/604-567-3856
Specialties: Traditional and working/using straight knives of his design. **Patterns:** Bowies, fighters and hunters. **Technical:** Grinds 440C; forges and grinds tool steels. Uses exotic handle and spacer material. File cut; prefers narrow tang. Sheaths available. **Prices:** $150 to $450; some to $1100. (Can.) **Remarks:** Full-time maker; first knife sold in 1976. Doing business as Lay's Custom Knives. **Mark:** Signature acid etched.

LAY'S CUSTOM KNIVES (See Lay, R.J.)

LAZO, ROBERT T., 11850 SW 181 St., Miami, FL 33177/305-232-1569
Specialties: Traditional working and using straight knives and folders in standard patterns. **Patterns:** Utility/camp knives, locking folders, fillet knives and some miniatures. **Technical:** Grinds 440C, ATS-34 and O1. All knives come with hand-tooled leather sheaths, some with fancy inlays. **Prices:** $90 to $250; some to $500. **Remarks:** Spare-time maker; first knife sold in 1990. **Mark:** Engraved or stamped name.

LDA/LAKELL (See C-G Tay, Larry)

LEACH, MIKE J., 5377 W. Grand Blanc Rd., Swartz Creek, MI 48473/810-655-4850
Specialties: Fancy working knives. **Patterns:** Hunters, fighters, Bowies and heavy-duty knives; slip-joint folders and integral straight patterns. **Technical:** Grinds D2, 440C and 154CM; buys Damascus. **Prices:** Start at $150. **Remarks:** Full-time maker; first knife sold in 1952. **Mark:** First initial, last name.

LEATHER BOX, THE (See Benjamin Jr., George)

LEAVITT JR., EARL F., Pleasant Cove Rd., Box 306, E. Boothbay, ME 04544/207-633-3210
Specialties: 1500-1870 working straight knives and fighters; pole arms. **Patterns:** Historically significant knives, classic/modern custom designs. **Technical:** Flat-grinds O1; heat-treats. Filework available. **Prices:** $90 to $350; some to $1,000. **Remarks:** Full-time maker; first knife sold in 1981. Doing business as Old Colony Manufactory. **Mark:** Initials in oval.

LeBATARD, PAUL M., 14700 Old River Rd., Vancleave, MS 39565/601-826-4137
Specialties: Sound working knives; lightweight folders. **Patterns:** Hunters, fillets, camp and kitchen knives, combat/survival utility knives, Bowies, toothpicks and one- and two-blade folders. **Technical:** Grinds ATS-34; forges carbon steel; machines folder frames from aircraft aluminum. **Prices:** $50 to $450. **Remarks:** Part-time maker; first knife sold in 1974. Offers knife repair, restoration and sharpening. **Mark:** Last name.

LEBER, HEINZ, Box 446, Hudson's Hope, BC VOC 1V0, CANADA/250-783-5304
Specialties: Working straight knives of his design. **Patterns:** 20 models, from capers to Bowies. **Technical:** Hollow-grinds D2 and M2 steel; mirror-finishes and full tang only. Likes moose, elk, stone sheep for handles. **Prices:** $175 to $1,000. **Remarks:** Full-time maker; first knife sold in 1975. **Mark:** Initials connected.

LeBLANC, JOHN, Rt. 2, Box 22950, Winnsboro, TX 75494/903-629-7745

LECK, DAL, Box 390, Hayden, CO 81639/303-276-3663
Specialties: Classic, traditional and working knives of his design and in standard patterns; period pieces. **Patterns:** Boots, daggers, fighters, hunters and push daggers. **Technical:** Forges O1 and 5160; makes his own Damascus. **Prices:** $175 to $700; some to $1,500. **Remarks:** Part-

time maker; first knife sold in 1990. Doing business as The Moonlight Smithy. **Mark:** Stamped initials.

LEDBETTER, RANDY R., P.O. Box 897, Payette, Idaho 83661/208-642-9833
Specialties: Fixed blade, working and art knives to customer specs. **Patterns:** Daggers, skinners, fighters, utility, Bowies, patch knives and letter openers. **Technical:** Stock removal; grinds Damascus, ATS-34, 440C, A2, planer and saw blades. **Prices:** $149 to $269. Sheaths are extra. **Remarks:** Part-time maker; first knife sold in 1991. **Mark:** Superimposed initials or first and middle initials and last name.

LEDFORD, BRACY R., 3670 N. Sherman Dr., Indianapolis, IN 46218/317-546-6176
Specialties: Art knives and fantasy knives; working knives upon request. **Patterns:** Bowies, locking folders and hunters; coil spring action folders. **Technical:** Files and sandpapers 440C by hand; other steels available upon request; likes exotic handle materials. **Prices:** Folders start at $350; fixed blades $225. **Remarks:** Full-time maker; first knife sold in 1983. **Mark:** First and middle initials, last name, city and state.

LEE, RANDY, P.O. Box 1873, St. Johns, AZ 85936/520-337-2594
Specialties: Traditional working and using straight knives of his design. **Patterns:** Bowies, fighters, hunters, daggers and professional throwing knives. **Technical:** Grinds ATS-34, 440C and D2. Offers sheaths. **Prices:** $175 to $500; some to $800. **Remarks:** Part-time maker; first knife sold in 1979. **Mark:** Full name, city, state.

LEE, TOMMY, 1180 Rd. 4, Powell, WY 82435/307-754-5404
Specialties: Working knives and period pieces. **Patterns:** Daggers, boots, fighters and folders. **Technical:** Forges and grinds 440C, ATS-34 and his own and commercial Damascus. **Prices:** $200 to $500; some to $2,000. **Remarks:** Full-time maker; first knife sold in 1974. **Mark:** Last name in capital block letters.

LEET, LARRY W., 14417 2nd Ave. S.W., Burien, WA 98166-1505
Specialties: Heavy-duty working knives. **Patterns:** Hunters, tantos, camp knives and Bowies. **Technical:** Grinds stainless steels; likes filework. **Remarks:** Full-time maker; first knife sold in 1970. **Mark:** Stylized initials.

LELAND HANDMADE KNIVES (See Leland, Steve)

LELAND, STEVE, P.O. Box 1173, Fairfax, CA 94978/415-457-0318; FAX: 415-457-0995
Specialties: Traditional and working straight knives and folders of his design and to customer specs. **Patterns:** Boots, hunters, fighters, Bowies and locking folders. **Technical:** Grinds O1, ATS-34 and 440C. **Prices:** $150 to $300; some to $750. **Remarks:** Part-time maker; first knife sold in 1987. Doing business as Leland Handmade Knives. **Mark:** Last name.

LEMAIRE, DENIS, 534 Verendrye St., Boucherville, P.Q. J4B 2Y1 CANADA

LEONE, NICK, 9 Georgetown, Pontoon Beach, IL 62040/618-797-1179
Specialties: Working straight knives and art daggers. **Patterns:** Bowies, skinners, hunters, camp/utility, fighters, daggers and primitive knives. **Technical:** Forges 5160, W2, O1, 1098, 52100 and his own Damascus and cable. **Prices:** $25 to $1000; some to $2500. **Remarks:** Full-time maker; first knife sold in 1987. Doing business as Anvil Head Forge. **Mark:** Last name or anvil head forge.

LEPORE, MICHAEL J., 66 Woodcutters Dr., Bethany, CT 06524/203-393-3823
Specialties: One-of-a-kind designs to customer specs; mostly handmade. **Patterns:** Fancy working straight knives and folders. **Technical:** Forges and grinds W2, W1 and O1; prefers natural handle materials. **Prices:** Start at $350. **Remarks:** Spare-time maker; first knife sold in 1984. **Mark:** Last name.

LERCH, MATTHEW, N88 W23462 North Lisbon Road, Sussex, WI 53089/414-246-6362
Specialties: Gentlemen's working and investment-grade folders. **Patterns:** Interframe and integral folders; lock backs, slip-joints, side locks, button locks. **Technical:** Grinds ATS-34, 1095, 440 and Damascus. Offers filework and embellished bolsters. **Prices:** $400 to $1,000; some to $2,000. **Remarks:** Part-time maker; first knife sold in 1995. **Mark:** Last name.

LETCHER, BILLY, 200 Milkyway, Fort Collins, CO 80525/970-223-9689
Specialties: Traditional working and using straight knives; fancy knives. **Patterns:** Boots, Bowies, daggers, fighters, hunters, letter openers. **Technical:** Grinds 440C, ATS-34 and D2. **Prices:** $70 to $350. **Remarks:** Part-time maker; first knife sold in 1983. **Mark:** Last name.

LEVENGOOD, BILL, 15011 Otto Rd., Tampa, FL 33624/813-961-5688
Specialties: Working straight knives and folders. **Patterns:** Hunters, Bowies, folders and collector pieces. **Technical:** Grinds ATS-34 and D2. **Prices:** $65 to $1,200. **Remarks:** Part-time maker; first knife sold in 1983. **Mark:** Last name, city, state.

LEVIN, JACK, 72-16 Bay Pkwy., Brooklyn, NY 11204/718-232-8574

LEVERETT, KEN, P.O. Box 696, Lithia, FL 33547/813-689-8578
Specialties: High-tech and working straight knives and folders of his design and to customer specs. **Patterns:** Bowies, hunters and locking folders. **Technical:** Grinds ATS-34, Damascus. **Prices:** $100 to $350; some to $1,500. **Remarks:** Part-time maker; first knife sold in 1991. **Mark:** Name, city, state.

LEVINE, BOB, 101 Westwood Dr., Tullahoma, TN 37388/615-454-9943
Specialties: Working left- and right-handed liner lock folders. **Patterns:** Hunters and folders. **Technical:** Grinds ATS-34, 440C, D2, O1 and some Damascus; hollow and some flat grinds. Uses sheephorn, fossil ivory, Micarta and exotic woods. Provides custom leather sheath with each knife. **Prices:** $105 to $500; some higher. **Remarks:** Full-time maker; first knife sold in 1984. **Mark:** Name and logo.

LEWIS, K.J., 374 Cook Rd., Lugoff, SC 29078/803-438-4343

LEWIS, MIKE, 111 W. Central Ave., Tracy, CA 95376/209-836-5753
Specialties: Traditional straight knives. **Patterns:** Swords and daggers. **Technical:** Grinds 440C, ATS-34 and 5160. Frequently uses cast bronze and cast nickel guards and pommels. **Prices:** $100 to $750. **Remarks:** Part-time maker; first knife sold in 1988. **Mark:** Dragon Steel and serial number.

LEWIS, RON, Box S-365, Edgewood, NM 87015/505-281-8343
Specialties: Classic straight knives. **Patterns:** Bowies, skinners, buckskinners, art and utility knives. **Technical:** Grinds and forges Damascus, 1084 and ATS-34. **Prices:** Start at $250. **Remarks:** Full-time maker; first knife sold in 1987. **Mark:** Logo with serial number.

LEWIS, TOM R., 1613 Standpipe Rd., Carlsbad, NM 88220/505-885-3616
Specialties: Traditional working straight knives and pocketknives. **Patterns:** Outdoor knives, hunting knives and Bowies and pocketknives. **Technical:** Grinds ATS-34 and CPM-T-440V; forges 52100. Makes wire, pattern welded and chainsaw Damascus. **Prices:** $75 to $650. **Remarks:** Part-time maker; first knife sold in 1980. Doing business as TRL Handmade Knives. **Mark:** Lewis family crest.

LICATA, STEVEN, 116 Front St., Mineola, NY 11501/516-248-8633; FAX: 914-779-4234
Specialties: Fantasy and high-art knives. **Patterns:** Daggers, fighters, axes and swords. **Technical:** Forges O1, 440C and Damascus. **Prices:** $200 to $5,000. **Remarks:** Full-time maker; first knife sold in 1989. **Mark:** Stylized initials.

LICORNE EDGED CREATIONS (See Van Schaik, Bastiaan)

LIEBENBERG, ANDRE, 8 Hilma Rd., Bordeauxrandburg 2196, SOUTH AFRICA/011-787-2303
Specialties: High-art straight knives of his design. **Patterns:** Daggers, fighters and swords. **Technical:** Grinds 440C and 12C27. **Prices:** $250 to $500; some $4,000 and higher. Giraffe bone handles with semi-precious stones. **Remarks:** Spare-time maker; first knife sold in 1990. **Mark:** Initials.

LIEGEY, KENNETH R., 132 Carney Dr., Millwood, WV 25262/304-273-9545
Specialties: Traditional working/using straight knives of his design and to customer specs. **Patterns:** Hunters, utility/camp knives, miniatures. **Technical:** Grinds 440C. **Prices:** $75 to $150; some to $300. **Remarks:** Spare-time maker; first knife sold in 1977. **Mark:** First and middle initials, last name.

LIGHTFOOT, GREG, 5502-45 Street, Lloydminster, AB T9V 0C2, CANADA/403-875-0789
Specialties: High-tech folders of his design. **Patterns:** Boots, fighters and locking folders. **Technical:** Grinds ATS-34, 440C and D2. Kydex or leather sheaths on fixed blades; titanium, G-10, Micarta and carbon fiber on folders. Offers engraving. **Prices:** $250 to $425; some to $850. **Remarks:** Full-time maker; first knife sold in 1988. Doing business as Lightfoot Knives. **Mark:** Shark with Lightfoot Knives below.

LIGHTFOOT KNIVES (See Lightfoot, Greg)

LIKARICH, STEVE, 26075 Green Acres Rd., Colfax, CA 95713/916-346-8480
Specialties: Fancy working knives; art knives of his design. **Patterns:** Hunters, fighters and art knives of his design. **Technical:** Grinds ATS-34, 154CM and 440C; likes high polishes and filework. **Prices:** $200 to $2,000; some higher. **Remarks:** Full-time maker; first knife sold in 1987. **Mark:** Name.

LILE, MARILYN (JIMMY), 2721 S. Arkansas Ave., Russellville, AR 72801/501-968-2011
Specialties: Fancy working knives. **Patterns:** Bowies, full line of straight knives, button-lock folders. **Technical:** Grinds D2 and 440C. **Prices:** $125 to $800; some higher. **Remarks:** Full-time maker; first knife sold in 1944. Creator of the original *First Blood* and *Rambo* survival knives. **Mark:** Last name with a dot between the I and L.

LINCOLN, JAMES, 5359 Blue Ridge Pkwy., Bartlett, TN 38134/901-372-5577
Specialties: Fancy and embellished automatics with unusual/hidden releases, in standard patterns. **Patterns:** Locking folders and automatics. **Technical:** Grinds ATS-34, CM154 and 440C. Filework on most knives. Most blades and bolsters hand-finished and polished. Prefers pearl and ivory for handle material, occasionally uses precious stones and gold. Offers engraving. **Prices:** $350 to $500; some to $950. **Remarks:** Part-time maker; first knife sold in 1994. Doing business as JBL Knives. **Mark:** Handmade by J.B. Lincoln.

LINDSAY, CHRIS A., 1324 N.E. Locksley Dr., Bend, OR 97701/541-389-3875
Specialties: Working knives in standard patterns. **Patterns:** Hunters and camp knives. **Technical:** Hollow- and flat-grinds 440C and ATS-34; offers brushed finishes, tapered tangs. **Prices:** $75 to $160; knife kits $60 to $80. **Remarks:** Part-time maker; first knife sold in 1980. **Mark:** Last name, town and state in oval.

LINKLATER, STEVE, 8 Cossar Drive, Aurora, Ontario, L4G3N8 CANADA/905-727-8929
Specialties: Traditional working/using straight knives and folders of his design. **Patterns:** Fighters, hunters and locking folders. **Technical:** Grinds ATS-34, 440V and D2. **Prices:** $125 to $350; some to $600. **Remarks:** Part-time maker; first knife sold in 1987. Doing business as Links Knives. **Mark:** LINKS, year and Ontario, Canada.

LINKS KNIVES (See Linklater, Steve)

LISTER JR., WELDON E., 9140 Sailfish Dr., Boerne, TX 78006/210-981-2210
Specialties: One-of-a-kind fancy and embellished folders. **Patterns:** Locking and slip-joint folders. **Technical:** Commercial Damascus and O1. All knives embellished. Engraves, inlays, carves and scrimshaws. **Prices:** Upscale. **Remarks:** Spare-time maker; first knife sold in 1991. **Mark:** Last name.

LITTLE, GARY M., HC84 Box 10301, P.O. Box 156, Broadbent, OR 97414/503-572-2656
Specialties: Fancy working knives. **Patterns:** Hunters, tantos, Bowies, axes and buckskinners; locking folders and interframes. **Technical:** Forges and grinds O1, L6, 1095; makes his own Damascus; bronze fittings. **Prices:** $85 to $300; some to $2,500. **Remarks:** Full-time maker; first knife sold in 1979. Doing business as Conklin Meadows Forge. **Mark:** Name, city and state.

LITTLE, JIMMY L., P.O. Box 871652, Wasilla, AK 99687/907-373-7831
Specialties: Working straight knives; fancy period pieces. **Patterns:** Bowies, bush swords and camp knives. **Technical:** Grinds 440C, 154CM and ATS-34. **Prices:** $100 to $1,000. **Remarks:** Full-time maker; first knife sold in 1984. **Mark:** First and middle initials, last name.

LIVELY, MARIAN (See Lively, Tim and Marian)

LIVELY, TIM AND MARIAN, P.O. Box 8784 CRB, Tucson, AZ 85738
Specialties: Multi-cultural primitive knives of their design on speculation. **Patterns:** Neo-tribal one-of-a-kinds. **Technical:** Hand forges using ancient techniques; hammer finish. **Prices:** Moderate. **Remarks:** Full-time makers; first knife sold in 1974. **Mark:** Last name with broken arrow.

LIVINGSTON, ROBERT C., P.O. Box 6, Murphy, NC 28906/704-837-4155
Specialties: Art letter openers to working straight knives. **Patterns:** Minis to machetes. **Technical:** Forges and grinds most steels. **Prices:** Start at $20. **Remarks:** Full-time maker; first knife sold in 1988. Doing business as Mystik Knifeworks. **Mark:** MYSTIK.

LOCKETT, LOWELL C., 116 South Mill Creek Ct., Woodstock, GA 30188/770-926-2998
Specialties: Traditional and working/using knives. **Patterns:** Bowies, hunters and utility/camp knives. **Technical:** Forges 5160, 1098, L6 and high-carbon. Makes his own guards; sewn or riveted sheaths. **Prices:** Start at $100. **Remarks:** Full-time maker; first knife sold in 1994. Doing business as Fire Forged Knives. **Mark:** Script initials.

LOCKETT, STERLING, 527 E. Amherst Dr., Burbank, CA 91504/818-846-5799
Specialties: Working straight knives and folders to customer specs. **Patterns:** Hunters and fighters. **Technical:** Grinds. **Prices:** Moderate. **Remarks:** Spare-time maker. **Mark:** Name, city with hearts.

LOERCHNER, WOLFGANG, P.O. Box 255, Bayfield, Ont. N0M 1G0, CANADA/519-565-2196
Specialties: Traditional straight knives, mostly ornate. **Patterns:** Small swords, daggers and stilettos; locking folders and miniatures. **Technical:** Grinds D2, 440C and 154CM; all knives hand-filed and flat-ground. **Prices:** $300 to $5,000; some to $10,000. **Remarks:** Part-time maker; first knife sold in 1983. Doing business as Wolfe Fine Knives. **Mark:** WOLFE.

LOFLIN, BOB, San Jose, Costa Rica; c/o Levi Strauss, 5979 N. West 151st St., Miami Lakes, FL 33014/011-506-799155
Specialties: Fancy working knives of his design. **Patterns:** Hunters, fighters and camp knives; locking folders. **Technical:** Grinds D2, 440C and ATS-34. **Prices:** $75 to $250; some to $700. **Remarks:** Part-time maker; first knife sold in 1983. **Mark:** Name.

LONE STAR CUSTOM KNIVES (See Richardson Jr., Percy)

LONESOME PINE KNIVES (See Harley, Larry W.)

LONEWOLF, J. AGUIRRE, Rt. 1 Box 1322A, Demorest, GA 30535/706-754-4660; FAX: 706-754-8470; WEB: http://www.cyberhighway.net/~lonewolf/
Specialties: High-art working and using straight knives of his design. **Patterns:** Bowies, hunters, utility/camp knives and fint steel blades. **Technical:** Forges Damascus and high-carbon steel. Most knives have hand-carved moose antler handles. **Prices:** $55 to $500; some to $2,000. **Remarks:** Full-time maker; first knife sold in 1980. Doing business as Lonewolf Trading Post. **Mark:** Stamp.

LONEWOLF TRADING POST (See Lonewolf, J. Aguirre)

LONG, GLENN A., 3601 Catalina, Palm Beach Gardens, FL 33410/561-622-1553
Specialties: Classic working and using straight knives of his design and to customer specs. **Patterns:** Hunters, Bowies, utility/camp knives and miniatures. **Technical:** Grinds ATS-34, 440C, D2 and 440V. **Prices:** $85 to $300; some to $800. **Remarks:** Part-time maker; first knife sold in 1990. **Mark:** Last name inside diamond.

LONGHORN KNIFE WORKS (See Hagwood, Kellie)

LONGWORTH, DAVE, 1811 SR 774, Hamersville, OH 45130/513-876-3637
Specialties: High-tech working knives. **Patterns:** Locking folders, hunters, fighters and elaborate daggers. **Technical:** Grinds O1, ATS-34, 440C; buys Damascus. **Prices:** $125 to $600; some higher. **Remarks:** Part-time maker; first knife sold in 1980. **Mark:** Last name.

LOOS, HENRY C., 210 Ingraham., New Hyde Park, NY 11040/516-354-1943

Specialties: Miniature fancy knives and period pieces of his design. **Patterns:** Bowies, daggers, swords and lockbacks. **Technical:** Grinds O1 and 440C. Uses sterling, 18K, rubies and emeralds. All knives come with handmade hardwood cases. **Prices:** $90 to $195; some to $250. **Remarks:** Spare-time maker; first knife sold in 1990. **Mark:** Script last initial.

LORD (See Sontheimer, G. Douglas)

LORO, GENE, summer: 2457 St. Rt. 93NE, Crooksville, OH 43731/614-982-4521; winter: 13745 Summerstar, Sun City W., AZ 85375/602-584-2461

LOVE, ED, 11146 Vance Jackson, #4003, San Antonio, TX 78230/210-691-1090
Specialties: Fancy working knives in standard patterns or to customer specs. **Patterns:** Hunters, Bowies and and one-of-a-kinds. **Technical:** Grinds ATS-34. **Prices:** $90 to $190; some to $500. **Remarks:** Part-time maker; first knife sold in 1980. **Mark:** Name in weeping heart.

LOVELESS, R.W., P.O. Box 7836, Riverside, CA 92503/909-689-7800
Specialties: Working knives, fighters and hunters of his design. **Patterns:** Contemporary hunters, fighters and boots. **Technical:** Grinds 154CM and ATS-34. **Prices:** $850 to $4950. **Remarks:** Full-time maker since 1969. **Mark:** Name in logo.

LOVESTRAND, SCHUYLER, 206 Bent Oak Cir., Harvest, AL 35749/205-430-0828
Specialties: Fancy working straight knives of his design and to customer specs; unusual fossil ivories. **Patterns:** Hunters, fighters, Bowies and fishing knives. **Technical:** Grinds ATS-34. **Prices:** $150 to $1,095; some higher. **Remarks:** Part-time maker; first knife sold in 1982. **Mark:** Name in logo.

LOZIER, DON, 5394 SE 168th Ave., Ocklawaha, FL 32179/352-625-3576
Specialties: Fancy and working straight knives of his design and in standard patterns. **Patterns:** Daggers, fighters, boot knives, and hunters. **Technical:** Grinds ATS-34 and Damascus. Most knives fileworked, custom pinned, exhibition grade handle materials. Handcarves and handsews all sheaths. **Prices:** Start at $250; some to $8,500. **Remarks:** Full-time maker. **Mark:** Name.

LUBRICH, MARK, P.O. Box 122, Matthews, NC 28106-0122/704-567-7692
Specialties: Traditional working and using straight knives of his design and to customer specs. **Patterns:** Hunters and utility/camp knives. Some woodcarving sets. **Technical:** Forges O1, 5160 and 1095; using some cable; forges 440C stainless, brass and silver inlaid handles. Differentially heat-treats; makes sheaths; hardwood/stag or leather/stag handles. **Prices:** $75 to $225; some to $500. **Remarks:** Part-time maker; first knife sold in 1980. Doing business as Handmade Knives by Mark Lubrich. **Mark:** Etched last name on stock removal; stamped logo on forged blades.

LUCHAK, BOB, 15705 Woodforest Blvd., Channelview, TX 77530/713-452-1779
Specialties: Presentation knives; start of The Survivor series. **Patterns:** Skinners, Bowies, camp axes, steak knife sets and fillet knives. **Technical:** Grinds 440C. Offers electronic etching; filework. **Prices:** $50 to $1,500. **Remarks:** Full-time maker; first knife sold in 1983. Doing business as Teddybear Knives. **Mark:** Full name, city and state with Teddybear logo.

LUCIE, JAMES R., 4191 E. Fruitport Rd., Fruitport, MI 49415/616-865-6390; FAX: 616-865-3170
Specialties: Hand-forges William Scagel-style knives. **Patterns:** Authentic Scagel-style knives and miniatures. **Technical:** Forges 5160. **Prices:** Start at $550. **Remarks:** Full-time maker; first knife sold in 1975. **Mark:** Scagel Kris with maker's name and address.

LUCK, GREGORY, 74-5602 Alapa St., #428, Kailua-Kona, HI 96740
Specialties: Forged straight knives. **Patterns:** Bowies, fighters, buckskinners and other working straight knives. **Technical:** Forges carbon steel and own cable Damascus; differential tempers; makes distinctive sheaths. **Prices:** $75 to $400; some higher. **Remarks:** Spare-time maker; first knife sold in 1988. **Mark:** Three runes or last name and dragon-knot logo.

LUCKETT, BILL, 108 Amantes Ln., Weatherford, TX 76088/817-613-9412
Specialties: Uniquely patterned robust straight knives. **Patterns:** Fighters, Bowies, hunters. **Technical:** Grinds 440C and commercial Damascus; makes heavy knives with deep grinding. **Prices:** $275 to $1,000; some to $2,000. **Remarks:** Part-time maker; first knife sold in 1975. **Mark:** Last name over Bowie logo.

LUDWIG, RICHARD O., 57-63 65 St., Maspeth, NY 11378
Specialties: Traditional working/using knives. **Patterns:** Boots, hunters and utility/camp knives. **Technical:** Grinds 440C, ATS-34 and 154CM. File work on guards and handles; silver spacers. Offers scrimshaw. **Prices:** $240 to $400; some to $600. **Remarks:** Full-time maker. **Mark:** Stamped first initial, last name, state.

LUI, RONALD M., 4042 Harding Ave., Honolulu, HI 96816/808-734-7746
Specialties: Working straight knives and folders in standard patterns. **Patterns:** Hunters, boots and liner locks. **Technical:** Grinds 440C and ATS-34. **Prices:** $100 to $700. **Remarks:** Spare-time maker; first knife sold in 1988. **Mark:** Initials connected.

LUM, ROBERT W., 901 Travis Ave., Eugene, OR 97404/503-688-2737
Specialties: High-art working knives of his design. **Patterns:** Hunters, fighters, tantos and folders. **Technical:** Grinds 440C, 154CM and ATS-34; plans to forge soon. **Prices:** $175 to $500; some to $800. **Remarks:** Full-time maker; first knife sold in 1976. **Mark:** Chop with last name underneath.

LUNDSTROM, JAN-AKE, Mastmostigen 8, 66010 Dals-Langed, SWEDEN/0531-41259
Specialties: Viking swords, axes and knives in cooperation with handlemakers. **Patterns:** All traditional styles, especially swords and inlaid blades. **Technical:** Forges his own Damascus and laminated steel. **Prices:** $200 to $1,000. **Remarks:** Full-time maker; first knife sold in 1985; collaborates with museums. **Mark:** Runic.

LUNN, LARRY A., 3432 State Route 580, #312, Safety Harbor, FL 34695/813-796-2386
Specialties: Art knives of his design, collector folders and straight knives. **Patterns:** Folders, straight knives and swords. **Technical:** Grinds stainless steel and forges own Damascus; makes own mokume. Offers filework; uses exotic handle materials. **Prices:** Start at $300. **Remarks:** Part-time maker; first knife sold in 1989. **Mark:** Name in script and small samurai helmet in a circle.

LUTES, ROBERT, 24878 U.S. #6 East (RR 1), Nappanee, IN 46550/219-773-4773
Specialties: Straight working knives of his design or to standard patterns. **Patterns:** Hunters, fighters, boots and axes. **Technical:** Grinds 440C and commercial Damascus. **Prices:** $50 to $1,500. **Remarks:** Full-time maker; first knife sold in 1980. **Mark:** Last name.

LUTZ, GREG, 149 Effie Dr., Greenwood, SC 29649/803-229-7340
Specialties: Working and using knives and period pieces of his design and to customer specs. **Patterns:** Fighters, hunters and swords. **Technical:** Forges 1095 and O1; grinds ATS-34. Differentially heat-treats forged blades; uses cryogenic treatment on ATS-34. **Prices:** $50 to $350; some to $1,200. **Remarks:** Full-time maker; first knife sold in 1986. Doing business as Scorpion Forge. **Mark:** First initial, last name.

LYLE III, ERNEST L., 4501 Meadowbrook Ave., Orlando, FL 32808/407-299-7227
Specialties: Fancy period pieces; one-of-a-kind and limited editions. **Patterns:** Arabian/Persian influenced fighters, military knives, Bowies and Roman short swords; several styles of hunters. **Technical:** Grinds 440C, D2 and 154CM. Engraves. **Prices:** Upscale. **Remarks:** Full-time maker; first knife sold in 1972. Doesn't accept orders. **Mark:** Last name in capital letters.

LYONS DEN, THE (See Lyons, Randy)

LYONS, RANDY, Rt. 3 Box 677A, Lumberton, TX 77656/409-755-3860
Specialties: Working straight knives and folders. **Patterns:** Bowies, hunters, locking folders and utility/camp knives. **Technical:** Grinds ATS-34, 440C and D2. **Prices:** $60 to $300; some to $600. **Remarks:** Full-time maker; first knife sold in 1989. Doing business as The Lyons Den. **Mark:** First and middle initials, last name, city and state.

LYTTLE, BRIAN, Box 5697, High River, AB T1V 1M7, CANADA/403-558-3638
Specialties: Fancy working straight knives and folders; art knives. **Patterns:** Hunters, Bowies, daggers, stilettos, fighters and miniatures. **Technical:** Forges his own Damascus, cable and motorcycle chain; offers scrimshaw and forged jewelry to Damascus bits and spurs. **Prices:** $350 to $800; some to $5,000. **Remarks:** Full-time maker; first knife sold in 1983. **Mark:** Last name, country.

m

MAC THE KNIFE (See MacDonald, John)

MacBAIN, KENNETH C., 30 Briarwood Ave., Norwood, NJ 07648/201-768-0652
Specialties: Fantasy straight knives and folders, some high-tech. **Patterns:** Swords, knife-rings, push daggers and some miniatures. **Technical:** Forges and grinds A2, W2 and O1. **Prices:** $200 to $500; some to $2,500. **Remarks:** Part-time maker; first knife sold in 1986. **Mark:** Initials.

MacDONALD, JOHN, 9 David Drive, Raymond, NH 03077/603-895-0918
Specialties: Working/using straight knives of his design and to customer specs. **Patterns:** Bowies, hunters and swords. **Technical:** Grinds O1, L6 and ATS-34. Swords have matching handles and scabbards with Japanese flair. **Prices:** $70 to $250; some to $500. **Remarks:** Part-time maker; first knife sold in 1988. Doing business as Mac the Knife. **Mark:** Initials.

MACKRILL, STEPHEN, P.O. Box 1580, Pinegowrie 2123, Johannesburg, SOUTH AFRICA/27-11-886-2893; FAX: 27-11-334-3729
Specialties: Fancy and working knives. **Patterns:** Fighters, hunters and utility/camp knives. **Technical:** N690, K110, 12C27. Silver and gold inlay on handles; wooden sheaths. **Prices:** $98 to $700; some to $1,800. **Remarks:** Full-time maker; first knife sold in 1978. **Mark:** First initial, last name.

MADISON II, BILLY D., 2295 Tyler Rd., Remlap, AL 35133/205-680-6722
Specialties: Traditional working and using straight knives and folders of his design. **Patterns:** Hunters, locking folders and utility/camp knives. **Technical:** Grinds 440C and ATS-34; forges 52100. Grinds and hand-sands to 1500 grit for mirror finish. Prefers natural handle material. Offers carving and sheaths. **Prices:** $100 to $400; some to $1000. **Remarks:** Part-time maker; first knife sold in 1978. Doing business as Madison Knives. **Mark:** Name and year.

MADSEN, JACK, 3311 Northwest Dr., Wichita Falls, TX 76305/817-322-4112
Specialties: Working straight knives in standard patterns. **Patterns:** Bowies, hunters, swords, tomahawks and heavy-duty camp knives. **Technical:** Forges W2, O1 and his own Damascus. **Prices:** $85 to $350; some to $1,000. **Remarks:** Full-time maker; first knife sold in 1975. **Mark:** Name and city.

MAESTRI BROS. (See Maestri, Peter A.)

MAESTRI, PETER A., S11251 Fairview Rd., Spring Green, WI 53588/608-546-4481
Specialties: Working straight knives in standard patterns. **Patterns:** Camp and fishing knives, utility green-river styled. **Technical:** Grinds 440C, 154CM and 440A. **Prices:** $15 to $45; some to $150. **Remarks:** Full-time maker; first knife sold in 1981. Provides professional cutler service to professional cutters. **Mark:** CARISOLO, MAESTRI BROS., or signature.

MAGNUS DESIGN STUDIO (See Jensen, John Lewis).

MAIENKNECHT, STANLEY, 38648 S.R. 800, Sardis, OH 43946

MAISEY, ALAN, P.O. Box 316, Toongabbie 2146, AUSTRALIA/Sydney 636-2183
Specialties: Daggers, especially krisses; period pieces. **Technical:** Offers knives and finished blades in Damascus and nickel Damascus. **Prices:** $75 to $2,000; some higher. **Remarks:** Part-time maker; provides complete restoration service for krisses. Trained by a Javanese kris smith. **Mark:** None, triangle in a box, or three peaks.

MALLOY, JOE, P.O. Box 156, 1039 Schwabe St., Freeland, PA 18224/717-636-2781
Specialties: Working knives; customer designs welcome. **Patterns:** Hunters, utility/camp knives, fighters Bowies, tantos and folders. **Technical:** Grinds 154CM, 440C, D2 and A2. **Prices:** $100 to $800. **Remarks:** Part-time maker; first knife sold in 1982. **Mark:** First and middle initials, last name, city and state.

MANABE, MICHAEL K., 3659 Tomahawk Lane, San Diego, CA 92117/619-483-2416
Specialties: Classic and high-art straight knives of his design or to customer specs. **Patterns:** Bowies, fighters, hunters, utility/camp knives; all knives one-of-a-kind. **Technical:** Forges and grinds 52100, 5160 amd 1095. Does multiple quenching for distinctive temper lines. Each blade triple-tempered. **Prices:** Start at $200. **Remarks:** Part-time maker; first knife sold in 1994. **Mark:** First and middle initials, last name and J.S. on other side.

MANEKER, KENNETH, RR 2, Galiano Island, B.C. V0N 1P0, CANADA/604-539-2084
Specialties: Working straight knives; period pieces. **Patterns:** Camp knives and hunters; French chef knives. **Technical:** Grinds 440C, 154CM and Vascowear. **Prices:** $50 to $200; some to $300. **Remarks:** Part-time maker; first knife sold in 1981. Doing business as Water Mountain Knives. **Mark:** Japanese Kanji of initials, plus glyph.

MARAGNI, DAN, R.D. 1, Box 106, Georgetown, NY 13072/315-662-7490
Specialties: Heavy-duty working knives, some investor class. **Patterns:** Hunters, fighters and camp knives, some Scottish types. **Technical:** Forges W2 and his own Damascus; toughness and edge-holding a high priority. **Prices:** $125 to $500; some to $1,000. **Remarks:** Full-time maker; first knife sold in 1975. **Mark:** Celtic initials in circle.

MARKLEY, KEN, 7651 Cabin Creek Lane, Sparta, IL 62286/618-443-5284
Specialties: Traditional working and using knives of his design and to customer specs. **Patterns:** Fighters, hunters and utility/camp knives. **Technical:** Forges 5160, 1095 and L6; makes his own Damascus; does filework. **Prices:** $150 to $800; some to $2,000. **Remarks:** Part-time maker; first knife sold in 1991. Doing business as Cabin Creek Forge. **Mark:** Last name, JS.

MARKS, CHRIS, 1061 Sherwood Dr., Breaux Bridge, LA 70517/318-332-3930
Specialties: Traditional straight knives of his design; period pieces. **Patterns:** Bowies, hunters and utility/camp knives. **Technical:** Forges W2, 5160 and his own Damascus. **Prices:** NA. **Mark:** Name in anvil logo and Master Smith, ABS.

MARLOWE, DONALD, 2554 Oakland Rd., Dover, PA 17315/717-764-6055
Specialties: Working straight knives in standard patterns. **Patterns:** Bowies, fighters, boots and utility knives. **Technical:** Grinds D2 and 440C. **Prices:** $120 to $525. **Remarks:** Spare-time maker; first knife sold in 1977. **Mark:** Last name.

MARSHALL, GLENN, P.O. Box 1099 (305 Hofmann St.), Mason, TX 76856/915-347-6207
Specialties: Working knives and period pieces. **Patterns:** Straight and folding hunters, fighters and camp knives. **Technical:** Forges and grinds O1, D2 and 440C. **Prices:** $90 to $150; some to $450. **Remarks:** Full-time maker; first knife sold in 1932. **Mark:** First initial, last name, city and state with anvil logo.

MARTIN, BRUCE E., Rt. 6, Box 164-B, Prescott, AR 71857/501-887-2023
Specialties: Fancy working straight knives of his design. **Patterns:** Bowies, camp knives, skinners and fighters. **Technical:** Forges 5160, 1095 and his own Damascus. Uses natural handle materials; filework available. **Prices:** $75 to $350; some to $500. **Remarks:** Full-time maker; first knife sold in 1979. **Mark:** Name in arch.

MARTIN CUSTOM KNIVES, JIM (See Martin, Jim)

MARTIN CUSTOM PRODUCTS (See Martin, Peter)

MARTIN, GENE, P.O. Box 396, Williams, OR 97544/541-846-6755
Specialties: Straight knives and folders. **Patterns:** Fighters, hunters, skinners, boot knives, spring back and lock back folders. **Technical:** Grinds ATS-34, 440C, Damascus and 154CM. Forges 5160; makes own Damascus; scrimshaws. **Prices:** Start at $100. **Remarks:** Full-time maker; first knife sold in 1993. Doing business as Provision Forge. **Mark:** Name and/or crossed staff and sword.

MARTIN, JIM, 1120 S. Cadiz Ct., Oxnard, CA 93035/805-985-9849
Specialties: Fancy and working/using folders of his design. **Patterns:** Automatics, locking folders and miniatures. **Technical:** Grinds 440C, AEB-L, 304SS and Damascus. **Prices:** $350 to $700; some to $1500. **Remarks:** Full-time maker; first knife sold in 1992. Doing business as Jim Martin Custom Knives.

MARTIN KNIVES, MICHAEL W. (See Martin, Michael W.)

MARTIN, MICHAEL W., Box 572, Jefferson St., Beckville, TX 75631/903-678-2161
Specialties: Classic working/using straight knives of his design and in standard patterns. **Patterns:** Hunters. **Technical:** Grinds ATS-34, 440C, O1 and A2. Bead blasted, Parkerized, high polish and satin finishes. Sheaths are handmade. **Prices:** $145 to $230. **Remarks:** Part-time maker; first knife sold in 1995. Doing business as Michael W. Martin Knives. **Mark:** Name and city, state in arch.

MARTIN, PETER, 28220 N. Lake Dr., Waterford, WI 53185/414-662-3629
Specialties: Fancy, fantasy and working straight knives and folders of his design and in standard patterns. **Patterns:** Bowies, fighters, hunters, locking folders and liner locks. **Technical:** Grinds ATS-34, 440C, A2 and D2; forges 1095, 5160, W1, 4340 and his own Damascus. Prefers natural handle material; offers filework and carved handles. **Prices:** $100 to $500; some to $2000. **Remarks:** Part-time maker; first knife sold in 1988. Doing business as Martin Custom Products. **Mark:** Martin Knives, city and state.

MARTIN, RANDALL J., 1477 Country Club Rd., Middletown, CT 06457/860-347-1161
Specialties: High-performance using knives. **Patterns:** Neck knives, tactical liner locks, survival, utility and Japanese knives. **Technical:** Grinds BG42, CPMM4, D2 and A2; aerospace composite materials; carbon fiber sheaths. **Prices:** Start at $150. **Remarks:** Part-time maker; first knife sold in 1976. Doing business as Martinsite Knives. **Mark:** First and middle initials, last name.

MARTIN, ROBB, 7 Victoria St., Elmira Ontario N3B 1R9, CANADA

MARTINSITE KNIVES (See Martin, Randall J.)

MARTRILDONNO, PAUL, 140 Debary Dr., Debary, FL 32713-3460
Specialties: One-of-a-kind fantasy knives. **Patterns:** "Knifelace"—necklace with push dagger, knuckle knives, fantasy tantos, etc. **Technical:** Grinds 440C and 154CM. Reforges commercial Damascus. **Prices:** $400 to $1,500; some to $5,000. **Remarks:** Full-time maker; first knife sold in 1982. **Mark:** PAULIE, or signature.

MARZITELLI, PETER, 19929 35A Ave., Langley, BC V3A 2R1, CANADA/604-532-8899
Specialties: Specializes in natural handle materials; bone, antler, prehistoric ivory, gemstones and shells. **Patterns:** Daggers, Bowies, tantos, hunters, folders and art knives. **Technical:** Grinds ATS-34, 440C, D2 and 12C27. **Prices:** $100 to $1,000. **Remarks:** Full-time maker; first knife sold in 1984. **Mark:** "Marz."

MASON, BILL, 1114 St. Louis, #33, Excelsior Springs, MO 64024/816-637-7335
Specialties: Combat knives; some folders. **Patterns:** Fighters to match knife types in book *Cold Steel.* **Technical:** Grinds O1, 440C and ATS-34. **Prices:** $115 to $250; some to $350. **Remarks:** Spare-time maker; first knife sold in 1979. **Mark:** Initials connected.

MASSEY, AL, Box 14, Site 15, RR#2, Mount Uniacke, Nova Scotia, B0N 1Z0 CANADA

MASSEY, ROGER, RR 19, Box 3300, Texarkana, AR 71854/870-779-1018
Specialties: Traditional and working straight knives and folders of his design and to customer specs. **Patterns:** Bowies, hunters, daggers and utility knives. **Technical:** Forges carbon steels and his own Damascus. Offers filework and silver wire inlay in handles. **Prices:** $150 to $500; some to $2,000. **Remarks:** Part-time maker; first knife sold in 1991. **Mark:** Last name, M.S.

MASTER DON KNIVES (See Miller, Don)

MATHERTON FORGE (See Cashen, Kevin R.)

MATTIS, JAMES K., 500 N. Central Ave., Suite 740, Glendale, CA 91203/818-247-3400, 818-353-4734; FAX: 818-353-7873; E-MAIL: jkmtsm@earthlink.net; WEB:http://home.earthlink.net/~jkmtsm/
Specialties: Working straight knives in standard patterns. **Patterns:** Hunters, kitchen knives and small utility or specialty patterns. **Technical:** Offers ATS-34, 440C and carbon; hand-rubbed finishes, hardwood and Micarta handles; mosaic pins. **Prices:** $75 to $250. **Remarks:** Spare-time maker; first knife sold in 1990. Usually uses blades by Bob Engnath. **Mark:** Last name plus Hebrew word for "life."

MAXFIELD, LYNN, 382 Colonial Ave., Layton, UT 84041/801-544-4176
Specialties: Sporting knives, some fancy. **Patterns:** Hunters, survival and fishing knives; some locking folders. **Technical:** Grinds 440C, ATS-34, 154CM, D2, 440V and Damascus. **Prices:** $125 to $400; some to $900. **Remarks:** Part-time maker; first knife sold in 1979. **Mark:** Name, city and state.

MAXWELL, DON, 3164 N. Marks, Suite 122, Fresno, CA 93722/209-497-8441
Specialties: Fancy working and using straight knives of his design. **Patterns:** Hunters, fighters, utility/camp knives, liner lock folders and fantasy knives. **Technical:** Grinds 440C, ATS-34, D2 and commercial Damascus. **Prices:** $100 to $500; some to $2,000. **Remarks:** Full-time maker; first knife sold in 1987. **Mark:** Last name, city, state.

MAY, JAMES E., 6513 State Rd. T., Auxvasse, MO 65231/573-386-2910
Specialties: Working straight knives of his design. **Patterns:** Hunters, Bowies, fighters, camp knives, boots and folders. **Technical:** Mosaic and pattern welded Damascus. **Prices:** $65 to $350; some to $450. **Remarks:** Full-time maker; first knife sold in 1978. Doing business as J.E.M. Knives. **Mark:** First initial in diamond.

MAYNARD, LARRY JOE, P.O. Box 493, Crab Orchard, WV 25827
Specialties: Fancy and fantasy straight knives. **Patterns:** Big knives; a Bowie with a full false edge; fighting knives. **Technical:** Grinds standard steels. **Prices:** $350 to $500; some to $1,000. **Remarks:** Full-time maker; first knife sold in 1986. **Mark:** Middle and last initials.

MAYNARD, WILLIAM N., 2677 John Smith Rd., Fayetteville, NC 28306/910-425-1615
Specialties: Traditional and working straight knives of all designs. **Patterns:** Bowies, fighters, hunters and utility knives. **Technical:** Grinds 440C, ATS-34 and commercial Damascus. Offers fancy filework; handmade sheaths. **Prices:** $100 to $300; some to $500. **Remarks:** Part-time maker; first knife sold in 1988. **Mark:** Last name.

MAYO JR., TOM, 67-420 Alahaka St., Waialua, HI 96791/808-637-6560
Specialties: Presentation grade working knives. **Patterns:** Combat knives, hunters, Bowies and folders. **Technical:** Uses ATS-34 and 440V. 440C, D2 and Stellite upon request. **Prices:** Start at $150. **Remarks:** Part-time maker; first knife sold in 1983. **Mark:** Volcano logo with name and state.

MAYVILLE, OSCAR L., 2130 E. County Rd. 910S., Marengo, IN 47140/812-338-3103
Specialties: Working straight knives; period pieces. **Patterns:** Kitchen cutlery, Bowies, camp knives and hunters. **Technical:** Grinds A2, O1 and 440C. **Prices:** $50 to $350; some to $500. **Remarks:** Full-time maker; first knife sold in 1984. **Mark:** Initials over knife logo.

MAZAKI, YOSHIO, Bl Fukoku Seimei Building 2-4, Komatu bara-cho Kita-ku, Osaka City, 530 JAPAN/06-313-2525; FAX: 06-313-2626
Specialties: Classic and working knives of his design. **Patterns:** Bowies, hunters and utility knives. **Technical:** Grinds ATS-34, Gingami 3 GO and Cowry X. **Prices:** $250 to $1,500. **Remarks:** Part-time maker; first knife sold in 1992. Doing business as World Gallery Co., Ltd. **Mark:** NA.

McBURNETTE, HARVEY, P.O. Box 227, Eagle Nest, NM 87718/505-377-6254; FAX: 505-377-6218
Specialties: Fancy working folders; some to customer specs. **Patterns:** Front-locking folders. **Technical:** Grinds D2, 440C and 154CM; engraves. **Prices:** $450 to $3,000. **Remarks:** Full-time maker; first knife sold in 1972. **Mark:** Last name, city and state.

McCARLEY, JOHN, 562 Union Brige Rd., Union Bridge, MD 21791
Specialties: Working straight knives; period pieces. **Patterns:** Hunters, Bowies, camp knives, miniatures, throwing knives. **Technical:** Forges W2, O1 and his own Damascus. **Prices:** $150 to $300; some to $1,000. **Remarks:** Part-time maker; first knife sold in 1977. **Mark:** Initials in script.

McCARTY, HARRY, 1121 Brough Ave., Hamilton, OH 45015
Specialties: Working straight knives; period pieces. **Patterns:** Bowies, camp knives, daggers and buckskinners. **Technical:** Forges and grinds O1. **Prices:** $75 to $350; some to $600. **Remarks:** Part-time maker; first knife sold in 1977. **Mark:** Stylized initials.

McCARTY, ZOLLAN, 101½ Ave. E, Thomaston, GA 30286/404-647-6869
Specialties: Working knives; period pieces. **Patterns:** Straight knives and folders; Scagel replicas; gut hook hatchets. **Technical:** Forges and grinds 440C, 154CM and ATS-34. **Prices:** $110 to $600. **Remarks:** Full-time maker; first knife sold in 1971. Doing business as Z Custom Knives. **Mark:** First initial, last name.

McCLURE, LEONARD, 212 S.W. Ave. I, Seminole, TX 79360/915-758-3929
Specialties: Traditional working/using straight knives of his design or in standard patterns. **Patterns:** Bowies, hunters and utility/camp knives. **Technical:** Grinds O1, D2 and ATS-34. **Prices:** $50 to $150; some to $500. **Remarks:** Spare-time maker; first knife sold in 1970. Doing business as Shamrock Knives. **Mark:** A shamrock.

McCLURE, MICHAEL, 803-17th Ave., Menlo Park, CA 94025/415-323-2596
Specialties: Working/using straight knives of his design and to customer specs. **Patterns:** Bowies, hunters, skinners, utility/camp and boot knives. **Technical:** Grinds ATS-34, 440C and D2. Makes sheaths. **Prices:** Start at $100. **Remarks:** Part-time maker; first knife sold in 1991. **Mark:** Full name.

McCOLL, JOHN, 35 Green St., Stonehouse, Lanarkshire, ML9-3LW SCOTLAND/01698-792223
Specialties: Traditional working straight knives and folders of his design. **Patterns:** Hunters, Bowies and locking folders. **Technical:** Forges his Damascus; grinds 440C, D2 and O1. **Prices:** $125 to $175; some to $590. **Remarks:** Full-time maker; first knife sold in 1980. **Mark:** Full name.

McCONNELL, CHARLES R., 158 Genteel Ridge, Wellsburg, WV 26070/304-737-2015
Specialties: Working straight knives. **Patterns:** Hunters, Bowies, daggers, minis and push knives. **Technical:** Grinds 440C and 154CM; likes full tangs. **Prices:** $65 to $325; some to $800. **Remarks:** Part-time maker; first knife sold in 1977. **Mark:** Name.

McCONNELL JR., LOYD A., 1712 Royalty, Odessa, TX 79761/915-363-8344
Specialties: Working straight knives and folders, some fancy. **Patterns:** Hunters, boots, Bowies, locking folders and slip-joints. **Technical:** Grinds A2, 154CM, CPM10V and commercial Damascus. **Prices:** $175 to $900; some to $10,000. **Remarks:** Full-time maker; first knife sold in 1975. Doing business as Cactus Custom Knives. **Mark:** Name, city and state in cactus logo.

McCOUN, MARK, 14212 Pine Dr., DeWitt, VA 23840/804-469-7631
Specialties: Working/using straight knives of his design and in standard patterns; custom miniatures. **Patterns:** Hunters and tantos. **Technical:** Grinds ATS-34 and 440C. **Prices:** $70 to $150. **Remarks:** Part-time maker; first knife sold in 1989. **Mark:** Name, city and state.

McCRACKIN and SON, V.J., 3720 Hess Rd., House Springs, MO 63051/314-677-6066
Specialties: Working straight knives in standard patterns. **Patterns:** Hunters, Bowies and camp knives. **Technical:** Forges L6, 5160, his own Damascus, cable Damascus. **Prices:** $75 to $400; some to $1,000. **Remarks:** Part-time maker; first knife sold in 1983. Son Kevin helps make the knives. **Mark:** Last name, M.S.

McDEARMONT, DAVE, 1618 Parkside Trail, Lewisville, TX 7567/214-436-4335
Specialties: Collector-grade knives. **Patterns:** Hunters, fighters, boots and folders. **Technical:** Grinds ATS-34; likes full tangs, mirror finishes. **Prices:** $200 to $1,000. **Remarks:** Part-time maker; first knife sold in 1981. **Mark:** Name.

McDONALD, RICH, 4590 Kirk Rd., Columbiana, OH 44408/330-482-0007; FAX: 330-482-0007
Specialties: Traditional working/using and art knives of his design. **Patterns:** Bowies, hunters, primitives and tomahawks. **Technical:** Forges 5160, 1095, 52100 and his own Damascus. Fancy filework. **Prices:** $125 to $500; some to $1,000. **Remarks:** Part-time maker; first knife sold in 1994. **Mark:** First and last initials connected.

McDONALD, ROBERT J., 14730 61 Court N., Loxahatchee, FL 33470/561-790-1470
Specialties: Traditional working straight knives to customer specs. **Patterns:** Fighters, swords and folders. **Technical:** Grinds 440C, ATS-34 and forges own Damascus. **Prices:** $150 to $1,000. **Remarks:** Part-time maker; first knife sold in 1988. **Mark:** Electro-etched name.

McDONALD, W.J. "JERRY," 7173 Wickshire Cove E., Germantown, TN 38138/901-756-9924
Specialties: Classic and working/using straight knives of his design and in standard patterns. **Patterns:** Bowies, hunters and kitchen knives. **Technical:** Grinds ATS-34, D2 and 440C. **Prices:** $65 to $400. **Remarks:** Full-time maker; first knife sold in 1989. **Mark:** First and middle initials, last name, maker, city and state.

McELHANNON, MARCUS, 310 Darby Trails, Sugar Land, TX 77479/713-494-1345
Specialties: Working straight knives and folders of his design and to customer specs. **Patterns:** Fighters, hunters and locking folders. **Technical:** Grinds ATS-34, 440C and 440V. **Prices:** $125 to $300; some to $1,500. **Remarks:** Spare-time maker; first knife sold in 1988. **Mark:** First name.

McFALL, KEN, P.O. Box 458, Lakeside, AZ 85929/602-537-2026
Specialties: Fancy working straight knives and some folders. **Patterns:** Daggers, boots, tantos, Bowies; some miniatures. **Technical:** Grinds D2, ATS-34 and 440C. **Prices:** $175 to $900. **Remarks:** Part-time maker; first knife sold in 1984. **Mark:** Name, city and state.

McFARLIN, ERIC E., P.O. Box 2188, Kodiak, AK 99615/907-486-4799
Specialties: Working knives of his design. **Patterns:** Bowies, skinners, camp knives and hunters. **Technical:** Flat and convex grinds 440C, A2 and AEB-L. **Prices:** Start at $150. **Remarks:** Part-time maker; first knife sold in 1989. **Mark:** Name and city in rectangular logo.

McFARLIN, J.W., 3331 Pocohantas Dr., Lake Havasu City, AZ 86404/520-855-8095

McGILL, JOHN, P.O. Box 302, Blairsville, GA 30512/404-745-4686
Specialties: Working knives. **Patterns:** Traditional patterns; camp knives. **Technical:** Forges L6 and 9260; makes Damascus. **Prices:** $50 to $250; some to $500. **Remarks:** Full-time maker; first knife sold in 1982. **Mark:** XYLO.

McGINNIS, TOM, 1188 W. State Hwy. NN, Ozark, MO 65721/417-581-8203
Specialties: Pattern welded Damascus straight knives to customer specs. **Patterns:** Hunters. **Technical:** Forges 1095, 440C and Damascus. Offers filework; carves handles. **Prices:** Start at $200. **Remarks:** Part-time maker; first knife sold in 1977. **Mark:** First and last name.

McGOVERN, JIM, 31 Scenic Dr., Oak Ridge, NJ 07438/201-697-4558
Specialties: Working straight knives and folders. **Patterns:** Hunters and boots. **Technical:** Hollow-grinds 440C, ATS-34; prefers full tapered tangs. Offers filework. **Prices:** Straight knives, $165 to $250; folders start at $325. **Remarks:** Full-time maker; first knife sold in 1985. **Mark:** Name.

McGOWAN, FRANK E., 12629 Howard Lodge Dr., Sykesville, MD 21784/410-489-4323
Specialties: Fancy working knives to customer specs. **Patterns:** Survivor knives, fighters, fishing knives and hunters. **Technical:** Grinds and forges O1, 440C, 5160 and ATS-34. **Prices:** $75 to $500; some to $1,000. **Remarks:** Full-time maker; first knife sold in 1986. **Mark:** Last name.

McGRODER, PATRICK J., 5725 Chapin Rd., Madison, OH 44057/216-298-3405; FAX: 216-298-3405
Specialties: Traditional working/using knives of his design. **Patterns:** Bowies, hunters and utility/camp knives. **Technical:** Grinds ATS-34, D2 and customer requests. Does reverse etching; heat-treats; prefers natural handle materials; custom made sheath with each knife. **Prices:** $125 to $250. **Remarks:** Part-time maker. **Mark:** First and middle initials, last name, maker, city and state.

McGUANE IV, THOMAS F., 410 South 3rd Ave., Bozeman, MT 59715/406-586-0248
Specialties: Traditional straight knives and folders of his design. **Patterns:** Tantos, swords and locking folders. **Technical:** Forges 1095 and L6; hand-smelted Japanese style steel. Silk and samé handles. **Prices:** $375 to $850; some to $3,000. **Remarks:** Full-time maker; first knife sold in 1988. **Mark:** Last name, city, state.

McHENRY, WILLIAM JAMES, Box 67, Wyoming, RI 02898/401-539-8353

Specialties: Fancy high-tech folders of his design. **Patterns:** Locking folders with various mechanisms. **Technical:** Forges and grinds commercial Damascus and his Damascus. Most pieces disassemble and feature top-shelf materials including gold, silver and gems. **Prices:** $2,500; some to five figures. **Remarks:** Full-time maker; first knife sold in 1988. Former goldsmith. **Mark:** Last name or first and last initials.

McINTOSH, DAVID L., P.O. Box 948, Haines, AK 99827/907-766-3673
Specialties: Working straight knives and folders of all designs. **Patterns:** All styles, except swords. **Technical:** Grinds ATS-34 and top name maker Damascus. Engraves; offers tooling on sheaths. Uses fossil ivory. **Prices:** $60 to $800; some to $2,000. **Remarks:** Full-time maker; first knife sold in 1984. **Mark:** Last name, serial number, steel type, city and state.

McKISSACK II, TOMMY, P.O. Box 991, Sonora, TX 76950/915-387-3253
Specialties: Plain to fancy folders. **Patterns:** Swords to folders, traditional to exotic. **Technical:** Grinds and forges D2, ATS-34, Vascowear, own Damascus and mokume. **Prices:** $100 to $1,500; some to $3,500. **Remarks:** Full-time maker; first knife sold in 1980. **Mark:** Name.

McLUIN, TOM, 36 Fourth St., Dracut, MA 01826/508-957-4899
Specialties: Working straight knives and folders of his design. **Patterns:** Boots, hunters and folders. **Technical:** Grinds ATS-34, 440C, O1 and Damascus; makes his own mokume. **Prices:** $100 to $400; some to $700. **Remarks:** Full-time maker; first knife sold in 1991. **Mark:** Last name.

McMAHON, JOHN P., 44871 Santa Anita #A, Palm Desert, CA 92260/619-341-4238
Specialties: Classic working and using straight knives of his design or to customer specs. **Patterns:** Hunters, Bowies and fighters. **Technical:** Grinds 5160 spring steel for large knives and O1 tool steel for small ones. Differentially tempers. **Prices:** $45 to $300; some to $1,000. **Remarks:** Full-time maker; first knife sold in 1989. Doing business as J.P.M. Knives. **Mark:** Initials.

McMANUS, DANNY, 413 Fairhaven Drive., Taylors, SC 29687/864-268-9849; FAX: 864-268-9699
Specialties: High-tech and traditional working/using straight knives of his design, to customer specs and in standard patterns. **Patterns:** Boots, Bowies, fighters, hunters and utility/camp knives. **Technical:** Forges stainless steel Damascus; grinds ATS-34. Offers engraving and scrimshaw. **Prices:** $300 to $2,000; some to $3,000. **Remarks:** Full-time maker; first knife sold in 1997. Doing business as Stamascus Knife-Works Corp. **Mark:** Stamascus N/V.

McNABB, TOMMY, P.O. Box 327, Bethania, NC 27010/919-759-0640
Specialties: Working and using straight knives of his design. **Patterns:** Hunters, fighters and utility/camp knives. **Technical:** Forges his own Damascus; grinds ATS-34. **Prices:** $100 to $550; some to $2,500. **Remarks:** Full-time maker; first knife sold in 1979. **Mark:** Carolina Custom Knives.

McNEIL, JIMMY, 1175 Mt. Moriah Rd., Memphis, TN 38117/901-544-0710 or 901-683-8133
Specialties: Fancy high-art straight knives of his design. **Patterns:** Bowies, daggers and swords. **Technical:** Grinds O1 and Damascus. Engraves, carves and inlays. **Prices:** $50 to $300; some to $2,000. **Remarks:** Spare-time maker; first knife sold in 1993. Doing business as McNeil's Minerals and Knives. **Mark:** Crossed mining picks and serial number.

McNEIL'S MINERALS AND KNIVES (See McNeil, Jimmy)

McWILLIAMS, SEAN, 311 Gem Lane, Bayfield, CO 81122/970-884-9854
Specialties: Stainless steel combat-survival and working knives of his own design. **Patterns:** Fighters, sub-hilts, utility and camp knives. **Technical:** Forges CPM-T-440V and ATS-34 stainless only. Offers high-tech Kydex-nylon sheaths and carry systems. **Prices:** $300 to $700. **Remarks:** Full-time maker; first knife sold in 1979. **Mark:** Stylized bear paw.

MECCHI, RICHARD, 4225 Gibraltar St., Las Vegas, NV 89121/702-435-7448; FAX: 702-435-7448
Specialties: Working straight knives, some fancy. **Patterns:** Hunters, daggers, Bowies and fillets. **Technical:** Grinds 440C, ATS-34 and 154CM. Exotic handle materials offered. **Prices:** $125 to $950. **Remarks:** Part-time maker; first knife sold in 1982. **Mark:** First initial, last name.

MEDIEVAL CUSTOMS (See Johns, Rob)

MEIER, DARYL, 75 Forge Rd., Carbondale, IL 62901/618-549-3234
Specialties: One-of-a-kind knives and swords. **Patterns:** Collaborates on blades. **Technical:** Forges his own Damascus, W1 and A203E, 440C, 431, nickel 200 and clad steel. **Prices:** $250 to $450; some to $6,000. **Remarks:** Full-time smith and researcher since 1974; first knife sold in 1974. **Mark:** Name or circle/arrow symbol or SHAWNEE.

MELOY, SEAN, 7148 Rosemary Lane, Lemon Grove, CA 91945-2105/619-465-7173
Specialties: Traditional working straight knives of his design. **Patterns:** Bowies, fighters and utility/camp knives. **Technical:** Grinds 440C, ATS-34 and D2. **Prices:** $125 to $300. **Remarks:** Part-time maker; first knife sold in 1985. **Mark:** Broz Knives.

MENSCH, LARRY, RD #3, Box 1444, Milton, PA 17847/717-742-9554; FAX: 717-742-2999
Specialties: Fancy and embellished working/using straight knives in standard patterns, of his design and to customer specs. **Patterns:** Bowies, daggers, hunters, tantos, short swords and miniatures. **Technical:** Grinds ATS-34, carbon and stainless steel Damascus; blade grinds hollow, flat and slack. Filework; bending guards and fluting handles with finger grooves. Offers engraving and scrimshaw. **Prices:** $100 to $300; some to $1,000. **Remarks:** Part-time maker; first knive sold in 1993. Doing business as Larry's Knife Shop. **Mark:** Connected capital "L" and small "m" in script.

MERCER, MIKE, 149 N. Waynesville Rd., Lebanon, OH 45036/513-932-2837
Specialties: Jeweled gold and ivory daggers; multi-blade folders. **Patterns:** 1¼" folders, hunters, axes, replicas. **Technical:** Uses O1 Damascus and mokume. **Prices:** $150 to $1,500. **Remarks:** Full-time maker since 1991. **Mark:** Last name in script.

MERCHANT, TED, 7 Old Garrett Ct., White Hall, MD 21161/410-343-0380
Specialties: Traditional and classic working knives. **Patterns:** Bowies, hunters, camp knives, fighters, daggers and skinners. **Technical:** Forges W2 and 5160; makes own Damascus. Makes handles with wood, stag, horn, silver and gem stone inlay; fancy filework. **Prices:** $125 to $600; some to $1,500. **Remarks:** Full-time maker; first knife sold in 1985. **Mark:** Last name.

MERZ III, ROBERT L., 20219 Prince Creek Dr., Katy, TX 77450/281-492-7337
Specialties: Working straight knives and folders, some fancy, of his design. **Patterns:** Hunters, skinners, fighters and camp knives. **Technical:** Flat-grinds 440C, 154CM, ATS-34, 440V and commercial Damascus. **Prices:** $150 to $450; some to $600. **Remarks:** Part-time maker; first knife sold in 1974. **Mark:** MERZ KNIVES, city and state, or last name in oval.

MESHEJIAN, MARDI, 33 Elm Dr., E. Northport, NY 11731/516-757-4541
Specialties: One-of-a-kind fantasy and high-art straight knives of his design. **Patterns:** Swords, daggers, finger knives and other edged weapons. **Technical:** Hand-forged chainsaw and timing chain Damascus. **Prices:** $150 to $2,500; some to $3,000. **Remarks:** Part-time maker; first knife sold in 1996. Doing business as Tooth and Nail Metalworks. **Mark:** Etched stylized "M."

MESSER, DAVID T., 134 S. Torrence St., Dayton, OH 45403-2044/513-228-6561
Specialties: Fantasy period pieces, straight and folding, of his design. **Patterns:** Bowies, daggers and swords. **Technical:** Grinds 440C, O1, 06 and commercial Damascus. Likes fancy guards and exotic handle materials. **Prices:** $100 to $225; some to $375. **Remarks:** Spare-time maker; first knife sold in 1991. **Mark:** Name stamp.

METAL POINT (See Carlsson, Mark Bjorn)

METHENY, H.A. "WHITEY," 7750 Waterford Dr., Spotsylvania, VA 22553/703-582-3228
Specialties: Working and using straight knives of his design and to customer specs. **Patterns:** Hunters and kitchen knives. **Technical:** Grinds 440C and ATS-34. Offers filework; tooled custom sheaths. **Prices:** $150 to $350. **Remarks:** Spare-time maker; first knife sold in 1990. **Mark:** Initials/full name football logo.

METTLER, J. BANJO, 129 S. Second St., North Baltimore, OH 45872/419-257-2210
Specialties: Fancy folders of his design. **Patterns:** Locking folders, interframes, "A-5" automatic and "L-3" lockbacks of his design, deer-foot-style lockbacks 1-inch closed. **Technical:** Grinds ATS-34, D2 and O1. **Prices:** Start at $100. **Remarks:** Part-time maker; first knife sold in 1988. **Mark:** Deer foot underlined with profile of knife.

MICHAEL'S HANDMADE KNIVES (See Bouse, D. Michael)

MICK'S CUSTOM KNIVES (See Sears, Mick)

MIDDLETON, KEN, Citrus Heights, CA 95621/916-966-6070
Specialties: Traditional and fantasy straight knives and folders of his design. **Patterns:** Hunters, Bowies and daggers. **Technical:** Grinds 440C, ATS-34 and D2. Likes natural handle materials. **Prices:** $150 to $800; some to $3,500. **Remarks:** Spare-time maker; first knife sold in 1986. **Mark:** Last name or Middleton Custom.

MILFORD, BRIAN A., RD 2 Box 294, Knox, PA 16232/814-797-2595; FAX: 814-226-4351
Specialties: Traditional and working/using straight knives of his design or to customer specs. **Patterns:** Fighters, hunters and utility/camp knives. **Technical:** Forges Damascus and 52100; grinds 440C. **Prices:** $50 to $300; some to $750. **Remarks:** Part-time maker; first knife sold in 1991. Doing business as BAM Forge. **Mark:** Full name or initials.

MILLARD, FRED G., 5317 N. Wayne, Chicago, IL 60640/773-769-5160
Specialties: Working/using straight knives of his design or to customer specs. **Patterns:** Bowies, hunters, utility/camp knives, kitchen/steak knives. **Technical:** Grinds ATS-34, O1, D2 and 440C. Makes sheaths. **Prices:** $80 to $250. **Remarks:** Full-time maker; first knife sold in 1993. Doing business as Millard Knives. **Mark:** Mallard duck in flight with serial number.

MILLARD KNIVES (See Millard, Fred G.)

MILLER, BOB, 7659 Fine Oaks Pl., Oakville, MO 63129/314-846-3851
Specialties: Mosaic Damascus; collector using straight knives and folders. **Patterns:** Hunters, Bowies, utility/camp knives, daggers. **Technical:** Forges own Damascus, mosaic-Damascus and 52100. **Prices:** $125 to $500. **Remarks:** Part-time maker; first knife sold in 1983. **Mark:** First and middle initials and last name, or initials.

MILLER JR., CHRIS, P.O. Box 15471, Gainesville, FL 32604-5471
Specialties: Fancy working straight knives. **Patterns:** Swords and large knives of all kinds. **Technical:** Grinds D2, 440C and 154CM. **Prices:** $100 to $500. **Remarks:** Full-time maker; first knife sold in 1976. **Mark:** Last initial.

MILLER CUSTOM KNIVES (See Miller, Michael E.)

MILLER, DON, 1604 Harrodsburg Rd., Lexington, KY 40503/606-276-3299

MILLER, HANFORD J., Box 97, Cowdrey, CO 80434/970-723-4708
Specialties: Working knives in Moran style; period pieces. **Patterns:** Bowies, fighters, camp knives and other large straight knives. **Technical:** Forges W2, 1095, 5160 and his own Damascus; differential tempers; offers wire inlay. **Prices:** $300 to $800; some to $2,000. **Remarks:** Full-time maker; first knife sold in 1968. **Mark:** Initials or name within Bowie logo.

MILLER, JAMES P., 9024 Goeller Rd., RR 2, Box 28, Fairbank, IA 50629/319-635-2294
Specialties: All tool steel Damascus; working knives and period pieces. **Patterns:** Hunters, Bowies, camp knives and daggers. **Technical:** Forges and grinds 1095, 52100, 440C and his own Damascus. **Prices:** $100 to $350; some to $1,500. **Remarks:** Full-time maker; first knife sold in 1970. **Mark:** First and middle initials, last name with knife logo.

MILLER, L. MAURICE, P.O. Box 3064, Missoula, MT 59806-3064/406-549-3276
Specialties: Personally designed knives. **Patterns:** Fighters, folders and skinners. **Technical:** Grinds Damascus and 440C, fileart standard. All knives sold with sheath or displayed on walnut base. **Prices:** Damascus $850 to $1,400; 440C $250 to $600; folders $85 to $400. **Remarks:** Professional/artist maker; first knife sold in 1980. **Mark:** Buffalo skull with last name.

MILLER, M.A., 8979 Pearl St., Apt. 2005, Thornton, CO 80229/303-427-8756
Specialties: Using knives for hunting. 3½"-4" Loveless drop-point. Made to customer specs. **Patterns:** Skinners and camp knives. **Technical:** Grinds 440C, D2, O1 and ATS-34 Damascus miniatures. **Prices:** $225 to $275; miniatures $75. **Remarks:** Part-time maker; first knife sold in 1988. **Mark:** Last name stamped in block letters or first and middle initials, last name, maker, city and state with triangles on either side etched.

MILLER, MICHAEL E., 1527 4th St., Monett, MO 65708/417-235-5955
Specialties: Traditional working/using knives of his design. **Patterns:** Bowies, hunters and kitchen knives. **Technical:** Grinds ATS-34; forges Damascus and cable Damascus. Prefers scrimshaw, fancy pins, basket weave and embellished sheaths. **Prices:** $60 to $175; some to $500. **Remarks:** Part-time maker; first knife sold in 1984. Doing business as Miller Custom Knives. **Mark:** First and middle initials, last name, maker, city and state.

MILLER, MICHAEL K., 28510 Santiam Hwy., Sweet Home, OR 97386/541-367-4927
Specialties: Specializes in kitchen cutlery of his design or made to customer specs. **Patterns:** Hunters, utility/camp knives and kitchen cutlery. **Technical:** Grinds ATS-34. Does special filework/tooling, leather work, and makes carved handles. Makes custom sheaths and holsters. **Prices:** $200. **Remarks:** Full-time maker; first knife sold in 1989. **Mark:** M&M Kustom Krafts.

MILLER, R.D., 10526 Estate Lane, Dallas, TX 75238/214-348-3496
Specialties: One-of-a-kind collector-grade knives. **Patterns:** Boots, hunters, Bowies, camp and utility knives, fishing and bird knives, miniatures. **Technical:** Grinds a variety of steels to include O1, D2, 440C, 154CM and 1095. **Prices:** $65 to $300; some to $900. **Remarks:** Full-time maker; first knife sold in 1984. **Mark:** R.D. Custom Knives with date or bow and arrow logo.

MILLER, RICK, RD 3 Box 273, Rockwood, PA 15557/814-926-2059
Specialties: Working/using straight knives of his design and in standard patterns. **Patterns:** Bowies, daggers, hunters and friction folders. **Technical:** Grinds L6. Forges 5160, L6 and Damascus. Patterns for Damascus are random, twist, rose or ladder. **Prices:** $75 to $250; some to $400. **Remarks:** Part-time maker; first knife sold in 1982. **Mark:** Initials.

MILLER, ROBERT, P.O. Box 2722, Ormond Beach, FL 32175/904-676-1193
Specialties: Working straight knives, some fancy, of his design or to customer specs. **Patterns:** Large Bowies, hunters, miniatures. **Technical:** Grinds O1, D2 and 440C. Offers inlay and fancy filework; inlaid military insignias. **Prices:** $35 to $750. **Remarks:** Full-time maker; first knife sold in 1986. Doing business as Holly Knives. **Mark:** Holly and date.

MILLER, RONALD T., 12922 127th Ave. N., Largo, FL 34644/813-595-0378 (after 5 p.m.)
Specialties: Working straight knives in standard patterns. **Patterns:** Combat knives, camp knives, kitchen cutlery, fillet knives, locking folders and butterflies. **Technical:** Grinds D2, 440C and ATS-34; offers brass inlays and scrimshaw. **Prices:** $45 to $325; some to $750. **Remarks:** Part-time maker; first knife sold in 1984. **Mark:** Name, city and state in palm tree logo.

MILLER, TED, P.O. Box 6328, Santa Fe, NM 87502/505-984-0338
Specialties: Carved antler display knives of his design. **Patterns:** Hunters, swords and miniatures. **Technical:** Grinds 440C. **Prices:** $110 to $350; some average $900. **Remarks:** Full-time maker; first knife sold in 1971. **Mark:** Initials and serial number.

MILLS, ANDY, 414 E. Schubert, Fredericksburg, TX 78624/512-997-8167
Specialties: Working straight knives and folders. **Patterns:** Hunters. **Technical:** Grinds 440C, D2, A2 and 154CM. Offers leatherwork, fabrication, heat-treating. **Prices:** Moderate. **Remarks:** Full-time maker; first knife sold in 1980. **Mark:** Name.

MILLS, LOUIS G., 9450 Waters Rd., Ann Arbor, MI 48103/313-668-1839
Specialties: High-art Japanese-style period pieces. **Patterns:** Traditional tantos, daggers and swords. **Technical:** Makes steel from iron; makes his own Damascus by traditional Japanese techniques. **Prices:** $900 to $2,000; some to $8,000. **Remarks:** Spare-time maker in partnership with Jim Kelso. **Mark:** Yasutomo in Japanese Kanji.

MINDS' EYE METALMASTER (See Smith, D. Noel)

MINERAL MOUNTAIN HATCHET WORKS (See Frizzell, Ted)

MINK, DAN, P.O. Box 861, 196 Sage Circle, Crystal Beach, FL 34681/813-786-5408; FAX: 813-787-2670
Specialties: Traditional and working knives of his design. **Patterns:** Bowies, fighters, folders and hunters. **Technical:** Grinds ATS-34, 440C and D2. Blades and tanges embellished with fancy filework. Uses natural and rare handle materials. **Prices:** $125 to $450. **Remarks:** Part-time maker; first knife sold in 1985. **Mark:** Name and star encircled by custom made, city, state.

MINNICK, JIM, 144 North 7th St., Middletown, IN 47356/317-354-4108
Specialties: Traditional working and using straight knives and folders; classic high-art and fancy/embellished knives of his design or to customer specs. **Patterns:** Hunters, Bowies, daggers, fighters, boots, art knives, locking folders and slip-joint folders. **Technical:** Grinds 440C and 154CM. **Prices:** $185 to $225; some to $1,800. **Remarks:** Part-time maker; first knife sold in 1976. **Mark:** Last name.

MISSION KNIVES & TOOLS, INC. (See Schultz, Richard A.)

MITCHELL, WM. DEAN, P.O. Box 183, Forgan, OK 73938
Specialties: Classic and high-art knives in standard patterns. **Patterns:** Bowies, daggers and swords. **Technical:** Forges 1095, 5160; makes pattern, composite and mosiac Damascus; offers filework and elecroplating. Makes wooden display cases. **Prices:** Mid to upper scale. **Remarks:** Part-time maker; first knife sold in 1986. Doing business as Pioneer Forge & Woodshop. **Mark:** Full name or initials, MS.

MITCHELL, JAMES A., P.O. Box 4646, Columbus, GA 31904/404-322-8582
Specialties: Fancy working knives. **Patterns:** Hunters, fighters, Bowies and locking folders. **Technical:** Grinds D2, 440C and commercial Damascus. **Prices:** $100 to $400; some to $900. **Remarks:** Part-time maker; first knife sold in 1976. Sells knives in sets. **Mark:** Signature and city.

MITCHELL, MAX, DEAN AND BEN, 3803 V.F.W. Rd., Leesville, LA 71440/318-239-6416
Specialties: One-of-a-kind hatchet and knife sets and classic folders. **Patterns:** Hatchet and knife sets with folders to match. **Technical:** L6 double-fired edge; soft backs. Oiled and waxed heavy basket weave sheaths. **Prices:** $125 to $500. **Remarks:** Part-time makers; first knife sold in 1965. Custom orders only; no stock. **Mark:** First names.

MITCHELL, R.W. "MITCH," 24530 Bundy Canyon Road, Wildomar, CA 92595-8732/909-244-4953
Specialties: Working straight knives with Indian influence. **Patterns:** Bowies, fighters, hunters with horseshoe guards, etc. **Technical:** Grinds 440C, O1 and ATS-34; prefers natural handle materials; heat-treats. **Prices:** $125 to $750. **Remarks:** Part-time maker; first knife sold in 1988. **Mark:** Mitch with arrow logo.

M.J.C. KNIVES (See Cashion, Mary Jane)

M&M KUSTOM KRAFTS (See Miller, Michael K.)

M&N ARTS LTD. (See Wattelet, Michael A.)

MOMCILOVIC, GUNNAR, Nordlysv, 16, N-30055 Krokstadelva, NORWAY/0111-47-3287-3586

MONK, NATHAN P., 1304 4th Ave. SE, Cullman, AL 35055/205-737-0463
Specialties: Traditional working and using straight knives of his design and to customer specs; fancy knives. **Patterns:** Bowies, daggers, fighters, hunters, utility/camp knives and one-of-a-kinds. **Technical:** Grinds ATS-34, 440C and A2. **Prices:** $50 to $175. **Remarks:** Spare-time maker; first knife sold in 1990. **Mark:** First and middle initials, last name, city, state.

MONTAÑO, GUS A., 3539 Luna Ave., San Diego, CA 92117/619-273-5357
Specialties: Traditional working/using straight knives of his design. **Patterns:** Boots, Bowies and fighters. **Technical:** Grinds 1095 and 5160; grinds and forges cable. Double or triple hardened and triple drawn; hand rubbed finish. Prefers natural handle materials. **Prices:** $200 to $400; some to $600. **Remarks:** Spare-time maker; first knife sold in 1997. **Mark:** First initial and last name.

MONTEIRO KNIVES S.C. (See Monteiro, Victor)

MONTEIRO, VICTOR, 31 Rue D'Opprebais, Maleve Ste. Marie-Perwez, BELGIUM/075 82 08 18
Specialties: Working and fancy straight knives, folders and integrals of his design. **Patterns:** Bowies, fighters and hunters. **Technical:** Grinds ATS-34, 440C and commercial Damascus. Offers heat-treating, embellishment, filework and domed pins. **Prices:** $300 to $1,000, some higher. **Remarks:** Full-time maker; first knife sold in 1989. Doing business as Monteiro Knives S.C. **Mark:** Logo with initials connected.

MONTJOY, CLAUDE, RR 2, Box 1280, Clinton, SC 29325/803-697-6160
Specialties: Fancy working knives. **Patterns:** Hunters, boots, fighters, some art knives and folders. **Technical:** Grinds ATS-34 and 440C. Offers inlaid handle scales. **Prices:** $100 to $500. **Remarks:** Part-time maker; first knife sold in 1982. **Mark:** Last name.

MOON, SIDNEY "PETE," 928 Bellevue Plantation Rd., Lafayette, LA 70503/318-981-7396; FAX: 318-984-1485
Specialties: Straight knives and folders of his design. **Patterns:** Hunters, automatics and locking folders. **Technical:** Grinds CPM-44-V, ATS-34 and Damascus. Does file work; offers engraving. **Prices:** $150 to $650; some to $1500. **Remarks:** Part-time maker; first knife sold in 1989. **Mark:** Man in the moon (half moon), name, city and state.

MOONLIGHT SMITHY, THE (See Leck, Dal)

MOORE, BILL, 806 Community Ave., Albany, GA 31705/912-438-5529
Specialties: Working and using folders of his design and to customer specs. **Patterns:** Bowies, hunters and locking folders. **Technical:** Grinds ATS-34, forges 5168 and cable Damascus. Filework. **Prices:** $100 to $400. **Remarks:** Part-time maker; first knife sold in 1988. **Mark:** Moore Knives.

MOORE, JAMES B., 1707 N. Gillis, Ft. Stockton, TX 79735/915-336-2113
Specialties: Classic working straight knives and folders of his design. **Patterns:** Hunters, Bowies, daggers, fighters, boots, utility/camp knives, locking folders and slip-joint folders. **Technical:** Grinds 440C, ATS-34, D2, L6, CPM and commercial Damascus. **Prices:** $85 to $700; exceptional knives to $1,500. **Remarks:** Full-time maker; first knife sold in 1972. **Mark:** Name, city and state.

MOORE, MERRILL, 7612 Sharps Rd. NE, Albuquerque, NM 87109

MORAN JR., WM. F., P.O. Box 68, Braddock Heights, MD 21714/301-371-7543
Specialties: High-art working knives of his design. **Patterns:** Fighters, camp knives, Bowies, daggers, axes, tomahawks, push knives and miniatures. **Technical:** Forges W2, 5160 and his own Damascus; puts silver wire inlay on most handles; uses only natural handle materials. **Prices:** $400 to $7,500; some to $9,000. **Remarks:** Full-time maker. **Mark:** First and middle initials, last name, M.S.

MORGAN, JEFF, 9200 Arnaz Way, Santee, CA 92071/619-448-8430
Specialties: Fancy working straight knives. **Patterns:** Hunters, fighters, boots, miniatures. **Technical:** Grinds D2, 440C and ATS-34; likes exotic handles. **Prices:** $65 to $140; some to $500. **Remarks:** Full-time maker; first knife sold in 1977. **Mark:** Initials connected.

MORGAN, TOM, 14689 Ellett Rd., Beloit, OH 44609/330-537-2023
Specialties: Working straight knives and period pieces. **Patterns:** Hunters, boots and presentation tomahawks. **Technical:** Grinds O1, 440C and 154CM. **Prices:** Knives, $65 to $200; tomahawks, $100 to $325. **Remarks:** Full-time maker; first knife sold in 1977. **Mark:** Last name and type of steel used.

MORGAN VALLEY FORGE (See Clark, Howard F.)

MORLAN, TOM, 30635 S. Palm, Hemet, CA 92343/714-767-0543
Specialties: Fancy working knives to customer specs. **Patterns:** Bowies, tantos, fishing knives and locking folders. **Technical:** Grinds 440C, 154CM and ATS-34. **Prices:** $75 to $250; some to $3,000. **Remarks:** Part-time maker; first knife sold in 1979. **Mark:** Initials connected.

MORRIS, C.H., 828 Meadow Dr., Atmore, AL 36502/334-368-2089
Specialties: Liner lock folders. **Patterns:** Interframe liner locks. **Technical:** Grinds 440C and ATS-34. **Prices:** Start at $350. **Remarks:** Full-time maker; first knife sold in 1973. Doing business as Custom Knives. **Mark:** First and middle initials, last name.

MORRIS, DARRELL PRICE, 92 Union, St. Plymouth, Devon, ENGLAND PL1 3EZ/0752 223546
Specialties: Traditional Japanese knives, Bowies and high-art knives. **Technical:** Nickel Damascus and mokamame. **Prices:** $1,000 to $4,000. **Remarks:** Part-time maker; first knife sold in 1990. **Mark:** Initials and Japanese name—Kuni Shigae.

MORRIS, ERIC, 306 Ewart Ave., Beckley, WV 25801/304-255-3951

MORSETH SPORTS EQUIPMENT CO. (See Russell, A.G.)

MORTENSON, ED, 2742 Hwy. 93 N, Darby, MT 59829/406-821-3146; FAX: 406-821-3146
Specialties: Period pieces and working/using straight knives of his design, to customer specs and in standard patterns. **Patterns:** Bowies, hunters and kitchen knives. **Technical:** Grinds ATS-34, 5160 and 1095. Sheath combinations—flashlite/knife, hatchet/knife, etc. **Prices:** $60 to $140; some to $300. **Remarks:** Full-time maker; first knife sold in 1993. Doing business as The Blade Lair. **Mark:** M with attached O.

MOSSER, GARY E., 11827 NE 102nd Place, Kirkland, WA 98033-5170/206-827-2279
Specialties: Working knives. **Patterns:** Hunters, skinners, camp knives, some art knives. **Technical:** Stock removal method; prefers ATS-34. **Prices:** $100 to $250; special orders and art knives are higher. **Remarks:** Part-time maker; first knife sold in 1976. **Mark:** Name.

MOULTON, DUSTY, 11385 W. Ardyce St., Boise, ID 83713/208-323-7911
Specialties: Fancy and working straight knives. **Patterns:** Hunters, fighters, fantasy and miniatures. **Technical:** Grinds exclusively ATS-34. **Prices:** $160 to $600; some to $1,500. **Remarks:** Full-time maker; first knife sold in 1991. **Mark:** Last name.

MOUNT, DON, 2117 Birch Leaf Circle, Las Vegas, NV 89115/702-438-1535
Specialties: High-tech working and using straight knives of his design. **Patterns:** Bowies, fighters and utility/camp knives. **Technical:** Uses 440C and ATS-34. **Prices:** $150 to $300; some to $1,000. **Remarks:** Part-time maker; first knife sold in 1985. **Mark:** Name below a woodpecker.

MOUNTAIN HOME KNIVES, P.O. Box 167, Jamul, CA 91935/619-669-0833
Specialties: High-quality working straight knives. **Patterns:** Hunters, fighters, skinners, tantos, utility and fillet knives, Bowies and *san-mai* Damascus Bowies. **Technical:** Hollow-grind 440C by hand. Feature linen Micarta handles, nickel-silver handle bolts and handmade sheaths. **Prices:** $65 to $270. **Remarks:** Company owned by Jim English. **Mark:** Mountain Home Knives.

MOUNTAIN MAN KNIVES (See Driscoll, Mark)

MOYER, RUSS, 277 71st Ave. NW, Havre, MT 59501/406-265-5116
Specialties: Working knives to customer specs. **Patterns:** Hunters, Bowies and survival knives. **Technical:** Forges W2. **Prices:** $150 to $350. **Remarks:** Part-time maker; first knife sold in 1976. **Mark:** Initials in logo.

MT. CROSBY ARTECH AND FORGE
(See Rowe, Stewart G. and Mullen, Annette

MULLEN, ANNETTE (See Rowe, Stewart G. and Mullen, Annette)

MULLIN, STEVE, 500 W. Center Valley Rd., Sandpoint, ID 83864/208-263-7492
Specialties: Damascus period pieces and folders. **Patterns:** Full range of folders, hunters and Bowies. **Technical:** Forges and grinds O1, D2, 154CM and his own Damascus. Engraves. **Prices:** $100 to $2,000. **Remarks:** Full-time maker; first knife sold in 1975. Sells line of using knives under Pack River Knife Co. **Mark:** Full name, city and state.

MURPHY, DAVE, P.O. Box 256, Gresham, OR 97030/503-665-8634
Specialties: Working knives of his design; small kitchen knives. **Patterns:** Hunters, fighters and boots. **Technical:** Grinds 440C, ATS-34 and L6; likes narrow tangs, composite handles. **Prices:** $44 to $12,500. **Remarks:** Full-time maker; first knife sold in 1940. **Mark:** Name, city and state with likeness of face on blade.

MURSKI, RAY, 12129 Captiva Ct., Reston, VA 22091-1204/703-264-1102
Specialties: Fancy working/using folders of his design. **Patterns:** Hunters, slip-joint folders and utility/camp knives. **Technical:** Grinds 440C, O1 and D2. **Prices:** $100 to $300. **Remarks:** Spare-time maker; first knife sold in 1996. **Mark:** Stamped last name above serial number; type of steel stamped on opposite side of tang.

MUSTANG FORGE (See Hinderer, Rick)

MYERS, MEL, 611 Elmwood Drive, Spencer, IA 51301/712-262-3383
Specialties: Working knives. **Patterns:** Hunters and small utilitarian knives. **Technical:** Uses 440C and no power tools except polisher. **Prices:** $75 to $150. **Remarks:** Spare-time maker; first knife sold in 1982. **Mark:** Signature.

MYERS, PAUL, 614 W. Airwood Dr., E. Alton, IL 62024
Specialties: Fancy working straight knives and folders. **Patterns:** Full range of folders, straight hunters and Bowies; tie tacks; knife and fork sets. **Technical:** Grinds D2, 440C, ATS-34 and 154CM. **Prices:** $100 to $350; some to $3,000. **Remarks:** Full-time maker; first knife sold in 1974. **Mark:** Initials with setting sun on front; name and number on back.

MYSTIK KNIFEWORKS (See Livingston, Robert C.)

n

NATEN, GREG, 1916 16th St. #B, Bakersfield, CA 93301-5005/805-861-0845
Specialties: Fancy and working/using folders of his design. **Patterns:** Fighters, hunters and locking folders. **Technical:** Grinds 440C, ATS-34 and CPM440V. Heat-treats; prefers desert ironwood, stag and mother of pearl. Designs and sews leather sheaths for straight knives. **Prices:** $175 to $600; some to $950. **Remarks:** Spare-time maker; first knife sold in 1992. **Mark:** Last name above battle-ax, handmade.

NEALY, BUD, 822 Thomas St., Stroudsburg, PA 18360/717-421-4040; FAX: 717-421-2593.
Specialties: Original design concealment knives with designer multi-concealment sheath system. **Patterns:** Concealment knives, boots, combat and collector pieces. **Technical:** Grinds ATS-34; uses Damascus. **Prices:** $175 to $1,200. **Remarks:** Full-time maker; first knife sold in 1980. **Mark:** Name, city, state or signature.

NEALEY, IVAN F. (FRANK), Anderson Dam Rd., Box 65, HC #87, Mt. Home, ID 83647/208-587-4060
Specialties: Working straight knives in standard patterns. **Patterns:** Hunters, skinners and utility knives. **Technical:** Grinds D2, 440C and 154CM. **Prices:** $90 to $135; some higher. **Remarks:** Part-time maker; first knife sold in 1975. **Mark:** Name.

NEDVED, DAN, 206 Park Dr., Kalispell, MT 59901/406-752-5060

NEELEY, VAUGHN, 666 Grand Ave., Mancos, CO 81328/303-533-7982
Specialties: High-tech working straight knives and folders. **Patterns:** High-tech approaches; locking folders and interframes. **Technical:** Grinds 440C, D2 and 154CM. **Prices:** Upscale. **Remarks:** Full-time maker; first knife sold in 1982. **Mark:** Name.

NEELY, GREG, 9605 Radio Rd., Houston, TX 77075-2238/713-991-2677; E-MAIL: gtneely@IX.netcom.com
Specialties: Traditional patterns and his own patterns for work and/or collecting. **Patterns:** Hunters, Bowies and utility/camp knives. **Technical:** Forges own Damascus, 1084, 5160 and some tool steels. Differentially tempers. **Prices:** $195 to $3,500. **Remarks:** Part-time maker; first knife sold in 1987. **Mark:** Last name or interlocked initials, MS.

NEERING, WALT AND REPKE, MIKE, 4191 N. Euclid Ave., Bay City, MI 48706/517-684-3111
Specialties: Traditional working and using straight knives of their design or to customer specs; classic knives; display knives. **Patterns:** Hunters, Bowies, skinners, fighters boots, axes and swords. **Technical:** Grind 440C. Offer variety of handle materials. **Prices:** $99 to $1,500. **Remarks:** Full-time makers. Doing business as Black Forest Blades. **Mark:** Knife logo.

NELSON, ROGER S., Box 294, Central Village, CT 06332/203-774-6749
Specialties: Working knives. **Patterns:** Hunters, fighters, camp knives, locking folders, butterflies. **Technical:** Grinds D2, 440C and 154CM. **Prices:** $90 to $140; some to $250. **Remarks:** Spare-time maker; first knife sold in 1975. **Mark:** First initial, last name.

NELSON'S CUSTOM KNIVES (See Gunn, Nelson L.)

NETO JR., NELSON AND DE CARVALHO, HENRIQUE M., R. Joao Margarido, No. 20-V, Guerra, Braganca Paulista, SP-12900-000, BRAZIL/011-7843-6889; FAX: 011-7843-6889
Specialties: Straight knives and folders. **Patterns:** Bowies, katanas, jambyias and others. **Technical:** Forges high carbon steels. **Prices:** $70 to $3,000. **Remarks:** Full-time makers; first knife sold in 1990. **Mark:** H&N

NEUHAEUSLER, ERWIN, Heiligenangerstrasse 15, 86179 Augsburg, GERMANY/0821-814997
Specialties: Traditional working/using straight knives of his design. **Patterns:** Boots, hunters and Japanese style knives. **Technical:** Grinds ATS-34, Damascus and HWL-34. **Prices:** $250 to $750. **Remarks:** Spare-time maker; first knife sold in 1991. **Mark:** Etched logo, last name and city.

NEWCOMB, CORBIN, 628 Woodland Ave., Moberly, MO 65270/816-263-4639
Specialties: Working straight knives and folders; period pieces. **Patterns:** Hunters, axes, Bowies, folders, buckskinner blades and boots. **Technical:** Hollow-grinds D2, 440C and 154CM; prefers natural handle materials. Makes own Damascus; offers cable Damascus. **Prices:** $100 to $500. **Remarks:** Full-time maker; first knife sold in 1982. Doing business as Corbin Knives. **Mark:** First name and serial number.

NEWTON, LARRY, 1758 Pronghorn Ct., Jacksonville, FL 32225/904-221-2340
Specialties: Traditional and slender high grade gentlemen's folders. **Patterns:** Front release locking folders and interframes. **Technical:** Grinds Damascus, ATS-34, 440C and D2. **Prices:** Start at $350. **Remarks:** Spare-time maker; first knife sold in 1989. **Mark:** Last name.

NICHOLSON, R. KENT, P.O. Box 204, Phoenix, MD 21131/410-323-6925
Specialties: Large using knives. **Patterns:** Bowies and camp knives in the Moran style. **Technical:** Forges W2, 9260, 5160; makes Damascus. **Prices:** $150 to $995. **Remarks:** Part-time maker; first knife sold in 1984. **Mark:** Name.

NIELSON, JEFF V., 610 S. 200 E., P.O. Box 365, Monroe, UT 84754/801-527-4242
Specialties: Classic folders of his design and to customer specs. **Patterns:** Fighters, hunters, locking folders; miniatures. **Technical:** Grinds 440C stainless. **Prices:** $80 to $500. **Remarks:** Part-time maker; first knife sold in 1991. Doing business as Fine Custom Knives. **Mark:** Name, location.

NIEMUTH, TROY, 3143 North Ave., Sheboygan, WI 53083/414-452-2927
Specialties: Period pieces and working/using straight knives of his design and to customer specs. **Patterns:** Hunters and utility/camp knives. **Technical:** Grinds 440C, 1095 and A2. **Prices:** $85 to $350; some to $500. **Remarks:** Full-time maker; first knife sold in 1995. **Mark:** Etched last name.

NIMO FORGE (See Sinyard, Cleston S.)

NIRO, FRANK, Box 552, Mackenzie, BC V0J 2C0, CANADA/604-997-6975
Specialties: Comfortable working straight knives and folders. **Patterns:** Hunters, Bowies, fishing knives, camp and kitchen knives. **Technical:** Grinds 440C, ATS-34 and CPM-T-440V. Specializes in "cross cut" 440C and ATS-34. **Prices:** $40 to $450. **Remarks:** Part-time maker; first knife sold in 1983. Doing business as Frank's Place. **Mark:** Name, city, province.

NISHIUCHI, MELVIN S., 6121 Forest Park Dr., Las Vegas, NV 89115/702-438-2327
Specialties: Working straight knives; collector pieces. **Patterns:** Hunters, fighters, utility knives and some fancy personal knives. **Technical:** Grinds ATS-34; prefers exotic wood and/or stone handle materials. **Prices:** $200 to $1,000; some to $2,000. **Remarks:** Part-time maker; first knife sold in 1985. **Mark:** Circle with a line above it.

NOBLE HOUSE ARMOURERS (See Kennedy, Kelly S.)

NOLEN, GEORGE (See Nolen, R.D. and George)

NOLEN, R.D. and GEORGE, 1110 Lakeshore Dr., Estes Park, CO 80517-7113/970-586-5814; FAX: 970-586-8827
Specialties: Working knives; display pieces. **Patterns:** Wide variety of straight knives, butterflies and buckles. **Technical:** Grind D2, 440C and 154CM. Offer filework; make exotic handles. **Prices:** $100 to $800; some higher. **Remarks:** Full-time makers; first knife sold in 1968. **Mark:** NK in oval logo.

NOLFI, TIM, P.O. Box P, Chapel Hill Rd., Dawson, PA 15428/412-529-2439
Specialties: High-art straight knives and folders of his design; working and using knives. **Patterns:** Hunters, Bowies, fighters and some locking folders. **Technical:** Forges and grinds his own Damascus, O1 and 1095. Also works with wrought iron and 200 nickel. **Prices:** $125 to $1,500; some to $4,000. **Remarks:** Full-time maker; first knife sold in 1988. **Mark:** Nolfi Forge or last name alone.

NORDELL, INGEMAR, Skarpå 2103, 82041 Färila, SWEDEN/0651-23347
Specialties: Classic working and using straight knives. **Patterns:** Hunters, Bowies and fighters. **Technical:** Forges and grinds ATS-34, D2 and Sandvik. **Prices:** $120 to $1,500. **Remarks:** Part-time maker; first knife sold in 1985. **Mark:** Initials or name.

NORFLEET, ROSS W., 3947 Tanbark Rd., Richmond, VA 23235/804-276-4169
Specialties: Classic, traditional and working/using knives of his design or in standard patterns. **Patterns:** Hunters and kitchen knives. **Technical:** Hollow-grinds 440C and ATS-34. **Prices:** $75 to $200; some to $400. **Remarks:** Part-time maker; first knife sold in 1993. **Mark:** Name in arch logo.

NORRIS CUSTOM KNIVES (See Norris, Don)

NORRIS, DON, 4711 N. Paseo Sonoyta, Tucson, AZ 85715/520-299-6531
Specialties: Classic and traditional working/using straight knives of his design, to customer specs and in standard patterns. **Patterns:** Bowies, daggers, fighters, hunters and utility/camp knives. **Technical:** Grinds and forges Damascus; grinds ATS-34 and 440C. Cast sterling guards and bolsters on Bowies. **Prices:** $300 to $1,000; some to $2,500. **Remarks:** Full-time maker; first knife sold in 1990. Doing business as Norris Custom Knives. **Mark:** Last name.

NORRIS, MIKE, 2115 W. Main St., Albemarle, NC 28001/704-982-8445
Specialties: Interframe folders and liner locks. **Patterns:** Hunters, fighters, and interframe folders. **Technical:** Grinds ATS-34, 440C, D2 and Damascus. **Prices:** $100 to $900; some to $3,000. **Remarks:** Full-time maker; first knife sold in 1982. **Mark:** Full name, maker, city and state.

NORTH, DAVID and PRATER, MIKE, 105 Sharp, Chickamauga, GA 30707/706-931-2396
Specialties: Variety of horn- and stag-handled belt knives. **Patterns:** Standard patterns in large and small narrow-tang construction. **Technical:** Grind O1, D2 and Damascus. **Prices:** $165 to $10,000. **Remarks:** First knife sold in 1980. **Mark:** Names, date, serial number.

NORTH TEXAS TECHNOLOGIES (See Smart, Steve)

NORTON, DENNIS, 5334 Ashland Dr., Ft. Wayne, IN 46835/219-486-3851
Specialties: Traditional working and using straight knives of his design; martial arts weapons. **Patterns:** Bowies, fighters and utility/camp knives. **Technical:** Grinds 440C, D2 and O1. Most knives have filework and exotic hardwood handles. **Prices:** $60 to $300; some to $750. **Remarks:** Part-time maker; first knife sold in 1985. **Mark:** Initials and last name.

NORTON, DON, 3206 Aspen Dr., Farmington, NM 87401/505-327-3604
Specialties: Fancy and plain straight knives. **Patterns:** Hunters, small Bowies, tantos, boot knives, fillets. **Technical:** Prefers 440C, Micarta, exotic woods and other natural handle materials. Hollow-grinds all knives except fillet knives. **Prices:** $85 to $1,000; average is $200. **Remarks:** Full-time maker; first knife sold in 1980. **Mark:** Full name, Hsi Shugi, city, state.

NOTT ENGRAVING, R.P. (See Nott, Ron P.)

NOTT, RON P., P.O. Box 281, Summerdale, PA 17093/717-732-2763; E-MAIL: neitznott@aol.com
Specialties: High-art folders and some straight knives. **Patterns:** Scale release folders. **Technical:** Grinds ATS-34, 416 and nickel silver. Engraves, inlays gold. **Prices:** $250 to $3,000. **Remarks:** Full-time maker; first knife sold in 1993. Doing business as R.P. Nott Engraving. **Mark:** First initial, last name and serial number.

NOWLAND, RICK, RR 1, Box 277, Waltonville, IL 62894/618-279-3170
Specialties: Traditional multi-blade folders with Damascus blades of his design. **Patterns:** Multi-blade slip-joints and lockback folders. **Technical:** Uses ATS-34, 440C; forges his own Damascus; makes mokume. **Prices:** $150 to $1,000. **Remarks:** Part-time maker; first knife sold in 1986. **Mark:** Last name.

NUNN, GREGORY, CVSR Box 2107, Moab, UT 84532/801-259-8607
Specialties: High-art working and using knives of his design; new edition Emperor's Choice knife with purple sheen obsidian handle; new edition knife with handle made from agatetized dinosaur bone—first ever made. **Patterns:** Flaked stone knives. **Technical:** Uses gem-quality agates, jaspers and obsidians for blades. **Prices:** $125 to $600; some to $1,000. **Remarks:** Full-time maker; first knife sold in 1989. **Mark:** Name, knife and edition numbers, year made.

NYMEYER, EARL, 2802 N. Fowler, Hobbs, NM 88240/505-392-2164
Specialties: One-of-a-kind working straight knives of his design. **Patterns:** Hunters and small and large belt knives. **Technical:** Hollow-grinds; offers filework. **Prices:** $75 to $95; some to $195. **Remarks:** Spare-time maker; first knife sold in 1983. **Mark:** Initials or first initial, last name.

OAKTREE FORGE (See Wagner, Dan)

O'CEILAGHAN, MICHAEL, 1623 Benhill Rd., Baltimore, MD 21226/410-355-1660; FAX: 410-355-1661
Specialties: High-art and traditional straight knives of his design and to customer specs. **Patterns:** Fighters, hunters and utility/camp knives. **Technical:** Forges 5160, O6, 1045 and railroad spikes. Blades are "Hamon" tempered and drawn; handles are either horn or hand-carved wood. **Prices:** $100 to $325; some to $750. **Remarks:** First knife sold in 1992. Doing business as Howling Wolf Forge. **Mark:** Howling Wolf Forge, signed signature, date forged.

OCHS, CHARLES F., 124 Emerald Lane, Largo, FL 33771/813-536-3827
Specialties: Working knives; period pieces. **Patterns:** Hunters, fighters, Bowies, buckskinners and folders. **Technical:** Forges 52100, 5160 and his own Damascus. **Prices:** $150 to $1,800; some to $2,500. **Remarks:** Full-time maker; first knife sold in 1978. **Mark:** OX Forge.

ODA, KUZAN, 629 W. 15th Ave., Anchorage, AK 99501-5005/907-746-3018
Specialties: High-tech Japanese-style knives; contemporary working knives. **Patterns:** Swords, fighters, hunters and folders. **Technical:** Forges and grinds BG42, 154CM, tamahagane and his own Damascus; offers traditional and authentic Japanese sword-smithing and polishing. **Prices:** $200 to $600; some to $8,000. **Remarks:** Full-time maker; first knife sold in 1957. Waiting list only. **Mark:** First name.

ODELL, PHILIP, 1303 Cobb St., San Mateo, CA 94401-3617/415-570-5360

OGG, ROBERT G., 537 Old Dug Mtn. Rd., Paris, AR 72855/501-963-2767
Specialties: Plain and fancy working knives. **Patterns:** One and two blade folders, hunters, military and kitchen knives. **Technical:** Grinds 440C, ATS-34 and high carbon. **Prices:** Folders start at $120; fixed blades start at $20. **Remarks:** Spare-time maker; first knife sold in 1964. **Mark:** Name.

OGLETREE JR., BEN R., 2815 Israel Rd., Livingston, TX 77351/409-327-8315
Specialties: Working/using straight knives of his design. **Patterns:** Hunters, kitchen and utility/camp knives. **Technical:** Grinds ATS-34, W1 and 1075; heat-treats. **Prices:** $200 to $400. **Remarks:** Part-time maker; first knife sold in 1955. **Mark:** Last name, city and state in oval with a tree on either side.

OKAYSU, KAZOU, 12-2 1 Chome Higashi Veno, Taito-Ku, Tokyo 110, JAPAN

OL BLUE KNIVES, INC. (See Burns, Dave)

OLD COLONY MANUFACTORY (See Leavitt Jr., Earl F.)

OLIVER, ANTHONY CRAIG, 1504 Elaine Pl., Ft. Worth, TX 76106/817-625-0825
Specialties: Fancy and embellished traditional straight knives of his design. **Patterns:** Hunters, full-size folders, Bowies, daggers and miniatures in stainless and nickel Damascus with tempered blades. **Technical:** Grinds 440C and ATS-34. **Prices:** $40 to $500. **Remarks:** Part-time maker; first knife sold in 1988. **Mark:** Initials and last name.

OLSON, DARROLD E., 28182 Lark Lane, Shedd, OR 97377/541-466-3202
Specialties: Straight knives and folders of his design and to customer specs. **Patterns:** Hunters, liner locks and locking folders. **Technical:** Grinds 440C, ATS-34 and 154CM. Uses anodized titanium; sheaths wet-moulded. **Prices:** $150 to $350. **Remarks:** Part-time maker; first knife sold in 1989. **Mark:** Initials and last name.

OLSON POCKET KNIVES (See Olson, Rod)

OLSON, ROD, 110 3rd Ave. NE, High River AB, CANADA T1V 1L9/403-652-2744; FAX: 403-652-3061
Specialties: Traditional and working/using folders of his design; period pieces. **Patterns:** Locking folders. **Technical:** Grinds ATs-34. Offers filework, sculptured steel frames. **Prices:** $300 to $750. **Remarks:** Part-time maker; first knife sold in 1979. Doing business as Olson Pocket Knives. **Mark:** Last name on blade; country, serial number inside frame.

OLSON, WAYNE C., 11655 W. 35th Ave., Wheat Ridge, CO 80033/303-420-3415
Specialties: High-tech working knives. **Patterns:** Hunters to folding lockers; some integral designs. **Technical:** Grinds 440C, 154CM and ATS-34; likes hand-finishes; precision-fits stainless steel fittings—no solder, no nickel silver. **Prices:** $275 to $600; some to $3,000. **Remarks:** Full-time maker; first knife sold in 1979. **Mark:** Name, maker.

OLYMPIC KNIVES (See Ball, Robert)

ONE OF A KIND KNIVES (See Wardian, Paul G.)

ONION, KENNETH J., 91-990 Oaniani St., Kapolei, HI 96707/808-674-1300; FAX: 808-674-1403
Specialties: Straight knives and folders. **Patterns:** Bowies, daggers, tantos, fighters, boots, hunters, utility knives and art knives. **Technical:** ATS-34, 440C, Damascus, 5160, D2. **Prices:** $135 to $1,500. **Remarks:** Part-time maker; first knife sold in 1991. All knives fully guaranteed. Call for availability. **Mark:** Name and state.

ORION (See Reed, Del)

ORTON KNIFE WORKS (See Orton, Richard)

ORTON, RICHARD, P.O. Box 7002, La Verne, CA 91750/909-596-8344
Specialties: Classic and traditional working and using straight knives of his design, to customer specs and in standard patterns. **Patterns:** Boots, daggers and hunters. **Technical:** Grinds ATS-34, 440C and file steel. Filework on blades and handle backs. Handles of exotic hardwoods, stag and mother-of-pearl with gemstones and silver inlay. Hand-stitched leather sheaths, some with tooling. **Prices:** $150 to $350; some to $750. **Remarks:** Full-time maker; first knife sold in 1992. Doing business as Orton Knife Works. **Mark:** Last name, city and state.

OSBORNE, MICHAEL, 585 Timber Ridge Dr., New Braunfels, TX 78132/210-609-0118
Specialties: Traditional and working/using straight knives of his design. **Patterns:** Bowies, fighters and hunters. **Technical:** Forges 5160, 52100 and 10. Tempers all blades. Some filework. Embellishes with silver wire inlay. **Prices:** $125 to $500; some to $1,000. **Remarks:** Part-time maker; first knife sold in 1988. **Mark:** Engraved signature and year.

OSBORNE, WARREN, 215 Edgefield, Waxahachie, TX 75165/972-937-0899; FAX: 972-937-9004
Specialties: Investment grade collectible, interframes, one-of-a-kinds; unique locking mechanisms. **Patterns:** Folders; bolstered and interframes; conventional lockers, frontlockers and backlockers; some slip-joints; some high-art pieces; fighters. **Technical:** Grinds ATS-34, 440 and 154; some Damascus and CPM400V. **Prices:** $400 to $2,000; some to $4,000. Interframes $650 to $1,500. **Remarks:** Full-time maker; first knife sold in 1980. **Mark:** Last name in boomerang logo.

OSTERMAN, DANIEL E., 1644 W. 10th, Junction City, OR 97448/541-998-1503
Specialties: One-third scale copies of period pieces, museum class miniatures. **Patterns:** Antique Bowies. **Technical:** Grinds all cutlery grade steels, engraves, etches, inlays and overlays. **Prices:** Start at

$2,500. **Remarks:** Full-time maker; first miniature knife sold in 1975. **Mark:** Initials.

OUTLAW, ANTHONY L., 4115 Gaines St., Panama City, FL 32404/904-769-7754
Specialties: Traditional working straight knives. **Patterns:** Tantos, Bowies, camp knives, etc. **Technical:** Grinds A2, W2, O1, L6, 1095 and stainless steels to mirror finish. **Prices:** $85 to $175; some to $300. **Remarks:** Part-time maker; first knife sold in 1984. **Mark:** Last name.

OVEREYNDER, T.R., 1800 S. Davis Dr., Arlington, TX 76013/817-277-4812; FAX: 817-860-5485
Specialties: Highly finished collector-grade knives. **Patterns:** Fighters, Bowies, daggers, locking folders, slip-joints and 90 percent collector-grade interframe folders. **Technical:** Grinds D2, 440C and 154CM. Has been making titanium-frame folders since 1977. **Prices:** $500 to $1,500; some to $7,000. **Remarks:** Part-time maker; first knife sold in 1977. Doing business as TRO Knives. **Mark:** T.R. OVEREYNDER KNIVES, city and state.

OWEN, BILL, 39965 Compher Road, Lovettsville, VA 20180/540-882-3004
Specialties: Working and using straight knives of his design. **Patterns:** Hunters, Bowies and utility/camp knives. **Technical:** Grinds D2; forges various spring steels. Heat-treats and makes sheaths. **Prices:** Start at $100. **Remarks:** Spare-time maker; first knife sold in 1990. **Mark:** Last name with three dots circling the top of the "O."

OWENS, JOHN, 6513 E. Lookout Dr., Parker, CO 80134
Specialties: Contemporary working straight knives; period pieces. **Patterns:** Hunters, Bowies and camp knives. **Technical:** Grinds and forges 440C, 154CM, ATS-34 and O1. **Prices:** $150 to $600. **Remarks:** Spare-time maker. **Mark:** Last name.

OWNBY HANDMADE KNIVES, JOHN C. (See Ownby, John C.)

OWNBY, JOHN C., 1716 Hastings Ct., Planto, TX 75023-5027
Specialties: Traditional working and using straight knives and folders of his design. **Patterns:** Hunters, locking folders and utility/camp knives. **Technical:** Grinds 440C, 1095, and ATS-34. Blades are flat ground. Prefers natural materials for handles—exotic woods, horn and antler. **Prices:** $125 to $250; some to $500. **Remarks:** Part-time maker; first knife sold in 1993. Doing business as John C. Ownby Handmade Knives. **Mark:** Name, city, state.

OX FORGE (See Ochs, Charles F.)

OYSTER, LOWELL R., RR #2, Box 5605, East Coringh, ME 04427/207-884-8663
Specialties: Traditional and original designed multi-blade slip-joint folders. **Patterns:** Hunters, minis, camp and fishing knives. **Technical:** Grinds O1; heat-treats. **Prices:** $55 to $450; some to $750. **Remarks:** Full-time maker; first knife sold in 1981. **Mark:** A scallop shell.

p

PACHI, FRANCESCO, Via Albisola 97B, 16162 Genova, ITALY/010-713050
Specialties: Fancy and working knives. **Patterns:** Hunters and skinners. **Technical:** Grinds ATS-34 and Damascus. **Prices:** $400 to $2,500. **Remarks:** Full-time maker; first knife sold in 1991. **Mark:** Logo with last name.

PACK RIVER KNIFE CO. (See Mullin, Steve)

PACKARD, BOB, P.O. Box 311, Elverta, CA 95626/916-991-5218
Specialties: Traditional working/using straight knives of his design and to customer specs. **Patterns:** Hunters, fishing knives, utility/camp knives. **Technical:** Grinds ATS-34, 440C; Forges 52100, 5168 and cable Damascus. **Prices:** $75 to $225. **Mark:** Engraved name and year.

PADGETT JR., EDWIN L., 845 Bank St., New London, CT 06320/860-443-2938
Specialties: Skinners and working knives of any design. **Patterns:** Straight and folding knives. **Technical:** Grinds ATS-34 or any tool steel upon request. **Prices:** $50 to $300. **Mark:** Name.

PADILLA, GARY, P.O. Box 741, Weimar, CA 95736/916-637-5182
Specialties: Native American influenced working and using straight knives of his design. **Patterns:** Hunters, kitchen knives, utility/camp knives and obsidian ceremonial knives. **Technical:** Grinds 440C, ATS-34, O1 and Damascus. **Prices:** $65 to $195; some to $500. **Remarks:** Part-time maker; first knife sold in 1977. Doing business as Bighorn Knifeworks. **Mark:** Stylized initials or name over company name.

PAGE, LARRY, 165 Rolling Rock Rd., Aiken, SC 29803/803-648-0001
Specialties: Working knives of his design; period pieces. **Patterns:** Hunters, boots and fighters. **Technical:** Grinds 154CM and ATS-34. **Prices:** Start at $85. **Remarks:** Part-time maker; first knife sold in 1983. **Mark:** Name, city and state in oval.

PAGE, REGINALD, 6587 Groveland Hill Rd., Groveland, NY 14462/716-243-1643
Specialties: High-art straight knives and one-of-a-kind folders of his design. **Patterns:** Hunters, locking folders and slip-joint folders. **Technical:** Forges O1, 5160 and his own Damascus. Prefers natural handle materials but will work with Micarta. **Remarks:** Spare-time maker; first knife sold in 1985. **Mark:** First initial, last name.

PANKIEWICZ, PHILIP R., RFD #1, Waterman Rd., Lebanon, CT 06249
Specialties: Working straight knives. **Patterns:** Hunters, daggers, minis and fishing knives. **Technical:** Grinds D2, 440C and 154CM. **Prices:** $60 to $125; some to $250. **Remarks:** Spare-time maker; first knife sold in 1975. **Mark:** First initial in star.

PANTHER CREEK FORGE (See Cook, Louise and Cook, Mike)

PAPP, ROBERT, P.O. Box 29596, Parma, OH 44129/216-888-9299
Specialties: Swords—broad and fantasy; variety of display knives. **Patterns:** Integral-designed hunters, fighters, minis and boots. **Technical:** Grinds D2, 440C, 154CM, ATS-34, CPM108 and CPM440C. **Prices:** $95 to $10,000; some higher. **Remarks:** Full-time maker; first knife sold in 1964. **Mark:** Full name, city and state.

PARDUE, MELVIN M., Rt. 1, Box 130, Repton, AL 36475/205-248-2686
Specialties: Fancy straight knives and folders. **Patterns:** Locking and push-button folders, tantos, krisses, liner locks, fighters and boots. **Technical:** Grinds D2, 440C, 154CM and UHB-A-EBL; uses anodized titanium. Likes coffin handles. **Prices:** $140 to $350. **Remarks:** Full-time maker; first knife sold in 1974. **Mark:** Last name.

PARKER, J.E., 1300 E. Main, Clarion, PA 16214/814-226-4837; FAX: 814-226-4351
Specialties: Fancy/embellished, traditional and working straight knives of his design and to customer specs. **Patterns:** Bowies and hunters. **Technical:** Grinds 440C, 440V, ATS-34 and nickel Damascus. Prefers mastadon, oosik, amber and malachite handle material. **Prices:** $90 to $550; some to $750. **Remarks:** Part-time maker; first knife sold in 1991. Doing business as Custom Knife. **Mark:** Name and city with knife stamped in blade.

PARKER, ROBERT NELSON, 5223 Wilhelm Rd. N.W., Rapid City, MI 49676
Specialties: Traditional working and using straight knives of his design. **Patterns:** Hunters, fighters, utility/camp knives; some Bowies. **Technical:** Grinds ATS-34; hollow and flat grinds, full and hidden tangs. Hand-stitched leather sheaths. **Prices:** $225 to $500; some to $1,000. **Remarks:** Part-time maker; first knife sold in 1986. **Mark:** Full name.

PARKS, BLANE C., 15908 Crest Dr., Woodbridge, VA 22191/703-904-2842
Specialties: Knives of his design. **Patterns:** Boots, Bowies, daggers, fighters, hunters, kitchen knives, locking and slip-joint folders, utility/camp knives, letter openers and friction folders. **Technical:** Grinds ATS-34, 440C, D2 and other carbon steels. Offers filework, silver wire inlay and wooden sheaths. **Prices:** Start at $150. **Remarks:** Part-time maker; first knife sold in 1993. Doing business as B.C. Parks Knives. **Mark:** First and middle initials, last name.

PARKS, JOHN, 3539 Galilee Church Rd., Jefferson, GA 30549/706-367-4916
Specialties: Traditional working and using straight knives of his design. **Patterns:** Trout knives, hunters and integral bolsters. **Technical:** Forges 1095 and 5168. **Prices:** $100 to $250; some to $600. **Remarks:** Part-time maker; first knife sold in 1989. **Mark:** Initials in script.

PARKS KNIVES, B.C. (See Parks, Blane C.)

PARLER, THOMAS O'NEIL, 11 Franklin St., Charleston, SC 29401/803-723-9433
Specialties: Period pieces and traditional straight knives of his design. **Patterns:** Bowies, utility/camp knives, Scottish dirks, skean dhu and other Celtic period pieces. **Technical:** Forges 5160, 1095 and W2. Prefers matte or satin finish, brass or German silver buttcaps and bolsters and some Celtic carving on handles. **Prices:** $300 to $1,000; some to $2,000. **Remarks:** Part-time maker; first knife sold in 1995. Doing business as Raven Forge. **Mark:** Last name in runic letters, rune for "protection."

PARRISH III, GORDON A., 940 Lakloey Dr., North Pole, AK 99705/907-488-0357
Specialties: Classic and high-art straight knives of his design and to customer specs.; working and using knives. **Patterns:** Bowies and hunters. **Technical:** Grinds tool steel and ATS-34. Uses mostly Alaskan handle materials. **Prices:** $125 to $750. **Remarks:** Spare-time maker; first knife sold in 1980. **Mark:** Last name, state.

PARRISH, ROBERT, 271 Allman Hill Rd., Weaverville, NC 28787/704-645-2864
Specialties: Heavy-duty working knives of his design or to customer specs. **Patterns:** Survival and duty knives; hunters and fighters. **Technical:** Grinds 440C, D2, O1 and commercial Damascus. **Prices:** $200 to $300; some to $6,000. **Remarks:** Full-time maker; first knife sold in 1970. **Mark:** Initials connected, sometimes with city and state.

PARSONS, MICHAEL R., 1600 S. 11th St., Terre Haute, IN 47802-1722/812-234-1679
Specialties: Fancy straight knives. **Patterns:** Railroad spike knives and variety of one-of-a-kinds including files. **Technical:** Forges and hand-files scrap steel. Engraves, carves, wire inlays and offers leatherwork. **Prices:** $150 to $1,500. **Remarks:** Full-time maker; first knife sold in 1965. **Mark:** Mc with key logo.

PATE, LLOYD D., 219 Cottontail Ln., Georgetown, TX 78626/512-863-7805
Specialties: Traditional working straight knives. **Patterns:** Hunters, fighters and Bowies. **Technical:** Hollow-grinds D2, 440C and ATS-34; likes mirror-finishes. **Prices:** $75 to $350; some to $500. **Remarks:** Part-time maker; first knife sold in 1983. **Mark:** Last name.

PATRICK, BOB, 12642 24A Ave., S. Surrey, B.C. V4A 8H9 CANADA/604-538-6214; FAX: 604-888-2683
Specialties: Field grade to presentation grade traditional straight knives and period pieces of his design. **Patterns:** Boots, Bowies and hunters. **Technical:** Grinds all available knife steels. Offers scrimshaw. **Prices:** Fair and reasonable. **Remarks:** Full-time maker; first knife sold in 1987. Doing business as Patrick Custom Knives. **Mark:** Name in oval logo.

PATRICK, CHUCK, P.O. Box 127, Brasstown, NC 28902/704-837-7627
Specialties: Period pieces. **Patterns:** Hunters, daggers, tomahawks, pre-Civil War folders. **Technical:** Forges all hardware, 5160, his own cable and Damascus, available in fancy pattern and mosaic. **Prices:** $150 to $1,000; some higher. **Remarks:** Full-time maker; first knife sold in 1980. **Mark:** Hand-engraved name, date and flying owl.

PATRICK CUSTOM KNIVES (See Patrick, Bob)

PATRICK, WILLARD C., P.O. Box 5716, Helena, MT 59604/406-458-6552
Specialties: Working straight knives and one-of-a-kind art knives of his design or to customer specs. **Patterns:** Hunters, Bowies, fish, patch and kitchen knives. **Technical:** Grinds ATS-34, 1095, O1, A2 and Damascus. **Prices:** $85 to $350; some to $600. **Remarks:** Full-time maker; first knife sold in 1989. Doing business as Wil-A-Mar Cutlery. **Mark:** Shield with last name and a dagger.

PATTAY KNIVES (See Pattay, Rudy)

PATTAY, RUDY, 510 E. Harrison St., Long Bch., NY 11561/516-431-0847
Specialties: Fancy and working straight knives of his design. **Patterns:** Bowies, hunters, utility/camp knives. **Technical:** Hollow-grinds ATS-34, 440C, O1. Offers stainless steel soldered guards; fabricates guard and buttcap on lathe and milling machine. Heat-treats. Prefers synthetic handle materials. Offers hand-sewn sheaths. **Prices:** $100 to $350; some to $500. **Remarks:** Part-time maker; first knife sold in 1990. Doing business as Pattay Knives. **Mark:** First initial, last name in sorcerer logo.

PATTERSON, ALAN W., Rt. 3, Box 131, Hayesville, NC 28904/704-389-9103
Specialties: Working straight knives and folders of his design or to customer specs; period pieces. **Patterns:** Forged knives, swords, tomahawks and folders. **Technical:** Damascus, cable and tool steels. Some custom leatherwork; wife offers scrimshaw. **Prices:** $125 to $5,000. **Remarks:** Full-time maker; first knife sold in 1990. **Mark:** Patterson Forge.

PATTERSON, KARL, 8 Madison Ave., Silver Creek, NY 14136/716-934-2578
Specialties: Working and using straight knives of his design or to customer specs. **Patterns:** Drop-point hunters, utility/camp knives and skinners. **Technical:** Grinds 440C, ATS-34 and O1. Prefers natural wood but will use Micarta, etc., for strength. **Prices:** Start at $75. **Remarks:** Spare-time maker; first knife sold in 1990. **Mark:** First name.

PATTON, DICK, 206F W. 38th St., Garden City, ID 83714/208-395-0896

PAVACK, DON, Elk Meadow Ranch, Leo Rt., Hanna, WY 82327/307-325-9245
Specialties: Working straight knives. Will work with customer designs. **Patterns:** Hunters and fillet knives; folders. **Technical:** Grinds ATS-34, 440C, 154CM and Damascus steel. Prefers natural handle materials; uses Micarta and diamond wood. **Prices:** $95 to $2,000. **Mark:** Signature and initials.

PEAGLER, RUSS, P.O. Box 1314, Moncks Corner, SC 29461/803-761-1008
Specialties: Traditional working straight knives of his design and to customer specs. **Patterns:** Hunters, fighters, boots. **Technical:** Hollow-grinds 440C, ATS-34 and O1; uses Damascus steel. Prefers bone handles. **Prices:** $85 to $300; some to $500. **Remarks:** Spare-time maker; first knife sold in 1983. **Mark:** Initials.

PEASE, W.D., Rt. 2 Box 37AA, Ewing, KY 41039/606-845-0387
Specialties: Display-quality working straight knives and folders. **Patterns:** Fighters, tantos and boots; locking folders and interframes. **Technical:** Grinds 440C, ATS-34 and commercial Damascus; has own side-release lock system. **Prices:** $300 to $500; some to $1,500. **Remarks:** Full-time maker; first knife sold in 1970. **Mark:** First and middle initials, last name.

PEELE, BRYAN, 219 Ferry St., P.O. Box 1363, Thompson Falls, MT 59873/406-827-4633
Specialties: Fancy working and using knives of his design. **Patterns:** Hunters, Bowies and fighters. **Technical:** Grinds 440C, ATS-34, D2, O1 and commercial Damascus. **Prices:** $110 to $300; some to $900. **Remarks:** Part-time maker; first knife sold in 1985. **Mark:** The Elk Rack, full name, city, state.

PENDLETON, LLOYD, 24581 Shake Ridge Rd., Volcano, CA 95689/209-296-3353; FAX: 209-296-3353
Specialties: Contemporary working knives in standard patterns. **Patterns:** Hunters, fighters and boots. **Technical:** Grinds 154CM and ATS-34; mirror finishes. **Prices:** $300 to $700; some to $2,000. **Remarks:** Full-time maker; first knife sold in 1973. **Mark:** First initial, last name logo, city and state.

PENDRAY, ALFRED H., Rt. 2, Box 1950, Williston, FL 32696/352-528-6124
Specialties: Working straight knives and folders; period pieces. **Patterns:** Fighters and hunters, axes, camp knives and tomahawks. **Technical:** Forges Wootz steel; makes his own Damascus; makes traditional knives from old files and rasps. **Prices:** $125 to $1,000; some to $3,500. **Remarks:** Part-time maker; first knife sold in 1954. **Mark:** Last intial in horseshoe logo.

PENNINGTON, C.A., 137 Riverlea Estate Dr., Stewarts Gully, Christchurch 9, NEW ZEALAND/03-323 7292; FAX: 03-323-7292
Specialties: Classic working/using straight knives of his design. **Patterns:** Hunters, kitchen knives, utility/camp knives. **Technical:** Grinds D2, 440C and ATS-34. Forges his own tool steel Damascus. **Prices:** $240 to $1,500. **Remarks:** Full-time maker; first knife sold in 1988. **Mark:** Name, country.

PEPIOT, STEPHAN, 73 Cornwall Blvd., Winnipeg, Manitoba, CANADA R3J-1E9/204-888-1499
Specialties: Working straight knives in standard patterns. **Patterns:** Hunters and camp knives. **Technical:** Grinds 440C and industrial hacksaw blades. **Prices:** $75 to $125. **Remarks:** Spare-time maker; first knife sold in 1982. Not currently taking orders. **Mark:** PEP.

PEPPER KNIVES (See Culpepper, John)

PERRY, CHRIS, 1654 W. Birch, Fresno, CA 93711/209-498-2342
Specialties: Traditional working/using straight knives of his design. **Patterns:** Boots, hunters and utility/camp knives. **Technical:** Grinds ATS-34 and 416 ss fittings. **Prices:** $190 to $225. **Remarks:** Spare-time maker. **Mark:** Name above city and state.

PERRY CUSTOM KNIVES (Perry, John)

PERRY, JOHN, 9 South Harrell Rd., Mayflower, AR 72106/501-470-3043
Specialties: Investment grade and working folders; some straight knives. **Patterns:** Front and rear lock folders, liner locks and hunters. **Technical:** Grinds CPM440V, D2 and Damascus. Offers filework. **Prices:** $250 to $750; some to $950. **Remarks:** Part-time maker; first knife sold in 1990. Doing business as Perry Custom Knives. **Mark:** Initials or last name in high relief set in a diamond shape.

PERSUADER (See Hill, Howard E.)

PETEAN, FRANCISCO AND MAURICIO, R. Dr. Carlos de Carvalho Rosa, 52, Centro, Birigui, SP-16200-000, BRAZIL/0186-424786
Specialties: Classic knives to customer specs. **Patterns:** Bowies, boots, fighters, hunters and utility knives. **Technical:** Grinds D6, 440C and high carbon steels. Prefers natural handle material. **Prices:** $70 to $500. **Remarks:** Full-time maker; first knife sold in 1985. **Mark:** Last name, hand made.

PETEAN, MAURICIO (See Petean, Francisco and Mauricio)

PETERSEN, DAN L., 3015 SW Clark Ct., Topeka, KS 66604
Specialties: Period pieces and forged integral hilts on hunters and fighters. **Patterns:** Texas style Bowies, boots and hunters in high carbon and Damascus steel. **Technical:** Austempers forged high-carbon blades. **Prices:** $200 to $3,000; some to $3,000. **Remarks:** First knife sold in 1978. **Mark:** Stylized initials, MS.

PETERSON, CHRIS, Box 143, 2175 W. Rockyford, Salina, UT 84654/801-529-7194
Specialties: Working straight knives of his design. **Patterns:** Large fighters, boots, hunters and some display pieces. **Technical:** Forges O1 and meteor. Makes and sells his own Damascus. Engraves, scrimshaws and inlays. **Prices:** $150 to $600; some to $1,500. **Remarks:** Full-time maker; first knife sold in 1986. **Mark:** A drop in a circle with a line through it.

PETERSON, ELDON G., 1395 Marjoria Ave., Columbia Falls, MT 59912/406-892-2068; FAX: 406-862-3103
Specialties: Fancy and working folders, any size. **Patterns:** Lockback interframes, integral bolster folders and two-bladers. **Technical:** Grinds 440C and ATS-34. Offers gold inlay work, gem stone inlays and engraving. **Prices:** $285 to $5,000. **Remarks:** Full-time maker; first knife sold in 1974. **Mark:** Name, city and state.

PHILLIPS, RANDY, 759 E. Francis St., Ontario, CA 91761/909-923-4381
Specialties: Hunters, collector-grade liner locks and high-art daggers. **Technical:** Grinds D2, 440C and 154CM; embellishes. **Prices:** Start at $200. **Remarks:** Part-time maker; first knife sold in 1981. Not currently taking orders. **Mark:** Name, city and state in eagle head.

PICKENS, SELBERT, Rt. 1, Box 216, Liberty, WV 25124/304-586-2190
Specialties: Using knives. **Patterns:** Standard sporting knives. **Technical:** Stainless steels; stock removal method. **Prices:** Moderate. **Remarks:** Part-time maker. **Mark:** Name.

PIENAAR, CONRAD, 19A Milner Rd., Bloemfontein 9300, REPUBLIC OF SOUTH AFRICA/051-314180
Specialties: Fancy working and using straight knives and folders of his design, to customer specs and in standard patterns. **Patterns:** Hunters, locking folders, cleavers, kitchen and utility/camp knives. **Technical:** Grinds 12C27, D2 and ATS-34. Uses some Damascus. Scrimshaws; inlays gold. Knives come with wooden box and custom-made leather sheath. **Prices:** $400 to $1,000. **Remarks:** Part-time maker; first knife sold in 1981. Doing business as C.P. Knifemaker. **Mark:** Initials and serial number.

PIERCE, HAROLD L., 106 Lyndon Lane, Louisville, KY 40222/502-429-5136
Specialties: Working straight knives, some fancy. **Patterns:** Big fighters and Bowies. **Technical:** Grinds D2, 440C, 154CM; likes sub-hilts. **Prices:** $150 to $450; some to $1,200. **Remarks:** Full-time maker; first knife sold in 1982. **Mark:** Last name with knife through the last initial.

PIERGALLINI, DANIEL E., 4011 N. Forbes Rd., Plant City, FL 33565/813-754-3908
Specialties: Traditional and fancy straight knives of my design or to customer's specs. **Patterns:** Hunters, fighters, three-fingered skinners, fillet, working and camp knives. **Technical:** Grinds 440C, O1, D2, ATS-34 and Damascus; forges his own mokume. Uses natural handle material. **Prices:** $150 to $500; some to $1,200. **Remarks:** Part-time maker; sold first knife in 1994. **Mark:** Last name, city, state.

PIESNER, DEAN, 30 King St., St. Jacobs, Ont. CANADA N0B 2N0/519-664-3622; FAX: 519-664-1828; E-MAIL: piesner@hookup.net
Specialties: Classic and period pieces of his design and to customer specs. **Patterns:** Bowies, skinners, fighters and swords. **Technical:** Forges 5160, 52100, steel Damascus and nickel-steel Damascus. Makes own mokume gane with copper, brass and nickel silver. Silver wire inlays in wood. **Prices:** Start at $125. **Remarks:** Full-time maker; first knife sold in 1990. **Mark:** First initial, last name, JS.

PIONEER FORGE & WOODSHOP (See Mitchell, Wm. Dean)

PIOREK, JAMES S., P.O. Box 5032, Missoula, MT 59806/406-728-0119
Specialties: Custom tailored, advanced concealment blades; sheaths and total body harness systems. **Patterns:** Tactical/personal defense fighters, swords, utility blades and custom patterns. **Technical:** Grinds A2; heat-treats. Sheaths are Kydex-lined leather laminated. Exotic materials available. **Prices:** $275 to $10,000. **Remarks:** Full-time maker; first knife sold in 1990. Doing business as Blade Rigger. **Mark:** Initials with abstract cutting edge.

PIRANHA KNIFE CO. (See Horton, Scot)

PITT, DAVID F., P.O. Box 1564, Pleasanton, CA 94566/415-846-9751
Specialties: Working straight knives. **Patterns:** Knives for deer and elk hunters, including hatchets and cleavers; small gut hook hunters and capers. **Technical:** Grinds A2, 440C and 154CM. **Prices:** $100 to $200; some to $450. **Remarks:** Full-time maker; first knife sold in 1972. **Mark:** Bear paw with name.

PLUNKETT, RICHARD, 29 Kirk Rd., West Cornwall, CT 06796/860-672-3419; TOLL-FREE: 888-KNIVES-8
Specialties: Traditional, fancy folders and straight knives of his design. **Patterns:** Slip-joint folders and small straight knives. **Technical:** Grinds O1 and stainless steel. Offers many different file patterns. **Prices:** $150 to $450. **Remarks:** Full-time maker; first knife sold in 1994. **Mark:** Signature and date under handle scales.

POAG, JAMES, RR 1, Box 212A, Grayville, IL 62844/618-375-7106
Specialties: Working straight knives and folders; period pieces; of his design or to customer specs. **Patterns:** Bowies and camp knives, lockers and slip-joints. **Technical:** Forges and grinds stainless steels and others; provides serious leather; offers embellishments; scrimshaws, engraves and does leather work for other makers. **Prices:** $65 to $1,200. **Remarks:** Full-time maker; first knife sold in 1967. **Mark:** Name.

POGREBA, LARRY, Box 861, Lyons, CO 80540/303-823-6691
Specialties: Steel and Damascus lightweight hunters; kitchen knives. **Patterns:** Fighters, hawks and spears. **Technical:** Forges/grinds his own Damascus. **Prices:** $40 to $1,000. **Remarks:** Part-time maker; first knife sold in 1976. Doing business as Cadillac Blacksmithing. **Mark:** Initials.

POLK, CLIFTON, 4625 Webber Creek Rd., Van Buren, AR 72956/501-474-3828
Specialties: Fancy working straight knives and folders. **Patterns:** Locking folders, slip-joints, two-blades, straight knives. **Technical:** Offers 440C, D2 ATS-34 and Damascus. **Prices:** $150 to $3,000. **Remarks:** Full-time maker. **Mark:** Last name.

POLKOWSKI, AL, 8 Cathy Ct., Chester, NJ 07930/908-879-6030
Specialties: High-tech straight knives and folders for adventurers and professionals. **Patterns:** Fighters, side-lock folders, boots and concealment knives. **Technical:** Grinds D2 and ATS-34; features satin and bead-blast finishes; Kydex sheaths. **Prices:** Start at $100. **Remarks:** Full-time maker; first knife sold in 1985. **Mark:** Full name, Handmade.

POLZIEN, DON, 1912 Inler Suite-L, Lubbock, TX 79407/806-791-0766 **Specialties:** Traditional Japanese-style blades; restores antique Japanese swords, scabbards and fittings. **Patterns:** Hunters, fighters, one-of-a-kind art knives. **Technical:** 1045-1050 carbon steels, 440C, D2, ATS-34, standard and cable Damascus. **Prices:** $150 to $2,500. **Remarks:** Full-time maker. First knife sold in 1990. **Mark:** Oriental characters inside square border.

PONZIO, DOUG, 3212 93rd St., Kenosha, WI 53142/414-694-3188

POOLE, MARVIN O., P.O. Box 5234, Anderson, SC 29623/803-225-5970 **Specialties:** Traditional working/using straight knives and folders of his design and in standard patterns. **Patterns:** Bowies, fighters, hunters, locking folders, bird and trout knives. **Technical:** Grinds 440C, D2, ATS-34. **Prices:** $50 to $150; some to $750. **Remarks:** Part-time maker; first knife sold in 1980. **Mark:** First initial, last name, year, serial number.

POOLE, STEVE L., 200 Flintlock Trail, Stockbridge, GA 30281/770-474-9154
Specialties: Traditional working and using straight knives and folders of his design, to customer specs and in standard patterns. **Patterns:** Bowies, fighters, hunters, utility and locking folders. **Technical:** Grinds ATS-34 and 440V; buys Damascus. Heat-treats; offers leatherwork. **Prices:** $85 to $350; some to $800. **Remarks:** Spare-time maker; first knife sold in 1991. **Mark:** Stylized first and last initials.

POPLIN, JAMES L., 103 Oak St., Washington, GA 30673/404-678-2729 **Specialties:** Contemporary hunters. **Patterns:** Hunters and boots. **Technical:** Hollow-grinds. **Prices:** Reasonable. **Mark:** POP.

POPP SR., STEVE, 6573 Winthrop Dr., Fayetteville, NC 28311/910-822-3151
Specialties: Working straight knives. **Patterns:** Hunters, Bowies and fighters. **Technical:** Forges and grinds his own Damascus, O1, L6 and spring steel. **Prices:** $75 to $600; some to $1,000. **Remarks:** Full-time maker; first knife sold in 1984. **Mark:** Initials and last name.

PORTER, JAMES E., P.O. Box 2583, Bloomington, IN 47402/812-859-4302
Specialties: Working straight knives; period pieces. **Patterns:** Outdoor knives; Bowies and short swords. **Technical:** Forges W2 and 1095; makes pattern-welded Damascus. Prefers Damascus for blades and fittings. **Prices:** $125 to $3,000. **Remarks:** Part-time maker; first knife sold in 1986. **Mark:** First and middle initials, MS.

POSKOCIL, HELMUT, Oskar Czeijastrasse 2, A-3340 Waidhofen/Ybbs, AUSTRIA/0043-7442-54519; FAX: 0043-7442-54519
Specialties: High-art and classic straight knives and folders of his design. **Patterns:** Bowies, daggers, hunters and locking folders. **Technical:** Grinds ATS-34 and stainless and carbon Damascus. Hardwoods, fossil ivory, horn and amber for handle material; silver wire and gold inlays; silver butt caps. Offers engraving and scrimshaw. **Prices:** $350 to $850; some to $3,500. **Remarks:** Part-time maker; first knife sold in 1991. **Mark:** Name.

POSNER, BARRY E., 12501 Chandler Blvd., Suite 104, N. Hollywood, CA 91607/818-752-8005; FAX: 818-752-8006
Specialties: Working/using straight knives. **Patterns:** Hunters, kitchen and utility/camp knives. **Technical:** Grinds ATS-34; forges 1095 and nickel. **Prices:** $100 to $250. **Remarks:** Part-time maker; first knife sold in 1987. Doing business as Posner Knives. Supplier of finished mosaic handle pin stock. **Mark:** First and middle initials, last name.

POSNER KNIVES (See Posner, Barry E.)

POSTON, ALVIN, 1197 Bass Rd., Pamplico, SC 29583/803-493-0066 **Specialties:** Working straight knives. **Patterns:** Hunters, Bowies and fishing knives; some miniatures. **Technical:** Grinds 154CM and ATS-34. **Prices:** Start at $100. **Remarks:** Part-time maker; first knife sold in 1979. **Mark:** Last name.

POTIER, TIMOTHY F., P.O. Box 711, Oberlin, LA 70655/318-639-2229 **Specialties:** Classic working and using straight knives to customer specs; some collectible. **Patterns:** Hunters, Bowies, utility/camp knives and belt axes. **Technical:** Forges carbon steel and his own Damascus; offers filework. **Prices:** $300 to $1,800; some to $4,000. **Remarks:** Part-time maker; first knife sold in 1981. **Mark:** Last name, MS.

POTOCKI, ROGER, Rte. 1, Box 333A, Goreville, IL 62939/618-995-9502

POYTHRESS, JOHN, P.O. Box 585, 625 Freedom St., Swainsboro, GA 30401/912-237-9233; 912-237-9478
Specialties: Traditional working and using straight knives of his design or to customer specs. **Patterns:** Hunters. **Technical:** Uses 440C, ATS-34 and D2. **Prices:** $75 to $250; some to $400. **Remarks:** Spare-time maker; first knife sold in 1983. **Mark:** J.W. Poythress Handcrafted, serial number.

PRATER, MIKE (See North, David and Prater, Mike)

PREHISTORIC EDGE, THE (See Stafford, Michael)

PRESSBURGER, RAMON, 59 Driftway Rd., Howell, NJ 07731/908-363-0816
Specialties: Traditional working knives to customer specs. **Patterns:** Hunters, skinners and utility/camp knives. **Technical:** Uses ATS-34, D2 and BG 42 and high-carbon steels. **Prices:** $70 to $500. **Remarks:** Full-time maker; first knife sold in 1970. **Mark:** NA.

PRICE, JERRY L., P.O. Box 782, Springdale, AR 72764
Specialties: Working straight knives in standard patterns. **Patterns:** Fighters, boots and Bowies. **Technical:** Grinds A2, 440C and 154CM; matte black oxide finish on fighters. Offers Kydex sheaths. **Prices:** $60 to $200; some to $400. **Remarks:** Full-time maker; first knife sold in 1975. **Mark:** First initial, last name.

PRICE, JIMMY, 2205 Highway 81 South, Covington, GA 30209/770-787-6526

PRICE, JOEL HIRAM, RR1, Box 18GG, Interlochen, FL 32148-9709 **Specialties:** Working straight knives to customer specs. **Patterns:** Variety of straight knives. **Technical:** Forges and grinds W2, O1, D2 and 440C—customer choice; buys Damascus. All knives have filework. **Prices:** $50 to $250; some $750 and higher. **Remarks:** Full-time maker; first knife sold in 1984. **Mark:** Hiram Knives in script.

PRICE, STEVE, 899 Ida Lane, Kamloops, BC V2B 6V2, CANADA/604-579-8932
Specialties: Working knives and fantasy pieces of his design or to customer specs. **Patterns:** Hunters, axes, tantos, survival knives, locking folders and some miniatures. **Technical:** Grinds D2, 440C and ATS-34; buys Damascus. **Prices:** $90 to $350; some to $1,200. **Remarks:** Full-time maker; first knife sold in 1982. **Mark:** First initial, last name.

PRINCE, JOE R., 5406 Reidville Rd., Moore, SC 29369/803-576-7479 **Specialties:** Traditional straight knives and folders of his design. **Patterns:** Boots and locking folders. **Technical:** Grinds ATS-34 and 154CM. **Prices:** $100 to $500. **Remarks:** Part-time maker; first knife sold in 1975. **Mark:** Last name.

PRITCHARD, RON, 613 Crawford Ave., Dixon, IL 61021/815-284-6005 **Specialties:** Plain and fancy working knives. **Patterns:** Variety of straight knives, locking folders, interframes and miniatures. **Technical:** Grinds 440C, 154CM and commercial Damascus. **Prices:** $100 to $200; some to $1,500. **Remarks:** Part-time maker; first knife sold in 1979. **Mark:** Name and city.

PRO-FLYTE, INC. (See Branton, Robert)

PROVENZANO, JOSEPH D., 3024 Ivy Place, Chalmette, LA 70043/504-279-3154
Specialties: Working straight knives and folders in standard patterns. **Patterns:** Hunters, Bowies, folders, camp and fishing knives. **Technical:** Grinds ATS-34, 440C, 154CM and Damascus. Hollow-grinds hunters. **Prices:** $75 to $300; some to $500. **Remarks:** Part-time maker; first knife sold in 1980. **Mark:** Joe-Pro.

PROVISION FORGE (See Martin, Gene)

PUEDO KNIFEWORKS (See Johnson, Randy)

PUGH, JIM, P.O. Box 711, Azle, TX 76020/817-444-2679; FAX: 817-444-5455
Specialties: Fancy/embellished limited editions by request. **Patterns:** 5- to 7-inch Bowies, wildlife art pieces, hunters, daggers and fighters; some commemoratives. **Technical:** Grinds 440C and ATS-34; casts guards and buttcaps in bronze, synthetic gold, silver and 14K gold. Offers engraving, fancy file etching and leather sheaths for wildlife art pieces. Ivory and cocobolo handle material on limited editions. Designs

animal head buttcaps and paws or bear claw guards; sterling silver heads and guards. **Prices:** $500 to $5,500; some to $20,000. **Remarks:** Full-time maker; first knife sold in 1970. **Mark:** Last name.

PULIS, VLADIMIR, Horna Ves 43/B/25, 96701 Kremnica, SLOVAKIA/421-857-757-214
Specialties: Fancy and high-art straight knives of his design. **Patterns:** Daggers and hunters. **Technical:** Forges Damast steel. All work done by hand. **Prices:** $250 to $3,000; some to $10,000. **Remarks:** Part-time maker; first knife sold in 1990. **Mark:** Initials in octagon.

PULLEN, MARTIN, 1701 Broken Bow Rd., Granbury, TX 76049/817-573-1784
Specialties: Working straight knives; period pieces. **Patterns:** Fighters, Bowies and daggers; locking folders. **Technical:** Grinds D2, 440C, ATS-34 and 154CM. **Prices:** Start at $150. **Remarks:** Full-time maker; first knife sold in 1978. **Mark:** Last name.

PULLIAM, MORRIS C., 560 Jeptha Knob Rd., Shelbyville, KY 40065/502-633-2261; FAX: 502-633-5294.
Specialties: Working knives; classic Bowies. **Patterns:** Bowies, hunters, Fort Meigs axes and tomahawks. **Technical:** Forges L6, W2, 1095, Damascus and nickel-sheet and bar 1000 to 16,000 layer Damascus. **Prices:** $165 to $1,200. **Remarks:** Full-time maker; first knife sold in 1974. Makes knives for Native American festivals. Doing business as Knob Hill Forge. **Mark:** Last name or last initial.

PURSLEY, AARON, Box 1037, Big Sandy, MT 59520/406-378-3200
Specialties: Fancy working knives. **Patterns:** Locking folders, straight hunters and daggers, personal wedding knives and letter openers. **Technical:** Grinds O1 and 440C; engraves. **Prices:** $300 to $600; some to $1,500. **Remarks:** Full-time maker; first knife sold in 1975. **Mark:** Initials connected with year.

PUTNAM, DONALD S., 590 Wolcott Hill Rd., Wethersfield, CT 06109/203-563-9718; FAX: 203-563-9718
Specialties: Working knives for the hunter and fisherman. **Patterns:** His design or to customer specs. **Technical:** Uses stock removal method, O1, W2, D2, ATS-34, 154CM, 440C and CPM REX 20; stainless steel Damascus on request. **Prices:** NA. **Remarks:** Full-time maker; first knife sold in 1985. **Mark:** Last name with a knife outline.

q

QUALITY CUSTOM KNIVES (See Fisher, Jay)

QUARTON, BARR, P.O. Box 4335, McCall, ID 83638/208-634-3641
Specialties: Plain and fancy working knives; period pieces. **Patterns:** Hunters, tantos and swords. **Technical:** Forges and grinds 154CM, ATS-34 and his own Damascus. **Prices:** $180 to $450; some to $4,500. **Remarks:** Full-time maker; first knife sold in 1978. Doing business as Barr Custom Knives and Deer Creek Forge. **Mark:** First name with bear logo.

QUATTLEBAUM, CRAIG, P.O. Box 983, Searcy, AR 72145-0983
Specialties: Traditional straight knives and one-of-a-kind knives of his design; period pieces. **Patterns:** Bowies and fighters. **Technical:** Forges 5168, 52100 and own Damascus. **Prices:** $100 to $1,200. **Remarks:** Part-time maker; first knife sold in 1988. **Mark:** Stylized initials.

QUICK, MIKE, 23 Locust Ave., Kearny, NJ 07032/201-991-6580
Specialties: Traditional working/using straight knives. **Patterns:** Bowies. **Technical:** 440C and ATS-34 for blades; Micarta, wood and stag for handles.

r

RACHLIN, LESLIE S., 1200 W. Church St., Elmira, NY 14905/607-733-6889
Specialties: Classic and working/using straight knives and folders of his design. **Patterns:** Hunters, locking folders and utility/camp knives. **Technical:** Grinds 440C and Damascus. **Prices:** $110 to $200; some to $450. **Remarks:** Spare-time maker; first knife sold in 1989. Doing business as Tinkermade Knives. **Mark:** Stamped initials or Tinkermade, city and state.

RADOS, JERRY F., 7523 E 5000 N Rd., Grant Park, IL 60940/815-472-3350; FAX: 815-472-3944
Specialties: Deluxe period pieces. **Patterns:** Hunters, fighters, locking folders, daggers and camp knives. **Technical:** Forges and grinds his own Damascus which he sells commercially; makes pattern-welded Turkish Damascus. **Prices:** Start at $900. **Remarks:** Full-time maker; first knife sold in 1981. **Mark:** Last name.

RAFTER KK CUSTOM KNIVES (See Kimsey, Kevin)

RAGSDALE, JAMES D., 3002 Arabian Woods Dr., Lithonia, GA 30038/770-482-6739
Specialties: Fancy and embellished working knives of his design or to customer specs. **Patterns:** Hunters, folders and fighters. **Technical:** Grinds 440C, ATS-34 and A2. **Prices:** $100 to $350; some to $800. **Remarks:** Full-time maker; first knife sold in 1984. **Mark:** Fish symbol with name above, town below.

RAINVILLE, RICHARD, 126 Cockle Hill Rd., Salem, CT 06420/203-859-2776
Specialties: Traditional working straight knives. **Patterns:** Outdoor knives, including fishing knives. **Technical:** Grinds O1, L6, 400C, ATS-34, 154CM. Custom fits handles. **Prices:** $85 to $600. **Remarks:** Full-time maker; first knife sold in 1982. **Mark:** Name, city, state in oval logo.

RALPH, DARREL, 7032 E. Livingston Ave., Reynoldsburg, OH 43068/614-577-1040
Specialties: Fancy, high-art, high-tech, collectible straight knives and folders of his design and to customer specs; unique mechanisms, some disassemble. **Patterns:** Daggers, fighters and swords. **Technical:** Forges his own Damascus, nickel and high carbon. Uses mokume and Damascus; mosaics and special patterns. Engraves and heat-treats. Prefers pearl, ivory and abolone handle material; uses stones and jewels. **Prices:** $250 to $2,500; some to $10,000. **Remarks:** Full-time maker; first knife sold in 1987. Doing business as Briar Knives. **Mark:** Hand-signed.

RAMEY, MARSHALL F., P.O. Box 2589, West Helena, AR 72390/501-572-7436, 501-572-6245
Specialties: Traditional working knives. **Patterns:** Designs military combat knives; makes butterfly folders, camp knives and miniatures. **Technical:** Grinds D2 and 440C. **Prices:** $100 to $500. **Remarks:** Full-time maker; first knife sold in 1978. **Mark:** Name with ram's head.

RANDALL, BILL, 765 W. Limberlost #30, Tucson, AZ 85705/502-887-9776
Specialties: High-art and period pieces of his design. **Patterns:** Fighters, hunters and neo-tribal. **Technical:** Forges A6 and carbon steel; forges and grinds Damascus. Hammer-finish on neo-tribal style knives. Uses natural handle material; makes own sheaths. **Prices:** $85 to $250; some to $500. **Remarks:** Part-time maker; first knife sold in 1995. Doing business as Bill Randall Knives. **Mark:** Last name.

RANDALL KNIVES, BILL (See Randall, Bill)

RANDALL MADE KNIVES, P.O. Box 1988, Orlando, FL 32802/407-855-8075; FAX: 407-855-9054; WEB: http://www.randallknives.com
Specialties: Working straight knives. **Patterns:** Hunters, fighters and Bowies. **Technical:** Forges and grinds O1 and 440B. **Prices:** $65 to $250; some to $450. **Remarks:** Full-time maker; first knife sold in 1937. **Mark:** Randall, city and state in scimitar logo.

RANKL, CHRISTIAN, Possenhofenerstr. 33, 81476 München, GERMANY/0171-3662679; FAX: 089-797010
Specialties: Tail-lock knives. **Patterns:** Fighters, hunters and locking folders. **Technical:** Grinds ATS-34, 4034 and stainless Damascus by F. Schneider. **Prices:** $450 to $950; some to $2,000. **Remarks:** Full-time maker; first knife sold in 1989. **Mark:** Electrochemical etching on blade.

RAPP, STEVEN J., 7479 S. Ramanee Dr., Midvale, UT 84047/801-567-9553
Specialties: Fancy Bowies and daggers; reproductions of antique knives. **Patterns:** Daggers, Bowies, fighters and San Francisco knives. **Technical:** Hollow- and flat-grinds 440C and Damascus. **Prices:** Start at $500. **Remarks:** Full-time maker; first knife sold in 1981. **Mark:** Name and state.

RAPPAZZO, RICHARD, 142 Dunsbach Ferry Rd., Cohoes, NY 12047/518-783-6843

Specialties: Damascus locking folders and straight knives. **Patterns:** Folders, dirks, fighters and tantos in original and traditional designs. **Technical:** Hand-forges all blades; specializes in Damascus; uses only natural handle materials. **Prices:** $400 to $1,500. **Remarks:** Part-time maker; first knife sold in 1985. **Mark:** Name, date, serial number.

RARDON, A.D., 1589 S.E. Price Dr., Polo, MO 64671/816-354-2330
Specialties: Working knives, miniatures, automatics and folders. **Patterns:** Hunters, buckskinners, Bowies, miniatures and daggers. **Technical:** Grinds O1, D2, 440C and ATS-34. **Prices:** $100 to $1,500; some higher. **Remarks:** Full-time maker; first knife sold in 1954. **Mark:** Name, address in running fox logo.

RARDON, ARCHIE F., Rt. 1, Box 79, Polo, MO 64671/816-354-2330
Specialties: Working knives. **Patterns:** Hunters, Bowies and miniatures. **Technical:** Grinds O1, D2, 440C, ATS-34, cable and Damascus. **Prices:** $50 to $500. **Remarks:** Part-time maker. **Mark:** Name and address in razor-back hog logo.

RATTLER BRAND KNIVES (See Selvidio, Ralph J.)

RAVEN FORGE (See Parler, Thomas O'Neil)

RAY, ALAN W., P.O. Box 479, Lovelady, TX 75851/409-636-2301
Specialties: Working straight knives and folders of his design. **Patterns:** Hunters, camp knives, folders, steak knives and carving sets. **Technical:** Forges L6 and 5160 for straight knives; grinds D2 and 440C for folders and kitchen cutlery. **Prices:** $200 to $500. **Remarks:** Full-time maker; first knife sold in 1989. **Mark:** Stylized initials.

RAYMOND, DONALD, P.O. Box 1141, Groveton, TX 75845/409-642-1707
Specialties: Traditional working and using straight knives and folders of his design and to customer specs. **Patterns:** Fighters, hunters, kitchen knives and locking folders. **Technical:** Grinds 440C and D2; forges his own Damascus. **Prices:** $150 to $550; some to $850. **Remarks:** Full-time maker; first knife sold in 1988. Doing business as DR Knives. **Mark:** Stylized initials.

RAZAVI-MEHR (See Farid)

R.D. CUSTOM KNIVES (See Miller, R.D.)

RECE, CHARLES V., P.O. Box 868, Paw Creek, NC 28130/704-391-0209
Specialties: Traditional straight knives and presentation knives. **Patterns:** Bowies, hunters and presentation knives. **Technical:** Grinds ATS-34, D2 and 440C. Scrimshawed handles are standard. **Prices:** $150 to $400. **Remarks:** Limited-production maker; first knife sold in 1986. Doing business as Uwharrie Rattler Knives and Wildwood Art. **Mark:** Engraved timber rattler.

REDDIEX, BILL, 27 Galway Ave., Palmerston North, NEW ZEALAND/06-357-0383; FAX: 06-358-2910
Specialties: Collector-grade working straight knives. **Patterns:** Traditional-style Bowies and drop-point hunters. **Technical:** Grinds 440C, D2 and O1; offers variety of grinds and finishes. **Prices:** $130 to $750. **Remarks:** Full-time maker; first knife sold in 1980. **Mark:** Last name around kiwi bird logo.

REDUCED REALITY (See Heasman, H.G.)

REED, DAVE, Box 132, Brimfield, MA 01010/413-245-3661
Specialties: Traditional styles. Makes knives from chains, rasps, gears, etc. **Patterns:** Bush swords, hunters, working minis, camp and utility knives. **Technical:** Forges 1075 and his own Damascus. **Prices:** Start at $50. **Remarks:** Part-time maker; first knife sold in 1970. **Mark:** Initials.

REED, DEL, 13765 SW Parkway, Beaverton, OR 97005
Specialties: Unusual configurations. **Patterns:** Swing-blade knives. **Technical:** Grinds stainless steel. **Prices:** $100 to $125. **Remarks:** First knife sold in 1988. **Mark:** ORION.

REEVE, CHRIS, 11624 W. President Dr., Apt. B, Boise, ID 83713/208-375-0367
Specialties: One-piece utility/military fixed blades. **Patterns:** Working and art folders; variety of fixed-blade shapes in one-piece design. **Technical:** Grinds folder blades of BG42, mostly titanium handles; A2 for fixed blades. Art knives are ATS-34, BG42 or Damascus blades; titanium or exotic handle material. **Prices:** $165 to $800; some to $4,000. **Remarks:** Full-time maker; first knife sold in 1982. Availability of art pieces very limited. **Mark:** Initials connected.

REEVES, WINFRED M., P.O. Box 300, West Union, SC 29696/803-638-6121
Specialties: Working straight knives; some elaborate pieces. **Patterns:** Hunters, tantos and fishing knives. **Technical:** Grinds D2, 440C and ATS-34. Does not solder joints; does not use buffer unless requested. **Prices:** $75 to $150; some to $300. **Remarks:** Part-time maker; first knife sold in 1975. **Mark:** Last name, Walhalla, state.

REGGIO JR., SIDNEY J., P.O. Box 851, Sun, LA 70463/504-886-5886
Specialties: Miniature classic and fancy straight knives of his design or in standard patterns. **Patterns:** Fighters, hunters and utility/camp knives. **Technical:** Grinds 440C, ATS-34 and commercial Damascus. Engraves; scrimshaws; offers filework. Hollow grinds most blades. Prefers natural handle material. Offers handmade sheaths. **Prices:** $85 to $250; some to $500. **Remarks:** Part-time maker; first knife sold in 1988. Doing business as Sterling Workshop. **Mark:** Initials.

REH, BILL, 2061 Tomlinson Rd., Caro, MI 48723/517-673-1195
Specialties: Traditional and working/using straight knives of his design and to customer specs. **Patterns:** Boots, hunters and Bowies. **Technical:** Stock removal; uses all kinds of steel. **Prices:** $100 to $180. **Remarks:** Spare-time maker; first knife sold in 1981. Doing business as Reh Custom Knives. **Mark:** Last name in sun-ray logo.

REH CUSTOM KNIVES (See Reh, Bill)

REMINGTON, DAVID W., 3608-17998 Syble Rd., Lincoln, AR 72744/501-846-3526
Specialties: Fancy and traditional straight knives of his design and to customer specs. **Patterns:** Bowies, daggers and hunters. **Technical:** Grinds ATS-34, A2 and D2. Makes own twist and random-pattern Damascus. Wholesale D2, A2, stag and ossic sheephorn. Rope and thorn pattern filework; tapered tangs; heat-treats. **Prices:** $65 to $250; some to $1,000. **Remarks:** Part-time maker; first knife sold in 1991. **Mark:** First and last name, Custom.

REPKE, MIKE (See Neering, Walt and Repke, Mike)

REPRODUCTION BLADES (See Kelley, Gary)

REVERDY, PIERRE, 21 AV Victor Hugo, 26100 Romans, FRANCE/334 75 05 10 15; FAX: 334 75 02 28 40; WEB: http://www.reverdy.com
Specialties: One-of-a-kind knives. **Patterns:** Daggers, Bowies, hunters and other large patterns. **Technical:** Forges his Damascus and "poetique Damascus"; works with his own EDM machine to create any kind of pattern inside the steel with his own touch. **Prices:** $200 to $40,000. **Remarks:** Full-time maker; first knife sold in 1986. **Mark:** Initials connected.

REVISHVILI, ZAZA, 7233 Cooper Ave., Glendale, NY 11385-7367
Specialties: Fancy/embellished and high-art straight knives and folders of his design. **Patterns:** Daggers, swords and locking folders. **Technical:** Uses Damascus; silver filigree inlay in wood; enameling. **Prices:** $1,000 to $9,000; some to $15,000. **Remarks:** Full-time maker; first knife sold in 1987. **Mark:** Initials, city.

REVISHVILI, ZAZA, P.O. Box 29, 125438 Moscow, RUSSIA/718-628-91-98; FAX: 7:095-402-75-74 (see above)

REXROAT, KIRK, 527 Sweetwater Circle, Box 224, Wright, WY 82732/307-464-0166
Specialties: Using and collectible straight knives and folders of his design or to customer specs. **Patterns:** Bowies, hunters, locking folders, utility/camp knives. **Technical:** Grinds 440C; forges cable, layered and Turkish Damascus; triple quenches 52100. Offers tapered tangs and dove-tailed guards. **Prices:** $150 to $450; some to $1,000. **Remarks:** Part-time maker; first knife sold in 1984. Doing business as Rexroat Knives. **Mark:** First initial, last name, city, state.

REXROAT KNIVES (See Rexroat, Kirk)

REYNOLDS, DAVE, Rt. 2, Box 36, Harrisville, WV 26362/304-643-2889
Specialties: Working straight knives of his design. **Patterns:** Bowies, kitchen and utility knives. **Technical:** Grinds and forges L6, 1095 and 440C. Heat-treats. **Prices:** $50 to $85; some to $175. **Remarks:** Full-time maker; first knife sold in 1980. Doing business as Terra-Gladius Knives. **Mark:** Mark on special orders only; serial number on all knives.

REYNOLDS, JOHN C., #2 Andover, HC77, Gillette, WY 82716/307-682-6076
Specialties: Working knives, some fancy. **Patterns:** Hunters, Bowies, tomahawks and buckskinners; some folders. **Technical:** Grinds D2, 440C and commerical Damascus. Scrimshaws. **Prices:** $100 to $320; some to $3,000. **Remarks:** Spare-time maker; first knife sold in 1969. **Mark:** Last name.

REX KNIVES (See Robinson III, Rex R.)

RHEA, DAVID, Rt. 1, Box 272, Lynnville, TN 38472/615-363-5993
Specialties: High-art fantasy knives. **Patterns:** Fighters, Bowies, survival knives and locking folders. **Technical:** Grinds D2, 440C, 154CM and Damascus. Embellishes; offers precious stones, metals and ivory. **Prices:** $300 to $2,000 and higher. **Remarks:** Part-time maker; first knife sold in 1982. **Mark:** Last name.

RHO, NESTOR LORENZO, Primera Junta 589, Junin (6000), Buenos Aires, ARGENTINA/(0362) 32247/21717
Specialties: Classic and fancy straight knives of his design. **Patterns:** Bowies, fighters and hunters. **Technical:** Grinds 420C, 440C and 1050. Offers semi-precious stones on handles, acid etching on blades and blade engraving. **Prices:** $60 to $300 some to $1,200. **Remarks:** Full-time maker; first knife sold in 1975. **Mark:** Name.

RHODES, JAMES D., 205 Woodpoint Ave., Hagerstown, MD 21740/301-739-2657
Specialties: Traditional working and using straight knives of his design. **Patterns:** Bowies, fighters, hunters and kitchen knives. **Technical:** Forges 5160, 1085 and 9260; makes own Damascus. Hard edges, soft backs, dead soft tangs. Heat-treats. **Prices:** $150 to $350. **Remarks:** Part-time maker. **Mark:** Last name, JS.

RIAL, DOUGLAS, Rt. 2, Box 117A, Greenfield, TN 38230/901-235-3994
Specialties: Working knives to customer specs; period pieces. **Patterns:** Hunters, fighters, boots, locking folders, slip-joints and miniatures. **Technical:** Grinds D2, 440C and 154CM. **Prices:** $60 to $100; some to $250. **Remarks:** Spare-time maker; first knife sold in 1978. **Mark:** Name and city.

RICE, ADRIENNE, P.O. Box 252, Lopez Island, WA 98261
Specialties: Folders and straight knives of her own and traditional designs; marine-oriented knives. **Patterns:** Traditional and neo-traditional folders; fillet and rigging knives; primitive inspired pieces. **Technical:** Grinds ATS-34, D2 and O1; forges old steel and Damascus. Uses natural handle materials. **Prices:** $150 to $750. **Remarks:** Full-time maker; first knife sold in 1981. Formerly Madrona Knives. **Mark:** Logo, name, handmade.

RICHARD, RON, 4875 Calaveras Ave., Fremont, CA 94538/510-796-9767
Specialties: High-tech working straight knives of his design. **Patterns:** Bowies, swords and locking folders. **Technical:** Forges and grinds ATS-34, 154CM and 440V. All folders have dead-bolt button locks. **Prices:** $650 to $850; some to $1,400. **Remarks:** Full-time maker; first knife sold in 1968. **Mark:** Full name.

RICHARDSON JR., PERCY, P.O. Box 973, Hemphill, TX 75948/409-787-2279
Specialties: Traditional and working straight knives and folders in standard patterns and to customer specs. **Patterns:** Bowies, daggers, hunters, automatics, locking folders, slip-joints and utility/camp knives. **Technical:** Grinds ATS-34, 440C and D2. **Prices:** $125 to $600; some to $1,800. **Remarks:** Full-time maker; first knife sold in 1990. Doing business as Lone Star Custom Knives. **Mark:** Lone Star with last name across it.

RICHTER FORGE (See Richter, John C.)

RICHTER, JOHN C., 932 Bowling Green Trail, Chesapeake, VA 23320
Specialties: Hand-forged knives in original patterns. **Patterns:** Hunters, fighters, utility knives and other belt knives, folders, swords. **Technical:** Hand-forges high carbon and his own Damascus; makes mokume gane. **Prices:** $75 to $1,500. **Remarks:** Part-time maker. **Mark:** Richter Forge.

RICHTER MADE (See Richter, Scott)

RICHTER, SCOTT, 516 E. 2nd St., S. Boston, MA 02127/617-269-4855
Specialties: Traditional working/using folders. **Patterns:** Locking folders, swords and kitchen knives. **Technical:** Grinds ATS-34, 5160 and A2. High-tech materials. **Prices:** $150 to $650; some to $1,500. **Remarks:** Full-time maker; first knife sold in 1991. Doing business as Richter Made. **Mark:** Last name, Made.

RICKE, DAVE, 1209 Adams, West Bend, WI 53095/414-334-5739
Specialties: Working knives; period pieces. **Patterns:** Hunters, boots, Bowies; locking folders and slip-joints. **Technical:** Grinds ATS-34, A2, 440C and 154CM. **Prices:** $75 to $260; some to $1,200. **Remarks:** Part-time maker; first knife sold in 1976. **Mark:** Last name.

RIETVELD, BERTIE, P.O. Box 53, Magaliesburg 2805, SOUTH AFRICA/27142-771294; E-MAIL: batavia@caseynet.co.za
Specialties: Damascus fighters, art daggers and button-lock folders. **Technical:** Makes his own stainless Damascus. **Prices:** $350 to $2,000. **Mark:** Elephant with last name.

RIGNEY JR., WILLIE, 191 Colson Dr., Bronston, KY 42518/606-679-4227
Specialties: High-tech period pieces and fancy working knives. **Patterns:** Fighters, boots, daggers and push knives. **Technical:** Grinds 440C and 154CM; buys Damascus. Most knives are embellished. **Prices:** $150 to $1,500; some to $10,000. **Remarks:** Full-time maker; first knife sold in 1978. **Mark:** First initial, last name.

RINGING CIRCLE, THE (See Fitzgerald, Dennis M.)

RINKES, SIEGFRIED, Am Sportpl 2, D 91459 Markterlbach, GERMANY

RIZZI, RUSSELL J., 6 King Arthur's Ct., E. Setauket, NY 11733/516-689-2698
Specialties: Fancy working and using straight knives and folders of his design or to customer specs. **Patterns:** Hunters, locking folders and fighters. **Technical:** Grinds 440C, D2 and commercial Damascus. **Prices:** $150 to $750; some to $2,500. **Remarks:** Part-time maker; first knife sold in 1990. **Mark:** Last name, Long Island, NY.

RL CUSTOM KNIVES (See Lambert, Ronald S.)

ROATH, DEAN, 3050 Winnipeg Dr., Baton Rouge, LA 70819/504-272-5562
Specialties: Classic working knives; specifically turkey hunting knives. **Patterns:** Hunters, boating/sailing and trail knives. **Technical:** Grinds 440C and ATS-34. **Prices:** $200 to $500; some to $1,500. **Remarks:** Part-time maker; first knife sold in 1978. **Mark:** Name, city and state.

ROBBIE KNIFE (See Robinson, Robert W.)

ROBBINS, HOWARD P., 1407 S. 217th Ave., Elkhorn, NE 68022/402-289-4121
Specialties: High-tech working knives with clean designs, some fancy. **Patterns:** Folders, hunters and camp knives. **Technical:** Grinds 440C and ATS-34. Heat-treats; likes mirror finishes. Offers leatherwork. **Prices:** $100 to $500; some to $1,000. **Remarks:** Full-time maker; first knife sold in 1982. **Mark:** Name, city and state.

ROBERTS, CHUCK, 5004 W. 92nd Ave., #207, Westminster, CO 80030/303-650-4563
Specialties: Traditional straight knives. **Patterns:** Bowies, hunters and California knives. **Technical:** Grinds 440C, 5160, Damascus and ATS-34. Handles made of stag, ivory or mother-of-pearl. **Prices:** Start at $350. **Remarks:** Full-time maker. **Mark:** Last initial or last name.

ROBERTS, GEORGE A., 93 Lewes Blvd., Apt. 207B, Whitehorse, Yukon Territories Y1A3J4, CANADA/403-667-7099; FAX: 403-668-5916
Specialties: Hunters, liner lockers and fancy fillet knives. **Patterns:** Bowies, hunters, liner lockers, fillet knives and ivory handled letter openers. **Technical:** Grinds ATS-34, 440C, Boye Dendritic, O1, mild Damascus and 440V. Liner lock liners are titanium. Etches, engraves and offers fancy filework on blades; scrimshaws and carves handles; makes leather sheaths. Uses fossilized mastadon ivory. **Prices:** $80 to $2,500. **Remarks:** Full-time maker; first knife sold in 1986. Doing business as Bandit Blades. **Mark:** Bandit.

ROBERTS, MICHAEL, 601 Oakwood Dr., Clinton, MS 39056/601-924-3154; PAGER: 601-978-8180
Specialties: Working and using knives in standard patterns and to customer specs. **Patterns:** Hunters, Bowies, tomahawks and fighters. **Technical:** Forges 5160, O1, 1095 and his own Damascus. Uses only natural handle materials. **Prices:** $145 to $500; some to $1,100. **Remarks:** Part-time maker; first knife sold in 1988. **Mark:** Last name or first and last name in Celtic script.

ROBINSON, CHARLES (DICKIE), P.O. Box 221, Vega, TX 79092/806-267-2629
Specialties: Classic and working/using knives. **Patterns:** Bowies, daggers, fighters, hunters and camp knives. **Technical:** Forges O1, 5160, 52100 and his own Damascus. **Prices:** $125 to $850; some to $2,500. **Remarks:** Part-time maker; first knife sold in 1988. Doing business as Robinson Knives. **Mark:** Last name, JS.

ROBINSON KNIVES (See Robinson, Charles [Dickie])

ROBINSON III, REX R., 10531 Poe St., Leesburg, FL 34788/352-787-4587
Specialties: One-of-a-kind high-art automatics of his design. **Patterns:** Automatics, liner locks and lock back folders. **Technical:** Uses tool steel and stainless Damascus and mokume; flat grinds. Hand carves folders. **Prices:** $1,000 to $2,600; some to $3,500. **Remarks:** First knife sold in 1988. **Mark:** First name inside oval.

ROBINSON, ROBERT W., 1569 N. Finley Pt., Polson, MT 59860/406-887-2259; FAX: 406-887-2259
Specialties: High-art straight knives, folders and automatics of his design. **Patterns:** Hunters and locking folders. **Technical:** Grinds ATS-34, 154CM and 440V. Inlays pearl and gold; engraves sheep horn and ivory. **Prices:** $150 to $500; some to $2,000. **Remarks:** Full-time maker; first knife sold in 1983. Doing business as Robbie Knife. **Mark:** Name on left side of blade.

ROCHFORD, MICHAEL R., P.O. Box 577, Dresser, WI 54009/715-755-3520
Specialties: Working straight knives and folders. **Patterns:** Bowies, hunters and camp knives. **Technical:** Grinds and forges W2, 440C, 154CM and his Damascus. **Prices:** $100 to $500; some to $800. **Remarks:** Part-time maker; first knife sold in 1984. **Mark:** Name.

ROCKY MOUNTAIN KNIVES (See Conklin, George L.)

RODKEY, DAN, 18336 Ozark Dr., Hudson, FL 34667/813-863-8264
Specialties: Traditional straight knives of his design and in standard patterns. **Patterns:** Boots, fighters and hunters. **Technical:** Grinds 440C, D2 and ATS-34. **Prices:** Start at $200. **Remarks:** Full-time maker; first knife sold in 1985. Doing business as Rodkey Knives. **Mark:** Etched logo on blade.

RODKEY KNIVES (See Rodkey, Dan)

ROE JR., FRED D., 4005 Granada Dr., Huntsville, AL 35802/205-881-6847
Specialties: Highly finished working knives of his design; period pieces. **Patterns:** Hunters, fighters and survival knives; locking folders; specialty designs like divers' knives. **Technical:** Grinds 154CM, ATS-34 and Damascus. Field-tests all blades. **Prices:** $125 to $250; some to $2,000. **Remarks:** Part-time maker; first knife sold in 1980. **Mark:** Last name.

ROGERS JR., ROBERT P., 3979 South Main St., Acworth, GA 30101/404-974-9982
Specialties: Traditional working knives. **Patterns:** Hunters, 4-inch trailing-points. **Technical:** Grinds D2, 154CM and ATS-34; likes ironwood and ivory Micarta. **Prices:** $125 to $175. **Remarks:** Spare-time maker; first knife sold in 1975. **Mark:** Name.

ROGERS, RODNEY, 602 Osceola St., Wildwood, FL 34785/352-748-6114
Specialties: Traditional straight knives and folders. **Patterns:** Fighters, hunters, skinners; some tactical knives. **Technical:** Flat-grinds ATS-34 and Damascus. Prefers natural materials. **Prices:** $150 to $1,400. **Remarks:** Full-time maker; first knife sold in 1986. **Mark:** Last name, Handmade.

ROGHMANS, MARK, 607 Virginia Ave., LaGrange, Georgia 30240/706-885-1273
Specialties: Classic and traditional knives of his design. **Patterns:** Bowies, daggers and fighters. **Technical:** Grinds ATS-34, D2 and 440C. **Prices:** $250 to $500. **Remarks:** Part-time maker; first knife sold in 1984. Doing business as LaGrange Knife. **Mark:** Last name and/or LaGrange Knife.

ROHN, FRED, W7615 Clemetson Rd., Coeur d'Alene, ID 83814/208-667-0774
Specialties: Working straight knives, some unusual. **Patterns:** Hunters, fighters, a unique Bowie design and locking folders. **Technical:** Grinds 440C and 154CM; stainless steel pins, bolsters and guards on all knives. **Prices:** $65 to $200; some to $450 and higher. **Remarks:** Part-time maker. **Mark:** Name in logo and serial number.

ROLAND, DAN, 1966 W. 13th Lane, Yuma, AZ 85364/520-343-2818

ROLLERT, STEVE, P.O. Box 65, Keenesburg, CO 80643-0065/303-732-4858
Specialties: Highly finished working knives. **Patterns:** Variety of straight knives; locking folders and slip-joints. **Technical:** Forges and grinds W2, 1095, ATS-34 and his pattern-welded, cable Damascus and nickel Damascus. **Prices:** $300 to $1,000; some to $3,000. **Remarks:** Full-time maker; first knife sold in 1980. Doing business as Dove Knives. **Mark:** Last name in script.

ROSA, PEDRO GULLHERME TELES, R. das Magnolias, 45, CECAP, Presidente Prudente, SP-19065-410, BRAZIL/0182-271769
Specialties: Using straight knives and folders to customer specs; some high-art. **Patterns:** Fighters, Bowies and daggers. **Technical:** Grinds and forges D6, 440C, high carbon steels and Damascus. **Prices:** $60 to $400. **Remarks:** Full-time maker; first knife sold in 1991. **Mark:** A hammer over "Hammer."

ROSENFELD, BOB, 955 Freeman Johnson Road, Hoschton, GA 30548/770-867-2647
Specialties: Fancy and embellished working/using straight knives of his design and in standard patterns. **Patterns:** Daggers, hunters and utility/camp knives. **Technical:** Forges 52100, A203E, 1095 and L6 Damascus. Offers engraving. **Prices:** $125 to $650; some to $1,000. **Remarks:** Full-time maker; first knife sold in 1984. **Mark:** Last name or full name, Knifemaker.

ROSS, D.L., 27 Kinsman St. Dunedin, NEW ZEALAND/(03) 464 0239; international, 64 3 464 0239
Specialties: Working straight knives of his design. **Patterns:** Hunters, various others. **Technical:** Grinds 440C. **Prices:** $100 to $450; some to $700 NZ dollars. **Remarks:** Part-time maker; first knife sold in 1988. **Mark:** Dave Ross, Maker, city and country.

ROSS, GREGG, 4556 Wenhart Rd., Lake Worth, FL 33463/407-439-4681
Specialties: Working/using straight knives. **Patterns:** Bowies, hunters and utility/camp knives. **Technical:** Forges and grinds ATS-34, Damascus and cable Damascus. Uses decorative pins. **Prices:** $125 to $250; some to $400. **Remarks:** Part-time maker; first knife sold in 1992. **Mark:** Name, city and state.

ROSS, STEPHEN, 534 Remington Dr., Evanston, WY 82930/307-789-7104
Specialties: One-of-a-kind collector-grade classic and contemporary straight knives and folders of his design and to customer specs; some fantasy pieces. **Patterns:** Combat and survival knives, hunters, boots and folders. **Technical:** Grinds stainless; forges spring and tool steel. Engraves, scrimshaws. Makes leather sheaths. **Prices:** $160 to $3,000. **Remarks:** Full-time maker; first knife sold in 1971. **Mark:** Last name in modified Roman; sometimes in script.

ROSS, TIM, 3239 Oliver Rd., RR #17, Thunder Bay, ON P7B 6C2, CANADA/807-935-2667
Specialties: Fancy working knives of his design. **Patterns:** Fishing and hunting knives, Bowies, daggers and miniatures. **Technical:** Uses D2, Stellite 6K and 440C; forges 52100 and Damascus. Makes antler handles and sheaths; has supply of whale teeth and moose antlers for trade. Prefers natural materials only. Wife Katherine scrimshaws. **Prices:** $100 to $350; some to $2,100. **Remarks:** Part-time maker; first knife sold in 1975. **Mark:** Last name stamped on tang.

ROTELLA, RICHARD A., 643—75th St., Niagara Falls, NY 14304
Specialties: Working knives of his design. **Patterns:** Various fishing, hunting and utility knives; folders. **Technical:** Grinds ATS-34. Prefers hand-rubbed finishes. **Prices:** $65 to $450; some to $900. **Remarks:** Spare-time maker; first knife sold in 1977. Not taking orders at this time; only sells locally. **Mark:** Name and city in stylized waterfall logo.

ROULIN, CHARLES, 113 B Rt. de Soral, 1233 Geneva, SWITZERLAND/022-757-4479; FAX: 022-757-4479
Specialties: Fancy high-art straight knives and folders of his design. **Patterns:** Bowies, locking folders, slip-joint folders and miniatures. **Technical:** Grinds 440C, ATS-34 and D2. Engraves; carves nature scenes and detailed animals in steel, ivory, on handles and blades. **Prices:** $500

to $3,000; some to $10,000. **Remarks:** Full-time maker; first knife sold in 1988. **Mark:** Symbol of fish with name or name engraved.

ROWE, STEWART G. and MULLEN, ANNETTE, 8-18 Coreen Court, Mt. Crosby, Brisbane 4306, AUSTRALIA/07-201-0906
Specialties: Designer knives—reproduction of ancient weaponry, traditional Japanese tantos and edged tools. **Patterns:** "Shark" blade range, defense weapons. **Technical:** Forges W1, W2, D2; creates own Tamahagne steel and composite pattern-welded billets. Gold, silver and ivory fittings available. **Prices:** $300 to $11,000. **Remarks:** Full-time maker; first knife sold in 1981. Doing business as Mt. Crosby Artech and Forge. **Mark:** Artech.

RP KNIVES (See Parrish, Robert)

RT CUSTOM KNIVES (See Tyser, Ross)

RUA, GARY (WOLF), 529 Osborn St., Fall River, MA 02724/508-677-2664
Specialties: Working knives of his design; 18th and 19th century period pieces. **Patterns:** Bowies, hunters, fighters, buckskinners and patch knives. **Technical:** Forges 5160, 1095, old files; uses only natural handle materials. **Prices:** $100 to $500; some to $1,000. **Remarks:** Part-time maker. Doing business as Harvest Moon Forge. **Mark:** Last name.

RUANA KNIFE WORKS, Box 520, Bonner, MT 59823/406-258-5368
Specialties: Working knives and period pieces. **Patterns:** Variety of straight knives. **Technical:** Forges 5160 chrome alloy for Bowies and 1095. **Prices:** $60 to $240; some to $300 and higher. **Remarks:** Full-time maker; first knife sold in 1938. **Mark:** Name.

RUBLEY, JAMES A., 5765 N. 500 W., Angola, IN 46703/219-833-1255
Specialties: Working American knives and collectibles for hunters, buckskinners and re-enactment groups from Pre-Revolutionary War through the Civil War. **Patterns:** Anything authentic, barring folders. **Technical:** Iron fittings, natural materials; forges files. **Prices:** $175 to $2,500. **Remarks:** Museum consultant and blacksmith for two decades. Offers classes in beginning, intermediate and advanced traditional knifemaking. **Mark:** Lightning bolt.

RUBY MOUNTAIN KNIVES (See Schirmer, Mike)

RUPERT, BOB, 301 Harshaville Rd., Clinton, PA 15026/412-573-4569
Specialties: Fantasy and traditional straight knives of his design. **Patterns:** Hunters, slip-joint and primitive folders and utility/camp knives. **Technical:** Forges 1095 and O1; grinds 440C. Offers pattern file work, some crown gargoyle carving and hand-sewn sheaths. **Prices:** $75 to $150; some to $500. **Remarks:** Part-time maker; first knife sold in 1980. **Mark:** Last initial etched or stamped.

RUPLE, WILLIAM H., P.O. Box 370, Charlotte, TX 78011/210-277-1371
Specialties: Traditional working and using straight knives and folders in standard patterns. **Patterns:** Hunters, locking folders and slip-joint folders. **Technical:** Grinds 440C, ATS-34 and D2. Offers filework on blade and spring. **Prices:** $100 to $300; some to $500. **Remarks:** Full-time maker; first knife sold in 1988. **Mark:** Last name.

RUSS, RON, 5351 NE 160th Ave., Williston, FL 32696/352-528-2603

RUSSELL, A.G., 1705 Hwy. 71 N., Springdale, AR 72764/501-751-7341
Specialties: Morseth knives; contemporary working knives. **Patterns:** Hunters and Bowies; personal utility knives in Morseth line, drop-points and boots in Russell line. **Technical:** Laminated blades in Morseth line; modern stainless steel in Russell line; classic shapes. **Prices:** Moderate. **Remarks:** Old name still at work. Doing business as Morseth Sports Equip. Co. **Mark:** Morseth or first and middle initials, last name.

RUSSELL, MICK, 4 Rossini Rd., Pari Park, Port Elizabeth 6070, SOUTH AFRICA
Specialties: Art knives. **Patterns:** Working and collectible bird, trout and hunting knives, defense knives and folders. **Technical:** Grinds D2, 440C, ATS-34 and Damascus. Offers mirror or satin finishes. Uses nickel-silver, 303 stainless and titanium fittings and a wide variety of African hardwoods; ivory, buffalo and antelope horn and bone handle materials. **Prices:** Start at $100. **Remarks:** Full-time maker; first knife sold in 1986. **Mark:** Stylized rhino incorporating initials.

RUSSELL, TOM, 6500 New Liberty Rd., Jacksonville, AL 36265/205-492-7866
Specialties: Straight working knives of his design or to customer specs. **Patterns:** Hunters, folders, fighters, skinners, Bowies and utility knives. **Technical:** Grinds D2, 440C and ATS-34; offers filework. **Prices:** $75 to $225. **Remarks:** Part-time maker; first knife sold in 1987. Full-time tool and die maker. **Mark:** Last name with tulip stamp.

RUST, CHARLES C., P.O. Box 374, Palermo, CA 95968/916-533-9389
Specialties: Working knives, some fancy; period pieces. **Patterns:** Hunters, Bowies, buckskinners, sets. **Technical:** All work done by hand; low production. **Prices:** $125 to $2,000; some to $3,500. **Remarks:** Full-time maker; first knife sold in 1972. Not currently taking orders. **Mark:** Rustway in logo.

RUSTWAY (See Rust, Charles C.)

RV KNIVES (See Vunk, Robert)

RYAN, C.O., 902-A Old Wormley Creek Rd., Yorktown, VA 23692/757-898-7797
Specialties: Working/using knives. **Patterns:** Hunters, kitchen knives, locking folders. **Technical:** Grinds 440C and ATS-34. **Prices:** $45 to $130; some to $450. **Remarks:** Part-time maker; first knife sold in 1980. **Mark:** Name.

RYAN, J.C., Rt. 5, Box 183-A, Lexington, VA 24450/703-348-5014

RYBAR JR., RAYMOND B., 277 Stone Church Road, Finleyville, PA 15332/412-348-4841
Specialties: Fancy/embellished, high-art and traditional working using straight knives and folders of his design and in standard patterns; period pieces. **Patterns:** Daggers, fighters and swords. **Technical:** Forges Damascus. All blades have etched biblical scripture or biblical significance. **Prices:** $120 to $1,200; some to $4,500. **Remarks:** Full-time maker; first knife sold in 1972. Doing business as Stone Church Forge. **Mark:** Last name or business name.

RYBERG, GOTE, Faltgatan 2, S-562 00 Norrahammar, SWEDEN, 4636-61678

RYDER, BEN M., P.O. Box 133, Copperhill, TN 37317/615-496-2750
Specialties: Working/using straight knives of his design and to customer specs. **Patterns:** Fighters, hunters, utility/camp knives. **Technical:** Grinds 440C, ATS-34, D2, commercial Damascus. **Prices:** $75 to $400. **Remarks:** Part-time maker; first knife sold in 1992. **Mark:** Full name in double butterfly logo.

S

SAINDON, R. BILL, 11 Highland View Rd., Claremont, NH 03743/603-542-9418
Specialties: Collector-quality folders of his design or to customer specs. **Patterns:** Latch release, liner lock and lockback folders. **Technical:** Offers limited amount of own Damascus; also uses Damas makers steel. Prefers natural handle material, gold and gems. **Prices:** $500 to $4,000. **Remarks:** Full-time maker; first knife sold in 1981. Doing business as Daynia Forge. **Mark:** Sun logo or engraved surname.

SAKAKIBARA, MASAKI, 20-8 Sakuragaoka, 2-Chome Setagaya-ku, Tokyo 156, JAPAN/03-420-0375

SAKMAR, MIKE, 1670 Morley, Rochester, MI 48307/810-852-6775
Specialties: Fancy and working straight knives of his design and to customer specs. **Patterns:** Bowies, fighters, hunters and integrals. **Technical:** Grinds ATS-34, Damascus and high-carbon tool steels. Uses mostly natural handle materials—elephant ivory, walrus, ivory stag, wildwood, oosic, etc. **Prices:** $150 to $2,500; some to $4,000. **Remarks:** Full-time maker; first knife sold in 1990. **Mark:** Last name.

SALAMANDER ARMOURY (See Hrisoulas, Jim)

SALLEY, JOHN D., 3965 Frederick-Ginghamsburg Rd., Tipp City, OH 45371/513-698-4588
Specialties: Fancy working knives and art pieces. **Patterns:** Hunters, fighters, daggers and some swords. **Technical:** Grinds ATS-34, 12C27 and W2; buys Damascus. **Prices:** $85 to $1,000; some to $6,000. **Remarks:** Part-time maker; first knife sold in 1979. **Mark:** First initial, last name.

SAMBAR CUSTOM KNIVES (See Giljevic, Branko)

SAMPSON, LYNN, 381 Deakins Rd., Jonesborough, TN 37659/423-348-8373
Specialties: Highly finished working knives, mostly folders. **Patterns:** Locking folders, slip-joints, interframes and two-blades. **Technical:** Grinds D2, 440C and ATS-34; offers extensive filework. **Prices:** Start at $300. **Remarks:** Full-time maker; first knife sold in 1982. **Mark:** Name and city in logo.

SANDERS, A.A., 3850 72 Ave. NE, Norman, OK 73071/405-364-8660
Specialties: Working straight knives and folders. **Patterns:** Hunters, fighters, daggers and Bowies. **Technical:** Forges his own Damascus; offers stock removal with ATS-34, 440C, A2, D2, O1, 5160 and 1095. **Prices:** $85 to $1,500. **Remarks:** Full-time maker; first knife sold in 1985. Formerly known as Athern Forge. **Mark:** Name.

SANDERS, BILL, 335 Bauer Ave., P.O. Box 957, Mancos, CO 81328/970-533-7223
Specialties: Working straight knives, some fancy and some fantasy, of his design. **Patterns:** Hunters, boots, utility knives, using belt knives. **Technical:** Grinds 440C, ATS-34 and commercial Damascus. Provides wide variety of handle materials. **Prices:** $170 to $350; some to $800. **Remarks:** Full-time maker. **Mark:** Name, city and state.

SANDERS, MICHAEL M., P.O. Box 1106, Ponchatoula, LA 70454/504-294-3601
Specialties: Working straight knives and folders, some deluxe. **Patterns:** Hunters, fighters, Bowies, daggers, large folders and deluxe Damascus miniatures. **Technical:** Grinds O1, D2, 440C, ATS-34 and Damascus. **Prices:** $75 to $650; some higher. **Remarks:** Full-time maker; first knife sold in 1967. **Mark:** Name and state.

SANDERSON, RAY, 4403 Uplands Way, Yakima, WA 98908/509-965-0128
Specialties: One-of-a-kind Buck knives; traditional working straight knives and folders of his design. **Patterns:** Bowies, hunters and fighters. **Technical:** Grinds 440C and ATS-34. **Prices:** $200 to $750. **Remarks:** Part-time maker; first knife sold in 1984. **Mark:** Sanderson Knives in shape of Bowie.

SANDLIN, LARRY, 4580 Sunday Dr., Adamsville, AL 35005/205-674-1816
Specialties: High-art straight knives of his design. **Patterns:** Boots, daggers, hunters and fighters. **Technical:** Forges 1095, L6, O1, carbon steel and Damascus. **Prices:** $200 to $1,500; some to $5,000. **Remarks:** Part-time maker; first knife sold in 1990. **Mark:** Chiseled last name in Japanese.

SASSER, JIM, 926 Jackson, Pueblo, CO 81004
Specialties: Working straight knives and folders of his design. **Patterns:** Makes elk hunters' tools, axes, camp knives, a variety of folders and limited editions. **Technical:** Grinds ATS-34. **Prices:** $75 to $300; some to $800. **Remarks:** Full-time maker; first knife sold in 1970. **Mark:** Last name or full name in circle.

SAWBY, SCOTT, 400 W. Center Valley Rd., Sandpoint, ID 83864/208-263-4171
Specialties: Folders, working and fancy. **Patterns:** Locking folders, patent locking systems and interframes. **Technical:** Grinds D2, 440C, 154CM, CPM-T-440V and ATS-34. **Prices:** $400 to $1,000. **Remarks:** Full-time maker; first knife sold in 1974. **Mark:** Last name, city and state.

SAYEN, MURAD, P.O. Box 127, Bryant Pond, ME 04219/207-665-2224
Specialties: Carved handles. **Patterns:** Fighters, boots, Bowies, daggers and fantasy knives. **Technical:** Forges carbon and Damascus steel only. Handles carved and inlaid, some with stones. **Prices:** $750 to $5,000. **Remarks:** Full-time maker; first knife sold in 1977. Doing business as Kemal. **Mark:** Last name with date.

SCARROW CUSTOM KNIFE WORKS (See Scarrow, Wil)

SCARROW, WIL, c/o L&W Mail Service, 16236 Chicago Ave., Bellflower, CA 90706/310-866-6384
Specialties: Working straight knives in standard patterns or to customer specs. **Patterns:** Hunters, fisherman's, skinners, utility, swords and Bowies. **Technical:** Forges and grinds W1, W2, 5160, 1095, 440C, AEB-L, ATS-34 and other steels on request; offers some filework. **Prices:** $85 to $750; some higher. Prices include leather sheath. **Remarks:** Full-time maker; first knife sold in 1983. Four- to six-month construction time on custom orders. Doing business as Scarrow Custom Knife Works and Gold Hill Knife Works in Oregon. **Mark:** SC with arrow and date/year made.

SCHALLER, ANTHONY BRETT, 5609 Flint Ct. NW, Albuquerque, NM 87120/505-899-0155
Specialties: Traditional working/using straight knives of his design and in standard patterns. **Patterns:** Boots, fighters and utility knives. **Technical:** Grinds 440C, ATS-34. Offers filework, mirror finishes and full and narrow tangs. Prefers exotic woods or Micarta for handle materials. **Prices:** $60 to $195; some to $285. **Remarks:** Part-time maker; first knife sold in 1990. **Mark:** Last name.

SCHEID, MAGGIE, 124 Van Stallen St., Rochester, NY 14621-3557
Specialties: Simple working straight knives. **Patterns:** Kitchen and utility knives; some miniatures. **Technical:** Forges 5160 high-carbon steel. **Prices:** $100 to $200. **Remarks:** Part-time maker; first knife sold in 1986. **Mark:** Full name.

SCHELL, CLYDE M., 4735 NE Elliott Circle, Corvallis, OR 97330/503-752-0235

SCHEMPP, ED, P.O. Box 1181, Ephrata, WA 98823/509-754-2963; FAX: 509-754-3212
Specialties: High-tech working/using straight knives; integral Damascus knives and tomahawks. **Patterns:** Fighters, hunters and utility/camp knives. **Technical:** Grinds CPM440V; forges 52100 and Damascus. Makes sheaths. **Prices:** $100 to $400; some to $2,000. **Remarks:** Part-time maker; first knife sold in 1991. Doing business as Ed Schempp Knives. **Mark:** Ed Schempp Knives over five heads of wheat, city and state.

SCHEMPP KNIVES, ED (See Schempp, Ed)

SCHEMPP, MARTIN, P.O. Box 1181, 5430 Baird Springs Rd. N.W., Ephrata, WA 98823/509-754-2963; FAX: 509-754-3212
Specialties: Fantasy and traditional straight knives of his design, to customer specs and in standard patterns; Paleolithic styles. **Patterns:** Fighters and Paleolithic designs. **Technical:** Uses opal, Mexican rainbow and obsidian. Offers scrimshaw. **Prices:** $15 to $100; some to $250. **Remarks:** Spare-time maker; first knife sold in 1995. **Mark:** Initials and date.

SCHEPERS, GEORGE B., Box 83, Chapman, NE 68827/308-986-2444
Specialties: Fancy period pieces of his design. **Patterns:** Bowies, swords, tomahawks; locking folders and miniatures. **Technical:** Grinds W1, W2 and his own Damascus; etches. **Prices:** $125 to $600; some higher. **Remarks:** Full-time maker; first knife sold in 1981. **Mark:** Schep.

SCHEURER, ALFREDO E. FAES, Rincon del Sur #15-21-7, Col. Bosque Res. del Sur, C.P. 16010 MEXICO
Specialties: Fancy and fantasy knives of his design. **Patterns:** Daggers. **Technical:** Grinds stainless steel; casts and grinds silver. Sets stones in silver. **Prices:** $2,000 to $3,000. **Remarks:** Spare-time maker; first knife sold in 1989. **Mark:** Symbol.

SCHIRMER, MIKE, 28 Biltmore Rd., P.O. Box 534, Twin Bridges, MT 59754/406-684-5868
Specialties: Working straight knives of his design or to customer specs; mostly hunters and personal knives. **Patterns:** Bowies, hunters, camp, fighters and boot knives. **Technical:** Grinds O1, D2, A2 and Damascus. **Prices:** $100 to $175; some higher. **Remarks:** Full-time maker; first knife sold in 1992. Doing business as Ruby Mountain Knives. **Mark:** Last name or signature.

SCHLOMER, JAMES E., 991 Hickory Ct., Kissimmee, FL 34743/407-348-8044
Specialties: Working and show straight knives. **Patterns:** Hunters, Bowies and skinners. **Technical:** Stock removal method, 440C and L6. Scrimshaws; carves sambar stag handles. Works on corean and Micarta. **Prices:** $75 to $500. **Remarks:** Full-time maker. **Mark:** Name and steel number.

SCHMIDT, JAMES A., 1167 Eastern Ave., Ballston Lake, NY 12019/518-882-9322
Specialties: High-art Damascus folders and collector-quality period pieces. **Patterns:** Schmidt patterns in folders; variety of investor-class straight knives. **Technical:** Forges W2 and his own Damascus; offers elaborate filework and etching; uses exotic handle materials. **Prices:** $900 to $2,200; some to $5,000. **Remarks:** Full-time maker; first knife sold in 1975. **Mark:** Last name.

SCHMIDT, RICK, P.O. Box 1318, Whitefish, MT 59937/406-862-6471; 406-862-6078
Specialties: Traditional working and using straight knives and folders of his design and to customer specs. **Patterns:** Fighters, hunters, cutlery and utility knives. **Technical:** Flat-grinds D2 and ATS-34. Custom leather sheaths. **Prices:** $120 to $250; some to $1,900. **Remarks:** Full-time maker; first knife sold in 1975. **Mark:** Stylized initials.

SCHNEIDER, CRAIG M., 285 County Rd. 1400 N., Seymour, IL 61875/217-687-2651
Specialties: Traditional working straight knives of his design or to customer specs. **Patterns:** Hunters, fighters, Bowies and utility/camp knives. **Technical:** Grinds 440C, 440V, ATS-34, D2 and O1; uses various animal horns, antlers, bones, jawbones, gold, silver, precious stones, minerals and fossil ivory for handle materials. **Prices:** $50 to $3,000. **Remarks:** Part-time maker; first knife sold in 1985. **Mark:** Stylized initials.

SCHNEIDER, HERMAN J., 10 Sun Hala Dr., Pittsburg, TX 75686-9318/903-856-9802; FAX: 903-856-9803
Specialties: Investor-class straight knives and fantasy pieces of his design. **Patterns:** Fully finished hunters, daggers, fighters and push knives. **Technical:** Forges and grinds 154CM, ATS-34 and his Damascus. Exotic materials are a specialty. **Prices:** Start at $800 for hunters. **Remarks:** Full-time maker; first knife sold in 1972. **Mark:** First and middle initials, last name.

SCHNEIDER, KARL A., 209 N. Brownleaf Rd., Newark, DE 19713/302-737-0277
Specialties: Traditional working and using straight knives of his design. **Patterns:** Hunters, kitchen and fillet knives. **Technical:** Grinds ATS-34. Shapes handles to fit hands; uses Micarta, Pakkawood and exotic woods. Makes hand-stitched leather cases. **Prices:** $95 to $225. **Remarks:** Part-time maker; first knife sold in 1984-85. **Mark:** Name, address; also name in shape of fish.

SCHOEMAN, CORRIE, Box 573, Bloemfontein 9300, SOUTH AFRICA/051-332982; FAX: 051-333472
Specialties: High-tech folders of his design or to customer's specs; fixed-blade knives on request. **Patterns:** Liner lock and lockback folders; some fixed blade knives. **Technical:** ATS-34 or Damascus blades with titanium frames; Prefers exotic materials for handles. **Prices:** $200 to $400. **Remarks:** Part-time maker; first knife sold in 1984. **Mark:** Etched name logo in knife shape.

SCHOENFELD, MATTHEW A., RR #1, Galiano Island, B.C. V0N 1P0, CANADA/604-539-2806
Specialties: Working knives of his design. **Patterns:** Kitchen cutlery, camp knives, hunters, swords. **Technical:** Grinds 440C buys Damascus. **Prices:** $85 to $500. **Remarks:** Part-time maker; first knife sold in 1978. **Mark:** Signature, Galiano Is. B.C., and date.

SCHOLL CUSTOM KNIVES, TIM (See Scholl, Tim)

SCHOLL, TIM, Rt. 3, Box 158-1A, Angier, NC 27501/910-897-2051
Specialties: Fancy and working/using straight knives and folders of his design and to customer specs. **Patterns:** Tomahawks, swords, tantos and fantasy knives. **Technical:** Grinds ATS-34; forges carbon and tool steel and Damascus. Offers filework, engraving and scrimshaw. **Prices:** $100 to $650; some to $1,500. **Remarks:** Part-time maker; first knife sold in 1990. Doing business as Tim Scholl Custom Knives. **Mark:** Last name or last initial with arrow.

SCHROEN, KARL, 4042 Bones Rd., Sebastopol, CA 95472/707-823-4057; FAX: 707-823-2914
Specialties: Using knives made to fit. **Patterns:** Sgian dubhs, carving sets, wood-carving knives, fishing knives, kitchen knives and new cleaver design. **Technical:** Forges A2, ATS-34 and D2. **Prices:** $100 to $800. **Remarks:** Full-time maker; first knife sold in 1968. Author of *The Hand Forged Knife*. **Mark:** Last name.

SCHULTZ, RICHARD A., P.O. Box 1616, San Juan Capistrano, CA 92693/714-661-3879
Specialties: Traditional working and using straight knives of his design, to customer specs and in standard patterns. **Patterns:** Fighters, hunters, Specwar and survival knives. **Technical:** Grinds 440C, ATS-34, tool steels and titanium. **Prices:** Start at $200. **Remarks:** Part-time maker; first knife sold in 1991. Manufactures specialized knives in titanium to U.S. Government Specwar teams as Mission Knives & Tools, Inc. **Mark:** First initial, last name, year.

SCHUSTER, STEVE, 3034 Brookgreen, Lawrenceville, GA 30043/770-682-9421
Specialties: Traditional working/using straight knives of his design and to customer specs. **Patterns:** Fighters, hunters and skinners. **Technical:** Forges and grinds O1; grinds D2. Handles from shedded India sambar stag; heat-treats; makes sheaths custom to each knife. **Prices:** $90 to $250. **Remarks:** Spare-time maker; first knife sold in 1993. Doing business as Steve's Knives. **Mark:** First name and Roman numeral of knife.

SCHWARZER, JAMES, P.O. Box 4, Pomona Park, FL 32181/904-649-5026; FAX: 904-649-8585
Specialties: Working straight knives of his design. **Patterns:** Capers and small hunters. **Technical:** Forges high-carbon steel and Damascus. **Prices:** $50 to $300. **Remarks:** Twelve-year-old part-time maker; first knife sold in 1989. Sells only at shows. **Mark:** Last name with anvil and first name underneath.

SCHWARZER, STEPHEN, P.O. Box 4, Pomona Park, FL 32181/904-649-5026; FAX: 904-649-8585
Specialties: Mosaic Damascus. **Patterns:** Hunters, fighters, locking folders, axes and buckskinners. **Technical:** Forges W2, O1, Wootz steel and his own Damascus; all knives have carving or filework. **Prices:** $150 to $500; some to $5,000. **Remarks:** Full-time maker; first knife sold in 1976. **Mark:** Name over anvil; folders marked inside liner.

SCOFIELD, EVERETT, 2873 Glass Mill Rd., Chickamauga, GA 30707/706-375-2790
Specialties: Historic and fantasy miniatures. **Patterns:** All patterns. **Technical:** Uses only the finest tool steels and other materials. Uses only natural, precious and semi-precious materials. **Prices:** $100 to $1,500. **Remarks:** Full-time maker; first knife sold in 1971. Doing business as Three Crowns Cutlery. **Mark:** Three Crowns logo.

SCORDIA, PAOLO, Via del Collettore Secondario 23, 00119 Ostia Antica, ROMA ITALY /06-5650717
Specialties: Plain working knives. **Patterns:** Skinners, hunters, utility and boot knives, fighters, daggers, bush swords, kitchen knives and liner lock folders. **Technical:** Grinds 420C, 440C, ATS-34; uses hardwoods and Micarta for handles, brass and nickel-silver for fittings. Makes sheaths. **Prices:** $80 to $500. **Remarks:** Part-time maker; first knife sold in 1988. **Mark:** Initials with sun and moon logo.

SCORPION FORGE (See Lutz, Greg)

SCOTT, AL, HC63 Box 802, Harper, TX 78631-0431
Specialties: High-art straight knives of his design. **Patterns:** Daggers, swords, early European, Middle East and Japanese knives. **Technical:** Uses ATS-34, 440C and Damascus. Hand engraves; does file work; cuts filigree in the blade; offers ivory carving and precious metal inlay. **Remarks:** Full-time maker; first knife sold in 1994. Doing business as Al Scott Maker of Fine Blade Art. **Mark:** Name engraved in old English, sometime inlaid in 24K gold.

SCOTT, WINSTON, Rt. 2, Box 62, Huddleston, VA 24104/703-297-6130
Specialties: Working knives. **Patterns:** Hunting and fishing knives. **Technical:** Grinds ATS-34, 440C and 154CM; likes full and narrow tangs, natural materials, sterling silver guards. **Prices:** $100 to $200; some to $400. **Remarks:** Part-time maker; first knife sold in 1984. **Mark:** Last name.

SCRATCHY HAND (See Anderson, Mel)

SEA-MOUNT KNIFE WORKS (See Wilson, Philip C.)

SEARS, MICK, 1697 Peach Orchard Rd., #302, Sumter, SC 29154/803-499-5074
Specialties: Scots and confederate reproductions; Bowies and fighters. **Patterns:** Bowies, fighters. **Technical:** Grinds 440C and 1095. **Prices:** $50 to $150; some to $300. **Remarks:** Part-time maker; first knife sold in 1975. Doing business as Mick's Custom Knives. **Mark:** First name.

SELENT, CHUCK, P.O. Box 1207, Bonners Ferry, ID 83805-1207/208-267-5807
Specialties: Period, art and fantasy miniatures; exotics; one-of-a-kinds. **Patterns:** Swords, daggers and others. **Technical:** Works in Damascus, meteorite, 440C and tool steel. Offers scrimshaw. Offers his own casting and leatherwork; uses jewelry techniques. Makes display cases for miniatures. **Prices:** $75 to $400. **Remarks:** Part-time maker; first

knife sold in 1990. **Mark:** Last name and bear paw print logo scrimshawed on handles or leatherwork.

SELF, ERNIE, 950 O'Neill Ranch Rd., Dripping Springs, TX 78620-9760/512-858-7133
Specialties: Traditional and working straight knives and folders of his design and in standard patterns. **Patterns:** Hunters, locking folders and slip-joints. **Technical:** Grinds 440C, D2, 440V, ATS-34 and Damascus. Offers fancy filework. **Prices:** $125 to $500; some to $1,500. **Remarks:** Full-time maker; first knife sold in 1982. **Mark:** Initials brand.

SELLEVOLD, HARALD, S.Kleivesmau:2, 5023 Dreggen, NORWAY/55-310682
Specialties: Norwegian styles; collaborates with other Norse craftsmen. **Patterns:** Distinctive ferrules and other mild modifications of traditional patterns; Bowies and friction folders. **Technical:** Buys Damascus blades; blacksmiths his own blades. Semi-gemstones used in handles; gemstone inlay. **Prices:** $350 to $2,000. **Remarks:** Full-time maker; first knife sold in 1980. **Mark:** Horseshoe last initial.

SELVIDIO, RALPH J., P.O. Box 248, 1135 Main St., #37, Warwick, RI 02888
Specialties: Collector-grade folders with unique mechanisms; straight and folding fantasy knives of his design. **Patterns:** Locking folders, swords and fighters. **Technical:** Grinds and forges Damascus and 1095; grinds O1. Handle material is mostly ivory and pearl. Uses exotic skin overlays on cases. **Prices:** $1,000 to $5,000; some to $7,500. **Remarks:** Full-time maker; first knife sold in 1986. Doing business as Rattler Brand Knives. **Mark:** RATTLER BRAND.

SENTZ GUNSMITHING, INC., M. CHARLES (See Sentz, Mark C.)

SENTZ, MARK C., 4084 Baptist Rd., Taneytown, MD 21787/410-756-2018
Specialties: Fancy straight working knives of his design. **Patterns:** Hunters, fighters, folders and utility/camp knives. **Technical:** Forges 1085, 1095, 5160, 5155 and his Damascus. Most knives come with wood-lined leather sheath or wooden presentation sheath. **Prices:** Start at $225. **Remarks:** Full-time maker; first knife sold in 1989. Doing business as M. Charles Sentz Gunsmithing, Inc. **Mark:** Last name.

SERAFEN, STEVEN E., 24 Genesee St., New Berlin, NY 13411/607-847-6903
Specialties: Traditional working/using straight knives of his design and to customer specs. **Patterns:** Bowies, fighters, hunters. **Technical:** Grinds ATS-34, 440C, high-carbon steel. **Prices:** $175 to $600; some to $1,200. **Remarks:** Part-time maker; first knife sold in 1990. **Mark:** First and middle initial, last name in script.

SERVEN, JIM, P.O. Box 1, Fostoria, MI 48435/517-795-2255
Specialties: Highly finished unique folders. **Patterns:** Fancy working folders, axes, miniatures and razors; some straight knives. **Technical:** Grinds 440C; forges his own Damascus. **Prices:** $150 to $800; some to $1,500. **Remarks:** Full-time maker; first knife sold in 1971. **Mark:** Name in map logo.

SHADLEY, EUGENE W., 645 Norway Dr., Bovey, MN 55709/218-245-3820; FAX: 218-245-1639; E-MAIL: bses@uslink.net
Specialties: Classic multi-blade folders. **Patterns:** Stockman, sowbelly, congress, trapper, etc. **Technical:** Grinds ATS-34, 416 frames. **Prices:** Start at $300. **Remarks:** Full-time maker; first knife sold in 1985. Doing business as Shadley Knives. **Mark:** Last name.

SHADLEY KNIVES (See Shadley, Eugene W.)

SHAMROCK KNIVES (See McClure, Leonard)

SHARP, MARGIE (See Sharp, Wes and Margie)

SHARP, WES and MARGIE, 1220 N. 18th Ave., Milton, FL 32583/904-994-3779
Specialties: Traditional and working straight knives of their design and to customer specs. **Patterns:** Bowies, hunters and fillet knives. **Technical:** Grind 440C and ATS-34. Offer filework and custom leather work. **Prices:** $75 to $300; some to $500. **Remarks:** Full-time maker; first knife sold in 1985. **Mark:** Last name.

SHARRIGAN, MUDD, RR4 Box 1164, Wiscasset, ME 04578-9330/207-882-9820; FAX: 207-882-9835
Specialties: Classic and using straight knives and folders of his design and to customer specs. **Patterns:** Daggers, fighters, hunters, buckskinner, Indian crooked knives and seamen working knives; traditional Scandinavian styles. **Technical:** Forges 1095, O1 and Rolls Royce steel. Laminates 1095 and mild steel. **Prices:** $50 to $325; some to $1,200. **Remarks:** Full-time maker; first knife sold in 1982. **Mark:** First name and swallow tail carving.

SHAWNEE (See Meier, Daryl)

SHELTON, PAUL S., 1406 Holloway, Rolla, MO 65401/314-364-3151
Specialties: Fancy working straight knives of his design or to customer specs. **Patterns:** All types from camp knives to miniatures, except folders. **Technical:** Grinds ATS-34 and commercial Damascus. Offers filework, texturing, natural handle materials and exotic leather sheaths. **Prices:** Start at $100. **Remarks:** Part-time maker; first knife sold in 1984. **Mark:** Last name and serial number.

SHIKAYAMA, TOSHIAKI, 259-2 Suka Yoshikawa Machi, Kitakatsushika, Saitama JAPAN/04-89-81-6605; FAX: 04-89-81-6605
Specialties: Folders in standard patterns. **Patterns:** Locking and slip-joint folders. **Technical:** Grinds ATS. **Prices:** $400 to $2,500; some to $8,000. **Remarks:** Full-time maker; first knife sold in 1952. **Mark:** First initial, last name.

SHINOSKY, ANDY, 134 N. Roanoke Ave., Youngstown, OH 44515/330-793-9810
Specialties: Collectible fancy folders and interframes. **Patterns:** Drop points, trailing points and daggers. **Technical:** Grinds ATS-34 and Damascus. Prefers natural handle materials. **Prices:** Start at $450. **Remarks:** Part-time maker; first knife sold in 1992. **Mark:** Name or bent folder logo.

SHOEMAKER, CARROLL, 380 Yellowtown Rd., Northup, OH 45658/614-446-6695
Specialties: Working/using straight knives of his design. **Patterns:** Hunters, utility/camp and early American backwoodsmen knives. **Technical:** Grinds ATS-34; forges old files, O1 and 1095. Uses some Damascus; offers scrimshaw and engraving. **Prices:** $100 to $175; some to $350. **Remarks:** Spare-time maker; first knife sold in 1977. **Mark:** Name and city or connected initials.

SHOEMAKER, SCOTT, 316 S. Main St., Miamisburg, OH 45342/513-859-1935
Specialties: Twisted, wire-wrapped handles on swords, fighters and fantasy blades; new line of seven models with quick-draw, multi-carry Kydex sheaths. **Patterns:** Bowies, boots and one-of-a-kinds in his design or to customer specs. **Technical:** Grinds A6 and ATS-34; buys Damascus. Hand satin finish is standard. **Prices:** $100 to $1,500; swords to $8,000. **Remarks:** Part-time maker; first knife sold in 1984. **Mark:** Angel wings with last initial, or last name.

SHOGER, MARK O., 14780 SW Osprey Dr., Suite 345, Beaverton, OR 97007/503-579-2495
Specialties: Working and using straight knives and folders of his design; fancy and embellished knives. **Patterns:** Hunters, Bowies, daggers and locking folders. **Technical:** Forges O1, W2 and his own pattern-welded Damascus. **Remarks:** Spare-time maker. **Mark:** Last name or stamped last initial over anvil.

SHORE, JOHN I., P.O. Box 5184, Ft. Richardson, AK 99505-5184/907-349-2355; FAX: 907-384-0565
Specialties: Traditional working/using straight knives and folders in standard patterns. **Patterns:** Fighters and hunters. **Technical:** Grinds 154CM, ATS-34 and 440C. **Prices:** $95 to $350; some to $1,200. **Remarks:** First knife sold in 1984. Doing business as Alaska Knifemaker. **Mark:** Name in logo, city and state.

SHOSTLE, BEN, 1121 Burlington, Muncie, IN 47302/317-282-9073
Specialties: Fancy high-art straight knives of his design. **Patterns:** Bowies, daggers and fighters. **Technical:** Uses 440C, ATS-34 and commercial Damascus. All knives are engraved. **Prices:** $900 to $3,200; some to $4,000. **Remarks:** Full-time maker; first knife sold in 1987. Doing business as The Gun Room (T.G.R.). **Mark:** Last name.

SHUFORD, RICK, Rt. 8, Box 256A, Statesville, NC 28677/704-873-0633
Specialties: Fancy working knives to customer specs. **Patterns:** Hunters, buckskinners, camp and fishing knives and miniatures. **Technical:** Forges and grinds O1, D2 and 440C. **Prices:** $125 to $250; some to $450. **Remarks:** Part-time maker; first knife sold in 1981. **Mark:** Last name and three dots.

SHUSHUNOV, SERGEI, P.O. Box 1304, Bath, OH 44210/216-665-4117

SHUSUI KANDA (See Kanda, Michio)

SIBRIAN, AARON, 4308 Dean Dr., Ventura, CA 93003/805-642-6950
Specialties: Tough working knives of his design and in standard patterns. **Patterns:** Makes a "Viper utility"—a kukri derivative—and a variety of straight using knives. **Technical:** Grinds 440C and ATS-34. Offers traditional Japanese blades; soft backs, hard edges, temper lines. **Prices:** $60 to $100; some to $250. **Remarks:** Spare-time maker; first knife sold in 1989. **Mark:** Initials in diagonal line.

SIDELINGER, ROBERT, 1365 St. Francis Rd., Bel Air, MD 21014/410-879-0963
Specialties: Folders only of his design. **Patterns:** Drop-points, trailing-points and daggers. **Technical:** Grinds ATS-34 and Damascus. Likes interframes, integral spring locks. Handle inlays made of ivory, horn, wood, coral and pearl. **Prices:** $950 to $3,500. **Remarks:** Part-time maker; first knife sold in 1990. **Mark:** Gothic last initial inside shield or last name.

SIGMAN, CORBET R., Rt. 1, Box 212-A, Liberty, WV 25124/304-586-9131
Specialties: Collectible working straight knives and folders. **Patterns:** Hunters, fighters, boots, camp knives and exotics such as sgian dubhs—distinctly Sigman lines; folders. **Technical:** Grinds D2, 154CM, plain carbon tool steel and ATS-34. **Prices:** $60 to $800; some to $4,000. **Remarks:** Full-time maker; first knife sold in 1970. **Mark:** Name or initials.

SIGMAN, JAMES P., 52474 Johnson Rd., Three Rivers, MI 49093/616-279-2508
Specialties: High-tech working knives of his design. **Patterns:** Daggers, hunters, fighters and folders. **Technical:** Forges and grinds L6, O1, W2 and his Damascus. **Prices:** $150 to $750. **Remarks:** Part-time maker; first knife sold in 1982. **Mark:** First initial, last name or SIG.

SIMMONDS, KURT BARNES, RSD 181, North Castlemaine, Vic. 3450, AUSTRALIA/054-705864
Specialties: Straight knives and folders; fancy period pieces. **Patterns:** Art daggers, traditional Bowies, fancy folders and miniatures. **Technical:** Grinds ATS-34, D2, 440C; offers filework, chisel work and inlays. **Prices:** $185 to $375; some to $2,500. **Remarks:** Full-time maker; first knife sold in 1983. **Mark:** Initials and address in Southern Cross motif.

SIMMONS, H.R., P.O. Box 176, Grantsboro, NC 28529/919-249-0094
Specialties: Working/using straight knives of his design. **Patterns:** Fighters, hunters and utility/camp knives. **Technical:** Forges and grinds Damascus and L6; grinds ATS-34. **Prices:** $150 to $250; some to $400. **Remarks:** Part-time maker; first knife sold in 1987. Doing business as HRS Custom Knives. **Mark:** Initials.

SIMONELLA, GIANLUIGI, 15, via Rosa Brustolo, 33085 Maniago, ITALY/01139-427-730350
Specialties: Traditional and classic folding and working/using knives of his design and to customer specs. **Patterns:** Bowies, fighters, hunters, utility/camp knives. **Technical:** Forges ATS-34, D2, 440C. **Prices:** $250 to $400; some to $1,000. **Remarks:** Full-time maker; first knife sold in 1988. **Mark:** Wilson.

SIMONICH, ROB, P.O. Box 278, Clancy, MT 59634/406-933-8274
Specialties: Working knives in standard patterns. **Patterns:** Hunters, combat knives, Bowies and small fancy knives. **Technical:** Grinds D2, ATS-34 and 440C; forges own cable Damascus. Offers filework on most knives. **Prices:** $75 to $300; some to $1,000. **Remarks:** Spare-time maker; first knife sold in 1984. Not currently taking orders. **Mark:** Last name in buffalo logo.

SIMONS, BILL, 6217 Michael Ln., Lakeland, FL 33811/941-646-3783
Specialties: Working folders. **Patterns:** Locking folders, liner locks, slip-joints in hunters; some straight camp knives. **Technical:** Grinds D2, ATS-34 and O1. **Prices:** Start at $100. **Remarks:** Full-time maker; first knife sold in 1970. **Mark:** Last name.

SIMS, BOB, P.O. Box 772, Meridian, TX 76665/817-435-6240
Specialties: Traditional working straight knives and folders in standard patterns; banana/sheepfoot blade combinations in trapper patterns. **Patterns:** Locking folders, slip-joint folders and hunters. **Technical:** Grinds D2, ATS-34 and O1. Offers filework on some knives. **Prices:** $150 to $275; some to $600. **Remarks:** Part-time maker; first knife sold in 1975. **Mark:** The division sign.

SINCLAIR, J.E., 520 Francis Rd., Pittsburgh, PA 15239/412-793-5778
Specialties: Working/using straight knives of his design. **Patterns:** Boots, daggers, fighters and hunters. **Technical:** Flat-grinds 440C, ATS-34 and spring steel. Uses natural handle materials; prefers mirror finishes. **Prices:** $65 to $200. **Remarks:** Part-time maker; first knife sold in 1995. **Mark:** First and middle initials, last name and maker.

SINYARD, CLESTON S., 27522 Burkhardt Dr., Elberta, AL 36530/334-987-1361
Specialties: Working straight knives and folders of his design. **Patterns:** Hunters, buckskinners, Bowies, daggers, fighters and all-Damascus folders. **Technical:** Makes Damascus from 440C, stainless steels, D2 and regular high-carbon steel; forges "forefinger pad" into hunters and skinners. **Prices:** In Damascus $450 to $1,500; some to $2,500. **Remarks:** Full-time maker; first knife sold in 1980. Doing business as Nimo Forge. **Mark:** Last name, U.S.A. in anvil.

SISKA, JIM, 6 Highland Ave., Westfield, MA 01085/413-568-9787; FAX: 413-568-6341
Specialties: Traditional working straight knives and folders. **Patterns:** Hunters, fighters, Bowies and one-of-a-kinds; folders. **Technical:** Grinds D2 and ATS-34; buys Damascus. Likes exotic woods. **Prices:** $195 to $2,500. **Remarks:** Part-time maker; first knife sold in 1983. **Mark:** Last name in Old English.

SJOSTRAND, KEVIN, 1541 S. Cain St., Visalia, CA 93292/209-625-5254
Specialties: Traditional and working/using straight knives and folders of his design or to customer specs. **Patterns:** Bowies, hunters, utility/camp knives, lockback, springback and liner lock folders. **Technical:** Grinds ATS-34, 440C and 1095. Prefers high polished blades and full tang. Natural and stabilized hardwoods, Micarta and stag handle material. **Prices:** $75 to $300. **Remarks:** Part-time maker; first knife sold in 1992. Doing business as Black Oak Blades. **Mark:** Oak tree, Black Oak Blades, name, or just last name.

SKELLERN, DR. M.J., P.O. Munster 4278, SOUTH AFRICA/03930-92537; FAX: 03931-76513
Specialties: Fancy high-tech folders of his design. **Patterns:** Locking and slip-joint folders. **Technical:** Grinds ATS-34 and Sandvick 12C27; uses Damascus. Inlays his stainless steel integral handles; offers rare African handle materials. **Prices:** $200 to $500; some to $700. **Remarks:** Part-time maker; first knife sold in 1986. **Mark:** Last name.

SLEE, FRED, 9 John St., Morganville, NJ 07751/908-591-9047
Specialties: Working straight knives, some fancy, to customer specs. **Patterns:** Hunters, fighters, boots, fancy daggers and folders. **Technical:** Grinds D2, 440C and ATS-34. **Prices:** $90 to $450; some to $1,200. **Remarks:** Part-time maker; first knife sold in 1980. **Mark:** Last name in old English.

SLOAN, SHANE, Rt. 1, Box 17, Newcastle, TX 76372/817-846-3290
Specialties: Collector-grade straight knives and folders. **Patterns:** Bowies, lockers, slip-joints, fancy folders, fighters and period pieces. **Technical:** Grinds D2 and ATS-34. Uses hand-rubbed satin finish. Prefers rare natural handle materials. **Prices:** $250 to $1,600. **Remarks:** Full-time maker; first knife sold in 1985. **Mark:** Name and city.

SLOBODIAN, SCOTT, 4101 River Ridge Dr., P.O. Box 1498, San Andreas, CA 95249/209-286-1980; FAX: 209-286-1982; E-MAIL: ghostridge@aol.com
Specialties: Japanese-style knives and swords, period pieces, fantasy pieces and miniatures. **Patterns:** Small kweikens, tantos, wakazashis, katanas, traditional samurai swords. **Technical:** Flat-grinds 1045, 1060 and commercial Damascus; differentially hardens blades with fireclay. **Prices:** $800 to $3,500; some to $7,500. **Remarks:** Full-time maker; first knife sold in 1987. **Mark:** Blade signed in Japanese characters and various scripts.

SMALL, ED, Rt. 1, Box 178-A, Keyser, WV 26726/304-298-4254
Specialties: Working knives of his design; period pieces. **Patterns:** Hunters, daggers, buckskinners and camp knives; likes one-of-a-kinds. **Technical:** Forges and grinds W2, L6 and his own Damascus. **Prices:** $150 to $1,500. **Remarks:** Full-time maker; first knife sold in 1978. Doing business as Iron Mountain Forge Works. **Mark:** Script initials connected.

SMART, STEVE, 1 Meadowbrook Cir., Melissa, TX 75454/214-837-4216; FAX: 214-837-4111
Specialties: Working/using straight knives and folders of his design, to customer specs and in standard patterns. **Patterns:** Bowies, hunters, kitchen knives, locking folders, utility/camp, fishing and bird knives. **Technical:** Grinds ATS-34, D2, 440C and O1. Prefers mirror polish or satin finish; hollow-grinds all blades. All knives come with sheath. Offers some filework. **Prices:** $95 to $225; some to $500. **Remarks:** Spare-time maker; first knife sold in 1983. **Mark:** Name, Custom, city and state in oval.

SMEDEFIRMA (See Strande, Poul)

SMIT, GLENN, 627 Cindy Ct., Aberdeen, MD 21001/410-272-2959
Specialties: Working and using straight and folding knives of his design or to customer specs. Customizes and repairs all types of cutlery. **Patterns:** Hunters, Bowies, daggers, fighters, utility/camp, folders, kitchen knives and miniatures. **Technical:** Grinds 440C, ATS-34, O1 and A2; reforges commercial Damascus and makes own Damascus. **Prices:** Miniatures start at $20; full-size knives start at $40. **Remarks:** Spare-time maker; first knife sold in 1986. Doing business as Wolf's Knives. **Mark:** G.P. SMIT, with year on reverse side.

SMITH, BOBBIE D., 802 W. Hwy. 90., Bonifay, FL 32425/904-547-5935
Specialties: Working straight knives and folders. **Patterns:** Bowies, hunters and slip-joints. **Technical:** Grinds 440C and ATS-34; custom sheaths for each knife. **Prices:** $75 to $250. **Remarks:** Part-time maker. **Mark:** NA.

SMITH, D. NOEL, P.O. Box 1363, Canon City, CO 81215-1363/719-275-2574; FAX: 719-275-2574
Specialties: Fantasy art knives of his own design or to standard patterns. **Patterns:** Daggers, hunters and art knives. **Technical:** Grinds O1, D2, 440C stainless and Damascus. Offers natural and synthetic carved handles, engraved and acid etched blades, sculptured guards, buttcaps and bases. **Prices:** Start at $250. **Remarks:** Full-time maker; first knife sold in 1990. Doing business as Minds' Eye Metalmaster. **Mark:** Signature.

SMITH, GREGORY H., 8607 Coddington Ct., Louisville, KY 40299/502-491-7439
Specialties: Traditional working straight knives and fantasy knives to customer specs. **Patterns:** Fighters and modified Bowies; camp knives and swords. **Technical:** Grinds O1, 440C and commercial Damascus bars. **Prices:** $55 to $300. **Remarks:** Part-time maker; first knife sold in 1985. **Mark:** JAGED, plus signature.

SMITH JR., JAMES B. "RED," Rt. 2, Box 1525, Morven, GA 31638/912-775-2844
Specialties: Folders. **Patterns:** Rotating rear-lock folders. **Technical:** Grinds ATS-34, D2 and Vascomax 350. **Prices:** Start at $350. **Remarks:** Full-time maker; first knife sold in 1985. **Mark:** GA RED in cowboy hat.

SMITH, J.D., 516 E. Second St., No. 38, S. Boston, MA 02127/617-269-1699
Specialties: Classic working and using straight knives and folders; period pieces mainly from his design. **Patterns:** Bowies, fighters and locking folders. **Technical:** Forges and grinds ATS-34, his Damascus, O1, 1095 and wootz-pattern hammer steel. **Prices:** $200 to $800; some to $1,500. **Remarks:** Full-time maker; first knife sold in 1987. Doing business as Hammersmith. **Mark:** Last initial alone or in cartouche.

SMITH, JOHN M., RR 6, Box 52A, Centralia, IL 62801/618-249-6444
Specialties: Art knives and some work knives. **Patterns:** Daggers, Bowies, fighters, boots, and folders. **Technical:** Forges Damascus. **Prices:** $700 to $3,000. **Remarks:** Full-time maker; first knife sold in 1980. **Mark:** Etched signature or logo.

SMITH, JOHN W., 1416 Cow Branch Rd., West Liberty, KY 41472/606-743-3599
Specialties: Fancy and working locking folders of his design or to customer specs. **Patterns:** Interframes, traditional and daggers. **Technical:** Grinds ATS-34, 440C and commercial Damascus. Offers gold inlay, engraving with gold inlay, hand-fitted mosaic pearl inlay and filework. Prefers hand-rubbed finish. Pearl and ivory available. **Prices:** $650 to $1,500; some higher. **Remarks:** Full-time maker. **Mark:** Initials engraved inside diamond.

SMITH, JOSH, Box 64, Lincoln, MT 59639/406-362-4485
Specialties: Working/using and hunting knives. **Patterns:** Hunters and skinners. **Technical:** Hand-forges 5160; stock removal 1095. **Prices:** Start at $100. **Remarks:** Part-time maker; first knife sold in 1992. **Mark:** First and last name and Custom Knives.

SMITH, MICHAEL J., 1501 Donald Ave., Royal Oak, MI 48073/810-583-1785
Specialties: Fancy and high-tech folders folders of his design. **Patterns:** Locking folders, fighters and daggers. **Technical:** Grinds ATS-34 and Damascus. Hand-rubbed satin finish. Prefers natural handle materials. Uses titanium on folders; silver casting and wire/silk wraps on daggers. **Prices:** $300 to $3,000. **Remarks:** Full-time maker; first knife sold in 1989. **Mark:** Name, city, state.

SMITH, NEWMAN L., 676 Glades Rd., Shop #3, Gatlinburg, TN 37738/423-436-3322
Specialties: Collector-grade and working knives. **Patterns:** Hunters, slip-joint and lock-back folders, some miniatures. **Technical:** Grinds O1 and ATS-34; makes fancy sheaths. **Prices:** $110 to $450; some to $1,000. **Remarks:** Full-time maker; first knife sold in 1984. Partners part-time to handle Damascus blades by Jeff Hurst; marks these with SH connected. **Mark:** First and middle initials, last name.

SMITH, RALPH L., 522 Hendrix Road, Greer, SC 29651-7950/864-848-1247
Specialties: Working knives. **Patterns:** Hunters, folders, fighters and boots. **Technical:** Grinds ATS-34 and D2. **Prices:** $140 to $600. **Remarks:** Part-time maker; first knife sold in 1971. **Mark:** Last name, handcrafted knives, in state map logo.

SMITH, RAYMOND L., Box 370, Breesport, NY 14816/607-739-3126
Specialties: Working/using straight knives and folders to customer specs and in standard patterns; period pieces. **Patterns:** Bowies, hunters, slip-joints. **Technical:** Forges 5160, 52100, 1018 Damascus and wire cable Damascus. Filework. **Prices:** $55 to $225; some to $500. **Remarks:** Part-time maker; first knife sold in 1991. Doing business as The Anvils Edge. **Mark:** Initials in script.

SMITH, W.M., 802 W. Hwy. 90, Bonifay, FL 32425/904-547-5935

SMOKER, RAY, 113 Church Rd., Searcy, AR 72143/501-796-2712
Specialties: Working/using fixed blades of his design only. **Patterns:** Hunters, skinners, utility/camp and flat-ground knives. **Technical:** Forges his own Damascus and 52100; makes sheaths. Uses improved multiple edge quench he developed. **Prices:** $140 to $200; price includes sheath. **Remarks:** Full-time maker; first knife sold in 1992. **Mark:** Last name.

SMYTHE, KEN, Box 494, Underberg 4590, SOUTH AFRICA/033-7011542
Specialties: Working and using straight knives of his design and to customer specs. **Patterns:** Fighters and hunters. **Technical:** Grinds 12C27 and 440C. Scrimshaws. **Prices:** $150 to $480. **Remarks:** Part-time maker; first knife sold in 1982. **Mark:** Sword lying on Bible.

SNARE, MICHAEL, 3352 E. Mescal St., Phoenix, AZ 85028

SNELL, JERRY L., 235 Woodsong Dr., Fayetteville, GA 30214/770-461-0586
Specialties: Working straight knives of his design and in standard patterns. **Patterns:** Hunters, boots, fighters, daggers and a few folders. **Technical:** Grinds 440C, ATS-34; buys Damascus. **Prices:** $175 to $1,000. **Remarks:** Part-time maker. **Mark:** Last name, or name, city and state.

SNOW, BILL, 4824 18th Ave., Columbus, GA 31904/706-576-4390
Specialties: Traditional working/using straight knives and folders of his design and to customer specs. Offers engraving and scrimshaw. **Patterns:** Bowies, fighters, hunters and folders. **Technical:** Grinds ATS-34, 440V and O1; forges if needed. Cryogenically quenches all steels; inlaid handles; some integrals; leather or Kydex sheaths. **Prices:** $125 to $700; some to $3,500. **Remarks:** Full-time maker; first knife sold in 1958. Doing business as Tipi Knifeworks. **Mark:** Old English scroll "S" inside a tipi.

SOLOMON, MARVIN, 23750 Cold Springs Rd., Ferndale, AR 72122/501-821-3170
Specialties: Traditional working and using straight knives of his design and to customer specs. **Patterns:** Bowies, hunters and utility/camp knives. **Technical:** Forges 5160, 1095, O1 and random Damascus. **Prices:** $100 to $500. **Remarks:** Part-time maker; first knife sold in 1990. Doing business as Cold Springs Forge. **Mark:** Last name.

SONTHEIMER, G. DOUGLAS, 12604 Bridgeton Dr., Potomac, MD 20854/301-963-3855
Specialties: Working straight knives of his design. **Patterns:** Fighters, backpackers, claws and straight edges. **Technical:** Grinds. **Price:** $275 to $900; some to $1,500. **Remarks:** Spare-time maker; first knife sold in 1976. **Mark:** LORD.

SOPPERA, ARTHUR, Morgentalstr. 37, P.O. Box 708, CH-8038 Zurich, SWITZERLAND/1-482 86 12
Specialties: High-art, high-tech knives of his design. **Patterns:** Locking folders, daggers and boots. **Technical:** Grinds ATS-34 and commercial Damascus. Folders have button lock of his own design; some are fancy folders in jeweler's fashion. Also makes jewelry with integrated small knives. **Prices:** $200 to $1,000; some $2,000 and higher. **Remarks:** Full-time maker; first knife sold in 1986. **Mark:** Stylized initials, name, country.

SORNBERGER, JIM, 25126 Overland Dr., Volcano CA 95689/209-295-7819
Specialties: Collectible straight knives. **Patterns:** Fighters, daggers, Bowies; locking folders and miniatures; hunters. **Technical:** Grinds 440C, 154CM and ATS-34; engraves, carves and embellishes. **Prices:** $500 to $1,500; some to $3,500. **Remarks:** Full-time maker; first knife sold in 1970. **Mark:** First initial, last name, city and state.

SOUTHERN PRIDE KNIVES (See Benjamin Jr., George)

SOVEREIGN KNIVES (See Humphreys, Joel)

SPANO, DOMINICK, 2726 Rice Ave., San Angelo, TX 76904/915-944-9630
Specialties: Working/using straight knives of his design and to customer specs. **Patterns:** Boots, hunters, slip-joints and lockbacks. **Technical:** Grinds ATS-34. Heat-treats. Makes sheaths. **Prices:** $145 to $300. **Remarks:** Part-time maker; first knife sold in 1989. Doing business as Spano Knives. **Mark:** Last name in script.

SPANO KNIVES (See Spano, Dominick)

SPECK, DOUG, 483 Nairn Ave., Toronto, ONT. M6E 4J3 CANADA/416-256-1638

SPECWAR KNIVES (See Emerson, Ernest R.)

SPENCER, JOHN E., HC63 Box 267, Harper, TX 78631/512-864-4216
Specialties: Working straight knives. **Patterns:** Hunters, fighters and survival knives; locking folders; axes. **Technical:** Grinds O1, D2 and 440C; commercial Damascus. **Prices:** $60 to $300; some to $500. **Remarks:** Full-time maker; first knife sold in 1982. **Mark:** Last name.

SPINALE, RICHARD, 4021 Canterbury Ct., Lorain, OH 44053/216-282-1565
Specialties: High-art working knives of his design. **Patterns:** Hunters, fighters, daggers and locking folders. **Technical:** Grinds 440C, ATS-34 and 07; engraves. Offers gold bolsters and other deluxe treatments. **Prices:** $300 to $1,000; some to $3,000. **Remarks:** Spare-time maker; first knife sold in 1976. **Mark:** Name, address, year and model number.

SPIVEY, JEFFERSON, 9244 W. Wilshire, Yukon, OK 73099/405-721-4442
Specialties: The Sabertooth: a combination hatchet, saw and knife. **Patterns:** Built for the wilderness, all are one-of-a-kind. **Technical:** Grinds chromemoly steel. The sawtooth spine curves with a double row of biangular teeth. **Prices:** Start at $300. **Remarks:** First knife sold in 1977. **Mark:** Name and serial number.

SPRAGG, WAYNE E., P.O. Box 508, 1314 3675 East Rd., Ashton, ID 83420
Specialties: Working straight knives, some fancy. **Patterns:** Hunters, skinners, kitchen knives, Bowies and miniatures. **Technical:** Grinds ATS-34, 440C, D2, O1 and commercial Damascus. Likes filework and fancy handlework. All blades heat-treated by Paul Bos. **Prices:** $110 to $400; some higher. **Remarks:** Spare-time maker; first knife sold in 1989. **Mark:** Name, city and state with bucking horse logo.

SPRINGFIELD® (See Greenfield, G.O.)

SPROUSE, TERRY, 1633 Newfound Rd., Asheville, NC 28806/704-683-3400
Specialties: Traditional and working straight knives of his design. **Patterns:** Bowies and hunters. **Technical:** Grinds ATS-34, 440C and D2. Makes sheaths. **Prices:** $85 to $125; some to $225. **Remarks:** Part-time maker; first knife sold in 1989. **Mark:** NA.

STAFFORD, MICHAEL, 3109 Todd Dr., Madison, WI 53713/608-273-3022
Specialties: Traditional and high-art stone-bladed knives of his design. **Patterns:** Bowies, daggers and fighters. **Technical:** Hand-chips Obsidian, English flint, Danish flint. Laminations and inlays on handles; specializes in stone handles. **Prices:** $80 to $225; some to $350. **Remarks:** Part-time maker; first knife sold in 1987. Doing business as The Prehistoric Edge. **Mark:** Engraved last name.

STAFFORD, RICHARD, 104 Marcia Ct., Warner Robins, GA 31088/912-923-6372
Specialties: High-tech straight knives and some folders. **Patterns:** Hunters in several patterns, fighters, boots, camp knives, combat knives and period pieces. **Technical:** Grinds ATS-34 and 440C; satin finish is standard. **Prices:** Starting at $75. **Remarks:** Part-time maker; first knife sold in 1983. **Mark:** Last name.

STALTER, HARRY L., 2509 N. Trivoli Rd., Trivoli, IL 61569/309-362-2306
Specialties: Fancy working knives of his design and in standard patterns; period pieces. **Patterns:** Hunters, fighters and Bowies; fancy daggers, miniatures—fancy swords, daggers, fantasy knives. **Technical:** Stock removal; 440C, D2, 154CM and Damascus. Currently makes 60 styles of miniatures with 440C, Damascus. **Prices:** $110 to $2,000. **Remarks:** Full-time maker; first knife sold in 1980. **Mark:** Last name.

STAMASCUS KNIFEWORKS CORP. (See McManus, Danny)

STAPEL, CHUCK, Box 1617, Glendale, CA 91209/213-66-KNIFE; FAX: 213-669-1577
Specialties: Working knives of his design. **Patterns:** Variety of straight knives—tantos, hunters, folders and utility knives. **Technical:** Grinds D2, 440C and AEB-L. **Prices:** $185 to $3,000. **Remarks:** Full-time maker; first knife sold in 1974. **Mark:** Last name or last name, U.S.A.

STAPEL, CRAIG, Box 1617, Glendale, CA 91209/213-668-2669
Specialties: Working knives. **Patterns:** Hunters, tantos and fishing knives. **Technical:** Grinds 440C and AEB-L. **Prices:** $80 to $150. **Remarks:** Spare-time maker; first knife sold in 1981. **Mark:** First and middle initials, last name.

STEEL MASTER, 847-473-9987
Specialties: Working and using straight knives to customer specs; period pieces. **Patterns:** Boots, Bowies, skinners, fighters and utility/camp knives. **Technical:** Forges Damascus and O1; grinds D2 and 440. **Prices:** $100 to $400. **Remarks:** Full-time maker; first knife sold in 1976. **Mark:** None.

STEEL TALON CUTLERY (See Gillis, C.R. "Rex")

STEGALL, KEITH, 2101 W. 32nd, Anchorage, AK 99517/907-276-6002
Specialties: Traditional working straight knives. **Patterns:** Most patterns. **Technical:** Grinds 440C and 154CM. **Prices:** $100 to $300. **Remarks:** Spare-time maker; first knife sold in 1987. **Mark:** Name and state with anchor.

STEGNER, WILBUR G., 9242 173rd Ave. SW, Rochester, Washington 98579/360-273-0937
Specialties: Working/using straight knives and folders of his design. **Patterns:** Hunters and locking folders. **Technical:** Grinds ATS-34 and other tool steels. Quenches, tempers and hardness tests each blade. **Prices:** $80 to $400; some to $3,000. **Remarks:** Full-time maker; first knife sold in 1979. **Mark:** First and middle initials, last name in bar over shield logo.

STEIGER, MONTE L., Box 186, Genesee, ID 83832/208-285-1769
Specialties: Traditional working/using straight knives of all designs. **Patterns:** Hunters, utility/camp knives. **Technical:** Grinds 1095, O1, 440C. Handles of stacked leather, natural wood, Micarta or Pakkawood. Each knife comes with right- or left-handed sheath. **Prices:** $70 to $220. **Remarks:** Spare-time maker; first knife sold in 1988. **Mark:** First initial, last name, city and state.

STEIGERWALT, KEN, P.O. Box 172, Orangeville, PA 17859/717-683-5156
Specialties: Fancy classic folders of his design. **Patterns:** Folders, but-

ton locks and rear locks. **Technical:** Grinds ATS-34, 440C and commercial Damascus. Experiments with unique filework. **Prices:** $200 to $600; some to $1,500. **Remarks:** Full-time maker; first knife sold in 1981. **Mark:** Initials.

STEINAU, JURGEN, Julius-Hart Strasse 44, Berlin 0-1162, GERMANY/372-6452512; FAX: 372-645-2512
Specialties: Fantasy and high-art straight knives of his design. **Patterns:** Boots, daggers and switch-blade folders. **Technical:** Grinds 440B, 2379 and X90 Cr.Mo.V. 78. **Prices:** $1,500 to $2,500; some to $3,500. **Remarks:** Full-time maker; first knife sold in 1984. **Mark:** Symbol, plus year, month, day and serial number.

STEINBERG, AL, 2499 Trenton Dr., San Bruno, CA 94066/415-583-8281
Specialties: Fancy working straight knives to customer specs. **Patterns:** Hunters, Bowies, fishing and camp knives, push knives. **Technical:** Grinds O1, 440C and 154CM. **Prices:** $60 to $2,500. **Remarks:** Full-time maker; first knife sold in 1972. **Mark:** Signature, city and state.

STEKETEE, CRAIG A., 871 N. Hwy. 60, Billings, MO 65610/417-744-2770
Specialties: Classic and working straight knives and swords of his design. **Patterns:** Bowies, Japanese style swords and hunters. **Technical:** Forges his own Damascus; bronze and silver cast fittings. Engraves; offers filework. Prefers exotic and natural handle materials. **Prices:** $125 to $4,000. **Remarks:** Full-time maker. **Mark:** STEK.

STEPHAN, DANIEL, 2201 S. Miller Rd., Valrico, FL 33594/813-684-2781

STERLING, MURRAY, 523 Round Peak Church Rd., Mounty Airy, NC 27030/910-352-5110

STERLING WORKSHOP (See Reggio Jr., Sidney J.)

STEVENS, BARRY B., Rt. 6, 901 Amherst, Cridersville, OH 45806/419-221-2446
Specialties: Small fancy folders of his design and to customer specs; mini-hunters and fighters. **Patterns:** Fighters, hunters, liner locks, lockback and bolster release folders. **Technical:** Grinds ATS-34, 440C, Damascus and SS Damascus. Prefers hand-rubbed finishes and natural handle materials—horn, ivory, pearls, exotic woods. **Prices:** $300 to $1,000; some to $2,500. **Remarks:** Part-time maker; first knife sold in 1991. Doing business as Bare Knives. **Mark:** First and middle initials, last name.

STEVE'S KNIVES (See Schuster, Steve)

STEWART, CHARLES, 2128 Garrick, Warren, MI 48091/810-757-4418
Specialties: Working knives of his design. **Patterns:** Exotic opening mechanisms for his folders; personally designed and patented release locks; straight knives, some fancy. **Technical:** Forges and grinds 440C, 154CM and ATS-34; offers finishes from gold to blueing. **Prices:** $250 to $11,500; some to $9,500. **Remarks:** Full-time maker; first knife sold in 1968. **Mark:** Stylized initials.

STICE, DOUGLAS, 223 S. Parkridge Ct., Wichita, KS 67209-4032
Specialties: Working straight knives. **Patterns:** Hunters, Bowies, fighters, tantos and fishing knives. **Technical:** Grinds 440C, ATS-34 and D2. **Prices:** $50 to $150; some to $225. **Remarks:** Part-time maker; first knife sold in 1985. **Mark:** Name.

STIPES, DWIGHT, 8089 SE Country Estates Way, Jupiter, FL 33458/407-743-0550
Specialties: Traditional and working straight knives in standard patterns. **Patterns:** Boots, Bowies, daggers, hunters and fighters. **Technical:** Grinds 440C, D2 and D3 tool steel. Handles of natural materials, animal, bone or horn. **Prices:** $75 to $150. **Remarks:** Full-time maker; first knife sold in 1972. **Mark:** Last name.

STODDART, W.B. "BILL," 917 Smiley, Forest Park, OH 45240/513-851-1543
Specialties: Sportsmen's working knives and multi-blade folders. **Patterns:** Hunters, camp and fish knives; multi-blade reproductions of old standards. **Technical:** Grinds A2, 440C and ATS-34; makes sheaths to match handle materials. **Prices:** $80 to $300; some to $850. **Remarks:** Part-time maker; first knife sold in 1976. **Mark:** Name, Cincinnati, state.

STOKES, ED, 22614 Cardinal Dr., Hockley, TX 77447/713-351-1319
Specialties: Working straight knives and folders of all designs. **Patterns:** Boots, Bowies, daggers, fighters, hunters and miniatures. **Technical:** Grinds ATS-34, 440C and D2. Offers decorative buttcaps, tapered spacers on handles and finger grooves, nickel-silver inlays, hand-made sheaths. **Prices:** $185 to $290; some to $350. **Remarks:** Full-time maker; first knife sold in 1973. **Mark:** First and last name, Custom Knives with apache logo.

STONE BIRDS (See Thompson, Tommy)

STONE CHURCH FORGE (See Rybar Jr., Raymond B.)

STONE, JERRY, P.O. Box 1027, Lytle, TX 78052/512-772-4502
Specialties: Traditional working and using folders of his design and to customer specs; fancy knives. **Patterns:** Fighters, hunters, locking folders and slip-joints. **Technical:** Grinds 440C and ATS-34. Offers filework. **Prices:** $125 to $375; some to $700. **Remarks:** Full-time maker; first knife sold in 1973. **Mark:** Initials.

STOUT, JOHNNY, 1205 Forest Trail, New Braunfels, TX 78132/210-629-1011; E-MAIL: jlstout@concentric.net
Specialties: Working knives, some fancy. **Patterns:** Hunters, tactical, Bowies, automatics, liner locks and slip-joints. **Technical:** Grinds stainless and carbon steels; forges own Damascus. **Prices:** $300 to $650; some to $2,500. **Remarks:** Full-time maker; first knife sold in 1983. **Mark:** Name and city in logo with serial number.

STOVER, TERRY "LEE," 1809 N. 300E., Kokomo, IN 46901/317-457-2809
Specialties: Damascus folders with filework; Damascus Bowies of his design or to customer specs. **Patterns:** Lockback folders and Sheffield-style Bowies. **Technical:** Forges 1095, Damascus using O2, 203E or O2, pure nickel. Makes mokume. Uses only natural handle material. **Prices:** $300 to $1,700; some to $2,000. **Remarks:** Part-time maker; first knife sold in 1984. **Mark:** First and middle initials, last name in knife logo; Damascus blades marked in Old English.

STRAIGHT, DON, P.O. Box 12, Points, WV 25437/304-492-5471
Specialties: Traditional working straight knives of his design. **Patterns:** Hunters, Bowies and fighters. **Technical:** Grinds 440C, ATS-34 and D2. **Prices:** $75 to $125; some to $225. **Remarks:** Spare-time maker; first knife sold in 1978. **Mark:** Last name.

STRANDE, POUL, Soster Svenstrup Byvej 16, Dastrup 4130 Viby Sj., DENMARK/46 19 43 05; FAX: 46 19 53 19
Specialties: Classic fantasy working knives. **Patterns:** Bowies, daggers, fighters, hunters and swords. **Technical:** Uses carbon steel and 15C20 steel. **Prices:** NA. **Remarks:** Full-time maker; first knife sold in 1985. **Mark:** First and last initials.

STRICKLAND, DALE, 1440 E. Thompson View, Monroe, UT 84754/801-896-8362
Specialties: Traditional and working straight knives and folders of his design and to customer specs. **Patterns:** Hunters, folders, miniatures and utility knives. **Technical:** Grinds Damascus and 440C. **Prices:** $120 to $350; some to $500. **Remarks:** Part-time maker; first knife sold in 1991. **Mark:** Oval stamp of name, Maker.

STRONG, SCOTT, 2138 Oxmoor, Beavercreek, OH 45431/937-426-9290
Specialties: Working knives, some deluxe. **Patterns:** Hunters, fighters, survival and military-style knives, art knives. **Technical:** Forges and grinds O1, A2, D2, 440C and ATS-34. Uses no solder; most knives disassemble. **Prices:** $75 to $450; some to $1,500. **Remarks:** Spare-time maker; first knife sold in 1983. **Mark:** Strong Knives.

STROYAN, ERIC, Box 218, Dalton, PA 18414/717-563-2603
Specialties: Classic and working/using straight knives and folders of his design. **Patterns:** Hunters, locking folders, slip-joints. **Technical:** Forges Damascus; grinds ATS-34, D2. **Prices:** $200 to $600; some to $2,000. **Remarks:** Part-time maker; first knife sold in 1968. **Mark:** Signature or initials stamp.

STUART, STEVE, Box 168, Gores Landing, Ontario, CANADA K0K 2E0/905-342-5617
Specialties: Straight knives. **Patterns:** Tantos, fighters, skinners, file and rasp knives. **Technical:** Uses 440C, files, Micarta and natural handle materials. **Prices:** $60 to $400. **Remarks:** Part-time maker. **Mark:** Interlocking SS with last name.

SUEDMEIER, HARLAN, RFD 2, Box 299D, Nebraska City, NE 68410/402-873-4372
Specialties: Working straight knives. **Patterns:** Hunters, fighters and Bowies. **Technical:** Grinds ATS-34 and 440C; forges 52100. **Prices:**

Start at $75. **Remarks:** Part-time maker; first knife sold in 1982. Not currently taking orders. **Mark:** First initial, last name.

SUGIHARA, KEIDOH, 4-16-1 Kamori-Cho, Kishiwada City, Osaka, F596 JAPAN

SUMMERS, ARTHUR L., 8700 Brigner Rd., Mechanicsburg, OH 43044/513-834-3776
Specialties: Collector-grade knives in drop points, clip points or straight blades. **Patterns:** Fighters, hunters, Bowies and personal knives. **Technical:** Grinds 440C, ATS-34, D2 and Damascus. **Prices:** $150 to $650; some to $2,000. **Remarks:** Part-time maker; first knife sold in 1987. **Mark:** Last name and serial number.

SUMMERS, DAN, 2675 NY Rt. 11, Whitney Pt., NY 13862

SUMMERS, DENNIS K., 827 E. Cecil St., Springfield, OH 45503/513-324-0624
Specialties: Working/using knives. **Patterns:** Fighters and personal knives. **Technical:** Grinds 440C, A2 and D2. Makes drop and clip point. **Prices:** $75 to $200. **Remarks:** Part-time maker; first knife sold in 1995. **Mark:** First and middle initials, last name, serial number.

SUN KNIFE CO. (See Sunderland, Richard)

SUNDERLAND, RICHARD, Box 248, Quathiaski Cove, British Columbia, CANADA/V0P 1N0/250-285-3038
Specialties: Personal and hunting knives with carved handles in oosic and ivory. **Patterns:** Hunters, Bowies, daggers, camp and personal knives. **Technical:** Grinds 440C, ATS 34 and O1. Handle materials of rosewoods, fossil mammoth ivory and oosic. **Prices:** $150 to $1,000. **Remarks:** Full-time maker; first knife sold in 1983. Doing business as Sun Knife Co. **Mark:** SUN.

SUTHERLAND, GREG, P.O. Box 23516, Flagstaff, AZ 86002-3516/520-774-6050
Specialties: Classic working/using straight knives of his design and in standard patterns. **Patterns:** Bowies, hunters, fighters, boots, kitchen, duty and utility/camp knives. **Technical:** Grinds ATS-34, O1. Offers occasional filework and some bronze guards and bolsters. Likes desert ironwood. Hunting and utility knives come with leather or Kydex sheath. **Prices:** $100 to $1,000. **Remarks:** Full-time maker; first knife sold in 1989. Doing business as Sutherland Knives Outdoors West. **Mark:** Last name, city, state.

SUTHERLAND KNIVES OUTDOORS WEST (See Sutherland, Greg)

SUTTON, S. RUSSELL, 4900 Cypress Shores Dr., New Bern, NC 28562/919-637-3963
Specialties: Straight knives and folders to customer specs and in standard patterns. **Patterns:** Boots, hunters and locking folders. **Technical:** Grinds ATS-34 and 440C. Makes own sheaths. **Prices:** $145 to $450; some to $625. **Remarks:** Part-time maker; first knife sold in 1992. **Mark:** Etched last name.

SWAIN, ROD, 1020 Avon Pl., South Pasadena, CA 91030/818-799-7666
Specialties: Working straight knives, some fancy, of his design and to customer specs. **Patterns:** Outdoor patterns, Bowies and push knives, utility drop-points. **Technical:** Grinds O1, 440C, AEB-L. **Prices:** $75 to $250; some to $450. **Remarks:** Part-time maker; first knife sold in 1981. **Mark:** Last name in logo.

SWYHART, ART, 509 Main St., P.O. Box 267, Klickitat, WA 98628/509-369-3451
Specialties: Traditional working and using knives of his design. **Patterns:** Bowies, hunters and utility/camp knives. **Technical:** Forges 52100, 5160 and Damascus 1084 mixed with either 15N20 or 0186. Blades differentially heat-treated with visible temper line. **Prices:** $75 to $250; some to $350. **Remarks:** Part-time maker; first knife sold in 1983. **Mark:** First name, last initial in script.

SYSLO, CHUCK, 3418 South 116 Ave., Omaha, NE 68144/402-333-0647
Specialties: High-tech working straight knives. **Patterns:** Hunters, daggers and survival knives; locking folders. **Technical:** Flat-grinds D2, 440C and 154CM; hand polishes only. **Prices:** $175 to $500; some to $3,000. **Remarks:** Part-time maker; first knife sold in 1978. **Mark:** CISCO in logo.

SZILASKI, JOSEPH, 29 Carroll Dr., Wappingers Falls, NY 12590/914-297-5397
Specialties: Straight knives, folders and tomahawks of his design, to customer specs and in standard patterns. Many pieces are one-of-a-kind. **Patterns:** Bowies, daggers, fighters, hunters, art knives and early American styles. **Technical:** Grinds 440C and 154CM; forges A2, D2, O1 and Damascus. **Prices:** $145 to $950; some to $3,000. **Remarks:** Full-time maker; first knife sold in 1990. **Mark:** Snake logo.

TAGLIENTI, ANTONIO J., 164 Rhodes Dr., Beaver Falls, PA 15010-1438
Specialties: Working straight knives in standard patterns. **Patterns:** Hunters—likes forefinger radius; Bowies, tantos and camp knives. **Technical:** Grinds D2, 440C and 154CM. Emphasizes full tangs; offers filework. **Prices:** $85 to $200; some to $350. **Remarks:** Part-time maker; first knife sold in 1985. **Mark:** Last name.

TAKAHASHI, MASAO, 39-3 Sekine-cho, Maebashi-shi, Gunma 371 JAPAN/0272-34-2223

TALLY, GRANT C., 14618 Cicotte, Allen Park, MI 48101/313-381-0100
Specialties: Straight knives and folders of his design. **Patterns:** Bowies, fighters and locking folders. **Technical:** Grinds ATS-34, 440C and D2. Offers filework. **Prices:** $125 to $500. **Remarks:** Part-time maker; first knife sold in 1985. Doing business as GT Knives. **Mark:** NA.

TALON BLADES (See Knuth, Joseph E.)

TAMBOLI, MICHAEL, 12447 N. 49 Ave., Glendale, AZ 85304/602-978-4308
Specialties: Miniatures, some full size. **Patterns:** Miniature hunting knives to fantasy art knives. **Technical:** Grinds 440C, 154CM and Damascus. **Prices:** $75 to $500; some to $1,000. **Remarks:** Part-time maker; first knife sold in 1978. **Mark:** Initials or last name, city and state.

TASAKI, SEICHI, 24 Shizuwa, Shimotsuga-Gun, Tochigi, JAPAN/0482-55-6066
Specialties: High-tech traditional straight knives and folders. **Patterns:** Variety of hunters, miniatures, interframe folders and more. **Technical:** Forges and grinds 440C and carbon steel. **Prices:** $230 to $850; some to $5,000. **Remarks:** Full-time maker; first knife sold in 1984. **Mark:** Initials connected.

"tat" (See Brack, Douglas D.)

TAY, LARRY C-G, Siglap P.O. Box 315, Singapore 9145, REPUBLIC OF SINGAPORE/65-2419421
Specialties: Working and using straight knives and folders of his design; Marble's Safety Knife with stained or albino Asian buffalo horn and bone or rosewood handles. **Patterns:** Fighters, locking folders and utility/camp knives. **Technical:** Forges and grinds 440C; uses Damascus USA billets, truck leaf springs. **Prices:** $50 to $200; some to $500. **Remarks:** Spare-time maker; first knife sold in 1957. **Mark:** LDA/LAKELL

TAYLOR, BILLY, 10 Temple Rd., Petal, MS 39465/601-544-0041
Specialties: Straight knives of his design. **Patterns:** Bowies, skinners, hunters and utility knives. **Technical:** Flat-grinds 440C, ATS-34 and 154CM. **Prices:** $60 to $300. **Remarks:** Part-time maker; first knife sold in 1991. **Mark:** Full name, city and state.

TAYLOR, C. GRAY, 137 Lana View Dr., Kingsport, TN 37664/423-288-5969
Specialties: High-art display knives; period pieces. **Patterns:** Fighters, Bowies, daggers, locking folders and interframes. **Technical:** Grinds 440C, 154CM and ATS-34. **Prices:** $200 to $3,000; some to $7,000. **Remarks:** Part-time maker; first knife sold in 1975. **Mark:** Name, city and state.

TAYLOR, DAVID, 232 Akard St., Bristol, TN 37620/423-764-3811
Specialties: Folders. **Patterns:** Slip-joint, lock-back and multi-blade folders. **Technical:** Grinds 440C, 154CM and ATS-34. **Prices:** $150 to $550; some higher. **Remarks:** Part-time maker; first knife sold in 1981. **Mark:** Name, city and state.

TAYLOR, SHANE, 18 Broken Bow, Miles City, MT 59312/406-232-7175
Specialties: One-of-a-kind fancy Damascus straight knives. **Patterns:** Bowies, daggers, skinners, hunters and miniatures. **Technical:** Forges

and creates own mosaic and pattern welded Damascus. **Prices:** $200 to $750; some to $1,500. **Remarks:** Part-time maker; first knife sold in 1982. **Mark:** First name.

TEDDER, MICKEY, Rt. 2, Box 22, Conover, NC 28613/704-464-9002
Specialties: Working folders. **Patterns:** Locking hunters, fighters and boots. **Technical:** Grinds D2, 440C and 154CM. Makes gold miniatures as jewelry. **Prices:** $150 to $300; some to $1,500. **Remarks:** Part-time maker. **Mark:** Last name.

TEDDYBEAR KNIVES (See Luchak, Bob)

TEDDYHAWK (See Goldenberg, T.S.)

TENNESSEE KNIFE MAKER—TKM (See Ward, W.C.)

TERAUCHI, TOSHIYUKI, 7649-13 219-11 Yoshida, Fujita-Cho Gobo-Shi, JAPAN

TERRA-GLADIUS KNIVES (See Reynolds, Dave)

TERRILL, STEPHEN, 21363 Rd. 196, Lindsay, CA 93247/209-562-4395
Specialties: Deluxe working straight knives and folders. **Patterns:** Fighters, tantos, boots, locking folders and axes; traditional oriental patterns. **Technical:** Forges 440C, 1084 and his Damascus. **Prices:** Moderate. **Remarks:** Part-time maker; first knife sold in 1972. **Mark:** Name, city, state in logo.

TERRY KNIVES (See Cohen, Terry A.)

TERZUOLA, ROBERT, Rt. 6, Box 83A, Santa Fe, NM 87501/505-473-1002; FAX: 505-438-8018
Specialties: Working folders of his design; period pieces. **Patterns:** High-tech utility, defense and gentleman's folders. **Technical:** Grinds ATS-34. Offers titanium and G10 composite for side-lock folders. **Prices:** $350 to $425. **Remarks:** Full-time maker; first knife sold in 1980. **Mark:** Mayan dragon head, name and motto meaning "second to none."

THAYER, DANNY, 4504 W. 660 S., Lafayette, IN 47905/765-538-3105
Specialties: Traditional working and using straight knives in standard patterns and to customer specs. **Patterns:** Hunters, Bowies, daggers, utility/camp and kitchen knives. **Technical:** Forges O1, W2, 1095 and 5160. **Prices:** $150 to $1,000. **Remarks:** Spare-time maker; first knife sold in 1988. **Mark:** Last name.

THILL, JIM, 10242 Bear Run, Missoula, MT 59803/406-251-5475
Specialties: Traditional and working/using knives of his design. **Patterns:** Fighters, hunters and utility/camp knives. **Technical:** Grinds D2 and ATS-34; forges 10-95-85. Offers hand cut sheaths with rawhide lace. **Prices:** $145 to $350; some to $1250. **Remarks:** Full-time maker; first knife sold in 1962. **Mark:** Running bear in triangle.

THOM'S CUSTOM KNIVES (See Broome, Thomas A.)

THOMAS, DANIEL, 1017 Rollins Dr. SW, Leesburg, VA 22075/703-442-6877
Specialties: Traditional working and using straight knives and folders of his design. **Patterns:** Hunters, slip-joint and locking folders. **Technical:** Grinds ATS-34, D2 and commercial Damascus. Offers fixed blade and folder repair and rebuilding. **Prices:** $125 to $200; some to $350. **Remarks:** Spare-time maker; first knife sold in 1983. **Mark:** Last name, Handcrafted.

THOMAS, DEVIN, 90 N. 5th St., Panaca, NV 89042/702-728-4363
Specialties: Traditional straight knives and folders in standard patterns. **Patterns:** Bowies, fighters, hunters. **Technical:** Forges stainless Damascus, nickel and 1095. Uses, makes and sells Mokume with brass, copper and nickel-silver. **Prices:** $300 to $1,200. **Remarks:** Full-time maker; first knife sold in 1979. **Mark:** First and last name, city and state with anvil, or first name only.

THOMAS IRON WORKS (See Thomas, Kim)

THOMAS, KIM, P.O. Box 13, Brunswick OH 44212/330-483-3416
Specialties: Fancy and traditional straight knives of his design and to customer specs; period pieces. **Patterns:** Boots, daggers, fighters, swords. **Technical:** Forges own Damascus from 5160, 1010 and nickel. **Prices:** $135 to $1,500; some to $3,000. **Remarks:** Part-time maker; first knife sold in 1986. Doing business as Thomas Iron Works. **Mark:** Initials.

THOMAS, ROCKY, 204 Columbia Dr., Ladson, SC 29456/803-553-6843
Specialties: Traditional working and using straight knives in standard patterns. **Patterns:** Hunters and utility/camp knives. **Technical:** Grinds 440C, ATS-34 and commercial Damascus. **Prices:** $75 to $125. **Remarks:** Spare-time maker; first knife sold in 1986. **Mark:** First name in script.

THOMPSON, KENNETH, 4887 Glenwhite Dr., Duluth, GA 30136/770-446-6730
Specialties: Traditional working and using knives of his design. **Patterns:** Hunters, Bowies and utility/camp knives. **Technical:** Forges 5168, O1, 1095 and 52100. **Prices:** $75 to $1,500; some to $2,500. **Remarks:** Part-time maker; first knife sold in 1990. **Mark:** P/W; or name, P/W, city and state.

THOMPSON, LEON, 1735 Leon Drive, Forest Grove, OR 97116/503-357-2573
Specialties: Working knives. **Patterns:** Locking folders, slip-joints and liner locks. **Technical:** Grinds ATS-34, D2 and 440C. **Prices:** $200 to $600. **Remarks:** Full-time maker; first knife sold in 1976. **Mark:** First and middle initials, last name, city and state.

THOMPSON, LLOYD, P.O. Box 1664, Pagosa Springs, CO 81147/303-264-5837
Specialties: Working and collectible straight knives and folders of his design. **Patterns:** Hunter drop-points, lockbacks and hawkbills. **Technical:** Hollow-grinds ATS-34, D2 and O1. Uses sambar stag and exotic woods. **Prices:** $125 to $400. **Remarks:** Full-time maker; first knife sold in 1985. Doing business as Trapper Creek Knife Co. **Mark:** Name.

THOMPSON, ROBERT L., P.O. Box 23992, Phoenix, AZ 85063/602-846-5102
Specialties: Fantasy and working straight knives of his design; miniatures as jewelry items. **Patterns:** Daggers, fighters and utility knives. **Technical:** Forges own Damascus, cable and meteorite; grinds everything else, including stone. **Prices:** $35 to $350; some to $2,000. **Remarks:** Full-time maker; first knife sold in 1989. **Mark:** Runic figure of initials.

THOMPSON, TOMMY, 4015 NE Hassalo, Portland, OR 97232-2607/503-235-5762
Specialties: Fancy and working knives; mostly liner lock folders. **Patterns:** Fighters, hunters and liner locks. **Technical:** Grinds D2, ATS-34, CPM440V and T15. Handles are either hardwood inlaid with wood banding and stone or shell, or made of agate, jasper, petrified woods, etc. **Prices:** $75 to $500; some to $1,000. **Remarks:** Part-time maker; first knife sold in 1987. Doing business as Stone Birds. **Mark:** First and last name, city and state.

THOMSEN, LOYD W., HCR-46, Box 19, Oelrichs, SD 57763/605-535-6162
Specialties: High-art and traditional working/using straight knives and folders of his design and to customer specs; period pieces. **Patterns:** Bowies, hunters, locking folders and utility/camp knives. **Technical:** Forges and grinds 1095HC, 440C stainless steel, nickel 200; special restoration process on period pieces. Makes sheaths. Uses natural materials for handles. **Prices:** $125 to $300; some to $600. **Remarks:** Full-time maker; first knife sold in 1995. Doing business as Horsehead Creek Knives. **Mark:** Initials and last name over a horse's head.

THOUROT, MICHAEL W., T-814, Co. Road 11, Napoleon, OH 43545/419-533-6832
Specialties: Working straight knives to customer specs. Designed two-handled skinning ax and limited edition engraved knife and art print set. **Patterns:** Fishing and fillet knives, Bowies, tantos and hunters. **Technical:** Grinds O1, D2, 440C and Damascus. **Prices:** $200 to $5,000. **Remarks:** Part-time maker; first knife sold in 1968. **Mark:** Initials.

THREE CROWNS CUTLERY (See Scofield, Everett)

THUESEN, ED, P.O. Box 79402, Houston, TX 77279-9402/281-493-3984
Specialties: Working straight knives. **Patterns:** Hunters, fighters and survival knives. **Technical:** Grinds D2, 440C, ATS-34 and Vascowear. **Prices:** $85 to $250; some to $600. **Remarks:** Part-time maker; first knife sold in 1979. Runs knifemaker supply business. **Mark:** Last name.

THUESEN, KEVIN, 10649 Haddington, Suite 180, Houston, TX 77043/713-461-8632

Specialties: Working straight knives. **Patterns:** Hunters, including upswept skinners, and custom walking sticks. **Technical:** Grinds D2, 440C, 154CM and ATS-34. **Prices:** $85 to $125; some to $200. **Remarks:** Part-time maker; first knife sold in 1985. **Mark:** Initials on slant.

THUNDER MOUNTAIN FORGE CLAIBORNE KNIVES (See Claiborne, Ron)

THUNDERBOLT ARTISANS (See Hilker, Thomas N.)

TICHBOURNE, GEORGE, 7035 Maxwell Rd. #5, Mississauga, Ontario CANADA L5S 1R5/905-670-0200; FAX: 905-670-0200
Specialties: Traditional working and using straight knives and folders of his design. **Patterns:** Bowies, hunters and locking folders. **Technical:** Grinds 440C, ATS-34 and D2. Does filework and scrimshaw. **Prices:** $80 to $175; some to $400. **Remarks:** Part-time maker; first knife sold in 1990. **Mark:** Full name above maple leaf.

TIGHE, BRIAN, RR 1 Ridgeville, L0S 1M0 Ontario, CANADA/905-892-2734
Specialties: Fancy/embellished and high tech folders of his design. **Patterns:** Boots, daggers, locking and slip-joint folders. **Technical:** Grinds 440C, ATS-34 and Damascus. Prefers natural handle material inlay; hand finishes. **Prices:** $350 to $800; some to $1,500. **Remarks:** Part-time maker; first knife sold in 1989. **Mark:** Etched signature.

TILL, CALVIN E. AND RUTH, 619 Mears St., Chadron, NE 69337
Specialties: Fantasy and traditional straight knives of his design and to customer specs. **Patterns:** Bowies, hunters and locking folders. **Technical:** Grinds spring steel only. Full or threaded tangs. Prefers mirror polishes. **Prices:** $80 to $120; some to $250. **Remarks:** Part-time maker; first knife sold in 1986. **Mark:** Name, date and serial number.

TILL, RUTH (See Till, Calvin E. and Ruth)

TINKER, THE (See Ladd, Jim S.)

TINKER, CAROLYN D., P.O. Box 5123, Whittier, CA 90607/213-696-9202
Specialties: Working straight knives of her design. **Patterns:** Hunters, kitchen and fishing knives; small tools. **Technical:** Grinds D2, 440C and 154CM. **Prices:** $85 to $125. **Remarks:** Full-time maker; first knife sold in 1974. Currently not taking orders. **Mark:** Name and city in logo.

TINKER'S BENCH, THE (See Andrews, Eric)

TINKERMADE KNIVES (See Rachlin, Leslie S.)

TIPI KNIFEWORKS (See Snow, Bill)

TKM—TENNESSEE KNIFE MAKER (See Ward, W.C.)

TODD, ED, 9 Woodlawn Rd., Putnam Valley, NY 10579

TOICH, NEVIO, Via Pisacane 9, Rettorgole di Caldogna, Vincenza, ITALY 36030/0444-985065; FAX: 0444-301254
Specialties: Working/using straight knives of his design or to customer specs. **Patterns:** Bowies, hunters, skinners and utility/camp knives. **Technical:** Grinds 440C, D2 and ATS-34. Hollow-grinds all blades and uses mirror polish. Offers hand-sewn sheaths. Uses wood and horn. **Prices:** $120 to $300; some to $450. **Remarks:** Spare-time maker; first knife sold in 1989. Doing business as Custom Toich. **Mark:** Initials and model number punched.

TOKAR, DANIEL, Box 1776, Shepherdstown, WV 25443
Specialties: Working knives; period pieces. **Patterns:** Hunters, camp knives, buckskinners, axes, swords and battle gear. **Technical:** Forges L6, 1095 and his Damascus; makes mokume, Japanese alloys and bronze daggers; restores old edged weapons. **Prices:** $25 to $800; some to $3,000. **Remarks:** Part-time maker; first knife sold in 1979. Doing business as The Willow Forge. **Mark:** Arrow over rune and date.

TOLLEFSON, BARRY A., 177 Blackfoot Trail, Gunnison, CO 81230-9720/970-641-0752
Specialties: Working straight knives, some fancy. **Patterns:** Hunters, skinners, fighters and camp knives. **Technical:** Grinds 440C, ATS-34 and D2. Likes mirror-finishes; offers some fancy filework. Handles made from elk, deer and exotic hardwoods. **Prices:** $75 to $300; some higher. **Remarks:** Part-time maker; first knife sold in 1990. **Mark:** Stylized initials.

TOMES, ANTHONY S., 8190 Loch Seaforth Ct., Jacksonville, FL 32244
Specialties: Working knives and period pieces. **Patterns:** Hunters, daggers, folders and liner locks. **Technical:** Grinds D2 and ATS-34. **Prices:** $50 to $500. **Remarks:** Part-time maker. **Mark:** Initials.

TOMES, P.J., 2061 Harvard St., Middleburg, FL 32068/904-282-7095; FAX: 904-291-7399
Specialties: Scagel reproductions. **Patterns:** Front lock folders. **Technical:** Forges 52100. **Prices:** $150 to $750. **Mark:** Last name, USA, MS, stamped in forged blades.

TOMKA ARMOURY (See Kaczor, Tom)

TOMPKINS, DAN, P.O. Box 398, Peotone, Illinois 60468/708-258-3620
Specialties: Working knives, some deluxe, some folders. **Patterns:** Hunters, boots, daggers and push knives. **Technical:** Grinds D2, 440C, ATS-34 and 154CM. **Prices:** $85 to $150; some to $400. **Remarks:** Part-time maker; first knife sold in 1975. **Mark:** Last name, city, state.

TONER, ROGER, 531 Lightfoot Place, Pickering, Ont. L1V 5Z8, CANADA/905-420-5555
Specialties: Exotic sword canes. **Patterns:** Bowies, daggers and fighters. **Technical:** Grinds 440C, D2 and Damascus. Scrimshaws and engraves. Silvercast pommels and guards in animal shapes; twisted silver wire inlays. Uses semi-precious stones. **Prices:** $200 to $2,000; some to $3,000. **Remarks:** Part-time maker; first knife sold in 1982. **Mark:** Last name.

TOOTH AND NAIL METALWORKS (See Meshejian, Mardi)

TOPLISS, M.W. "IKE," 1668 Hermosa Ct., Montrose, CO 81401/970-249-4703
Specialties: Working/using straight knives of his design and to customer specs. **Patterns:** Boots, hunters, utility/camp knives. **Technical:** Grinds ATS-34, 440C, D2. Prefers natural hardwoods, antler and Micarta. All sheaths hand-made. **Prices:** $125 to $250; some to $600. **Remarks:** Part-time maker; first knife sold in 1984. **Mark:** Name, city, state.

TOWELL, DWIGHT L., Rt. 1, Box 66, Midvale, ID 83645/208-355-2419
Specialties: Solid, elegant working knives; art knives. **Patterns:** Hunters, Bowies, daggers; folders in several weights. **Technical:** Grinds 154CM; some engraving. **Prices:** $250 to $800; some $3,500 and higher. **Remarks:** Part-time maker; first knife sold in 1970. **Mark:** Last name.

TOWNSEND, J.W., 2073 Highway 200, Trout Creek, MT 59874/406-847-2667
Specialties: One-of-a-kinds. **Patterns:** Fantasy knives and fighters. **Technical:** Grinds 440C, O1, commercial Damascus and ATS-34. **Prices:** $175 to $1,200; some higher. **Remarks:** Full-time maker; first knife sold in 1985. **Mark:** First and middle initials and last name, or stylized last name.

TRABBIC, R.W., 4550 N. Haven, Toledo, OH 43612/419-478-9578
Specialties: Working knives. **Patterns:** Hunters, Bowies, locking hunters and springbacks in standard patterns. **Technical:** Grinds D2, 440C and 154CM. **Prices:** $80 to $250. **Remarks:** Part-time maker; first knife sold in 1973. **Mark:** First and middle initials, last name.

TRACKERS FORGE (See Alderman, Robert)

TRACY, BUD, 15500 Fawn Ln., Reno, NV 89511

TRAPPER CREEK KNIFE CO. (See Thompson, Lloyd)

TREIBER KNIVES (See Treiber, Leon)

TREIBER, LEON, P.O. Box 342, Ingram, TX 78025/210-367-2246
Specialties: Folders of his design and to customer specs. **Patterns:** Locking folders. **Technical:** Grinds CPM-T-440V, D2, 440C. **Prices:** $250 to $600. **Remarks:** Part-time maker; first knife sold in 1992. Doing business as Treiber Knives. **Mark:** First initial, last name, city, state.

TREML, GLENN, RR #14, Site 11-10, Thunder Bay, Ontario, CANADA P7B 5E5/807-767-1977
Specialties: Working straight knives of his design and to customer specs. **Patterns:** Hunters, kitchen knives and double-edged survival knives. **Technical:** Grinds 440C, ATS-34 and O1; stock removal

method. Uses various woods and Micarta for handle material. **Prices:** $60 to $400; some higher. **Mark:** Stamped last name.

TRINDLE, BARRY, 1660 Ironwood Trail, Earlham, IA 50072-8611/515-462-1237
Specialties: Engraved folders. **Patterns:** Mostly small folders, classical styles and pocket knives. **Technical:** 440 only. Engraves. Handles of wood or mineral material. **Prices:** Start at $750. **Mark:** Name on tang.

TRITZ, JEAN JOSE, Schopstrasse 23, 20255 Hamburg, GERMANY/040-49 78 21
Specialties: Japanese kitchen knives and Scandinavian knives. **Patterns:** Puukkos, Koyatanas, Hoche, Tollekniven, kitchen knives and friction folders. **Technical:** Forges carbon steels, tool steels, ball bearing steel, file steel, *san-mai* and his own pattern Damascus. Makes own Mokume. Prefers natural handle material; does leatherwork, some exotic. **Prices:** $150 to $1,000; some higher. **Remarks:** Part-time maker; first knife sold in 1989. **Mark:** Initials in monogram.

TRL HANDMADE KNIVES (See Lewis, Tom R.)

TRO KNIVES (See Overeynder, T.R.)

TROLL HAMMER FORGE (See Dube, Paul)

TRUCKEE KNIFEWORKS (See Fronefield, Mike)

TRUJILLO, ADAM, 3001 Tanglewood Dr., Anchorage, AK 99517/907-243-6093
Specialties: Working/using straight knives of his design. **Patterns:** Hunters and utility/camp knives. **Technical:** Grinds 440C, ATS-34 and O1; ice tempers blades. Sheaths are dipped in wax and oil base. **Prices:** $200 to $500; some to $1,000. **Remarks:** Spare-time maker; first knife sold in 1995. Doing business as Alaska Knife & Service Co. **Mark:** NA.

TRUJILLO, MIRANDA, 3001 Tanglewood Dr., Anchorage, AK 99517/907-243-6093
Specialties: Working/using straight knives of her design. **Patterns:** Hunters and utility/camp knives. **Technical:** Grinds ATS-34 and 440C. Sheaths are water resistant. **Prices:** $145 to $400; some to $600. **Remarks:** Spare-time maker; first knife sold in 1989. Doing business as Alaska Knife & Service Co. **Mark:** NA.

TRUJILLO, THOMAS A., 3001 Tanglewood Dr., Anchorage, AK 99517/907-243-6093
Specialties: High-end art knives. **Patterns:** Hunters, Bowies, daggers and locking folders. **Technical:** Grinds to customer choice, including rock and commercial Damascus. Inlays jewels and carves handles. **Prices:** $150 to $900; some to $6,000. **Remarks:** Full-time maker; first knife sold in 1976. Doing business as Alaska Knife & Service Co. **Mark:** Alaska Knife and/or Thomas Anthony.

TSCHAGER, REINHARD, Piazza Parrocchia 7, I-39100 Bolzano, ITALY/0471-970642; FAX: 0471-970642
Specialties: Classic, high-art, collector-grade straight knives of his design. **Patterns:** Hunters. **Technical:** Grinds ATS-34, D2 and Damascus. Oval pins. Gold inlay. Offers engraving. **Prices:** $500 to $1,200; some to $4,000. **Remarks:** Spare-time maker; first knife sold in 1979. **Mark:** Gold inlay stamped with initials.

TURCOTTE, LARRY, 1707 Evergreen, Pampa, TX 79065/806-665-9369, 806-669-0435
Specialties: Fancy and working/using knives of his design and to customer specs. **Patterns:** Hunters, kitchen knives, utility/camp knives. **Technical:** Grinds 440C, D2, ATS-34. Engraves, scrimshaws, silver inlays. **Prices:** $150 to $350; some to $1,000. **Remarks:** Part-time maker; first knife sold in 1977. Doing business as Knives by Turcotte. **Mark:** Last name.

TURECEK, JIM, P.O. Box 882, Derby, CT 06418/203-734-8406
Specialties: Exotic folders, art knives and some miniatures. **Patterns:** Trout and bird knives with split bamboo handles and one-of-a-kind folders. **Technical:** Grinds and forges stainless and carbon Damascus. **Prices:** $750 to $1,500; some to $3,000. **Remarks:** Full-time maker; first knife sold in 1983. **Mark:** Last initial in script, or last name.

TURNBULL, RALPH A., 5722 Newburg Rd., Rockford, IL 61108/815-398-3799
Specialties: Plain or fancy working knives. **Patterns:** Hunters, fighters, boots, folders and Bowies. **Technical:** Grinds ATS-34, 440C, 154CM, CPM and other's Damascus. Makes wood inlay handles. **Prices:** $100 to $300; some to $2,000. **Remarks:** Full-time maker; first knife sold in 1973. **Mark:** Signature or initials.

TURNER, KEVIN, 17 Hunt Ave., Montrose, NY 10548/914-739-0535
Specialties: Working straight knives of his design and to customer specs; period pieces. **Patterns:** Daggers, fighters and utility knives. **Technical:** Forges 5160 and 52100. **Prices:** $90 to $500. **Remarks:** Part-time maker; first knife sold in 1991. **Mark:** Acid-etched signed last name and year.

TWIG (See Davis, K.M. "Twig")

TWILIGHT FORGE (See Champagne, Paul)

TWISTED NICKEL KNIVES (See Ferguson, Jim [Temecula, CA])

TYC, WILLIAM J., 14 Hob St., Newburgh, NY 12550/914-562-5165
Specialties: Traditional and working straight knives of all designs. **Patterns:** Bowies, fighters and utility knives. **Technical:** Grinds 440C, ATS-34 and O1. Satin finishes blades. **Prices:** $80 to $300; some to $500. **Remarks:** Spare-time maker; first knife sold in 1989. **Mark:** First and last name.

TYCER, ART, 3807 Hillside Dr., North Little Rock, AR 72118/501-753-7637
Specialties: Fancy working/using straight knives of his design, to customer specs and standard patterns. **Patterns:** Boots, Bowies, daggers, fighters, hunters, kitchen and utility knives. **Technical:** Grinds ATS-34, 440C, D2 and A2. Uses exotic woods with spacer material, stag and water buffalo. Offers filework. **Prices:** $100 to $175; some to $400. **Remarks:** Part-time maker; first knife sold in 1990. **Mark:** Flying "T" over first initial.

TYSER, ROSS, 1015 Hardee Court, Spartanburg, SC 29303/864-585-7616
Specialties: Traditional working and using straight knives and folders of his design and in standard patterns. **Patterns:** Bowies, hunters and slip-joint folders. **Technical:** Grinds 440C and commercial Damascus. Mosaic pins; stone inlay. Does filework and scrimshaw. Offers engraving and cut-work and some inlay on sheaths. **Prices:** $45 to $125; some to $400. **Remarks:** Part-time maker; first knife sold in 1995. Doing business as RT Custom Knives. **Mark:** Stylized initials.

u

UEKAMA, NOBUYUKI, 3-2-8-302 Ochiai, Tama City, Tokyo, JAPAN

UWHARRIE RATTLER KNIVES (See Rece, Charles V.)

v

VACHON, YVON, 98, Lehoux St., Robertsonville, Quebec, CANADA G0N 1L0/418-338-6601
Specialties: Functional miniatures and micro straight knives in standard patterns. **Patterns:** Automatics, daggers, folders, locking folders, swords and knife pistols. **Technical:** Grinds 440C, 316 and Damascus. Uses gold, exotic wood, malachite, buffalo horn, mother-of-pearl and abalone. **Prices:** $100 to $700; some to $6,000. **Remarks:** Full-time maker; first knife sold in 1982. Doing business as Creations Yvon Vachon. **Mark:** Initials punched.

VAGNINO, MICHAEL, P.O. Box 67, Visalia, CA 93279/209-528-2800
Specialties: Traditional working and using straight knives of his design and to customer specs. **Patterns:** Hunters, kitchen knives and utility/camp knives. **Technical:** Forges and grinds A2 and ATS-34; grinds 420. Etched blades, rust brown and blued. **Prices:** $100 to $175; some to $250. **Remarks:** Part-time maker; first knife sold in 1995. **Mark:** Logo and name.

VALLOTTON, BUTCH AND AREY, 621 Fawn Ridge Dr., Oakland, OR 97462/503-459-2216
Specialties: Heavy-duty folders with complicated mechanisms to cus-

tomer specs. **Patterns:** Fighters, gentleman's knives and working folders. **Technical:** Grinds ATS-34, 440C, Damascus, titanium, 416 and nickel-silver. Prefers bead-blasted, mirror or anodized finishes. **Prices:** $350 to $2,500. **Remarks:** Full-time maker; first knife sold in 1981. **Mark:** Name, area and state.

VALLOTTON, RAINY D., 621 Fawn Ridge Dr., Oakland, OR 97462/503-459-2216
Specialties: Folders and one-handed openers. **Patterns:** Hunters, fighters, folders and sheath knives. **Technical:** Stock removal all steels; uses titanium liners and bolsters; uses all finishes. **Prices:** $250 to $1,000. **Remarks:** Full-time maker. **Mark:** Name.

VALLOTTON, SHAWN, 621 Fawn Ridge Dr., Oakland, OR 97462/503-459-2216
Specialties: Left-hand knives. **Patterns:** All styles. **Technical:** Grinds 440C, ATS-34 and Damascus. Uses titanuim. Prefers bead-blasted or anodized finishes. **Prices:** $250 to $1,400. **Remarks:** Full-time maker. **Mark:** Name and specialty.

VALOIS, A. DANIEL, 3552 W. Lizard Ck. Rd., Lehighton, PA 18235/717-386-3636
Specialties: Big working knives; various sized lock-back folders with new safety releases. **Patterns:** Fighters in survival packs, sturdy working knives, belt buckle knives, military-style knives, swords. **Technical:** Forges and grinds A2, O1 and 440C; likes full tangs. **Prices:** $65 to $240; some to $600. **Remarks:** Full-time maker; first knife sold in 1969. **Mark:** Anvil logo with last name inside.

VAN DE MANAKKER, THIJS, Koolweg 34, 5759 px Helenaveen, HOLLAND/0493539369
Specialties: Classic high-art knives. **Patterns:** Swords, utility/camp knives and period pieces. **Technical:** Forges soft iron, carbon steel and Bloomery Iron. Makes own Damascus, Bloomery Iron and patterns. **Prices:** $20 to $2,000; some higher. **Remarks:** Full-time maker; first knife sold in 1969. **Mark:** Stylized "V."

VAN DEN ELSEN, GERT, Purcelldreef 83, 5012 AJ Tilburg, NETHERLANDS/013-4563200
Specialties: Fancy, working/using, miniatures and integral straight knives of the maker's design or to customer specs. **Patterns:** Bowies, fighters and hunters. **Technical:** Grinds ATS-34 and 440C; forges Damascus. Offers filework, differentially tempered blades and some mokume-gane fittings. **Prices:** $170 to $500; some to $2500. **Remarks:** Part-time maker; first knife sold in 1982. Doing business as G-E Knives. **Mark:** Initials GE in lozenge shape.

VAN ELDIK, FRANS, Ho Flaan 3, 3632BT Loenen, NETHERLANDS/0031 294 233 095; FAX: 0031 294 233 095
Specialties: Fancy collector-grade straight knives and folders of his design. **Patterns:** Hunters, fighters, boots and folders. **Technical:** Forges and grinds D2, 154CM, ATS-34 and stainless Damascus. **Prices:** Start at $225. **Remarks:** Spare-time maker; first knife sold in 1979. **Mark:** Lion with name and Amsterdam.

VAN HOY, ED, 413 Fairhaven Rd., Taylors, SC 29687/864-268-9849
Specialties: Traditional and working/using straight knives of his design. **Patterns:** Fighters, folders, hunters and art knives. **Technical:** Grinds ATS-34 and 440V; forges D2. Offers filework, engraves, acid etching, mosaic pins, decorative bolsters and custom fitted English bridle leather sheaths. **Prices:** $250 to $3,000. **Remarks:** Full-time maker; first knife sold in 1977. Wife also engraves. Doing business as Van Hoy Knives. **Mark:** Acid etched last name.

VAN HOY KNIVES (See Van Hoy, Ed)

VAN RIJSWIJK, AAD, Oberonweg 284, 3208 PG Spijkenisse, HOLLAND/0181-640334; FAX: 0181-640334
Specialties: High-art interframe folders of his design and in standard patterns. **Patterns:** Hunters and locking folders. **Technical:** ATS-34 and stainless Damascus. Uses semi-precious stones. Handle materials include ivory, mammoth ivory, iron wood. Offers hand-made sheaths. **Prices:** $400 to $1,200; some to $2,000. **Remarks:** Full-time maker; first knife sold in 1993. **Mark:** NA.

VAN SCHAIK, BASTIAAN, Post Box 75269, 1070 AG, Amsterdam, NETHERLANDS/31-20-633-80-25; FAX: 31-20-679-72-19
Specialties: Working/using straight knives and axes of his design. **Patterns:** Daggers, fighters, push daggers and battle axes. **Technical:** Grinds ATS-34 and 440C; forges high-carbon steel. Uses Damascus and high-tech coatings. **Prices:** $400 to $1,500; some to $2,000. **Remarks:** Full-time maker; first knife sold in 1993. Doing business as Licorne Edged Creations. **Mark:** Unicorn head.

VANDERFORD, CARL G., Rt. 9, Box 238B, Columbia, TN 38401/615-381-1488
Specialties: Traditional working straight knives and folders of his design. **Patterns:** Hunters, Bowies and locking folders. **Technical:** Forges and grinds 440C, O1 and wire Damascus. **Prices:** $60 to $125. **Remarks:** Part-time maker; first knife sold in 1987. **Mark:** Last name.

VEATCH, RICHARD, 2580 N. 35th Pl., Springfield, OR 97477/541-747-3910
Specialties: Traditional working and using straight knives of his design and in standard patterns; period pieces. **Patterns:** Daggers, hunters, swords, utility/camp knives and minis. **Technical:** Forges and grinds his own Damascus; uses L6 and O1. Prefers natural handle materials; offers leatherwork. **Prices:** $50 to $300; some to $500. **Remarks:** Full-time maker; first knife sold in 1991. **Mark:** Stylized initials.

VEIT, MICHAEL, 3289 E. Fifth Rd., LaSalle, IL 61301/815-223-3538
Specialties: Period pieces—fancy straight knives and Damascus folders. **Technical:** Forges his own Turkish Damascus. Engraves. **Prices:** $1,500 to $2,500. **Remarks:** Part-time maker; first knife sold in 1985. **Mark:** Name in script.

VELARDE, RICARDO, 746 E. 200 N., Provo, UT 84606/801-375-0519; FAX: 801-375-2742
Specialties: Working and using straight knives of his design and in standard patterns. **Patterns:** Boots, fighters and hunters; flat or hollow grind. **Technical:** Grinds ATS-34, 440C and D2. **Prices:** Start at $250. **Remarks:** First knife sold in 1992. **Mark:** First initial, last name on blade; city, state, U.S.A. at bottom of tang.

VENSILD, HENRIK, Gl Estrup, Randersvei 4, DK-8963 Auning, DENMARK/+45 86 48 44 48
Specialties: Classic and traditional working and using knives of his design; Scandinavian influence. **Patterns:** Hunters and using knives. **Technical:** Forges Damascus. Hand makes handles, sheaths and blades. **Prices:** $350 to $1,000. **Remarks:** Part-time maker; first knife sold in 1967. **Mark:** Initials.

VIALLON, HENRI, Les Belins, 63300 Thiers, FRANCE/(33)-73-80-24-03; FAX: 73-51-02-02
Specialties: Traditional straight knives and folders of his design. **Patterns:** Hunters, folders, boots and utility knives. **Technical:** Forges and grinds 12C27, D2, 440C, ATS-34 and his own Damascus; mosaic Damascus. **Prices:** $175 to $375; some to $1,500. **Remarks:** Full-time maker; first knife sold in 1985. **Mark:** First initial, last name.

VIELE, H.J., 88 Lexington Ave., Westwood, NJ 07675/201-666-2906
Specialties: Folding knives of distinctive shapes. **Patterns:** High-tech folders. **Technical:** Grinds 440C and ATS-34. **Prices:** Start at $350. **Remarks:** Full-time maker; first knife sold in 1973. **Mark:** Last name with stylized throwing star.

VIKING KNIVES (See Eriksen, James Thorlief)

VILLA, LUIZ, R. Com. Miguel Calfat, 398, Itaim Bibi, Sao Paulo, SP-04537-081, BRAZIL/011-8290649
Specialties: One-of-a-kind straight knives and jewel knives of all designs. **Patterns:** Bowies, hunters, utility/camp knives and jewel knives. **Technical:** Grinds D6, Damascus and 440C; forges 5160. Prefers natural handle material. **Prices:** $70 to $200. **Remarks:** Part-time maker; first knife sold in 1990. **Mark:** Last name and serial number.

VILLAR, RICARDO, Al. dos Jasmins, 243, Mairipora, S.P. 07600-000, BRAZIL/011-4851649; WEB: http://www.visual.net.com/blade web
Specialties: Straight working knives to customer specs. **Patterns:** Bowies, fighters and utility/camp knives. **Technical:** Grinds D6, ATS-34 and 440C stainless. **Prices:** $80 to $200. **Remarks:** Part-time maker; first knife sold in 1993. **Mark:** Percor over sword and circle.

VISTNES, TOR, N-6930 Svelgen, NORWAY/047-57795572
Specialties: Traditional and working knives of his design. **Patterns:** Hunters and utility knives. **Technical:** Grinds Uddeholm Elmax. Handles made of rear burls of different Nordic stabilized woods. **Prices:** $300 to $1100. **Remarks:** Part-time maker; first knife sold in 1988. **Mark:** Etched name and deer head.

VOSS, BEN, 362 Clark St., Galesburg, IL 61401/309-342-6994
Specialties: Fancy working knives of his design. **Patterns:** Bowies, fighters, hunters, boots and folders. **Technical:** Grinds 440C, ATS-34 and D2. **Prices:** $35 to $1,200. **Remarks:** Part-time maker; first knife sold in 1986. **Mark:** Name, city and state.

VOTAW, DAVID P., Box 327, Pioneer, OH 43554/419-737-2774
Specialties: Working knives; period pieces. **Patterns:** Hunters, Bowies, camp knives, buckskinners and tomahawks. **Technical:** Grinds O1 and D2. **Prices:** $100 to $200; some to $500. **Remarks:** Part-time maker; took over for the late W.K. Kneubuhler. Doing business as W-K Knives. **Mark:** WK with V inside anvil.

VULTURE CUTLERY (See Goers, Bruce)

VUNK, ROBERT, 4408 Buckeye Ct., Orlando, FL 32804/407-628-3970
Specialties: Working knives, some fancy; period pieces. **Patterns:** Variety of tantos, fillet knives, kitchen knives, camp knives and folders. **Technical:** Grinds O1, 440C and ATS-34; provides mountings, cases, stands. **Prices:** $55 to $1,300. **Remarks:** Part-time maker; first knife sold in 1985. Doing business as RV Knives. **Mark:** Initials.

W

WADA, YASUTAKA, Fujinokidai 2-6-22, Nara City Nara prefect, 631 JAPAN/0742 46-0689
Specialties: Fancy and embellished one-of-a-kind straight knives of his design. **Patterns:** Bowies, daggers and hunters. **Technical:** Grinds ATS-34, Cowry X and Cowry X L-30 laminate. **Prices:** $400 to $2,500. **Remarks:** Part-time maker; first knife sold in 1990. **Mark:** Owl eyes with initial and last name underneath.

WADE, JAMES M., 812 Tamarack Dr., Apt. 8304, Fayetteville, NC 28311/919-483-3548
Specialties: Working straight knives. **Patterns:** Gut-hook hunters, boots, Bowies, fighters. **Technical:** Grinds D2, 440C, 154CM and ATS-34. **Prices:** $100 to $450; some to $1,000. **Remarks:** Spare-time maker; first knife sold in 1982. **Mark:** Name.

WAGAMAN, JOHN K., 903 Arsenal Ave., Fayetteville, NC 28305/910-485-7860
Specialties: Fancy working knives. **Patterns:** Bowies, miniatures, hunters, fighters and boots. **Technical:** Grinds D2, 440C, 154CM and commercial Damascus; inlays mother-of-pearl. **Prices:** $110 to $2,000. **Remarks:** Part-time maker; first knife sold in 1975. **Mark:** Last name.

WAGNER, DAN, 112 Delaware St., New Castle, DE 19720-4814
Specialties: Fantasy and working/using straight knives of his design and to customer specs. **Patterns:** Daggers, fighters, hunters. **Technical:** Grinds ATS-34, 52100, CPM440V. Offers full or tapered tangs, fancy filework. Uses expensive burls and exotic woods for handles. Offers custom leather work. **Prices:** $75 to $250; some to $650. **Remarks:** Part-time maker; first knife sold in 1991. **Mark:** Oaktree Forge or acorn.

WAHLSTER, MARK DAVID, 1404 N. Second St., Silverton, OR 97381/503-873-3775
Specialties: Automatics, antique and high tech folders in standard patterns and to customer specs. **Patterns:** Hunters, fillets and combat knives. **Technical:** Flat grinds 440C, ATS-34, D2 and Damascus. Uses titanium in folders. **Prices:** $100 to $1,000. **Remarks:** Full-time maker; first knife sold in 1981. **Mark:** Name, city and state or last name.

WALDROP, MARK, 14562 SE 1st Ave. Rd., Summerfield, FL 34491/352-347-9034
Specialties: Period pieces. **Patterns:** Bowies and daggers. **Technical:** Uses stock removal. Engraves. **Prices:** Moderate to upscale. **Remarks:** Part-time maker; first knife sold in 1978. **Mark:** Last name.

WALKER, GEORGE A., Star Route, Alpine, WY 83128/307-883-2372
Specialties: Deluxe working knives. **Patterns:** Hunters, boots, fighters, Bowies and folders. **Technical:** Forges his own Damascus and cable; engraves, carves, scrimshaws. Makes sheaths. **Prices:** $125 to $750; some to $1,000. **Remarks:** Full-time maker; first knife sold in 1979. Partners with wife. **Mark:** Name, city and state.

WALKER, JIM, 22 Walker Lane, Morrilton, AR 72110/501-354-3175
Specialties: Period pieces and working/using knives of his design and to customer specs. **Patterns:** Bowies, fighters and hunters. **Technical:** Forges 5160, O1 and L6. **Prices:** Start at $225. **Remarks:** Part-time maker; first knife sold in 1993. **Mark:** Three arrows with last name/MS.

WALKER, JOHN W., 10620 Moss Branch Rd., Bon Aqua, TN 37025/615-670-4754
Specialties: Straight knives and short daggers. **Patterns:** Hunters, boots, etc., some with precious stones. **Technical:** Grinds 440C, ATS-34, L6, etc. **Prices:** $100 to $450; some to $800. **Remarks:** Part-time maker; first knife sold in 1982. **Mark:** Hohenzollern Eagle emblem with name, or last name.

WALKER, MICHAEL L., 2925 Powell St., Eugene, OR 97405/541-465-LOCK (5625); FAX: 541-465-8973
Specialties: High-tech folders of his design. **Patterns:** Locking folders, patent locks, interframes—engraved, scrimmed, anodized in titanium colors, furnished with rich materials. **Technical:** Grinds AEB-L, 6K and commercial Damascus. **Prices:** $1,200 to $12,000. **Remarks:** Full-time maker; first knife sold in 1980. Has trademarked words "blade lock" and "Zipper" blades for advertising use. Most knives a team effort with Patricia Walker. **Mark:** Walker's Lockers by M.L. Walker, or initials.

WALKER, PATRICIA (See Walker, Michael L.)

WALKER'S LOCKERS (See Walker, Michael L.)

WALLACE, ROGER L., 4902 Collins Lane, Tampa, FL 33603/813-239-3261
Specialties: Working straight knives, Bowies and camp knives to customer specs. **Patterns:** Hunters, skinners and utility knives. **Technical:** Forges high-carbon steel. **Prices:** Start at $75. **Remarks:** Part-time maker; first knife sold in 1985. **Mark:** First initial, last name.

WALTERS, A.F., 609 E. 20th St., Tifton, GA 31794/912-382-1282
Specialties: Working knives, some to customer specs. **Patterns:** Locking folders, straight hunters, fishing and survival knives. **Technical:** Grinds D2, 154CM and 13C26. **Prices:** Start at $150. **Remarks:** Part-time maker. Label: "The jewel knife." **Mark:** "J" in diamond and knife logo.

WANO KNIVES (See Ware, Tommy)

WARD, CHUCK, 1010 E. North St., Benton, AR 72015/501-778-4329
Specialties: Traditional working and using straight knives and folders of his design. **Technical:** Grinds 440C, D2, A2 and O1; uses natural and composite handle materials. **Prices:** $90 to $400, some higher. **Remarks:** Full-time maker; first knife sold in 1990. **Mark:** First initial, last name.

WARD CUSTOM KNIVES (See Ward, Ron)

WARD, J.J., 7501 S.R. 220, Waverly, OH 45690/614-947-5328
Specialties: Traditional and working/using straight knives and folders of his design. **Patterns:** Hunters and locking folders. **Technical:** Grinds ATS-34, 440C and Damascus. Offers handmade sheaths. **Prices:** $125 to $250; some to $500. **Remarks:** Spare-time maker; first knife sold in 1980. **Mark:** Etched name.

WARD, KEN, 1188 Wesley Lane, Auburn, CA 95603/916-885-8908
Specialties: Working knives, some to customer specs. **Patterns:** Straight and folding hunters, axes, Bowies, buckskinners and miniatures. **Technical:** Grinds ATS-34, Damascus and Stellite 6K. **Prices:** $100 to $700. **Remarks:** Part-time maker; first knife sold in 1977. **Mark:** Name.

WARD, RON, 409 Arrowhead Trails, Loveland, OH 45140/513-683-8729
Specialties: Classic working and using straight knives of his design or to customer specs. **Patterns:** Bowies, hunters and utility/camp knives. **Technical:** Grinds 440C, 154CM, and ATS-34. Multi-metal guards; exotic natural wood handles. **Prices:** $65 to $150; some to $500. **Remarks:** Part-time maker; first knife sold in 1992. Doing business as Ward Custom Knives. **Mark:** Last name.

WARD, W.C., 817 Glenn St., Clinton, TN 37716/615-457-3568
Specialties: Working straight knives; period pieces. **Patterns:** Hunters, Bowies, swords and kitchen cutlery. **Technical:** Grinds O1. **Prices:** $85 to $150; some to $500. **Remarks:** Part-time maker; first knife sold in 1969. He styled the Tennessee Knife Maker. **Mark:** TKM.

WARDELL, MICK, 85 Coneybury, Bletchingley, Surrey RH1 4PR ENGLAND/01883742918
Specialties: Folders of his design. **Patterns:** Locking and slip-joint folder, hunters and Bowies. **Technical:** Grinds CPM-T-440V, D2 and Dam-

ascus. Heat-treats. **Prices:** £80 to £500; some to £700. **Remarks:** Full-time maker; first knife sold in 1986. **Mark:** Last name or initials.

WARDEN, ROY A., 275 Tanglewood Rd., Union, MO 63084/314-583-8813 **Specialties:** Working straight knives of his design and in standard patterns. **Patterns:** Hunters, bird and trout knives, camp knives. **Technical:** Forges 5160. Makes own pattern-welded steel Damascus and mosaic Damascus; Damascus billets rough-forged and patterned to order; makes cable Damascus knives and belt buckles. Heat-treats and embellishes. Makes individual knife display stands from woods, steel and horns. **Prices:** Start at $65. **Remarks:** Part-time maker; first knife sold in 1987. **Mark:** Last name.

WARDIAN, PAUL G., 460 SW Halsey Loop, Troutdale, OR 97060/503-661-4324
Specialties: Fancy straight knives and miniatures. **Patterns:** Bowies, daggers, fighters and miniatures. **Technical:** Grinds 5160, tool steel and Damascus. Carves antler and wood, sculpts blades, engraves and scrimshaws. **Prices:** $55 to $225; some to $1,600. **Remarks:** Part-time maker; first knife sold in 1988. Doing business as One Of A Kind Knives. **Mark:** Engraved initials in logo.

WARE, TOMMY, P.O. Box 488, Datil, NM 87821/505-772-5817
Specialties: Traditional working and using straight knives, folders and automatics of his design and to customer specs. **Patterns:** Hunters, automatics and locking folders. **Technical:** Grinds ATS-34, 440C and D2. Offers engraving and scrimshaw. **Prices:** $225 to $575; some to $1,000. **Remarks:** Full-time maker; first knife sold in 1990. Doing business as Wano Knives. **Mark:** Last name inside oval, business name above, city and state below, year on side.

WARENSKI, BUSTER, P.O. Box 214, Richfield, UT 84701/801-896-5319 **Specialties:** Investor-class straight knives. **Patterns:** Daggers, swords, fighters and Bowies. **Technical:** Grinds, engraves and inlays; offers surface treatments. **Prices:** Upscale. **Remarks:** Full-time maker. Not currently taking orders. **Mark:** First or last name.

WARREN, AL, 1423 Sante Fe Circle, Roseville, CA 95678/916-784-3217 **Specialties:** Working straight knives and folders, some fancy. **Patterns:** Hunters, Bowies, daggers, short swords, fillets and kitchen knives. **Technical:** Grinds D2, ATS-34 and 440C. **Prices:** $110 to $950. **Remarks:** Part-time maker; first knife sold in 1978. **Mark:** First and middle initials, last name.

WARREN, DELLANA, P.O. Box 9511, Schenectady, NY 12309/518-370-0101; FAX: 518-370-0101
Specialties: Fancy/embellished and high-art folders of her design. **Patterns:** Locking folders. **Technical:** Forges her own Damascus and W2. Engraves; does stone setting, filework and carving. Prefers exotic, high karat gold, silver and gemstone handle material. **Prices:** $1,600 to $3,800; some to $5,500. **Remarks:**Full-time maker; first knife sold in 1994. Doing business as Dellana. **Mark:** Engraved in gold: first name, number of knife, name of knife, date.

WARTHER, DALE, 331 Karl Ave., Dover, OH 44622/216-343-7513
Specialties: Working knives; period pieces. **Patterns:** Kitchen cutlery, daggers, hunters and some folders. **Technical:** Forges and grinds O1, D2 and 440C. **Prices:** $250 to $7,000. **Remarks:** Full-time maker; first knife sold in 1967. Takes orders only at shows or by personal interviews at his shop. **Mark:** Warther Originals.

WARTHER ORIGINALS (See Warther, Dale)

WARZOCHA, STANLEY, 32540 Wareham Dr., Warren, MI 48092/810-939-9344
Specialties: Working straight knives; some period pieces. **Patterns:** Hunters, buckskinners, fighters and fishing knives. **Technical:** Grinds 440C and ATS-34 **Prices:** $125 to $1,200. **Remarks:** Spare-time maker; first knife sold in 1978. **Mark:** Last name.

WATANABE, WAYNE, P.O. Box 3563, Montebello, CA 90640/213-728-6867
Specialties: Straight knives in Japanese styles. One-of-kind designs; welcomes customer designs. **Patterns:** Tantos to katanas, Bowies. **Technical:** Flat grinds A2, O1 and ATS-34. Offers hand-rubbed finishes and wrapped handles. **Prices:** Start at $200. **Remarks:** Part-time maker. **Mark:** Name in characters with flower.

WATER MOUNTAIN KNIVES (See Maneker, Kenneth)

WATSON, BERT, P.O. Box 26, Westminster, CO 80030-0026/303-426-7577
Specialties: Working/using straight knives of his design and to customer specs. **Patterns:** Fighters, hunters, utility/camp knives. **Technical:** Grinds O1, ATS-34, 440C, D2, A2 and others. **Prices:** $50 to $250. **Remarks:** Full-time maker; first knife sold in 1974. Doing business as Game Trail Knives. **Mark:** GTK stamped or etched, sometimes with first or last name.

WATSON, BILLY, 440 Forge Rd., Deatsville, AL 36022/334-365-1482 **Specialties:** Working and using straight knives and folders of his design; period pieces. **Patterns:** Hunters, Bowies and utility/camp knives. **Technical:** Forges and grinds his own Damascus, 1095, 5160 and 52100. **Prices:** $20 to $900. **Remarks:** Full-time maker; first knife sold in 1970. Doing business as Billy's Blacksmith Shop. **Mark:** Last name.

WATSON, DANIEL, 350 Jennifer Ln., Driftwood, TX 78619/512-847-9679; WEB: http://www.angelsword.com; E-MAIL: a.sword@ccsi.com
Specialties: One-of-a-kind knives and swords. **Patterns:** Hunters, daggers, swords and miniatures. **Technical:** Hand-purify and carbonize his own high-carbon steel, pattern-welded Damascus, cable and carbon-induced crystalline Damascus. European and Japanese tempering. **Prices:** $90 to $4,000; swords to $25,000. **Remarks:** Full-time maker; first knife sold in 1979. **Mark:** "Angel Sword" on forged pieces; "Bright Knight" for stock removal.

WATSON, PETER, 66 Kielblock St., La Hoff 2570, SOUTH AFRICA/018-84942
Specialties: Traditional working and using straight knives and folders of his design. **Patterns:** Hunters, locking folders and utility/camp knives. **Technical:** Sandvik and 440C. **Prices:** $120 to $250; some to $1,500. **Remarks:** Part-time maker; first knife sold in 1989. **Mark:** Buffalo head with name.

WATSON, TOM, 1103 Brenau Terrace, Panama City, FL 32405/850-785-9209; FAX: 850-763-6034
Specialties: Lockback folders with G10 or Micarta handles. **Patterns:** Folding drop-point hunters, folding boot knives, fixed blade hunters, boots and small fighters. **Technical:** Flat-grinds ATS-34, 440C and 440V. Heat-treats with multiple tempering and hardness testing. Prefers satin finishes. **Prices:** Starting at $150. **Remarks:** Full-time maker; first knife sold in 1978. **Mark:** Name and city.

WATT III, FREDDIE, P.O. Box 1372, Big Spring, TX 79721/915-263-6629 **Specialties:** Working straight knives, some fancy. **Patterns:** Hunters, fighters and Bowies. **Technical:** Grinds A2, D2, 440C and ATS-34; prefers mirror finishes. **Prices:** $150 to $350; some to $750. **Remarks:** Full-time maker; first knife sold in 1979. **Mark:** Last name, city and state.

WATTELET, MICHAEL A., P.O. Box 649, 125 Front, Minocqua, WI 54548/715-356-3069
Specialties: Working and using straight knives of his design and to customer specs; fantasy knives. **Patterns:** Daggers, fighters and swords. **Technical:** Grinds 440C and L6; forges and grinds O1. Silversmith. **Prices:** $75 to $1,000; some to $5,000. **Remarks:** Full-time maker; first knife sold in 1966. Doing business as M&N Arts Ltd. **Mark:** First initial, last name.

WATTS, MIKE, Rt. 1 Box 81, Gatesville, TX 76528

WATTS, WALLY, 9560 Hwy. 36, Gatesville, TX 76528/817-487-2866
Specialties: Unique traditional folders of his design. **Patterns:** One- to five-blade folders and single-blade gents in various blade shapes. **Technical:** Grinds ATS-34; D2 and 440C on request. **Prices:** $150 to $250; some to $500. **Remarks:** Full-time maker; first knife sold in 1986. **Mark:** Last name.

WEBER, FRED E., 517 Tappan St., Forked River, NJ 08731/609-693-0452
Specialties: Working knives in standard patterns. **Patterns:** Hunters, slip-joint and lock-back folders, Bowies and various-sized fillets. **Technical:** Grinds D2, 440V and ATS-34. **Prices:** $125 to $250; some to $500. **Remarks:** Full-time maker; first knife sold in 1973. **Mark:** First and middle initials, last name.

WEDDLE JR., DEL, 2703 Green Valley Rd., St. Joseph, MO 64505/816-364-1981
Specialties: Working knives; some period pieces. **Patterns:** Hunters, fighters, locking folders, push knives. **Technical:** Grinds D2 and 440C;

can provide precious metals and set gems. Offers his own forged wire-cable Damascus in his finished knives. **Prices:** $80 to $250; some to $2,000. **Remarks:** Full-time maker; first knife sold in 1972. **Mark:** Signature with last name and date.

WEHNER, RUDY, Rt. 4, Box 364 A1, Collins, MS 39428/601-765-4997
Specialties: Reproduction antique Bowies and contemporary Bowies in full and miniature. **Patterns:** Skinners, camp knives, fighters, axes and Bowies. **Technical:** Grinds 440C, ATS-34, 154CM and Damascus. **Prices:** $100 to $500; some to $850. **Remarks:** Full-time maker; first knife sold in 1975. **Mark:** Last name on Bowies and antiques; full name, city and state on skinners.

WEILAND JR., J. REESE, 612 Superior Ave., Tampa, FL 33606/813-971-5378 (7:30 a.m.-5:00 p.m.); 813-671-0661 (after 6:00 p.m.); FAX: 813-972-5336
Specialties: Traditional working straight knives and folders; liner locks and Hawk bills. **Patterns:** Hunters, tantos, Bowies, fantasy knives, spears and some swords. **Technical:** Grinds ATS-34 and Damascus bars. Offers titanium hardware on his liner locks and button locks. Distinctive bird-shaped handle on some models. **Prices:** $100 to $4,000. **Remarks:** Full-time maker; first knife sold in 1983. **Mark:** RW slant.

WEILER, DONALD E., P.O. Box 1576, Yuma, AZ 85366-9576/520-782-1159
Specialties: Working straight knives; period pieces. **Patterns:** Dirks, daggers, fighters, survival, throwing and camp knives; scramasax; buckskinner and Norse designs. **Technical:** Forges O1, W2, 5160, ATS-34, D2 and cable Damascus. Makes his own high-carbon steel Damascus. **Prices:** $80 to $1,000. **Remarks:** Full-time maker; first knife sold in 1952. **Mark:** Last name, city.

WEINAND, GEROME M., 14440 Harpers Bridge Rd., Missoula, MT 59802/406-543-0845
Specialties: Working straight knives. **Patterns:** Bowies, fishing and camp knives, large special hunters. **Technical:** Grinds O1, 440C, ATS-34, 1084 and L6; makes all-tool steel Damascus; Dendritic D2 from powdered steel. Heat-treats. **Prices:** $30 to $100; some to $500. **Remarks:** Full-time maker; first knife sold in 1982. **Mark:** Last name.

WEINSTOCK, ROBERT, Box 39, 520 Frederick St., San Francisco, CA 94117/415-731-5968
Specialties: Fancy and high-art straight knives of his design. **Patterns:** Daggers, folders, poignards and miniatures. **Technical:** Grinds A2, O1 and 440C. Chased and hand-carved blades and handles. **Prices:** $1,500 and $4,000; some to $5,000 or $6,000. **Remarks:** Full-time maker; first knife sold in 1994. **Mark:** Carved last name.

WEISS, CHARLES L., 18847 N. 13th Ave., Phoenix, AZ 85027/602-582-6147
Specialties: High-art straight knives and folders; deluxe period pieces. **Patterns:** Daggers, fighters, boots, push knives and miniatures. **Technical:** Grinds 440C, 154CM and ATS-34. **Prices:** $300 to $1,200; some to $2,000. **Remarks:** Full-time maker; first knife sold in 1975. **Mark:** Name and city.

WELCH, WILLIAM H., 8232 W. Red Snapper Dr., Kimmell, IN 46760/219-856-3577
Specialties: Working knives; deluxe period pieces. **Patterns:** Hunters, tantos, Bowies. **Technical:** Grinds ATS-34, D2 and 440C. **Prices:** $100 to $600. **Remarks:** Part-time maker; first knife sold in 1976. **Mark:** Last name.

WERNER KNIVES (See Werner Jr., William A.)

WERNER JR., WILLIAM A., 336 Lands Mill, Marietta, GA 30067/404-988-0074
Specialties: Fantasy and working/using straight knives. **Patterns:** Bowies, daggers, fighters. **Technical:** Grinds 440C stainless, 10 series carbon and Damascus. **Prices:** $150 to $400; some to $750. **Remarks:** Part-time maker. Doing business as Werner Knives. **Mark:** Last name.

WERTH, GEORGE W., 5223 Woodstock Rd., Poplar Grove, IL 61065/815-544-4408
Specialties: Period pieces, some fancy. **Patterns:** Straight fighters, daggers and Bowies. **Technical:** Forges and grinds O1, 1095 and his Damascus, including mosaic patterns. **Prices:** $200 to $650; some higher. **Remarks:** Full-time maker. Doing business as Fox Valley Forge. **Mark:** Name in logo or initials connected.

WESCOTT, CODY, 5330 White Wing Rd., Las Cruces, NM 88012/505-382-5008
Specialties: Fancy and presentation-grade working knives. **Patterns:** Hunters, locking folders and Bowies. **Technical:** Hollow-grinds D2 and ATS-34; all knives fileworked. Offers some engraving. Makes sheaths. **Prices:** $80 to $300; some to $950. **Remarks:** Full-time maker; first knife sold in 1982. **Mark:** First initial, last name.

WEST, CHARLES A., 1315 S. Pine St., Centralia, IL 62801/618-532-2777
Specialties: Classic, fancy, high tech, period pieces, traditional and working/using straight knives and folders. **Patterns:** Bowies, fighters and locking folders. **Technical:** Grinds ATS-34, O1 and Damascus. Prefers hot blued finishes. **Prices:** $100 to $1,000; some to $2,000. **Remarks:** Full-time maker; first knife sold in 1963. Doing business as West Custom Knives. **Mark:** Name or name, city and state.

WEST CUSTOM KNIVES (See West, Charles A.)

WEST, PAT, P.O. Box 9, Charlotte, TX 78011/210-277-1290
Specialties: Classic working and using straight knives and folders. **Patterns:** Hunters, kitchen knives, slip-joint folders. **Technical:** Grinds ATS-34, D2 and Vascowear. Offers filework and decorates liners on folders. **Prices:** $300 to $600. **Remarks:** Spare-time maker; first knife sold in 1984. **Mark:** Name.

WESTBERG, LARRY, 305 S. Western Hills Dr., Algona, IA 50511/515-295-9276
Specialties: Traditional and working straight knives of his design and in standard patterns. **Patterns:** Bowies, hunters, utility knives and miniatures. **Technical:** Grinds 440C, D2 and 1095. Heat-treats. Uses natural handle materials. **Prices:** $85 to $600; some to $1,000. **Remarks:** Part-time maker; first knife sold in 1987. **Mark:** Last name.

WHIPPLE, WESLEY A., P.O. Box 47, Thermopolis, WY 82443/307-864-2255
Specialties: Working straight knives, some fancy. **Patterns:** Hunters, Bowies, camp knives, fighters. **Technical:** Forges 5168, 52100, W2; makes cable and pattern Damascus; offers silver-wire inlay. **Prices:** $125 to $450; some higher. **Remarks:** Part-time maker; first knife sold in 1989. **Mark:** Last name.

WHISKERS (See Allen, Mike "Whiskers")

WHITE CUSTOM KNIVES, S.H. (See White, Scottie H.)

WHITE, GENE E., 6620 Briarleigh Way, Alexandria, VA 22315/703-924-1268
Specialties: Small utility/gents knives. **Patterns:** Eight standard hunters; most other patterns on commission basis. Currently no swords, axes and fantasy knives. **Technical:** Stock removal 440C and D2; others on request. Mostly hollow grinds; some flat grinds. Prefers natural handle materials. Makes own sheaths. **Prices:** Start at $85. **Remarks:** Part-time maker; first knife sold in 1971. **Mark:** First and middle intials, last name.

WHITE, ROBERT J., RR 1, 641 Knox Rd. 900 N., Gilson, IL 61436/309-289-4487
Specialties: Working knives, some deluxe. **Patterns:** Bird and trout knives, hunters, survival knives and locking folders. **Technical:** Grinds A2, D2 and 440C; commercial Damascus. Heat-treats. **Prices:** $125 to $250; some to $600. **Remarks:** Full-time maker; first knife sold in 1976. **Mark:** Last name in script.

WHITE JR., ROBERT J. "BUTCH," RR 1, Gilson, IL 61436/309-289-4487
Specialties: Folders of all sizes. **Patterns:** Hunters, fighters, boots and folders. **Technical:** Forges Damascus; grinds tool and stainless steels. **Prices:** $500 to $1,800. **Remarks:** Full-time maker; first knife sold in 1980. **Mark:** Last name in block letters.

WHITE, SCOTTIE H., Rt. 2, Box 556G, Pecks Mill, WV 25547/304-752-0239
Specialties: Working and using straight knives of his design and to customer specs. **Patterns:** Daggers, fighters and hunters. **Technical:** Grinds ATS-34 and 440C. Offers engraving. **Prices:** $175 to $1,200. **Remarks:** Full-time maker; first knife sold in 1986. Doing business as S.H. White Custom Knives. **Mark:** First and middle initials, and last name.

WHITEHEAD, JAMES D., 204 Cappucino Way, Sacramento, CA 95838/916-641-7309; FAX: 916-641-1941

Specialties: Highly detailed straight and folding miniatures. **Patterns:** Traditional and fancy. **Technical:** Forges and grinds O1 and commercial Damascus. **Prices:** $1,500 to $5,000. **Remarks:** Part-time maker; first knife sold in 1985. **Mark:** Initials.

WHITENECT, JODY, Elderbank, Halifax County, Nova Scotia, CANADA, B0N 1K0/902-384-2511
Specialties: Fancy and embellished working/using straight knives of his design and to customer specs. **Patterns:** Bowies, fighters and hunters. **Technical:** Forges 1095 and O1; forges and grinds ATS-34. Various filework on blades and bolsters. **Prices:** $200 to $400; some to $800. **Remarks:** Part-time maker; first knife sold in 1996. **Mark:** Longhorn stamp or engraved.

WHITLEY, WAYNE, 210 E. 7th St., Washington, NC 27889/919-946-5648
Specialties: Working/using straight knives of his design and to customer specs. **Patterns:** Bowies, hunters, utility/camp knives. **Technical:** Grinds ATS-34, D2, 440C; forges own Damascus and cable and high-carbon tool steels. **Prices:** $65 to $650; some to $1,500. **Remarks:** Part-time maker; first knife sold in 1990. Doing business as WW Custom Knives. **Mark:** Name, city, state or stylized initials.

WHITLEY, WELDON G., 6316 Jebel Way, El Paso, TX 79912/915-584-2274
Specialties: Working knives of his design or to customer specs. **Patterns:** Hunters, folders and various double-edged knives. **Technical:** Grinds 440C, 154CM and ATS 34. **Prices:** $150 to $1250. **Mark:** Name, address, road-runner logo.

WHITMAN, JIM, 21044 Salem St., Chugiak, AK 99567/907-688-4575; 907-688-4278
Specialties: Working straight knives; some art pieces. **Patterns:** Hunters, skinners, Bowies, camp knives, working fighters, swords and hatchets. **Technical:** Grinds AEB-L Swedish, 440C, ATS-34 and commercial Damascus in full convex. Prefers natural and native handle materials—whale bone, antler, ivory and horn. **Prices:** Start at $85. **Remarks:** Part-time maker; first knife sold in 1983. **Mark:** Name, city, state.

WHITMIRE, EARL T., 725 Colonial Dr., Rock Hill, SC 29730/803-324-8384
Specialties: Working straight knives, some to customer specs; some fantasy pieces. **Patterns:** Hunters, fighters and fishing knives. **Technical:** Grinds D2, 440C and 154CM. **Prices:** $40 to $200; some to $250. **Remarks:** Full-time maker; first knife sold in 1967. **Mark:** Name, city, state in oval logo.

WHITTAKER, ROBERT E., P.O. Box 204, Mill Creek, PA 17060
Specialties: Using straight knives. Has a line of knives for buckskinners. **Patterns:** Hunters, skinners and Bowies. **Technical:** Grinds O1, A2 and D2. Offers filework. **Prices:** $35 to $100. **Remarks:** Part-time maker; first knife sold in 1980. **Mark:** Last initial or full initials.

WHITTAKER, WAYNE, 2900 Woodland Ct., Metamore, MI 48455/810-797-5315
Specialties: High-art working/using straight knives of his design. **Patterns:** Bowies, daggers and hunters. **Technical:** Grinds O1 tool steel. **Prices:** $150 to $250; some to $2,000. **Remarks:** Spare-time maker; first knife sold in 1985. **Mark:** Initials, year on other side.

WHITWORTH, KEN J., 41667 Tetley Ave., Sterling Heights, MI 48078/313-739-5720
Specialties: Working straight knives and folders. **Patterns:** Locking folders, slip-joints and boot knives. **Technical:** Grinds 440C, 154CM and D2. **Prices:** $100 to $225; some to $450. **Remarks:** Part-time maker; first knife sold in 1976. **Mark:** Last name.

WICKER, DONNIE R., 2544 E. 40th Ct., Panama City, FL 32405/904-785-9158
Specialties: Traditional working and using straight knives of his design or to customer specs. **Patterns:** Hunters, fighters and slip-joint folders. **Technical:** Grinds 440C, ATS-34, D2 and 154CM. Heat-treats and does hardness testing. **Prices:** $90 to $200; some to $400. **Remarks:** Part-time maker; first knife sold in 1975. **Mark:** First and middle initials, last name.

WIGGINS, HORACE, 203 Herndon, Box 152, Mansfield, LA 71502/318-872-4471 (evenings)
Specialties: Fancy working knives. **Patterns:** Straight and folding hunters. **Technical:** Grinds O1, D2 and 440C. **Prices:** $90 to $275. **Remarks:** Part-time maker; first knife sold in 1970. **Mark:** Name, city and state in diamond logo.

WIL-A-MAR CUTLERY (See Patrick, Willard C.)

WILCHER, WENDELL L., RR3, Box 3341, Palestine, TX 75801/903-549-2530
Specialties: Fantasy, miniatures and working/using straight knives and folders of his design and to customer specs. **Patterns:** Fighters, hunters, locking folders. **Technical:** Grinds 440C, ATS-34, O1. Some filework. **Prices:** $75 to $250; some to $600. **Remarks:** Part-time maker; first knife sold in 1987. **Mark:** Initials, year, serial number.

WILD BILL & SONS (See Caldwell, Bill)

WILDWOOD ART (See Rece, Charles V.)

WILLEY, W.G., R.D. 1, Box 235-B, Greenwood, DE 19950/302-349-4070
Specialties: Fancy working straight knives. **Patterns:** Small game knives, Bowies and throwing knives. **Technical:** Grinds 440C and 154CM. **Prices:** $225 to $600; some to $1,500. **Remarks:** Part-time maker; first knife sold in 1975. Owns retail store. **Mark:** Last name inside map logo.

WILLIAMS, JASON L., P.O. Box 67, Wyoming, RI 02898/401-539-8353; FAX: 401-539-0252
Specialties: Fancy and high-tech folders of his design. **Patterns:** Fighters, locking folders, automatics and fancy pocketknives. **Technical:** Forges Damascus and other steels by request. Uses exotic handle materials and precious metals. Offers inlaid spines and gemstone thumb knobs. **Prices:** $1,000 to $2,500; some to $3,500. **Remarks:** Full-time maker; first knife sold in 1989. **Mark:** First and last initials on pivot.

WILLIAMS, MICHAEL L., Rt. 4, P.O. Box 64-1, Broken Bow, OK 74728/405-494-6326
Specialties: Plain to fancy working and dress knives. **Patterns:** Hunters, Bowies, camp knives and others. **Technical:** Forges 5160, L6, 52100, cable and pattern-welded steel. **Prices:** Start at $140. **Remarks:** Part-time maker; first knife sold in 1989. **Mark:** Last name.

WILLIAMS JR., RICHARD, 1440 Nancy Circle, Morristown, TN 37814/615-581-0059
Specialties: Working and using straight knives of his design or to customer specs. **Patterns:** Hunters, dirks and utility/camp knives. **Technical:** Forges 5160 and uses file steel. Hand-finish is standard; offers filework. **Prices:** $80 to $180; some to $250. **Remarks:** Spare-time maker; first knife sold in 1985. **Mark:** Last initial or full intials.

WILLIAMSON, TONY, Rt. 3, Box 503, Siler City, NC 27344/919-663-3551
Specialties: Flint knapping—knives made of obsidian flakes and flint with wood, antler or bone for handles. **Patterns:** Skinners, daggers and flake knives. **Technical:** Blades have width/thickness ratio of at least 4 to 1. Hafts with methods available to prehistoric man. **Prices:** $58 to $160. **Remarks:** Student of Errett Callahan. **Mark:** Initials and number code to identify year and number of knives made.

WILLOW FORGE, THE (See Tokar, Daniel)

WILLSON CUSTOM CUTLERY, HARLAN (See Willson, Harlan M.)

WILLSON, HARLAN M., P.O. Box 2113, Lompoc, CA 93436/805-735-0085; FAX: 805-735-0085
Specialties: Working, fantasy and art straight knives of his design and to customer specs. **Patterns:** Various styles. **Technical:** Grinds ATS-34, 440C, 1095 and O1. Prefers bone and natural handle materials; some exotic woods. Carves custom handle designs. **Prices:** $200 to $500; some to $1,000. **Remarks:** Full-time maker; first knife sold in 1990. Doing business as Harlan Willson Custom Cutlery. **Mark:** Initials and last name or heart within bear paw.

WILSON (See Simonella, Gianluigi)

WILSON, JAMES G., P.O. Box 4024, Estes Park, CO 80517/303-586-3944
Specialties: Bronze Age knives; Medieval and Scottish styles; tomahawks. **Patterns:** Bronze knives, daggers, swords, spears and battle axes; 12-inch steel Misericorde daggers, sgian dubhs, "his and her" skinners, bird and fish knives, capers, boots and daggers. **Technical:** Casts bronze; grinds D2, 440C and ATS-34. **Prices:** $49 to $400; some to $1,300. **Remarks:** Part-time maker; first knife sold in 1975. **Mark:** WilsonHawK.

WILSON, JAMES R., Rt. 2 Box 175HC, Seminole, OK 74868/405-382-7230
Specialties: Traditional working knives. **Patterns:** Bowies, hunters, skinners, fighters and camp knives. **Technical:** Forges 5160, 1095, O1 and his Damascus. **Prices:** Start at $125. **Remarks:** Part-time maker; first knife sold in 1994. **Mark:** First initial, last name.

WILSON, JON J., 1826 Ruby St., Johnstown, PA 15902/814-266-6410
Specialties: Miniatures only. **Patterns:** Bowies, daggers and hunters. **Technical:** Grinds Damascus, 440C and O1. Scrimshaws and carves. **Prices:** $65 to $175; some to $250. **Remarks:** Full-time maker; first knife sold in 1988. **Mark:** First and middle initials, last name.

WILSON, MIKE, 2619 Fork Creek Ln., Bowman, GA 30624/706-245-0823
Specialties: Fancy working and using straight knives of his design or to customer specs. **Patterns:** Hunters, Bowies, utility knives, gut hooks, skinners, fighters and miniatures. **Technical:** Hollow-grinds 440C, ATS-34 and D2. Mirror finishes are standard. Offers filework. **Prices:** $70 to $300. **Remarks:** Full-time maker; first knife sold in 1985. **Mark:** Last name.

WILSON, PHILIP C., 1064 Lomitas Ave., Livermore, CA 94550/510-455-9474
Specialties: Working knives; emphasis on salt water fillet knives and utility hunters of his design. **Patterns:** Fishing knives, hunters, kitchen knives. **Technical:** Grinds CPM420V and CPM440V. Prefers hollow grinds and hand-rubbed satin finishes. Heat-treats and Rockwell tests all blades. **Prices:** Start at $120. **Remarks:** Part-time maker; first knife sold in 1985. Doing business as Sea-Mount Knife Works. **Mark:** Signature.

WILSON, RON, 2289 Falcon Ridge Ln., Los Osos, CA 93402/805-528-5645
Specialties: Classic and fantasy straight knives of his design. **Patterns:** Daggers, fighters, swords and axes—mostly all miniatures. **Technical:** Forges and grinds Damascus and various tool steels; grinds meteorite. Uses gold, precious stones and exotic woods. **Prices:** Vary. **Remarks:** Part-time maker; first knife sold in 1995. **Mark:** Stamped first and last initials.

WILSON, R.W., P.O. Box 2012, Weirton, WV 26062/304-723-2771
Specialties: Working straight knives; period pieces. **Patterns:** Bowies, tomahawks and patch knives. **Prices:** $85 to $175; some to $1,000. **Technical:** Grinds 440C; scrimshaws. **Remarks:** Part-time maker; first knife sold in 1966. Knifemaker supplier. Offers free knifemaking lessons. **Mark:** Name in tomahawk.

WILSONHAWK (See Wilson, James G.)

WIMPFF, CHRISTIAN, P.O. Box 700526, 70574 Stuttgart, 70 GERMANY/711-764324; FAX: 711-7656960
Specialties: High-tech folders of his design. **Patterns:** Boots, locking folders and liner locks. **Technical:** Grinds CPM-T-440V, ATS-34 and Schneider stainless Damascus. Offers pantographing and meteorite bolsters and blades. **Prices:** $1,000 to $2,800; some to $4,000. **Remarks:** Full-time maker; first knife sold in 1984. **Mark:** First initial, last name.

WIND RIVER KNIVES (See Bridges, Justin W.)

WINE, MICHAEL, 265 S. Atlantic Ave., Cocoa Beach, FL 32931/407-784-2187
Specialties: Traditional working straight knives. **Patterns:** Fishing, hunting and kitchen knives. **Technical:** Grinds carbon, high-chrome tool steels, Stellite; casts 440C. **Prices:** Start at $145. **Remarks:** Spare-time maker; first knife sold in 1971. **Mark:** First initial, last name with palm tree.

WINGO, PERRY, 22 55th St., Gulfport, MS 39507/601-863-3193
Specialties: Traditional working straight knives. **Patterns:** Hunters, skinners, Bowies and fishing knives. **Technical:** Grinds 440C. **Prices:** $75 to $1,000. **Remarks:** Full-time maker; first knife sold in 1988. **Mark:** Last name.

WINKLER, DANIEL, P.O. Box 2166, Blowing Rock, NC 28605/704-295-9156, 704-295-0133 (message); FAX: 704-295-0133
Specialties: Period pieces, some made to look old; buckskinner working knives. **Patterns:** Buckskinners, axes, tomahawks, patch knives, daggers, folders, skinners and fighters. **Technical:** Forges and grinds 52100, L6, O1, old files and his Damascus. **Prices:** $200 to $2,500. **Remarks:** Full-time maker; first knife sold in 1984. **Mark:** Initials connected.

WINN, TRAVIS A., 558 E. 3065 S., Salt Lake City, UT 84106/801-467-5957
Specialties: Fancy working knives and knives to customer specs. **Patterns:** Hunters, fighters, boots, Bowies and fancy daggers, some miniatures, tantos and fantasy knives. **Technical:** Grinds D2 and 440C. Embellishes. **Prices:** $100 to $500; some higher. **Remarks:** Part-time maker; first knife sold in 1976. **Mark:** TRAV stylized.

WINSTON, DAVID, 1671 Red Holly St., Starkville, MS 39759/601-323-1028
Specialties: Fancy and traditional knives of his design and to customer specs. **Patterns:** Bowies, daggers, hunters, boot knives and folders. **Technical:** Grinds 440C, ATS-34 and D2. Offers filework; heat-treats. **Prices:** $40 to $750; some higher. **Remarks:** Part-time maker; first knife sold in 1984. Offers lifetime sharpening for original owner. **Mark:** Last name.

WISE, DONALD, 304 Bexhill Rd., St. Leonardo-On-Sea, East Sussex TN3 8AL ENGLAND
Specialties: Fancy and embellished working straight knives to customer specs. **Patterns:** Hunters, Bowies and daggers. **Technical:** Grinds Sandvik 12C27, D2, D3 and O1. Scrimshaws. **Prices:** $110 to $300; some to $500. **Remarks:** Full-time maker; first knife sold in 1983. **Mark:** KNIFECRAFT.

WISE, JOHN, P.O. Box 994, Winchester, OR 97495
Specialties: Classic high-art straight knives and folders to customer specs. **Patterns:** Daggers, fighters, locking folders, miniatures. **Technical:** Grinds 440C, ATS-34, commercial Damascus. **Prices:** $150 to $350; some to $1,000. **Remarks:** Part-time maker; first knife sold in 1989. **Mark:** Stylized name.

WITSAMAN, EARL, 3957 Redwing Circle, Stow, OH 44224/330-688-4208
Specialties: Straight and fantasy miniatures. **Patterns:** Wide variety—Randalls to D-guard Bowies. **Technical:** Grinds O1, 440C and 300 stainless; buys Damascus; highly detailed work. **Prices:** $70 to $200. **Remarks:** Part-time maker; first knife sold in 1974. **Mark:** Initials.

WITT, DOUGLAS, P.O. Box 520, North Bend, WA 98045
Specialties: Traditional and working/using knives and folders; historical pieces. **Patterns:** Locking folders, personals and guarded butcher knives. **Technical:** Uses O1 tool steel only, precision ground with certs; heat-treats, tempers; Rc hardness testing. Uses Micarta or nylon for handle material; hand-sewn cowhide sheaths. **Prices:** $100 to $400. **Remarks:** Full-time maker; first knife made in 1965. **Mark:** Last name above city and state.

W-K KNIVES (See Votaw, David P.)

WOLF, BILL, 4618 N. 79th Ave., Phoenix, AZ 85033/602-846-3585
Specialties: Investor-grade folders and straight knives. **Patterns:** Lockback, slip joint and sidelock interframes. **Technical:** Grinds ATS-34 and 440C. **Prices:** $650 to $4,000. **Remarks:** Full-time maker; first knife sold in 1989. **Mark:** Name.

WOLF, BOB, PSC-76, Box 4091, APO-AP, Tempe, AZ 96319-4091
Specialties: Small and medium straight knives and lockback folders. **Patterns:** Utility, hunters and fighters. **Technical:** Forges 5160; grinds 1095 and other steels upon request. Uses natural handle materials. **Prices:** $75 to $250. **Remarks:** Part-time maker; first knife sold in 1988. Doing business as L&H Knife Works. **Mark:** L&H (with Doc Gundersen).

WOLF'S KNIVES (See Smit, Glenn)

WOLFE FINE KNIVES (See Loerchner, Wolfgang)

WOMACK, A.M. "BABE," 1718 Rebecca, Conroe, TX 77301/409-539-9373
Specialties: Classic and traditional straight knives and folders of his design. **Patterns:** Hunters, locking folders and utility/camp knives. **Technical:** Grinds ATS-34, 440C and D2. Makes sheaths. **Prices:** $150 to $350; some to $1,000. **Remarks:** Part-time maker; first knife sold in 1989. **Mark:** Name and city.

WOOD, ALAN, Greenfield Villa, Greenhead, Carlisle, CA6 7HH ENGLAND/016977-47303
Specialties: High-tech working straight knives of his design. **Patterns:** Hunters, utility/camp and woodcraft knives. **Technical:** Grinds Sandvik 12C27, D2 and O1. Blades are cryogenic treated. **Prices:** $150 to $400; some to $750. **Remarks:** Full-time maker; first knife sold in 1979. **Mark:** First initial, last name and country.

WOOD, BARRY B. and IRIE, MICHAEL L., 3002 E. Gunnison St., Colorado Springs, CO 80909/719-578-9226
Specialties: High-tech working folders with patented locking system. **Patterns:** Thirty-four variations of five designs. **Technical:** Blades mainly made of ATS-34, some of commercial Damascus. Handles investment-cast in 17-4PH. **Prices:** $175 to $460; some higher. **Remarks:** Full-time makers; first knife sold in 1969. **Mark:** Two sets of initials in script with linked triangles of arcs.

WOOD, LARRY B., 6945 Fishburg Rd., Huber Heights, OH 45424/513-233-6751
Specialties: Fancy working knives of his design. **Patterns:** Hunters, buckskinners, Bowies, tomahawks, locking folders and Damascus miniatures. **Technical:** Forges 1095, file steel and his own Damascus. **Prices:** $125 to $500; some to $2,000. **Remarks:** Full-time maker; first knife sold in 1974. Doing business as Wood's Metal Studios. **Mark:** Variations of last name, sometimes with blacksmith logo.

WOOD, LEONARD J., 84 Anderson St., Beacon, NY 12508/914-838-1637
Specialties: Traditional working/using straight knives of all designs. **Patterns:** Boots, Bowies, hunters, miniatures. **Technical:** Grinds ATS-34, 440C, commercial Damascus. **Prices:** $85 to $375; some to $450. **Remarks:** Spare-time maker; first knife sold in 1993. Doing business as Wood's Custom Knives. **Mark:** Last initial with wings.

WOOD, OWEN DALE, P.O. Box 515, Honeydew 2040 (Transvaal), SOUTH AFRICA/011-958-1789
Specialties: Fancy working knives. **Patterns:** Hunters and fighters; variety of big knives; sword canes. **Technical:** Forges and grinds 440C, 154CM and his own Damascus. Uses rare African handle materials. **Prices:** $280 to $450; some to $3,000. **Remarks:** Full-time maker; first knife sold in 1976. **Mark:** Initials.

WOOD, WEBSTER, 22041 Shelton Trail, Atlanta, MI 49709/517-785-2996
Specialties: Fancy working knives. **Patterns:** Hunters, survival knives, locking folders and slip-joints. **Technical:** Grinds O1, 440C and 154CM; engraves and scrimshaws. **Prices:** $100 to $500; some to $3,000. **Remarks:** Full-time maker; first knife sold in 1980. **Mark:** Initials inside shield and name.

WOOD, WILLIAM W., P.O. Box 606, Seymour, TX 76380/817-888-5832
Specialties: Exotic working knives with Middle-East flavor. **Patterns:** Fighters, boots and some utility knives. **Technical:** Grinds D2 and 440C; buys Damascus. Prefers hand-rubbed satin finishes; uses only natural handle materials. **Prices:** $300 to $600; some to $2,000. **Remarks:** Full-time maker; first knife sold in 1977. **Mark:** Name, city and state.

WOOD'S CUSTOM KNIVES (See Wood, Leonard J.)

WOOD'S METAL STUDIOS (See Wood, Larry B.)

WOODCOCK, DENNIS "WOODY," P.O. Box 76, Wheeler, OR 97147/503-368-7511
Specialties: Working knives; miniatures. **Patterns:** Hunters, Bowies, skinners, miniatures. **Technical:** Grinds ATS-34, 154CM, D2 and 440C. Offers filework. Scrimshaws; makes sheaths. **Prices:** $45 to $475. **Remarks:** Full-time maker; first knife sold in 1982. Doing business as Knife Emporium. **Mark:** Nickname, last name, city, state.

WORKMAN JR., HUBERT L., Tyree Rd., Williamsburg, WV 24991/304-645-4815
Specialties: Working knives of his design and to customer specs; period pieces. **Patterns:** Daggers, fighters and hunters. **Technical:** Uses obsidian, flint and chert; prefers natural materials. **Prices:** $25 to $150; some to $250. **Remarks:** Part-time maker; first knife sold in 1989. **Mark:** NA.

WORLD GALLERY CO., LTD.
(See Yoshio, Mazaki; Ueda, Masaharu)

WRIGHT, KEVIN, 671 Leland Valley Rd. W, Quilcene, WA 98376-9517/360-765-3589
Specialties: Fancy working or collector knives to customer specs. **Patterns:** Hunters, boots, buckskinners, miniatures. **Technical:** Forges and grinds L6, 1095, 440C and his own Damascus. **Prices:** $75 to $500; some to $2,000. **Remarks:** Part-time maker; first knife sold in 1978. **Mark:** Last initial in anvil.

WRIGHT, TIMOTHY, P.O. Box 3746, Sedona, AZ 86340/520-282-4180; FAX: 520-282-4180
Specialties: High-tech folders and working knives. **Patterns:** Interframe locking folders, non-inlaid folders, straight hunters and kitchen knives. **Technical:** Grinds BG-42, AEB-L, K190 and Cowry X; works with new steels. All folders can disassemble and are furnished with tools. **Prices:** $150 to $1,800; some to $3,000. **Remarks:** Full-time maker; first knife sold in 1975. **Mark:** Last name and type of steel used.

WW CUSTOM KNIVES (See Whitley, Wayne)

WYATT, WILLIAM R., Box 237, Rainelle, WV 25962/304-438-5494
Specialties: Classic and working knives of all designs. **Patterns:** Hunters and utility knives. **Technical:** Forges and grinds saw blades, files and rasps. Prefers stag handles. **Prices:** $45 to $95; some to $350. **Remarks:** Part-time maker; first knife sold in 1990. **Mark:** Last name in star with knife logo.

WYVERN (See Ferdinand, Don)

x, y

XYLO (See McGill, John)

YASUTOMO (See Louis G. Mills)

YEATES, JOE A., 730 Saddlewood Circle, Spring, TX 77381/281-367-2765
Specialties: Bowies and period pieces. **Patterns:** Bowies, toothpicks and combat knives. **Technical:** Grinds 440C, D2 and ATS-34. **Prices:** $250 to $1,500; some to $2,000. **Remarks:** Full-time maker; first knife sold in 1975. **Mark:** Last initial within outline of Texas; or last initial.

YORK, DAVID C., P.O. Box 1342, Crested Butte, CO 81224/970-349-5826
Specialties: Working straight knives and folders. **Patterns:** Prefers small hunters and skinners; locking folders, buckskinner and survival knives. **Technical:** Grinds D2 and 440C; buys Damascus. **Prices:** $75 to $300; some to $600. **Remarks:** Full-time maker; first knife sold in 1975. **Mark:** Last name.

YOUNG, BUD, Box 336, Port Hardy, BC V0N 2P0, CANADA/604-949-6478
Specialties: Working straight knives, some fancy. **Patterns:** Hunters from drop-points to skinners. **Technical:** Grinds O1, L6, 1095 and 5160; uses 154CM and ATS-34 when available. Likes satin and glass bead finishes and natural handle materials. **Prices:** $200 to $400; some higher. **Remarks:** Spare-time maker; first knife sold in 1985. **Mark:** Name.

YOUNG, CLIFF, Fuente De La Cibeles No. 5, Atascadero, San Miguel De Allende, GTO., Mexico, 37700/011-52-415-2-57-11
Specialties: Working knives. **Patterns:** Hunters, fighters and fishing knives. **Technical:** Grinds all; offers D2, 440C and 154CM. **Prices:** Start at $250. **Remarks:** Part-time maker; first knife sold in 1980. **Mark:** Name.

YOUNG, ERROL, 4826 Storey Land, Alton, IL 62002/618-466-4707
Specialties: Traditional working straight knives and folders **Patterns:** Wide range, including tantos, Bowies, miniatures and multi-blade folders. **Technical:** Grinds D2, 440C and ATS-34. **Prices:** $75 to $650; some to $800. **Remarks:** Part-time maker; first knife sold in 1987. **Mark:** Last name with arrow.

YOUNG, GEORGE, 713 Pinoak Dr., Kokomo, IN 46901; 765-457-8893
Specialties: Fancy/embellished and traditional straight knives and folders of his design and to customer specs. **Patterns:** Hunters, fillet/camp knives and locking folders. **Technical:** Grinds 440C, CPM440V, and Stellite 6K. Fancy ivory, black pearl and stag for handles. Filework—all Stellite construction (6K and 25 alloys). Offers engraving. **Prices:** $350 to $750; some $1,500 to $3,000. **Remarks:** Full-time maker; first knife sold in 1954. Doing business as Young's Knives. **Mark:** Last name integral inside Bowie.

YOUNG, PAUL A., 168 Elk Ridge Rd., Boone, NC 28607/704-264-7048
Specialties: Working straight knives and folders of his design or to customer specs; some art knives. **Patterns:** Small boot knives, skinners, 18th century period pieces and folders. **Technical:** Forges O1 and file steels. Full-time embellisher—engraves and scrimshaws. Prefers floral designs; any design accepted. Does not engrave hardened metals. **Prices:** Determined by type and design. **Remarks:** Full-time maker; first knife sold in 1978. **Mark:** Initials in logo.

YOUNG'S KNIVES (See Young, George)

YUNES, YAMIL R., P.O. Box 573, Roma, TX 78584/512-849-1001
Specialties: Traditional straight knives and folders. **Patterns:** Locking folders, slip-joints, hunters, fighters and utility knives. **Technical:** Grinds 440C, O1 and D2. Has patented cocking design for folders. **Prices:** $45 to $140; some to $300. **Remarks:** Part-time maker; first knife sold in 1975. **Mark:** Last name.

YURCO, MIKE, P.O. Box 712, Canfield, OH 44406/330-533-4928
Specialties: Working straight knives. **Patterns:** Hunters, utility knives, Bowies and fighters, push knives, claws and other hideouts. **Technical:** Grinds 440C, ATS-34 and 154CM; likes mirror and satin finishes. **Prices:** $20 to $500. **Remarks:** Part-time maker; first knife sold in 1983. **Mark:** Name, steel, serial number.

Z

Z CUSTOM KNIVES (See McCarty, Zollan)

ZACCAGNINO JR., DON, P.O. Box 583, Pahokee, FL 33476/407-924-7844
Specialties: Working knives and some period pieces of their designs. **Patterns:** Heavy-duty hunters, axes and Bowies; a line of light-weight hunters, fillets and personal knives. **Technical:** Grinds 440C and 17-4 PH—highly finished in complex handle and blade treatments. **Prices:** $165 to $500; some to $2,500. **Remarks:** Part-time maker; first knife sold in 1969 by Don Zaccagnino Sr. **Mark:** ZACK, city and state inside oval.

ZACK KNIVES (See Zaccagnino Jr., Don)

ZAHM, KURT, 488 Rio Casa, Indialantic, FL 32903/407-777-4860
Specialties: Working straight knives of his design or to customer specs. **Patterns:** Daggers, fancy fighters, Bowies, hunters and utility knives. **Technical:** Grinds D2, 440C; likes filework. **Prices:** $75 to $1,000. **Remarks:** Part-time maker; first knife sold in 1985. **Mark:** Last name.

ZAKABI, CARL S., P.O. Box 893161, Mililani Town, HI 96789-0161/808-626-2181
Specialties: Working and using straight knives of his design. **Patterns:** Fighters, hunters and utility/camp knives. **Technical:** Grinds 440C and ATS-34. **Prices:** $55 to $200. **Remarks:** Spare-time maker; first knife sold in 1988. Doing business as Zakabi's Knifeworks. **Mark:** Last name and state.

ZAKABI'S KNIFEWORKS (See Zakabi, Carl S.)

ZAKHAROV, CARLOS, R. Sergipe, 68, Rio Comprido, Jacarel, SP-12300-000, BRAZIL/0123-515192; FAX: 0123-515192
Specialties: Using straight knives of his design. **Patterns:** Hunters, kitchen and utility/camp knives. **Technical:** Grinds his own "secret steel." **Prices:** $60 to $200. **Remarks:** Full-time maker. **Mark:** Archip.

ZEMBKO III, JOHN, 140 Wilks Pond Rd., Berlin, CT 06037/860-828-3503
Specialties: Working knives of his design or to customer specs. **Patterns:** Variety of working straight knives. **Technical:** Grinds ATS-34, A2 and O1; forges O1. **Prices:** $50 to $400; some higher. **Remarks:** First knife sold in 1987. **Mark:** Name.

ZEMITIS, JOE, 14 Currawong Rd., Cardiff Hts., 2285 Newcastle, AUSTRALIA/049-549907
Specialties: Traditional working straight knives. **Patterns:** Hunters, Bowies, tantos, fighters and camp knives. **Technical:** Grinds O1, D2, W2 and 440C; makes his own Damascus. Embellishes; offers engraving and scrimshaw. **Prices:** $150 to $3,000. **Remarks:** Full-time maker; first knife sold in 1983. **Mark:** First initial, last name and country, or last name.

ZIMA, MICHAEL F., 732 State St., Ft. Morgan, CO 80701/970-867-6078
Specialties: Working straight knives and folders. **Patterns:** Hunters; utility, locking and slip-joint folders. **Technical:** Grinds D2, 440C and ATS-34. **Prices:** $150 to $300; some higher. **Remarks:** Full-time maker; first knife sold in 1982. **Mark:** Last name.

ZINSMEISTER, PAUL D., HC 63, Box 53B, Harper, TX 78631/210-864-4574
Specialties: Traditional working and using straight knives and folders of his design. **Patterns:** Automatics, hunters, locking folders, slip-joint folders, daggers, Bowies and miniatures. **Technical:** Uses 440C and ATS-34 stainless steel. **Prices:** $85 to $250; some to $1,500. **Remarks:** Full-time maker; first knife sold in 1982. **Mark:** Handmade with stylized last initial.

ZIRBES, RICHARD, Neustrasse 15, D-54526 Niederkail, GERMANY/01149-6575 1371.
Specialties: Fancy/embellished, classic and traditional working and using straight knives of his design. **Patterns:** Boots, fighters and hunters. **Technical:** Grinds ATS-34, CPM-T-440V, 440 and D2; forges and grinds Damascus. Scrimshaws; makes sheaths. **Prices:** $250 to $650; some to $1,600. **Remarks:** Part-time maker; first knife sold in 1991.

ZOWADA, TIM, 4509 E. Bear River Rd., Boyne Falls, MI 49713/616-348-5416; E-MAIL: tzowada@freeway.net
Specialties: Working knives, some fancy. **Patterns:** Hunters, camp knives, boots, swords, fighters, tantos and locking folders. **Technical:** Forges O2, L6, W2 and his own Damascus. **Prices:** $150 to $1,000; some to $5,000. **Remarks:** Full-time maker; first knife sold in 1980. **Mark:** Lower case gothic letters for initials.

ZSCHERNY, MICHAEL, 2512 "N" Ave. NW, Cedar Rapids, IA 52405/319-396-3659
Specialties: Folders and daggers. **Patterns:** Slip-joints, lock-back folders, fancy daggers. **Technical:** Grinds 440C and 154CM; prefers natural handle materials. **Prices:** $150 to $1,000; some to $1,700. **Remarks:** Part-time maker. Not currently taking orders. **Mark:** Last name.

knifemakers state-by-state

alabama

Andress, Ronnie	Satsuma
Barrett, R.W.	Madison
Batson, James	Madison
Bell, Frank	Huntsville
Bullard, Bill	Andalusia
Coffman, Danny	Jacksonville
Conn Jr., C.T.	Attalla
Connell, Steve	Adamsville
Cutchin, Roy D.	Seale
Daniels, Alex	Town Creek
DiMarzo, Richard	Birmingham
Edwards, Fain E.	Jacksonville
Faulkner, Allan	Jasper
Fikes, Jimmy L.	Jasper
Fogg, Don	Jasper
Gilbreath, Randall	Dora
Gilpin, David	Alabaster
Hammond, Jim	Arab
Hodge, J.B.	Huntsville
Howard, Durvyn M.	Hokes Bluff
Howell, Len	Opelika
Howell, Ted	Wetumpka
Hulsey Jr., Hoyt	Steele
Lawless, Charles	Arab
Lovestrand, Schuyler	Harvest
Madison II, Billy D.	Remlap
Monk, Nathan P.	Cullman
Morris, C.H.	Atmore
Pardue, Melvin M.	Repton
Roe Jr., Fred D.	Huntsville
Russell, Tom	Jacksonville
Sandlin, Larry	Adamsville
Sinyard, Cleston S.	Elberta
Watson, Billy	Peatsville

alaska

Amoureux, A.W.	Anchorage
Brennan, Judson	Delta Junction
Breuer, Wayne	Wasilla
Broome, Thomas A.	Kenai
Bucholz, Mark A.	Eagle River
Cannon, Raymond W.	Homer
Chamberlin, John A.	Anchorage
Dempsey, Gordon W.	N.Kenai
DuFour, Arthur J.	Anchorage
England, Virgil	Anchorage
Gouker, Gary B.	Sitka
Grebe, Gordon S.	Anchor Point
Hibben, Westley G.	Anchorage
Johnson, David L.	Talkeetna
Kommer, Russell	Anchorage
Kubaiko, Hank	Palmer
Lance, Bill	Eagle River
Little, Jimmy L.	Wasilla
McFarlin, Eric E.	Kodiak
McIntosh, David L.	Haines
Oda, Kuzan	Anchorage
Parrish III, Gordon A.	North Pole
Shore, John I.	Ft. Richardson
Stegall, Keith	Anchorage
Trujillo, Adam	Anchorage
Trujillo, Miranda	Anchorage
Trujillo, Thomas A.	Anchorage
Whitman, Jim	Chugiak

arizona

Beaver, Devon	Phoenix
Boye, David	Dolan Springs
Cheatham, Bill	Laveen
Choate, Milton	Yuma
Craft III, John M.	Williams
Draper, Bart	Phoenix
Edge, Tommy	Cash
Genovese, Rick	Sedona
Goo, Tai	Tucson
Guignard, Gib	Quartzsite
Gundersen, D.F. "Doc"	Tempe
Hancock, Tim	Scottsdale
Hoel, Steve	Pine
Holder, D'Alton	Peoria
Hull, Michael J.	Cottonwood
Kopp, Todd M.	Apache Junction
Lampson, Frank G.	Rimrock
Lee, Randy	St. Johns
Lively, Tim	Tucson
McFall, Ken	Lakeside
McFarlin, J.W.	Lake Havasu City
Norris, Don	Tucson
Oliver, Milford	Prescott
Randall, Bill	Tucson
Roland, Dan	Yuma
Snare, Michael	Phoenix
Sutherland, Greg	Flagstaff
Tamboli, Michael	Glendale
Thompson, Robert L. (Bob)	Phoenix
Weiler, Donald E.	Yuma
Weiss, Charles L.	Phoenix
Wolf, Bill	Phoenix
Wolf, Bob	Tempe
Wright, Timothy	Sedona

arkansas

Anders, David	Center Ridge
Brown, Jim	Little Rock
Cook, James Ray	Nashville
Crawford, Pat	West Memphis
Crowell, James L.	Mountain View
Dozier, Bob	Springdale
Dungy, Lawrence	Little Rock
DuVall, Fred	Benton
Ferguson, Lee	Hindsville
Fisk, Jerry	Lockesburg
Flournoy, Joe	El Dorado
Foster, Al	Dogpatch
Frizzell, Ted	West Fork
Gaston, Bert	N. Little Rock
Grigsby, Ben	Mt. View
Hicks, Vernon G.	Bauxite
Lane, Ben	No. Little Rock
Lawrence, Alton	DeQueen
Lile, James B. (Marilyn)	Russelville
Martin, Bruce E.	Prescott
Massey, Roger	Texarkana
Ogg, Robert G.	Paris
Perry, John	Mayflower
Polk, Clifton	Van Buren
Price, Jerry L.	Springdale
Quattlebaum, Craig	Searcy
Ramey, Marshall F.	West Helena
Remington, David W.	Lincoln
Russell, A.G.	Springdale
Smoker, Ray	Searcy
Solomon, Marvin	Ferndale
Tycer, Art	N. Little Rock
Walker, Jim	Morrilton
Ward, Chuck	Benton

california

Abernathy, Paul J.	Eureka
Barlow, Ken	Fortuna
Barron, Brian	San Mateo
Benson, Don	Escalon
Berger, Max A.	Carmichael
Blum, Chuck	Brea
Blum, Roy	Covington
Boyd, Francis	Berkeley
Brack, Douglas	Camirillo
Breshears, Clint	Manhattan Beach
Brown, Ted	Downey
Browne, Rick	Upland
Brunetta, David	Laguna Beach
Chelquist, Cliff	Arroyo Grande
Clark, W.R.	Santa Fe Springs
Cohen, Terry A.	Laytonville
Collins, A.J.	Arleta
Connolly, James	Oroville
Davis, Charlie	Santee
Dillon, Earl E.	Arleta
Dion, Greg	Oxnard
Dixon Jr., Ira E.	Ventura
Donovan, Patrick	San Jose
Doolittle, Mike	Novato
Driscoll, Mark	La Mesa
Dugan, Brad M.	San Diego
Eaton, Al	Clayton
Eaton, Rick	Strawberry Valley
Ellis, David	San Diego
Ellis, William Dean	Fresno
Emerson, Ernest R.	Torrance
English, Jim	Jamul
Engnath, Bob	Glendale
Essegian, Richard	Fresno
Ferguson, Jim	Acton
Ferguson, Jim	Downey
Fisher, Ted	Montague
Fox, Jack L.	Citrus Heights
Fraley, Ierek	Dixon
Francis, Vance	Alpine
Freeman, Arthur F.	Citrus Heights
Freer, Ralph	Seal Beach
Fronefield, Mike	Truckee
Fulton, Mickey	Willows
Gamble, Frank	Fremont
George, Tom	Magalia
Gofourth, Jim	Santa Paula
Golding, Robin	Lathrop
Hardy, Scott	Placerville
Harris, Jay	Redwood City
Hartsfield, Phill	Newport Beach
Hayes, Dolores	Los Angeles
Helton, Roy	Bakersfield
Hermes, Dana E.	Fremont
Herndon, Wm. R. Bill	Acton
Hink, Less	Stockton
Hoy, Ken	North Fork
Hume, Don	Sherman Oaks
Humenick, Roy	Rescue
Jacks, Jim	Covina
Johnson, Dave	Jamul
Johnson, Randy	Turlock
Jones, Curtis J.	Palmdale
Keyes, Dan	Chino
Kozlow, Kelly	Ridgecrest
Kreibich, Donald L.	San Jose
Kruse, Martin	Reseda
Larson, Richard	Turlock
Leland, Steve	Fairfax
Levine, Norman	Lake Elsinore

Lewis, Mike — Tracy
Likarich, Steve — Colfax
Lockett, Sterling — Burbank
Loveless, R.W. — Riverside
Manabe, Michael K. — San Diego
Martin, Jim — Oxnard
Mattis, James K. — Glendale
Maxwell, Don — Fresno
McClure, Michael — Menlo Park
McMahon, John — Palm Dessert
Meloy, Sean — Lemon Grove
Middleton, Ken — Citrus Heights
Mitchell, R.W. — Wildomar
Montano, Gus A. — San Diego
Morgan, Jeff — Santee
Morlan, Tom — Hemet
Naten, Greg — Bakersfield
Odell, Philip — San Mateo
Orton, Richard — LaVerne
Packard, Bob — Elverta
Pendleton, Lloyd — Volcano
Perry, Chris — Fresno
Phillips, Randy — Ontario
Pitt, David F. — Pleasanton
Posner, Barry E. — N. Hollywood
Reed, Wyle Fred — Sacramento
Richard, Ron — Fremont
Rust, Charles C. — Palermo
Scarrow, Lin — Bellflower
Scarrow, Will — Bellflower
Schroen, Karl — Sebastopol
Schultz, Richard — San Juan Capistrano
Sibrian, Aaron — Ventura
Sjostrand, Kevin — Visalia
Slobodian, Scott — San Andreas
Sornberger, Jim — Volcano
Stapel, Chuck — Glendale
Stapel, Craig — Glendale
Steel, Ray — San Diego
Steinberg, Al — San Bruno
Swain, Rod — South Pasadena
Tamboli, Michael — Glendale
Terrill, Stephen — Lindsay
Tinker, Carolyn D. — Whittier
Vagnino, Michael — Visalia
Ward, Ken — Auburn
Warren, Al — Roseville
Watanabe, Wayne — Montebello
Weinstock, Robert — San Francisco
Whitehead, James D. — Sacramento
Williams, Sherman A. — Simi Valley
Willson, Harlan M. — Lompoc
Wilson, Philip C. — Livermore
Wilson, Ron — Los Osos
Wylefred, Reed — Sacramento

colorado

Anderson, Mel — Cedaredge
Appleton, Ray — Byers
Barrett, Cecil Terry — Colorado Springs
Booco, Gordon — Hayden
Brock, Kenneth L. — Allenspark
Brown, E.H. — Grand Junction
Campbell, Dick — Conifer
Davis, Don — Loveland
Dennehy, John D. — Wellington
Dawson, Barry — Durango
DeLong, Dick — Aurora
Dennehy, Dan — Del Norte
Dill, Robert, Bonnie and Chris — Loveland
Eckerson, Charley — Pueblo
Genge, Roy E. — Eastlake
High, Tom — Alamoso
Hockensmith, Dan — Drake
Hodgson, Richard J. — Boulder
Hughes, Ed — Grand Junction
Kitsmiller, Jerry — Montrose
Lampson, Frank G. — Fruita
Leck, Dal — Hayden
Letcher, Billy — Fort Collins
McWilliams, Sean — Bayfield
Miller, Hanford J. — Cowdrey
Miller , M.A. — Thornton
Neeley, Vaughn — Mancos
Nolen, R.D. and George — Estes Park
Olson, Wayne C. — Wheat Ridge
Owens, John — Parker
Peasley, David S. — Alamosa
Pogreba, Larry — Lyons
Robbins, Howard P. — Estes Park
Roberts, Chuck — Westminster
Rollert, Steve — Keenesburg
Sanders, Bill — Mancos
Sasser, Jim — Pueblo
Smith, D. Noel — Canon City
Thompson, Lloyd — Pagosa Springs
Tollefson, Barry A. — Gunnison
Topliss, M.W. "Ike" — Montrose
Watson, Bert — Westminster
Wilson, James G. — Estes Park
Wood, Barry B. — Colorado Springs
York, David C. — Crested Butte
Zima, Michael F. — Ft. Morgan

connecticut

Buebendorf, Robert E. — Monroe
Chapo, William G. — Wilton
Coughlin, Michael M. — New Milford
Hubbard, Arthur J. — Monroe
Jean, Gerry — Manchester
Lepore, Michael J. — Bethany
Martin, Randall J. — Middletown
Nelson, Roger S. — Central Village
Padgett, Jr., Edwin L. — New London
Pankiewicz, Philip R. — Lebanon
Plunkett, Richard — West Cornwall
Putnam, Donald S. — Wethersfield
Rainville, Richard — Salem
Turecek, Jim — Derby
Zembko III, John — Berlin

delaware

Dugan, Brad M. — Milford
Schneider, Karl A. — Newark
Wagner, Dan — New Castle
Willey, W.G. — Greenwood

district of columbia

Cumming, R.J. — Washington

florida

Adams, Les — Hialeah
Atkinson, Dick — Wausau
Barry, James J. — West Palm Beach
Bartrug, Hugh E. — St. Petersburg
Benjamin Jr., George — Kissimmee
Blackton, Andrew — Bayonet Point
Bosworth, Dean — Key Largo
Bradley, John — Pomona Park
Bray Jr., W. Lowell — New Port Richey
Brown, Harold E. — Arcadia
Burns, Dave — Boynton Beach
Chase, Alex — Deland
Cobb, Lowell D. — Daytona Beach
Cross, John M. — Bryceville
Davenport, Jack — Dade City
DeGraeve, Richard — Sebastian
Dietzel, Bill — Middleburg
Dotson, Tracy — Baker
Ek, Gary Whitney — North Miami
Ellerbe, W.B. — Geneva
Embry, Brad — Plant City
Enos III, Thomas M. — Orlando
Fagan, James A. — Lake Worth
Farrts, Cal — Altoona
Faulkner, Allan — St. Petersburg
Ferrara, Thomas — Naples
Fowler, Charles R. — Ft. McCoy
Gamble, Roger — St. Petersburg
Garcia, Tony — Palm Beach
Garner Jr., William O. — Pensacola
Gibson, Jim "Hoot" — Bunnell
Goers, Bruce — Lakeland
Griffin Jr., Howard A. — Davie
Grospitch, Ernie — Orlando
H&W Knives — Pace
Harris, Ralph Dewey — Brandon
Heitler, Henry — Tampa
Hennon, Robert — Ft. Walton Beach
Hill, Steven E. — Orlando
Hodge III, John — Palatka
Hoffman, Kevin L. — Winter Park
Hughes, Dan — West Palm Beach
Humphries, Joel — Bowling Green
Hytovick, Joe "Hy" — Dunnellon
Jernigan, Steve — Milton
Johnson, Durrell Carmon — Sparr
Kelly, Lance — Edgewater
King, Bill — Tampa
Krapp, Denny — Apopka
Lazo, Robert T. — Miami
Levengood, Bill — Tampa
Leverett, Ken — Lithia
Loflin, Bob — Miami Lakes
Long, Glenn A. — Palm Beach Gardens
Lozier, Don — Ocklawaha
Lunn, Larry A. — Safety Harbor
Lyle III, Ernest L. — Orlando
Martrildonno, Paul — Debary
McDonald, Robert J. — Loxahatchee
Miller Jr., Chris — Gainesville
Miller, Robert — Ormond Beach
Miller, Ronald T. — Largo
Mink, Dan — Crystal Beach
Ochs, Charles F. — Largo
Outlaw, Anthony L. — Panama City
Pendray, Alfred H. — Williston
Piergallini, Daniel E. — Plant City
Price, Joel Hiram — Palatka
Randall, Gary T. — Orlando
Robinson, Rex — Leesburg
Rodkey, Dan — Hudson
Rogers, Rodney — Wildwood
Ross, Gregg — Lake Worth
Russ, Ron — Williston
Schlomer, James E. — Kissimmee
Schwarzer, James — Pomona Park
Schwarzer, Stephen — Pomona Park
Sharp, Wes & Margie — Milton
Simons, Bill — Lakeland
Smith, Bobbie D. — Bonifay
Smith, W.M. — Bonifay
Stephan, Daniel — Valrico
Stipes, Dwight — Jupiter

Tomes, Anthony	Jacksonville
Tomes, P.J.	Middleburg
Vunk, Robert Bob	Orlando
Waldrop, Mark	Summerfield
Wallace, Roger L.	Tampa
Watson, Tom	Panama City
Weiland Jr., J. Reese	Tampa
Wicker, Donnie R.	Panama City
Wine, Michael	Cocoa Beach
Zaccagnino, Don & Don Jr.	Pahokee
Zahm, Kurt	Indialantic

georgia

Arrowwood, Dale	Sharpsburg
Ashworth, Boyd	Powder Springs
Barker, Robert G.	Bishop
Black, Scott	Covington
Bradley, Dennis	Blairsville
Buckner, Jimmie H.	Putney
Carey Jr., Charles W.	Griffin
Chamblin, Joel	Concord
Cofer, Ron	Loganville
Cole, Welborn I.	Atlanta
Cosby, E. Blanton	Columbus
Crockford, Jack	Chamblee
Davis, Steve	Powder Springs
DeYong, Clarence	Kennesaw
Dunn, Charles K.	Shiloh
Ford, Allen	Smyrna
Fuller, John W.	Douglasville
Greene, David	Covington
Halligan, Ed	Sharpsburg
Harmon, Jay	Woodstock
Harmon, Joe	Jonesboro
Hawkins, Rade	Fayetteville
Haynie, Charles	Toccoa
Hegedus Jr., Lou	Cave Spring
Hegwood, Joel	Summerville
Hensley, Wayne	Conyers
Hinson, R. and Son	Columbus
Holland, John	Calhoun
Hyde, Jimmy	Ellenwood
Johnson, Harold Harry C.	Chickamauga
Kilby, Keith	Jefferson
Kimsey, Kevin	Cartersville
King, Fred J.	Cartersville
Landers, John	Newnan
Lockett, Lowell C.	Woodstock
Lonewolf, J. Aguirre	Demorest
Love, Ed	Stockbridge
McCarty, Zollan	Thomaston
McGill, John	Blairsville
Mitchell, James A.	Columbus
Moore, Bill	Albany
North, David	Chickamauga
Parks, John	Jefferson
Pittman, Leon	Pendergrass
Poole, Steve L.	Stockbridge
Poplin, James L.	Washington
Poythress, John	Swainsboro
Prater, Mike	Chickamauga
Ragsdale, James D. Jim	Lithonia
Rogers Jr., Robert P.	Acworth
Roghmans, Mark	Lagrange
Rosenfeld, Bob	Hoschton
Royal, B.M. "Red"	Helen
Schuster, Steve	Lawrenceville
Scofield, Everett	Chickamauga
Smith Jr., James B.	Morven
Snell, Jerry L.	Fayetteville
Snow, Bill	Columbus
Stafford, Richard	Warner Robins
Thompson, Kenneth	Duluth
Walters, A.F.	Tifton
Werner, William A. Jr.	Marietta
Wilson, Robert M.	Bowman

hawaii

Dolan, Robert L.	Kula
Evans, Vincent K.	Keaau
Fujisaka, Stanley	Kaneohe
Luck, Gregory	Kailua-Kona
Lui, Ronald	Honolulu
Mayo Jr., Thomas H.	Waialua
Onion, Kenneth J.	Kapolei
Zakabi, Carl S.	Mililani Town

idaho

Alderman, Robert	Sagle
Andrews, Don	Coeur D'Alene
Hawk, Gavin	Idaho City
Hawk, Grant	Idaho City
Horton, Scot	Buhl
Kranning, Terry L.	Pocatello
Ledbetter, Randy R.	Payette
Moulton, Dusty	Boise
Mullin, Steve	Sandpoint
Nealy, Ivan F.	Mountain Home
Patton, Dick	Garden City
Quarton, Barr	McCall
Reeve, Chris	Boise
Rohn, Fred	Coeur d'Alene
Sawby, Scott	Sand Point
Selent, Chuck	Bonners Ferry
Shockey, Joel	Boise
Spragg, Wayne E.	Ashton
Steiger, Monte L.	Genesee
Towell, Dwight L.	Midvale

illinois

Abbott, William M.	Chandlerville
Bloomer, Allan T.	Maquon
Brandsey, Edward P.	Woodstock
Brannan, Ralph	Frankfort
Bridgnardello, E.D.	Crete
Bulawski, Rick	Sandwich
Caudell, Richard M.	Lawrenceville
Cook, Louise	Ozark
Cook, Mike	Ozark
Detmer, Phillip	Breese
Eaker, Allen	Paris
Guth, Kenneth	Chicago
Hill, Rick	Maryville
James, Peter	Hoffman Estates
Knuth, Joseph E.	Rockford
Kovar, Eugene	Evergreen Park
Lang, Kurt	McHenry
Leone, Nick	Pontoon Beach
Markley, Ken	Sparta
Meier, Daryl	Carbondale
Millard, Fred G.	Chicago
Myers, Paul	East Alton
Nowland, Rick	Waltonville
Poag, James	Grayville
Potocki, Roger	Goreville
Pritchard, Ron	Dixon
Rados, Jerry F.	Grant Park
Schneider, Craig M.	Seymour
Smith, John M.	Centralia
Stalter, Harry L.	Trivoli
Steelmaster	Waukegan
Tompkins, Dan	Peotone
Turnbull, Ralph A.	Rockford
Veit, Michael	LaSalle
Voss, Ben	Galesburg
Werth, George W.	Poplar Grove
West, Charles A.	Centralia
White, Robert J. Bob	Gilson
White Jr., Robert J. "Butch"	Gilson
Young, Errol	Alton

indiana

Allen, Joe	Princeton
Ball, Ken	Mooresville
Birt, Sid	Nashville
Bose, Reese	Lewis
Bose, Tony	Shelburn
Broughton, Don R.	Floyd Knob
Chaffee, Jeff L.	Morriss
Clay, Richard S.	Winchester
Damlovac, Sava	Indianapolis
Darby, Jed	Greensburg
Fitzgerald, Dennis	Fort Wayne
Flynn, Bruce	Middletown
Imel, Billy Mace	New Castle
Johnson, C.E. Gene	Portage
Keeslar, Steven C.	Hamilton
Keeton, William L.	Laconia
Largin, Ken	Batesville
Ledford, Bracy R.	Indianapolis
Lutes, Robert	Nappanee
Mayville, Oscar	Marengo
Minnick, Jim	Middletown
Norton, Dennis G.	Fort Wayne
Parsons, Michael R.	Terre Haute
Porter, James E.	Bloomington
Rigney, Willie	Shelbyville
Rubley, James A.	Angola
Shostle, Ben	Muncie
Stover, Terry "Lee"	Kokomo
Thayer, Danny	Lafayette
Welch, William H.	Kimmell
Young, George	Kokomo

iowa

Brooker, Dennis	Derby
Brower, Max	Boone
Clark, Howard	Runnells
Lainson, Tony	Council Bluffs
Miller, James P.	Fairbank
Myers, Mel	Spencer
Trindle, Barry	Earlham
Westberg, Larry	Algona
Zscherny, Michael	Cedar Rapids

kansas

Ames, Mickey L.	Lebo
Bradburn, Gary	Wichita
Chard, Gordon R.	Iola
Courtney, Eldon	Wichita
Craig, Roger L.	
Culver, Steve	Mayetta
Dugger, Dave	Westwood
Dunn, Melvin T.	Rossville
George, Les	Wichita
Hegwald, J.L.	Humboldt
Herman, Tim	Overland Park
Kennelley, J.C.	Arkansas City
Kraft, Steve	Abilene
Petersen, Dan L.	Topeka
Stice, Douglas	Wichita

kentucky

Barr, A.T.	Nicholasville
Baskett, Lee Gene	Eastview
Bodner, Gerald "Jerry"	Louisville
Brumagen, Jerry	Lexington
Bugden, John	Murray
Bybee, Barry J.	Cadiz
Carson, Harold J. Kit	Vine Grove
Clay, J.D.	Greenup
Coil, Jimmie J.	Owensboro
Corbit, Gerald E. "Jerry"	Elizabethtown
Downing, Larry	Bremen
Dunn, Steve	Smiths Grove
Fannin, David A.	Lexington
Finch, Ricky D.	West Liberty
Fister, Jim	Simpsonville
France, Dan	Cawood
Gevedon, Hanners	Crab Orchard
Greco, John	Greensburg
Hemphill, Jesse	Berea
Hibben, Daryl	LaGrange
Hibben, Gil	LaGrange
Hibben, Joleen	LaGrange
Holbrook, H.L.	Olive Hill
Howser, John C.	Frankfort
Keeslar, Joseph F.	Almo
Pease, W.D.	Ewing
Pierce, Harold L.	Louisville
Pulliam, Morris C.	Shelbyville
Smith, Gregory H.	Louisville
Smith, John W.	West Liberty
Waddle, Thomas	Louisville

louisiana

Blaum, Roy	Covington
Caldwell, Bill	West Monroe
Camp, Jeff	Ruston
Capdepon, Randy	Carencro
Capdepon, Robert	Carencro
Chauvin, John	Scott
Culpepper, John	Monroe
Dake, C.M.	New Orleans
Durio, Fred	Opelousas
Elkins, R. Van	Bonita
Faucheaux, Howard J.	Loreauville
Forstall, Al	Slidell
Gorenflo, James T.	Baton Rouge
Graffeo, Anthony I.	Chalmette
Holmes, Robert	Baton Rouge
Howard, Seth	Baton Rouge
Ki, Shiva	Baton Rouge
Laurent, Kermit	LaPlace
Marks, Chris	Breaux Bridge
Mitchell, Max and Dean	Leesville
Moon, Sidney "Pete"	Lafayette
Potier, Timothy F.	Oberlin
Provenzano, Joseph D.	Chalmette
Reggio Jr., Sidney J.	Sun
Roath, Dean	Baton Rouge
Sanders, Michael M.	Ponchatoula
Smith, W.F. Red	Slidell
Wiggins, Horace	Mansfield

maine

Bohrmann, Bruce	Yarmouth
Coombs Jr., Lamont	Bucksport
Courtois, Bryan	Saco
Fuegen, Larry	Wiscasset
Leavitt, Earl F.	E. Boothbay
Oyster, Lowell R.	East Corinth
Sayen, Murad	Bryant Pond
Sharrigan, Mudd	Wiscasset

maryland

Antonio, William J.	Golts
Barnes, Aubrey G.	Hagerstown
Barnes, Gary L.	New Windsor
Beers, Ray	Monkton
Bouse, D. Michael	Waldorf
Cohen, N.J. Norm	Baltimore
Corkum, Steve	Frederick
Freiling, Albert J.	Finksburg
Fuller, Jack A.	New Market
Hart, Bill	Pasadena
Hendrickson, E.J. Jay	Frederick
Hudson, Robbin C.	Rock Hall
Hurt, William R.	Frederick
Kremzner, Raymond L.	Stevenson
Kretsinger Jr., Philip W.	Boonsboro
McCarley, John	Union Bridge
McGowan, Frank	Sykesville
Merchant, Ted	White Hall
Moran, Wm. F.	Braddock Heights
Nicholson, Kent R.	Phoenix
O'Ceilaghan, Michael	Baltimore
Rhodes, James D.	Hagerstown
Sentz, Mark C.	Taneytown
Sidelinger, Robert	Bel Air
Smit, Glenn	Aberdeen
Sontheimer, Douglas G.	Potomac

massachusetts

Banaitis, Romas	So. Boston
Dailey, G.E.	Seekonk
DaConceicao	ReHoboth
Flechtner, Chris	Fitchburg
Gaudette, Linden L.	Wilbraham
Grossman, Stewart	Clinton
Gwozdz, Bob	Attleboro
Halpern, Les	Monson
Jarvis, Paul M.	Cambridge
Khalsa, Jot Singh	Millis
Kubasek, John A.	Easthampton
Lapen, Charles	W. Brookfield
McLuin, Tom	Dracut
Reed, Dave	Brimfield
Richter, Scott	South Boston
Rua, Gary (Wolf)	Fall River
Siska, Jim	Westfield
Sloan, John	Foxboro
Smith, J.D.	Boston
Tsoulas, Jon J.	Peabody

michigan

Andrews, Eric	Grand Ledge
Beckwith, Michael R.	New Baltimore
Behnke, William	Lake City
Bethke, Lora	Grand Haven
Booth, Philip W.	Ithaca
Buckbee, Donald M.	Grayling
Carlisle, Frank	Detroit
Cashen, Kevin R.	Hubbardston
Cook, Mike A.	Portland
Cousino, George	Onsted
Cowles, Don	Royal Oak
Dilluvio, Frank J.	Warren
Enders, Robert	Cement City
Erickson, Walter E.	Warren
Garbe, Bob	Fraser
Gottage, Dante	Clinton Township
Hartman, Arlan	N. Muskegon
Hughes, Daryle	Nunica
Kalfayan, Edward N.	Ferndale
Krause, Roy W.	St. Clair Shores
Lankton, Scott	Ann Arbor
Leach, Mike J.	Swartz Creek
Lucie, James R.	Fruitport
Mills, Louis G. Yasutomo	Ann Arbor
Parker, Robert Nelson	Rapid City
Reh, Bill	Caro
Repke, Mike	Bay City
Sakmar, Mike	Rochester
Serven, Jim	Fostoria
Sigman, James P.	Three Rivers
Smith, Michael J.	Royal Oak
Stewart, Charles Chuck	Warren
Tally, Grant C.	Allen Park
Warzocha, Stanley	Warren
Whittaker, Wayne	Metamore
Whitworth, Ken J.	Sterling Heights
Wood, Webster	Atlanta
Zowada, Tim	Boyne Falls

minnesota

Dingman, Scott	Bemidji
Dube, Paul N.	Chaska
Fiorini, Bill	LaCrescent
Goltz, Warren L.	Ada
Griffin, Thomas J.	Windom
Hagen, Philip L.	Pelican Rapids
Hansen, Robert W.	Cambridge
Holland, Dale J.	Chanhassen
Janiga, Matthew A.	Andover
Johnson, Ronald B.	Clearwater
Knipschield, Terry	Rochester
Lange, Donald G.	Pelican Rapids
McGinnis, Tom	Ozark
Shadley, Eugene W.	Bovey
Voorhies, Les	Lonsdale

mississippi

Boleware, Dave	Carson
Craft, Richard C.	Jackson
Davis, Jesse W.	Sarah
Dees, Jay	Collins
Fowler, Ricky	Richton
Greco, John	Bay St. Louis
Hand, James E., M.D.	Gloster
Landrum, Leonard	Lumberton
LeBatard, Paul M.	Vancleave
Roberts, Michael	Clinton
Taylor, Billy	Petal
Wehner, Rudy	Collins
Wingo, Perry	Gulfport
Winston, David	Starkville

missouri

Bolton, Charles B.	Jonesburg
Burrows, Stephen R.	Kansas City
Cover, Raymond A.	Mineral Point
Cox, Colin	Raymore
Davis, W.C.	Raymore
Dippold, A.W.	Perryville
Driskill, Beryl	Braggadocio
Duvall, Larry E.	Gallatin
Engle, William	Boonville
Garcia Jr., Raul	Aberdeen
Glaser, Ken	Purdy
Kennedy, Jerry	Blue Springs
Kinnikin, Todd	House Springs

Knickmeyer, Hank	Cedar Hill
Mason, Bill	Excelsior Springs
May, James E.	Auxvasse
McCrackin and Son, V.J.	House Springs
Miller, Bob	Oakville
Miller, Michael E.	Monett
Newcomb, Corbin	Moberly
Rardon, A.D.	Polo
Rardon, Archie F.	Polo
Shelton, Paul	Rolla
Steketee, Craig A.	Billings
Warden, Roy A.	Union
Weddle Jr., Del	St. Joseph

montana

Barnes, Jack	Whitefish
Beam, John R.	Kalispell
Brooks, Steve R.	Big Timber
Caffrey, Edward J.	Great Falls
Colter, Wade	Colstrip
Conklin, George	Fort Benton
Crowder, Robert	Thompson Falls
DesJardines, Dennis	Plains
Dunkerley, Rick	Lincoln
Ellefson, Joel	Manhattan
Fassio, Melvin G.	Bonner
Forthofer, Pete	Whitefish
Gallagher, Barry	Lewistown
Harkins, J.A.	Conner
Hill, Howard	Polson
Hintz, Gerald M.	Helena
Kauffman, Dave	Helena
Kraft, Elmer	Big Arm
McGuane IV, Thomas F.	Bozeman
Miller, Larry	Missoula
Mortenson, Ed	Darby
Moyer, Russ	Havre
Nedved, Dan	Kalispell
Patrick, Willard	Helena
Peele, Bryan	Thompson Falls
Peterson, Eldon G.	Columbia Falls
Piorek, James S.	Missoula
Pursley, Aaron	Big Sandy
Robinson, Robert W.	Polson
Ruana Knife Works	Bonner
Schirmer, Mike	Twin Bridges
Schmidt, Rick	Whitefish
Simonich, Bob	Clancy
Smith, Josh	Lincoln
Taylor, Shane	Angela
Thill, Jim	Missoula
Townsend, J.W.	Trout Creek
Weinand, Gerome W.	Missoula

nebraska

Brown, David B.	Fairbury
Gutekunst, Ralph	Fremont
Hielscher, Guy	Alliance
Jensen Jr., Carl A.	Blair
Jokerst, Charles	Omaha
Schepers, George B.	Chapman
Suedmeier, Harlan	Nebraska City
Syslo, Chuck	Omaha
Till, Calvin E.	Chadron

nevada

Blanchard, Gary	Las Vegas
Cameron, Ron G.	Logandale
Defeo, Robert A.	Henderson
Duff, Bill	Virginia City
Hrisoulas, Jim	Las Vegas
Mecchi, Richard	Las Vegas
Mount, Don	Las Vegas
Nishiuchi, Melvin S.	Las Vegas
Thomas, Devin	Las Vegas
Tracy, Bud	Reno

new hampshire

Gunn, Nelson L.	Epping
Hitchmough, Howard	Peterborough
MacDonald, John	Raymond
Saindon, R. Bill	Claremont

new jersey

D'Andrea, John	Wayne
Foley, Barney	Somerset
Grussenmeyer, Paul	Lindenwold
MacBain, Kenneth	Norwood
McGovern, Jim	Oak Ridge
Polkowski, Al	Chester
Pressburger, Ramon	Howell
Quick, Mike	Kearny
Slee, Fred	Morganville
Viele, H.J.	Westwood
Weber, Fred E.	Forked River

new mexico

Becket, Norman L.	Farmington
Black, Tom	Albuquerque
Coleman, Keith E.	Los Lunas
Cordova, Joseph G.	Peralta
Digangi, Joseph M.	Santa Cruz
Duran, Jerry T.	Albuquerque
Dyess, Eddie	Roswell
Fisher, Jay	Magdalena
Goode, Bear	Navajo Dam
Gunter, Brad	Tijeras
Hethcoat, Don	Clovis
Homer, Glen	Bloomfield
Jones, Bob	Albuquerque
Lewis, Ron	Edgewood
Lewis, Tom R.	Carlsbad
McBurnette, Harvey	Eagle Nest
Miller, Ted	Santa Fe
Norton, Don	Farmington
Nymeyer, Earl	Hobbs
Pagnard, Philip E.	Albuquerque
Schaller, Antony B.	Albuquerque
Terzuola, Robert	Santa Fe
Walker, Michael	Taos
Ware, Tommy	Datil
Wescott, Jim	Las Cruces

new york

Anderson, Edwin	Glen Cove
Baker, Bill	Boiceville
Champagne, Paul	Mechanicville
Cute, Thomas	Cortland
Davis, Barry L.	Castleton
Eneboe, James	Schenectady
Levin, Al	Brooklyn
Levin, Jack	Brooklyn
Licata, Steven	Mineola
Loos, Henry C.	New Hyde Park
Ludwig, Richard O.	Maspeth
Maragni, Dan	Georgetown
Meshejian, Mardi	E. Northport
Page, Reginald	Groveland
Pattay, Rudy	Long Beach
Patterson, Karl	Silver Creek
Rachlin, Leslie S.	Elmira
Rappazzo, Richard	Cohoes
Revishvili, Zaza	Glendale
Rizzi, Russell	East Setauket
Rotella, Richard A.	Niagara Falls
Scheid, Maggie	Rochester
Schmidt, James A.	Ballston Lake
Serafen, Steven E.	New Berlin
Smith, Raymond L.	Breesport
Summers, Dan	Whitney Point
Szilaski, Joseph	Wappingers Falls
Todd, Ed	Putnam Valley
Turner, Kevin	Montrose
Tyc, William J.	Newburgh
Warren, Dellana	Schenectady
Wood, Leonard J.	Beacon

north carolina

Baker, Herb	Eden
Britton, Tim	Kinston
Brown, Tom	Greensboro
Busfield, John	Roanoke Rapids
Chastain, Wade	Horse Shoe
Clark, Dave	Andrews
Daniel, Travis E.	Winston-Salem
Folts, Alan C.	Clayton
Fox, Paul	Claremont
Gaddy, Gary Lee	Washington
Goguen, Scott	Newport
Goldenberg, T.S.	Fairview
Gross, W.W.	High Point
Gurganus, Carol	Colerain
Gurganus, Melvin H.	Colerain
Guthrie, George B.	Bessemer City
Harless, Walt	Stoneville
King, Randall	Asheville
Livingston, Robert C.	Murphy
Lubrich, Mark	Matthews
Maynard, William N. (Bill)	Fayetteville
McNabb, Tommy	Winston-Salem
Norris, Mike	Albemarle
Parrish, Robert	Weaverville
Patrick, Chuck	Brasstown
Patterson, Alan W.	Hayesville
Popp Sr., Steve F.	Fayetteville
Rece, Charles V.	Paw Creek
Scholl, Tim	Angier
Greene, Chris	Shelby
Shuford, Rick	Statesville
Simmons, H.R.	Grantsboro
Sprouse, Terry	Asheville
Sterling, Murray	Mount Airy
Sutton, S. Russell	New Bern
Tedder, Mickey	Conover
Wade, J.M.	Fayetteville
Wagaman, John K.	Fayetteville
Whitley, Wayne	Washington
Williamson, Tony	Siler City
Winkler, Daniel	Boone
Young, Paul A.	Boone

north dakota

Ennis, Ray W.	Grand Forks
Keidel, Gene W.	Dickinson
Keidel, Scott J.	Dickinson

ohio

Babcock, Raymond G.	Vincent
Busse, Jerry	Wauseon

Click, Joe	Liberty Center
Collins, Harold A.	West Union
Collins, Lynn M.	Elyria
Corwin, Don	Monclova
Cottrill, James I.	Columbus
Darby, Rick	Youngstown
Downing, Tom	Cortland
Downs, Jim	Londonderry
Etzler, John	Grafton
Foster, R.L. (Bob)	Mansfield
Franklin, Mike	Aberdeen
Geisler, Gary	Clarksville
Glover, Ron	Cincinnati
Greiner, Richard	Green Springs
Grubb, Richard A.	Columbus
Guess, Raymond L.	Mechanicstown
Hetmanski, Thomas S.	Mansfield
Hinderer, R.	Wooster
Imboden II, Howard L.	Dayton
Johnson, W.C. "Bill"	New Carlisle
Kiefer, Tony	Pataskala
Koutsopoulos, George	LaGrange
Koval, Michael T.	New Albany
Layton, Jim	Portsmouth
Longworth, Dave	Hamersville
Loro, Gene	Crooksville
Maienknecht, Stanley	Sardis
McCarty, Harry	Hamilton
McDonald, Rich	Columbiana
McGroder, Patrick J.	Madison
Mercer, Mike	Lebanon
Messer, David T.	Dayton
Mettler, J. Banjo	No. Baltimore
Morgan, Tom	Beloit
Papp, Robert Bob	Parma
Ralph, Darrel	Reynoldsburg
Salley, John D.	Tipp City
Shinosky, Andy	Youngstown
Shoemaker, Carroll	Northup
Shoemaker, Scott	Miamisburg
Shushunov, Sergei	Bath
Spinale, Richard	Lorain
Steven, Barry B.	Cridersville
Stoddart, W.B. Bill	Forest Park
Strong, Scott	Beaver Creek
Summers, Arthur L.	Mechanicsburg
Summers, Dennis K.	Springfield
Thomas, Kim	Brunswick
Thourot, Michael W.	Napoleon
Trabbic, R.W.	Toledo
Votaw, David P.	Pioneer
Ward, J.J.	Waverly
Ward, Ron	Loveland
Warther, Dale	Dover
Witsaman, Earl	Stow
Wood, Larry B.	Huber Heights
Yurco, Mike	Canfield

oklahoma

Baker, Ray	Sapulpa
Barngrover, Jerry	Afton
Brown, Troy L.	Park Hill
Burke, Dan	Edmond
Crenshaw, Al	Eufaula
Dill, Dave	Bethany
Englebretson, George	Oklahoma City
Gepner, Don	Norman
Johns, Rob	Enid
Kennedy Jr., Bill	Yukon
Mitchell, Wm. Dean	Forgan
Sanders, Athern Al	Norman
Spivey, Jefferson	Yukon
Williams, Michael L.	Broken Bow

oregon

Alverson, Tim	Klamath Falls
Anderson, Virgil W.	Portland
Bell, Michael	Coquille
Bochman, Bruce	Grants Pass
Buchman, Bill	Bend
Buchner, Bill	Idleyld Park
Coats, Eldon M.	Beatty
Coon, Raymond C.	Gresham
Corrado, Jim	Glide
Davis, Terry	Sumpter
Dowell, T.M.	Bend
Draper, Kent	Cheshire
Eck, Larry A.	Terrebonne
Ferdinand, Don	Shady Cove
Fox, Wendell	Springfield
Frank, Heinrich H.	Seal Rock
Goddard, Wayne	Eugene
Harsey, William W.	Creswell
Hilker, Thomas N.	Williams
Horn, Jess	Florence
Huey, Steve	Junction City
Kelley, Gary	Aloha
Lake, Ron	Eugene
Lindsay, Chris A.	Bend
Little, Gary M.	Broadbent
Lum, Robert W.	Eugene
Martin, Gene	Williams
Miller, Michael K.	Sweet Home
Murphy, Dave	Gresham
Olson, Darrold E.	Shedd
Osterman, Daniel E.	Junction City
Reed, Del	Beaverton
Saddle Mountain Knife	Vernonia
Schell, Clyde M.	Corvallis
Shoger, Mark O.	Beaverton
Thompson, Leon	Forest Grove
Thompson, Tommy	Portland
Vallotton, Butch	Oakland
Vallotton, Rainy D.	Oakland
Vallotton, Shawn	Oakland
Veatch, Richard	Springfield
Wahlster, Mark David	Silverton
Walker, Michael L.	Eugene
Walker, Patricia	Eugene
Wardian, Paul G.	Troutdale
Wise, John	Winchester
Woodcock, Dennis "Woody"	Wheeler
Zeller, Dennis J.	Gresham

pennsylvania

Amor Jr., Miguel	Lancaster
Anderson, Gary D.	Spring Grove
Besedick, Frank E.	Ruffsdale
Candrella, Joe	Warminster
Clark, D.E. Lucky	Mineral Point
Ellenberg, William C.	Melrose Park
Frey Jr., W. Fredrick	Milton
Goldberg, David	Blue Bell
Gottschalk, Gregory J.	Carnegie
Malloy, Joe	Freeland
Marlowe, Donald	Dover
Mensch, Larry	Milton
Milford, Brian A.	Knox
Miller, Rick	Rockwood
Nealy, Bud	Stroudsburg
Nolfi, Tim	Dawson
Nott, Ron P.	Summerdale
Parker, J.E.	Clarion
Rupert, Robert	Clinton
Rybar Jr., Raymond B.	Finleyville
Sinclair, J.E.	Pittsburgh
Steigerwalt, Ken	Orangeville
Stroyan, Eric	Dalton
Taglienti, Antonio J.	Beaver Falls
Valois, A. Daniel	Lehighton
Whittaker, Robert E.	Mill Creek
Wilson, Jon J.	Johnstown

rhode island

Bardsley, Norman P.	Pawtucket
Black, Robert	N. Kingstown
Gentile, Al	Warwick
Jensen, John Lewis	Providence
Lambert, Ronald S.	Johnston
McHenry, William James	Wyoming
Selvidio, Ralph	Wyoming
Williams, Jason L.	Wyoming

south carolina

Barefoot, Joe W.	Liberty
Batchelor, Ritchie	Salley
Beatty, Gordon H.	Seneca
Branton, Robert	Awendaw
Brend, Walter J.	Walterboro
Bridwell, Richard A.	Taylors
Cannady, Daniel L.	Allendale
Cox, Sam	Gaffney
Davis, Dixie	Clinton
Defreest, William G.	Barnwell
Easler, Paula	Woodruff
Easler Jr., Russell O.	Woodruff
Fecas, Stephen J.	Anderson
Gainey, Hal	Greenwood
Gaston, Ron	Woodruff
George, Harry	Aiken
Gregory, Michael	Belton
Hendrix, Wayne	Allendale
Herron, George	Springfield
Kaufman, Scott	Anderson
Kay, J. Wallace	Liberty
Kessler, Ralph A.	Marietta
Knott, Steve	Clinton
Langley, Gene H.	Florence
Lewis, K.J.	Lugoff
Lutz, Greg	Greenwood
McManus, Danny	Taylors
Montjoy, Claude	Clinton
Owens, Dan	Blacksburg
Page, Larry	Aiken
Parler, Thomas O'Neil	Charleston
Peagler, Russ	Moncks Corner
Poole, Marvin	Anderson
Poston, Alvin	Pamplico
Prince, Joe R.	Moore
Reeves, Winfred M.	West Union
Sears, Mick	Sumter
Smith, Ralph L.	Greer
Thomas, Rocky	Ladson
Tyser, Ross	Spartanburg
Van Hoy, Ed	Taylors
Whitmire, Earl T.	Rock Hill

south dakota

Thomsen, Loyd W.	Oelrichs

tennessee

Bailey, Joseph D.	Nashville
Baker, Vance	Riceville
Bartlow, John	Norris

Canter, Ronald E.	Jackson
Cargill, Bob	Ocoee
Casteel, Dianna	Monteagle
Casteel, Douglas	Monteagle
Centofante, Frank & Tony	Madisonville
Claiborne, Ron	Knoxville
Clay, Wayne	Pelham
Conley, Bob	Jonesboro
Coogan, Robert	Smithville
Copeland, George A. Steve	Alpine
Corby, Harold	Johnson City
Crisp, Harold	Cleveland
Ewing, John H.	Clinton
Eldridge, Allan L.	Gallatin
Harley, Larry W.	Bristol
Hurst, Jeff	Rutledge
Johnson, Ryan M.	Hixson
Langston, Bennie E.	Memphis
Levine, Bob	Tullahoma
Lincoln, James B.	Bartlett
McDonald, W.J. "Jerry"	Germantown
McNeil, Jimmy	Memphis
Rhea, David	Lynnville
Rial, Douglas	Greenfield
Ryder, Ben M.	Copperhill
Sampson, Lynn	Jonesborough
Smith, Newman L.	Gatlinburg
Taylor, C. Gray	Kingsport
Taylor, David	Bristol
Vanderford, Carl G.	Columbia
Walker, John W.	Bon Aqua
Ward, W.C.	Clinton
Williams Jr., Richard T.	Morristown
Wright, Harold C.	Centerville

texas

Adams, William D.	Houston
Allen, Mike Whiskers	Malakoff
Allred, Elvan	Wichita Falls
Anderson, Michael D.	Arlington
Ashby, Douglas	Dallas
Bailey, Kirby C.	Lytle
Barbee, Jim	Ft. Stockton
Barnes, Jim	San Angelo
Batts, Keith	Hooks
Blasingame, Robert	Kilgore
Blum, Kenneth	Brenham
Boatright, Basel	New Braunfels
Brayton, Jim	Burkburnett
Brightwell, Mark	Leander
Broadwell, David	Wichita Falls
Brooks, Michael	Lubbock
Bullard, Randall	Canyon
Bullard, Tom	Comfort
Burden, James M.	Burkburnett
Byrd, Don E.	Roanoke
Callahan, F. Terry	Boerne
Carter, Fred	Wichita Falls
Cashion, Mary Jane	Ennis
Champion, Robert	Amarillo
Chase, John E.	Aledo
Churchman, T.W.	San Antonio
Clark, Roger	Rockdale
Collett, Jerry D.	Castroville
Connor, Michael	Winters
Costa, Scott	Spicewood
Crain, Jack W.	Weatherford
Davis, Vernon	Waco
Dean, Harvey J.	Rockdale
Dietz, Howard	New Braunfels
Dominy, Chuck	Colleyville
Edwards, Lynn	West Columbia
Elishewitz, Allen	Dallas
Eriksen, James Thorlief	Garland
Ferguson, Jim	San Angelo
Fischer, Clyde E.	Nixon
Fowler, Jerry	Hutto
Franks, Joel	Lubbock
Fritz, Jesse	Slaton
Fuller, Bruce A.	Baytown
Gardner, Rob	Port Aransas
Gartman, M.D.	Gatesville
Gault, Clay	Lexington
Green, Bill	Garland
Green, Roger M.	Joshua
Griffin, Rendon and Mark	Houston
Hagwood, Kellie	San Antonio
Hajovsky, Robert J.	Scotland
Hamlet Jr., Johnny	Clute
Hand, Bill	Spearman
Hays, Mark	Carrollton
Hesser, David	Dripping Springs
Hollett, Jeff	Rockwall
Howell, Robert L.	Kilgore
Hudson, Robert	Humble
Hueske, Chubby	Bellaire
Hughes, Lawrence	Plainview
Jetton, Cay	Winnsboro
Johnson, Gorden W.	Houston
Johnson, Ruffin	Houston
Johnson, Ryan M.	Hixson
Kennedy, Kelly S.	Odessa
Kious, Joe	Kerrville
Knipstein, Robert C.	Arlington
Ladd, Jim	Deer Park
Ladd, Jimmie L.	Deer Park
Lambert, Jarrell D.	Ganado
LaPlante, Brett	McKinney
Laughlin, Don	Vidor
Lay, L.J.	Burkburnett
LeBlanc, John	Winnsboro
Lister Jr., Weldon E.	Boerne
Love, Ed	San Antonio
Luchak, Bob	Channelview
Luckett, Bill	Weatherford
Lyons, Randy	Lumberton
Madsen, Jack	Wichita Falls
Marshall, Glenn	Mason
Martin, Michael W.	Beckville
McClure, Leonard	Seminole
McConnell Jr., Loyd A.	Odessa
McDearmont, Dave	Lewisville
McElhannon, Marcus	Sugarland
McKissack II, Tommy	Sonora
Merz III, Robert L.	Katy
Miller, R.D.	Dallas
Mills, Andy	Fredericksburg
Neely, Greg	Houston
Moore, James B.	Ft. Stockton
Ogletree Jr., Ben R.	Livingston
Oliver, Anthony Craig	Ft. Worth
Osborne, Michael	New Braunfels
Osborne, Warren	Waxahachie
Overeynder, T.R.	Arlington
Ownby, John C.	Plano
Pate, Lloyd D.	Georgetown
Polzien, Don	Lubbock
Pugh, Jim	Azle
Pullen, Martin	Granbury
Ray, Alan W.	Lovelady
Raymond, Donald	Groveton
Richardson Jr., Percy	Hemphill
Robinson, Charles	Vega
Ruple, William H.	Charlotte
Schneider, Herman J.	Pittsburg
Scott, Al	Kerrville
Self, Ernie	Dripping Springs
Sims, Bob	Meridian
Sloan, Shane	Newcastle
Smart, Steve	Melissa
Spano, Dominick	San Angelo
Spencer, John E.	Harper
Stokes, Ed	Hockley
Stone, Jerry	Lytle
Stout, Johnny	New Braunfels
Thuesen, Ed	Houston
Thuesen, Kevin	Houston
Treiber, Leon	Ingram
Turcotte, Larry	Pampa
Watson, Daniel	Driftwood
Watt III, Freddie	Big Spring
Watts, Mike	Gatesville
Watts, Wally	Gatesville
West, Pat	Charlotte
Whitley, Weldon G.	El Paso
Wilcher, Wendell L.	Palestine
Womack, A.M. "Babe"	Conroe
Wood, William W.	Seymour
Yeates, Joe A.	Spring
Yunes, Yamil R.	Roma
Zinsmeister, Paul	Harper

utah

Black, Earl	Salt Lake City
Davis, Greg	Redmond
Ence, Jim	Richfield
Erickson, Curt	Ogden
Erickson, L.M.	Liberty
Hatch, Ken	Jensen
Hunter, Hyrum and Kellie	Aurora
Johnson, Steve R.	Manti
Maxfield, Lynn	Layton
Nielson, Jeff	Monroe
Nunn, Gregory R.	Moab
Peterson, Chris	Aurora
Rapp, Steven J.	Midvale
Strickland, Dale	Monroe
Velarde, Ricardo	Provo
Warenski, Buster	Richfield
Winn, Travis A.	Salt Lake City

vermont

Haggerty, George S.	Jacksonville
Kelso, Jim	Worcester

virginia

Ballew, Dale	Bowling Green
Barber, Robert E.	Charlottesville
Batson, Richard G.	Rixeyville
Beverly II, Larry H.	Spotsylvania
Blakley II, William E.	Fredericksburg
Callahan, Errett	Lynchburg
Chamberlain III, Chas. R.	Barren Springs
Compton, William E.	Sterling
Conkey, Tom	Nokesville
Davidson, Edmund	Goshen
Douglas, John J.	Lynch Station
Fielder, William V.	Richmond
Frazier, Ron	Powhatan
Hawk, Jack L.	Ceres
Hawk, Joe	Ceres
Hawk, Joey K.	Ceres
Hedrick, Don	Newport News
Hendricks, Samuel J.	Maurertown
Holloway, Paul	Norfolk

Jones, Barry	Danville
Jones, Enoch	Warrenton
Jones, Phillip G.	Danville
Kellogg, Brian R.	New Market
McCoun, Mark	DeWitt
Metheny, H.A."Whitey"	Spotsylvania
Murski, Ray	Reston
Norfleet, Ross W.	Richmond
Owen, Bill	Lovettsville
Parks, Blane C.	Dale City
Richter, John C.	Chesapeake
Ryan, C.O.	Yorktown
Scott, Winston	Huddleston
Thomas, Daniel	Leesburg
White, Gene E.	Alexandria

washington

Baldwin, Phillip	Snohomish
Ball, Robert	Port Angeles
Ber, Dave	San Juan Island
Blomberg, Gregg	Lopez
Boguszewski, Phil	Tacoma
Boyer, Mark	Bothell
Brothers, Robert L.	Colville
Brunckhorst, Lyle	Bothell
Chamberlain, John B.	East Wenatchee
Chamberlain, Jon A.	East Wenatchee
Conti, Jeffrey D.	Port Orchard
Crain, Frank	Spokane
D'Angelo, Laurence	Vancouver
Davis, John	Selah
Davis, K.M. Twig	Monroe
Goertz, Paul S.	Renton
Gray, Bob	Spokane
Greenfield, G.O.	Everett
Huddleston, Joe D.	Yelm
Hurst, Cole	East Wenatchee
Kramer, Bob	Seattle
Leet, Larry W.	Burien
Mosser, Gary E.	Kirkland
Rice, Adrienne	Lopez Island
Sanderson, Ray	Yakima
Schempp, Ed	Ephrata
Schempp, Martin	Ephrata
Stegner, Wilbur G.	Rochester
Witt, Douglas	North Bend
Wright, Kevin	Quilcene

west virginia

Barnett, Van	New Haven
Bowen, Tilton	Baker
Dent, Douglas M.	South Charleston
Derr, Herbert	Clendenin
Drost, Jason D.	French Creek
Drost, Michael B.	French Creek
Elliott, Jerry P.	Charleston
Jeffries, Robert W.	Red House
Liegey, Kenneth R.	Millwood
Maynard, Larry Joe	Crab Orchard
McConnell, Charles R.	Wellsburg
Morris, Eric	Beckley
Pickens, Selbert	Liberty
Reynolds, Dave	Harrisville
Sigman, Corbet R.	Liberty
Small, Ed	Keyser
Straight, Don	Points
Tokar, Daniel	Shepherdstown
White, Scottie H.	Pecks Mill
Williams, Leonard	Meadow Bridge
Wilson, R.W.	Weirton
Workman, Jr., Hubert L.	Williamsburg
Wyatt, William R.	Rainelle

wisconsin

Brdlik, Dan E.	Prescott
Dahl, Cris	Lake Geneva
Gannaway, Woodson	Madison
Genske, Jay	Fond du Lac
Hanson, Travis	Mosinee
Hembrook, Ron	Neosho
Johnson, Kenneth B.	Mindoro
Kolitz, Robert	Beaver Dam
Lary, Ed	Mosinee
Lerch, Matthew	Sussex
Maestri, Peter A.	Spring Green
Martin, Peter	Waterford
Niemuth, Troy	Sheboygan
Ponzio, Doug	Kenosha
Ricke, Dave	West Bend
Rochford, Michael R.	Dresser
Stafford, Michael	Madison
Wattelet, Michael A.	Minocqua

wyoming

Alexander, Darrel	Ten Sleep
Ankrom, W.E.	Cody
Banks, David L.	Riverton
Bridges, Justin W.	Dubois
Draper, Audra	Riverton
Fowler, Ed A.	Riverton
Friedly, Dennis	Cody
Iiams, Richard D.	Mills
Kinkade, Jacob	Carpenter
Lee, Tommy	Powell
Pavack, Don	Hanna
Rexroat, Kirk	Wright
Reynolds, John C.	Gillette
Ross, Stephen	Evanston
Walker, George A.	Alpine
Whipple, Wesley A.	Thermopolis

foreign countries

argentina

Ayarragaray, Cristian L.	La Paz
Kehiayan, Alfredo	Buenos Aires
Rho, Nestor Lorenzo	Junin B.A.
Schonhals, Gualberto G.	Diamante

australia

Bennett, Peter	Engadine
Brown, Peter	Emerald Beach
Cross, Robert	Tamworth
Crawley, Bruce R.	Croyden
Gerus, Gerry	Cairns
Giljevic, Branko	Queanbeyan
Green, William	View Bank
Harvey, Max	Perth
Husiak, Myron	Altona
Jones, John	Manly
Maisey, Alan	Toongabbie
Rowe, Stewart G.	Mt. Crosby
Simmonds, Kurt Barnes	N. Castlemaine
Zemitis, Joe	Cardiff Hts.

austria

Poskocil, Helmut	Waidhofen/Ybbs

belgium

Monteiro, Victor	Maleve Ste. Marie-Perwez

botswana

Dauberman, Desmond P.	Gaborone

brazil

Bodolay, Antal	Belo Horizonte
Boscoli, Melquisede Ricci	Presidente Prudente
Bossaerts, Carl	Ribeirao Preto
DeCarvalho, Henrique M.	Braganca Paulista
Gaeta, Angelo	Jali
Gaeta, Roberto	Sao Paulo
Garcia, Mario Eiras	Sao Paulo
Ikoma, Flavio	Presidente Prudente
Lala, Paulo Ricardo	Presidente Prudente
Lala, Roberto P.	Presidente Prudente
Neto Jr., Nelson	Braganca Paulista
Petean, Francisco	Birigui
Petean, Mauricio	Birigui
Rosa, Pedro Guillermo Teles	Presidente Prudente
Villa, Luiz	Sao Paulo
Villar, Ricardo	Mairipora
Zakharov, Carlos	Vanderhoof

canada

Arnold, Joe	London
Beauchamp, Gaetan	Stoneham
Bell, Donald	Bedford
Bold, Stu	Sarnia
Boos, Ralph	Edmonton
Bourbeau, Jean Yves	Ile Perrot
Cote, Yves	Ste-Foy
DeBraga	Val Belair
Deringer, Christoph	Sherbrooke
Doussot, Laurent	Montreal
Downie, James T.	Port Franks
Dublin, Dennis	Enderby
Fraser, Grant	Foresters Falls
Freeman, John	Cambridge
Gilbert, Chantal	St. Romuald
Grenier, Roger	Saint Jovite
Hartmann, Bruce James	Port Elgin
Hayes, Wally	Orleans
Haynes, Chap	Tatamagouche
Hoffmann, Uwe H.	Vancouver
Jobin, Jacques	Levis
Kaczor, Tom	Upper London
Lay, R.J. (Bob)	Vanderhoof
Leber, Heinz	Hudson Hope
Lemaire, Denis	Boucherville
Lightfoot, Greg	Lloydminster
Linklater, Steve	Aurora
Loerchner, Wolfgang	Bayfield
Lyttle, Brian	High River
Maneker, Kenneth	Galiano Island
Martin, Robb	Elmira
Marzitelli, Peter	Langley
Massey, Al	Nova Scotia
Niro, Frank	Mackenzie
Olson, Rod	High River
Patrick, Bob	S. Surrey
Pepiot, Stephan	Winnipeg
Piesner, Dean	St. Jacobs
Price, Steve	Kamloops
Roberts, George A.	White Horse
Ross, Tim	Thunder Bay
Schoenfeld, Matthew A.	Galiano Island
Speck, Doug	Toronto
Stuart, Steve	Gores Landing
Sunderland, Richard	Quathiakski Cove
Tichbourne, George	Mississauga
Tighe, Brian	Ridgeville
Toner, Roger	Pickering
Treml, Glenn	Thunder Bay
Vachon, Yvon	Robertsonville
Whitenect, Jody	Elderbank
Young, Bud	Port Hardy

denmark

Andersen, Henrik Lefolii	Fredensborg
Carlsson, Mark	Copenhagen

Dyrnoe, Per	Hilleroed
Henriksen, Hans J.	Helsinge
Strande, Poul	Viby Sj.
Vensild, Henrik	Auning

england

Boden, Harry	Bonsall
Elliott, Marcus	Llandudno
Farid	Kent
Hague, Geoff	Marlborough
Heasman, H.G.	Llandudno
Henry, Peter and Son	Wokingham
Jackson, Jim	Berkshire
Jones, Charles Anthony	No. Devon
Lamprey, Mike	Devon
Morris, Darrell Price	Devon
Wardell, Michael Ronald	Bletchingley
Wise, Donald	St. Leonards-On-Sea
Wood, Alan	Greenhead

france

Bertholus, Bernard	Antibes
Doursin, Gerard	Pernes les Fontainas
Ganster, Jean-Pierre	Strasbourg
Graveline, Pascal & Isabelle	Ris
Reverdy, Pierre	Valence
Viallon, Henri	Thiers

germany

Balbach, Markus	Weilmünster-Laubuseschbach
Becker, Franz	Marktl/Inn
Boehlke, Guenter	Grossholbach
Borger, Wolf	Graben-Neudorf
Bürger, Günter	Castrop-Rauxel
Dell, Wolfgang	Owen-Teck
Greiss, Jockl	Gutenberg
Faust, Joachim	Goldkronach
Fruhmann, Ludwig	Burghausen
Hehn, Richard Karl	Dörrebach
Herbst, Peter	Lauf d.d.Pegn.
Joehnk, Bernd	Kiel
Kaluza, Werner	Nurnberg
Kersten, Michael	Berlin
Kressler, D.F.	Puchheim
Neuhaeusler, Erwin	Augsburg
Rankl, Christian	Munich
Rinkes, Siegfrien	Markterlbach
Steinau, Jurgen	Berlin
Tritz, Jean Jose	Hamburg
Wimpff, Christian	Stuttgart
Zirbes, Richard	Niederkail

italy

Albericci, Emilio	Bergamo
Ameri, Mauro	Genova
Ballestra, Santino	Ventimiglia
Bertuzzi, Ettore	Bergamo
Bonassi, Franco	Pordenone
Fogarizzu, Boiteddu	Pattada
Giagu, Salvatore e Deroma Maria Rosario	Pattada
Pachi, Francesco	Genoa
Scordia, Paolo	Roma
Simonella, Gianluigi	Maniago
Toich, Nevio	Vicenza
Tschager, Reinhard	Bolzano

japan

Aida, Yoshihito	Tokyo
Fujikawa, Shun	Osaka
Fukuta, Tak	Seki-City
Hara, Kouji	Seki-City
Hirayama, Harumi	Warabi City
Ishihara, Nobuhiko (Hank)	Sakura City
Kagawa, Koichi	Kanagawa
Kanda, Michio	Yamaguehi
Kawasaki, Akihisa	Kobe
Mazaki, Yoshio	Osaka City
Okaysu, Kazou	Tokyo
Sakakibara, Masaki	Tokyo
Shikayama, Toshiaki	Saitama
Sugihara, Keidoh	Osaka
Takahashi, Masao	Gunma
Tasaki, Seiichi	Tochigi
Terauchi, Toshiyuki	Wakayama-Ken
Uekama, Nobuyuki	Tokyo
Wada, Yasutaka	Nara City

mexico

Scheurer, Alfredo Faes	Bosque
Young, Cliff	San Miguel de Allende

netherlands

Van de Manakker, Thys	Helenaveen
Van den Elsen, Gert	A.J. Tilburg
Van Eldik, Frans	Loenen
Van Rijswijk, Aad	Spijkenisse
Van Schaik, Bastiaan	Amsterdam

new zealand

Pennington, C.A.	Christchurch
Reddiex, Bill	Palmerston North
Ross, D.L. (Dave)	Dunedin

norway

Bache-Wiig, Tom	Eivindvik
Holum, Morton	Oslo
Jorgensen, Gerd	Stokke
Momcilovic, Gunnar	Krokstadelva
Sellevold, Harald	Dreggen
Vedaa, Vidar	Flaqtveit
Vistnes, Tor	Kjelhenes

russia

Kharlamov, Yuri	Tula
Revishvili, Zaza	Moscow

scotland

McColl, John	Stonehouse

singapore

Tay, Larry C-G	Singapore

slovak republic

Bojtos, Arpad	Lucenec
Pulis, Vladimir	Kremnica

south africa

Bauchop, Peter	Germiston
Bauchop, Robert	Elsburg
Beukes, Tinus	Vereeniging
Bezuidenhout, Buzz	Queensburgh
Boardman, Guy	New Germany
Brown, Robert E.	Port Elizabeth
Burger, Fred	Munster
Dickerson, Gavin	Petit
Frankland, Andrew	Wilderness
Grey, Piet	Silverton
Kojetin, W.	Germiston
Lackovic, Niko	Port Elizabeth
LaGrange, Fanie	Bellville
Lancaster, C.G.	Sasowburg
Liebenberg, Andre	Bordeaux
Mackrill, Stephen	Pinegowrie
Pienaar, Conrad	Bloemfontein
Rietveld, Bertie	Magaliesburg
Russell, Mick	Port Elizabeth
Schoeman, Corrie	Bloemfontein
Skellern, Dr. M.J.	Munster
Smythe, Ken	Underberg
Watson, Peter	Klerksdorp
Wood, Owen	Honeydew

sweden

Eklund, Maihkel	Färila
Embretsen, Kaj	Edsbyn
Johansson, Anders	Väasterås
Lundstrom, Jan-Ake	Dals-Langed
Nordell, Ingemar	Färila
Ryberg, Gote	Norrahammar

switzerland

Roulin, Charles	Geneva
Soppera, Arthur	Zurich

uruguay

Gonzales, Leonardo Williams	Maldonado

wales

Elliott, Marcus	Llandudno

zimbabwe

Burger, Pon	Bulawayo

knifemakers membership lists

Not all knifemakers are organization-types, but those listed here are in good standing with these organizations.

knifemakers guild

1998 voting membership

a **Les Adams,**, Yoshihito Aida, Mike "Whiskers" Allen, R.V. Alverson, Michael Anderson, W.E. Ankrom, Joe Arnold, Dick Atkinson.

b **Joseph D. Bailey**, Phillip Baldwin, Norman Bardsley, A.T. Barr, C. T. Barrett, James Barry III, John Bartlow, Gene Baskett, James Batson, Butch & Judy Beaver, Raymond Beers, Tom Black, Andrew Blackton, Alan Bloomer, Michel Blum, Arpad Bojtos, Philip Boguszewski, Wolf Borger, Dennis Bradley, Edward Brandsey, Bobby Branton, W. Lowell Bray Jr., Judson Brennan, Clint Breshears, Mark Anthony Brightwell, Tim Britton, David Broadwell, Don Broughton, David Brown, Harold Brown, Rick Browne, John Busfield.

c **Bill Caldwell,** Ronald Canter, Bob Cargill, Harold J. "Kit" Carson, Fred Carter, Dianna Casteel, Douglas Casteel, Frank Centofante, Joel Chamblin, William Chapo, Gordon Chard, Alex Chase, William Cheatham, David Clark, Howard F. Clark, Wayne Clay, Lowell Cobb, Keith Coleman, Vernon Coleman, Alex Collins, Blackie (Walter) Collins, Bob Conley, Harold Corby, Joe Cordova, Leonard Corlee, Jim Corrado, George Cousino, Raymond Cover, Colin Cox, John Craft III, Pat Crawford, John M. Cross, Bob Crowder, James Crowell, Dan Cruze, Roy Cutchin.

d **Charles M. Dake**, Alex Daniels, Jack Davenport, Edmund Davidson, Barry Davis, Terry Davis, Vernon M. Davis, W.C. Davis, Harvey Dean, Bill DeFreest, Dan Dennehy, William Dietzel, Robert Dill, Frank Dilluvio, Allen Dippold, T.M. Dowell, Larry Downing, Tom Downing, James Downs, Bill Duff, Melvin Dunn, Steve Dunn, Jerry Duran.

e **Paula K. Easler,** Al Eaton, Rick Eaton, Allen Elishewitz, Joel Ellefson, Kaj Embretsen, Brad Embry, Jim Ence, Virgil England, William Engle, Robert Engnath, James T. Eriksen.

f **Stephen Fecas,** Lee Ferguson, Thomas M. Ferrara, Bill Fiorini, Jay Fisher, Jerry Fisk, Joe Flournoy, Don Fogg, Pete Forthofer, Paul Fox, Henry Frank, Michael H. Franklin, Ron Frazier, Dennis Friedly, Larry Fuegen, Stanley Fujisaka, Tak Fukuta, John W. Fuller, Shiro Furukawa.

g **Frank Gamble,** Roger Gamble, Robert Garbe, William Garner, Ronald Gaston, Clay Gault, Roy Genge, Harry George, James "Hoot" Gibson Sr., Wayne Goddard, Bruce Goers, David Goldberg, Warren Goltz, Dante & Judith Gottage, Greg Gottschalk, Roger M. Green, Carol Gurganus, Melvin Gurganus, Kenneth Guth.

h **Philip L. "Doc" Hagen,** Robert Hajovsky, Ed Halligan & Son, Jim Hammond, Tim Hancock, James E. Hand, M.D., Kouji Hara, Walt Harless, Larry Harley, Jay Harmon, Ralph Harris, Rade Hawkins, Richard Hehn, Henry Heitler, Roy L. Helton, Earl Jay Hendrickson, Wayne Hendrix, Wayne Hensley, Peter Herbst, Tim Herman, George Herron, Don Hethcoat, Thomas S. Hetmanski, Daryl Hibben, Gil Hibben, Howard Hill, Steven Hill, R. Hinson & Son, Harumi Hirayama, Howard Hitchmough, Steve Hoel, Kevin Hoffman, D'Alton Holder, Jess Horn, Durvyn Howard, Arthur Hubbard, Rob Hudson, Joel Humphreys.

i **Billy Mace Imel.**

j **Jim Jacks,** Paul Jarvis, Steve Jernigan, Steve Johanning, Brad Johnson, Ronald Johnson, Ruffin Johnson, Steve Johnson, W.C. Johnson, Enoch D. Jones, Robert Jones.

k **Edward N. Kalfayan,** William Keeton, Bill Kennedy Jr., Ralph Kessler, Jot Khalsa, Keith Kilby, Bill King, Joe Kious, Jon Kirk, Terry Knipschield, R.C. Knipstein, Michael Koval, Dennis G. Krapp, Roy Krause, D.F. Kressler.

l **Ron Lake,** Frank Lampson, Gene Langley, Scott Lankton, Ken Largin, Edward Lary, Kermit Laurent, Mike Leach, Bracy Ledford, Tommy Lee, Bill Levengood, Lile Handmade Knives (Marilyn Lile), Wolfgang Loerchner, R.W. Loveless, Schuyler Lovestrand, Don Lozier, Bob Luchak, Robert Lum, Ernest Lyle, Brian Lyttle.

m **Joe Malloy,** Dan Maragni, Randall J. Martin, James May, Zollan McCarty, Charles McConnell, Loyd McConnell, Marcus McElhannon, Ken McFall, J.J. McGovern, Frank McGowan, W.J. McHenry, David McIntosh, Tommy McNabb, Mike Mercer, Ted Merchant, Robert Merz III, James Miller, Steve Miller, Louis Mills, Dan Mink, Jim Minnick, James B. Moore, Jeff Morgan, C.H. Morris, Paul Myers.

n **Bud Nealy,** Corbin Newcomb, Larry Newton, R.D. & George Nolen, Mike Norris, Don Norton.

o **Charles Ochs,** Ben R. Ogletree Jr., Warren Osborne, T.R. Overeynder, John Owens.

p **Larry Page,** Robert Papp, Melvin Pardue, Russ Peagler, W.D. Pease, Alfred Pendray, Eldon Peterson, Kenneth Pfeiffer, David Pitt, Leon Pittman, Tracy Pittman, Clifton Polk, Al Polkowski, Joe Prince, Jim Pugh, Martin Pullen, Morris Pulliam.

r **Jerry Rados,** James D. Ragsdale, Steven Rapp, A. D. Rardon, Bill Reddiex, Chris Reeve, Pierre Reverdy, John Reynolds, Ron Richard, David Ricke, Willie Rigney, Dean Roath, Howard Robbins, Rex Robinson III, Robert Robinson, Daniel Rodkey, Fred Roe, Rodney Rogers, Charles Roulin, A.G. Russell, Gote Ryberg.

s **Bill Saindon,** Masaki Sakakibara, Mike Sakmar, John Salley, A.A. Sanders, Scott Sawby, James Schmidt, Herman Schneider, Maurice & Alan Schrock, Steve Schwarzer, Mark C. Sentz, James Serven, Eugene W. Shadley, Paul Sheehan, Scott Shoemaker, Ben Shostle, Robert Sidelinger, Bill Simons, R.J. Sims, Cleston Sinyard, Jim Siska, Fred Slee, Scott Slobodian, J.D. Smith, John Smith, Ralph Smith, Jerry Snell, Marvin Solomon, Arthur Soppera, Jim Sornberger, Richard Stafford, Harry Stalter, Ken Steigerwalt, Jurgen Steinau, Charles Stewart, Scott Strong, Arthur Summers, S. Russell Sutton, Charles Syslo, Joseph Szilaski.

t **David A. Taylor,** Gray Taylor, Robert Terzuola, Leon Thompson, Carolyn Tinker, P.J. Tomes, Dan Tompkins, Dwight Towell, Leon Treiber, Barry Trindle, Reinhard Tschager, Jim Turecek, Ralph Turnbull, William Tyc.

v **Butch Vallotton,** Frans Van Eldik, Michael Veit, Howard Viele.

w **Mark Waldrop**, George Walker, Michael Walker, Charles Ward, Buster Warenski, Dellana Warren, Dale Warther, Thomas J. Watson, Reese Weiland, Charles Weiss, Wayne Whittaker, Weldon Whitley, Donnie R. Wicker, Jason Williams, Gordon Wilson, R.W. Wilson, Christian Wimpff, Daniel Winkler, Earl B. Witsaman, William Wolf, Owen Wood, Wood, Irie & Company, Webster Wood, Tim Wright.

y **Joe Yeates,** Yoshindo Yoshihara, George Young, Mike Yurco.

z **Don Zaccagnino Jr.,** Tim Zowada.

probationary members, 1997

Van Barnett, Gaetan Beauchamp, Charlie Bennica, Gary Blanchard, Tony Bose, Bob Dozier, Fain Edwards, Jockl Greiss, Jeffrey Harkins, Dave Kauffman, Peter Martin, Robert J. McDonald, Gunnar Momcilovic, Dusty Moulton, Hiroyuki Sakurai, John W. Smith, Michael J. Smith, Daniel Stephan, Barry Stevens, Johnny Lee Stout, Terry Lee Stover, John W. Walker, Charles Weeber, Levin Yakov.

american bladesmith society (MS) = Master Smith

a **Robin Eileen Ackerson**, Bill Adams, Richard L. Adkins, Eugene Alexander, Mickey L. Ames, David Anders **(MS)**, Autumn D. Anderson, Brian Anderson, Gary D. Anderson **(MS)**, Ronnie A. Andress, Sr., Alan H. Arrington M.D., Doug, Asay, Boyd Ashworth

b **Vance L. Baker,** Robert Ball, Romas Banaitis, David L. Banks, C. David Barker, R.G. Barker, Aubrey G. Barnes **(MS)**, Eric Barnes, Gary Barnes **(MS)**, Marlen R. Barnes, Richard Barney, Almon T. Barton, Hugh E. Bartrug **(MS)**, James L. Batson **(MS)**, Robert K. Batts, Geneo Beasley, James S. Beaty III, Robert B. Beaty, William H. Behnke, George Benjamin, Jr., C.L. (Larry) Bentley, Lara Sue Bethke, Hal Bish, Scott Black, William A. Black, R. Gordon Bloomquist, Kenneth Blum, Geoffrey W. Boos, John P. Boots, Raymond A. Boysen, Garrick A. Bradford, John C. Bradley, Robert Branton, W. Lowell Bray, Jr., Don Broughton **(MS)**, John T. Brown, Troy L. Brown, Thomas L. Browning, Lisa Broyles, Jimmie Buckner (MS), John F. Buffington, Bill Bullard, Jay Burger, Paul E. Burke, Stephan R. Burrows, Owen John C. Bush, John Butler, Dee Button-Inman, Sue G. Button.

c **Michael Cabbage**, Buddy Cabe, Edward J. Caffrey, Terry F. Callahan, Robert W. Calvert, Jeff Camp, Courtenay M. Campbell, Robert D. Carignan, Ron Carpenter, Murray M. Carter, Kevin R. Cashen **(MS)**, Chris Cawthorne, Tom S. Cellum, Frank Cherry, Ron Clairborne, Peter John Clapp, Howard F. Clark **(MS)**, James R. Coker, Harold A. Collins, Wade Colter, Larry D. Coltrain, Roger Comar, Roger Combs, John W. Conner, Michael L. Connor **(MS)**, James R. Cook **(MS)**, George S. Cook, Louise Cook, J. Michael Cook, Rachel Cook, Raymond C. Coon, Todd A. Cooper Joseph G. Cordova **(MS)**, James H. Corry, Mike Corvin, Dr. Timothy L. Costello, Billy W. Cothran Sr., Houston L. Cotton, Monty L. Crain, Dawnavan M. Crawford, John M. Cross **(MS)**, James L. Crowell **(MS)**, William M. Culnon, Steven M. Culver.

d **Mary H. Dake,** Benjamin M. Daland, Sava Damlovac, Barry Davis, Don Davis, Dudley L. Dawkins, Harvey J. Dean, Jr. **(MS)**, Marco A.M. de Castro, Anthony Del Giorno, John C. Delavan, Larry Russell Dement, Mike de Punte, Christoph Deringer **(MS)**, Herbert Derr, Dennis E. DesJardins, John Thomas Devardo, Steven Deweese, Gordon S. Dickerson, William J. Dietzel, A.W. Dippold, Audra L. Draper, Mike Draper, Joseph D. Drouin, Paul Dube, Philip F. Duffy, Brad M. Dugan, Rick Dunkerley, Steve Dunn **(MS)**, Kenneth Durham, Fred Durio, Oliver H. Durrell.

e **Robert A. Ebersole,** Roger Echols, Hugh E. Eddy, Lynn Edwards, Mitch Edwards, Perry B. Elder Jr., Ronald V. Elkins, Terry W. Ellerbee, Dave Ellis, Kaj Embretsen, James Eneboe, David Etchieson, Ronald B. Evans, Vincent K. Evans, Wyman Ewing.

f **James A. Fagan,** George Fant Jr., Jack S. Feder, Gregory K. Ferrier, Ioannis-Minas Filippou, Edward Finn, William R. Fiorini, Clyde E. Fischer, Don Fisher, Jerry Fisk **(MS)**, Jim Fister **(MS)**, John S. Fitch, Joe Flournoy**(MS)**, Don Fogg, Gerald J. Fontenot, Norvell C. Foster, Ronnie E. Foster, Charles Ronald Fowler, Ed A. Fowler **(MS)**, Jerry B. Fowler, Ricky Fowler, Wendell Fox, Walter P. Framski, Daniel Frank, Ralph Freer, Larry Friedrich, Daniel Fronefield, DeWayne Frost, Larry Fuegen **(MS)**, Bruce A. Fuller **(MS)**, Jack A. Fuller **(MS)**.

g **Peter Gagstaher,** Yvon Gagueche, Barry Gallagher, Sean Gallagher, Timothy P. Garrity, Bert Gaston **(MS)**, Leslie George, Thomas Gerner, Richard Gerson, Bruymimx Gert, John Glasscock, Sherwood M. Glotfelty, Jim Gofourth, Wayne L. Goddard **(MS)**, Scott K. Goguen, David Goldberg, Robert Golden, Phillipe Gontier, Gabe Gorenflo, James T. Gorenflo, Greg Gottschalk, Gordon Graham, Walter M. Graves, Bob Gray, Don Greenaway, Chris L. Greene, David Greene, Richard F. Greiner, D.F. Gundersen, Ralph Gutekunst.

h **Philip L. Hagen**, Ed Halligan **(MS)**, N.P. Pete Hamilton, Phil Hammond, Timothy J. Hancock **(MS)**, Bill Hand, Scott Hardy, Larry Harley, Paul W. Harm, R.L. Harper, Cass Harris, Jeffrey A. Harris, Tom Harrison, Rade Hawkins, Scotty Hayes, Wally Hayes **(MS)**, Charles E. Haynes **(MS)**, Mary Margaret Haynes, Bob Dale Hays, John Heinz, Earl J. Hendrickson **(MS)**, Shawn E. Hendrickson, Carl E. Henkle, A.J. Hermann, Bill Herndon, Jay Heselschwerdt, Don Hethcoat **(MS)**, Jerry Hewitt, B.W. Hicks, Kent Hicks, Gene R. Hobart, Dan Hockensmith, Thomas R. Hogan, Bob Hollar, Robert A. Howes, C. Robbin Hudson **(MS)**, Bill R. Hughes, Daryle Hughes, Lawrence H. Hulett, Richard D. Hunter, William Hurt, Joe Hytovick.

i **Paul R. Inman III,** Carole Ivie.

j **Charlton R. (Jack) Jackson**, Jim L. Jackson, John R. Johnson, Randy Johnson, Robert Johnston, Enoch (Nick) Jones, Franklin W. Jones, Andrew S. Jordan.

k **Al J. Kajin**, J. Michael Keeney II, Michael Keeney, Joseph F. Keeslar **(MS)**, John C. Keller, Jerry Kennedy, Kelly S. Kennedy, R.W. Kern, Hyman S. Kessler, Shiva Ki, Keith Kilby **(MS)**, Richard L. Kimberley, Fred King, Todd Kinnikin, Ray Kirk, Russell K. Klingbeil, Hank Knickmeyer**(MS)**, Kurt Knickmeyer, Charles Ray Knowles, Bob Kramer, Lefty Kreh, Raymond Kremzner, Phillip W. Kretsinger **(MS)**, Danny L. Kyle.

l **Cliff Lacey**, Christian Laferriere, Curtis J. Lamb, Jarrell D. Lambert, Leonard Landrum, Bud Lang, Donald G. Lange **(MS)**, Kermit J. Laurent, Charles A. Lawless, Alton Lawrence, Dal Leck, Rick Leeson, Nick Leone III, Bernard Levine, H. Stephen Lewis, Jack Lewis, Peter Lin, Wayne B. Lindsey, Guy A. Little, Lowell C. Lockett, J.A. Lonewolf, Aldo Lorenzi, Eugene F. Loro, Mark Lubrich, James R. Lucie, Gerard P. Lukaszevicz, Larry A. Lunn, Greg Lutz, William R. Lyons.

m **Clent Mackay,** Robert Mackay, Raymond J. Malaby, Michael K. Manabe, Ken Mankel, James Maples, Dan Maragni **(MS)**, Ken Markley, Chris Marks **(MS)**, Stephen R. Marshall, Bruce E. Martin, Gene Martin, John Alexander Martin, Peter Martin, Bill Mason, Alan Robert Massey, Roger D. Massey **(MS)**, Frederick L. McCoy, Kevin McCrackin, Victor J. McCrackin **(MS)**, Richard McDonald, Robert J. McDonald, Frank McGowan, David Brian McKenzie, Tommy McNabb, Mardi Meshecian, James L. Meyers, Bob Miller, Hanford J. Miller **(MS)**, Kent Miller, Richard Miller, Delbert Mills, Stephen J. Mischke, W. Dean Mitchell **(MS)**, Gustav Moertensson, Michael Steven Moncus, Gus A. Montano, Billy R. Moore, Marve Moore, William F. Moran, Jr. **(MS)**, Dennis L. Morris, Franklin D. Morris, Jan Muchnikoff, Dawn Mulbery, Jack W. Muse.

knifemakers membership lists

n **Angelo Navagato,** Gregory T. Neely **(MS)**, Carl Nelson, Robert M. Newhouse, Ron Newton, Tim Nolfi.

o **Winston Oakes**, Charles F. Ochs III **(MS)**, Clyde O'Dell, Vic Odom, Randy W. Ogden, Michael E. Olive, Ben M. Ortega, Dr. Michael R. Osborne, Stephen H. Overstreet, Donald Owens.

p **Jeff Pacelt,** Beuford M. Pardue, John Parks, Thomas O. Parler, Chuck Patrick, Michael D. Pemberton, Alfred H. Pendray **(MS)**, Frederic Perrin, Jim Perry, Johnny Perry, Dan L. Peterson **(MS)**, Lloyd C. Peterson, Clay C. Peyton, Edward W. Phillips, James M. Phillips, Dean Piesner, David Pitman, Dietmar Pohl, James P. Poling, Douglas Ponzio, James E. Porter **(MS)**, Timothy F. Potier **(MS)**, Karlis A. Povisils, James Powell, Houston Price, Terry Primos, Jonathan K. Purviance.

q **Thomas C. Quakenbush,** Craig Quattlebaum.

r **R. Wayne Raley,** Darrel Ralph, Richard A. Ramsey, Gary Randall, Ralph Randow, Robert Renkoski, Kirk Rexroat, James D. Rhodes, Douglas R. Rice, Stephen E. Rice, Alvin C. Richards, Jr., David M. Rider, E. Ray Roberts, Michael Roberts, Charles R. Robinson, Michael R. Rochford, Walter D. Rollick, Jerry Romig, Bob Rosenfeld, Robert N. Rossdeutscher Jr., Charles Roulin, Kenny Rowe, Gary Rua, J. Ken Rudder Jr., Al Runyon, Bob Rupert, Ronald S. Russ, Raymond B. Rybar Jr., Gerald Rzewnicki.

s **Bill Saindon**, Reisuke Saitoh, Ed Schempp, Tom Schilling, James S. Schippnick, James A. Schmidt **(MS)**, Raymond E. Schmitz, Randy Schmoker, Tim Scholl, Charles E. Schultz, Robert W. Schultz, Steven C. Schwarzer **(MS)**, Barry Scott, James A. Scroggs, Robert J. Scroggs, W.P. Semon Jr., Mark C. Sentz **(MS)**, Steve Shackleford, William B. Shackleford, Thomas J. Sheehy, Steven Sheets, Tom Siess, James P. Sigman, Harland R. Simmons, S. Ted Sketos, Wayne Smallwood, J.D. Smith, John M. Smith, Joshua J. Smith, Lenerd C. Smith, Raymond L. Smith, Timothy E. Smock, Marvin Solomon, Gregory Noble Spickler, Thomas K. St. Clair, H. Red St. Cyr, Chuck Stancer, Udo Stegemann, Craig Steketee, Edward L. Stewart, Gary Kenneth Stine, Marc Stokeld, Johnnie L. Stout, Howard Stover, James K. Stover, Terry Lee Stover, Kenneth J. Straight, Frank Stratton III, Terry Stults, Harlan Suedmeier, Cynthia Ann Summers, Daniel L. Summers, Mike Sweany, Arthur Swyhart, Daniel L. Syrcle, Mark G. Szarek, Joseph Szilaski, Joseph G. Szopa.

t **Scott Taylor,** Shane Taylor, Jimmy D. Tharp, Danny Thayer, Jean-Paul Thevenot, Devin Thomas, Kenneth Thompson, P.J. Tomes **(MS)**, Samuel L. Torgeson, Kenneth W. Trisler, Kevin Turner, Randall W. Turner, Jerry L. Tyer.

v **Wayne Valachovic, (MS)**, James N. Van Riper, Jonny David Vasquez, Jan Vaughan, Arthur V. Velasco, Patrik Vogt, Lew Von Lossberg, Bruce Voyles.

w **Bill Walker**, Don Walker, James L. Walker **(MS)**, John Wade Walker III, Roger L. Wallace, Charles W. Wallingford, Wellington Tu Wang, Charles B. Ward, Michael B. Ward, Ken Warner, Dellana Warren, Robert Lee Washburn Jr., Herman Harold Waters, Lu Waters, Billy Watson, Daniel Watson, Haines R. (Dick) Wendell, Jim Weyer, Robert R. Wheeler, Wesley Whipple, Richard T. White, Stephen Whitham, Lenwood W. Whitley, Randy Whittaker, A.L. Williams, Larry D. Williams, Michael L. Williams, Richard T. Williams, Wayne Willson, Jesse Allen Wilmer, George H. Wilson, James R. Wilson, Dan Winkler **(MS)**, George Winter, Donald Witzler, Jim Woods, Randy Wootton, Bill Worthen, Travis Wuertz.

y **Yasuhiro Yamanaka,** Todd Yelverton, Yoshindo Yoshihara.

z **William H. Zeanon.**

miniature knifemaker's society

Paul Abernathy, Mel Anderson, Mary W. Bailey, Paul Charles Basch, Jesse J. Bass, Ray Beers, John Biggers, Blade Magazine, Dennis Blaine, Gerald Bodner, Gary F. Bradburn, Mary Bray, Brock Custom Knives, David Bullard, Dan Carlson, Fred Carter, Eddie Contreras, Kenneth W. Corey, Thomas A. Counts, Damascus USA, Gary Demns, Diana Duff, Paula K. Easler, Albert Eaton, Jay Eisenberg, Allan Eldridge, Gwen Flournoy, Jean Pierre Ganster, Les George, Wayne Goddard, Donald Gossens, Art Grossman, Tommie F. Guinn, Melvin and Carol Gurganus, Ralph Dewey Harris, Terry Ann Hayes, Richard Heise, Bob Hergert, Tom Hetmanski, Albert Izuka, Roger Jones, Wallace J. Kay, Gary Kelley, Shiva Ki, R.F. Koebbeman, Terry Kranning, Gary Ladd, Bernard Levine, Les Levinson, Jack Lewis, Kenneth R. Liegey, Henry C. Loos, Jim Martin, Marlene Marton, Ken McFall, McMullen & Yee Publishing, M.C. "Mal" Mele, Mike Mercer, Paul Meyers, Wayne Morrison, Rateep Mosrie, Allen R. Olsen, Charles Ostendorf, Daniel E. Osterman, Houston Price, Jim Pugh, John Rakusan, Sidney Reggio, Stephan Ricketts, Cindy Rogers, Mark Rogers, David J. Schwan, Al Sears, Paul C. Sheffield, Glen Paul Smit, Sporting Blades, Harry Stalter, Wilson Streeter, Mike Tamboli, Jim Turacek, Yvon Vachon, Rudy Wehner, Jim Weyer, James D. Whitehead, Michael Whittingham, Will Wickliffe, Ron Wilson, Dennis Windmiller, Earl Witsaman, Errol & Mary Young.

professional knifemakers association

Darrel D. Alexander, Melvin Anderson, Don Andrews, Jerry J. Barngrover, Cecil T. Barrett, Norman L. Beckett, Robert Blasingame, Justin Bridges, Robert L. Brothers, C. Lyle Brunckhorst, Stephen R. Burrows, Jerry Busse, Thomas P. Calawa, Danniel L. Cannady, Raymond W. Cannon, Matt K. Carlil, Jeffrey L. Chaffee, Curt D. Childs, Howard F. Clark, David Clouse, Alex Collins, C.M. Dake, Sava Damlovac, Jed Darby, Don Davis, Dan Dennehy, Robert Dill, Melvin T. Dunn, Rick Eaton, Charley Eckerson, Ray W. Ennis, James Thorlief Eriksen, Ralph M. Freer, Barry C. Gallagher, Bob Garbe, Bruce E. Goers, Paul S. Goertz, Kenneth G. Henschel, Tom High, Dan Hockensmith, Scot Horton, Ken Hoy, Robert Hudson, Michael J. Hull, Robert James Hunter, Michael L. Irie, R.B. Johnson, Steven R. Johnson, Jerry Kennedy, Matt Klyczynski, Frank Lampson, James Largent, Norman Levine, W. Tim Lively, Randy Lyons, Guy MacEwan, Mike Mann, Glenn Marshall, Jim Martin, Osa & JB McDowell, David L. McIntosh, Clayton Miller, Jr., J.P. Moss, Dusty Moulton, Bud Nealy, Donald A. Norris, Robert K. Patrick, Willard C. Patrick, Eldon G. Peterson, Cecil W. Quier, Lee Reeves, Wayne A. Reno, Chuck Roberts, Robert Robinson, Steve Rollert, R. Bill Saindon, Clint Sampson, Michael J. Schirmer, Ernie Self, Eugene W. Shadley, James Sigg, Noel Smith, Craig Steketee, Greg A. Sutherland, Hal Tarpley, John E. Toner, John W. Townsend, Tommy J. Ware, Michael A. Wattelet, Gerome M. Weinand, Charles A. West, Bill Wolf, Barry Wood, Joe A. Yeates, Mike Zima.

state/regional associations

alaska knifemakers association (1996 data)
A.W. Amoureux, John Arnold, Bud Aufdermauer, Robert Ball, J.D. Biggs, Lonnie Breuer, Tom Broome, Mark Bucholz, Irvin Campbell, Virgil Campbell, Raymond Cannon, Christopher Cawthorne, John Chamberlin, Bill Chatwood, George Cubic, Bob Cunningham, Gordon S. Dempsey, J.L. Devoll, James Dick, Art Dufour, Alan Eaker, Norm Grant, Gordon Grebe, Dave Highers, Alex Hunt, Dwight Jenkins, Hank Kubaiko, Bill Lance, Bob Levine, Michael Miller, John Palowski, Gordon Parrish, Mark W. Phillips, Frank Pratt, Guy Recknagle, Ron Robertson, Steve Robertson, Red Rowell, Dave Smith, Roger E. Smith, Gary R. Stafford, Keith Stegall, Wilbur Stegner, Norm Story, Robert D. Shaw, Thomas Trujillo, Ulys Whalen, Jim Whitman, Bob Willis.

arizona knifemakers association (1996 data)
D. "Butch" Beaver, Bill Cheatham, Dan Dagget, Tom Edwards, Anthony Goddard, Steve Hoel, Ken McFall, Milford Oliver, Jerry Poletis, Merle Poteet, Mike Quinn, Elmer Sams, Jim Sornberger, Glen Stockton, Bruce Thompson, Sandy Tudor, Charles Weiss.

arkansas knifemakers association (1996 data)
David Anders, Robert Bailey, Reggie Barker, Cecil Barnes, Keith Batts, Larry Beason, James Black, R.P. Black, Joel Bradford, Mike Brannan, Gary Braswell, J.C. Brown, Paul Brown, Richard Brown, Troy L. Brown, Jim Butler, Buddy Cabe, James Cook, Pat Crawford, Ed Crawley, Jim Crowell, Ben Daland, Harvey Dean, Lawrence Dungy, Steve Dunn, Fred Duvall, Jack East, Rodger Echols, David Etchieson, George Fant Jr., Lee Ferguson, Joe Finch, Jerry Fisk, John Fitch, Joe Flournoy, Dewayne Forrester, John Fortenbury, Ronnie Foster, Roger Freeze, Dewayne Funderburg, Bert Gaston, Ed Gentis, Roger George, Paul Giller, Walter M. Graves, Don Greenwaway, Arthur J. Gunn, Jr., Bobby J. Hamilton, John Heuston, Don Hicks, Larry Holler, H. Steven Holliman, Mark A. Hoyt, B.R. Hughes, Terry Johnson, Thomas Kirksey, Ben Lane, Alton Lawrence, Ronald Lichlyter, Roger D. Massey, Douglas Mays, Kim McClusky, Mike McCollum, John McKeehan, Joe McVay, Bart Messina, Richard C. Meyer, Clyde O'Dell, Henry Parker, John Perry, Pete Peterson, Cliff Polk, Ted Quandt, Craig Quattlebaum, Randy Rains, Vernon Red, Tim Richardson, Charles R. Robinson, J.D. Robson, Scott J. Robson, George R. Roth, Kenny Rowe, Pat Ryan, James Seale, Terry Shurtleff, Carroll Shoffner, Charles Sisemore, Roy Slaughter, Richard D. Smith, Scott Smith, Ray Smoker, Marvin Solomon, James W. Spears, Charles Stout, Arthur Tycer, Jerry L. Tyer, James Walker, Chuck Ward, Bryce White, David Wilson, Rick Wilson, Randy Wootton, Jimmy Worden, George Zimmerman.

australian knifemakers guild inc.
Peter Allan, Tim Anson, Peter Bald, Wayne Barrett, David Bassett, Leighton Beamsley, Alf Bennett, Peter Bennett, Wayne Bennett, Wally Bidgood, Peter Binns, Kenneth Bradford, David Brodziak, Stuart Burdett, Neil Charity, Gregory Chow, Bruce Crawley, John Creedy, Mark Crowley, Jamie Culpitt, Les Curry, Lance Davison, Steve Dawson, Brandon DeBomford, Jim Deering, Peter Del Raso, Glen Duncan, Chris Erickson, Marcus Everett, Steve Fulham, Thomas Gerner, Branko Giljevic, Eric Gillard, Russ Gillard, Peter Gordon, Judy Gottage, Stephen Gregory-Jones, Ronald Hansen, Frank Harbottle, Lloyd Harding, Ray Harris, Rod Harris, Max Harvey, Barry Hosking, John Hounslowe-Robinson, Michael Hunt, Myron Husiak, Zen Imports, Raymond Jenkins, Ross Johnston, John Jones, Jason Jonker, Simeon Jurkijevic, Wolf Kahrau, Peter Kandavnieks, Roger Keagle, Peter Kenny, Tasman Kerley, Max Kershaw, John Kilby, Murray Lanthois, Mitchell Lowe, Greg Lyell, Brian Mackle, Paul Maffi, Gerald Maybus, Maurice McCarthy, John Minogue, Peter Moncrieff, Dave Myhill, Donald Neil, George Nisselle, Peter Owen, Charles Parsons, John Pattison, Adrian Pearce, Chris Pennington, Mike Petersen, Peter Reardon, Daveid Ross, Fred Rowley, Murray Shanaughan, Gary Siemer, Kurt Simmonds, Warrick Smith, Keith Spencer, Jim Steele, Chuck Stewart, Jason Stone, David Strickland, Peter Tarling, Kelvin Thomas, Jim Thom, Doug Timbs, Len Van Dongen, Andre Ver Eecke, David Walford, Hardy Wangemann, Brendon Ware, Glen Waters, Sharyn Wells, David Whisker, Bob Wilhelm, Laurie Wilson, Joe Zemitis, David Zerbe.

california knifemakers association
Arnie Abegg, George J. Antinarelli, Everett Archer, Elmer Art, Gregory Barnes, Gordon Bishop, Russell Blackburn, Roger Bost, Doug "Tat" Brack, Clint Breshears, Buzz Brooks, Scot Brown, David Brunetta, Steven E. Bunyea, Darrell Campbell, David Cavallero, Frank Clay, T.C. Collins, ELR Cooper, James N. Copeland, Ewell M. Curtis, Jim Engman, Bob Engnath, Alex Felix, Jim Ferguson, John Ferguson, Dave Flowers, Ralph M. Freer, Bill Fried, Buster Gaston, Logwood Gion, Tony Goldbach, Russ Green, Richard A. Gutowski, Jerome Harris, Dolores Hayes, Bill Herndon, F. Mallory Hicklin, Neal A. Hodges, William D. Horner, Josh Hoy, Jim Jacks, Lawrence Johnson, Curtis J. Jones, Richard D. Keyes, John Kray, Bud Lang, Stephen Lindberg, R.W. Loveless, Lawrence Lund, "KC" Lund, John Mackie, Thomas Markey, Jade Marsh, James K. Mattis, John McGaughy, Jim Merritt, Jack Mills, Walt Modest, Emil Morgan, Gerald Morgan, Mike Murphy, William B. Murray, Thomas Orth, Bob Packard, Barry Evan Posner, John Radovich, Terry J. Ramey, Jeffrey Robertson, James L. Rodebaugh, Clark D. Rozas, Jack Rutigliano, Brian Saffran, Tom R. Smith, Gregg P. Songer, H. (Red) St. Cyr, James Stankovich, W.R. Stroman, Tony Swatton, Ken Tallent, Scott Taylor, Carolyn D. Tinker, Tru-Grit Inc., Michael P. Wallace, Jessie C. Ward, Wayne Watanabe, Troy L. Wellington, Harlan M. Willson, Doug Winberg, Barry B. Wood, Lee E. Wuchner.

knifemakers' guild of southern africa
George Baartman, Francois Basson, Peter Bauchop, Arno Bernard, Gert Bezuidenhout, Wolf Borger, Peet Bronkhorst, Rob Brown, Fred Burger, William Burger, Jacobus De Wet Coetzee, Z. André De Beer, André De Villiers, Gavin Dickerson, Roy H. Dunseith, Charl Du Plooy, J.M. Du Plooy, Dries Esterhuizen, Leigh Fogarty, Andrew Frankland, Ettoré Gianferrari, John Grey, Piet Grey, J.C. Greyling, Kevin Harvey, Howard Hitchmough, Des Horn, Ben Kleynhans, Willibald Kojetin, Mark Kretschmer, Fanie LaGrange, Garry Lombard, Steve Lombard, Theo Martins, Francois Massyn, Edward G. Mitchell, Willie Paulsen, Conrad Pienaar, David Schalk Pienaar, Jan Potgieter, Neels Pretorius, Hilton Purvis, Derek Rausch, Chris Reeve, Bertie Rietveld, Dean Riley, John Robertson, Mick Russel, Corrie Schoeman, Elke Schönert, Michael J. Skellern, Toi Skellern, Carel Smith, Ken Smythe, Brent E. Sandow, Graham Sparks, J.H. Stander, André E. Thorburn, Fanie Van Der Linde, Marius Van Der Vyver, Boekoe Van Rensburg, Marlene Van Schalkwyk, Sias Van Schalkwyk, Danie Van Wyk, Shalk Van Wyk, Ben Venter, Willie Venter, Gert Vermaak, René Vermeulen, Tony Victor, Peter Watson, Ted Whitfield, John Wilmot, Armin Winkler, Wollie Wolfaardt, Owen Wood.

midwest knifemakers association
E.R. Andrews III, Michael Ballinger, Frank Berlin, Charles Bolton, Stephen F. Burrows, Tony Cates, Mike Chesterman, Jim Cornelius, Larry Duvall, Bobby Eades, Jackie Emanuel, William Engle, David Feyh, George Gibson, James Haynes, Jerry Johnson, John A. Jones, Harvey King, Mickey Koval, Carl LeBlanc, Ron Lichlyter, George Martoncik, James May, Victor J. McCrakin, Gene Millard, William Miller, Corbin Newcomb, Chris Owen, A.D. Rardon, Archie Rardon, Max Smith, Ed Stewart, Charles Syslo, Ward Westbrook, Melvin Williams.

montana knifemaker's association
Angelique Adamson, Mike Alber, Robert Alderman, Darrel Alexander, Bruce Althoff, Mel Anderson, Doug and Connie Asay, Donald Babcock, Lyle Bainbridge, Jack Barnes, Wendell Barnes, Steve Becker, Robert Bizzell, Allen Blade, Gene Bland, R.J. (Ric) Bosshardt, Mark Boyer, Chuck Bragg, Paul Bray, Peter Bromley, Glenn Brown, Lyle Brunckhorst, Ed Caffrey, Jeff Carlisle, Alex Chase, Michael Clancy, Jake Clouse, Foy Cochran, Wade Colter, Jack Cory, Bob Crowder, Gary Debrock, Dennis DesJardins, Frank Dobesh, Elizabeth Dolbare, Audra Draper, Rick Dunkerley, Hugh Eddy M.D., Joel Ellefson, Joel Ellefson, Bruce Emery, Ray Ennis, Melvin Fassio, Gary Flohr, Wendell Fox, Barry Gallagher, Frank Gamble, Wayne Goddard, Jack Gohn, Bob Gray, James Hand, Barry Hands, Jeff Harkins, Scott Higginbotham, Howard Hill, Bob Hollar, Ken Hoy, Steve Hulett, Randy Janisko, Travis Johnson, Al Kajin, Dave Kauffman, George Kirtley, James Largent, Einar Larsen, Randy Liv-

ingston, Mel Long, Mike Mann, Turning Bear Mason, David McGonagle, Thomas McGuane, Larry Miller, Jim Minnick, Ed Mortenson, Louis Morton, Russell Moyer, Dick Murphy, David Neagle, Dan Nedved, Vaughn Oligny, Willard Patrick, Brian Peele, Eldon Peterson, Tony Piondexter, Joe Rapier, Raymond Rasmussen, Bill Reh, Kirk Rexroat, Jim Riddle, Lori Ristinen, Wayne Robbins, Gary Rodewald, Ed Schempp, Bob Schopp, Dean Schroeder, Randy Simon, Harry Smith, Josh Smith, Alfred St. Pierre, Art Swyhart, Shane Taylor, Jim Thill, Leon Thompson, Jack Todd, J.W. Townsend, Frank Towsley, Butch Vollotton, Bill Waldrup, Jim Walker, Ken Ward, Gerome Weinand, Daniel Winkler.

new england bladesmiths guild (1996 data)
Phillip Baldwin, Gary Barnes, Paul Champagne, Jimmy Fikes, Don Fogg, Larry Fuegen, Rob Hudson, Midk Langley, Louis Mills, Dan Maragni, Jim Schmidt, Wayne Valachovic and Tim Zowada.

north carolina custom knifemakers' guild (1996 data)
Dr. James Batson, Tim Britton, Thomas Brown, Dr. Robert Charlton, Donald Daniel, Travis Daniel, Billy Downs, Gary Gaddy, Major Garris, Mark Gottesman, Robert Grooms, Carol & Melvin Gurganus, George Guthrie, Jack Hyer, Barry Jones, Phillip Jones, Tony Kelly, Charles Ray Knowles, Robert Livingston, Danny Masser, Bill Maynard, Tommy McNabb, Alex Moss, James Parker, Alan Patterson, Charles Rece, Ben Ryder, J.D. Sams, Ellis Sawyer, Tim Scholl, H.R. Simmons, Russel Sutton, Robert Thomas, Mike Weaver, Wayne Whitley, Michael Wise.

ohio knifemakers association (1996 data)
Raymond Babcock, Van Barnett, Harold A. Collins, Larry Detty, Tom Downing, Jim Downs, Patty Ferrier, Jeff Flannery, James Fray, Bob Foster, Raymond Guess, Scott Hamrie, Rick Hinderer, Curtis Hurley, Ed Kalfayan, Michael Koval, Judy Koval, Larry Lunn, Stanley Maienknecht, Dave Marlott, Mike Mercer, David Morton, Patrick McGroder, Charles Pratt, Darrel Ralph, Roy Roddy, Carroll Shoemaker, John Smith, Clifton Smith, Art Summers, Jan Summers, Donald Tess, Dale Warther, John Wallingford, Earl Witsaman, Joanne Yurco, Mike Yurco.

south carolina association of knifemakers (1996 data)
Robert Branton, Richard Bridwell, Dan Cannady, Charles S. Cox, William DeFreest, Paula Easler, Russell Easler, Hal Gainey, Ron Gaston, Harry George, Dick Gillenwater, Mike Gregory, Wayne Hendrix, George Herron, Jerry Hucks, Ralph Kessler, Gene Langley, Dan Owens, Larry Page, Russ Peagler, Alvin Poston, Joe Prince, Ralph Smith, Rocky Thomas.

tennessee knifemakers association (1996 data)
John Bartlow, Doug Casteel, Harold Crisp, Larry Harley, John W. Walker, Harold Woodward, Harold Wright.

knife photo index

knives '98

directory

engravers

scrimshanders

leatherworkers/sheathmakers

etchers/carvers

handle artisans

knife photo index

knives '93-'97

The Knife Photo Index includes only the last five editions of photos.

a

b

c

d

e

f

g

h

i

j

k

l

m

n

o

p

q

r

s

t

u

v

w

y

z

engravers

scrimshanders

etchers/carvers

leatherwork/sheathmakers

handle artisans

specialty cutlers

The firms listed here are special in the sense that they make or market special kinds of knives made in facilities they own or control either in the U.S. or overseas. Or they are special because they make knives of unique design or function.

ACE OF BLADES
P.O. Box 1778
Herndon, VA 22070-1778
Phone: 703-904-8629
Specialties: Discreet personal defense cutlery by John Mitchell, owner and designer.

ADAMS INTERNATIONAL KNIFEWORKS
(See Importers & Foreign Cutlers)

ANZA FILE KNIVES
(See Blair Blades & Accessories—Mail-Order Sales)

B&D TRADING CO.
3935 Fair Hill Rd.
Fair Oaks, CA 95628
Phone: 916-967-9366;800-334-3790
FAX: 916-967-4873
Specialties: Carries the full line of Executive Edge—Brazil's locking folders.

BARTEAUX MACHETES, INC.
1916 S.E. 50th St.
Portland, OR 97215
Phone: 503-233-5880
FAX: 503-233-5838
Specialties: Machetes of high-carbon and stainless steel. Line greatly expanded of late.

BAY KNIFE COMPANY
37780 Hills Tech Drive
Farmington Hills, MI 48331
Phone: 810-848-0590
FAX: 810-848-6883
Specialties: Camping and survival knives; "The Cobra"

BENCHMADE KNIFE CO. INC.
300 Beaver Creek Rd.
Oregon City, OR 97045
Phone: 503-655-6004
FAX: 503-655-6223
Specialties: Balisong knives, tactical patterns in folders, axes and big knives. U.S. production.

BENCHMARK KNIVES
(See Gerber Legendary Blades—General Cutlers)

BERETTA U.S.A. CORP.
17601 Beretta Dr.
Accokeek, MD 20607
Phone: 301-283-2191
Specialties: A variety of Beretta-only designs, including folding tactical knives.

BROWNING
Rt. 1
Morgan, UT 84050
Phone: 800-333-3288
Specialties: Has its own name on sports knives of all kinds, all in Browning finish.

BRUNTON/LAKOTA U.S.A.
620 E. Monroe Ave.
Riverton, WY 82501
Phone: 307-856-6559
FAX: 307-856-8282
Specialties: Heavy-duty sports knives, straight and folding, on a distinctive design theme.

BULLFROG BRAND (See Lake & Walker)

BUSSE COMBAT KNIFE CO.
19203 12th
Wauseon, OH 43567
Phone: 419-923-6471
Specialties: Simple and very strong straight knife designs for tactical and expedition use.

COLD STEEL, INC.
2128-D Knoll Dr.
Ventura, CA 93003
Phone: 800-255-4716
FAX: 805-642-9727
Specialties: Variety of urban survival instruments—big in tantos. Bowie and Hunter; several new and exclusive specialty designs.

COLONIAL KNIFE CO., INC. (See General Cutlers)

CRIPPLE CREEK KNIVES
Rt. 1, Box 501B
Oldfort, TN 37362
Phone: 615-338-8418
Specialties: The same old maker, same old buffalo, same kind of knives, and Po' Boys under $50 besides.

CTECH PLASTICS ENGINEERING
Shaun Cavanaugh
266 Calle Pintoresco
San Clemente, CA 92672-7504
Specialties: Knives in thermosets and thermoplastics. Custom injection molding, prototype tooling and engineering services.

CUTCO KNIVES
(See Alcas Company, General Cutlers)

EMERSON KNIVES, INC.
P.O. Box 4325
Redondo Beach, CA 90278
Phone: 310-542-3050
Specialties: Production versions of original tactical bladeware from a top designer of such.

GATCO (GREAT AMERICAN TOOL CO., INC.)
P.O. Box 600
Getzville, NY 14068
Phone: 716-877-2200
Specialties: Besides their sharpeners, they now own and market Timberline knives and other Neely designs.

GENUINE ISSUE INC.
949 Middle Country Rd.
Selden, NY 11784
Phone: 516-696-3802
FAX: 516-696-3802

GRIZZLY KNIFE AND TACKLE CO.
P.O. Box 2219
Bellingham, WA 98227
Phone: 800-883-6423
Specialties: Wide variety in sports cutlery, including the Junglee line, mostly made overseas; direct-markets as Gorilla & Sons.

GT KNIVES
7716 Anjos Dr.
San Diego, CA 92126
Phone: 619-566-1511
FAX: 619-530-0734
WEB: http://www.coherent data.com/GTknives
Specialties: High-tech machined folders.

H&B FORGE CO.
235 Geisinger Rd.
Shiloh, OH 44878
Phone: 419-895-1856
Specialties: Tomahawks and throwing knives.

HONEYCUTT MARKETING, INC., DAN
3165 A-2 So. Campbell
St. Louis, MO 65807
Phone: 417-886-2888
FAX: 417-886-5664
Specialties: Manufacturer of the Honeycomb.

IMPERIAL SCHRADE CORP.
(See General Cutlers)

IRON MOUNTAIN KNIFE CO.
1270 Greg St.
Sparks, NV 89431-6005
Phone: 702-356-3632
FAX: 702-356-3640
Specialties: Line of fixed-blade hunters based on special patented handle shape.

KA-BAR KNIVES
(See Alcas Company, General Cutlers)

KATZ KNIVES, INC.
P.O. Box 730
Chandler, AZ 85224-0730
Phone: 602-786-9334
FAX: 602-786-9338

KELLAM KNIVES CO.
3422 Old Capitol Trail, Suite 831
Wilmington, DE 19808
Phone: 302-996-3386
FAX: 516-232-1747
Specialties: Makers of Lapp folders; extensive selection of hand-made Finnish knives.

KERSHAW/KAI CUTLERY CO.
25300 SW Parkway
Wilsonville, OR 97070
Phone: 503-682-1966; 800-325-2891
FAX: 503-682-7168
WEB: http://www.kershawknives.com
Specialties: Former Gerber designer's heavy-duty sports knives made overseas; also smaller "pocket jewelry"; handsome scrimshaw; new designs in using knives.

KNIVES OF ALASKA, INC.
715 N. Tone
Denison, TX 75020 (Southern office)
P.O. Box 675
Cordova, AK 99574 (Northern office)
Phone: 800-572-0980
FAX: 903-463-7165
Specialties: Husky edged tools for big game hunting and fishing.

LAKE & WALKER
P.O. Box 1210
Veneta, OR 97487-1210
Phone: 541-935-1635
FAX: 541-465-8973
Specialties: Bullfrog brand.

LAKOTA U.S.A. (See Brunton/Lakota U.S.A.)

LEATHERMAN TOOL GROUP, INC.
P.O. Box 20595
Portland, OR 97294
Phone: 503-253-7826
FAX: 503-253-7830
Specialties: All-in-one pocket tool in two sizes.

MAR KNIVES, INC., AL
5755 SW Jean Rd., Suite 101
Lake Oswego, OR 97035
Phone: 503-635-9229
FAX: 503-223-0467
Specialties: Founded by the late Al Mar, a designer, the company continues to market Mar's designs under the direction of Ann Mar.

MARBLE ARMS
420 Industrial Park
Gladstone, MI 49837
Phone: 906-428-3710
Specialties: The grand old Marble's knives again from the grand old U.P. stand.

MICRO TECHNOLOGY
932 36th Ct. SW
Vero Beach, FL 32968
Phone: 561-569-3058
Specialties: High-tech folders in their own works; some double-action liner locks.

MISSION KNIVES & TOOLS, INC.
P.O. Box 1616
San Juan Capistrano, CA 92693
Phone: 714-951-3879
Specialties: Titanium blade knives and all titanium folders. Currently supplying certified non-magnetic SPECWAR knives to the U.S. Navy SEALS and EOD teams.

MOKI (See Spyderco, Inc.)

MORTY THE KNIFE MAN, INC.
P.O. Box 630007
Little Neck, NY 11363-0007
Phone: 516-491-5764/800-247-2511
Specialties: Everything for the fish trade; own and make both U.S. and import brands; includes many working knives not easily found, as well as chain mesh protection gloves and aprons.

MUSEUM REPLICAS LTD.
2143 Gees Mill Rd., Box 840XZ
Conyers, GA 30207
Phone: 404-922-3703
Specialties: Authentic edged weapons of the ages, battle-ready—over 50 models; subsidiary of Atlanta Cutlery; catalog $2.

MYERCHIN MARINE CLASSICS
850 W. Randall Ave.
P.O. Box 911
Rialto, CA 92377
Phone: 909-875-3592
FAX: 909-874-6058
E-MAIL: myerchin@aol.com
Specialties: The Myerchin Offshore System—a quality cutlery package for the yachtsman or deep water sailor; supplier to the U.S. Navy and Coast Guard.

OUTDOOR EDGE CUTLERY CORP.
2888 Bluff St., Suite 130
Boulder, CO 80301
Phone: 303-652-8212
FAX: 303-652-8238
Specialties: All-in-one tools for preparing game and all-purpose field use.

PARAGON CUTLERY CO.
2015 Asheville Hwy.
Hendersonville, NC 28791

Phone: 704-697-8833
Specialties: Now selling automatic folders through appropriate channels; has other sports designs.

PILTDOWN PRODUCTIONS
Errett Callahan
2 Fredonia Ave.
Lynchburg, VA 24503
Phone: 804-528-3444
Specialties: Makes obsidian scalpels and knives; replicates Stone Age tools and weapons—all types—for museums and academia. $3 for catalog.

REMINGTON ARMS CO., INC.
870 Remington Drive
P.O. Box 700
Madison, NC 27025
Phone: 800-243-9700
Specialties: Old and new patterns in the Remington style and more to come.

SANTA FE STONEWORKS
3790 Cerrillos Rd.
Santa Fe, NM 87505
Phone:505-471-3953
FAX: 505-471-0036
Specialties: Embellished personal and gift cutlery and desk accessories.

SKYLINE TECHNOLOGY INC.
2 Pennsylvania Ave.
Malvern, PA 19355
Phone: 610-296-7501
Specialties: The current source for the swell old Woodsman's Pal.

SMITH & WESSON KNIVES
(See Taylor Cutlery, Importers)

SOG SPECIALTY KNIVES & TOOLS, INC.
6521 212th St. S.W.
Lynwood, WA 98036
Phone: 206-771-6230
FAX: 206-771-7689
Specialties: High-quality folding and combat knives, and a multi-tool, as well.

SPYDERCO, INC.
P.O. Box 800
Golden, CO 80402-0800
Phone: 303-279-8383; 800-525-7770
FAX: 303-278-2229
Specialties: Clipit folding knives; sharpening gear. Has kitchen and diving knives and new stuff every year. Sells Moki knives.

SWISS ARMY BRANDS LTD.
(See Importers & Foreign Cutlers)

TIMBERLINE (See GATCO)

TRU-BALANCE KNIFE CO.
P.O. Box 140555
Grand Rapids, MI 49514
Phone: 616-453-3679
Specialties: The late Harry McEvoy's full line of throwers—a design for any throwing job. Can provide custom-made throwing knives. Catalog and throwing instructions can be had with a SASE.

TURNER, P.J., KNIFE MFG., INC.
P.O. Box 1549
Afton, WY 83110
Phone: 307-886-3423
Specialties: A fold-up pick axe for elk hunters and other deep-woods travellers.

WYOMING KNIFE CORP.
101 Commerce Dr.
Ft. Collins, CO 80524
Phone: 303-224-3454
Specialties: A tool for dealing with game animals—gutting and skinning. Also makes a short folding saw, and the Powder River folders.

general cutlers

These are, plain and simple, knife factories. Some are giants; some not so big; some are a century old; some just two decades in existence. All market very complete lines of knives, generally through standard mercantile channels.

ALCAS COMPANY
1125 E. State St.
Olean, NY 14760
Phone: 716-372-3111
Specialties: Owns Cutco, a direct marketer of specialty household knives and KA-BAR Knives, now launched once again.

AMERICAN CONSUMER PRODUCTS, INC.
(See Ka-Bar Knives, Specialty Cutlers)

BEAR MGC CUTLERY
1111 Bear Blvd. SW
Jacksonville, AL 36265
Phone: 205-435-2227
FAX: 205-435-9348
Specialties: General line of traditional folders and belt knives—wide range of patterns.

BUCK KNIVES
1900 Weld Blvd.
El Cajon, CA 92020
Phone: 619-449-1100
FAX: 619-562-5774
Specialties: Creators of the belt folder syndrome; sturdy, solid working knives widely sold.

CAMILLUS CUTLERY CO.
54 Main St.
Camillus, NY 13031
Phone: 315-672-8111
FAX: 315-672-8832
Specialties: Long-time competitor in all phases of cutlery; military knife contractor; some neat pocketknife designs. Makes and markets Western knives.

CASE CUTLERY
Owens Way
Bradford, PA 16701
Phone: 800-523-6350
Specialties: At the same old stand producing the good base patterns, and widely advertised these days.

CHICAGO CUTLERY CO.
1536 Beech St.
Terre Haute, IN 47804
Phone: 800-457-2665
Specialties: Solid utility knives; a full line of kitchen cutlery; owned by General Housewares Corp.

COAST CUTLERY (See Importers & Foreign Cutlers)

COLONIAL KNIFE CO., INC.
Steve Paolantonio
Agnes at Magnolia St.
Providence, RI 02909
Phone: 800-556-7824
FAX: 401-421-2047
Specialties: Commercial pocketknives for competitive pricing; some belt knives.

FISKARS (See Gerber Legendary Blades)

GERBER LEGENDARY BLADES
14200 SW 72nd Ave.
Portland, OR 97223
Phone: 503-639-6161
FAX: 503-684-7008
Specialties: Well-known sports and dining cutlery line, plus Fiskars cutlery and Benchmark specialty knives.

GIESSER MESSERFABRIK GMBH, JOHANNES
(See Importers & Foreign Cutlers)

IMPERIAL SCHRADE CORP.
7 Schrade Ct.
Ellenville, NY 12428
Phone: 914-647-7601
FAX: 914-647-8701
Specialties: Probably the biggest; owns Imperial and Schrade. Sells many labels in several brands, U.S.-made and imported.

MORTY THE KNIFE MAN (See Specialty Cutlers)

ONTARIO KNIFE CO.
P.O. Box 145
Franklinville, NY 14737
Phone: 716-676-5527
FAX: 716-676-5535
Specialties: Some pocketknives; many styles of utility knives for household and restaurant use. Brands, both Hickory and Colonial Forge. Excellent values.

QUEEN CUTLERY
P.O. Box 500
Franklinville, NY 14737
Phone: 716-676-5527
FAX: 716-676-5535
Specialties: Old name. The line is growing, moving toward collector appeal.

SCHRADE CUTLERY CORP.
(See Imperial Schrade Corp.)

SWISS ARMY BRANDS LTD.
(See Importers & Foreign Cutlers)

UTICA CUTLERY CO.
820 Noyes St.
Utica, NY 13503
Phone: Outside NY 800-888-4223; 315-733-4663
FAX: 315-733-6602
Specialties: Nice line of pocketknives, including Barlows and hunters and working pattern knives. Brands: Kutmaster, Walco.

WESTERN CUTLERY (See Camillus Cutlery Co.)

importers & foreign cutlers

Knives are imported by almost every sort of commercial cutler, but the names here are those whose specialty is importing, whether it be their brand, famous overseas brands, or special knives for special purposes best made overseas. Every effort is made to keep the list updated, but importing is sometimes an uncertain endeavor.

ADAMS INTERNATIONAL KNIFEWORKS
8710 Rosewood Hills
Edwardsville, IL 62025
Phone: 618-656-9868
FAX: 618-656-9868
Specialties: Antique or current automatic knives designed for law enforcement, military and collectors. Largest dealer of Linder-Solingen, Germany knives; offers Muela, Cold Steel, SOG, Kershaw, Ka-Bar-Boker and Henckels to name a few.

AITOR-CUCHILLERIA DEL NORTE, S.A.
P.O. Box No. 1
48260 Ermua (Vizcaya)
SPAIN
Phone: 34-43-17 00 01
Specialties: Full range of Aitor products from jungle knives to folding pocketknives.

ARISTOCRAT (See Degen Knives, Inc.)

ATLANTA CUTLERY CORP.
2143 Gees Mill Rd.
Box 839XZ
Conyers, GA 30207
Phone: 404-922-3700
Specialties: Carefully chosen inventory from all over the world; selected Indian, Pakistani, Spanish, Japanese, German, English and Italian knives; often new ideas—a principal source for kukris.

BAILEY'S
P.O. Box 550
Laytonville, CA 95454
Specialties: Importers of Tuatahi brand axes from New Zealand.

BAKER, B.W. (See Svord Knives)

BELTRAME, FRANCESCO
Coltellerie F.lli Beltrame F&A
di Francesco & Armando snc
Via dei Fabbri 15
I-33085 Maniago (PN), ITALY
Phone: 011-39-427-71338
FAX: 011-39-427-71338

BOKER USA, INC.
1550 Balsam St.
Lakewood, CO 80215-3117
Phone: 303-462-0662
FAX: 303-462-0668
Specialties: Tree Brand knives and a host of new knives in the Boker USA label.

CAMPOS, IVAN DE ALMEIDA
Custom and Old Knives Trader
R. Stelio M. Loureiro, 206
Centro, Tatui, BRAZIL
Phone: 0152-512102 or 51-6952
FAX: 0152-514896
Specialties: Knives of all Brazilian makers.

C.A.S. IBERIA, INC./MUELA KNIVES
650 Industrial Blvd.
Sale Creek, TN 37373
Phone: 423-332-4700
FAX: 423-332-7248
Specialties: Knives made in Spain by people with an eye on U.S. custom makers.

CATOCTIN CUTLERY
P.O. Box 188
Smithsburg, MD 21783
Phone: 301-824-7416
FAX: 301-824-6138
Specialties: Full line of Aitor knives from Spain, others from Italy, Germany, the Philippines; wholesale only. Has own brands—Fox and Koncept, the latter U.S.-made.

CHRISTOPHER MFG., E. (See Knifemaking Supplies)

CLASSIC INDUSTRIES
1325 Howard Ave., Suite 408
Burlingame, CA 94010
Phone: 415-343-7196
FAX: 415-401-6061
Specialties: Hunting, sportsmen, pocket and kitchen knives and leather sheaths, manufactured in Pakistan factory.

COACH MARKETING (See Degen Knives, Inc.)

COAST CUTLERY CO.
2045 SE Ankeny St.
Portland, OR 97214
Phone: 503-234-4545
FAX: 503-234-4422
Specialties: Long-time large wholesaler now national Puma reps; exclusive Puma importer.

COLUMBIA PRODUCTS CO.
P.O. Box 1333
Sialkot 51310, PAKISTAN
Phone: 011-92-432-86921
FAX: 011-92-432-558417
Specialties: See Columbia Products Int'l.

COLUMBIA PRODUCTS INT'L
P.O. Box 8243
New York, NY 10116-8243
Phone: 201-854-8504
FAX: 201-854-7058
Specialties: Lockblade and slip-joint folders in old and new U.S.-style patterns; heavy-duty belt knives; low prices.

COMPASS INDUSTRIES, INC.
104 E. 25th St.
New York, NY 10010
Phone: 212-473-2614; 800-221-9904
FAX: 212-353-0826
Specialties: Imports for dealer trade from all over at many price and quality levels; two hot brands are Silver Falcon and Sportster.

CONAZ COLTELLERIE
dei F.lli Consigli-Scarperia
Via G. Giordani, 20
50038 Scarperia (Firenze), ITALY
Phone: 055-846197
FAX: 055-846603
Specialties: Handmade, handsharpened knives with horn handles.

CONFEDERATE STATES ARMORY
2143 Gees Mill Rd.
Box 839XZ
Conyers, GA 30207
Phone: 800-241-3664
Specialties: Replicas of Confederate arms of the Civil War.

CONSOLIDATED CUTLERY CO., INC.
696 NW Sharpe St.
Port St. Lucie, FL 34983
Phone: 407-878-6139/800-288-6288
Specialties: Hunting knives, wood-carving tools, stag-handled steak/carving sets, camping axes, knife sharpening steels.

CRAZY CROW TRADING POST
P.O. Box H-K96
Pottsboro, TX 75020
Phone: 903-463-1366
FAX: 903-463-7734
Specialties: Mountain man cutlery and fixings. Knife blades, books, knifemaking supplies; $3 for catalog.

DEGEN KNIVES, INC.
1701 W. Wernsing Ave.
Effingham, IL 62401
Phone: 800-953-3436
FAX: 217-347-3083
Specialties: Imports Degen Knives, locking folders and multi-function outdoorsman knives; and Aristocrat knives, premium sports and action cutlery made in the U.S. and in Seki, Japan.

DER FLEISSIGEN BEAVER
(The Busy Beaver)
Harvey Silk
P.O. Box 1166
64343 Griesheim, GERMANY
Phone: 06155-2232
FAX: +49-6155-2433
Specialties: Specialized importer/wholesaler of American custom-made knives; displays at 40 German antique knife fine arts exhibitions each year.

EKA (See Nichols Co.)

EMPIRE CUTLERY CORP.
12 Kruger Ct.
Clifton, NJ 07013
Phone: 201-472-5155; 800-325-6433
FAX: 201-779-0759
Specialties: Imports Frost knives from Mora in Sweden, including the new Swedish soldier's knives. Knives are priced to sell.

EXECUTIVE EDGE (See B&D Trading Co.)

FALLKNIVEN AB
Box 204
S-961 23 Boden, SWEDEN
Phone: Int. 011-46-921-54422
FAX: 011-46-921-54433
Specialties: Folders and hunting knives.

FORSCHNER GROUP, INC., THE
(See Swiss Army Brands Ltd.)

FREDIANI COLTELLI FINLANDESI
Via Lago Maggiore 41
I-21038 Leggiuno, ITALY
Phone: 0039 332 647 362
Specialties: Purveyors from Italy of fine Finnish knives, some with Italian decorative touches.

FROST CUTLERY CO. (See Mail-Order Sales)

FROSTS KNIFE MANUFACTURING (Mora, SWEDEN)
(See Scandia International)

GIESSER MESSERFABRIK GMBH, JOHANNES
P.O. Box 168; Waiblingerstr. 5+7
D-71349 Winnenden, GERMANY
Phone: 0049-7195-1808-0
FAX: 0049-7195-64466
Specialties: Manufacturer of professional and kitchen cutlery. See Illinois Cutlery and Markuse Corp.

GORILLA & SONS
(See Grizzly Knife and Tackle Co., Specialty Cutlers)

HENCKELS ZWILLINGSWORK, INC., J.A.
171 Saw Mill River Road
Hawthorne, NY 10532
Phone: 914-747-0300
FAX: 914-747-1850
Specialties: U.S. office of world-famous Solingen cutlers—high-quality pocket and sportsman's knives with the "twin" logo.

HIMALAYAN IMPORTS
225 W. Moana Ln., Suite 226
Reno, NV 89509
Specialties: Just one: Nepalese-made kukris, which they spell *khukuri*, hand-forged in that mountain kingdom.

ILLINOIS CUTLERY
P.O. Box 607
Barrington, IL 60011-0607
Phone: 847-426-5002
FAX: 847-426-4942
Specialties: Illinois Cutlery knives.

INTERNATIONAL CUTLERY LTD.
127 W. 25th - 5th Floor
New York, NY 10001
Phone: 212-924-7300

JOY ENTERPRISES
1104 53rd Court South
Mangonia Park, FL 33407
Phone: 561-863-3205
FAX: 561-863-3277
Specialties: Sporting and combat-style cutlery under the Fury label—full range. Folders and swords. Wholesale only.

JUNGLEE KNIVES
(See Grizzly Knife and Tackle Co., Specialty Cutlers)

KA-BAR KNIVES, Collector's Division
(See Alcas Company, General Cutlers)

KELLAM KNIVES CO.
3422 Old Capitol Trail, Suite 831
Wilmington, DE 19808
Phone: 302-996-3386
FAX: 516-232-1747
Specialties: Largest selection of Finnish knives; over 300 models from over 30 makers, everyday use to fancy collectibles.

KLÖTZLI (See Messer Klötzli)

KNIFE COLLECTORS ASSN.-JAPAN (See Murakami, Ichiro)

KNIFE IMPORTERS, INC.
P.O. Box 1000
Manchaca, TX 78652
Phone: 512-282-6860
FAX: 512-282-7504
Specialties: Eye Brand cutlery.

KOPROMED, USA
1701 Broadway, Suite 282
Vancouver, WA 98663
Phone: 360-695-8864
FAX: 360-690-8576
Specialties: U.S. distributor for Kopromed forged 440C hunting knives and table cutlery from Poland.

LEISURE PRODUCTS CORP.
P.O. Box 1171
Sialkot-51310, PAKISTAN
Phone: 92-432-86921/592009
FAX: 92-432-588417/591030
Specialties: A wide range of lockblade and slip-joint folders in old and new U.S.-style patterns; heavy-duty belt knives; low prices.

LINDER, CARL NACHF.
Erholungstr. 10
42699 Solingen, GERMANY
Phone: 0212-330856
FAX: 0212-337104

MARKUSE CORP., THE
10 Wheeling Ave.
Woburn, MA 01801
Phone: 617-932-9444
FAX: 617-933-1930
Specialties: U.S. agent for Johannes Giesser Messerfabrik GmbH's "Creative Collection" range of knives.

MARTTIINI KNIVES
P.O. Box 44 (Marttiinintie 3)
96101 Rovaniemi, FINLAND
Phone: 358-60-330330
FAX: 358-60-3303399
Specialties: Finnish knives straight from Finland's biggest cutler. Includes fancy Finn-type hunters.

MATTHEWS CUTLERY
4401 Sentry Dr., Suite K
Tucker, GA 30084
Phone: 404-939-6915
Specialties: Wholesalers only. Carries all major brands which include over 2,800 patterns. Has U.S. distribution for Linder-Solingen and others. Catalog $2.

MESSER KLÖTZLI
P.O. Box 104
CH-3400 Burgdorf, SWITZERLAND
Phone: 0041-34-422-2378
FAX: 0041-34-422-7693
Specialties: High-tech locking liner knives in carbon fiber; OEM manufacturing.

MORTY THE KNIFE MAN, INC. (See Specialty Cutlers)

MUELA (See C.A.S. Iberia, Inc./Muela)

MURAKAMI, ICHIRO
Knife Collectors Assn. Japan
Tokuda Nishi 4 chome, 76 banchi, Ginancho
Hashimagun, Gifu, JAPAN
Phone: 81 58 274 1960
FAX: 81 58 273 7369
Specialties: Buys collector-grade and commercial U.S. knives for sale in Japan.

MUSEUM REPLICAS LIMITED
2143 Gees Mill Rd., Box 839 XZ
Conyers, GA 30207
Phone: 404-922-3703
Specialties: Battle-ready hand-forged edged weapons. Carry swords, daggers, halberds, dirks and axes. Catalog $2.

NICHOLS CO.
P.O. Box 473, #5 The Green
Woodstock, VT 05091
Phone: 802-457-3970
FAX: 802-457-2051
Specialties: Importer/distributor of precision-engineered EKA pocketknives from Sweden; also fixed-blade knives from Norway and Finland.

NORMARK CORP.
Craig Weber
10395 Yellow Circle Drive
Minnetonka, MN 55343
Phone: 612-933-7060
FAX: 612-933-0046
Specialties: Scandinavian-made sturdy knives for fishermen; puuko-style belt knives for hunters; fillet knives. Good stainless steel.

PRECISE INTERNATIONAL
15 Corporate Dr.
Orangeburg, NY 10962
Phone: 800-431-2996
FAX: 914-425-4700
Specialties: Wenger Swiss Army knives.

PRO CUT
P.O. Box 2189
Downey, CA 90242
Phone: 800-356-8507
FAX: 310-803-4261
Specialties: Wholesale only. Imports historical medieval and samurai swords; armor and weapons, over 100 different models.

PUUKKO CUTLERY
P.O. Box 303
Wolf Lake, MN 56593
Phone: 218-538-6633
FAX: 218-538-6633
Specialties: A full and complete Finnish cutlery line, including the Puukko cutlery line, all custom/hand-forged. Offers Scandinavian or Nordic expertise on makers and knife values.

PUMA CUTLERY (See Coast Cutlery)

REFLECTIONS OF EUROPE
Peter Ward
151 Rochelle Ave.
Rochelle Park, NJ 07662
Phone: 201-845-8120
FAX: 201-843-8419
Specialties: Importer for Eberhard Schaaf kitchen cutlery and professional chef knives.

RUSSELL CO., A.G.
1705 Highway 71 North
Springdale, AR 72764
Phone: 501-751-7341
Specialties: Morseth knives; Russell-marked special designs—"Woods Walker," Sting, CIA letter opener, Russell One-Hand knives, lots more every year.

SCANDIA INTERNATIONAL, INC.
118 English Neighborhood Rd., P.O. Box 218
East Woodstock, CT 06244-0218
Phone: 860-928-9525
FAX: 860-928-1779
Specialties: U.S. importer of Frosts Knife Manufacturing AB of Mora, Sweden—over 800 models.

SPYDERCO, INC. (See Specialty Cutlers)

STAR SALES CO., INC.
1803 N. Central St., P.O. Box 1503
Knoxville, TN 37901
Phone: 615-524-0771
FAX: 615-524-4889
Specialties: New collector pocketknives; imports Star knives and Kissing Crane knives.

SUOMI SHOP (See Puukko Cutlery)

SVORD KNIVES
Smith Rd., RD 2
Waiuku, South Auckland, NEW ZEALAND
Phone: +64 9 235 8846
FAX: +64 9 298 7670
Specialties: New Zealand private cutler makes belt knives and commercial knives.

SWISS ARMY BRANDS LTD.
The Forschner Group, Inc.
One Research Drive
Shelton, CT 06484
Phone: 800-243-4032
FAX: 800-243-4006
Specialties: This is the Victorinox headquarters in the U.S.; all current production comes through here; manages service center also. Group also manages flow of excellent Forschner commercial and household cutlery.

TAYLOR CUTLERY
P.O. Box 1638
1736 N. Eastman Rd.
Kingsport, TN 37662
Phone: 423-247-2406, 800-251-0254
FAX: 423-247-5371
Specialties: Taylor-Seto folders and straight knives, a line of scrimshaw knives, stag handles and many other imports; mfg. Smith & Wesson knives.

UNITED CUTLERY CORP.
1425 United Blvd.
Sevierville, TN 37876
Phone: 423-428-2532
FAX: 423-428-2267
Specialties: Wholesale only. Purchases for resale only; manufacture a number of items in the U.S. now.

VALOR CORP.
5555 N.W. 36th Ave.
Miami, FL 33142
Phone: 305-633-0127
FAX: 305-634-4536
Specialties: Emphasizes lockback folders from overseas in popular styles. Over 100 knife models imported.

ZEST INTERNATIONAL
1500 NE Jackson St.
Minneapolis, MN 55413
Phone: 800-453-8937/612-781-5036
FAX: 612-781-1452
Specialties: Full line of sports cutlery—dozens of models—with Zest trademark in 440A steel.

ZWILLINGSWORK (See Henckels, J.A.)

knifemaking supplies

The firms listed here specialize in furnishing knifemaking supplies in small amounts. Professional knifemakers have their own sources for much of what they use, but often patronize some of these firms. All the companies listed below have catalogs of their products, some available for a charge. For information about obtaining one, send a self-addressed and stamped envelope to the company. Firms are listed here by their request. New firms may be included by sending a catalog or the like to our editorial offices. We cannot guarantee the company's performance.

AFRICAN IMPORT CO.
Alan Zanotti
20 Braunecker Rd.
Plymouth, MA 02360
Phone: 508-746-8552
Specialties: Exotic African handle materials such as elephant and fossil ivory; exotic skins and leathers.

ALASKAN ANTLERCRAFT & IVORY
Roland and Kathy Quimby
Apr. to Oct.: P.O. Box 350
Ester, AK 99725
Nov. to Mar.: Box 3175-RB
Casa Grande, AZ 85222
Phone: Summer: 907-479-9335; Winter: 520-723-5827
Specialties: Mammoth and fossil walrus ivory, oosick and antler.

AMERICAN SIEPMANN CORP.
65 Pixley Industrial Parkway
Rochester, NY 14624
Phone: 716-247-1640
Specialties: Manufactures Siepmann grinders.

ART JEWEL ENTERPRISES, LTD.
460 Randy Rd.
Carol Stream, IL 60188
Phone: 708-260-0400
FAX: 708-260-0486
Specialties: Handles—stag, ivory, pearl, horn, rosewood, ebony.

ATLANTA CUTLERY CORP.
2143 Gees Mill Rd., Box 839XE
Conyers, GA 30207
Phone: 800-241-3595
Specialties: Many blades and fixings to choose from; occasional special buys in cutlery handles, pocketknife blades and the like; complete kits for buckskinner knives, small pocketknives. Catalog $2.

BATAVIA ENGINEERING
P.O. Box 53
Magaliesburg, 2805, SOUTH AFRICA
Phone: +27142-771294
E-MAIL: batavia@www.caseynet.co.za
Specialties: Belt grinders (Cutlermatic and Mini Cutlermatic); Discmatic disc grinder; contact wheels. Damascus steel in various blends and patterns and stainless steel Damascus. Price sheet.

BILL'S CUSTOM CASES
P.O. Box 2
Dunsmuir, CA 96025
Phone: 916-235-0177 or 235-2455
FAX: 916-235-4959
Specialties: Soft knife cases made of Cordura, Propex, pig suede and leather.

BLADEMASTER GRINDERS
P.O. Box 812
Crowley, TX 76036
Phone: 817-473-1081
Specialties: Manufactures knifemaking machine called "Blademaster." Wholesale and retail.

BLADES "N" STUFF
1019 E. Palmer Ave.
Glendale, CA 91205
Phone: 818-956-5110
FAX: 818-956-5120
Specialties: Full line of supplies and equipment, including excellent selection of tropical woods. Does big business in custom-ground heat-treated blades in dozens of shapes. Catalog $5.

BOONE TRADING CO., INC.
Box BB
Brinnon, WA 98320
Phone: 206-796-4330
Specialties: Exotic handle materials including elephant, fossil walrus, mastodon, warthog and hippopotamus ivory. Also sambar stag, oosic, impala and sheephorn.

BORGER, WOLF
Benzstrasse 8
76676 Graben-Neudorf
GERMANY
Phone: 07255-8314
FAX: 07255-6921
Specialties: Supplies European knifemakers, and others. German text catalog—write for details.

BOYE KNIVES
P.O. Box 1238
Dolan Springs, AZ 86441
Phone: 520-767-4273
FAX: 520-767-3030
Specialties: Casts dendritic blades and bar stock for knifemaking. Information $1.

BRIAR KNIVES
Darrel Ralph
7032 E. Livingston Ave.
Renoldsburg, OH 43068
Phone: 614-577-1040, 614-241-9793 (pager)
Specialties: Sells commercial Damascus, titanium and carbon fiber.

BRONK'S KNIFEWORKS
C. Lyle Brunckhorst
23716 Bothell-Everett Hwy.
Country Village, Suite B
Bothell, WA 98021
Phone: 206-402-3484
WEB: http://www.net-tech.com/~bronks/bronks.htm
Specialties: Knifemaking school, supplies, blades and kits; professional sharpening and heat treating.

CHARLTON, LTD. (See Damascus-USA)

CHRISTOPHER MFG., E.
P.O. Box 685
Union City, TN 38281
Phone: 901-885-0374
FAX: 901-885-0440
Specialties: Knife supplies for buckskinners; much early American hardware; blades; catalog $5 (outside U.S. $6). Also has knives made overseas, including Bowie replicas.

COLLECTOR'S GALLERY (See Stover, Jeff)

CUSTOM FURNACES
P.O. Box 353
Randvaal, 1873, SOUTH AFRICA
Phone: +27 16 365 5723
FAX: +27 16 365 5738
E-MAIL: jj300155@cls.co.za
Specialties: Hardening and tempering furnaces.

CUSTOM KNIFEMAKER'S SUPPLY
Bob Schrimsher
P.O. Box 308
Emory, TX 75440
Phone: 903-473-3330
FAX: 903-743-2235
Specialties: Big catalog full of virtually everything for knifemaking. Their 21st year in business.

CUSTOM KRAFT
14919 Nebraska Ave.
Tampa, FL 33613
Phone: 813-972-5336
Specialties: Knifemakers Ron Miller and Reese Weiland make up Custom Craft; they specialize in hard-to-find knifemaking supplies like titanium naltex, safety gear, mills, taps, Fuller brand files, and Allen/spline drive screws, to name a few. Catalog $1.

CUTLERY SPECIALTIES
Dennis Blaine
22 Morris Ln.
Great Neck, NY 11024-1707
Phone: 516-829-5899
FAX: 516-773-8076
E-MAIL: dennis13@aol.com
Specialties: Sole agent for "Renaissance" wax/polish and other restoration and preservation materials. Also buy, sell and trade antique to custom made knives. Price list.

DAMASCUS-USA
149 Deans Farm Rd.
Tyner, NC 27980-9718
Phone: 919-221-2010
FAX: 919-221-2009
Specialties: Manufactures carbon and stainless Damascus bar stocks and blanks.

DAN'S WHETSTONE CO., INC.
130 Timbs Place
Hot Springs, AR 71913
Phone: 501-767-1616
FAX: 501-767-9598
Specialties: Traditional sharpening materials and abrasive products.

DIAMOND MACHINING TECHNOLOGY, INC.
85 Hayes Memorial Dr.
Marlborough, MA 01752
Phone: 508-481-5944
FAX: 508-485-3924
Specialties: Quality diamond sharpening tools to hone all knife edges, including a unique serrated knife sharpener for all serration sizes.

DIXIE GUN WORKS, INC.
P.O. Box 130
Union City, TN 38281
Phone: 901-885-0700
FAX: 901-885-0440
Specialties: Knife division sold to E. Christopher Mfg.

EKLUND
P.O. Box 483
Nome, AK 99762-0483
Phone: NA
Specialties: Exotic handle materials like fossil walrus ivory, fossil whale and mammoth bone, mammoth ivory, oosic horn and antler. Eskimo artifacts and trophy tusks; price sheet $1.

EZE-LAP DIAMOND PRODUCTS
3572 Arrowhead Dr.
Carson City, NV 89706
Phone: 800-843-4815, 702-888-9500
FAX: 702-888-9555
Specialties: Diamond-coated sharpening instruments, various sizes.

FIELDS, RICK B.
26401 Sandwich Pl.
Mt. Plymouth, FL 32776
Phone: 352-383-6270
FAX: 352-383-6270
Specialties: Fossil walrus, mammoth ivory and ancient bone. Price list.

FLITZ INTERNATIONAL, LTD.
821 Mohr Ave.
Waterford, WI 53185
Phone: 800-558-8611
FAX: 414-534-2991
Specialties: General line of polishers.

FORTUNE PRODUCTS, INC.
HC 04, Box 303
Hwy. 1431 E. (Smithwick)
Marble Falls, TX 78654
Phone: 210-693-6111
FAX: 210-693-6394
Specialties: "Accu-sharp" sharpeners.

GILMER WOOD CO.
2211 NW St. Helens Rd.
Portland, OR 97210
Phone: 503-274-1271
FAX: 503-274-9839
Specialties: They list 112 varieties of natural woods.

GOLDEN AGE ARMS CO.
115 E. High St.
P.O. Box 366
Ashley, OH 43003
Phone: 614-747-2488
Specialties: Many types of blades; stag for handles; cast items—much for the buckskinner. Catalog $4.

GRS CORP.
Don Glaser
P.O. Box 1153
900 Overlander St.
Emporia, KS 66801
Phone: 316-343-1084 (Kansas); 800-835-3519
FAX: 316-343-9640
Specialties: Engraving products such as the Gravermeister and the Gravermax.

HALPERN TITANIUM
Leslie Halpern
14 Maxwell Road
Monson, MA 01057
Phone: 888-23-8627
FAX: 888-283-8627
Specialties: Full line of titanium sheet and rod; G-10 and carbon fiber sheet; titanium pocket clip blanks; Kydex sheet. Call or fax for free brochure and price list.

HARMON, JOE T.
8014 Fisher Drive
Jonesboro, GA 30236
Phone: 770-471-0024
Specialties: Maker of mini mills, surface grinders, pin routers.

HAWKINS CUSTOM KNIVES & SUPPLIES
110 Buckeye Rd.
Fayetteville, GA 30214
Phone: 770-964-1177
FAX: 770-306-2877
Specialties: Various size steel blanks, belts, buffing compounds and wheels; stag and drill bits.

HAYDU, THOMAS G.
2507 Bimini Lane
Ft. Lauderdale, FL 33312
Phone: 305-792-0185
Specialties: Deluxe boxes for knives that stay at home—some from Tomway Corp. have tambour covers.

HILTARY INDUSTRIES
7117 Third Ave.
Scottsdale, AZ 85251
Phone: 602-994-5752
FAX: 602-994-3680
Specialties: Gemstones, Damascus, meteorite and exotic steels.

HOUSE OF MUZZLE LOADING, THE (See Blades "N" Stuff)

HOUSE OF TOOLS LTD.
#136, 8228 MacLeod Tr. S.E.
Calgary, AB T2H 2B8, CANADA
Phone: 403-258-0005
FAX: 403-252-0149
Specialties: 440C and ATS34 handle and bolster material, sand belts, buff wheels and a large selection of tools.

HoV KNIVES & SUPPLIES
Box 8005
S-700 08 Orebro, SWEDEN
Phone: 46-19-187466
FAX: 46-19-100685
Specialties: Blades, exotic woods, stabilized woods, Amber, MoP, Abalone, horn, recon, stone and steel. Catalog $3.

INDIAN JEWELERS SUPPLY CO.
Mlg: P.O. Box 1774
Gallup, NM 87305-1774
Shpg: 601 East Coal Ave.
Gallup, NM 87301-6005
Phone: 505-722-4451
FAX: 505-722-4172
Specialties: Native American jewelry stones, castings and findings at the professional level; jeweler tools and supplies; catalogs.

INDIAN RIDGE TRADERS (See Koval Knives, Inc.)

INTERAMCO INC.
5210 Exchange Dr.
Flint, MI 48507
Phone:810-732-8181
Specialties: Manufacturers Berger grinding machines.

JANTZ SUPPLY
P.O. Box 584-GD
Davis, OK 73030-0584
Phone: 405-369-2316
FAX: 405-369-3082
E-MAIL: jantz@brightok.net
WEB: http://www.jantzsupply.com
Specialties: Polishing and finishing supplies, engraving tools, abrasives and bluing equipment. Price list.

JOHNSON, R.B.
I.B.S. Int'l. Folder Supplies
Box 11
Clearwater, MN 55320
Phone: 320-558-6128
Specialties: Folder supplies, threaded pivot pins, stainless and black oxide screws, taps and compasses.

JOHNSON WOOD PRODUCTS
34968 Crystal Rd.
Strawberry Point, IA 52076
Phone: 319-933-4930 or 933-6504
Specialties: Fancy domestic and imported knife handle woods. Price list.

K&G FINISHING SUPPLIES
P.O. Box 980
Lakeside, AZ 85929
Phone: 800-972-1192
Specialties: Belts, buffers, compounds, grinders, knife blanks, steel, sharpeners, handle material.

KNIFE & CUTLERY PRODUCTS, INC.
4122 N. Troost Ave.
Kansas City, MO 64116
Phone: 816-454-9879
Specialties: Offers 14 pages of knifemaking supplies such as exotic woods, wheels, bar stock and blades in a variety of shapes. Catalog $2; list of pocketknives $1.

KNIFE AND GUN FINISHING SUPPLIES
P.O. Box 458
Lakeside, AZ 85929
Phone: 520-537-8877
FAX: 520-537-8066
Specialties: Complete line of machine and materials for knifemaking and metal finishing. Custom ground blades and lots of factory blades to choose from. Specializing in rare and exotic handle materials—oosic, ivory, rare hardwoods, horn, stag and stabilized woods. Catalog $2.

KNIVES, ETC.
2522 N. Meridian
Oklahoma City, OK 73107
Phone: 405-943-9221
FAX: 405-943-4924
Specialties: Exotic woods; variety of blade steels; stag.

KOVAL KNIVES, INC.
5819 Zarley St.
New Albany, OH 43054
Phone: 614-855-0777
FAX: 614-855-0945
Specialties: Full range of Micarta and other materials for handles; brass, nickel silver, steels; machines and supplies for all knifemaking; some knife kits; catalog.

KWIK-SHARP
350 N. Wheeler St.
Ft. Gibson, OK 74434

Phone: 918-478-2443
Specialties: Ceramic rod knife sharpeners.

LINDER-SOLINGEN KNIFE PARTS
4401 Sentry Dr., Suite K
Tucker, GA 30084
Phone: 404-939-6915
Specialties: German-made knifemaking parts and blades. Wholesale catalog—send $2.

LITTLE GIANT POWER HAMMER
420 4th Corso
Nebraska City, NE 68410
Phone: 402-873-6602
Specialties: Little Giant Power Hammer parts and service; rebuilt power hammers.

LIVESEY, NEWT
202 Raines Rd.
Siloam Springs, AR 72761
Phone: 501-549-3356
FAX: 501-549-3357

LOGISTICAL SOLUTION
P.O. Box 211961
Augusta, GA 30917
Phone: 650-0252
FAX: 706-860-1623
Specialties: Modular component knife carry/storage systems.

LOHMAN CO., FRED
3405 N.E. Broadway
Portland, OR 97232
Phone: 503-282-4567
FAX: 503—288-3533
Specialties: Sword polishing and handle wrapping service, quality replacement parts, for the restoration of Japanese-style swords, both new and old. Catalog $5.

MARKING METHODS, INC.
Laura Jimenez
301 S. Raymond Ave.
Alhambra, CA 91803-1531
Phone: 818-282-8823
FAX: 818-576-7564
Specialties: Manufacturer of electro-chemical etching equipment and supplies for the knifemaking trade—power units & kits, long life photo stencils, and accessories.

MASECRAFT SUPPLY CO.
170 Research Pkwy #3
P.O. Box 423
170 Research Pkwy. #3
Meriden, CT 06450
Phone: 800-682-5489, 203-238-3049
FAX: 203-238-2373
Specialties: Handle materials.

MEIER STEEL
Daryl Meier
75 Forge Rd.
Carbondale, IL 62901
Phone: 618-549-3234
FAX: 618-549-6239
Specialties: Supplier and creator of "Meier Steel." Price sheet.

MOTHER OF PEARL CO.
D.A. Culpepper
P.O. Box 445, 401 Old GA Rd.
Franklin, NC 28734
Phone: 704-524-6842;
FAX: 704-369-7809
Specialties: Pearl, black pearl, abalone, pink pearl, sheephorn, bone, buffalo horn, stingray skin, exotic leathers, snake skin.

NICHOLAS EQUIPMENT CO.
730 E. Washington St.
Sandusky, OH 44870
Phone: 419-626-6342
Specialties: Manufactures commercial grinding machines.

NORTHWEST KNIFE SUPPLY
525-L S.W. Calapooia Ave.
Sutherlin, OR 97479
Phone: 541-459-2216
FAX: 541-459-4460
Specialties: Coote grinders, Klingspor abrasives, exotic woods, Micarta, stag, other supplies. Catalog $2; foreign $4.

OREGON ABRASIVE & MFG. CO.
11303 NE 207th Ave.
Brush Prairie, WA 98606
Phone: 206-254-5400
FAX: 206-892-3025
Specialties: Sharpening stones made under their own roof, and sharpening systems based on those.

OZARK KNIFE
3165 S. Campbell
Springfield, MO 65807
Phone: 417-886-3888
FAX: 417-886-5664
Specialties: Offers list of custom knives for sale, plus general cutlery collectibles; Randall knives, shining Wave Damascus and mokume.

PAPAI, ABE
5013 N. 800 E.
New Carlisle, IN 46552
Specialties: Knife sharpeners.

PARAGON INDUSTRIES, INC.
2011 South Town East Blvd.
Mesquite, TX 75149-1122
Phone: 800-876-4328; 972-288-7557
FAX: 972-222-0646
Specialties: Manufacturer of knifemaker's heat-treating furnaces in five available sizes.

POPLIN, JAMES/POP KNIVES & SUPPLIES
103 Oak St.
Washington, GA 30673
Phone: 404-678-2729
Specialties: Sanding belts, handle screws, buffing wheels and compound woods for knife handles, etc.

PUGH, JIM
Mlg: P.O. Box 711
Azle, TX 76098
Shpg: 917 Carpenter St.
Azle, TX 76020
Phone: 817-444-2679
FAX: 817-444-5455
Specialties: Kydex sheath material; limited.

RADOS, JERRY
P.O. Box 531
7523E 5000 N. Rd.
Grant Park, IL 60940
Phone: 815-472-3350
FAX: 815-472-3944
Specialties: Offers many distinct patterns of Damascus in forged-to-shape blades or customer designs.

REACTIVE METALS STUDIO, INC.
P.O. Box 890
Clarkdale, AZ 86324
Phone: 520-634-3434
FAX: 520-634-6734
E-MAIL: reactive@sedona.net
Specialties: Phil Baldwin heads up another business and this is a source for titanium and like exotic metals plus the equipment for coloring or anodizing them.

REAL WOOD
36 Fourth St.
Dracut, MA 01826
Phone: 508-957-4899
Specialties: Exotic wood for knife handles; carry over 60 different species and are always adding more; catalog $1.

REPRODUCTION BLADES
17485 SW Pheasant Ln.
Beaverton, OR 97006
Phone: 503-848-9313
Specialties: Custom cast blades.

RIVERSIDE KNIFE & FORGE SUPPLY
205 W. Stillwell
DeQueen, AR 71832
Phone: 501-642-7643
FAX: 501-642-4023
Specialties: Grinders, belts, wood, steel, blade stamps, Riverside Stampmaster, trip hammer repair, parts and sales.

ROCKY MOUNTAIN KNIVES
George L. Conklin
P.O. Box 902, 615 Franklin
Ft. Benton, MT 59442
Phone: 406-622-3268
FAX: 406-622-5670
Specialties: Knife sharpening; supplies.

RUMMELL, HANK
10 Paradise Lane
Warwick, NY 10990
Phone: 914-469-9172
FAX: 914-469-5968

SANDPAPER, INC. OF ILLINOIS
270 Eisenhower Ln. N., Unit 5B
Lombard, IL 60148
Phone: 630-629-3320
FAX: 630-629-3324
Specialties: Coated abrasives in belts, sheets, rolls, discs or any coated abrasive specialty.

SCHELL, CLYDE M.
4735 N.E. Elliott Circle
Corvallis, OR 97330
Phone: 503-752-0235
Specialties: Knife and exotic wood material.

SCHEP'S FORGE
Box 83
Chapman, NE 68827
Phone: 308-986-2444
Specialties: Damascus steel made in Nebraska.

SHEFFIELD KNIFEMAKERS SUPPLY, INC.
P.O. Box 741107
Orange City, FL 32774-1107
Phone: 904-775-6453
FAX: 904-774-5754
Specialties: Full line of knifemaking materials and machinery. Includes large inventory of steels, handle materials, N.S., brass, copper, aluminum, abrasives and much more. Catalog $5.

SHINING WAVE METALS
P.O. Box 563
Snohomish, WA 98290-0563
Phone: 425-334-5569
FAX: 425-334-5569
Specialties: Phil Baldwin makes and sells mokume, Damascus and a variety of Japanese alloys (for furniture, not blades) to order or from stock. Wholesale only.

SMEDEFIRMA (See Strande, Poul)

SMITH ABRASIVES, INC.
1700 Sleepy Valley Rd.
Hot Springs, AR 71901
Phone: 501-321-2244
FAX: 501-321-9232

SMITH WHETSTONE, INC.
1700 Sleepy Valley Rd.
Hot Springs, AR 71901
Phone: 501-321-2244
FAX: 501-321-9232
Specialties: Sharpeners of every kind, ceramic sharpeners, oils, kits and polishing creams.

SMOLEN FORGE, INC.
Nick Smolen
Rt. 2, Box 191A
Westby, WA 54667
Phone: 608-634-3569
FAX: 608-634-3569
Specialties: Makes custom Damascus steel. Various patterns and steel combinations and mokume available. Makes jigs, fixtures and hydraulic presses.

STOVER, JEFF
Mlg: P.O. Box 43
Torrance, CA 90507
Shpg: 833 W. Torrance Blvd.
Torrance, CA 90502
Phone: 310-328-8904, 310-532-2166 (Gallery)
Specialties: Unique items for collectors and investors.

STRANDE, POUL
Soster Svenstrup Byvej 16
Dastrup 4130 Viby Sj
DENMARK
Phone: 01-45-46194305
FAX: 01-45-46195319
Specialties: Blades and Damascus blade stock.

SUEDMEIER, HARLAN "SID"
(See Little Giant Power Hammer)

TEXAS KNIFEMAKERS SUPPLY
10649 Haddington, Suite 180
Houston, TX 77043
Phone: 713-461-8632
FAX: 713-461-8221
Specialties: Bar stock, factory blades, much handle material; offers heat-treating; catalog $3.

TRIPLE GRIT (See Oregon Abrasive & Mfg. Co.)

TRU-GRIT, INC.
760 E. Francis St. #N
Ontario, CA 91761
Phone: 909-923-4116, 800-532-3336
Specialties: Complete selection of 3M, Norton, Klingspor and Hermes belts for grinding and polishing, also Burr-King and square wheel grinders, Baldor buffers and an excellent line of machines for knifemakers; ATS-34 and 440C steel.

WASHITA MOUNTAIN WHETSTONE CO.
P.O. Box 378
Lake Hamilton, AR 71951
Phone: 501-525-3914
Specialties: Knife sharpeners.

WILD WOODS
Jim Fray
P.O. Box 104

Monclova, OH 43542
Phone: 419-866-0435
FAX: 419-867-0656
Specialties: Stabilized woods in a variety of colors in four grades.

WILSON, R.W.
113 Kent Way
Weirton, WV 26062
Phone: 304-723-2771
Specialties: Full range of supplies, but sells nothing he doesn't use himself.

WOOD CARVERS SUPPLY, INC.
P.O. Box 7500-K
Englewood, FL 34295-7500
Phone: 941-698-0123
Specialties: Carving tools, etc.

WYVERN INDUSTRIES
P.O. Box 1564
Shady Cove, OR 97539-1564
Phone: NA
E-MAIL: dufiron1@aol.com
Specialties: Purveyors of the hard-to-get for those who use anvils in their work.

ZOWADA CUSTOM KNIVES
Tim Zowada
4509 E. Bear River Rd.
Boyne Falls, MI 49713
Phone: 616-348-5416
FAX: 616-348-5416
E-MAIL: tzowada@freeway.net
Specialties: Damascus bars and billets, mokume and gas forge kits.

mail-order sales

The firms listed here have come to our attention over a period of years. All publish lists or catalogs. Their specialties are listed; send a self-addressed and stamped envelope for information. Firms are included here upon request. New firms wishing to be included should send a catalog or the like to our editorial offices. We cannot guarantee the company's performance.

ADAMS INTERNATIONAL KNIFEWORKS
(See Importers & Foreign Cutlers)

AFRICAN IMPORT CO.
(See Knifemaking Supplies)

AMERICAN TARGET KNIVES
1030 Brownwood NW
Grand Rapids, MI 49504
Phone: 616-453-1998
Specialties: Throwing knives

ARIZONA CUSTOM KNIVES
Jay and Karen Sadow
8617 E. Clydesdale
Scottsdale, AZ 85258
Phone: 602-951-0699
Specialties: Custom and factory made knives, tactical and/or investment grade. Color catalog of wide selection, always available: $3 US/$5 INT'L. Buy, sell, trade, consign.

ARTHUR, GARY B.
Rt. 7 Box 215
Forest, VA 24551
Phone: 804-525-8315
FAX: 804-525-8364
Specialties: Sells, buys and trades custom-made, investment-grade knives.

ATLANTA CUTLERY CORP.
2143 Gees Mill Rd., Box 839XZ
Conyers, GA 30207
Phone: 404-922-3700
Specialties: Catalog on request; wide selection of knives; aims to provide working-quality knives and give good value; showroom. Catalog $2.

ATLANTIC BLADESMITHS/PETER STEBBINS
32 Bradford St.
Concord, MA 01742
Phone: 508-369-3608
Specialties: Factory and custom-made knives, over 100 in stock at all times, for immediate sale. List $3.

BALLARD CUTLERY
1495 Brummel Ave.
Elk Grove Village, IL 60007
Phone: 708-228-0070
FAX: 708-228-0077
Specialties: Special-purchase knives, all types. Tries for good buys.

BARRETT-SMYTHE, LTD.
127 East 69th St., 1A
New York, NY 10021
Phone: 212-249-5500
FAX: 212-249-5550
Specialties: One-of-a-kind folding knives on sale in uptown Manhatten at prices suitable for their station.

BASCH ENTERPRISES, PAUL CHARLES
111 W. Del Amo Blvd., Suite 1
Long Beach, CA 90805
Phone: 562-423-5362
FAX: 562-423-5792
Specialties: Buys, sells and trades handmade knives only; large stock; sets up 45 shows a year.

BECK'S CUTLERY SPECIALTIES
748F East Chatham St.
Cary, NC 27511
Phone: 919-460-0203
FAX: 919-460-1684
Specialties: South African Peter Bauchop's tactical designs; other U.S. big-ticket tactical names.

BELL SR., R.T. "BOB"
P.O. Box 690147
Orlando, FL 32869
Phone: 407-352-1082
Specialties: Wide range of quality knives.

BILL'S CUSTOM CASES (See Knifemaking Supplies)

BLADES "N" STUFF (See Knifemaking Supplies)

BLAIRS BLADES & ACCESSORIES
531 Main St., Suite 651
El Segundo, CA 90245
Phone: 310-322-1063
FAX: 310-322-3112
Specialties: Sales reps for Anza File Knives.

BLUE RIDGE KNIVES
Rt. 6, Box 185
Marion, VA 24354-9351
Phone: 540-783-6143
FAX: 540-783-9298
Specialties: Wholesale only; top brand knives.

BOONE TRADING CO., INC.
P.O. Box BB
Brinnon, WA 98320
Phone: 206-796-4330
Specialties: Ivory; catalog features scrimshawed and carved ivory-handled knives.

CARMEL CUTLERY
Dolores & 6th; P.O. Box 1346
Carmel, CA 93921
Phone: 408-624-6699
FAX: 408-624-6780
Specialties: Knife retailer; factory and custom knives.

CHRISTOPHER MFG., E.
P.O. Box 685
Union City, TN 38281
Phone: 901-885-0374
FAX: 901-885-0440

CLASSIC CUTLERY
39 Roosevelt Ave.
Hudson, NH 03051-2828
Phone: 603-883-1199
FAX: 603-883-1199
Specialties: Factory knives and accessories, all discounted. Also custom, rare and discontinued knives. Genuine stone handle materials, jigged bone and mother-of-pearl; from the common to the unusual. Huge catalog $5 (refundable).

COHEN & NEAL CUSTOM KNIVES
P.O. Box 831
Cockeysville, MD 21030
Phone: 410-628-6262

CORRADO CUTLERY
Otto Pomper
26 N. Clark St.
Chicago, IL 60602
Phone: 312-368-8450
FAX: 312-368-8451
WEB: http://www.otto-corrado.com
E-MAIL: info@otto-corrado.com
Specialties: Premier fine cutlery, gifts and gadgets.

CREATIVE SALES & MFG.
Box 550
Whitefish, MT 59937
Phone: 406-862-5533
FAX: 406-862-6229
Specialties: Patent knife sharpeners.

CUTLERY SHOPPE
P.O. Box 610
Meridian, ID 83680-0610
Phone: 800-231-1272; 208-884-7575
Specialties: Discounts; custom and unusual balisongs; fighting and military-type knives; catalog $1.

DAMASCUS-USA (See Knifemaking Supplies)

DENTON, J.W.
102 N. Main St., Box 429
Hiawassee, GA 30546
Phone: 706-896-2292
FAX: 706-896-1212
Specialties: Buys and sells Loveless knives—has lists.

EDGE CO. KNIVES
P.O. Box 826
Brattleboro, VT 05302
Phone: 800-732-9976
FAX: 802-257-1967
Specialties: A variety of opportunity knives.

EUROCHASSE
398 Greenwich Ave.
Greenwich, CT 06830
Phone: NA

FAZALARE, ROY
P.O. Box 1335
Agoura Hills, CA 91376
Phone: 818-879-6161
Specialties: Specializing in custom handmade multi-blade folders by makers such as Tony Bose, Eugene Shadley and Terry Davis.

FROST CUTLERY CO.
P.O. Box 22636
Chattanooga, TN 37422
Phone: 423-894-6079
FAX: 423-894-9576
Specialties: Domestic and imported cutlery, especially folders and pocketknives; Hen & Rooster brand.

GENUINE ISSUE, INC.
949 Middle Country Rd.
Selden, NY 11784
Phone: 516-696-3802
FAX: 516-696-3803
Specialties: Representing the Digby line.

GILMER WOOD CO. (See Knifemaking Supplies)

GODWIN, INC., G. GEDNEY
2139 Welsh Valley Rd.
Valley Forge, PA 19481
Phone: 610-783-0670
Specialties: Reenactment gear—18th and 19th century complete.

GOLDEN AGE ARMS CO. (See Knifemaking Supplies)

HAWKINS CUSTOM KNIVES & SUPPLIES
(See Knifemaking Supplies)

HAWTHORN GALLERIES, INC.
P.O. Box 6071
Branson, MO 65616
Phone: 417-335-2170
FAX: 417-335-2011
Specialties: Buys, sells and trades collector-grade knives by mail and at major shows.

HERITAGE ANTIQUE KNIVES
Bruce Voyles
P.O. Box 22171
Chattanooga, TN 37422
Phone: 423-894-8319
Specialties: Deals in old knives, mostly U.S. and English and mostly folders; some Bowies. List.

HOUSE OF TOOLS LTD.
#136, 8228 MacLeod Tr. SE

Calgary, Alberta, CANADA T2H 2B8
Phone: 403-258-0005
FAX: 403-252-0149
Specialties: 440C and ATS-34 handle and bolster material, sand belts, buff wheels and a large selection of tools.

HUNTER SERVICES
Fred Hunter
P.O. Box 14241
Parkville, MD 64152
Phone: 816-587-9959
FAX: 816-746-5680
E-MAIL: fhunter@kcnet.net
Specialties: Quality antique pocketknives and related items. Select custom and military cutlery. $6 for four lists per year, refunded on first order.

IRONSTONE DISTINCTIVE BLADEWARE
16350 S. Golden Rd.
Golden, CO 80401
Phone: 800-828-1925
FAX: 303-278-2057
Specialties: Carry full line of Spyderco products, as well as many other quality knives and sharpeners.

JARVIS, PAUL M.
30 Chalk St.
Cambridge, MA 02139
Phone: 617-547-4355
FAX: 617-491-2900
Specialties: Custom knives, Japanese sword fittings, metal carving.

JENCO SALES, INC.
P.O. Box 1000
Manchaca, TX 78652
Phone: 512-282-6860
FAX: 512-282-7504
Specialties: Full line of domestic and imported knives and accessories.

KELLEM KNIVES CO.
3422 Old Capitol Trail, Ste. 831
Wilmington, DE 19808
Phone: 302-996-3386
FAX: 516-232-1747
Specialties: Handmade Finnish knives; 18-page color brochure, $4 (refundable).

KENEFICK, DOUG
29 Leander St.
Danielson, CT 06239
Phone: 203-774-8929
Specialties: Excellent selection of Randall Made knives and custom knives at list prices; catalog on request.

KNIFE-AHOLICS UNANIMOUS
P.O. Box 831
Cockeysville, MD 21030
Phone: 410-628-6262
Specialties: David Cohen—purveyor of custom knives.

KNIFE & CUTLERY PRODUCTS, INC.
P.O. Box 12480
North Kansas City, MO 64116
Phone: 816-454-9879
Specialties: Sells brand-name commercial cutlery, some collectibles; 14-page list $2

KNIFE IMPORTERS, INC.
P.O. Box 1000
Manchaca, TX 78652
Phone: 512-282-6860
FAX: 512-282-7504
Specialties: Eye Brand cutlery.

KNIFEMASTERS CUSTOM KNIVES/J&S FEDER
P.O. Box 2419
Westport, CT 06880
Phone: 203-226-5211
FAX: 203-226-5312
Specialties: Dealers in fine investment grade custom knives.

KRIS CUTLERY
P.O. Box 133 KN
Pinole, CA 94564
Phone: 510-758-9912
FAX: 510-223-8968
Specialties: Medieval swords and daggers, Indonesian and Moro krisses, Damascus balisongs.

LDC CUSTOM KNIVES
P.O. Box 211961
Augusta, GA 30917
Phone: 706-650-0252
FAX: 706-860-1623
Specialties: Specializing in collectible custom combat knives.

LES COUTEAUX CHOISSIS DE ROBERTS
Ron Roberts
P.O. Box 273
Mifflin, PA 17058
Phone: 717-436-5010
FAX: 717-436-9691
Specialties: Handles all types of manufacturers knives and related items for collectors and users.

LONDON, RICK
P.O. Box 21303
Oakland, CA 94620
Phone: 510-482-2775
Specialties: Purveyor of collectible knives. A special eye for fine crafted folders.

LOVELESS KNIVES (See Denton, J.W.)

MATTHEWS CUTLERY
4401 Sentry Dr., Suite K
Tucker, GA 30084
Phone: 404-939-6915
Specialties: Wholesale only. Carries major brands; monthly sale lists. Catalog (96 pages) $2.

MORTY THE KNIFE MAN, INC.
4 Manorhaven Blvd.
Port Washington, NY 11050
Phone: 516-767-2357
FAX: 516-767-7058
Specialties: The world's fish knives—all of them.

MURAKAMI, ICHIRO (See Importers & Foreign Cutlers)

MUSEUM REPLICAS LTD.
2143 Gees Mill Rd., Box 840XZ
Conyers, GA 30207
Phone: 404-922-3703
Specialties: Authentic edged weapons of the ages, battle-ready—over 50 models; subsidiary of Atlanta Cutlery; catalog $2.

NASHOBA VALLEY KNIFEWORKS
373 Langen Rd., Box 35
Lancaster, MA 01523
Phone: 508-365-6593
FAX: 508-368-4171
Specialties: Custom sales, emphasis on Guild members knives, plus Randall and Ruana. Large inventory; 6 lists a year. List $2.

NORDIC KNIVES
1634CZ Copenhagen Dr.
Solvang, CA 93463
Phone: 805-688-3612
Specialties: Custom and Randall knives; custom catalog $3; Randall catalog $2; both catalogs $4.

PARKER'S KNIFE COLLECTOR SERVICE
6715 Heritage Business court
Chattanooga, TN 37422
Phone: 423-892-0448
Specialties: Highly specialized into limited run case folders for modern collectors.

PEN AND THE SWORD LTD., THE
1833 E. 12th St.
Brooklyn, NY 11229
Phone: 718-382-4847
FAX: 718-376-5745
Specialties: Custom knives in a wide price range.

PLAZA CUTLERY, INC.
3333 S. Bristol St., South Coast Plaza
Costa Mesa, CA 92626
Phone: 714-549-3932
Specialties: List of custom knives for collectors, many top names every time; $1.

RAMSHEAD ARMOURY, INC.
P.O. Box 85
Maryville, IL 62062-0085
Phone: 888-ARMOURY
FAX: 888-ARMOURY
Specialties: Stocks swords, daggers and such for the Renaissance dragon-slaying-tournament trade. Catalog $2.

REPRODUCTION BLADES (See Knifemaking Supplies)

RIVERSIDE MACHINE (See Knifemaking Supplies)

ROBERTSON'S CUSTOM CUTLERY
P.O. Box 211961
Augusta, GA 30917
Phone: 706-650-0252
FAX: 706-860-1623
Specialties: Combat cutlery, investment grade knives and one-of-a-kind pieces. Catalog $5 US/$10 INTL.

ROBINSON, ROBERT W.
1569 N. Finley Pt.
Polson, MT 59860
Phone: 406-887-2259
FAX: 406-887-2259
Specialties: Investment grade modern, ancient, fixed and folding.

RUMMELL, HANK
10 Paradise Lane
Warwick, NY 10990
Phone: 914-469-9172
FAX: 914-469-5968

RUSSELL CO., A.G.
1705 Highway 71 North
Springdale, AR 72764
Phone: 501-751-7341; 800-255-9034
Specialties: Regularly lists custom knives by all makers; sold on consignment; also commemoratives, Russell and Morseth knives.

SHAW, GARY
24 Central Ave.
Ridgefield Park, NJ 07660
Phone: 201-641-8801
Specialties: Investment-grade knives of all kinds.

SMOKY MOUNTAIN KNIFE WORKS
P.O. Box 4430
Sevierville, TN 37864
Phone: 800-251-9306
Specialties: Retail and wholesale sales of all kinds of knives and supplies.

STIDHAM'S KNIVES
Rhett and Janie Stidham
P.O. Box 570
Roseland, FL 32957-0570
Phone: 561-589-0618
FAX: 561-589-3162
Specialties: Purveyors of fine custom knives—antique knives, military knives. Founders of Randall Knife Collectors Society.

STODDARD'S, INC.
Copley Place
100 Huntington Ave.
Boston, MA 02116
Phone: 617-536-8688
FAX: 617-357-8263
Specialties: Oldest cutlery retailer in the country; handmade and Randall knives, other fine production knives—Spyderco and Al Mar knives, etc. Manager: Steven Weingrad. Two additional stores in MA area.

STONEWORKS
P.O. Box 211961
Augusta, GA 30917
Phone: 706-650-0252
FAX: 706-860-1623
Specialties: Exclusively designed custom knives with exotic stone handles.

TEXAS KNIFEMAKERS SUPPLY
10649 Haddington, Suite 180
Houston, TX 77043
Phone: 713-461-8632
Specialties: Bar stock, factory blades, much handle material; offers heat-treating; catalog $3.

WASHITA MOUNTAIN WHETSTONE CO.
P.O. Box 378
Lake Hamilton, AR 71951
Phone: 501-525-3914
Specialties: Manufactures sharpening stones and wood products for custom wood boxes for many knife companies.

knife services

engravers

Adlam, Tim, 1705 Witzel Ave., Oshkosh, WI 54901/414-235-4589
Alfano, Sam, 36180 Henry Gaines Rd., Pearl River, LA 70452/504-863-3364; FAX: 504-863-7715
Allard, Gary, Creek Side Metal & Wood, 2395 Battlefield Rd., Fishers Hill, VA 22626/540-465-3903
Allred, Scott, 2403 Lansing Blvd., Wichita Falls, TX 76309/817-691-9563
Alpen, Ralph, 7 Bentley Rd., West Grove, PA 19390/215-869-9493
American Etching (See Miller, James K. and Vicky)
Baron Technology, Inc., David Baron, 62 Spring Hill Rd., Trumbull, CT 06611/203-452-0515; FAX: 203-452-0663
Barnett, Van, P.O. Box 1012, New Haven, WV 25265/304-882-3481
Bates, Billy, 2302 Winthrop Dr. SW, Decatur, AL 35603/205-355-3690
Beaver, Judy, 48835 N. 25 Ave., Phoenix, AZ 85027/602-465-7831; FAX: 602-465-7077
Becker, Franz, Am Kreuzberg 2, 84533 Marktl/Inn, GERMANY/08678-8020
Bettenhausen, Merle L., 17358 Ottawa, Tinley Park, IL 60477/708-532-2179
Blair, Jim, P.O. Box 64, 59 Mesa Verde, Glenrock, WY 82637/307-436-8115
Blanchard, Gary, 3025 Las Vegas Blvd. S., #120, Las Vegas, NV 89109/702-733-8333; FAX: 702-732-0333
Bleile, C. Roger, 5040 Ralph Ave., Cincinnati, OH 45238/513-251-0249
Bonshire, Benita, 1121 Burlington, Muncie, IN 47302/317-282-9073
Boster, A.D., 3744 Pleasant Hill Dr., Gainesville, GA 30504/404-535-8811
Bratcher, Dan, 311 Belle Aire Pl., Carthage, MO 64836/417-356-1518
Brooker, Dennis B., Rt. 1 Box 12A, Derby, IA 50068/515-533-2103
Churchill, Winston G., RFD Box 29B, Proctorsville, VT 05153/802-226-7772
Coffey, Barbara, RR 3 Box 662, Monroe, VA 24574-9600
Collins, David, Rt. 2 Box 425, Monroe, VA 24574/804-922-7465
Collins, Michael, Rt. 3075, Batesville Rd., Woodstock, GA 30188/404-475-7410
Creek Side Metal & Wood (See Allard, Gary)
Cupp, Alana, P.O. Box 207, Annabella, UT 84711/801-896-4834
Dashwood, Jim, 255 Barkham Rd., Wokingham, Berkshire RG11 4BY, ENGLAND/0734-781761
Davidson, Jere, Rt. 1, Box 132, Rustburg, VA 24588/804-821-3637
Dean, Bruce, 13 Tressider Ave., Haberfield, N.S.W. 2045, AUSTRALIA/02-797-7608
DeLorge, Ed, 2231 Hwy. 308, Thibodaux, LA 70301/504-447-1633
Dickson, John W., P.O. Box 49914, Sarasota, FL 34230/941-952-1907
Dolbare, Elizabeth, P.O. Box 222, Sunburst, MT 59482/403-647-2479
Downing, Jim, P.O. Box 4224, Springfield, MO 65808/417-865-5953
Drain, Mark, SE 3211 Kamilche Pt. Rd., Shelton, WA 98584/206-426-5452
Duarte, Carlos, 108 Church St., Rossville, CA 95678
Dubben, Michael, 414 S. Fares Ave., Evansville, IN 47714
Dubber, Michael W., P.O. Box 4365, Estes Park, CO 80517-4365/303-586-2388
Duguet, Thierry D., Rt. 250 W., Box 288, Ivy, VA 22945/804-977-4138
Eklund, Maihkel, Föne 1155, S-82041 Färila, SWEDEN/+46 651 24192
Eldridge, Allan, 1424 Kansas Lane, Gallatin, TN 37066/615-452-6027
Engel, Terry (Flowers), P.O. Box 96, Midland, OR 97634/503-882-1323
Eyster, Ken, Heritage Gunsmiths, Inc., 6441 Bishop Rd., Centerburg, OH 43011/614-625-6131
Fisher, Jay, 104 S. Main St., P.O. Box 267, Magdela, NM 87825/505-854-2407
Flannery Engraving Co., Jeff, 11034 Riddles Run Rd., Union, KY 41091/606-384-3127
Foster Enterprises, Norvell Foster, P.O. Box 200343, San Antonio, TX 78220/210-333-1675
Fountain Products, 492 Prospect Ave., West Springfield, MA 01089/413-781-4651; FAX: 413-733-8217
French, J.R., 1712 Creek Ridge Ct., Irving, TX 75060/214-254-2645
George, Tim and Christy, Rt. 1, Box 45, Evington, VA 24550
Gipe, Sandi, Rt. 2, Box 1090A, Kendrick, ID 83537
Glimm, Jerome C., 19 S. Maryland, Conrad, MT 59425/406-278-3574
Gournet, Geoffroy, 820 Paxinosa Ave., Easton, PA 18042/610-559-0710
Hands, Barry Lee, 26192 E. Shore Rte., Bigfork, MT 59911/406-837-0035
Harrington, Fred A., Winter: 3725 Citrus, St. James City, FL 33956/941-283-0721; Summer: 2107 W. Frances Rd., Mt. Morris, MI 48458/810-686-3008
Henderson, Fred D., 569 Santa Barbara Dr., Forest Park, GA 30297/770-968-4866
Hendricks, Frank, HC03, Box 434, Dripping Springs, TX 78620/512-858-7828
Heritage Gunsmiths, Inc. (See Eyster, Ken)
Holder, Pat, 7148 W. Country Gables Dr., Peoria, AZ 85381/602-878-3064; FAX: 602-878-3964
Houser, Jesse, P.O. Box 993, Biscoe, NC 27209
Hudson, Tommy, P.O. Box 2046, Monroe, NC 28110/704-283-8556
Ingle, Ralph W., 112 Manchester Ct., Centerville, GA 31028/912-953-5824
Jiantonio, Robert, P.O. Box 986, Venice, FL 34284/941-497-0347
Johns, Bill, 7927 Ranch Rd. 965, Fredericksburg, TX 78624/210-997-6795
Kelly, Lance, 1723 Willow Oak Dr., Edgewater, FL 32132/904-423-4933
Kelso, Jim, RD 1, Box 5300, Worcester, VT 05682/802-229-4254
Koevenig's Engraving Service, Koevenig, Eugene and Eve, Rabbit Gulch, Box 55, Hill City, SD 57745-0055/605-574-2239
Kostelnik, Joe and Patty, RD #4, Box 323, Greensburg, PA 15601/412-832-0365
Kraft, Brenda, Box 1143, Polson, MT 59860
Kudlas, John M., 622 14th St. SE, Rochester, MN 55904/507-288-5579
Lee, Ray, 209 Jefferson Dr., Lynchburg, VA 24502/804-237-2918
Limings Jr., Harry, 959 County Rd. 170, Marengo, OH 43334-9625
Lindsay, Steve, 3714 West Cedar Hills Drive, Kearney, NE 68847/308-236-7885; WEB:http://www.nyx.net/~slindsay; E-MAIL:slindsay@nyx.cs.du.edu
Lister, Weldon, Rt. 1, Box 1517, Boerne, TX 78006/210-755-2210
Lyttle, Brian, Box 5697, High River, AB T1V 1M7, CANADA/403-558-3638
Lytton, Simon M., 19 Pinewood Gardens, Hemel Hempstead, Herts. HP1 1TN, ENGLAND/01442-255542
McCombs, Leo, 1862 White Cemetery Rd., Patriot, OH 45658/614-256-1714
McDonald, Dennis, 8359 Brady St., Peosta, IA 52068/319-556-7940
McKenzie, Lynton, 6940 N. Alvernon Way, Tucson, AZ 85718/602-299-5090
Meyer, Chris, 39 Bergen Ave., Wantage, NJ 07461
Miller, James K. and Vicky, American Etching, 22500 Hwy. 72 W., Tuscumbia, AL 35674/205-381-1747
Montgomery, Charles, 4517 Summer Ave., Memphis, TN 38122/901-763-3053
Morgan, Tandie, P.O. Box 693, 30700 Hwy. 97, Nucla, CO 81424/303-864-7985
Morton, David A., 1110 W. 21st St., Lorain, OH 44052/216-245-3419
Moschetti, Mitch, 1435 S. Elizabeth, Denver, CO 80210/303-765-2843
Mountain States Engraving (See Warren, Kenneth)
Nelida, Toniutti, via G. Pasconi 29/c, Maniago 33085 (PN), ITALY
Norton, Jeff, 2009 65th St., Lubbock, TX 79412/806-744-2436
Nott, Ron, Box 281, Summerdale, PA 17093/717-732-2763
Parsons, Michael R., 1600 S. 11th St., Terre Haute, IN 47802-1722/812-234-1679
Patterson, W.H., P.O. Drawer DK, College Station, TX 77841/409-846-9257
Perdue, David L., Rt. 1 Box 657, Gladys, VA 24554/804-283-5300
Peri, Valerio, Via Meucci 12, Gardone V.T. 25063, ITALY
Pilkington Jr., Scott, P.O. Box 97, Monteagle, TN 37356/615-924-3475
Poag, James, RR1, Box 212A, Grayville, IL 62844/618-375-7106
Potts, Wayne, 912 Poplar St., Denver, CO 80220/303-355-5462
Poulakis, Jon, 58 Redfern Dr., Rochester, NY 14620-4618
Rabeno, Martin, Spook Hollow Trading Co., 92 Spook Hole Rd., Ellenville, NY 12428/914-647-4567
Raftis, Andrew, 2743 N. Sheffield, Chicago, IL 60614/312-871-6699
Reed, Chris, 4399 Bonny Mede Ct., Jackson, MI 49201/517-764-4387
Roberts, J.J., 7808 Lake Dr., Manassas, VA 22111/703-330-0448
Robidoux, Roland J., DMR Fine Engraving, 25 N. Federal Hwy. Studio 5, Dania, FL 33004/305-926-8040; FAX: 305-926-7955
Robyn, Jon, 232 Meriweather Rd., Lynchburg, VA 24503/804-384-7240
Rosser, Bob, Hand Engraving, 1824 29th Ave. South, Suite 214, Birmingham, AL 35209/205-870-4422; FAX: 205-870-4421

Rudolph, Gil, 386 Mariposa Dr., Ventura, CA 93001/805-643-4005
Rundell, Joe, 6198 W. Frances Rd., Clio, MI 48420/810-687-0559
Schickl, L., Ottingweg 497, A-5580 Tamsweg, AUSTRIA/0043-6474-8583
Schlott, Harald, Zingster Str. 26, 13051 Berlin, GERMANY/ +49(030)9293346
Schönert, Elke, 18 Lansdowne Pl., Central, Port Elizabeth, SOUTH AFRICA
Shaw, Bruce, P.O. Box 545, Pacific Grove, CA 93950/408-646-1937
Shelor, Ben, Rte. 1, Box 118 E 2A, Newtown, VA 23126/804-769-1103
Sherwood, George, 46 North River Dr., Roseburg, OR 97470/541-672-3159
Shostle, Ben, 1121 Burlington, Muncie, IN 47302/317-282-9073
Sinclair, W.P., 3, The Pippins, Warminster, Wiltshire BA12 8TH, ENGLAND/44 985 218544; FAX: 44 985 214111
Smith, Jerry, 7029 East Holmes Rd., Memphis, TN 38125/901-755-2648
Smith, Ron, 5869 Straley, Ft. Worth, TX 76114/817-732-6768
Smitty's Engraving, 800 N. Anderson Rd., Choctaw, OK 73020/405-769-3031
Spode, Peter, Tresaith, Newland, Malvern, Worcestershire WR13 5AY, ENGLAND/01886-832249
Steduto, Giovanni, Gardone, V.T. ITALY
Swartley, Robert D., 2800 Pine St., Napa, CA 94558/707-255-1394
Takeuchi, Shigetoshi, 21-14-1-Chome kamimuneoka Shiki shi, 353 Saitama, JAPAN
Theis, Terry, P.O. Box 535, 135 E. Main, Fredericksburg, TX 78624/210-997-6778
Thierry, Ivan, 15 Côte de Villancé, 28350 Saint-Lubin-des-Joncherets, FRANCE/33 232 582865; FAX: 33 232 583831
Valade Engraving, Robert B., 931 3rd Ave., Seaside, OR 97138/503-738-7672
VanHoy, Tanya, 1389 Hogan Farm Road, Star, NC 27356/910-428-4390
Waldrop, Mark, 14562 SE 1st Ave. Rd., Summerfield, FL 34491/904-347-9034
Walker, Patricia, 2925 Powell St., Eugene, OR 97405/541-484-5625; FAX: 541-465-8973
Wallace, Terry, 385 San Marino, Vallejo, CA 94589/707-642-7041
Warenski, Julie, 590 East 500 N., Richfield, UT 84701/801-896-5319; E-MAIL: jewel@inqua.net
Warren, Kenneth W., Mountain States Engraving, P.O. Box 2842, Wenatchee, WA 98807-2842/509-663-6123; FAX: 509-663-6123
Watson, Silvia, 350 Jennifer Lane, Driftwood, TX 78619/512-847-9679
Whitehead, James D., 204 Cappucino Way, Sacramento, CA 95838/916-641-7309; FAX: 916-641-1941
Whitmore, Jerry, 1740 Churchill Dr., Oakland, OR 97462/541-459-5497; FAX: 541-459-4854
Wilkerson, Dan, 2032 Westover Ave., Roanoke, VA 24105
Williams, Gary, 221 Autumn Way, Elizabeth, KY 42701
Willig, Claus, Siedlerweg 17, 97422 Schweinfurt, GERMANY/01149-9727-41446; FAX: 01149-9727-44413
Winn, Travis A., 558 E. 3065 S., Salt Lake City, UT 84106/801-467-5957, 801-328-0573
Wood, Mel, P.O. Box 1255, Sierra Vista, AZ 85636/602-455-5541
Zietz, Dennis, 5906 40th Ave., Kenosha, WI 53144/414-654-9550

heat-treaters

Aoun, Charles, Galeb Knives, 570 Massachusetts Ave., Boston, MA 02118/617-247-2431
Barbee, Jim, RR1 Box B, Fort Stockton, TX 79735-8507/915-336-2882
Bay State Metal Treating Co., 6 Jefferson Ave., Woburn, MA 01801/617-935-4100
Bos Heat Treating, Paul, Shop: 1900 Weld Blvd., El Cajon, CA 92020/619-562-2370; Home: 2320 Yucca Hill Dr., Alpine, CA 91901/619-445-4740
El Monte Steel, 355 SE End Ave., Pomona, CA 91766
Galeb Knives (See Aoun, Charles)
Hauni Richmond, Inc., 2800 Charles City Rd., Richmond, VA 23231/804-222-5262; FAX: 804-236-5284
Holt, B.R., 1238 Birchwood Drive, Sunnyvale, CA 94089/408-736-8500
Lamprey, Mike, 32 Pathfield, Great Torrington, Devon EX38 TBX, ENGLAND/01805-622651
Metal Treating, Inc., 710 Burns St., Cincinnati, OH 45204/513-921-2300; FAX: 513-921-2536
O&W Heat Treat, Inc., One Bidwell Rd., South Windsor, CT 06074/ 860-528-9239; FAX: 860-291-9939
Texas Heat Treating, Inc., 303 Texas Ave., Round Rock, TX 78664/ 512-255-5884
Texas Knifemakers Supply, 10649 Haddington, Suite 180, Houston, TX 77043/713-461-8632
The Tinker Shop, 1120 Helen, Deer Park, TX 77536/713-479-7286
Valley Metal Treating, Inc., 355 S. East End Ave., Pomona, CA 91766/ 909-623-6316; FAX: 909-620-7304
Wilson, R.W., P.O. Box 2012, Weirton, WV 26062/304-723-2771

leatherworkers

Anonymous Leather & Mfg., Vary Ltd., 519 Castro St., #M38, San Francisco, CA 94114/415-431-4555
The Astorian Ltd. (See Noone, George S.)
Baker, Don and Kay, 5950 Foxfire Dr., Zanesville, OH 43701/614-849-3044
Beadwork & Buckskin (See Niedenthal, John Andre)
Blade-Tech (See Wegner, Tim)
Bonder, Dirk J., Kwartel Voning F, 3403 ZN, Usselstein, HOLLAND/ 030-6889232
Cheramie, Grant, 4260 West Main, Rt. 3, Box 940, Cut Off, LA 70345/ 504-632-5770
Clements' Custom Leathercraft, Chas, 1741 Dallas St., Aurora, CO 80010-2018/303-364-0403; FAX: 303-739-9824
Congdon, David, Congdon Blade Leather 1063 Whitchurch Ct., Wheaton, IL 60187/630-665-8825
Congdon Blade Leather (See Congdon, David)
Cooper, Harold, 136 Winding Way, Frankfort, KY 40601/502-227-8151
Cooper, Jim, 2148 Cook Pl., Ramona, CA 92065-3214/619-789-1097
Corby, Harold, 218 Brandonwood Drive, Johnson City, TN 37604/423-926-9781
Cow Catcher Leatherworks, 3006 Industrial Ave., Raleigh, NC 27609/919-833-8262
Cubic, George, GC Custom Leather Co., 10561 E. Deerfield Pl., Tuscon, AZ 85749/520-760-5988
Custom Leather Knife Sheath Co. (See Schrap, Robert G.)
Dawkins, Dudley, 221 N. Broadmoor, Topeka, KS 66606-1254/913-235-0468
Dennehy, John D., John-D Custom Leatherworks and Handmade Knives, P.O. Box 431, 3926 Hayes Ave., Wellington, CO 80549-0431/970-568-9055
Fannin, David A., 2050 Idle Hour Center #191, Lexington, KY 40502
Foley, Barney, 3M Reler Lane, Somerset, NJ 08873/908-297-1880
GC Custom Leather Co. (See Cubic, George)
Genske, Jay, 262½ Elm St., Fond du Lac, WI 54935/414-921-6505
Graves, Dave, Miracle Valley Leather, P.O. Box 383, Lerona, WV 25971/304-384-9137
Harris, Tom, 519 S. 1st St., Mount Vernon, WA 98273/206-336-2713
Hawk, Ken, Western Leather, Rt. 1, Box 770, Ceres, VA 24318-9630/703-624-3219
Hendryx Design, Scott, 5997 Smokey Way, Boise, ID 83714/208-377-8044
Homyk, David N., 8047 Carriage Ln., Wichita Falls, TX 76306/817-855-8425
John-D Custom Leatherworks and Handmade Knives (See Dennehy, John D.)
John's Custom Leather (See Stumpf, John R.)
K&J Leatherworks, P.O. Box 609, Watford, Ont., N0M 2S0 CANADA
Kravitt, Chris, Treestump Leather, 18 State St., Ellsworth, ME 04605-9805/207-667-8756
Lamprey, Mike, 32 Pathfield, Great Torrington, Devon EX38 7BX, ENGLAND/0805-622651

Larson, Richard, 549 E. Hawkeye, Turlock, CA 95380
Lay, Judy M., RR #2 Braeside Rd., Vanderhoof B.C. VOJ 3AO CANADA/604-567-3856
Layton, Jim, 2710 Gilbert Avenue, Portsmouth, OH 45662/614-353-6179
Leathercrafters (See Mobley, Martha)
Lee, Sonja, P.O. Box 1873, St. Johns, AZ 85936/520-337-2594
Lefaucheux, Jean-Victor, Saint-Denis-Le-Ferment, 27140 Gisors, FRANCE/16.32.55-1410; FAX: 16.32.55-5087
Luck, Gregory, 749 S. Lemay Ave., #A3-207, Fort Collins, CO 80524-3251/303-686-7223
M&M Kustom Krafts (See Miller, Michael K.)
Mason, Arne, Mesa Case, 125 Wimer St., Ashland, OR 97520/503-482-2260; 800-326-9078
McGowan, Liz, 12629 Howard Lodge Dr., Sykesville, MD 21784/410-489-4323
Mesa Case (See Mason, Arne)
Metheny, H.A. "Whitey," 7750 Waterford Dr., Spotsylvania, VA 22553/703-582-3228
Miller, Michael K., M&M Kustom Krafts, 28510 Santiam Highway, Sweet Home, OR 97386/541-367-4927
Milton Gomes Cristine, Jose, R. Natal Meira de Barros, 194, Jd. Aricanduva, Sao Paulo, SP-03454-030, BRAZIL/011-8866895
Miracle Valley Leather (See Graves, Dave)
Mobley, Martha, Leathercrafters, 240 Alapaha River Road, Chula, GA 31733/912-831-4837
Morrissey, Martin, 4578 Stephens Rd., Blairsville, GA 30512
Niedenthal, John Andre, Beadwork & Buckskin, Studio 3955 NW 103 Dr., Coral Springs, FL 33065-1551/954-345-0447
NQ Leatherworks (See Qvist, Niels)
Poag, James H., RR #1 Box 212A, Grayville, IL 62844/618-375-7106
Pratt, Charles, 1953 Fillmans Bottom Rd., Port Washington, OH 43837/614-498-5404
Qvist, Niels, Leestrupvej #2, Hyllede, DK-4683 Roennede, DENMARK/(45)53 82 57 52
Ravon Industries, P.O. Box 670, Denton, TX 76202/817-382-1831
Red's Custom Leather, Ed Todd, 9 Woodlawn Rd., Putnam Valley, NY 10579/914-528-3783
Riney, Norm, 6212 S. Marion Way, Littleton, CO 80121/303-794-1731
Rowe, Kenny, Rowe's Leather, 1306 W. Ave. C, Hope, AR 71801/870-777-8216 or 870-777-2974
Rowe's Leather (See Rowe, Kenny)
Ruiz Industries, Inc., 1513 Gardena Ave., Glendale, CA 91204/818-242-4239
Schrap, Robert G., Custom Leather Knife Sheath Co., 7024 W. Wells St., Wauwatosa, WI 53213-3717/414-771-6472; FAX: 414-784-2996; E-MAIL:RSCHRAP@AOL.COM
Spragg, Wayne E., P.O. Box 508, Ashton, ID 83420/915-944-9630
Strahin, Robert, 401 Center Ave., Elkins, WV 26241/304-636-0128
Stuart, V. Pat, Rt. 1, Box 447-S, Greenville, VA 24440/703-377-2596
Stumpf, John R., John's Custom Leather, 523 S. Liberty St., Blairsville, PA 15717/412-459-6802; FAX: 412-459-5996
Tierney, Mike, 447 Rivercrest Dr., Woodstock, ON N4S 5W5, CANADA/519-539-8859
Todd, Ed (See Red's Custom Leather)
Treestump Leather (See Kravitt, Chris)
Turner, Kevin, 17 Hunt Ave., Montrose, NY 10548/814-739-0535
Velasquez, Gil, 7120 Madera Dr., Goleta, CA 93117/805-968-7787
Walker, John, 17 Laber Circle, Little Rock, AR 72209/501-228-0888
Watson, Bill, #1 Presidio, Wimberly, TX 78676/512-847-2531
Wegner, Tim, Blade-Tech Industries Inc., 8818-158th St. E., Puyallup, WA 98373/206-840-0447; FAX: 206-840-0447
Western Leather (See Hawk, Ken)
Whinnery, Walt, 1947 Meadow Creek Dr., Louisville, KY 40218/502-458-4361
Wilder, W. Barry (See Cow Catcher Leatherworks)
Williams, Sherman A., 1709 Wallace St., Simi Valley, CA 93065/805-583-3821

photographers

A Bar V Studio (See Rhoades, Cynthia J.)
Alfano, Sam, 36180 Henery Gaines Rd., Pearl River, LA 70452
Allen, John, Studio One, 3823 Pleasant Valley Blvd., Rockford, IL 61114
Berchtold, Robert, Berchtold Studios, 820 Greenbriar Circle, Suite #26, Chesapeake, VA 23320/757-366-0653; FAX: 757-366-0122; E-MAIL: bsiphoto@eorls.com
Berchtold Studios (See Berchtold, Robert)
Berisford, Bob, 505 West Adams St., Jacksonville, FL 32202/904-356-4780
Bilal, Mustafa, 908 NW 50th St., Seattle, WA 98107-3634
Bittner, Rodman, 3444 North Apache Circle, Chandler, AZ 85224/602-730-5088
Bloomer, Peter L., Horizons West, 427 S. San Francisco St., Flagstaff, AZ 86001/520-779-1014; FAX: 520-774-3925
Bogaerts, Jan, Regenweg 14, 5757 Pl., Liessel HOLLAND/04934-1580; FAX: 04934-2664
Box Photography, Doug, 1700 West Main, Brenham, TX 77833/409-836-1700
Brown, Charles, P.O. Box 671, Clayton, NC 27520/919-553-4688
Brown, Tom, 6048 Grants Ferry Rd., Brandon, MS 39042-8136
Buffaloe, Edwin, 104 W. Applegate, Austin, TX 78753/512-837-9746
Burdette, Roger W., Custom Images, 1516 E. 19th St., Des Moines, IA 50316-2708/515-266-4743
Burger, Gunter, Horststr. 55, 44581 Castrop-Rauseel GERMANY/02305-77145
Butman, Steve, P.O. Box 5106, Abilene, TX 79608/915-695-2341
Calidonna, Greg, 205 Helmwood Dr., Elizabethtown, KY 42701/502-769-2463
Campbell, Jim, 7935 Ranch Rd., Port Richey, FL 34668
Carter, Art, 818 Buffin Bay Rd., Columbia, SC 28210/802-772-2148
Casey, Robert, 3590 Polk Ave., Ogden, UT 84403/801-394-9114
Catalano, John D., 56 Kingston Ave., Hicksville, NY 11801/516-938-1356
Chan, Stanley B., 550 Weddell Dr., #7, Sunnyvale, CA 94089/408-734-8738; FAX: 408-734-8739
Chastain, Christopher, B&W Labs, 1462 E. Michigan St., Orlando, FL 32806/407-898-0266
Clark, John W., 604 Cherry St., Des Moines, IA 50309/515-280-3954; FAX: 515-280-7725
Clark, Ryerson, P.O. Box 1193, Dartmouth, NS B2Y 4B8, CANADA/902-466-5608
Corbett Photography, Charles, 126 Wilcocks Rd., Bloemfontein 9301, REPUBLIC OF SOUTH AFRICA/051-366-565; FAX: 051-366-565
Cotton, William A., 749 S. Lemay Ave. A3-211, Fort Collins, CO 80524/303-221-5071
Country Visions Photography (See Wells, Carlene L.)
Courtice, Bill, P.O. Box 1776, Duarte, CA 91010-4776/818-358-5715
Criscooli, Walter, Via Aquilzia 14, 33100 Udine, ITALY/0432-26819
Crosby, Doug, RFD 1, Box 1111, Stockton Springs, ME 04981
Custom Images (See Burdette, Roger W.)
Danko, Michael, Jay Verno Studio, 3030 Jane Street, Pittsburgh, PA 15203/412-381-5350; FAX: 412-381-8338
Davis, Marshall B., P.O. Box 3048, Austin, TX 78764/512-443-4030
Dikeman Photo, Lawrence, 2169 Arbor Ave., Muskegon, MI 49441/616-755-1881
Durant, Ross, 316 E. 1st Ave., Vancouver, B.C. V5t 1A9, CANADA/604-872-2717
Earley, Don, 1241 Ft. Bragg Rd., Fayetteville, NC 28305/910-485-6660
Eggly, Eric R. Point Seven Studios, 810 Seneca St., Toledo, OH 43608/419-243-8880; FAX: 419-243-3893
Ehrlich, Linn M., 2643 N. Clybourn Ave., Chicago, IL 60614/312-472-2025
Ellison, Troy, P.O. Box 94393, Lubbock, TX 79493/800-554-7097
Elvens Foto AB (See Eriksson, Stig)
Eriksson, Stig, Elvens Foto AB, Box 103, S-828 00 Edsbyn, SWEDEN/0271-20197
Etzler, John, 11200 N. Island Rd., Grafton, OH 44044/216-748-2460
Everett, David, White Lotus Studio, 258 Hartford Ave., Newington, CT 06111-2077

Fahrner Photographics, Dave, 1623 Arnold St., Pittsburgh, PA 15205/412-921-6861
Faul, Jan W., 903 Girard St. NE, Rr. Washington, DC 20017/202-526-1122; FAX: 202-526-0905
Fedorak, Allan, 28 W. Nicola St., Amloops, B.C. V2C 1J6, CANADA/604-372-1255
Fisher, Jay, P.O. Box 267, Magdalena, NM 87825
Fitzgerald, Dan, P.O. Box 198, Beverly Hills, CA 90213/818-507-8418
Forster, Jenny, 1112 N. McAree, Waukegan, IL 60085/708-244-7928
Foster's, Star Rt., Box 259A, Topton, NC 28781/704-321-3561
Foto NUTZ, Unterer Stadtplatz 23, 3340 Waidhofen a.d. Ybbs, AUSTRIA/07442-52320
Fotostudio ton Hartjens, Stationsstraat 35, 5751 hb Deurne, NETHERLANDS/0493-31 36 43; FAX: 0493-31 36 43
Fox, Daniel, Lumina Studios, 2570 Superior Ave., Cleveland, OH 44114/216-589-9090; FAX: 216-589-9612; E-MAIL: lumina@ix.netcom.com
Gallagher, Barry, 714 8th Ave. N., Lewistown, MT 59457/406-538-7056
Gardner, Chuck, 116 Quincy Ave., Oak Ridge, TN 37830/615-483-9411
Gawryla, Don, 1105 Greenlawn Dr., Pittsburgh, PA 15220/412-344-0787
Godby, Ronald E., 204 Seven Hollys Dr., Yorktown, VA 23692/804-898-4445
Goffe Photographic Associates, 3108 Monte Vista Blvd., N.E., Albuquerque, NM 87106/505-262-1421
Graham, James, 7452 Brentcove Circle, Dallas, TX 75214/214-828-9368; FAX: 214-828-9604
Graley, Gary W., RR2 Box 556, Gillett, PA 16925/717-537-6652
Gray, Corey, 760 Warehouse Rd., Suite D, Toledo, OH 43615/419-382-3222
Griggs, Dennis, Tannery Hill Studios, Inc., RR 1 Box 44A, Topsham, ME 04086-9705/207-725-5689
G Squared Photography (See Graley, Gary W.)
Gustavsson, Hakan, Box 182, S-828 00 Edsbyn, SWEDEN/0271-236 00
Hanusin, John, 3306 Commercial, Northbrook, IL 60062/708-564-2706
Hardy Photographics, Scott, 639 Myrtle Ave., Placerville, CA 95667/916-622-5780; E-MAIL: shardy@spider.lloyd.com
Hodge, Tom, P.O. Box 4444, Highland Park, NJ 08904/201-247-8869
Holter, Wayne V., 125 Larking Ave., Boonsboro, MD 21713
Horizons West (See Bloomer, Peter L.)
Impress by Design (See Robertson, Kathy)
Integrated Arts (See Bradley, Steven)
Kelley Photography, Gary, 17485 SW Pheasant Lane, Aloha, OR 97006/503-848-9313
Kerns, Bob, 18723 Birdseye Dr., Germantown, MD 20874/301-916-9092
Korsnes, Egil, Brakehaugen 2A, N-5050 Nesttun, NORWAY/55-135630
LaFleur, Gordon, 111 Hirst, Box 1209, Parksville, BC, CANADA V0R 270/604-248-8585
Landis, George E., Landis Associates, Inc., 16 Prospect Hill Rd., Cromwell, CT 06416/860-635-4720
Lasting Images Photography (See Stittleburg, Jan)
Lautman, Andy, 4906 41st N.W., Washington, D.C. 20016
Lear Photography, Dale, 848 2nd Ave., Gallipolis, OH 45631
LeBlanc, Paul, No. 3 Meadowbrook Cir., Melissa, TX 75454/214-838-4290
Lenz Photography, 939 S. 48th St., Suite 206, Tempe, AZ 85281/602-894-1229
Lester, Dean, 2801 Junipero Ave, Suite 212, Long Beach, CA 90806-2140/310-426-3960
Levinson, Lester, 13038 S. Brandon Ave., Chicago, IL 60633/773-646-1060; FAX: 773-646-1060
Leviton, David A., P.O. Box 2871, Silverdale, WA 98383/360-697-3452; FAX: 360-697-3452
Lewis, K.J., 374 Cook Rd., Lugoff, SC 29078
Long, Gary W., 3556 Miller's Crossroad Rd., Hillsboro, TN 37342/615-596-2275, 888-795-5700
Long, Jerry, 402 E. Gladden Dr., Farmington, NM 87401
Lum, Billy, 16307 Evening Star Ct., Crosby, TX 77532/713-328-3521
Lumina Studios (See Fox, Daniel)
Mardo Foto's, Park Heights No. 2, Railway Straat, Vereeniging, REPUBLIC OF SOUTH AFRICA/22-4021/4
Marshall Arts Photography (See Davis, Marshall B.)
McCollum, Tom, P.O. Box 933, Lilburn, GA 30226/404-972-8552
McCrackin, Kevin, 3720 Hess Rd., House Springs, MO 63051/314-677-6066
Moake, Jim, 18 Council Ave., Aurora, IL 60504/312-898-7184
Moya, Inc., 4212 S. Dixie Hwy., West Palm Beach, FL 33405/407-832-8457
Nevada Commercial Photography (See Parker, T.C.)
Newton, Thomas D., 136 1/2 W. 2nd St., Reno, NV 89501/702-232-0971
Norman's Studio, 322 S. 2nd St., Vivian, LA 71082/318-375-2932
Owens, William T., Box 99, Williamsburg, WV 24991/304-645-4114
Palmer Studio, 2008 Airport Blvd., Mobile, AL 36606/205-471-3523
Parker, T.C., Nevada Commercial Photography, 1720 Pacific, Las Vegas, NV 89104/702-457-0179
Parsons, 15 South Mission, Suite 3, Wenatchee, WA 98801/509-662-9576
Payne, Robert G., P.O. Box 141471, Austin, TX 78714/512-272-4554
Peders, Foto Atelier, Markevn 4A, 5012 Bergen, NORWAY/55-90-00-44
Peterson Photography, Kent, 230 Polk St., Eugene, OR 97402
Photographic Multi-Services (See Smith, Earl W.)
Pigott, John, 231 Heidelberg Drive, Loveland, OH 45140/513-683-6108
Point Seven Studios (See Eggly, Eric R.)
Rasmussen, Eric L., 1121 Eliason, Brigham City, UT 84302/801-734-9710
Reinders, Rick, 1707 Spring Place, Racine, WI 53404/414-634-1246
Rhoades, Cynthia J., A Bar V Studio, Box 195, Clearmont, WY 82835/307-758-4380
Rice Photography, Tim, 310 Wisconsin Ave., Whitefish, MT 59937/406-862-5416
Richardson, Kerry, 2520 Mimosa St., Santa Rosa, CA 95405/707-575-1875
Ridolfi's Photographics, 830 Central Ave., Tracy, CA 95376/209-835-7551; 209-835-7587
Robertson, Kathy, 304 Timberidge Dr., Martinez, GA 30907/706-650-0982; FAX: 706-860-1623
Ross, Bill (See Ross Commercial Photographics)
Ross Commercial Photographics, 28364 S. Western Ave., Suite 464, Rancho Palos Verdes, CA 90275/310-732-0000; FAX: 310-732-0000
Rubicam, Stephen, 14 Atlantic Ave., Boothbay Harbor, ME 04538-1202/207-633-4125
Ruby, Tom, Holiday Inn University, 11200 E. Goodman Rd., Olive Branch, MS 38654/601-895-2941
Rush, John D., 2313 Maysel, Bloomington, IL 61701/309-663-6766
Schreiber, Roger, 429 Boren Ave. N., Seattle, WA 98109/206-622-3525
Sellick, Rachel, 92 The Glebe, Glebe Estate, Norton, Stockton-On-Tees, Cleveland, TS20 1RL ENGLAND
Semmer, Charles, 7885 Cyd Dr., Denver, CO 80221/303-429-6947
Silver Fox Studio, Silver Images Photography, 21 E. Aspen Ave., Flagstaff, AZ 86001/520-774-6604; FAX: 520-774-7408
Silver Images Photography, 21 E. Aspen Ave., Flagstaff, AZ 86001/520-774-6604
Sims Photography, 461 Breezy Dr., Marietta, GA 30064/404-428-1698
Slobodian, Scott, 4101 River Ridge Dr., P.O. Box 1498, San Andreas, CA 95249/209-286-1980; FAX: 209-286-1982
Smith, Earl W., Photographic Multi-Services, 5121 Southminster Rd., Columbus, OH 43221/614-771-6487
Smith, Randall, 1720 Oneco Ave., Winter Park, FL 32789/407-628-5447
Stenzel Photography, P.O. Box 1504, Bozeman, MT 59771/406-586-4699
Storm Photo, 334 Wall St., Kingston, NY 12401
Strauss, Hans J., Bahnhofstr. 2, D-8262 Altotting, GERMANY/086 71-6979
Studio Elfin, Box 515, Bethlehem 9700, SOUTH AFRICA/058-3034830; FAX: 058-3038287
Surles, Mark, P.O. Box 147, Falcon, NC 28342/919-483-8814
Tardiolo, 9381 Wagon Wheel, Yuma, AZ 85365/520-348-1402
Teger, Allan I., 248 Tremont St., Newton, MA 02158/617-527-0798
Terra Photographic, P.O. Box 978, Newport, NH 03773/603-863-7735
Third Eye Photos, 140 E. Sixth Ave., Helena, MT 59601/406-443-4688
Thurber, David, P.O. Box 1006, Visalia, CA 93279/209-732-2798
Tighe, Brian, RR 1, Ridgeville, Ontario, L0S 1M0 CANADA/905-892-2734
Tocci, Tony, 41 Ellwood Rd., East Brunswick, NJ 08816/908-238-2289
Towell, Steven L., 3720 N.W. 32nd Ave., Camas, WA 98607/360-834-9049
Troutman, Harry, 107 Oxford Dr., Lititz, PA 17543/717-626-0685
Tsutsumi, Naganori, World Photo Press, 3-39-2, Nakano, Nakano-ku, Tokoyo 164, JAPAN/03-5358-1341; FAX: 03-5385-1347

Valley Photo, 2100 Arizona Ave., Yuma, AZ 85364/602-783-3522
Vallini, Massimo, Via Dello Scalo 2/3, 40131 Bologna ITALY/0039-51-522-087; FAX: 0039-51-522-087
Vara, Lauren, 4412 Waples Rd., Granbury, TX 76049
Verhoeven, Jon, 106 San Jose Dr., Springdale, AR 72764-2538/501-751-5040
Verno Studio, Jay, 3030 Jane Street, Pittsburgh, PA 15203/412-381-5350; FAX: 412-381-8338
Wabnik, Jochen, Otto-Dix-Ring 66, 01219 Dresden, GERMANY/275-3035
Wells, Carlene L., Country Visions Photography, 1060 S. Main, Sp. 52, Colville, WA 99114/509-684-2954
Weyer International, 2740 Nebraska Ave., Toledo, OH 43607/419-534-2020; FAX: 419-534-2697
White Lotus Studio (See Everett, David)
Wise, Harriet, 242 Dill Ave., Frederick, MD 21701
Worley, Holly, 4186 W. Grand Ave., Littleton, CO 80123/303-794-5832
Ziegler, Larry, 303 Oakwood Dr., Mt. Holly, NC 28120/704-827-6598

scrimshanders

Adlam, Tim, 1705 Witzel Ave., Oshkosh, WI 54901/414-235-4589
American Etching (See Miller, James K. and Vicky)
Anderson, Terry Jack, 10076 Birnamwoods Way, Riverton, UT 84065-9073
Art of Scrimshaw (See Velasquez, Gil)
Bailey, Mary W., 3213 Jonesboro Dr., Nashville, TN 37214/615-889-3172
Baker, Duane, 2145 Alum Creek Dr., Cambridge Park Apt. #10, Columbus, OH 43207/614-236-0915
Barndt, Kristen A., RR3, Box 72, Kunkletown, PA 18058/610-381-4048
Barrows, Miles, 524 Parsons Ave., Chillicothe, OH 45601/614-775-9627
Beauchamp, Gaetan, 125, de la Riviere, Stoneham, PQ CANADA
Beaver, Judy, 48835 N. 25 Ave., Phoenix, AZ 85027/602-465-7831; FAX: 602-465-7077
Bellet, Connie, Misty Valley Ranch, 103 Blunt Rd., Steelville, MO 65565/573-786-2331 or 2267; FAX: 573-775-2626
Benade, Lynn, 2567 Edgewood Rd., Beechwood, OH 44122/216-464-0777
Bonshire, Benita, 1121 Burlington Dr., Muncie, IN 47302/317-282-9073; FAX:317-282-9073
Boone Trading Co., Inc., P.O. Box BB, Brinnon, WA 98320/360-796-4330; FAX: 360-796-4511
Bowles, Rick, 1416 Debbs Rd., Chesapeake, VA 23320
Brady, Sandra, P.O. Box 104, Monclova, OH 43542/419-866-0435; FAX: 419-867-0656
Bruce, Lisa, c/o Joe Arnold, 47 Patience Cres., London, Ont. N6E 2K7, CANADA/519-686-2623; FAX: 519-686-9859
Bryan, Bob, 1120 Oak Hill Rd., Carthage, MO 64836/417-358-6331
Burdette, Bob, 4908 Maplewood Dr., Greenville, SC 29615/803-288-0976
Byrne, Mary Gregg, 1018 15th St., Bellingham, WA 98225-6604/206-676-1413
Cable, Jerry, 332 Main St., Mt. Pleasant, PA 15666/412-547-8282
Caudill, Lyle, 7626 Lyons Rd., Georgetown, OH 45121/513-876-2212
Clark, Inna, Pankova- (See Pankova-Clark, Inna)
Collins, Michael, Rt. 3075, Batesville Rd., Woodstock, GA 30188/404-475-7410
Conover, Juanita Rae, P.O. Box 70442, Eugene, OR 97401/541-747-1726
Cosimini, René (See McDonald, René Cosimini-)
Courtnage, Elaine, Box 473, Big Sandy, MT 59520/406-378-2492
Cover Jr., Raymond A., Rt. 1, Box 194, Mineral Point, MO 63660/314-749-3783
Cox, J. Andy, 116 Robin Hood Lane, Gaffney, SC 29340/803-489-1892
Davenport, Susan, 36842 Center Ave., Dade City, FL 33525/352-521-4088; FAX: 352-521-4088
DeYoung, Brian, 4140 Cripple Creek Way, Kennesaw, GA 30144/404-928-8051
Dietrich, Roni, Wild Horse Studio, 5821 Linglestown Rd., Harrisburg, PA 17112/717-469-0587 or 717-671-5553
DiMarzo, Richard, 2357 Center Place, Birmingham, AL 35205/205-252-3331
Dolbare, Elizabeth, P.O. Box 222, Sunburst, MT 59482/403-647-2479
Eklund, Maihkel, Föne 1155, S-82041 Färila, SWEDEN/+46 651 24192
Eldridge, Allan, 1424 Kansas Lane, Gallatin, TN 37066/615-452-6027
Eubank, Mary Ann, Rt. 1, Box 196, Pottsboro, TX 75076/903-786-3596; FAX: 903-786-3501
Evans, Rick M., 2717 Arrowhead Dr., Abilene, TX 79606/915-698-2620
Fields, Rick B., 26401 Sandwich Pl., Mt. Plymouth, FL 32776/352-383-6270; FAX: 352-383-6270
Fisk, Dale, Box 252, Council, ID 83612/208-253-4582
Foster Enterprises, Norvell Foster, P.O. Box 200343, San Antonio, TX 78220/210-333-1675
Fountain Products, 492 Prospect Ave., West Springfield, MA 01089/413-781-4651; FAX: 413-733-8217
Frazier, W.C., RR 3, Box 8720, Mansfield, LA 71052/318-872-1732
Garbe, Sandra, 1246 W. Webb, DeWitt, MI 48820/517-669-6022
Gill, Scott, 925 N. Armstrong St., Kokomo, IN 46901/317-452-3657
Halligan, Ed & Shawn, 14 Meadow Way, Sharpsburg, GA 30277/770-251-7720 (Phone & FAX)
Hands, Barry Lee, 26192 East Shore Route, Bigfork, MT 59911/406-837-0035
Hargraves Sr., Charles, RR 3 Bancroft, Ontario, K0L 1C0 CANADA/613-339-2302
Harless, Star, c/o Arrow Forge, P.O. Box 845, Stoneville, NC 27048-0845/910-573-9768; E-MAIL:StarScrim@msn.com
Harrington, Fred A., Winter: 3725 Citrus, St. James City, FL 33956/813-283-0721; Summer: 2107 W. Frances Rd., Mt. Morris, MI 48458/810-686-3008
Hawkins, Stan, 2230 El Capitan, Arcadia, CA 91006/818-445-3054
Henry, Michael K., Intarsia and Scrimshaw Art, Rte. 2, Box 161-J, Robbinsville, NC 28771/704-479-1034
Hergert, Bob, 12120 SW 9th, Beaverton, OR 97005/503-641-6924
hi II Originals (See Imboden II, Howard L.)
Hielscher, Vickie, HC34, P.O. Box 992, Alliance, NE 69301
High, Tom, Rocky Mountain Scrimshaw & Arts, 5474 S. 112.8 Rd., Alamosa, CO 81101/719-589-2108; FAX: 719-589-8324
Himmelheber, David R., 11289 40th St. N., Royal Palm Beach, FL 33411/407-795-1264
Holland, Dennis K., 4908-17th Place, Lubbock, TX 79416/806-799-8427
Hoover, Harvey, 5750 Pearl Dr., Paradise, CA 95969-4829
Houser, Jesse, P.O. Box 993, Biscoe, NC 27209
Images In Ivory (See Stahl, John)
Imboden II, Howard L., hi II Originals, 620 Deauville Dr., Dayton, OH 45429/513-439-1536
Intarsia and Scrimshaw Art (See Henry, Michael K.)
Johnson, Corinne, W3565 Lockington, Mindora, WI 54644/608-857-3035
Johnston, Kathy, W. 1134 Providence, Spokane, WA 99205/509-326-5711
Karst, Linda K., 402 Hwy. 27 E., Ingram, TX 78025/830-367-3350; FAX: 830-367-3350
Kelso, Jim, RD 1, Box 5300, Worcester, VT 05682/802-229-4254
Kiracofe, Gary, 1012 Trillium Ln., Sister Bay, WI 54234/414-854-5407
Kirk, Susan B., 1340 Freeland Rd., Merrill, MI 48637/517-839-9131
Koevenig's Engraving Service, Eugene and Eve Koevenig, Rabbit Gulch, Box 55, Hill City, SD 57745-0055/605-574-2239
Kostelnik, Joe and Patty, RD #4, Box 323, Greensburg, PA 15601/412-832-0365
Kudlas, John M., 622 14th St. SE, Rochester, MN 55904/507-288-5579
Land, John W., P.O. Box 917, Wadesboro, NC 28170/704-694-5141, 704-694-2001
Lemen, Pam, 3434 N. Iroquois Ave., Tucson, AZ 85705/520-887-3095
Letschnig, Franz, RR1, Martintown, Ont., CANADA/613-528-4843
Lovestrand, Erik, 206 Bent Oak Circle, Harvest, AL 35749-9334/205-430-0828
Martin, Diane, 28220 N. Lake Dr., Waterford, WI 53185/414-662-3629
McDonald, René Cosimini-, 14730 61 Court N., Loxahatchee, FL 33470/561-790-1470
McFadden, Berni, 1402 E. Best Ave., Coeur d'Alene, ID 83814/208-664-2686
McGowan, Frank, 12629 Howard Lodge Dr., Sykesville, MD 21784/410-489-4323

McGrath, Gayle, 12641 Panasoffkee, N. Ft. Meyers, FL 33903/813-997-2215
McKissack II, Tommy, P.O. Box 991, Sonora, TX 76950/915-387-3253
McLaran, Lou, 603 Powers St., Waco, TX 76705/817-799-2234
McWilliams, Carole, P.O. Box 693, Bayfield, CO 81122/303-884-0320
Mead, Faustina L., 2550 E. Mercury St., Inverness, FL 34453-0514/352-344-4751
Miller, James K. and Vicky, American Etching, 22500 Hwy. 72 W., Tuscumbia, AL 35674/205-381-1747
Minnick, Joyce, 144 N. 7th St., Middletown, IN 47356/317-354-4108
Mitchell, James, 1026 7th Ave., Columbus, GA 31901/404-576-4014
Moore, James B., 1707 N. Gillis, Stockton, TX 79735/915-336-2113
Morris, Darrel, 29 Hawksmoor, Aliso Viejo, CA 92656
Ochonicky, Michelle "Mike," Stone Hollow Scrimshaw Studio, 31 High Trail, Eureka, MO 63025/314-938-9570
Ochs, Belle, 124 Emerald Lane, Largo, FL 33771/813-530-3826
Pachi, Mirella, Via Abisola, 97B, 16162 Genoa, ITALY/010-713050
Pankova-Clark, Inna, P.O. Box 597, Andrews, NC 28901/704-321-2230
Parish, Vaughn, 103 Cross St., Monaca, PA 15061/412-495-3024
Peck, Larry H., 4021 Overhill Rd., Hannibal, MO 63401/314-221-5994
Peterson, Lou, 514 S. Jackson St., Gardner, IL 60424/815-237-8432
Petree, Linda A., Rt. 14, Box 2364A, Kennewick, WA 99337/509-586-9596
Poag, James H., RR #1 Box 212A, Grayville, IL 62844/618-375-7106
Polk, Trena, 4625 Webber Creek Rd., Van Buren, AR 72956/501-474-3828
Purvis, Hilton, P.O. Box 371, Noordhoek, 7985, REP. OF SOUTH AFRICA/021-891114
Raoux, Serge, 22 rue de Nohanent, 63100 Clermont-FD, FRANCE
Ramsey, Richard 8525 Trout Farm Rd., Neosho, MO 64850/417-451-1493
Rece, Charles V., Wildwood Art & Engraving, P.O. Box 868, Paw Creek, NC 28130/704-391-0209; FAX:704-351-8134
Riffe, Glen, 4430 See Saw Cir., Colorado Springs, CO 80917/719-574-8568
Ristinen, Lori, P.O. Box 41, Wolf Lake, MN 56593/218-538-6608; E-MAIL: grist@means.net; WEB: http://www.digitmaster.com/mnpro/lori/index.html
Roberts, J.J., 7808 Lake Dr., Manassas, VA 22111/703-330-0448
Rocky Mountain Scrimshaw & Arts (See High, Tom)
Rodkey, Sheryl, 18336 Ozark Dr., Hudson, FL 34667/813-863-8264
Rundell, Joe, 6198 W. Frances Rd., Clio, MI 48420/810-687-0559
Saggio, Joe, 1450 Broadview Ave. #12, Columbus, OH 43212/614-481-1967
Sahlin, Viveca, Scrim Art, Lövhagsgatan 39, S-724 71 Västerås, SWEDEN/+46 21 358778; FAX: +46 21 358778/WEB: http://www.algonet.se/~scrimart; E-MAIL: scrimart@algonet.se
Satre, Robert, 518 3rd Ave. NW, Weyburn, Sask. S4H 1R1, CANADA/306-842-3051
Schlott, Harald, Zingster Str. 26, 13051 Berlin, GERMANY/+49(030), 929 33 46
Schulenburg, E.W., 25 North Hill St., Carrollton, GA 30117
Schwallie, Patricia, 4614 Old Spartanburg Rd. Apt. 47, Taylors, SC 29687/803-292-8975
Scrim Art (See Sahlin, Viveca)
Selent, Chuck, P.O. Box 1207, Bonners Ferry, ID 83805/208-267-5807
Semich, Alice, 10037 Roanoke Dr., Murfreesboro, TN 37129/615-890-5146
Sherwood, George, 46 N. River Dr., Roseburg, OR 97470/541-672-3159
Shostle, Ben, 1121 Burlington, Muncie, IN 47302/317-282-9073 (Phone & FAX)
Sinclair, W.P., 3, The Pippins, Warminster, Wiltshire BA12 8TH, ENGLAND/U.K. Code (44-985) 218544; FAX: (44-985) 214111
Smith, Jerry, 7029 East Holmes Rd., Memphis, TN 38125/901-755-2648
Smith, Peggy, 676 Glades Rd., #3, Gatlinburg, TN 37738/423-436-3322 or 423-436-3567
Smith, Ron, 5869 Straley, Ft. Worth, TX 76114/817-732-6768
Stahl, John, Images in Ivory, 2049 Windsor Rd., Baldwin, NY 11510/516-223-5007
Stearns, Glen, 209 N. Detroit St., Kenton, OH 43326
Steigerwalt, Jim, RD#3 Sunbury, PA 17801/717-286-5806
Stone Hollow Scrimshaw Studio (See Ochonicky, Michelle "Mike")
Stuart, Stephen, 8080 Sunrise Lakes Dr. N., Building 28, Apt. 106, Sunrise, FL 33322/954-748-5151
Talley, Mary Austin, 2499 Countrywood Parkway, Cordova, TN 38018/901-372-2263
Thompson, Larry D., 23040 Ave. 197, Strathmore, CA 93267/209-568-2048
Tisdale, Gerald, 10013 Album Ave., El Paso, TX 79925-5442/915-590-4188
Tong, Jill, P.O. Box 572, Tombstone, AZ 85638/602-457-9268
Toniutti, Nelida, Via G. Pascoli, 33085 Maniago-PN, ITALY/24-0594
Tucker, Steve, 3518 W. Linwood, Turlock, CA 95380/309-682-2606
Tyser, Ross, 1015 Hardee Court, Spartanburg, SC 29303/864-585-7616
Veenstra, Gerry, 420 Wellington St., Apt. 206, St. Thomas, Ont. N5R 5P4, CANADA
Velasquez, Gil, Art of Scrimshaw, 7120 Madera Dr., Goleta, CA 93117/805-968-7787
Walker, Karen, Star Route, Alpine, WY 83128/307-883-2372
Walker, Patricia, P.O. Box 2343, 555 Este Es Rd., Taos, NM 87571/505-758-0233; FAX: 505-758-4133
Warren, Al, 1423 Santa Fe Circle, Roseville, CA 95678/916-784-3217
Wildwood Art & Engraving (See Rece, Charles V.)
Williams, Gary, (Garbo), 221 Autumn Way, Elizabethtown, KY 42701/502-765-6963
Winn, Travis A., 558 E. 3065 S., Salt Lake City, UT 84106/801-467-5957 or 801-328-0573
Young, Mary, 4826 Storeyland Dr., Alton, IL 62002/618-466-4707
Zima, Russell, 7291 Ruth Way, Denver, CO 80221/303-657-9378

miscellaneous

custom grinders

American Etching (See Miller, James K. and Vicky)
Elk Rack, The (See Peele, Bryan)
Engnath, Bob, 1019 E. Palmer Ave., Glendale, CA 91205/818-956-5710; FAX: 818-956-5120
Forosisky, Nicholas, 1414 Solomon St., Johnstown, PA 15902-4203/814-288-4543
hi II Originals (See Imboden II, Howard L.)
High, Tom, Rocky Mountain Scrimshaw & Arts, 5474 S. 112.8 Rd., Alamosa, CO 81101/719-589-2108; FAX: 719-589-8324
Holden, Larry, 1544 Strecker Street, Ridgecrest, CA 93555/619-377-3579
Imboden II, Howard L., hi II Originals, 620 Deauville Dr., Dayton, OH 45429/937-439-1536
Kelgin Knives (See Largin, Ken)
Kwik-Sharp Optronics, Inc., 350 N. Wheeler St., Ft. Gibson, OK 74434/918-683-9514
Lamprey, Mike, 32 Pathfield, Great Torrington, Devon EX38 TBX, ENGLAND/01805-622651
Largin, Ken, Kelgin Knives, 67 Arlington Dr., Batesville, IN 47006/812-934-5938
McGowan Manufacturing Company, 25 Michigan St., Hutchinson, MN 55350/320-587-2222; FAX: 320-587-7966 (mfg. sharpeners)
McLuin, Tom, 36 Fourth St., Dracut, MA 01826/508-957-4899
Miller, James K. and Vicky, American Etching, 22500 Hwy. 72, Tuscumbia, AL 35674/205-381-1747
Peele, Bryan, The Elk Rack, 215 Ferry St., P.O. Box 1363, Thompson Falls, MT 59873/406-827-4633
Rece, Charles V., Wilwood Art & Engraving, P.O. Box 868, Paw Creek, NC 28130/704-391-0209; FAX: 704-351-8134
Rocky Mountain Scrimshaw & Arts (See High, Tom)
Wildwood Art & Engraving (See Rece, Charles V.)
Wilson, R.W., P.O. Box 2012, Weirton, WV 26062/304-723-2771

custom handle artisans

Anderson, Mel, Scratchy Hand, 1718 Lee Ln., Cedaredge, CO 81413/970-856-6465
Barnett, Van, P.O. Box 1012, New Haven, WV 252651/304-882-3481

Beaver, Judy, 48835 N. 25 Ave., Phoenix, AZ 85027/602-465-7831; FAX: 602-465-7077
Clements' Custom Leathercraft, Chas, 1741 Dallas St., Aurora, CO 80010/303-364-0403
Cooper, Jim, 2148 Cook Pl., Ramona, CA 92065-3214/619-789-1097
Cover Jr., Raymond A., Rt. 1, Box 194, Mineral Point, MO 63660/314-749-3783
DiMarzo, Richard, 2357 Center Pl. S., Birmingham, AL 35205/205-252-3331
Draghi, Juan Jose, Gral Alvear 345, CP 2760-San Antonio de Areco, Pcia. de Bs Aires, ARGENTINA
Eccentric Endeavors, Michel Santos and Peggy Quinn, P.O. Box 97, Douglas Flat, CA 95229/209-728-9023
Eldridge, Allan, 1424 Kansas Lane, Gallatin, TN 37066/615-452-6027
Eubank, Mary Ann, Rt. 1 Box 196, Pottsboro, TX 75076/903-786-3596
Francis, Roger, 5419 Miller Ave., Dallas, TX 75206/214-824-8468 or 214-387-1209
Greco Knives (See Lott, Sherry)
Grussenmeyer, Paul G., 101 S. White Horse Pike, Lindenwold, NJ 08021-2304/609-435-1500; FAX: 609-435-3786
Harrison, Ed, 10125 Palestine, Houston, TX 77029/713-673-6893
hi II Originals (See Imboden II, Howard L.)
High, Tom, Rocky Mountain Scrimshaw & Arts, 5474 S. 112.8 Rd., Alamosa, CO 81101/719-589-2108; FAX: 719-589-8324
Hill, Russell S., 2384 Second Ave., Grand Island, NY 14072/716-773-0084
Holden, Larry, P.O. Box 2017, Ridgecrest, CA 93556-2017/760-375-7955
Holder, Pat, 4412 W. Diana Ave., Glendale, AZ 85302/602-435-9589; FAX: 602-939-4408
Holland, Dennis K., 4908-17th Pl., Lubbock, TX 79416/806-799-8427
Imboden II, Howard L., hi II Originals, 620 Deauville Dr., Dayton, OH 45429/937-439-1536
Kelso, Jim, RD 1, Box 5300, Worcester, VT 05682/802-229-4254
Knack, Gary, 309 Wightman, Ashland, OR 97520/503-482-2108
Krogman, Pam, 838 Merlarkkey St., Winnemucca, NV 89445/702-623-1299
Lee, Ray, 209 Jefferson Dr., Lynchburg, VA 24502/804-237-2918
Lefaucheux, Jean-Victor, Saint-Dennis-Le-Ferment, 27140 Gisors, FRANCE/32-55-1410; FAX: 32-55-5087
Letschnig, Franz, RR1, Martintown, Ont., CANADA/613-528-4843
Lott, Sherry, Greco Knives, 100 Mattie Jones Rd., Greensburg, KY 42743/502-932-3335
Marlatt, David, 67622 Oldham Rd., Cambridge, OH 43725/614-432-7549
Mead, Dennis, 2250 E. Mercury St., Inverness, FL 34453-0514/904-344-4751
Miller, Robert, 216 Seminole Ave., Ormond Beach, FL 32176/904-676-1193
Minds' Eye Metalmaster (See Smith, D. Noel)
Miteaif, Oleg, Oboronnay 46/2, 300007 Tula, RUSSIA
Myers, Ron, 6202 Marglenn Ave., Baltimore, MD 21206/301-866-8435
Northwest Knife Supply (See Vallotton, A.)
Rocky Mountain Scrimshaw & Arts (See High, Tom)
Saggio, Joe, 1450 Broadview Ave. #12, Columbus, OH 43212/614-481-1967
Sayen, Murad, P.O. Box 127, Bryant Pond, ME 04219/207-665-2224
Schlott, Harald, Zingster Str. 26, 13051 Berlin, GERMANY/+49(030) 9293346
Scratchy Hand (See Anderson, Mel)
Smith, Glen, 1307 Custer Ave., Billings, MT 59102/406-252-4064
Smith, D. Noel, P.O. Box 1363, Canon City, CO 81215-1363/719-275-2574; FAX: 719-275-2574
Snell, Barry A., 4801 96th St. N., St. Petersburg, FL 33708-3740
Vallotton, A., Northwest Knife Supply, 621 Fawn Ridge Dr., Oakland, OR 97462/503-459-2216
Watson, Silvia, 350 Jennifer Lane, Driftwood, TX 78619/512-847-9679
Williams, Gary, (GARBO), 221 Autumn Way, Elizabethtown, KY 42701/502-765-6963
Willson, Harlan M., P.O. Box 2113, Lompoc, CA 93438/805-735-0085; FAX: 805-735-0085

display cases and boxes

American Display Company, 55 Cromwell St., Providence, RI 02904/401-331-2464
Bill's Custom Cases, P.O. Box 2, Dunsmuir, CA 96025/916-235-0177 or 916-235-2455; FAX: 916-235-4959 (soft knife cases)
Brooker, Dennis, Rt. 1, Box 12A, Derby, IA 50068/515-533-2103
Clements' Custom Leathercraft, Chas. 1741 Dallas St., Aurora, CO 80010-2018/303-364-0403; FAX: 303-739-9824
Dennehy, John D., John-D Custom Leatherworks and Handmade Knives, P.O. Box 431, 3926 Hayes Ave., Wellington, CO 80549-0431/970-568-9055
Gimbert, Nelson, P.O. Box 787, Clemmons, NC 27012/919-766-5216
Haydu, Thomas G., Tomway Corp., 2507 Bimini Lane, Ft. Lauderdale, FL 33312/305-792-0185; FAX: 305-792-0115
John-D Custom Leatherworks and Handmade Knives (See Dennehy, John D.)
M&M Kustom Krafts (See Miller, Michael K.)
Mason, Arne (See Mesa Case)
Mesa Case, Arne Mason, 125 Wimer St., Ashland, OR 97520/503-4872-2260
Miller, Michael K., M&M Kustom Krafts, 28510 Santiam Highway, Sweet Home, OR 97386/503-367-4927
Miller, Robert, P.O. Box 2722, Ormond Beach, FL 32176/904-676-1193
Retichek, Joseph L., W9377 Co. TK. D, Beaver Dam, WI 53916/414-887-8061
Robbins, Wayne, 11520 Inverway, Belvidere, IL 61008/815-885-3712; FAX: 815-885-3709
S&D Enterprises, 20 East Seventh St., Manchester, OH 45144/937-549-2602; FAX: 937-549-2709
Tomway Corp. (See Haydu, Thomas G.)

etchers

American Etching (See Miller, James K. and Vicky)
Baron Technology, Inc., David Baron, 62 Spring Hill Rd., Trumbull, CT 06611/203-452-0515; FAX: 203-452-0663
David Boye Knives Gallery (See Martin, Francine)
Eubank, Mary Ann, Rt. 1, Box 196, Pottsboro, TX 75076/903-786-3596; FAX: 903-786-3501
Fountain Products, 492 Prospect Ave., West Springfield, MA 01089/413-781-4651; FAX: 413-733-8217
Hayes, Dolores, P.O. Box 41405, Los Angeles, CA 90041/213-258-9923
Holland, Dennis, 4908 17th Pl., Lubbock, TX 79416/806-799-8427
Kelso, Jim, RD1, Box 5300, Worcester, VT 05682/802-229-4254
Lefaucheux, Jean-Victor, Saint-Denis-Le-Ferment, 27140 Gisors, FRANCE/16-32-55-14-10; FAX: 16-32-55-50-87
Leibowitz, Leonard, 1025 Murrayhill Ave., Pittsburgh, PA 15217/412-361-5455
MacBain, Kenneth C., 30 Briarwood Ave., Norwood, NJ 07648/201-768-0652
Martin, Francine, David Boye Knives Gallery, P.O. Box 81, Davenport, CA 95017/408-426-6046; FAX: 408-426-6046; E-MAIL: larstein@cruzio.com
Miller, James K. and Vicky, American Etching, 22500 Hwy. 72, Tuscumbia, AL 35674/205-381-1747
Myers, Ron, 6202 Marglenn Ave., Baltimore, MD 21206/301-866-8435
Northwest Knife Supply (See Vallotton, A.)
Sayen, Murad, P.O. Box 127, Bryant Pond, ME 04219/207-665-2224
Smith, Glen, 1307 Custer Ave., Billings, MT 59102/406-252-4064
Vallotton, A., Northwest Knife Supply, 621 Fawn Ridge Dr., Oakland, OR 97462/503-459-2216
Watson, Silvia, 350 Jennifer Lane, Driftwood, TX 78619/512-847-9679

knife appraisers

Clements' Custom Leathercraft, Chas, 1741 Dallas St., Aurora, CO 80010-2018/303-364-0403; FAX: 303-739-9824
Levine, Bernard, P.O. Box 2404, Eugene, OR 97402/541-484-0294
Russell, A.G., 1705 Hwy. 71 North, Springdale, AR 72764/501-751-7341
Vallini, Massimo, Via Dello Scalo 2/3, 40131 Bologna ITALY/0039-51-522-087

organizations & publications

organizations

AMERICAN BLADESMITH SOCIETY
c/o Joseph G. Cordova, P.O. Box 977, Peralta, NM 87042/505-869-3912
If you're interested in the forged blade, you are welcome here. The Society has a teaching program, East and West, and awards stamps to Journeymen and Master Smiths after they pass tests—tough tests at a hot forge. You don't have to make knives to belong. A list of knifemaker members appears on page 275.

AMERICAN KNIFE THROWERS ALLIANCE
c/o Bobby Branton, 4976 Seewee Rd., Awendaw, SC 29429

ART KNIFE COLLECTOR'S ASSOCIATION
c/o Mitch Weiss, Pres., 2211 Lee Road, Suite 104, Winter Partk, FL 32789/407-740-8778; FAX: 407-649-7273; http://www.artknife.com; E-MAIL: mitch@artknife.com
The high-grade knife on the Internet with Web sites for everyone interested—makers and collectors.

AUSTRALIAN KNIFEMAKERS GUILD INC.
P.O. Box 659, Belgrave 3160, Victoria, Australia
The guild was formed by a group of dedicated custom knifemakers in 1984, with the express purpose of fostering the design, manufacture, sale and use of Australian made custom knives. A list of members appears on page 277.

CALIFORNIA KNIFEMAKERS ASSOCIATION
c/o Barry Evan Posner, Mbrshp. Chairman., 5222 Beeman Ave., N. Hollywood, CA 91607/818-980-7689. A list of members appears on page 277.

CANADIAN KNIFEMAKERS GUILD
c/o John Freeman, Sec./Treas., 160 Concession St., Cambridge, Ont. N1R 2H7 Canada/519-740-2767. Newly formed group—1994.

JAPANESE SWORD SOCIETY OF THE U.S.
P.O. Box 712, Breckenridge, TX 76424
They publish a newsletter bi-monthly and a bulletin once a year.

KANSAS KNIFE COLLECTORS ASSOCIATION
c/o Bill Davis, Pres., P.O. Box 1125, Wichita, KS 67201-1125/316-838-0540
Offers knife club since 1989.

KNIFEMAKERS GUILD
c/o Billy Mace Imel, Sec./Treas., 1616 Bundy Ave., New Castle, IN 47362/317-529-1651; FAX: 317-521-8696
This continues to be the big one. The Guild has prospered, as have its members. It screens prospects to ensure they are serious craftsmen; and it runs a big show in Orlando each July where over 250 Guild members show their best work, all in one room. Not all good knifemakers belong; some joined and later left for their own reasons; the Guild drops some for cause now and again. The Knifemakers Guild is an organization with a function. A list of Guild members appears on page 274.

KNIFEMAKERS GUILD OF SOUTHERN AFRICA, THE
c/o Bertie Rietveld, Chairman, P.O. Box 53, Magaliesburg, South Africa/+27142-771294. A list of members appears on page 277.

MIDWEST KNIFEMAKERS ASSOCIATION
c/o Corbin Newcomb, Pres., 628 Woodland Ave., Moberly, MO 65270/816-263-4639
The MKA currently has a membership of 49 makers from 10 states in the Midwest. A list appears on page 277.

MINIATURE KNIFEMAKERS' SOCIETY
c/o Gary F. Bradburn, Sec., 1714 Park Pl., Wichita, KS 67203/316-269-4273
The MKS is dedicated to improving the quality of custom miniature knives. The MKS welcomes miniature makers and collectors as members, publishes a bi-monthly newsletter, and awards miniature collectors who publicly show their collections. Send $1 for a list of members and an application. A list of knifemaker members appears on page 276.

THE MONTANA KNIFEMAKERS' ASSOCIATION
2608 Central Ave. West, Great Falls, MT 59404/406-727-9102. A list of members appears on page 277.

NORTH CAROLINA CUSTOM KNIFEMAKERS GUILD
c/o Tommy McNabb, Pres., 4015 Brownsboro Rd., Winston-Salem, NC 27106/910-759-0640. A list of members appears on page 278.

PROFESSIONAL KNIFEMAKERS ASSOCIATION
2905 N. Montana Ave., Ste. 30027, Helena, MT 59601/406-458-6552; E-MAIL: dondavis@csn.net; WEB: www.web2.com/pka. A list of members appears on page 276.

NEO-TRIBAL METALSMITHS
P.O. Box 44095, Tucson, AZ 85773-4095
The Neo-Tribal approach to metalsmithing combines ancient and modern tools, materials and techniques. It relies heavily on salvaged and recycled materials and the efficient use of both. The emphasis is on high quality and traditional hand craftsmanship.

REGIONAL ASSOCIATIONS
There are a number of state and regional associations with goals possibly more directly related to promotion of their members' sales than the Guild and the ABS. Among those known to us are the American Knife Throwers Alliance; Arizona Knifemakers Association; the Arkansas Knifemakers Association; the California Knifemakers Association; the Montana Knifemaker's Association; the South Carolina Association of Knifemakers; the Midwest Knifemakers Association; the New England Bladesmiths Guild; North Carolina Knifemaker's Guild; Ohio Knifemakers Association; and the Association of Southern Knifemakers. Lists of members of most of these may be found on page 277 .

UNITED KINGDOM BLADE ASSOCIATION (UKBA)
P.O. Box 1, Brampton, CA6 7GD, England
Promotes the study of knives as a sensible and fascinating pastime.

publications

BLADE MAGAZINE
Krause Publications, 700 E. State St., Iola, WI 54945/800-272-5233
Editor: Steve Shackleford. Monthly. Official magazine of the Knifemakers Guild. $3.25 on newsstand; $19.95 per year. Also publishes *Edges*, a quarterly ($12.95 for six issues); *Blade Trade*, a cutlery trade magazine; and knife books.

DBI BOOKS, a division of Krause Publications, Inc.
935 Lakeview Pkwy., Vernon Hills, IL 60061/847-573-8530; FAX: 847-573-8534
In addition to this *Knives* annual, DBI publishes *Gun Digest Book of Knives*, by Jack Lewis and Roger Combs; *Knifemaking*, also by Lewis and Combs; and *Levine's Guide to Knives and Their Values*, by Bernard Levine.

KNIFE WORLD
P.O. Box 3395, Knoxville, TN 37927/800-828-7751
Editor: Mark Zalesky. Monthly. Tabloid size on newsprint. Covers custom knives, knifemakers, collecting, old factory knives, etc. General coverage for the knife enthusiast. Subscription $15 year.

KNIVES ILLUSTRATED
265 S. Anita Dr., Ste. 120, Orange, CA 92868/714-939-9991
Editor: Bud Lang. $3.50 on newsstands; $14.95 for six issues. Plenty of four-color, all on cutlery; concentrates on handmade knives.

NATIONAL KNIFE MAGAZINE
P.O. Box 21070, Chattanooga, TN 37424/423-899-9456
For members of the National Knife Collectors Association. Emphasis on pocketknife collecting, of course, together with association show news. Membership $25 year; $28 for new members.

TACTICAL KNIVES
Harris Publications, 1115 Broadway, New York, NY 10010/212-807-7100; FAX: 212-627-4678
Editor: Steve Dick. Aimed at emergency-service knife designs and users, this new publication has made a great start. Price: $4.95; $14.95 for six issues. On newsstands.

TRIBAL NOW!
Neo-Tribal Metalsmiths, P.O. Box 44095, Tucson, AZ 85733-4095
Editor: Bill Randall. (See Neo-Tribal Metalsmiths under Organizations.) Price: $10 per year for four issues with two- to four-page supplements sent out on a regular basis.

UK BLADE
United Kingdom Blade Association, P.O. Box 1, Brampton CA6 7GD ENGLAND
On a base of UK knifemakers, the UKBA seeks to sweep the knife fancy of Britain all into one tent. Membership dues: Ordinary £16 year; husband and wife (one magazine) £20 year; trade £30 year. And they have no phone yet.

WEYER INTERNATIONAL BOOK DIVISION
2740 Nebraska Ave., Toledo, OH 43607, 419-534-2020, 419-534-2697
Publishers of the *Knives: Points of Interest* series. Sells knife-related books at attractive prices; has other knife-publishing projects in work.

STRAIGHT-FORWARD REFERENCE FOR THE SERIOUS COLLECTOR

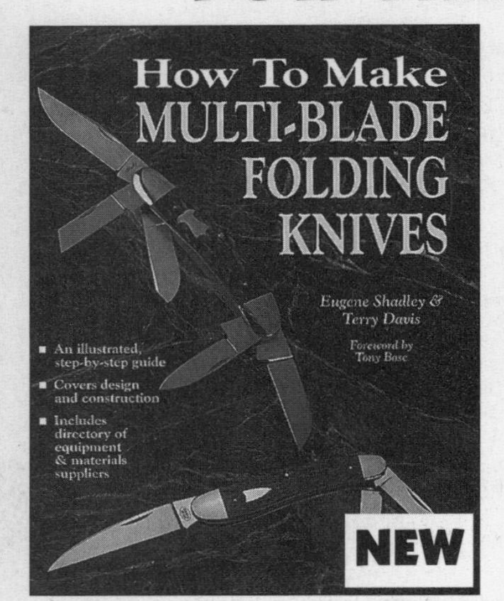

How to Make Multi-Blade Folding Knives
by Eugene Shadley & Terry Oates
This illustrated, step-by-step instructional book teaches knifemakers how to craft multiple-blade folding knives. Every aspect of construction-from design to completion-is carefully explained and clearly shown in precise illustrations. No other how-to on multi-blades exists! By the publisher of the world's #1 knife magazine, **Blade.** Softcover • 8-1/2 x 11 • 192 pages • 200 b&w photos • **MBK01 • $19.95**

The Gun Digest Book of Knives
5th Edition
by Jack Lewis & Roger Combs
The many topics explored include: the world of military knives; knife designs form Europe and the Far East; swords and sabers; collecting and investing; knife restoration; scrimshawing; engraving and etching; and forging knives the old-fashioned way. There are biographies of some of the great makers, as well as bright newcomers to the art. Also included is a directory of the knife trade.
Softcover • 8-1/2x11 • 256 pages • 500 b&w photos • **GDK5 • $19.95**

LEVINE'S GUIDE TO KNIVES AND THEIR VALUES
EXTENSIVELY REVISED 4TH EDITION
$27.95
THE COMPLETE
NEW EDITION

Levine's Guide to Knives and Their Values
The Complete Handbook of Knife Collecting, 4th Edition
by Bernard Levine
Stock the one book that's suitable for any knife collector. This handbook partners the latest knife values with pertinent historical overviews and expanded brand lists. Sets the standard for knife collectors worldwide. Numerous additions, significant pricing revisions and completely reworked sections head up the 4th edition that groups folding and fixed blades for simple identification. A traditional bible for collectors with a reputation for accuracy and excellence. Softcover • 8-1/2 x 11 • 512 pages • 1500 b&w photos • **LGK4 • $27.95**

Credit Card Calls Toll-free
800-258-0929 Dept. KAB1
Mon.-Fri., 7 a.m.-8 p.m. • Sat., 8 a.m.-2 p.m., CST
Visit our web site: http://www.krause.com
45 years kp

To order by mail send selection list and quantity with payment to:
Krause Publications Book Dept. KAB1
700 E. State St., Iola, WI 54990-0001
Please add appropriate shipping, handling and state tax charges as follows:
Shipping & Handling: $3.25 1st book; $2 ea. add'l. Foreign: $10 1st book; $5 ea. add'l.
Call for Overnight or UPS delivery rates.
Sales tax: WI res. 5.5%, IL res. 6.5%